German Idealism

German Idealism

An Anthology and Guide

Edited by

BRIAN O'CONNOR AND GEORG MOHR

Edinburgh University Press

Introductions, selections and editorial material © Brian O'Connor and Georg Mohr, 2006

The texts are reprinted by permission of other publishers; the acknowledgements on page vii constitute an extension of this copyright page

Edinburgh University Press Ltd
22 George Square, Edinburgh

Typeset in 10.5/12.5 Bembo and Frutiger
by TechBooks, India, and printed and
bound in Great Britain by
The Cromwell Press,
Trowbridge, Wilts

A CIP record for this book is available
from the British Library

ISBN-10 0 7486 1554 7 (hardback)
ISBN-13 978 0 7486 1554 4 (hardback)
ISBN-10 0 7486 1555 5 (paperback)
ISBN-13 978 0 7486 1555 1 (paperback)

Published with the support of the Edinburgh University Scholarly Publishing Initiatives Fund

Contents

Acknowledgements

The editors wish to thank all of those many friends and colleagues who made suggestions about which texts to select for this Anthology and who commented on the editorial material. We are grateful in particular to Bärbel Frischmann, Michael Inwood, Michael Rosen, Hans Jörg Sandkühler and David Wood.

Grateful acknowledgement is made to the following sources for permission to reproduce material in this book previously published elsewhere. Every effort has been made to trace copyright holders, but if any have been inadvertently overlooked the publisher will be pleased to make the necessary arrangement at the first opportunity.

Extracts from *Critique of Pure Reason* by Immanuel Kant, translated by Norman Kemp Smith, Macmillan Publishers Ltd, 1929. © 1929 by Macmillan Publishers Ltd. Reproduced with the permission of the publisher.

Extracts from *The Science of Knowledge, With the First and Second Introductions* by J.G. Fichte, edited by Peter Heath and John Lachs, Cambridge University Press, 1982. © 1982 by Cambridge University Press. Reproduced with the permission of the editors and publisher.

Extracts from 'Of the I as Principle of Philosophy, or On the Unconditional in Human Knowledge,' in *The Unconditional in Human Knowledge: Four Early Essays (1794–1796)* by F.W.J. Schelling, translated by Fritz Marti, Associated University Presses, 1980. © 1980 by Associated University Presses. Reproduced with the permission of the publisher.

Extracts from *Phenomenology of Spirit* by G.W.F. Hegel, translated by A.V. Millar, Oxford University Press, 1977. © 1977 by Oxford University Press. Reproduced with the permission of the publisher.

Extracts from *Of Human Freedom* by F.W.J. Schelling, translated by James Gutmann, Open Court Publishing Company, 1936. © 1936 by Open Court Publishing Company. Reproduced with the permission of Open Court Publishing Company, a division of Carus Publishing Company, Peru, IL.

Extracts from *Metaphysics of Morals* by Immanuel Kant, edited by Mary J. Gregor, Cambridge University Press, 1996. © 1996 by Cambridge University Press. Reproduced with the permission of the editor and publisher.

Extracts from *Foundations of Natural Right* by J.G. Fichte, edited by Frederick Neuhouser, translated by Michael Baur, Cambridge University Press, 2000. © 2000 by Cambridge University Press. Reproduced with the permission of the editor, translator and publisher.

Extracts from *Elements of the Philosophy of Right* by G.W.F. Hegel, edited by Allen W. Wood, translated by H.B. Nisbet, Cambridge University Press, 1996. © 1996 by Cambridge University Press. Reproduced with the permission of the editor, translator and publisher.

Extracts from *On the Aesthetic Education of Man* by F. Schiller, edited and translated by E.M. Wilkinson and I.A. Willoughby, Oxford University Press, 1967. © 1967 by Oxford University Press. Reproduced with the permission of the publisher.

Extracts from *System of Transcendental Idealism* by F.W.J. Schelling, translated by Peter Heath, University of Virginia Press, 1978. © 1978 by University of Virginia Press. Reproduced with the permission of the publisher.

Extracts from *Philosophy of Nature* by G.W.F. Hegel, edited and translated by A.V. Millar, Oxford University Press, 1970. © 1970 by Oxford University Press. Reproduced with the permission of the publisher.

Extracts from *The Ages of the World* by F.W.J. Schelling, the State University of New York Press, 2000. © 2000 by State University of New York. Reproduced with the permission of the publisher.

Abbreviations

The following abbreviations have been used to indicate where in the collected German editions a particular text can be found. The collections which are most easily available are cited:

KAA   Immanuel Kant, *Gesammelte Schriften*, edited by the Royal Prussian Academy of Sciences (Berlin: Walter de Gruyter, 1900ff), 29 volumes ("Akademie Ausgabe")

FW   J. G. Fichte, *Werke*, edited by Immanuel Herman Fichte (Berlin: de Gruyter, 1971), 11 volumes

SSW   F. W. J. Schelling, *Sämmtliche Werke*, edited by K. F. A. Schelling (Stuttgart: Cotta, 1856-61), 14 volumes. A selection of these volumes can be found in *Ausgewählte Schriften*, edited by Manfred Frank (Frankfurt: Suhrkamp, 1985), 6 volumes

HW   G. W. F. Hegel, *Werke in zwanzig Bänden: Theorie-Werkausgabe*, edited by Eva Moldenhauer and Karl Markus Michel (Frankfurt: Suhrkamp, 1971), 20 volumes

In the texts the abbreviation is followed by the volume number and then the page numbers of the relevant German edition.

Introduction

German Idealism: Historical Issues

In histories of philosophy the term 'German Idealism' has served conventionally as the collective name for the philosophies of Immanuel Kant (1724–1804), Johann Gottlieb Fichte (1762–1814), Friedrich Wilhelm Joseph Schelling (1775–1854) and Georg Wilhelm Friedrich Hegel (1770–1831). By as early as 1837–38, only a few years after Hegel's death, and still during Schelling's lifetime, Carl Ludwig Michelet published the two-volume *Geschichte der letzten Systeme der Philosophie in Deutschland von Kant bis Hegel* (*History of the Latest Systems of Philosophy in Germany from Kant to Hegel*), thereby grouping these four philosophers and their works within a determinate epoch of German philosophy.[1] Clearly, Michelet's conception continues to inform an approach to the history of philosophy. The implication of this approach is that an answer to the question of *what we should consider to be the philosophy of German Idealism* should be *the ideas found in the writings of these philosophers.* And in line with this approach we could organise the dates of German Idealism as beginning in 1781, with the publication of Kant's *Critique of Pure Reason,* and ending in 1831, with Hegel's sudden death, one week after he had signed the Preface to the second edition of his *Science of Logic.*[2] This Anthology largely follows that conception of German Idealism in taking selections from many of the major publications of Kant, Fichte, Schelling and Hegel on the grounds that these texts mark out the great achievements of a particular period of German philosophy.

As with all classifications, the historiographical category of 'German Idealism' may have pragmatic advantages, but it leaves open some significant historical issues. First of all, it is legitimate to question whether Kant can be reckoned amongst the German Idealists. Some, in fact, have suggested that he cannot be. Rather, Kant might be seen to occupy the position of the philosopher who ends one epoch (rationalism, empiricism, enlightenment) and smoothes the way for a new 'critical' philosophy, which in its turn becomes the key reference point for the following

[1] Another early presentation of post-Kantian philosophy, from around the same time, as directly shaped by Kant is Karl Rosenkranz's *Geschichte der Kant'schen Philosophie,* which appeared in 1840 as volume 12 of Immanuel Kant's *Sämmtliche Werke,* edited by Karl Rosenkranz and Friedrich Wilhelm Schubert.

[2] Richard Kroner sees the end of 'the development of the German Idealism from Kant to Hegel' as 1821, since that was the year of 'publication of Hegel's last great writing, his *Philosophy of Right': Von Kant bis Hegel* (Mohr: Tübingen, 2nd edition, 1961), p. 1.

generations of philosophers. Indeed, in terms of content, the basic approaches of the post-Kantian philosophers are distinguished in some fundamental respects by a direct departure from distinctions and principles which Kant regarded as the essential achievements of his 'transcendental idealism'. Kant's successors believed that his framework needed to be superseded in order to bring about what they regarded as the 'consistent realisation' of Kantian discoveries. But in so doing they departed ultimately from the basis of Kant's philosophy, arriving at an 'absolute idealism' whose beginnings with Fichte Kant himself had expressly rejected. All of this would suggest that Kant is neither explicitly nor implicitly (in terms of philosophical ambition) compatible with the post-Kantian direction of thought, designated as German Idealism, which Kant himself had nevertheless stimulated.

A further complication in the conventional conception of German Idealism is that it does not give explicit appropriate recognition to the rich and vibrant intellectual context of the period. Key to understanding the genesis of what today are regarded as the central works of Fichte, Schelling and Hegel – the three 'great' post-Kantian philosophers – is an appreciation of the significance of a series of further philosophers and their writings, even if these philosophers came later to be virtually neglected. Their theories and the arguments they provided for them served either as foils for contrast or as valuable philosophical contributions that entered positively into the theoretical conceptions of the German Idealists. Yet in both cases the positions of these other philosophers were absorbed by the 'great works' and thereby almost entirely removed from the further attentions of the history of philosophy. We can take the case of Fichte's philosophy in relation to its appropriation of and debate with Kant's philosophy. Fichte does not directly, as it were, take hold of Kant, but develops both his understanding of Kant as well as his own conception of philosophy under the influence of those philosophers who had for their part already reacted to Kant: Friedrich Heinrich Jacobi (1743–1819), Karl Leonhard Reinhold (1758–1823), Salomon Maimon (1753–1800), Gottlob Ernst 'Aenesidemus' Schulze (1761–1833), Jacob Sigismund Beck (1761–1840). These philosophers, sometimes known as the 'minor Kantians', defended or problematised Kant's transcendental philosophy from what were indeed differing perspectives which would lead to distinctive conclusions. All in all this prepared, however, for the further development of German Idealism's distinctive views of the problems of Kant's legacy. Johann Georg Hamann (1730–1788) and Johann Gottfried Herder (1744–1803), amongst Kant's earliest critics, remain of importance.

And with regard to the philosophical developments of Schelling and Hegel there are also numerous significant contemporaneous intellectuals. Amongst these belong, most prominently, Friedrich Schiller (1759–1804), Friedrich Hölderlin (1770–1843), the early Romantics Novalis (Friedrich von Hardenberg; 1772–1801) and Friedrich Schlegel (1772–1829), Johann Friedrich Herbart (1776–1841) and Jakob Friedrich Fries (1773–1843). Of particular and direct significance is Hölderlin who, as their fellow student and friend at Tübingen, shared in the earliest philosophical impulses of Schelling and Hegel.[3] Which of the three wrote the (subsequently titled) 'The Oldest Systematic Programme of German Idealism' (1796 or 1797) is still disputed today, but on the basis of their intellectual outlook any one of them is certainly the possible author.[4] A precise reconstruction of the forms of idealism that developed after Kant would have to set out the ideas of a series of further philosophers working in Tübingen and Jena from 1790 to 1794, amongst them, in particular, Johann Benjamin Erhard (1766–1826), Friedrich Immanuel Niethammer (1766–1848) and Immanuel Carl Diez (1766–1796), philosophers who prepared the way for the development of thought from Kant to Hölderlin, Schelling and Hegel.[5]

A further complication with the delimitation and characterisation of the development of German Idealism relates specifically to Schelling, in particular to his late philosophy. The early Schelling certainly agreed with Fichte on some fundamental issues, and in standard accounts of the period is placed between Fichte and Hegel. The later Schelling cannot be so ordered both on the basis of the content of his material and chronologically: he continued to produce significant and original philosophical ideas long after Hegel's death. Some of these texts, in fact, were specifically aimed against Hegel's Idealism.[6] So no matter what way one might interpret the philosophy of German Idealism, beyond any basic study of its works, it is clear these days that focusing on Hegel in a quasi-teleological narrative of thought *from Kant to Hegel*, as Richard Kroner in his two-volume work of 1921 and 1924 suggested, is inadequate.[7] This dramatic setting of Hegel's philosophy – a presentation in which Hegel's own teleological version of the history of philosophy is complicit – which presents and reduces a collection of thinkers around 1800 exclusively in terms of how they lead up to Hegel, has been challenged, not least from the quarter of Schelling scholarship.[8]

For many years this interpretative focus on Hegel has also served to push philosophical Romanticism into the background. It is really only in the past few years that the meaning of early Romanticism (Hölderlin, Novalis and Schlegel) has been appreciated, both indeed in the context of the development of German Idealism as well as, more originally, a consideration of its alternative forms of philosophical

---

[3] On Hölderlin as a philosopher, see especially Dieter Henrich, *Der Grund im Bewusstsein. Untersuchungen zu Hölderlins Denken (1794–1795)* (Stuttgart: Klett-Cotta, 1992).

[4] A translation of this text – 'Ältestes Systemprogramm des deutschen Idealismus' – can be found in the collection *The Philosophy of German Idealism* (New York: Continuum, 1987), edited by Ernst Behler.

[5] On this question see Dieter Henrich's comprehensive, two-volume work, *Grundlegung aus dem Ich. Untersuchungen zur Vorgeschichte des Idealismus. Tübingen – Jena 1790–1794* (Frankfurt: Suhrkamp, 2004), the product of many years of research into the intellectual paths from Kant to German Idealism.

[6] Cf. F. W. J. Schelling, trans. and ed. Andrew Bowie, *On the History of Modern Philosophy* (Cambridge: Cambridge University Press, 1994) (*Zur Geschichte der neueren Philosophie, SSW* X).

[7] See note 2.

[8] Walter Schultz's *Die Vollendung des deutschen Idealismus in der Spätphilosophie Schellings* (*The Completion of German Idealism in Schelling's Late Philosophy*) (Pfullingen: Neske, 2nd edition, 1975) strongly disputes the notion behind the Kant to Hegel to narrative. See also Andrew Bowie, *Schelling and Modern European Philosophy* (London: Routledge, 1993).

enquiry, an appreciation independent of, yet directly competitive with, current interests in German Idealism.[9]

We can see, then, that there are serious reasons against simply equating the term 'German Idealism' with the four names Kant, Fichte, Schelling and Hegel and with a single linear consecutive development of philosophical theory. Beside the standard account:

(a) 1781 to 1831: Kant – Fichte – Schelling – Hegel,

at least two further conceptions of this period of German philosophy are proposed, one more restrictive, which leaves out Kant, and starts with Fichte:

(b) 1793 to 1831: Fichte – Schelling – Hegel

and a maximal variant which begins with the first published document marking the emergence of transcendental idealism, *De mundi sensibilis atque intelligibilis forma et principiis* (Kant), and which also takes account of the late Schelling, Schleiermacher and Schopenhauer:

(c) 1770 to *c*.1860: Kant – Fichte – Schelling I – Hegel – Schelling II – Schleiermacher – Schopenhauer.

In recent years important English language scholarship that analyses the philosophical context of German Idealism has appeared. Frederick C. Beiser, in *The Fate of Reason*, follows the path from Kant to Fichte, dealing in particular with Hamann, Jacobi, Mendelssohn, Herder, Reinhold, Schulze and Maimon.[10] And in his extensive work, *German Idealism: The Struggle against Subjectivism*, he considers Kant, Fichte and Schelling as well as Hölderlin, Novalis and Schlegel during the years 1781 to 1801.[11] Apart from the four 'greats', Terry Pinkard's presentation, in his book *German Philosophy 1760–1860: The Legacy of Idealism*, explicitly includes Jacobi, Reinhold, Hölderlin, Novalis, Schlegel, Schleiermacher and Fries, and also, indeed, Schopenhauer and Kierkegaard.[12] A contribution to the *Cambridge Companion to German Idealism* gives further view to the place of Feuerbach, Marx and Kierkegaard in this tradition.[13] A comprehensive panorama of German Idealism, it is clear, would have to deal with all the thinkers named

---

[9] As examples of this new appreciation of the philosophical contribution of Romanticism, see, for instance, Manfred Frank, *Einführung in die frühromantische Ästhetik: Vorlesungen* (Frankfurt: Suhrkamp Verlag, 1989), *'Unendliche Annäherung': Die Anfänge der philosophischen Frühromantik* (Frankfurt: Suhrkamp, 1997); Bärbel Frischmann, *Vom transzendentalen zum frühromantischen Idealismus: J. G. Fichte und Fr. Schlegel* (Paderborn/München/Wien: Ferdinand Schöningh, 2004), Charles Larmore, *The Romantic Legacy* (New York: Columbia University Press, 1996).

[10] Frederick C. Beiser, *The Fate of Reason: German Philosophy from Kant to Fichte* (Cambridge, MA/London: Harvard University Press, 1987).

[11] Frederick C. Beiser, *German Idealism: The Struggle against Subjectivism, 1781–1801* (Cambridge, MA/London: Harvard University Press, 2002).

[12] Terry Pinkard, *German Philosophy 1760–1860* (Cambridge: Cambridge University Press, 2002).

[13] Karl Ameriks, 'The Legacy of Idealism in the Philosophy of Feuerbach, Marx, and Kierkegaard', *The Cambridge Companion to German Idealism* (Cambridge: Cambridge University Press, 2000), edited by Karl Ameriks.

above, as well as with the political and scientific conditions of the early nineteenth century.

In view of the enormously demanding and complex thoughts of all these philosophers, it is extremely difficult to strike a good balance between, on the one hand, working out a common horizon of problems within which they operate and, on the other, a differentiated appreciation of their heterogeneous styles and ways of thought. Undoubtedly the philosophical starting point of the salient philosophers of this period is substantially provided by Kant's project of a *transcendental philosophy* founded on a *critique of reason*. It is at this point that we find their commonality, the basis of a common intellectual context. At the same time, however, their different forms and ways of interpreting and developing this common point have to be appreciated in their distinctiveness. This contrasts with the approach in which some of their central thoughts have been reconstructed to fit a progressive narrative path which is, in effect, a development from the critical Kant through the early Fichte and the early Schelling up to Hegel's system. But it is obviously missing something to consider the philosophical conceptions of these four authors as a whole as the consecutive genesis of a system. Each of them takes his own path, following only in part the thought-process of a respective 'predecessor', which, however, is further developed in other directions.

An Anthology such as this one, which introduces readings from the central texts of German Idealism, cannot meet the demand of fully documenting the complexity of the developing theories of the period. It can take only a small selection, and this should be representative. The concentration on Kant, Fichte, Schelling and Hegel is, all in all, the best way of doing justice to this requirement. The consensus, from German Idealism scholarship, remains, with due regard to the contributions of other philosophers, that the most influential and important authors are indeed Kant, Fichte, Schelling and Hegel. This Anthology therefore takes selections, in English translations, from many of the major texts of these four philosophers (and, additionally, a selection from Friedrich Schiller, 1759–1805).

Despite the individuality of philosophical personalities, and the variety of their particular and heterogeneous theories, fundamental issues both essential and common to German Idealism can be identified. As 'idealists' they take up the concept of reason (*Vernunft*), understood in the broadest sense as covering all epistemic (cognitive, rational) structures, capacities and performances. All the supposed determinations of reason are to be fully developed from the inherent moments of reason itself. And in Kant's sense of the 'Copernican turn' – the turn to knowledge as such; the turn away from the world as it is supposed to be 'in-itself' – the principles lying behind the fundamental formal constitution of the world – that is, the most general principles of the 'laws of nature' – are to be located in determinations developed by reason itself. This notion is based on the belief in the *autonomy of reason*, that is, that human beings can accept as knowledge only those propositions which can be made transparent to reason. Knowledge, in other words, is not determined by parts of the world which stand beyond reason but by a coherent system of fundamental categories and principles generated by reason itself.[14] In this way the *autonomy of reason* becomes visible through the *systematic unity* of all of its determining moments. And for the German Idealists these 'self-determinations' are understood as the ground of a contentful and rationally explicated concept of *freedom* precisely in that they give human reason authority over what should count as true.

The German Idealists, in their very differing ways, were of course not satisfied with explanations of this basic project of the autonomy of reason in merely programmatic form, but rather, in more or less systematic ways, worked through the spectrum of the different disciplines and basic areas of philosophy. This Anthology reflects that range of concerns: we have assembled texts by Kant, Fichte, Schelling and Hegel on the following topics: epistemology, moral philosophy, political and social philosophy, aesthetics (with a contribution from Schiller's work), philosophy of history, philosophy of nature and philosophy of religion. The individual introductions to each piece deal with the content, motivation and situation of the particular text in the work and the immediate intellectual context of the philosopher concerned. However, with a view to setting out the broader context of the specific philosophical concerns it is useful to supplement the individual introductions to each text with more general considerations of the essential and fundamental thoughts of the German Idealists on these areas of philosophy, starting with the historical context of modern philosophy and in particular with the constellation of theories developed by Kant.

Subjectivity and Metaphysics: The Foundations and Method of Knowledge

Modernity

This Anthology opens with a passage from a famous chapter of Kant's *Critique of Pure Reason*, entitled 'Transcendental Deduction of the Pure Concepts of Understanding [Categories]'. Its main argument introduces the notion of the 'I think' and provides an analysis of the conditions of self-consciousness. Subjectivity is placed at the 'highest point' of philosophy in this text. Although Kant's theory of the 'I' represents a revolutionary development in the history of philosophy, the basic thought of a philosophy of subjectivity has a pre-history which it is important to consider. During the modern period the question of the foundation of knowledge claims, a question linked to the emergence of the modern empirical sciences, moved firmly to the centre of philosophical theory. The method of epistemological analysis was reflection on the cognitive capacities of the knowing

---

[14] A matter of some controversy between Kant, Fichte, Schelling and Hegel is that of whether reason has to apply its principles (conceived of as 'forms') to a 'given' external world (the 'material') or whether the principles of reason are sufficient determinations of the world as a whole.

subject. Perception and thought were analysed as the immanent conditions of the subject. Significant sources of the beginnings of the early modern philosophy of the subject in this sense are found in René Descartes' (1596–1650) *Meditationes de prima philosophia* (1641) and John Locke's (1632–1704) *Essay on Human Understanding* (1690). Knowing has epistemic authority on the basis of criteria anchored in the understanding of the subject, or the knower, and in the correct application of these criteria. Right into the twentieth century modern philosophy is to a large extent marked by the concern for a *theory of subjectivity*.

But it was not only in epistemology that this turn towards the subject was carried out. It is the case too in political philosophy. In the contract theory of the state, as developed most significantly by Thomas Hobbes (1588–1679) in his *Leviathan* (1651),[15] the foundation of legitimate political rule relates back to the will and the capacity for free agreement of the subjects (individuals) concerned. The political authority of states is anchored in normative criteria, which are themselves bound to the rationality of subjects.

In the modern era a fundamental conceptual controversy runs through epistemology and metaphysics: the controversy between rationalism and empiricism. Whilst Baruch de Spinoza (1632–1677), Gottfried Wilhelm Leibniz (1646–1716) and Christian Wolff (1679–1754) – to name only the most influential – developed comprehensive *systems* of rationalistic metaphysics, following after Descartes, the Anglo-Saxon empirical theory of knowledge, connected with Locke, led into a *critique* of metaphysics. And then concepts such as identity, substance and causality, soul, freedom and God were exposed by David Hume (1711–1776) as 'fictions' (extrapolations, imaginations) without epistemological foundations.

Kant: Transcendental Philosophy

Kant saw himself compelled by reason to undertake a revision of the 'method of metaphysics' as it was clear to him that under the methodological presuppositions of previous philosophy no end was in sight to the controversy – between the essentially rationalist and empiricist approaches – which had dragged on for centuries.[16] The end result is the *Critique of Pure Reason*. The title originally planned was *The Limits of Sensibility and Reason*.[17] Both titles provide us with information on two fundamental features of the method employed by Kant. (*a*) Philosophy must be self-critique: it is an examination of the presuppositions and powers of reason by reason itself. There cannot be any other instance of the critique of reason than what reason itself provides. Reason must make itself intelligible to itself from out of its own resources. It is in this principle that there lies the fundamental sense of

---

[15] The basic framework of the contractualist theory of the state was in fact already set out by Hobbes in his earlier *De Cive* (1642).

[16] See *Untersuchung über die Deutlichkeit der Grundsätze der natürlichen Theologie und der Moral* (Investigation into the Clarity of the Principles of Natural Theology and of Morality) (1764), *KAA* II, 286, Letter to Johann Heinrich Lambert (1728–1777) 31 December 1765, *KAA* X, 56.

[17] See Letter to Marcus Herz, 7 June 1771, *KAA* X, 123.

autonomy, which Kant ascribes to reason. (*b*) Philosophy must explain the *origin* and the *objective validity* of the concepts used by us. The question of whether a concept has its origin in representations of sensibility or has emerged exclusively from the understanding depends on whether the concept is objectively valid and how far its validity extends. For Kant, *critique* means carrying out a precise *demarcation* between sensibility and understanding as well as an appropriate *delimitation* of the claims of validity for our concepts. We must look at this issue briefly, in order to see the philosophical constellation established by Kant with which philosophers after 1781 were confronted.

For Kant what critique needs to negotiate above all are those concepts and principles we do not gain inductively from experience (empirical concepts), but are available to us *a priori*. Amongst these concepts are, in particular, those of classical metaphysics: space, time, identity, substance and causality, as well as freedom, soul and God. Metaphysics consists precisely in developing *a priori* systems of principles with such concepts. According to Kant the main objective of a *critical* philosophy must therefore be analysis of the *conditions of the possibility* of non-empirical knowledge. A philosophy built on a critique of the conditions of knowledge is what Kant calls *transcendental philosophy*. Since it is exactly this objective which establishes many of the presuppositions for the further development of German Idealism we need to look more closely at the fundamentals of the method and the systematicity of Kant's conception of transcendental philosophy.

The history of philosophy provided Kant with numerous examples of systems of reason, from Plato right up to his own time. The seventeenth and eighteenth centuries were times of blossoming for the rationalistic systems of metaphysics. But, thanks to the acute criticism of the empiricist Hume, it had become questionable whether and to what extent the *a priori* concepts and principles, which were used in these systems, could be deemed to be objectively valid and the extent to which they amounted to knowledge. And beyond that it was also unclear, from a methodological point of view, how a sound basis for alleged *a priori* principles could be established.

The first and most important step in addressing these issues is, according to Kant's philosophy, the precise *distinction* between, and respective epistemological delimitation of, sensibility and understanding, perceptions and concepts, empirical and *a priori* propositions, analytic and synthetic propositions. Kant's view that previous systems of metaphysics had no plausible methodology led him to try to set out these distinctions and delimitations. The metaphysical systems claimed an *a priori* knowledge without being able to indicate exactly what constituted or gave rise to this kind of knowledge, what Kant termed 'synthetic *a priori* judgements'. Kant therefore places at the centre of his critical transcendental philosophy the question '[h]ow are *a priori* synthetic judgments possible?'[18]

The doubtful possibility of such judgements depends on whether the *a priori* concepts, which are used in such judgements, can be demonstrated to be objectively

[18] Immanuel Kant, trans. Norman Kemp Smith, *Critique of Pure Reason* (London: Macmillan, 1927), B19.

valid. Not only metaphysics as a special discipline, but both philosophy in general and each science, in respect of its basic principles, has justified its existence only if the legitimacy of the use of *a priori* concepts can be shown. Kant uses the term 'deduction' for this method of demonstrating the legitimacy of the use of non-empirical concepts. According to Kant 'deduction' has two functions. It must, on the one hand, show which *a priori* concepts are epistemically fundamental. This involves pointing out the *origin* and *range* of these concepts. On the other hand, the deduction must also show that these concepts are *necessary conditions of all knowing* of states of affairs and of the experience of objects of one world, and that as such they are objectively valid. This implies setting out the systematic foundational connection of this epistemic necessity. Kant names the first part of the deduction the 'metaphysical deduction' and the second part is designated the 'transcendental deduction'.

Those fundamental *a priori* concepts – through whose deduction Kant takes up the philosophical tradition – are, as briefly mentioned above, in particular (*a*) space and time, (*b*) substance and causality, and (*c*) soul, freedom and God. Kant makes a rigorous distinction between these three kinds of fundamental *a priori* concepts. According to Kant space and time (*a*) are forms of sensuous intuition. Substance and causality (*b*) are two of twelve (in total) 'pure concepts of the understanding', which, like Aristotle, he calls 'categories'. Soul, freedom and God (*c*) are, Kant says, 'ideas' of pure reason. And what is required for a 'future metaphysics that will be able to come forward as science' (as the subtitle of Kant's *Prolegomena* puts it) is the development of the *systematicity* of these fundamental *a priori* concepts into a *comprehensive inventory* and the establishment of the *knowledge function* of these concepts.

Kant's two-part deduction is intended to meet these requirements of a 'scientifically' defensible metaphysics. In seeing how he goes about this we must, in this Introduction, limit ourselves to (*b*), that is, to Kant's deduction of the categories. In the *metaphysical* deduction, the first part, Kant proceeds from the 'capacity to judge' as the 'common principle' of the categories. He sets out the twelve moments of the 'logical function of thinking in judgements' as a table, which he takes initially from formal logic, but which, in addition, he modifies and supplements. Since rational thinking is nothing other than judging, this table is the inventory of all the elementary forms of thinking. The sought categories, according to Kant, result from, as he writes in the *Prolegomena*, 'relating the functions of judging to objects in general'.[19] Kant, then, insists that the categories be systematic, that is, comprehensive, determined and their order derived. His approach is different from Aristotle's, whose categories he accuses of having been 'rhapsodically' put together, in that Aristotle unsystematically places together concepts of different origin (modes of sensibility and concepts of the understanding) and different epistemic status (elementary terms and derived concepts).

---

[19] Immanuel Kant, trans. Gary Hatfield, *Prolegomena to Any Future Metaphysics* (Cambridge: Cambridge University Press, 1997), §39 (*KAA* IV, 324).

Kant wants to show in the *transcendental* deduction (the second part of the deduction) that the concepts he has set out in the metaphysical deduction are *objectively valid*, that is, are applicable to objects and states-of-affairs, as well as the extent of the region of their application. He sets about this task with an analysis of thinking, of the 'I think', which 'must be able to accompany all my representations', and its attendant presuppositions.[20] Kant's result, in summary, is that consciousness, which is a subject (an agent of thought) of itself and of its representations, is possible only as *identical self-consciousness* when its representations are connected under concepts of unity by a *synthesis* of the understanding. An 'original synthetic unity of apperception' is based on these unifying concepts, the 'categories'. The categories as the 'vehicle' of this transcendental apperception are at the same time necessary conditions for bringing representations to the unity of the *intuition of objects*. Kant's transcendental deduction contains proof, of huge significance for the further history of philosophy, that *self-consciousness* and *object-consciousness* mutually condition each other and that this constellation is determined through an apperceptive-categorial basic structure of subjectivity.

The concept of the 'I think' (in the second edition of the Transcendental Deduction of 1787) takes on, in Kant's philosophy, theoretical and argumentative dimensions which contrast with the *Cogito* thesis of Descartes. We can perhaps consider the 'I think' as in one way more and as in another less than Descartes' thesis. Kant's 'I think' in one respect takes on more than Descartes' *Cogito* since it is not to be conceived merely as the epistemic criterion of certainty, but is the expression of the unity of a subject, a subject which produces this unity through its own synthesising activity. The thesis of the 'I think' in another respect, however, claims less than Descartes' *Cogito*, since it provides no criterion for an ontological dualism of mind and body.

What Kant registers with the term 'deduction' is therefore nothing less than the procedure of a systematically secured derivation of all 'core concepts' and principles of the human capacities for knowledge (sensibility, understanding, reason) by means of an elemental analysis of (*a*) the notion of a judgement as the activity of understanding and its reference to objects, as well as (*b*) the conditions of the self-consciousness of a subject ('I'), connected with (*c*) the proof that nature, as an object of knowledge, is constituted necessarily in accordance with these *a priori* principles. A central result of Kant's transcendental philosophy is the 'highest principle of all synthetic judgements', which fulfils the Copernican turn: 'the conditions of the *possibility of experience* in general are likewise conditions of the *possibility of the objects of experience*'.[21] This, then, is also Kant's answer to the question about the possibility of synthetic *a priori* judgements.

This conception of a systematic *deduction* of all the epistemologically underpinned basic determinations of thinking and knowing is of the greatest importance for the development of German Idealism. The cohesive grounding requirements

---

[20] Kant, *Critique of Pure Reason*, §16, B131.
[21] Kant, *Critique of Pure Reason*, A158/ B197.

of the Deduction, which Kant declares to be substantial progress over the systems of his predecessors, would preoccupy his successors for decades to follow.

Subjectivity and Metaphysics: The Grounding and Method of Knowledge

Kant's Reconstruction of Metaphysics

The epochal effect of Kant's theory was not caused only by the exposition of this fundamental programme, but above all by its consequences for the history of metaphysics as a whole. On the basis of the systematicity of the functions of judgement and categories of the understanding Kant develops the systematicity of the '*ideas* of pure reason'. This allows him in turn to reconstruct metaphysics in the systematicity of its disciplines. The development of *general metaphysics*, ontology and the three disciplines of *special metaphysics* – rational psychology, rational cosmology, rational theology – is not a contingent historical fact, but is deduced from the logic of reason itself.

The diagnosis of the illusory knowledge of metaphysics, which Kant discusses in the Transcendental Dialectic, is not achieved inductively by way of a critique of specific theories; nor is it a critique of the contingent inadequacies of this or that author. Kant's critique of metaphysics is rather a proof of the breakdowns that necessarily occur when we overstep the limits of possible experience, that is, in Kant's terminology, with a 'transcendent' (not transcede*ntal*) use of reason. Transcendent thinking attempts to reach beyond the conditions of objectively valid knowledge. To think something corresponding to the logical *functions* does not in fact mean that one *knows* an existent object which corresponds to this thought. The point is that thinking and knowing are not the same activity of reason since only knowing must work within the conditions of the possibility of knowledge. It lies indeed in the 'nature' of reason to seek the ultimate conditions of all conditioned things, to seek *the* Unconditioned or *the* Absolute: the *idea* of an Unconditioned or Absolute may be *thought*, but *objects* allegedly corresponding to this idea cannot be *known*. Reason, however, errs necessarily so long as it has not clarified the origin of its concepts and the limits of validity of its principles.

The thesis that all non-empirical concepts and all *a priori* principles of the pure understanding are objectively valid only in relation to both the forms of sensuous intuition (space and time) and to objects of possible experience – in short, that categories may be applied only to *appearances*, not to *things-in-themselves* – is what Kant calls *transcendental idealism*. A consequence of this thesis is that the ideas of pure reason – soul, freedom, God – are not concepts of particular super-empirical, transcendent objects (things-in-themselves, unconditioned things, Absolutes), but are concepts of the *unity* of our *knowledge*. In the area of theoretical knowledge the 'ideas of pure reason' are 'regulative' research maxims of reason, on whose basis achieved knowledge develops as scientific theories, which trace back the manifold phenomena to uniform laws. The far-reaching point of Kant's theory of ideas is however that in these ideas the 'actual interest' of reason in the 'highest purposes of mankind' is expressed and this interest is a *practical* one. Kant's reconstruction of the highest unity concepts of metaphysics (soul, God) into 'postulates of practical reason' already points beyond theoretical reason to the context of the *Groundwork of the Metaphysics of Morals* (1785) and the *Critique of Practical Reason* (1788). This fundamental thought of the unity of theoretical and practical reason is then implemented in the *Critique of Judgement* (1790) in the context of a new logic of the judgement of taste and an equally innovative teleology of nature.

Fichte, Schelling, Hegel

Kant influenced the philosophical agenda of the generation around 1800 like no other philosopher of this period. This agenda, however, was far from being accepted without alteration. Some, such as Reinhold, Beck, Fichte and the early Schelling, understood themselves to be continuing or even completing the Kantian philosophy, whilst others, such as Jacobi, Maimon, Schulze and also Hamann, Herder and Hegel, turned critically against it. It was both Kant's methods of procedure (discussed above) and his philosophical theses which, in the 1780s and 1790s, were the focal centre of the reaction of philosophy to the *Critique of Pure Reason*: transcendental idealism with the distinction between the thing-in-itself and appearance, the dualism of intuition and concept, sensibility and understanding/reason, the theory of space and time as forms of intuition, the deduction of the categories from the logic of judgement; the foundation of the objectivity of the categories in the conditions of self-consciousness.

The distinction between *thing-in-itself* and *appearance*, as well as the corresponding limits of validity of the categories, was attacked by Jacobi and discussed polemically by his contemporaries, Reinhold, Maimon, Beck and Schulze. According to Maimon and Schulze, Kant did not succeed in refuting scepticism, but in fact encouraged it. Kant's acceptance of the thing-in-itself was rejected by Fichte, Schelling and Hegel as plain dogmatism. The dualism of *intuition* and *concept*, sensibility and understanding was thoroughly denied. Post-Kantian German Idealism can be considered in this respect as an attempt to preserve the rational critical achievements of Kant's philosophy whilst, at the same time, overcoming residues of alleged dogmatism, such as the thing-in-itself, without thereby falling back into a pre-critical metaphysical dogmatism.

Areas of Enquiry

Self and Knowledge

Kant's successors reacted strongly to his deduction of the categories and thesis of the 'I think'. It was alleged that in the Transcendental Deduction Kant had only claimed but not demonstrated the first premises of the foundational notions of the I–subject and categorially determined objectivity. This assessment lies at the basis of Reinhold's so-called 'philosophy of the elements' (*Attempt at a New Theory of the Faculty of Representations*, 1789), Fichte's 'Science of Knowledge' (*Wissenschaftslehre*) (*Foundations of the Entire Science of Knowledge*, 1794; First Introduction to the *Science of Knowledge*, 1797) and Schelling's philosophy of the subject ('On the I as the Principle of Philosophy', 1795). Fichte radicalises Kant's thesis of the spontaneity of understanding into a theory of the 'I' as 'deed-action' (*Tathandlung*) and 'intellectual intuition'. Consciousness, according to this radicalised position, must be explained as deriving from an original action of the I, which is constitutive for all epistemic (cognitive) achievements of consciousness. Hence Fichte terms this action 'deed-action' (*Tathandlung*) characterising it as a 'self-reverting activity' of the I.[22] Fichte's theory of 'fact-act', right from the first *Science of Knowledge* of 1794 (as well as in his later attempts at new foundations), is essentially led by the intention to demonstrate the genesis of the self-constitution of reason, of self-consciousness (which remained unexplained by Kant), as the result of transcendental apperception (interpreted as deed-action). Kant had 'never laid it down specifically *as* the basic principle'.[23] Fichte's 'science of knowledge' is supposed to '*discover* the primordial, absolutely unconditioned first principle of human knowledge'.[24] This principle 'is intended to express that deed-action which . . . lies at the basis of all consciousness and alone makes it possible'.[25] Schelling later abandoned his Fichtean style of philosophy of the subject in favour of a move towards a 'philosophy of nature'.[26]

Hegel takes up Fichte's *dialectic* of 'I' and 'not-I', as well as his method of a 'historiography of spirit',[27] and transforms it in the *Phenomenology of Spirit* (1807) into a 'science of the experience of Consciousness', and in the *Science of Logic* (1812, 1831) into a theory of the 'movement of concepts', out of which the system of all categorical determinations of thought are unfolded, which as such are also at once the determinations of being. Hegel's speculative dialectic of concepts is conceived by him as *absolute* idealism and it rescinds Kant's de-ontologicisation of subjectivity.

---

[22] J. G. Fichte, trans. Peter Heath and John Lachs, *The Science of Knowledge* (Cambridge: Cambridge University Press, 1982), p. 227 (*FW* I, 257). See also J. G. Fichte, trans. and ed. Daniel Breazeale *Foundations of Transcendental Philosophy (Wissenschaftslehre) nova methodo*, (Ithaca, NY: Cornell University Press, 1992), §1, and J. G. Fichte, trans. Michael Baur, *Foundations of Natural Right* (Cambridge: Cambridge University Press, 2000), §1, p. 18 (*FW* III, §1, 17).

[23] Fichte, *The Science of Knowledge*, p. 100 (*FW* I, 100).

[24] Fichte, *The Science of Knowledge*, p. 93 (*FW* I, 91).

[25] Fichte, *The Science of Knowledge*, p. 93 (terminology altered) (*FW* I, 91).

[26] Schelling presented his last significant systematic version of 'transcendental idealism' in his major work from 1800 entitled *System of Transcendental Idealism*. But even by 1797 he had begun developing his 'philosophy of nature', which marked a decisive separation from Fichte and indeed from Hegel.

[27] 'The Science of Knowledge is to be a pragmatic history of the human spirit': Fichte, *The Science of Knowledge*, pp. 198–9 (terminology altered) (*FW* I, 222).

Freedom and Morality

That German idealism is no linearly developing and homogeneous philosophical school is clearly revealed in the area of moral philosophy. Kant's view of the disciplines of philosophy and the systematic nature of its questions is to a large extent influenced by German 'School-Philosophy' as already inventoried by Christian Wolff.[28] Even the young Fichte, who for his part regarded his philosophy as the completion of Kant's transcendental philosophy, presents two parts of his three-part 'original system' (as Baumanns it calls[29]) under the classical designations: 'natural right' (*Naturrecht*) and 'science of ethics' (*Sittenlehre*). In Kant the corresponding disciplines are respectively 'the doctrine of right' (*Rechtslehre*) and 'the doctrine of virtue' (*Tugendlehre*).[30] For both philosophers moral philosophy is an important part of their system, expounded in extensive works.

In the *Groundwork of the Metaphysics of Morals* and the *Critique of Practical Reason* Kant develops and grounds the 'basic law of pure practical reason', that Kant himself frequently names as the 'ethical law' or 'moral law': 'So act that the maxim of your will could always hold at the same time as a principle establishing universal law'.[31] Kant's thesis, which he sets against all ethics based on the happiness principle, is that the moral law must be a *categorical imperative* and only the rational lawfulness of a maxim of action can make it into an object of duty. This thesis sets a new focal point for post-Kantian moral philosophy. Fichte's position is hugely indebted to Kant's moral philosophy, though he reformulates the ethical law with a subjective emphasis: 'Act only according to the best conviction of your duty; or: act according to your conscience'.[32] In his *System of Transcendental Idealism* (1800) Schelling also explicitly takes up Kant's ethical law only, again, to recast it: 'thou shalt will only what all pure intelligences are able to will'.[33] The sense of this requirement is explained by Schelling as follows: 'the *self* (*Ich*) shall will nothing else than pure self-determining itself'.[34] For Kant, Fichte and Schelling freedom lies in this autonomy of beings equipped with reason to determine themselves according to rational laws of practical action common to all subjects.

Although freedom is also at the centre of Schelling's and Hegel's philosophy moral philosophy specifically loses some of the status it had gained in Kant and

---

[28] 'School-Philosophy' is the name given to philosophy in Germany during the period between Leibniz and Kant, particularly to Wolff and his disciples.

[29] This is the title of Peter Baumanns' book, *Fichtes ursprüngliches System. Sein Standort zwischen Kant und Hegel* (Stuttgart-Bad Cannstatt: Frommann Holzboog, 1972).

[30] In the two parts of Kant's *Metaphysics of Morals* (1797), 'morals' (*Sitten*), in the traditional terminology used by Kant, is the general term for law (legal duties) *and* morals in the narrow sense (moral duties). See further explanations below.

[31] Immanuel Kant, trans. Lewis White Beck, *Critique of Practical Reason* (London: Macmillan, 1956), p. 30 (*KAA* V, 30).

[32] *FW* IV, 156 (*Das System der Sittenlehre nach den Principien der Wissenschaftslehre* / *System of the Science of Ethics*).

[33] F. W. J. Schelling, trans. Peter Heath, *System of Transcendental Idealism* (Charlottesville, VA: University Press of Virginia, 1978), p. 188 (*SSW* III, 574).

[34] Schelling, *System of Transcendental Idealism*, p. 188 (*SSW* III, 573).

Fichte. Schelling, uniquely amongst the German Idealists, made freedom the explicit theme of an entire work (the last work he saw to publication): *Philosophical Investigations into the Essence of Human Freedom* of 1809. But in that book he turns from the formal-rational interpretation of freedom which he, following Kant and Fichte, had earlier pursued in the *System of Transcendental Idealism*, and begins to understand freedom only as a 'capacity' of living beings for good and evil. Freedom, in this context, is the possibility of a will that can also be directed *against* reason.

With Hegel 'morality' is a theme of one of the chapters of his philosophy of right (or law). Right and history as the objectivisation of reason move to the foreground and the particular notion of reason on which the moral philosophies of Kant and Fichte are based is discredited, by Hegel, as 'abstract'. Practical philosophy as a theory of principles of reason, to be set 'against' a deficient historical reality, is thereby transformed into a philosophy of 'reason in history'. Kant, however, it should be noted, had given the decisive impulse for a philosophy of history understood as a theory of reason in history, which Fichte then adopted.[35] Part of the outcome of Fichte's engagement with this question was that he devises a concept of dialectics in the sense of a philosophical method as later adapted by Hegel. Historical thinking then achieves what in Hegel is of such fundamental significance, the historicisation of morality, in that morality is integrated into a rational-philosophical reconstruction of the traditions of right and morality: it is 'the sublation of morality into ethics'.[36]

But beyond all the divergences between the four major philosophers a basic idea can be seen throughout the complex constellation of the philosophies of German Idealism: the explanation of *freedom as autonomy*. Not only in the field of moral philosophy is this thesis clearly present, but for Kant, Fichte, Schelling and Hegel philosophy as a whole *has to do with freedom*. And philosophy is thereby the exercise (as can be seen below) of autonomous reason.

In the *Social Contract* of 1762 Jean-Jacques Rousseau, in passing and without comment, formulated the connection of freedom and autonomy, as it would be understood and systematically developed in German Idealism, as follows: 'obedience to a law which we prescribe to ourselves is liberty'.[37] In contrast with 'natural' freedom (*liberté naturelle*) and 'civil' freedom (*liberté civile*), Rousseau terms this form of freedom 'ethical' freedom (*liberté morale*). And it is this freedom that for Rousseau specifically distinguishes humans as humans. It alone 'makes man the effective master of himself'. It is this momentous intellectual innovation, the thought, apparently intuitively grasped but not developed systematically by Rousseau, that

---

[35] Cf. Kant's works, 'Idea for a Universal History from a Cosmopolitan Point of View' (1784) (reprinted in this Anthology), 'Conjectures on the Beginnings of Human History' (1786) and the *Conflict of Faculties* (1798). Cf. Fichte's *Characteristics of the Present Age* (1806) (an extract of which is reprinted in this Anthology), and *Addresses to the German Nation* (1808).

[36] Ludwig Siep, *Praktische Philosophie im Deutschen Idealismus* (Frankfurt: Suhrkamp, 1992), p. 10.

[37] Jean-Jacques Rousseau, trans. G. D. H. Cole, *The Social Contract* (London: J. M. Dent, 1993), Book I, Chapter 8, p. 196.

freedom is to be understood as *self-legislation, autonomy*, which Kant takes up and develops into a comprehensive theory of practical reason. Fichte and Hegel like-wise make Rousseau's thought of freedom, in the form which Kant's systematic interpretation had given it, a basic notion of their philosophies. German Idealism presents itself as the philosophically systematic formulation of the Rousseauean notion of freedom. This notion of freedom as autonomy would probably not have had such an effect had Kant not tied it to the actual interest in metaphysics, thereby allowing a notion that had started out in a purely moral philosophy context to take on significance for broader philosophical questions. Through Kant's pen freedom proved itself to be the essence of *reason* and to be primarily *practical*.

Of course, the appropriation of historically influential conceptions of moral philosophy is also important to the German Idealist development of this area of philosophy. Ancient ethics (Plato, Aristotle, Stoicism, Epicureanism) is in fact as great a presence as modern moral philosophies, such as the British philosophies of the seventeenth and eighteenth centuries (those of Francis Hutcheson [1694–1746], David Hume [1757–1838], Adam Smith [1723–1790], to name only the most immediate of Kant's predecessors) or the German rationalism of this time (especially Christian Wolff and Alexander Gottlieb Baumgarten [1714–1762]). There is, however, no philosophical thought with so great an effect on the authors, whom today we designate the German Idealists, as Kant's thought of *self-legislation as the principle of reason*.

Law and State

Introductions or overviews of German Idealism often neglect the philosophies of law and state. However, the renewal of the philosophy of law and state was a task of some priority in this period. Questions of law, justice and a free life had become urgent since the French Revolution of 1789. Kant's and Hegel's philosophies of law and state were of great significance in their historical context, but they remain influential in today's debates. That holds for theses regarding the general foundation of law and state with respect to their legitimation and function as much as for the philosophical concretisation of different areas of law. The theories that Kant, Fichte and Hegel offer in the areas of the philosophy of, for instance, fundamental rights, constitutional law, criminal law and international law are still in many respects amongst the leading contributions.

The universal principle of law or right which Kant presents in the first part of the *Metaphysics of Morals* is that '[a]ny action is *right* (*recht*) if it can coexist with everyone's freedom in accordance with a universal law, or if on its maxim the freedom of choice of each can coexist with everyone's freedom in accordance with a universal law'.[38] It is obvious that this law of right is structurally analogous to the 'fundamental law of pure practical reason' from the *Critique of Practical Reason*. The

---

[38] Immanuel Kant, trans. Mary Gregor, *Metaphysics of Morals* (Cambridge: Cambridge University Press, 1991), p. 56 (*KAA* VI, 230).

basic law of practical reason is the *universal* principle of practical validity, that is, the principle of *all duties*. It establishes the general criterion of what is *obligatory*. This universal criterion or principle is to be applied in two specific areas: morality and law. The *moral* assessment of an action refers to the 'motive': whether the 'attention to law' determines the action 'out of duty'. The *lawful* assessment, however, refers to the agreement of an action with the external freedom of each other acting subject equipped with reason. The law of right is in that way an application of the ethical law to the sphere of external freedom. Therefore, the basic laws of right (jurisprudence) and state (as the collective substance of all legally determined institutions) are likewise grounded in *a priori* reason and therefore just as necessarily and universally valid as the basic laws of the natural sciences.

Given that Kant also names the 'basic law' as 'the moral law' or 'ethical law' there could be the misunderstanding that right, for Kant, is determined through morality. We should not, however, be confused by the terminology. By 'morality' or 'ethics' Kant understands, in a way different from us, today's readers, the entire area of binding imperative duty. In Kant's use of language the terms 'morality' and 'ethics' do not designate anything specifically contrary to areas of norms demarcated by 'right', but name the comprehensive area of the *obligatory grounds for actions*, thus *everything that can count as a duty*. In the *Groundwork*, as well as in the *Critique of Practical Reason*, Kant grounds in rationality the obligatory character of duties in general. The *Metaphysics of Morals* then goes on to cover the doctrine of 'virtues' (moral philosophy in today's narrower sense) *and* the doctrine of 'right'. (In the text Kant actually places these two parts in reverse order.)

Contrary to the cliché of the 'I-philosopher', who makes the world and other persons the product of an all producing 'I', we can find first in Fichte an argument, systematically set out, which presents the constitutive function of corporeality and interpersonality in the existence and actions of persons as self-conscious, self-determining beings. (See Section 10 of this Anthology.) The outcome of Fichte's analyses is that the concept of the person implies the reciprocal recognition of limited personal spheres of freedom. Persons recognise each other as the sort of people in whom they reciprocally recognise their freedom and its limitation. From this concept of the person Fichte develops his entire philosophy of right. Right is deduced from the 'mere concept of the person as such'; it is the quintessence of what it means 'that someone is free in general, or is a person'.[39] The concept of right is thus tied to the basic idea that '[e]ach is said only to be free in general, to be a person'.[40] This idea contains two moments: the idea of the fundamental rights of the person as such and considered only for himself, as well as the compatibility of mutually granted spheres of freedom.

Hegel in his early works, taking up from Fichte, establishes a recognition-based concept of right.[41] For Fichte and Hegel right is that sphere through which

---

[39] Fichte, *Foundations of Natural Right*, p. 87 (*FW* III, 94).

[40] Fichte, *Foundations of Natural Right*, p. 86 (*FW* III, 93).

[41] See especially Ludwig Siep, *Anerkennung als Prinzip der praktischen Philosophie: Untersuchungen zu Hegels Jenaer Philosophie des Geistes* (Freiburg i. Br. / München: Alber, 1987), and also his *Praktische Philosophie*

freedom as the reciprocal recognition of rational beings as persons is realised.[42] Right is the determinate existence of freedom. Hegel understands the philosophy of right as an analysis of the concept of the will, of its determinations and forms. Considered systematically, Hegel's philosophy of right is a metaphysics of the will in that the concept of right itself, as well as the institutions of right ('abstract right'), morality and the state ('ethics') is also to be developed in the process of a categorial self-unfolding of the concept of the will. Personality is the basic condition and basic norm of all right or legality. From it results the grounding of the capacity for right: 'rights of every kind can belong only to a person'.[43] And the person is the object of the commandment of right: 'the commandment of right is therefore: *be a person and respect others as persons*'.[44] Personality is also at the same time the guiding idea of the order of right, as this must be constituted in such a way as to enable personality.

Beauty and Art

It was mentioned above that one of the elements required for a comprehensive examination of the history of the period of German Idealism is an account of the influence of romanticism on the development of the key texts of Fichte, Schelling and Hegel. This is nowhere more the case than in the field of aesthetics. Hegel's philosophy of art, for example – a towering achievement of the entire period – in certain ways bears the impact of the contributions of Friedrich Schlegel, Novalis and Friedrich Schiller, whose various reflections on the nature of art and its relation to culture all take their place in Hegel's considerable system. The task of setting this out is beyond what can be done here.[45]

Another of the historiographical challenges in the interpretation of German Idealism becomes evident in the field of aesthetics in that the philosophy of beauty during this period is particularly resilient to the conventional narrative which leads 'from Kant to Hegel'. The contributions to aesthetics of the four philosophers selected in this Anthology – Kant, Schiller, Schelling and Hegel – are quite distinct

---

im *Deutschen Idealismus* (particularly Chapter 3: 'Philosophische Begründung des Rechts bei Fichte und Hegel').

[42] On the concept of the 'person' and on the idea of a concept of right founded on a theory of interpersonality in Fichte, cf. Bärbel Frischmann and Georg Mohr, 'Leib und Person bei Descartes und Fichte', in Volker Schürmann (ed.), *Menschliche Körper in Bewegung. Philosophische Modelle und Konzepte der Sportwissenschaft* (Frankfurt / New York: Peter Lang, 2001), and also Georg Mohr, 'Der Begriff der Person bei Kant, Fichte und Hegel', in Dieter Sturma (ed.), *Person. Philosophiegeschichte – Theoretische Philosophie – Praktische Philosophie* (Paderborn: Mentis, 2001).

[43] G. W. F. Hegel, trans. H. B. Nisbett, *Elements of the Philosophy of Right* (Cambridge: Cambridge University Press, 1991), p. 72 (*HW* VII, §40, 100).

[44] Hegel, *Elements of the Philosophy of Right*, §36, p. 69 (*HW* VII, §36, 95).

[45] For further background, see Frederick Beiser, *The Romantic Imperative: The Concept of Early German Romanticism* (Cambridge, MA: Harvard University Press, 2004), Andre Bowie, *Aesthetics and Subjectivity: From Romanticism to Critical Theory* (Manchester: Manchester University Press, 2003), and the collection of texts in *Classic and Romantic German Aesthetics* (Cambridge: Cambridge University Press, 2003), edited by J. M. Bernstein.

and they propose really very differing ways of thinking about the nature of aesthetic experience and the nature of beauty. But what is historiographically illuminating, if we can be allowed to take these four philosophers as exemplifying the development of aesthetic theory (over a period of three decades), is that in aesthetics the demarcation between the general framework of the first period of German Idealism (Kantian transcendentalism) and the second period (which Hegel styled 'objective idealism') is quite apparent.

Kant's analysis of aesthetic experience (which can be seen in Section 12 of this Anthology) is based essentially on the point of view of 'aesthetic judgement'. For Kant an aesthetic judgement expresses what he thinks of as the 'subjective generality' of a perceiver's view of the beautiful object, and is strictly differentiated from an objective epistemic judgement in which one can claim to be saying something about the objective properties of the object. The analysis is therefore restricted to the object not as an object of objective knowledge, but in so far as it produces a certain relation, 'harmony', between the activities of the subject's capacities for knowledge: sense, imagination and understanding. The object – considered from the point of view of its supposed beauty as opposed to its objective qualities (say, its shape or size) – remains outside the realm of objective knowledge.

Through a complex synthesis of the notions of the formality of the moral law (from Kant's moral theory) and the formality of beauty (from Kant's theory of aesthetic judgement) Schiller believes that certain kinds of aesthetic experience may have 'educative' potential. (Again, the details of this can be seen in Section 13.) In one way Schiller seems to be fundamentally aligned with Kantian transcendentalism: the analysis of formalism, for instance, remains at the level of the judgement, and therefore experience, of the perceiver. But in another sense he opens up questions about the cultural location of aesthetic experiences which encourages him to determine the value of certain kinds of art, that is, to make judgements of artworks which relate to their objective, and, for Schiller, 'educative' qualities precisely as artworks. Whereas beauty, for Kant, is a 'symbol of morality' art, for Schiller, is the way to freedom.

However, it is amongst the 'objective idealists' that the meaning of artworks is systematically explored. Schelling, indeed, was the first philosopher to produce a book bearing the title, 'philosophy of art'.[46] In the *System of Transcendental Idealism* – which from a Kantian point of view is no transcendental idealism at all – he offers an account of the unique position of artworks: it is not their surface which determines their aesthetic properties, but the special activity of the artist who produces them, as he or she stands in a unique tension between freedom and necessity. Schelling examines, then, the activity of the artist, whereas Kant had examined the activity of the perceiver. This is a daring hypothesis, and it was not taken up by Hegel. But Hegel pushes the notion of the objectivity of art in another direction in seeing artworks as objects with a special capacity – along with religion and philosophy –

---

[46] F. W. J. Schelling, trans. Douglas W. Stott, *The Philosophy of Art* (Minneapolis, MN: Minnesota University Press, 1989) (*Philosophie der Kunst,* 1803) (*SSW* V).

to express the 'spirit' of the culture in which they are produced. In other words, artworks as such contain objective meanings which can be made available through the right form of interpretation.

History and Reason

The period of German Idealism witnessed many notable contributions to the philosophy of history. In addition to the works of the four main philosophers, there were books by other prominent thinkers, such as Herder and Friedrich Schlegel. No doubt each contribution developed the notion of history in distinctive ways, but it should also be noted that significant and influential theories of history preceded the period of German Idealism. This should tell us that the philosophy of German Idealism cannot be understood simply as the outcome of a debate between several contemporaneous or near contemporaneous figures.

As early as the sixteenth century optimistic theories of history were developed. The optimism was grounded in a providential thesis, namely that history is, in effect, the realisation of God's purposes. The providential thesis entails the intervention by God in the affairs of human beings. However, this thesis gave way during the Age of Enlightenment, in the eighteenth century, to the notion that although history bears the mark of God's intentions we are provided by God with a rational historical structure in which a fully enlightened world, that is free and rational, can be realised through human efforts. Montesquieu (1689–1755) and Voltaire (1694–1778) in France, the Scottish Enlightenment philosophers Adam Ferguson (1723–1816), John Millar (1745–1801) and Adam Smith (1723–1790), and in Germany, Gotthold Ephraim Lessing (1729–1781), to take just a sample, proposed this view.[47] Political normativity lies behind the optimists' theories of history in that they give us ground for regarding our present society as not yet complete, as unrealised or partially immature. The German Idealists in many respects continue with and extend a debate that had already attained high levels of sophistication in the Enlightenment period. And all four philosophers specify historical progress in terms of the ever-increasing realisation of freedom and law.

It is clear that Kant's contribution – which was influential within German philosophical circles – is quite in line with the Enlightenment standpoint of some decades earlier. Kant was a key advocate of the Enlightenment in Germany, and in a series of polemical and accessible papers proposed the view that the possibility of human progress could be discerned through a teleological analysis of the potential of human nature to attain full realisation. This was a view that continued to be argued outside Germany also, notably by Antoine-Nicolas de Condorcet (1743–1794) in his *Sketch for a Historical Picture of the Progress of the Human Mind* (1794).

Schelling and Hegel recast the notion of historical progress within a theory of the 'Absolute'. For them, it is at the realisation or full expression of the Absolute

---

[47] Cf. 'Die Geschichte', in *Handbuch Deutscher Idealismus* (Stuttgart: Metzler Verlag, 2005), ed. Hans Jörg Sandkühler, pp. 218–248.

that history aims. According to Schelling, history is the 'progressive, gradually self-disclosing revelation of the absolute', in which a series of epochs are unfolded.[48] Hegel sees history as the self-realisation of the world-spirit. The latter can be largely though not exclusively understood as the increasing growth of sophistication of human social consciousness. What is especially notable about Schelling's and Hegel's position is that the notion of the Absolute entails the element of agency, an agency that seeks to realise itself, producing history in the process.

This challenging thesis of the 'Absolute' certainly marks out a specific characteristic of post-Kantian philosophy of history. But yet more distinctive is the development by Fichte, Schelling and Hegel of a logic of history. It is Schelling, rather than Hegel, who developed the notion of a progressive notion of parts or epochs set out in the form of thesis, antithesis and synthesis; Fichte's account of the relation between the 'epochs' was an anticipation of the concept of dialectic that would become quite central to Hegel's narrative of 'philosophical history'.

Nature and Science

One of the enduring misperceptions of the German Idealist philosophy of nature is that it stands in some kind of opposition to the findings of the natural sciences. The root of this misperception is a confusion about what the idealists – in particular Fichte, Schelling and Hegel – thought they were doing when they attempted to clarify the basis or grounds or even rationality of science. The project was to demonstrate *not* that science must give way to some alleged higher insight of philosophy or accept that it remains aimless until philosophers have somehow validated it. Rather, the methods of science and the 'laws' of nature established through those findings can be understood to have been achieved through the application of frameworks that are ultimately traceable back to self-grounding reason. Science, or nature as it is understood by scientists, was thereby explicated by philosophy within the project of the autonomy of reason.

Kant's notion of science has three main principles which would determine the agenda for the idealist conception of nature. The first can be sourced back to the *Critique of Pure Reason* in which Kant's distinction between the phenomenal and noumenal realm is presented. The distinction is between (*a*) the world as it appears to us and as it can be known by us (phenomena) and (*b*) the world conceived as it is beyond our experience and ways of knowing, as it is 'in-itself' (noumenon). The principle is this: the world as it can be known – the world of appearances – lies within the region of our modes of understanding and knowledge. The structure of the world as we experience it, in other words, can be traced back to our ways of knowing it, a position which contrasts with the thesis that we are passive with regard to the world as it is in itself, merely registering it as it affects us.

This principle relates to the world as we understand it in its objective forms. But knowledge is not simply the practice of registering shapes, sizes and causes.

---

[48] Schelling, *System of Transcendental Idealism*, p. 211 (*SSW* III, 603).

Knowledge, and science is knowledge at its most rigorous, also involves the effort to bring our knowledge into systematic form, to concepts and principles, and to organise phenomena under categories. Kant's second major principle of the notion of science as the exercise of autonomous reason emerges at this point. In the Transcendental Dialectic section of the *Critique of Pure Reason* he argues – as briefly indicated above – that 'reason' seeks to give systematic form to knowledge, to find unity amongst phenomena. He writes: '[t]he law of reason which requires us to seek for this unity is a necessary law',[49] and '[i]f, therefore, the logical principle of genera is to be applied to nature (by which I here understand those objects only which are given to us), it presupposes a transcendental principle. And in accordance with this latter principle, homogeneity is presupposed in the manifold of possible experience . . .'[50]

Kant's third principle relates to the way in which science attempts to understand phenomena as operating according to some purpose. Purpose is not given in the phenomena, and Kant therefore regards this idea of purpose as arising from human reason itself. (See Section 20 of this Anthology.)

Kant's three principles provide an extremely attractive framework within which to conceive of nature in terms of a concept infused with the potential of human reason, as opposed to an alien world which we may or may not be able to describe through concepts that 'correspond to it'. What seemed problematic in Kant, however, was that he had so comprehensively set out the rational character of experience that he made redundant the very notion of a thing-in-itself: the thing-in-itself in no way entered our knowledge or determined our knowledge and it did not seem, therefore, to warrant a position within a system of reason. The forms of transcendental idealism that followed soon after Kant – Fichte's most notably – attempted to systematise Kant's various claims. But the end-result was unsuccessful as it involved ultimately tracing the external world (the 'not-I') back to the productivity of the 'I', a thesis crippled by a series of obvious questions it could not answer. Hence the conceptual shift away from transcendental idealism, in the Fichtean sense, seemed necessary to do justice to nature. But the principles set out by Kant regarding the fundamental reasonableness of nature were retained.

Schelling and Hegel were clearly inspired by the idea that it is possible to account for nature as a complex totality governed by a set by laws. This is not, of course, a view unique to philosophers: but it acquired a philosophical character when explanations were sought regarding the conditions under which we could defend the very principle that nature operates under determinate laws and principles. Schelling and Hegel both attempt to explain the ground of these laws. The ways in which Schelling and Hegel departed from the Kantian position can be seen Sections 21 and 22 below, but a general remark might serve to characterise the shift from the earlier 'transcendental idealist' philosophy of nature to the 'objective idealist' philosophy of nature. If we no longer conceive Kant's three principles – (*i*) that

---

[49] Kant, *Critique of Pure Reason*, A651/B679.
[50] Kant, *Critique of Pure Reason*, A654/B682.

nature conforms to the forms of understanding, (*ii*) that reason seeks homogeneity in knowledge, (*iii*) that reason seeks purpose in objects – as simply 'our ways'
of knowing but features intrinsic to nature itself, we introduce a new means of
meeting the challenge of a philosophy of nature (though Schelling, in particular,
was aware that the earlier rationalist tradition contained useful resources in this
particular domain of philosophy). What seemed to be missing in Kant's position,
as Schelling argued, was the dimension of the *productivity* of nature. And Hegel
held that it was not possible to account adequately for nature without conceiving
of it as a living totality. It is clear that such a notion represents terrain onto which
Kant would have refused to tread, since the very notion of the productivity of
nature seems to entail the notion of nature as a subject, possessing therefore an
inner nature not relative to our modes of understanding and reason. Instead, Kant
sees the task of philosophy as that of explaining how it is that we understand nature, and what precisely can be said to be reasonable about this activity. The issue
is dealt with, in a sense then, from the point of view of the knowing, judging
agent.

God and Religion

Nowhere was the application of the programme of the autonomy of reason to
produce such controversy as it did in the field of religion. And it is worth noting
how a variety of positions offered by the German Idealists were sometimes taken
as challenges to religious orthodoxy. All of the major philosophers during the
period of German Idealism were interested in laying out a notion of God which
is compatible though not necessarily coextensive with the notion of the God of
practised religion.

Kant was determined, indeed, to undermine what he saw as the fruitless and in
any case inappropriate metaphysical analysis of God in which the existence of God
was to be demonstrated on strictly rational grounds. He offers his transcendental
philosophy as an effort to refute the metaphysical approach and thereby, as he
puts it, 'to make room for faith'.[51] This notion of faith is further elaborated in
his practical philosophy where he argues that the notion of God is a postulate of
practical (not theoretical) reason. This does not mean that the existence of God
is 'posited' by practical reason, but rather that the very notion of practical reason
entails the notion of God, just as it entails the notion of freedom. Fichte in his
Attempt at a Critique of All Revelation (1792) (his first important work) and his
'On the Foundation of Our Belief in a Divine Government of the World' (1798)
develops this notion in ways that stay close to Kant's fundamental thesis. However,
Kant and Fichte were both suspected of some form of atheism or offence against
orthodox religion. This accusation is, in fact, quite false, but its motivations are not
difficult to understand. The God of the philosophers is a concept whose nature is
specified with regard to a particular purpose (a postulate of morality), an abstract

[51] Kant, *Critique of Pure Reason*, Bxxx.

concept which finds itself at a distance from the notion of a personal relationship with God, as achieved through prayer or some kind of religious devotion. To the orthodox reader the subtlety of the notion of God as a postulate of practical reason might lead them to the misapprehension that God was 'merely' a postulate of practical reason, or, worse still, that God was merely an idea useful to the exercise of morality. It could seem that the very programme of German Idealism – to affirm the autonomy of reason – could not accommodate the notion of a God who, according to the orthodox practices, exists beyond all reason.

Schelling's conception of God represents a new direction that moves away from a conception of God as a postulate of ethics. Schelling's writings on the nature of God and religion are more diverse and more difficult to characterise than those of the other German Idealists. However, a central theme runs through the writings from his Master's degree dissertation right up to the last writings on revelation and mythology, namely, that questions of religion cannot be posed outside the context of a philosophy of history. In his early writings he adopted a hermeneutic approach in which he viewed religious texts as historical, though their truth was not reducible to history. In the *System of Transcendental Idealism* the notion of God is presented, albeit briefly, as a being who 'continually reveals himself', and that '[m]an, through his history, provides a continuous demonstration of God's presence, a demonstration, however, which only the whole of history can render complete'.[52] In this way history comes to be understood as a process of revelation (a theme which would continue to fascinate Schelling into his later works). And then in the *Lectures on the Method of Academic Study* (1803) he again insists that religion is historically located and theology therefore must be conceived as an historical science. However, Schelling's writings continued with diverse reflections. For instance, in the *Philosophical Investigations into the Essence of Human Freedom* he is concerned with understanding human freedom in the context of a world created by a benevolent God. And various drafts of the *Ages of the World* developed complex notions of predication as a means of grasping the nature of God.

Hegel was clearly influenced by Schelling's writings on religion, and the influence is evident right up to the late *Lectures on the Philosophy of Religion* in that he tries to reconcile the competing givens of, on the one hand, the revealed eternal truths of religion and, on the other, the historical factuality of revelation. Like Kant and Fichte, Hegel found that his philosophical notion of God would arouse suspicion. He does not pursue the moral framework within which Kant provides the concept of God with a systematic location. Indeed, he does not follow Kant's idea that the nature of God could never be intelligibly discussed from within a purely theoretical framework. In this regard he launched a number of agenda-setting attacks against F. H. Jacobi, the latter who proposed that we could have a direct, unmediated, non-conceptual relationship with God. For Hegel, instead, God is intelligible within a complex of concepts. In some way this must seem

---

[52] Schelling, *System of Transcendental Idealism*, p. 211 (*SSW* III, 603).

alarming to the orthodox view, but Hegel's project is to demonstrate the utter centrality of God to the world which we can rationally reconstruct. Through the familiar method of unfolding the Absolute (which in the texts on metaphysics, the *Logics*, seems close to a conception of God, a pantheist – or 'panentheist', God-in-being, who is the whole of being – conception), through an analysis of its immanent moments, Hegel wants to show nothing less then that we cannot undertake metaphysics – the study of the structures of reality – without a notion of God: 'This elevation (*Erhebung*) of the spirit means that although being certainly does pertain to the world, it is only semblance, not genuine being, not absolute truth; for, on the contrary, the truth is beyond that appearance, in God alone, and only God is genuine being'.[53] (It might not be too fanciful to suggest that God, in this way, is a postulate of theoretical reason.) But this is not necessarily a satisfactory position from the perspective of practical religion: the God whose existence is rationally validated though a complex dialectic of the Absolute seems to be either a philosopheme or, worse still, a God whose existence is provisional until demonstrated by philosophical reason. (Neither of these accusations, however, could be based on conscientious readings of Hegel's rather precise formulations.) A further source of controversy was Hegel's Schellingian view that the forms of religion are expressive of a particular historical 'spirit'. It is clear that atheistic use could be made of this notion (as it was, most famously, by the young Karl Marx) in that it could also be taken to imply that the very principles of religion might turn out to be the contingent expressions of a group, rather than response to revelation.

In the period of German Idealism, then, the concept of God is not developed in increasing stages of sophistication leading from Kant to Hegel. The theories are many and various, each developing contrasting notions in differing frameworks. However, it is also clear that even the concept of God cannot be allowed to be thought without the application of reason: the revealed (Christian) religion may be true as far as all four are concerned, but that does not entail that we cannot make certain features of it transparent to reason. The accusation against the Idealists, however, was that they attempt not to make parts of religion transparent to reason but to produce them by reason and thereby uproot them from their revealed sources.

★

The general background that this Introduction sketches out can obviously be only a highly tentative and provisional appreciation of the complex issues and innovative concepts at work in the German Idealist tradition. The next steps for the reader are the individual introductions to each Section below and a study of the selected texts. Fully aware of the vast diversity of ideas and texts in the German Idealist period

---

[53] G. W. F Hegel, trans. T. F. Geraets, W. A. Suchting and H. S. Harris, *The Encyclopaedia Logic* (Indianapolis, IN: Hackett Publishing Company, 1991), §50, p. 96 (*HW* VIII, §50, 131).

the editors of this Anthology believe, however, that it is possible to appreciate what marks out German Idealism as a philosophical movement as well as understanding the tensions that lie within the very concept of German Idealism itself. *German Idealism: An Anthology and Guide* aims to be a contribution to the study of this rich and frequently misunderstood period of the history of philosophy.

I
_____

Self and Knowledge

1.

Immanuel Kant, Critique of Pure Reason (Kritik der reinen Vernunft): *Transcendental Deduction B (1787)*

The Transcendental Deduction section of the *Critique of Pure Reason* can be considered amongst the most influential texts of modern philosophy. Shortly after its publication it was to become a key resource for the so-called philosophy of the subject, which emerged in German philosophical circles after Kant, and then quite unexpectedly in the twentieth century it seemed to provide Anglo-American philosophy with an exciting contribution to the refutation of scepticism.

The Transcendental Deduction contains a number of important and inter-locking concepts. Indeed, entirely different theories of what the Transcen-dental Deduction is attempting to achieve can be generated by stressing any one of these concepts over others. Karl Ameriks has pointed out that in recent times the Transcendental Deduction has been read variously as an effort to give an account of a rationalist ontology, of a philosophy of the subject, of the fundamental condition of self-knowledge, and of the notion of synthesis.[1] (All of these readings, alarmingly enough, can claim significant textual support.)

The early German Idealists were in no doubt that the Transcendental Deduction is the basis of a theory of the freedom of the self. It seemed to them that the Transcendental Deduction could allow us to articulate an account of that part of human cognition which is irreducible to the world of ordinary causal events, namely, our capacity for free and rational judgement. To read the Transcendental Deduction in these terms, however, one had to read it alongside some of Kant's thoughts on freedom in the *Critique of Practical Reason*. The latter text made explicit the need for a differentiation between the self which would be deterministically subject to the laws of the empirical world and a self which would somehow be capable of acting subject to reason, rather than to empirical causality. For the early German Idealists the Transcendental Deduction seemed to provide the theoretical underpinnings of this practical position. It must be said that the philosophers who drew some inspiration from the Deduction did not seem always to be

[1] Karl Ameriks, 'Kant and the Self: A Retrospective', p. 56, in *Figuring the Self: Subject, Absolute, and Others in Classical German Philosophy* (Albany, NY: State University of New York Press, 1997), edited by David E. Klemm and Günter Zöller.

masters of its detail. However, their re-casting of an epistemological tract in terms of a philosophy of freedom drew out something powerful in Kant's text.

In the Introduction to the *Critique of Pure Reason* Kant had stated suggestively that 'though all our knowledge begins with experience, it by no means follows that all arises out of experience'. The Transcendental Deduction, in a way, can be seen to explain what part of knowledge does not arise out of experience. Its intention is to demonstrate that certain conditions must necessarily be in place – in particular, a certain form of consciousness – if we are to explain the phenomena of ordinary experience.

A number of key terms need to be understood. Broadly put, Kant uses the term 'representation' (*Vorstellung*, also translated at times as 'presentation') to mean anything that can come before the mind, or, as he puts it himself, as the 'inner determinations of our mind'. Representations may be received by us in so far as we, as sensuous beings, are in passive relation to the world. Kant associates the term intuition with this mode of passivity. But in this passive state representations come to us as a disparate manifold, not of the elements of an apparent whole. (Kant obviously enough follows the atomistic assumptions of his time.) The manifold of representations, however, is combined in some way in order to become an experience of an object. Of crucial significance here is the claim that combination – and the related idea of synthesis – is not a passive, but a spontaneous act. Spontaneity, in a way, names the origin of those parts of our knowledge which do not arise out of experience. Through this spontaneous act the manifold is synthesised into a coherent experience which we as experiencers understand. To put this another way, through synthesis experience is organised under general and necessary features. Earlier in the text of the *Critique* Kant had identified twelve categories – the chief amongst which are substance and causality – as the most basic logical functions which constitute the possibility of a judgement that '*x* is an object'. In the Transcendental Deduction he sees these categories as the modes through which the manifold is spontaneously synthesised.

But one further piece is required for this theory. All of the talk about passivity and receptivity presupposes a subject of experience, that is, an 'I'. Kant argues that a particular conception of 'I' is a necessary condition of rational experience. This 'I' must at least in some special sense be the agent of synthesis: it must provide the condition in which disparate and manifold representations become experiences of objects. In order for the 'I' – the 'I think' as Kant calls it – to serve this function it must be identical throughout experience. A continuity of experience of an object, for example, requires continuity of an 'I' which thinks it. Having set out these various different requirements Kant discusses the culminating idea of the Deduction, the transcendental unity of apperception (self-consciousness). This idea brings together notions of synthesis and thinking. In so far as I think an object a certain unity of consciousness must be in place. And in so far as thinking is a condition of experience all experience has reference back to a self which thinks whatever contents it has before the mind (self-consciousness). The necessity of the 'I think', then, is that it is the condition of the synthesis of the manifold, and thereby of coherent experience.

Some critics of developments in post-Kantian idealism seem to see Kant's discussion of the 'I think' and spontaneity as the forbidden fruits which after misappropriation led to a fall of a philosophical kind, a fall into an illicit metaphysics. It is clear that Kant is working hard to avoid any sense that the 'I think' is some kind of non-material entity magically controlling the shape of empirical reality. None of the post-Kantian idealists wanted to deny this, but they could not resist the idea that this 'I think' might somehow be equivalent to the same agency which is supposedly the source of moral freedom.

Actually, the Transcendental Deduction was one of the sections which Kant chose to revise in a second edition of the *Critique of Pure Reason* (the second edition version is the one reprinted here). The first edition version (the so-called A version) argued that the reproductive imagination was the synthesising faculty. It soon became clear to Kant that the necessary conditions of knowledge could not be sustainably attributed to psychological activities (such as imagination). But the grounds were thereby laid for the distinctly psychological resonances in Fichte's, Schopenhauer's and others' re-casting of Kant's transcendental idealism.

DEDUCTION OF THE PURE CONCEPTS
OF THE UNDERSTANDING†

[*As restated in 2nd edition*]

Section 2

TRANSCENDENTAL DEDUCTION OF THE PURE CONCEPTS
OF THE UNDERSTANDING

§15
The Possibility of Combination in General

The manifold of representations can be given in an intuition which is purely sensible, that is, nothing but receptivity; and the form of this intuition can lie *a priori* in our faculty of representation, without being anything more than the

---

†*KAA* IV, B129–B146. *Critique of Pure Reason* (London: Macmillan, 1929).

mode in which the subject is affected. But the combination (*conjunctio*) of a manifold in general can never come to us through the senses, and cannot, therefore, be already contained in the pure form of sensible intuition. For it is an act of spontaneity of the faculty of representation; and since this faculty, to distinguish it from sensibility, must be entitled understanding, all combination – be we conscious of it or not, be it a combination of the manifold of intuition, empirical or non-empirical,[1] or of various concepts – is an act of the understanding. To this act the general title 'synthesis' may be assigned, as indicating that we cannot represent to ourselves anything as combined in the object which we have not ourselves previously combined, and that of all representations *combination* is the only one which cannot be given through objects. Being an act of the self-activity of the subject, it cannot be executed save by the subject itself. It will easily be observed that this action is originally one and is equipollent [*gleichgeltend*] for all combination, and that its dissolution, namely, *analysis*, which appears to be its opposite, yet always presupposes it. For where the understanding has not previously combined, it cannot dissolve, since only as having been combined *by the understanding* can anything that allows of analysis be given to the faculty of representation.

But the concept of combination includes, besides the concept of the manifold and of its synthesis, also the concept of the unity of the manifold. Combination is representation of the *synthetic* unity of the manifold.[2] The representation of this unity cannot, therefore, arise out of the combination. On the contrary, it is what, by adding itself to the representation of the manifold, first makes possible the concept of the combination. This unity, which precedes *a priori* all concepts of combination, is not the category of unity (§ 10); for all categories are grounded in logical functions of judgment, and in these functions combination, and therefore unity of given concepts, is already thought. Thus the category already presupposes combination. We must therefore look yet higher for this unity (as qualitative, § 12), namely in that which itself contains the ground of the unity of diverse concepts in judgment, and therefore of the possibility of the understanding, even as regards its logical employment.

§16
The Original Synthetic Unity of Apperception

It must be possible for the 'I think' to accompany all my representations; for otherwise something would be represented in me which could not be thought at all,

---

[1] Reading, with Mellin, *empirischen oder nicht empirischen* for *sinnlichen oder nicht sinnlichen*.
[2] Whether the representations are in themselves identical, and whether, therefore, one can be analytically thought through the other, is not a question that here arises. The *consciousness* of the one, when the manifold is under consideration, has always to be distinguished from the consciousness of the other; and it is with the synthesis of this (possible) consciousness that we are here alone concerned.

and that is equivalent to saying that the representation would be impossible, or at least would be nothing to me. That representation which can be given prior to all thought is entitled intuition. All the manifold of intuition has, therefore, a necessary relation to the 'I think' in the same subject in which this manifold is found. But this representation is an act of *spontaneity*, that is, it cannot be regarded as belonging to sensibility. I call it *pure apperception*, to distinguish it from empirical apperception, or, again, *original [ursprüngliche] apperception*, because it is that self-consciousness which, while generating the representation '*I think*' (a representation which must be capable of accompanying all other representations, and which in all consciousness is one and the same), cannot itself be accompanied by any further representation. The unity of this apperception I likewise entitle the *transcendental* unity of self-consciousness, in order to indicate the possibility of *a priori* knowledge arising from it. For the manifold representations, which are given in an intuition, would not be one and all *my* representations, if they did not all belong to one self-consciousness. As *my* representations (even if I am not conscious of them as such) they must conform to the condition under which alone they *can* stand together in one universal self-consciousness, because otherwise they would not all without exception belong to me. From this original combination many consequences follow.

This thoroughgoing identity of the apperception of a manifold which is given in intuition contains a synthesis of representations, and is possible only through the consciousness of this synthesis. For the empirical consciousness, which accompanies different representations, is in itself diverse and without relation to the identity of the subject. That relation comes about, not simply through my accompanying each representation with consciousness, but only in so far as I *conjoin* one representation with another, and am conscious of the synthesis of them. Only in so far, therefore, as I can unite a manifold of given representations in *one consciousness*, is it possible for me to represent to myself the *identity of the consciousness in [i.e. throughout] these representations.* In other words, the *analytic* unity of apperception is possible only under the presupposition of a certain *synthetic* unity.[3]

The thought that the representations given in intuition one and all belong to me, is therefore equivalent to the thought that I unite them in one self-consciousness, or can at least so unite them; and although this thought is not itself the consciousness of the *synthesis* of the representations, it presupposes the possibility of that synthesis. In other words, only in so far as I can grasp the manifold of the representations

---

[3] The analytic unity of consciousness belongs to all general concepts, as such. If, for instance, I think red in general, I thereby represent to myself a property which (as a characteristic) can be found in something, or can be combined with other representations; that is, only by means of a presupposed possible synthetic unity can I represent to myself the analytic unity. A representation which is to be thought as common to *different* representations is regarded as belonging to such as have, in addition to it, also something *different*. Consequently it must previously be thought in synthetic unity with other (though, it may be, only possible) representations, before I can think in it the analytic unity of consciousness, which makes it a *conceptus communis*. The synthetic unity of apperception is therefore that highest point, to which we must ascribe all employment of the understanding, even the whole of logic, and conformably therewith, transcendental philosophy. Indeed this faculty of apperception is the understanding itself.

in one consciousness, do I call them one and all *mine*. For otherwise I should have as many-coloured and diverse a self as I have representations of which I am conscious to myself. Synthetic unity of the manifold of intuitions, as generated[4] *a priori*, is thus the ground of the identity of apperception itself, which precedes *a priori* all *my* determinate thought. Combination does not, however, lie in the objects, and cannot be borrowed from them, and so, through perception, first taken up into the understanding. On the contrary, it is an affair of the understanding alone, which itself is nothing but the faculty of combining *a priori*, and of bringing the manifold of given representations under the unity of apperception. The principle of apperception is the highest principle in the whole sphere of human knowledge.

This principle of the necessary unity of apperception is itself, indeed, an identical, and therefore analytic, proposition; nevertheless it reveals the necessity of a synthesis of the manifold given in intuition, without which the thoroughgoing identity of self-consciousness cannot be thought. For through the 'I', as simple representation, nothing manifold is given; only in intuition, which is distinct from the 'I', can a manifold be given; and only through *combination* in one consciousness can it be thought. An understanding in which through self-consciousness all the manifold would *eo ipso* be given, would be *intuitive*; our understanding can only *think*, and for intuition must look to the senses. I am conscious of the self as identical in respect of the manifold of representations that are given to me in an intuition, because I call them one and all *my* representations, and so apprehend them as constituting *one* intuition. This amounts to saying, that I am conscious to myself *a priori* of a necessary synthesis of representations — to be entitled the original synthetic unity of apperception — under which all representations that are given to me must stand, but under which they have also first to be brought by means of a synthesis.

§ 17
The Principle of the Synthetic Unity is the Supreme Principle of all Employment of the Understanding

The supreme principle of the possibility of all intuition in its relation to sensibility is, according to the Transcendental Aesthetic, that all the manifold of intuition should be subject to the formal conditions of space and time. The supreme principle of the same possibility, in its relation to understanding, is that all the manifold of intuition should be subject to conditions of the original synthetic unity of apperception.[5] In

---

[4] [Reading, with Vaihinger, *hervorgebracht* for *gegeben*.]

[5] Space and time, and all their parts, are *intuitions*, and are, therefore, with the manifold which they contain, singular representations (*vide* the Transcendental Aesthetic). Consequently they are not mere concepts through which one and the same consciousness is found to be contained in a number of representations. On the contrary, through them many representations are found to be contained in one representation, and

so far as the manifold representations of intuition are *given* to us, they are subject to the former of these two principles; in so far as they must allow of being *combined* in one consciousness, they are subject to the latter. For without such combination nothing can be thought or known, since the given representations would not have in common the act of the apperception 'I think', and so could not be apprehended together in one self-consciousness.

Understanding is, to use general terms, *the faculty of knowledge.* This knowledge consists in the determinate relation of given representations to an object; and an *object* is that in the concept of which the manifold of a given intuition is *united.* Now all unification of representations demands unity of consciousness in the synthesis of them. Consequently it is the unity of consciousness that alone constitutes the relation of representations to an object, and therefore their objective validity and the fact that they are modes of knowledge; and upon it therefore rests the very possibility of the understanding.

The first pure knowledge of understanding, then, upon which all the rest of its employment is based, and which also at the same time is completely independent of all conditions of sensible intuition, is the principle of the original *synthetic* unity of apperception. Thus the mere form of outer sensible intuition, space, is not yet [by itself] knowledge; it supplies only the manifold of *a priori* intuition for a possible knowledge. To know anything in space (for instance, a line), I must *draw* it, and thus synthetically bring into being a determinate combination of the given manifold, so that the unity of this act is at the same time the unity of consciousness (as in the concept of a line); and it is through this unity of consciousness that an object (a determinate space) is first known. The synthetic unity of consciousness is, therefore, an objective condition of all knowledge. It is not merely a condition that I myself require in knowing an object, but is a condition under which every intuition must stand in order *to become an object for me.* For otherwise, in the absence of this synthesis, the manifold would *not* be united in one consciousness.

Although this proposition makes synthetic unity a condition of all thought, it is, as already stated, itself analytic. For it says no more than that all *my* representations in any given intuition must be subject to that condition under which alone I can ascribe them to the identical self as *my* representations, and so can comprehend them as synthetically combined in one apperception through the general expression [*allgemeinen Ausdruck*], 'I think'.

This principle is not, however, to be taken as applying to every possible understanding, but only to that understanding through whose pure apperception, in the representation 'I am', nothing manifold is given. An understanding which through its self-consciousness could supply to itself the manifold of intuition – an understanding, that is to say, through whose representation the objects of the representation should at the same time exist – would not require, for the unity of

in the consciousness of that representation; and they are thus composite. The unity of that consciousness is therefore synthetic and yet is also original. The *singularity* of such intuitions is found to have important consequences (*vide* §25).

consciousness, a special act of synthesis of the manifold. For the human under-standing, however, which thinks only, and does not intuit, that act is necessary. It is indeed the first principle of the human understanding, and is so indispensable to it that we cannot form the least conception of any other possible understand-ing, either of such as is itself intuitive or of any that may possess an underly-ing mode of sensible intuition which is different in kind from that in space and time.

§18
The Objective Unity of Self-Consciousness

The transcendental unity of apperception is that unity through which all the mani-fold given in an intuition is united in a concept of the object. It is therefore entitled *objective*, and must be distinguished from the *subjective* unity of consciousness, which is a *determination* of *inner sense* – through which the manifold of intuition for such [objective] combination is empirically given. Whether I can become *empirically* conscious of the manifold as simultaneous or as successive depends on circum-stances or empirical conditions. Therefore the empirical unity of consciousness, through association of representations, itself concerns an appearance, and is wholly contingent. But the pure form of intuition in time, merely as intuition in general, which contains a given manifold, is subject to the original unity of consciousness, simply through the necessary relation of the manifold of the intuition to the one '*I think*', and so through the pure synthesis of understanding which is the *a priori* underlying ground of the empirical synthesis. Only the original unity is objectively valid; the empirical unity of apperception, upon which we are not here dwelling, and which besides is merely derived from the former under given conditions *in concreto*, has only subjective validity. To one man, for instance, a certain word suggests one thing, to another some other thing; the unity of consciousness in that which is empirical is not, as regards what is given, necessarily and universally valid.

§19
The Logical Form of all Judgments consists in the Objective Unity of the Apperception of the Concepts which they contain

I have never been able to accept the interpretation which logicians give of judgment in general. It is, they declare, the representation of a relation between two concepts. I do not here dispute with them as to what is defective in this interpretation – that in any case it applies only to *categorical*, not to hypothetical and disjunctive judgments (the two latter containing a relation not of concepts but of judgments), an oversight from which many troublesome consequences have followed.[6] I need only point out that the definition does not determine in what the asserted *relation* consists.

But if I investigate more precisely the relation of the given modes of knowledge [*Erkenntnisse*] in any judgment, and distinguish it, as belonging to the understanding, from the relation according to laws of the reproductive imagination, which has only subjective validity, I find that a judgment is nothing but the manner in which given modes of knowledge are brought to the objective unity of apperception. This is what is intended by the copula [*Verhältniswörtchen*] 'is'. It is employed to distinguish the objective unity of given representations from the subjective. It indicates their relation to original apperception, and its *necessary unity*. It holds good even if the judgment is itself empirical, and therefore contingent, as, for example, in the judgment, 'Bodies are heavy'. I do not here assert that these representations *necessarily* belong *to one another* in the empirical intuition, but that they belong to one another *in virtue of the necessary unity* of apperception in the synthesis of intuitions, that is, according to principles of the objective determination of all representations, in so far as knowledge can be acquired by means of these representations – principles which are all derived from the fundamental principle of the transcendental unity of apperception. Only in this way does there arise from this relation a *judgment*, that is, a relation which is *objectively valid*, and so can be adequately distinguished from a relation of the same representations that would have only subjective validity – as when they are connected according to laws of association. In the latter case, all that I could say would be, 'If I support a body, I feel an impression of weight'; I could not say, 'It, the body, is heavy'. Thus to say 'The body is heavy' is not merely to state that the two representations have always been conjoined in my perception, however often that perception be repeated; what we are asserting is that they are combined *in the object*, no matter what the state of the subject may be.

§20
All Sensible Intuitions are subject to the Categories, as Conditions under which alone their Manifold can come together in one Consciousness

The manifold given in a sensible intuition is necessarily subject to the original synthetic unity of apperception, because in no other way is the *unity* of intuition possible (§17). But that act of understanding by which the manifold of given

[6] The lengthy doctrine of the four syllogistic figures concerns categorical syllogisms only; and although it is indeed nothing more than an artificial method of securing, through the surreptitious introduction of immediate inferences (*consequentiae immediatae*) among the premises of a pure syllogism, the appearance that there are more kinds of inference than that of the first figure, this would hardly have met with such remarkable acceptance, had not its authors succeeded in bringing categorical judgments into such exclusive respect, as being those to which all others must allow of being reduced – teaching which, as indicated in §9, is none the less erroneous.

representations (be they intuitions or concepts) is brought under one apperception, is the logical function of judgment (cf. §19). All the manifold, therefore, so far as it is given in a single empirical intuition, is *determined* in respect of one of the logical functions of judgment, and is thereby brought into one consciousness. Now the *categories* are just these functions of judgment, in so far as they are employed in determination of the manifold of a given intuition (cf. §13). Consequently, the manifold in a given intuition is necessarily subject to the categories.

§21
Observation

A manifold, contained in an intuition which I call mine, is represented, by means of the synthesis of the understanding, as belonging to the *necessary* unity of self-consciousness; and this is effected by means of the category.[7] This [requirement of a] category therefore shows that the empirical consciousness of a given manifold in a single intuition is subject to a pure self-consciousness *a priori*, just as is empirical intuition to a pure sensible intuition, which likewise takes place *a priori*. Thus in the above proposition a beginning is made of a *deduction* of the pure concepts of understanding; and in this deduction, since the categories have their source in the understanding alone, *independently of sensibility*, I must abstract from the mode in which the manifold for an empirical intuition is given, and must direct attention solely to the unity which, in terms of the category, and by means of the understanding, enters into the intuition. In what follows (cf. §26) it will be shown, from the mode in which the empirical intuition is given in sensibility, that its unity is no other than that which the category (according to §20) prescribes to the manifold of a given intuition in general. Only thus, by demonstration of the *a priori* validity of the categories in respect of all objects of our senses, will the purpose of the deduction be fully attained.

But in the above proof there is one feature from which I could not abstract, the feature, namely, that the manifold to be intuited must be given prior to the synthesis of understanding, and independently of it. How this takes place, remains here undetermined. For were I to think an understanding which is itself intuitive (as, for example, a divine understanding which should not represent to itself given objects, but through whose representation the objects should themselves be given or produced), the categories would have no meaning whatsoever in respect of such a mode of knowledge. They are merely rules for an understanding whose whole power consists in thought, consists, that is, in the act whereby it brings the synthesis of a manifold, given to it from elsewhere in intuition, to the unity of apperception – a faculty, therefore, which by itself knows nothing whatsoever, but

---

[7] The proof of this rests on the represented *unity of intuition*, by which an object is given. This unity of intuition always includes in itself a synthesis of the manifold given for an intuition, and so already contains the relation of this manifold to the unity of apperception.

merely combines and arranges the material of knowledge, that is, the intuition, which must be given to it by the object. This peculiarity of our understanding, that it can produce *a priori* unity of apperception solely by means of the categories, and only by such and so many, is as little capable of further explanation as why we have just these and no other functions of judgment, or why space and time are the only forms of our possible intuition.

Translated by Norman Kemp Smith

2.

Johann Gottlieb Fichte, Science of Knowledge
(Versuch einer neuen Darstellung der
Wissenschaftslehre) : *First Introduction (1797)*

Fichte's *Wissenschaftslehre* of 1794 – the *Science of Knowledge* as it is usually translated – is a seminal text in the history of German Idealist thought.
It is a comprehensive effort to bring together two aspects of selfhood
which had, in Fichte's view, been sundered without systematic justification in Kant's philosophy: namely, the theoretical and practical aspects of
selfhood (the 'I think' of the Transcendental Deduction of the *Critique of
Pure Reason* and the moral self of the *Critique of Practical Reason* and other
works on freedom and morality respectively).

Fichte had unshakable confidence that the *Wissenschaftslehre* had rigorously achieved just that reconciliation of subjectivity, but was greatly troubled by what he perceived as his readers' reluctance to acknowledge the
validity of his conclusions. Over a period of years he added introductions to
the *Wissenschaftslehre*, and wrote supporting articles, eventually redrafting
the book in an effort to bring ever greater intelligibility to his ideas. We can
get a vivid picture of Fichte's frustration with his readership from the im-
ploring title of an 1801 work, 'A Crystal Clear Report to the General Public
Concerning the Actual Essence of the Newest Philosophy: An Attempt to
Force the Reader to Understand'.

The *Wissenschaftslehre* might not have succeeded in being recognised as
the new critical philosophy – as its author seemed to hope it would be – but
it did unquestionably stimulate new ways of thinking about the directions
in which Kant's philosophy might be taken. The *Wissenschaftslehre* covers
more exhaustively the themes that we can see in Schelling's 'Of the I as
Principle of Philosophy'. It makes similarly daring claims on behalf of the
subject as the ground of all experience, supporting these claims with radical
theories of the unique character of the 'I'. It is in the *Wissenschaftslehre*
that Fichte announces his term for the absolute 'I', the *Tathandlung* (the
complex notion literally, of a 'deed-action', which attempts to avoid the
sense of an entity or object that acts). The *Tathandlung* expresses the unique
characteristic of the 'I' – one not shared by any other aspect of reality – as
that of pure activity.

Fichte proclaimed himself a Kantian (though Kant rather publicly dis-
associated himself from Fichte's philosophy) but he did not always feel

constrained to theorise within the framework set out by Kant, rejecting, at times, some of what seemed to the carefully established conclusions of the critical philosophy. To be a Kantian meant, for him, taking what was 'true' in Kant – namely, the idea that the 'I' gives shape and form to the physical and moral world (the *Wissenschaftslehre* was to be an argument for an idealist theory of realism, as opposed to a materialist theory of realism) – and isolating it from other apparently less progressive ideas contained in the critical philosophy.

Fichte starts with the thesis that in our ordinary experience subject and object are united. But if we want to give a philosophical account of experience we have to abstract from experience, in the sense of seeking the principles which underpin it. For Fichte that means selecting either the subject or the object as the ground of experience. (This strategy is paralleled in Schelling's 'Of the I'.) If we opt for idealism, then we must explain our experience of external 'real' objects – those representations which are accompanied by the feeling of necessity, as Fichte put it – from within the intellect: the intellect must somehow give itself the feeling of necessity for those representations. (Later in the *Wissenschaftslehre* Fichte describes this activity of the intellect as 'positing'.) The feeling of necessity is that component of experience over which, in our ordinary empirical existences, we *feel* we have no control (the existence of certain laws being pre-eminent amongst them). If we opt for materialism – polemically labelled 'dogmatism' by Fichte on account of its unprovable first principle – we will argue that the object is responsible for the feeling of necessity which accompanies those representations. Fichte contends that the object, which is the alleged ground of experience in dogmatism, is a mere fabrication: it is the 'invention' of philosophy. Why? Because it supposedly lies behind all experience, and if it lies beyond all experience it is unknowable – a thing-in-itself apart from all knowledge – and hence is a dogmatic assertion. If it is a fabrication, then it cannot serve as the cause of our representations: our representations of 'outer objects' are accompanied by the feeling of necessity (that *I have to* think them), but a fabrication could not produce this feeling. The initially implausible idealist route becomes the preferred one simply by elimination of the only alternative Fichte is willing to conceive.

However, supporting concepts are offered. If idealism is true, there must be an aspect of 'self' which is free of the empirical world (otherwise it could not shape or determine the empirical world). This 'I' must therefore be 'presupposed' in all experience (derived clearly enough from the Kantian 'I think' which must accompany all representations.) And it is on this ground – on the 'I' – that Fichte wants positively to build the programme of idealism. But this 'I' is never available for observation: as it is activity, and not entity, it is known to us only through our free and rational actions.

One must always bear in mind, when examining Fichte's critiques, that he has also what we might term a romantic criterion of successful argument. In effect, the value of a system is for him as important as its coherence or rationality. The value that lies behind any philosophical position – what it is trying to say about the fundamentals of the human condition – is the most basic issue in that philosophy. The effect of this, however, is to introduce a curious relativism to philosophical disputes: a position is not defended simply in terms of its rationality, but also in terms of the values it embodies. And how we consider the values that a system embodies is a personal matter: they are relative to the person who considers them. Reason – understood as a mechanism of argument – cannot make the decision: 'the decision is determined by *inclination* and *interest'*.

Fichte believed that the *Wissenschaftslehre* had validated a set of fundamental concepts by means of which he might investigate further areas of human experience. This is particularly evident in the works published around the time of the *Wissenschaftslehre* itself: *The Foundation of Natural Right according to the Principles of the Wissenschaftslehre* (1796) and *The System of Ethics according to the Principles of the Wissenschaftslehre* (1798) (extracts from both of which are included in this Anthology).

FIRST INTRODUCTION TO THE SCIENCE OF KNOWLEDGE[†]

Prefatory Note

De re, quae agitur, petimus, ut homines, eam non opinionem sed opus esse, cogitent, ac pro certo habeant, non sectae nos alicujus, aut placiti, sed utilitatis et amplitudinis humanae fundamenta moliri. Deinde, ut suis commodis aequi, in commune consulant, et ipsi in partem veniant.

Baco de Verulamio

On a modest acquaintance with the philosophical literature since the appearance of the Kantian *Critiques* I soon came to the conclusion that the enterprise of this great man, the radical revision of our current conceptions of philosophy, and hence of all science, has been a complete failure; since not a single one of his numerous followers perceives what is really being said. Believing that I did, I decided to dedicate my life to a presentation, quite independent of Kant, of that great discovery, and will not relent in this determination. Whether I shall have greater success in making myself intelligible to my own generation, only time will tell. In any case, I know that nothing true or useful is lost again once it has entered the world of men; even if only a remote posterity may know how to use it.

[†]*FW* I, 419–449. *Science of Knowledge* (Cambridge: Cambridge University Press, 1982).

In pursuit of my academic duties, I at first wrote for my students in the classroom, where I had it in my power to continue with verbal explanations until I was understood.

> . . . in behalf of the matter which is in hand I entreat men to believe that it is not an opinion to be held, but a work to be done; and to be well assured that I am laboring to lay the foundation, not of any sect or doctrine, but of human utility and power. Next I ask that they fairly consult their common advantage, . . . and themselves participate in the remaining labors . . .
>
> Francis Bacon, *The Great Instauration*, Preface.

I need not here attest how many reasons I have for being satisfied with my students and for entertaining of very many of them the highest hopes for science. The manuscript in question also became known outside the university, and there are numerous ideas about it among the learned. Except from my students, I have neither read nor heard a judgment in which there was even a pretense of argument, but plenty of derision, abuse, and general evidence that people are passionately opposed to this theory, and also that they do not understand it. As to the latter, I take full responsibility for it, until people have become familiar with the content of my system in a different form and may find perchance that the exposition there is not, after all, so wholly unclear; or I shall assume the responsibility unconditionally and forever if this may incline the reader to study the present account, in which I shall endeavor to achieve the utmost clarity. I shall continue this exposition until I am convinced that I am writing wholly in vain. But I do write in vain, if no one examines my arguments.

I still owe the reader the following reminders. I have long asserted, and repeat once more, that my system is nothing other than the *Kantian*; this means that it contains the same view of things, but is in method quite independent of the *Kantian* presentation. I have said this not to hide behind a great authority, nor to seek an external support for my teaching, but to speak the truth and to be just.

After some twenty years it should be possible to prove this. Except for a recent suggestion, of which more anon, Kant is to this day a closed book, and what people have read into him is precisely what will not fit there, and what he wished to refute.

My writings seek neither to explain *Kant* nor to be explained by him; they must stand on their own, and *Kant* does not come into it at all. My aim – to express it directly – is not the correction and completion of the philosophical concepts now in circulation, whether anti-Kantian or Kantian; it is rather the total eradication and complete reversal of current modes of thought on these topics, so that in all seriousness, and not only in a manner of speaking, the object shall be posited and determined by the cognitive faculty, and not the cognitive faculty by the object. My system can therefore be examined on its own basis alone, not on the presuppositions of some other philosophy; it is to agree only with itself, it can be explained, proved, or refuted in its own terms alone; one must accept or reject it as a whole.

'If this system were true, certain propositions cannot hold' gets no reply from me: for I certainly do not consider that anything should hold, if this system contradicts it.

'I do not understand this work' means nothing more to me than just that; and I consider such an admission most uninteresting and uninstructive. My writings cannot be understood, and ought not to be understood by those who have not studied them; for they do not contain the repetition of a lesson already learned beforehand, but, since *Kant* has not been understood, something that is quite new in our day.

Unreasoned disparagement tells me no more than that this theory is not liked, and such an avowal is also extremely unimportant; the question is not whether it pleases you or not, but whether it has been demonstrated. In order to assist the testing of its foundations, I shall add indications throughout this exposition as to where the system needs to be attacked. I write only for those who still retain an inner feeling for the certainty or dubiousness, the clarity or confusion of their knowledge, to whom science and conviction matter, and who are driven by a burning zeal to seek them. I have nothing to do with those who, through protracted spiritual slavery, have lost themselves and with themselves their sense of private conviction, and their belief in the conviction of others; to whom it is folly for anyone to seek independently for truth; who see nothing more in the sciences than a comfortable way of earning a living, and who shrink back from any extension of knowledge, as from a new burden of work; to whom no means are shameful to suppress the destroyer of their trade.

I would be sorry if they understood me. Until now it has gone according to my wishes with these people; and I hope even now that this exordium will so bewilder them that from now on they see nothing but letters on the page, while what passes for mind in them is torn hither and thither by the caged anger within.

Introduction

1

Attend to yourself: turn your attention away from everything that surrounds you and towards your inner life; this is the first demand that philosophy makes of its disciple. Our concern is not with anything that lies outside you, but only with yourself.

Even the most cursory introspection will reveal to anyone a remarkable difference between the various immediate modifications of his consciousness, or what we may also call his presentations (*Vorstellungen*). Some of them appear to us as completely dependent on our freedom, but it is impossible for us to believe that there is anything answering to them outside us, independently of our activity. Our imagination and will appear to us to be free. Others of our presentations we refer to a reality which we take to be established independently of us, as to their model;

and we find ourselves limited in determining these presentations by the condition that they must correspond to this reality. In regard to the content of cognition, we do not consider ourselves free. In brief, we may say that some of our presentations are accompanied by the feeling of freedom, others by the feeling of necessity.

The question, 'Why are the presentations which depend on freedom determined precisely as they are, and not otherwise?' cannot reasonably arise, because in postulating that they depend on freedom all application of the concept of 'wherefore' is rejected; they are so because I have so determined them, and if I had determined them otherwise, they would be otherwise.

But the question, 'What is the source of the system of presentations which are accompanied by the feeling of necessity, and of this feeling of necessity itself?' is one that is surely worthy of reflection. It is the task of philosophy to provide an answer to this question, and in my opinion nothing is philosophy save the science which performs this task. The system of presentations accompanied by the feeling of necessity is also called *experience*, both internal and external. Philosophy, in other words, must therefore furnish the ground of all experience.

Only three objections may be brought against the above. A person might deny that presentations occur in consciousness which are accompanied by the feeling of necessity and referred to a reality which is taken to be determined without our assistance. Such a person would either deny against his better knowledge or be differently constituted from other people; if so, there would actually be nothing there for him to deny, and no denial, and we could disregard his objection without further ado. Secondly, someone might say that the question thus raised is completely unanswerable, for we are, and must remain, in insurmountable ignorance on this issue. It is quite unnecessary to discuss arguments and counterarguments with such a person. He is best refuted by providing the actual answer to the question, and then nothing remains for him to do but to examine our attempt and to indicate where and why it does not appear to him sufficient. Finally, someone might lay claim to the name and maintain that philosophy is entirely different from what has been indicated, or that it is something over and above this. It would be easy to show him that precisely what I have set forth has from the earliest been considered to be philosophy by all competent exponents, that everything he might wish to pass off as such has a different name already, and that if this word is to designate anything specific, it must designate precisely this science.

However, since we are not inclined to engage in this essentially fruitless controversy about a word, we have ourselves long ago surrendered this name and called the science which is expressly committed to solving the problem indicated, *the Science of Knowledge*.

2

One can ask for a reason only in the case of something judged to be contingent, viz., where it is assumed that it could also have been otherwise, and yet is not a matter of determination through freedom; and it is precisely the fact that he inquires as to its ground that makes it, for the inquirer, contingent. The task of seeking the ground of something contingent means: to exhibit some other thing whose properties reveal why, of all the manifold determinations that the explicandum might have had, it actually has just those that it does. By virtue of its mere notion, the ground falls outside what it grounds; both ground and grounded are, as such, opposed and yet linked to each other, so that the former explains the latter.

Now philosophy must discover the ground of all experience; thus its object necessarily lies outside all experience. This proposition holds good of all philosophy, and really did hold universally until the time of the Kantians and their facts of consciousness, and thus of inner experience.

There can be no objection at all to the proposition here established: for the premise of our argument is the mere analysis of our proposed concept of philosophy, and it is from this that our conclusion follows. Should someone say perhaps that the concept of ground ought to be explained in some other way, we certainly cannot prevent him from thinking what he likes in using this expression: however, it is our right to declare that under the above description of philosophy *we* wish nothing to be understood beyond what has been said. If this meaning be not accepted, the possibility of philosophy in our sense would accordingly have to be denied; and we have already attended to that alternative above.

3

A finite rational being has nothing beyond experience; it is this that comprises the entire staple of his thought. The philosopher is necessarily in the same position; it seems, therefore, incomprehensible how he could raise himself above experience.

But he is able to abstract; that is, he can separate what is conjoined in experience through the freedom of thought. *The thing*, which must be determined independently of our freedom and to which our knowledge must conform, and *the intelligence*, which must know, are in experience inseparably connected. The philosopher can leave one of the two out of consideration, and he has then abstracted from experience and raised himself above it. If he leaves out the former, he retains an intelligence in itself, that is, abstracted from its relation to experience, as a basis for explaining experience; if he leaves out the latter, he retains a thing-in-itself, that is, abstracted from the fact that it occurs in experience, as a similar basis of explanation. The first method of procedure is called *idealism*, the second *dogmatism*.

The present discussion should have convinced anyone that these two are the only philosophical systems possible. According to the former system, the presentations accompanied by the feeling of necessity are products of the intelligence which must be presupposed in their explanation; according to the latter, they are products of a thing-in-itself which must be assumed to precede them.

Should someone wish to deny this proposition, he would have to prove either that there is a way, other than that of abstraction, by which to rise above experience, or that the consciousness of experience consists of more constituents than the two mentioned.

Now in regard to the first system, it will indeed become clear later on that what is to rank as intelligence is not something produced merely by abstraction, but under a different predicate really has its place in consciousness; it will nonetheless emerge, however, that the consciousness thereof is conditioned by an abstraction, of a kind that is, of course, natural to man.

It is not at all denied that a person might fuse together a whole from fragments of these heterogeneous systems, or that idle work of this nature has in fact very often been done: but it is denied that, given a consistent procedure, there are any other systems possible besides these two.

4

Between the objects − we shall call the explanatory ground of experience that a philosophy establishes *the object of that philosophy*, since only through and for the latter does it appear to exist − between the object of *idealism* and that of *dogmatism*, there is, in respect of their relation to consciousness in general, a remarkable difference. Everything of which I am conscious is an object of consciousness. Such an object may stand in three relations to the subject. The object appears either as having first been created by the presentation of the intellect, or as existing without the aid of the intellect; and, in the latter case, either as determined in its nature, as well, or as present merely in its existence, while its essence is determinable by the free intellect.

The first relation amounts to a mere inventing, with or without an aim, the second to an object of experience, the third to a single object only, as we shall demonstrate forthwith.

I can freely determine myself to think this or that; for example, the thing-in-itself of the dogmatic philosophers. If I now abstract from what is thought and observe only myself, I become to myself in this object the content of a specific presentation. That I appear to myself to be determined precisely so and not otherwise, as thinking, and as thinking, of all possible thoughts, the thing-in-itself, should in my opinion depend on my self-determination: I have freely made myself into such an object. But I have not made myself as it is in itself; on the contrary, I am compelled to presuppose myself as that which is to be determined by self-determination. I myself, however, am an object for myself whose nature depends, under certain conditions, on the intellect alone, but whose existence must always be presupposed.

Now the object of idealism is precisely this self-in-itself.[1] The object of this system, therefore, actually occurs as something real in consciousness, not as a *thing-in-itself*, whereby idealism would cease to be what it is and would transform itself into dogmatism, but as a *self-in-itself*; not as an object of experience, for it is not determined but will only be determined by me, and without this determination

---

[1] I have avoided this expression until now, in order not to engender the idea of a self as a *thing*-in-itself. My caution was in vain: for this reason I now abandon it, for I do not see whom I should need to protect.

is nothing, and does not even exist; but as something that is raised above all experience.

By contrast, the object of dogmatism belongs to those of the first group, which are produced solely by free thought; the thing-in-itself is a pure invention and has no reality whatever. It does not occur in experience: for the system of experience is nothing other than thinking accompanied by the feeling of necessity, and not even the dogmatist, who like any other philosopher must exhibit its ground, can pass it off as anything else. The dogmatist wants, indeed, to assure to that thing reality, that is, the necessity of being thought as the ground of all experience, and will do it if he proves that experience can really be explained by means of it, and cannot be explained without it; but that is the very question at issue, and what has to be proved should not be presupposed.

Thus the object of idealism has this advantage over the object of dogmatism, that it may be demonstrated, not as the ground of the explanation of experience, which would be contradictory and would turn this system itself into a part of experience, but still in general in consciousness; whereas the latter object cannot be looked upon as anything other than a pure invention, which expects its conversion into reality only from the success of the system.

This is adduced only to promote clear insight into the differences between the two systems, and not in order to infer from it something against dogmatism. That the object of every philosophy, as the ground of the explanation of experience, must lie outside experience, is demanded simply by the nature of philosophy, and is far from proving a disadvantage to a system. We have not as yet found the reasons why this object should furthermore occur in a special manner in consciousness.

Should somebody be unable to convince himself of what has just been asserted, then, since this is only a passing remark, his conviction as to the whole is not yet made impossible thereby. Nevertheless, in accordance with my plan, I shall consider possible objections even here. One could deny the claim that there is immediate self-consciousness involved in a free action of the spirit. We would only have to remind such a person once more of the conditions of self-consciousness we have detailed. This self-consciousness does not force itself into being and is not its own source; one must really act freely and then abstract from objects and concentrate only upon oneself. No one can be compelled to do this, and even if he pretends to, one can never know if he proceeds correctly and in the requisite way. In a word, this consciousness cannot be demonstrated to anyone; each person must freely create it in himself. One could only object to the second assertion, viz., that the thing-in-itself is a sheer invention, by reason of having misunderstood it. We would refer such a person to the above description of the origin of this concept.

5

Neither of these two systems can directly refute its opposite, for their quarrel is about the first principle, which admits of no derivation from anything beyond it; each of the two, if only its first principle is granted, refutes that of the other; each denies everything in its opposite, and they have no point at all in common from which they could arrive at mutual understanding and unity. Even if they appear to agree about the words in a sentence, each takes them in a different sense.[2]

First of all, idealism cannot refute dogmatism. As we have seen, the former, indeed, has this advantage over the latter, that it is able to exhibit the presence in consciousness of the freely acting intellect, which is the basis of its explanation of experience. This fact, as such, even the dogmatist must concede, for otherwise he disqualifies himself from any further discussion with the idealist; but through a valid inference from his principle he converts it into appearance and illusion, and thereby renders it unfit to serve as an explanation of anything else, since in his philosophy it cannot even validate itself. According to him, everything that appears in our consciousness, along with our presumed determinations through freedom and the very belief that we are free, is the product of a thing-in-itself. This latter belief is evoked in us by the operation of the thing, and the determinations which we deduce from our freedom are brought about by the same cause: but this we do not know, and hence we attribute them to no cause, and thus to freedom. Every consistent dogmatist is necessarily a fatalist: he does not deny the fact of consciousness that we consider ourselves free, for that would be contrary to reason; but he demonstrates, on the basis of his principle, the falsity of this belief. – He completely denies the independence of the self upon which the idealist relies, and construes the self merely as a product of things, an accident of the world; the consistent dogmatist is necessarily also a materialist. He could be refuted only on the basis of the postulate of the freedom and independence of the self; but it is precisely this that he denies.

The dogmatist is no less incapable of refuting the idealist.

The thing-in-itself, which is the fundamental principle of the dogmatist, is nothing and has no reality, as even its exponents must concede, apart from what it is alleged to acquire through the circumstance that experience can be explained only on its basis. The idealist destroys this proof by explaining experience in another way: thus he denies precisely what the dogmatist relies on. The thing-in-itself becomes completely chimerical; there no longer appears to be any reason at all to assume one; and with this the entire edifice of dogmatism collapses.

From what has been said the absolute incompatibility of the two systems appears at once, in that what follows from one of them annihilates the conclusions of

---

[2] This is why *Kant* has not been understood and the Science of Knowledge has not found favor and is not soon likely to do so. The Kantian system and the Science of Knowledge are, not in the usual vague sense of the word, but in the precise sense just specified, idealistic; the modern philosophers, however, are one and all *dogmatists*, and firmly determined to remain so. *Kant* has been tolerated only because it was possible to make him into a dogmatist; the Science of Knowledge, which does not admit of such a transformation, is necessarily intolerable to these sages. The rapid diffusion of *Kantian* philosophy, once understood – as best it has been – is a proof not of the profundity, but of the shallowness of the age. In part, in its current form, it is the most fantastic abortion that has ever been produced by the human imagination, and it reflects little credit on the perspicacity of its defenders that they do not recognize this: in part, it is easy to prove that it has recommended itself only because people have thereby thought to rid themselves of all serious speculation and to provide themselves with a royal charter to go on cultivating their beloved, superficial empiricism.

the other; hence their fusion necessarily leads to inconsistency. Wherever it is attempted, the parts do not mesh, and at some juncture an immense hiatus ensues. Whoever would wish to take issue with what has just been asserted would have to demonstrate the possibility of such a combination, which presupposes a continued passage from matter to spirit or its reverse, or what is the same, a continued passage from necessity to freedom.

So far as we can yet see, from the speculative point of view the two systems appear to be of equal value: they cannot coexist, but neither one can make any headway against the other. In this light, it is interesting to ask what might motivate the person who sees this – and it is easy enough to see – to prefer one of the systems over the other, and how it is that skepticism, as the total surrender of the attempt to solve the problem presented, does not become universal.

The dispute between the idealist and the dogmatist is, in reality, about whether the independence of the thing should be sacrificed to the independence of the self or, conversely, the independence of the self to that of the thing. What is it, then, that motivates a reasonable man to declare his preference for one over the other?

From the given vantage point, which a person must necessarily adopt if he is to be counted a philosopher, and to which one comes sooner or later, even without meaning to, in the course of reflection, the philosopher finds nothing but *that he must present himself as free* and that there are determinate things outside him. It is impossible for a person to rest content with this thought; the thought of a mere presentation is only a half-thought, the fragment of a thought; something must be superadded which corresponds to the presentation independently of the presenting. In other words, the presentation cannot exist for itself alone: it is something only when conjoined with something else, and for itself it is nothing. It is precisely this necessity of thought which drives us on from that standpoint to the question, 'What is the ground of presentations?' or, what comes to the very same, 'What is it that corresponds thereto?'

Now the presentation of the independence of the self, and that of the thing, can assuredly coexist, but not the independence of both. Only one of them can be the first, the initiatory, the independent one: the second, by virtue of being second, necessarily becomes dependent on the first, with which it is to be conjoined.

Now which of the two should be taken as primary? Reason provides no principle of choice; for we deal here not with the addition of a link in the chain of reasoning, which is all that rational grounds extend to, but with the beginning of the whole chain, which, as an absolutely primary act, depends solely upon the freedom of thought. Hence the choice is governed by caprice, and since even a capricious decision must have some source, it is governed by *inclination* and *interest*. The ultimate basis of the difference between idealists and dogmatists is thus the difference of their interests.

The highest interest and the ground of all others is self-interest. This is also true of the philosopher. The desire not to lose, but to maintain and assert himself in the rational process, is the interest which invisibly governs all his thought. Now there are two levels of humanity, and before the second level is reached by everyone in the progress of our species, two major types of man. Some, who have not yet raised themselves to full consciousness of their freedom and absolute independence, find themselves only in the presentation of things; they have only that dispersed self-consciousness which attaches to objects, and has to be gleaned from their multiplicity. Their image is reflected back at them only by things, as by a mirror; if these were taken from them, their self would be lost as well; for the sake of their self they cannot give up the belief in the independence of things, for they themselves exist only if things do. Everything they are, they have really become through the external world. Whoever is in fact a product of things, will never see himself as anything else; and he will be right so long as he speaks only of himself and of others like him. The principle of the dogmatists is belief in things for the sake of the self: indirect belief, therefore, in their own scattered self sustained only by objects.

The man who becomes conscious of his self-sufficiency and independence of everything that is outside himself, however — and this can be achieved only by making oneself into something independently of everything else — does not need things for the support of himself, and cannot use them, because they destroy that self-sufficiency, and convert it into mere appearance. The self which he possesses, and which is the subject of his interest, annuls this belief in things; he believes in his independence out of inclination, he embraces it with feeling. His belief in himself is direct.

This interest also explains the emotions which usually enter into the defense of philosophical systems. The attack on his system in fact exposes the dogmatist to the danger of losing his self; yet he is not armed against this attack, because there is something within him that sides with the attacker; hence he defends himself with passion and animosity. By contrast, the idealist cannot readily refrain from regarding the dogmatist with a certain contempt, for the latter can tell him nothing save what he has long since known and already discarded as erroneous; for one reaches idealism, if not through dogmatism itself, at least through the inclination thereto. The dogmatist flies into a passion, distorts, and would persecute if he had the power: the idealist is cool and in danger of deriding the dogmatist.

What sort of philosophy one chooses depends, therefore, on what sort of man one is; for a philosophical system is not a dead piece of furniture that we can reject or accept as we wish; it is rather a thing animated by the soul of the person who holds it. A person indolent by nature or dulled and distorted by mental servitude, learned luxury, and vanity will never raise himself to the level of idealism.

We can show the dogmatist the inadequacy and incoherence of his system, of which we shall speak in a moment: we can bewilder and harass him from all sides; but we cannot convince him, because he is incapable of calmly receiving and coolly assessing a theory which he absolutely cannot endure. If idealism should prove to be the only true philosophy, it is necessary to be born, raised, and self-educated as a philosopher: but one cannot be made so by human contrivance. Our science expects few converts, therefore, among those *already formed*; if it may have any hopes at all, they are set, rather, upon the young whose innate power has not yet foundered in the indolence of our age.

6

But dogmatism is completely unable to explain what it must, and this demonstrates its untenability.

It must explain the fact of presentation, and undertakes to render it intelligible on the basis of the influence of the thing-in-itself. Now it must not deny what our immediate consciousness tells us about presentation. – What, then, does it say about presentation? It is not my intention here to conceptualize what can only be intuited internally, nor to treat exhaustively of that to whose discussion a large part of the Science of Knowledge is dedicated. I merely wish to recall what everybody who has taken just one good look into himself must have discovered long ago.

The intellect as such *observes itself*; and this self-observation is directed immediately upon its every feature. The nature of intelligence consists in this *immediate unity of being and seeing*. What is in it, and what it is in general, it is *for itself*; and it is that, *qua* intellect, only in so far as it is that for itself. I think of this or that object: what, then, does this involve, and how, then, do I appear to myself in this thinking? In no other way than this: when the object is a merely imaginary one, I create certain determinations in myself; when the object is to be something real, these determinations are present without my aid: *and I observe that creation and this being.* They are in me only in so far as I observe them: seeing and being are inseparably united. – A thing, to be sure, is supposed to have a diversity of features, but as soon as the question arises: '*For whom*, then, is it to have them?' no one who understands the words will answer: 'For itself'; for we must still subjoin in thought an intellect *for* which it exists. The intellect is, by contrast, necessarily what it is for itself, and requires nothing subjoined to it in thought. By being posited as intellect, that for which it exists is already posited with it. In the intellect, therefore – to speak figuratively – there is a double series, of being and of seeing, of the real and of the ideal; and its essence consists in the inseparability of these two (it is synthetic); while the thing has only a single series, that of the real (a mere being posited). Intellect and thing are thus exact opposites: they inhabit two worlds between which there is no bridge.

It is by the principle of causality that dogmatism wishes to explain this constitution of intellect in general, as well as its particular determinations: it is to be an effect and the second member in the series.

But the principle of causality holds of a single *real* series, not of a double one. The power of the cause is transferred to something else that lies outside it, opposed to it, and creates a being therein and nothing more; a being for a possible intellect outside it and not for the being itself. If you endow the object acted upon with mechanical power only, it will transfer the received impulse to its neighbor, and thus the motion originating in the first member may proceed through a whole series, however long you wish to make it; but nowhere in it will you find a member which reacts upon itself. Or if you endow the object acted upon with the highest quality you can give to a thing, that of sensitivity, so that it governs itself on its own account and in accordance with the laws of its own nature, not according to the law given it by its cause, as in the series of mere mechanism, then it certainly reacts back upon the stimulus, and the determining ground of its being in this action lies not in the cause, but only in the requirement to be something at all; yet it is and remains a bare, simple being: a being for a possible intellect outside of itself. You cannot lay hold of the intellect if you do not subjoin it in thought as a *primary absolute*, whose connection with that being independent of it may be difficult for you to explain. – The series is simple, and after your explanation it remains so, and what was to be explained is not explained at all. The dogmatists were supposed to demonstrate the passage from being to presentation; this they do not, and cannot, do; for their principle contains only the ground of a being, but not that of presentation, which is the exact opposite of being. They take an enormous leap into a world quite alien to their principle.

They seek to conceal this leap in a variety of ways. Strictly – and that is the procedure of consistent dogmatism, which becomes materialism at once – the soul should not be a thing at all, and should be nothing whatever but a product, simply the result of the interaction of things among themselves.

But by this means there arises something in the things only, and never anything apart from them, unless an intellect, which observes things, is supplied in thought. The analogies the dogmatists present to make their system intelligible – that of harmony, for example, which arises out of the concord of several instruments – actually make its irrationality apparent. The concord and the harmony are not in the instruments; they are only in the mind of the listener who unifies the manifold in himself; and unless such a listener is supplied, they are nothing at all.

And yet, who is to prevent the dogmatist from assuming a soul as one of the things-in-themselves? This would then belong among the postulates he assumes for the solution of the problem, and only so is the principle of the action of things on the soul applicable, for in materialism there is only an interaction among things whereby thought is supposed to be produced. In order to make the inconceivable thinkable, he has sought to postulate the active thing, or the soul, or both, to be such that through their action presentations could result. The *acting thing* was to be such that its actions could become presentations, much like *God* in *Berkeley's* system (which is a dogmatic, and not at all an idealistic one). This leaves us no better off; we understand only mechanical action, and it is absolutely impossible for us to think of any other; the above proposal, therefore, consists of mere words without any sense. Or again, the soul is to be such that every action upon it becomes a presentation. But with this we fare exactly as with the previous principle: we simply cannot understand it.

This is the course dogmatism takes everywhere and in every form in which it appears. In the immense hiatus left to it between things and presentations, it inserts some empty words instead of an explanation. To be sure, these words can be memorized and repeated, but nobody at all has ever had, nor ever will have, a thought connected to them. For if one tries to conceive distinctly *how* the above occurs, the whole notion vanishes in an empty froth.

Thus dogmatism can only repeat its principle, and then reiterate it under various guises; it can state it, and then state it again; but it cannot get from this to the explanandum, and deduce the latter. Yet philosophy consists precisely of this deduction. Hence dogmatism, even from the speculative viewpoint, is no philosophy at all, but merely an impotent claim and assurance. Idealism is left as the only possible philosophy.

What is here established has nothing to do with the objections of the reader, for there is absolutely nothing to be said against the latter; its concern is, rather, with the absolute incapacity of many to understand it. Nobody who even understands the words can deny that all causation is mechanical and that no presentation comes about through mechanism. But this is precisely where the difficulty lies. A grasp of the nature of intelligence as depicted, upon which our entire refutation of dogmatism is founded, presupposes a degree of independence and freedom of mind. Now many people have progressed no further in their thinking than to grasp the simple sequence of the mechanism of nature; so it is very natural that presentations, if they wish to think of them, should also fall for them in this series, the only one that has entered their minds. The presentation becomes for them a kind of thing: a singular confusion, of which we find traces in the most famous of philosophical authors. Dogmatism is enough for such men; there is no hiatus for them, because for them the opposing world does not even exist. – Hence the dogmatist cannot be refuted by the argument we have given, however clear it may be; for it cannot be brought home to him, since he lacks the power to grasp its premise.

The manner in which we deal here with dogmatism also offends against the indulgent logic of our age, which, though uncommonly widespread in every period, has only in our own been raised to the level of a maxim expressed in words: one need not be so strict in reasoning, proofs are not to be taken so rigorously in philosophy as they are, say, in mathematics. Whenever thinkers, of this type observe even a couple of links in the chain of reasoning, and catch sight of the rule of inference, they at once supply the remainder pell-mell by imagination, without further investigation of what it consists of. If an Alexander perforce tells them: Everything is determined by natural necessity: our presentations are dependent upon the disposition of things and our will upon the nature of our presentations; hence all our volitions are determined by natural necessity and our belief in free will is an illusion; they find this wonderfully intelligible and clear, and go off convinced and amazed at the brilliance of this demonstration, in spite of the fact that there is no sense to it. I beg to observe that the Science of Knowledge neither proceeds from nor counts upon this indulgent logic. If even a single member of the long chain that it must establish be not rigorously joined to the next, it will have proved nothing whatever.

7

As already stated above, idealism explains the determinations of consciousness on the basis of the activity of the intellect. The intellect, for it, is only active and absolute, never passive; it is not passive because it is postulated to be first and highest, preceded by nothing which could account for a passivity therein. For the same reason, it also has no *being* proper, no subsistence, for this is the result of an interaction and there is nothing either present or assumed with which the intellect could be set to interact. The intellect, for idealism, is an *act*, and absolutely nothing more; we should not even call it an *active* something, for this expression refers to something subsistent in which activity inheres. But idealism has no reason to assume such a thing, since it is not included in its principle and everything else must first be deduced. Now out of the activity of this intellect we must deduce *specific* presentations: of a world, of a material, spatially located world existing without our aid, etc., which notoriously occur in consciousness. But a determinate cannot be deduced from an indeterminate: the grounding principle, which is the rule of all deduction, is inapplicable here. Hence this primordial action of the intellect must needs be a determinate one, and, since the intellect is itself the highest ground of explanation, an action determined by the intellect and its nature, and not by something outside it. The presupposition of idealism will, therefore, be as follows: the intellect acts, but owing to its nature, it can act only in a certain fashion. If we think of this necessary way of acting in abstraction from the action itself, we shall call it, most appropriately, the law of action: hence there are necessary laws of the intellect. – This, then, also renders immediately intelligible the feeling of necessity that accompanies specific presentations: for here the intellect does not register some external impression, but feels in this action the limits of its own being. So far as idealism makes this one and only rationally determined and genuinely explanatory assumption, that the intellect has necessary laws, it is called critical, or also transcendental idealism. A transcendent idealism would be a system that deduced determinate presentations from the free and totally lawless action of the intellect; a completely contradictory hypothesis, for surely, as has just been remarked, the principle of grounding is inapplicable to such an action.

As surely as they are to be grounded in the unitary being of the intellect, the intellect's assumed laws of operation themselves constitute a system. This means that the fact that the intellect operates in just such a way under this specific condition can be further explained by the fact that it has a definite mode of operation under a condition in general; and the latter in turn may be explained on the basis of a single fundamental law: the intellect gives its laws to itself in the course of its operation; and this legislation itself occurs through a higher necessary action, or presentation. The law of causality, for example, is not a primordial law, but is merely one of several ways of connecting the manifold, and can be deduced from the fundamental law of this connection: and the law of this connection of the manifold, along with the manifold itself, can again be deduced from higher laws.

In accordance with this remark, critical idealism itself can now proceed in two different ways. On the one hand, it may really deduce the system of the necessary modes of operation, and with it concurrently the objective presentations created thereby, from the fundamental laws of the intellect, and so allow the whole compass of our presentations to come gradually into being before the eyes of its readers or listeners. On the other hand, it may conceive these laws as already and immediately applied to objects, that is, as applied somewhere, upon their lowest level (at which stage they are called categories), and then maintain that it is by means of them that objects are ordered and determined.

Now how can the critical philosopher of the latter sort, who does not deduce the accepted laws of the intellect from the nature thereof, obtain even a mere material knowledge of them – the knowledge that they are precisely these, viz., the laws of substantiality and causality? For I will not yet burden him with the question of how he knows that they are mere immanent laws of the intellect. They are the laws that are applied directly to objects: and he can have formed them only by abstraction from these objects, and hence only from experience. It avails nothing if he borrows them in some roundabout way from logic; for logic itself has arisen for him no otherwise than by abstraction from objects, and he merely does indirectly what, if done directly, would too obviously catch our eyes. Hence he can in no way confirm that his postulated laws of thought are really laws of thought, really nothing but immanent laws of the intellect. The dogmatist maintains against him that they are universal properties of things grounded in the nature of the latter, and it is past seeing why we should give more credence to the unproved assertion of the one than to the unproved assertion of the other. – This method yields no knowledge that the intellect must act precisely thus, nor why it must do so. In order to promote such understanding, something would have to be set forth in the premises that is the unique possession of the intellect, and those laws of thought would have to be deduced from these premises before our very eyes.

It is especially difficult to see, how, according to this method, the object itself arises; for, even if we grant the critical philosopher his unproved postulate, it explains nothing beyond the *dispositions* and *relations* of the thing; that, for example, it is in space, that it manifests itself in time, that its accidents must be related to something substantial, and so on. But whence comes that which has these relations and dispositions; whence the stuff that is organized in these forms? It is in this stuff that dogmatism takes refuge, and you have merely made a bad situation worse.

We know well enough that the thing comes into being surely through an action in accord with these laws, that it is nothing else but the *totality of these relations unified by the imagination*, and that all these relations together constitute the thing; the object is surely the original synthesis of all these concepts. Form and matter are not separate items; the totality of form is the matter, and it is through analysis that we first obtain individual forms. But the critical philosopher who follows the present method can only assure us of this; and it is in fact a mystery how he knows it himself, if indeed he does. So long as the thing is not made to arise as a whole in front of the thinker's eyes, dogmatism is not hounded to its last refuge. But this is possible only by dealing with the intellect in its total, and not in its partial conformity to law.

Such an idealism is, therefore, unproved and unprovable. It has no other weapon against dogmatism save the assurance that it is right; and against the higher, perfected critical philosophy, nothing save impotent rage and the assertion that one can go no further, the assurance that beyond it there is no more ground, that from there one becomes unintelligible to *it*, and the like; all of which means nothing whatever.

Finally, in such a system only those laws are established whereby the purely subsumptive faculty of judgment determines the objects of external experience alone. But this is by far the smallest part of the system of reason. Since it lacks insight into the whole procedure of reason, this halfhearted critical philosophy gropes around in the sphere of practical reason and reflective judgment just as blindly as the mere imitator and copies out, just as artlessly, expressions totally unintelligible to it.[3]

In another place[4] I have already set forth in full clarity the methods of the perfected transcendental idealism established by the Science of Knowledge. I cannot explain how people could have failed to understand that exposition; at any rate, it is asserted that some have not understood it.

I am forced, therefore, to repeat what has been said before, and warn that in this science everything turns on the understanding thereof.

This idealism proceeds from a single fundamental principle of reason, which it demonstrates directly in consciousness. In so doing it proceeds as follows. It calls upon the listener or reader to think a certain concept freely; were he to do so, he would find himself obliged to proceed in a certain way. We must distinguish two things here: the required mode of thinking – this is accomplished through freedom, and whoever does not achieve it with us will see nothing of what the

[3] Such a critical idealism has been propounded by *Professor Beck* in his *Einzig möglichen Standpunkte.* . . . Although I find in this view the weaknesses objected to above, that should not deter me from the public expression of due respect to the man who, on his own account, has raised himself out of the confusion of our age to the insight that the philosophy of Kant is not a dogmatism but a transcendental idealism, and that, according to it, the object is given neither in whole nor in half, but is rather made; and from expecting that in time he will raise himself even higher. I consider the above work as the most suitable present that could have been made to our age, and recommend it as the best preparation for those who wish to study the Science of Knowledge from my writings. It does not lead to this latter system; but destroys the most powerful obstacle which closes it off for many people. – Some have fancied themselves insulted by the tone of that work, and just recently a well-meaning reviewer in a famous journal demands in clear terms: *crustula, elementa velit ut discere prima.* For my part, I find its tone, if anything, too mild: for I truly do not think that we should, of all things, thank certain writers for having confused and debased the richest and noblest teaching for a decade or more, nor see why we should first ask their permission to be right. – As regards the hastiness with which the same author, in another group, which is far below him, pounces upon books that his own conscience ought to tell him he does not understand, and cannot even rightly know how deep their matter may go, I can feel sorry only on his own account.

[4] In the work, *Über den Begriff der Wissenschaftslehre.* Weimar, 1794.

Science of Knowledge reveals – and the necessary manner in which it is to be accomplished, which latter is not dependent on the will, being grounded in the nature of the intellect; it is something *necessary*, which emerges, however, only in and upon the occurrence of a free action; something *found*, though its discovery is conditioned by freedom.

So far idealism demonstrates its claims in our immediate consciousness. But that the above necessity is the fundamental law of all reason, that from it one can deduce the whole system of our necessary presentations – not only of a world whose objects are determined by the subsuming and reflective judgment, but also of ourselves as free practical beings under laws – this is a mere hypothesis. Idealism must prove this hypothesis by an actual deduction, and this precisely is its proper task.

In so doing it proceeds in the following fashion. *It shows that what is first set up as fundamental principle and directly demonstrated in consciousness, is impossible unless something else occurs along with it, and that this something else is impossible unless a third something also takes place, and so on until the conditions of what was first exhibited are completely exhausted, and this latter is, with respect to its possibility, fully intelligible.* Its course is an unbroken progression from conditioned to condition; each condition becomes, in turn, a conditioned whose condition must be sought out.

If the hypothesis of idealism is correct and the reasoning in the deduction is valid, the system of all necessary presentations or the entirety of experience (this identity is established not in philosophy but only beyond it) must emerge as the final result, as the totality of the conditions of the original premise.

Now idealism does not keep this experience, as the antecedently known goal at which it must arrive, constantly in mind; in its method it knows nothing of experience and takes no account of it at all; it proceeds from its starting point in accordance with its rule, unconcerned about what will emerge in the end. It has been given the right angle from which to draw its straight line; does it then still need a point to draw it to? In my opinion, all the points on its line are given along with it. Suppose that you are given a certain number. You surmise it to be the product of certain factors. Your task then is simply to seek out, by the rule well known to you, the product of these factors. Whether or not it agrees with the given number will turn out later, once you have the product. The given number is the entirety of experience; the factors are the principle demonstrated in consciousness and the laws of thought; the multiplication is the activity of philosophizing. Those who advise you always to keep an eye on experience when you philosophize are recommending that you change the factors a bit and multiply falsely on occasion, so that the numbers you get may, after all, match: a procedure as dishonest as it is superficial.

To the extent that these final results of idealism are viewed as such, as consequences of reasoning, they constitute the a priori in the human mind; and to the extent that they are regarded, where reasoning and experience really agree, as given in experience, they are called a posteriori. For a completed idealism the a priori and the a posteriori are by no means twofold, but perfectly unitary; they are merely two points of view, to be distinguished solely by the mode of our approach. Philosophy anticipates the entirety of experience and *thinks* it only as necessary, and to that extent it is, by comparison with real experience, a priori. To the extent that it is regarded as given, the number is a posteriori; the same number is a priori insofar as it is derived as a product of the factors. Anyone who thinks otherwise, simply does not know what he is talking about.

A philosophy whose results do not agree with experience is surely false, for it has not fulfilled its promise to deduce the entirety of experience and to explain it on the basis of the necessary action of the intellect. Either the hypothesis of transcendental idealism is, therefore, completely false, or it has merely been wrongly handled in the particular version which fails to perform its task. Since the demand for an explanation of experience is surely founded in human reason; since no reasonable man will accept that reason can impose a demand whose satisfaction is absolutely impossible; since there are only two roads to its satisfaction, that of dogmatism and that of transcendental idealism, and it can be proved without further ado that the former cannot fulfill its promise; for these reasons, the resolute thinker will always prefer the latter, holding that the hypothesis as such is completely right and that error has occurred only in the reasoning; nor will any vain attempt deter him from trying again, until finally success is achieved.

The course of this idealism runs, as can be seen, from something that occurs in consciousness, albeit only as the result of a free act of thought, to the entirety of experience. What lies between these two is its proper field. This latter is not a fact of consciousness and does not lie within the compass of experience; how could anything that did so ever be called philosophy, when philosophy has to exhibit the ground of experience, and the ground lies necessarily outside of what it grounds. It is something brought forth by means of free but law-governed thought. – This will become entirely clear as soon as we take a closer look at the fundamental assertion of idealism.

The absolutely postulated is impossible, so idealism shows, without the condition of a second something, this second without a third, and so on; that is, of all that it establishes nothing is possible alone, and it is only in conjunction with them all that each individual item is possible. Hence, by its own admission, only the whole occurs in consciousness, and this totality is in fact experience. Idealism seeks a closer acquaintance with this whole, and so must analyze it, and this not by a blind groping, but according to the definite rule of composition, so that it may see the whole take form under its eyes. It can do this because it can abstract; because in free thought it is surely able to grasp the individual alone. For not only the necessity of presentations, but also their freedom is present in consciousness: and this freedom, again, can proceed either lawfully or capriciously. The whole is given to it from the standpoint of necessary consciousness; it discovers it, just as it discovers itself. The series created by the unification of this whole emerges only through freedom. Whoever performs this act of freedom will come to be aware of it, and lay out, as it were, a new field in his consciousness: for one who does not perform it, that which the act conditions does not exist at all. – The chemist synthesizes a body, say a certain metal, from its elements. The ordinary man sees the metal familiar to him; the chemist, the union of these specific elements. Do they then see different things? I should think not! They see the same thing, though in different ways. What the chemist sees is the a priori, for he sees the individual elements: what the common man sees is the a posteriori, for he sees the whole. – But there is this difference here: the chemist must first analyze the whole before he can compound it, since he is dealing with an object whose rule of composition he cannot know prior to the analysis; but the philosopher can synthesize without prior analysis, because he already knows the rule that governs his object, reason.

No reality other than that of necessary thought falls, therefore, within the compass of philosophy, given that one wishes to think about the ground of experience at all. Philosophy maintains that the intellect can be thought only as active, and active only in this particular way. This reality is completely adequate for it; since it follows from philosophy that there is in fact no other.

It is the complete critical idealism here described that the Science of Knowledge intends to establish. What has just been said contains the concept of this former, and I shall entertain no objections to it, for no one can know better than I what I propose to do. Proofs of the impossibility of a project that will be accomplished, and in part already is so, are simply ridiculous. One has only to attend to the course of the argument, and examine whether or not it fulfills its promise.

Translated by Peter Heath
and John Lachs

3.

F. W. J. Schelling, 'Of the I as the Principle of Philosophy'
('Vom Ich als Princip der Philosophie oder über das
Unbedingte im menschlichen Wissen') (1795)

It is often said of Schelling that he was one of those rare things in philosophy, a prodigy. Born in 1775 he had by 1794 published his first essay ('On the Possibility of a Form of Philosophy in General'). The following year 'Of the I as the Principle of Philosophy' appeared.

This early essay shows the marked influence of Fichte's 1794 development of the idealist explanation of knowledge and experience (in the *Wissenschaftslehre* or *Science of Knowledge*). The essay sets out the ambitious thesis that the 'I' – understood in a quite specific sense – is the ground of all possible experience. What Schelling wants to show eventually is that his account of the 'I' could support our basic belief in freedom of the will.

In key respects Schelling was sticking to the post-Kantian agenda which had been announced in a series of texts by K. L. Reinhold. As Frederick Beiser has pointed out, Reinhold drew up for philosophy the following requirements: (i) that philosophy be systematic, (ii) that it 'should begin with a single, self-evident first-principle', and (iii) that 'only a phenomenology can realize the ideal of a *prima philosophia*', that is, a philosophy which could act as the foundational discipline of all rational enquires must somehow be grounded in some immediate experience of consciousness.[1] It is interesting to note that Reinhold's work received a shattering critical response from G. E. Schulze (1792) (writing under the pseudonym *Aenesidemus*) in which Reinhold's – and indeed Kant's – claims for the constitutive role in experience of the faculty of representation as 'the cause and ground of the actual presence of representations' was rigorously rejected.[2] However, rather than deterring Fichte and Schelling from some appropriation of the 'critical' philosophy of Kant it appeared to drive them more deeply into a theory of subjectivity in the search for more defensible account of what might be seen as 'the cause and ground of the actual presence of representations'.

Schelling's main target in the 'I as the Principle of Philosophy' was, however, determinism, rather than Schulze, or any other opponent of the critical

---

[1] Frederick C. Beiser, *The Fate of Reason: German Philosophy from Kant to Fichte* (Cambridge, Ma/London: Harvard University Press, 1987), p. 228.
[2] G. E. Schulze, *Aenesidemus*, p. 107, in *Between Kant and Hegel: Texts in the Development of Post-Kantian Idealism* (Indianapolis: Hackett, 2000) edited by George di Giovanni and H. S. Harris.

philosophy. The most potent version of determinism had been presented by Spinoza through his theory that nature – including human beings – was a radically determinist mechanism. Spinoza's world was a place in which human spontaneity was alleged to be nothing more than an illusion. He put it famously this way:

> Further conceive, I beg, that a stone, while continuing in motion, should be capable of thinking and knowing, that it is endeavouring, as far as it can, to continue to move. Such a stone, being conscious merely of its own endeavour and not at all indifferent, would believe itself to be completely free, and would think that it continued in motion solely because of its own wish. This is that human freedom, which all boast that they possess, and which consists solely in the fact, that men are conscious of their own desire, but are ignorant of the causes whereby that desire has been determined.[3]

In radical contrast Schelling set himself no less a task than to show that the essence of human beings is, in fact, freedom. Since the problem of determinism arises from commitments to naturalistic explanations of experience Schelling begins his defence of the grounds of human freedom through a rejection of the pre-eminent form of naturalistic ontology, materialism.

With a clarity by no means common in this period of philosophy Schelling works his way through some of the apparent facts of experience, analysing them to see whether any of them can serve as, what he sees as, the unconditioned element of experience. He is committed to the view that knowledge and experience would be impossible unless there were some foundational element, since without that element representations or ideas would be something like what John McDowell has described as a 'frictionless spinning in the void'. The desired element is immediately characterised by contrast with what is available to us as a representation, or idea: it is, in effect, non-inferential, and it is not dependent on some other concept for its meaning. For Schelling this element is eventually identified as the absolute I, not the empirical I which is possessed in uniquely different ways by each of us as contingent empirical realities.

Schelling is quite aware that Kant had sought to direct philosophy away from what he regarded as the fruitless search for the unconditioned. Kant's critical philosophy had concluded that 'the unconditioned cannot be thought without contradiction' since what can be coherently understood must be grounded in the spatio-temporal ('conditional') reality of our material experience. But Schelling was clearly tempted by other thoughts contained in Kant's critical philosophy: those which concerned the unique characteristics of the 'I think' (that which must accompany all representations, and that which is spontaneous in experience). It is not unfaithful to Kant to say that he too, albeit in a quite different manner, characterised this aspect of consciousness – the 'I think' – by contrast

---

[3] Spinoza, *Correspondence*. Letter to Schüller.

with 'determinable' objects. This contrast was, however, deepened by the post-Kantians – Fichte and Schelling and later Schopenhauer – who attributed ever more active powers to the 'I'. Schelling argues – as Fichte had on behalf of his famous *Tathandlung* – that the 'I' is a unity of being and seeing in that 'it produces itself by its own thinking'. Statements like these are designed to distinguish the notion of the absolute I from that of the empirical consciousness. Empirical consciousness, the argument goes, is subject to determination by whatever objects it happens to experience. In that respect I passively have, say, landscape thoughts as I gaze at a landscape, and my thoughts will change as the objects with which I am in a perceptual relation change. But the absolute I is self-producing. In so far as the 'I' can be seen as absolute – as self-producing – it serves Schelling's purpose as a refutation of determinism, as it provides against Spinozism a characterisation of the non-naturalistic agency of human beings.

A key point at which Schelling is explicitly and irreconcilably at odds with Kant is with respect to his idea of intellectual intuition. Intellectual intuition is the claim that there is awareness of the unconditioned I – that non-empirically determined part of our thinking – in all experience. This notion was utterly rejected by Kant, who insisted that the 'I think' is a logical condition of experience, but not as such available to any sort of experience. However Schelling's claim is not dogmatic if we consider phenomenologically the content of our thinking: it is by no means obvious that we can attribute all of its features to some empirical determination from sources outside us. (It is, of course, disputable whether this gives us any reason to describe it as absolute.)

In a later part of the essay (not reprinted here) Schelling tries to show that the 'I' is in fact responsible for the entirety of experience. One may give such claims a weak reading and argue that Schelling is explaining experience simply as that engagement with the world of which we are consciously aware and which we determine through our concepts. But there are passages – and they can be found in Fichte too – where Schelling seems to suggest that the very ontology of the world – that which we ordinarily experience as objects – can be understood as in some way grounded in the I.

By the end of the essay Schelling largely achieves a position structured in accordance with Reinhold's three criteria: (i) it systematically deduces the absoluteness of the I by exposing the inadequacy of the alternatives, (ii) that it begins with 'a single, self-evident first-principle' in the form of the 'I', and (iii) and this 'I' is phenomenologically validated by means of 'intellectual intuition'.

It was not long before Schelling himself began to doubt that it might be possible to found a theory of freedom on a subjective idealism. Later he developed a philosophy which took a more positive account of nature. However, 'Of the I' remains a key statement of the philosophy of the subject at this early phase of German Idealist philosophy.

OF THE I AS THE PRINCIPLE OF PHILOSOPHY[†]

§1

He who wants to know something, wants to know at the same time that what he knows is real. Knowledge without reality is not knowledge. What follows from that?

Either our knowledge has no reality at all and must be an eternal round of propositions, each dissolving in its opposite, a chaos in which no element can crystallize – or else there must be an ultimate point of reality on which everything depends, from which all firmness and all form of our knowledge springs, a point which sunders the elements, and which circumscribes for each of them the circle of its continuous effect in the universe of knowledge.

There must be something in which and through which everything that is reaches existence, everything that is being thought reaches reality, and thought itself reaches the form of unity and immutability. This something (as we can problematically call it for the time being) should be what completes all insights within the whole system of human knowledge, and it should reign – in the entire cosmos of our knowledge – as original ground [*Urgrund*] of all reality.

If there is any genuine knowledge at all, there must be knowledge which I do not reach by way of some other knowledge, but through which alone all other knowledge is knowledge. In order to reach this last statement I do not have to presuppose some special kind of knowledge. If we know anything at all, we must be sure of at least one item of knowledge which we cannot reach through some other knowledge and which contains the real ground of all our knowledge.

This ultimate in human knowledge must therefore not search for its own real ground in something other. Not only is it itself independent of anything superior but, since our knowledge rises from any consequence to the reason thereof and in reverse descends from that reason to the consequence, that which is the ultimate and for us the principle of all knowledge cannot be *known* in turn through another principle. That is, the principle of its being and the principle of its being known[1] must coincide, must be one, since it can be thought only because it itself is, not because there is something else. Therefore it must be thought simply because it is, and it must be because it itself is being thought, not because something else is thought. Its assertion must be contained in its thought; it must create itself through its being thought. If we had to think something else in order to reach its thought,

---

[†] *SSW* I, 162–195. 'Of the I as the Principle of Philosophy, Or on the Unconditional in Human Knowledge', in F.W.J. Schelling, *The Unconditional in Human Knowledge: Four Early Essays (1794–1796)* (Lewisburg, PN: Bucknell University Press/London: Associated University Presses, 1980).
[1] Footnote of the first edition: May this expression be taken here in its broadest sense, as long as the something we are looking for is determined only problematically.

then that other entity would be superior to the ultimate, which is a contradiction. In order to reach the ultimate I need nothing but the ultimate itself. The absolute can be given only by the absolute.

Now the investigation is becoming more definite. Originally I posited nothing but an ultimate ground of any real knowledge. Now this criterion that it must be the last absolute ground of knowledge permits us at the same time to establish its existence [*Sein*]. The last ground for all reality is something that is thinkable only through itself, that is, it is thinkable only through its being [*Sein*]; it is thought only inasmuch as it is. In short, *the principle of being and thinking is one and the same.* The question can now be expressed quite clearly and the investigation has a clue which can never fail.

§2

Knowledge which I can reach only through other knowledge is *conditional*. The chain of our knowledge goes from one conditional [piece of] knowledge to another. Either the whole has no stability, or one must be able to believe that this can go on ad infinitum, or else that there must be a some ultimate point on which the whole depends. The latter, however, in regard to the principle of its being, must be the direct opposite of all that falls in the sphere of the conditional, that is, it must be not only unconditional but altogether *unconditionable*.

All possible theories of the unconditional must be determinable a priori, once the only correct one has been found. As long as it has not been established, one must follow the empirical progress of philosophy. Whether that progress contains all possible theories will be seen only at the end.

As soon as philosophy begins to be a science, it must at least *assume* an ultimate principle and, with it, something unconditional.

To look for the unconditional in an *object*, in a *thing*, cannot mean to look for it in the generic character of things, since it is evident that a genus cannot be something that is unconditional. Therefore it must mean to look for the unconditional in an *absolute* object which is neither genus nor species nor individual. (Principle of consummate *dogmatism*.)

Yet, whatever is a thing is at the same time an *object* of knowing, therefore a link in the chain of our knowledge. It falls into the sphere of the knowable. Consequently it cannot contain the basis for the reality [*Realgrund*] of all knowledge and knowing. In order to reach an object *as* object I must already have another object with which it can be contrasted, and if the principle of all knowledge were lying in an object I would in turn have to have a new principle in order to find that ostensibly ultimate principle.

Moreover, the unconditional (by §1) should realize itself, create itself through its own thought; the principle of its being and its thinking should coincide: But no object ever realizes itself. In order to reach the existence of an object I must go beyond the mere concept of the object. Its existence is not a part of its reality. I can think its reality without positing it as existing. Suppose, for instance, that God, insofar as some define Him as an object, were the ground of the reality of our knowledge; then, insofar as He is an object, He would fall into the sphere of our knowledge; therefore He could not be for us the ultimate point on which the whole sphere depends. Also the question is not what God is for Himself, but what He is for us in regard to our knowledge. Even if we let God be the ground of the reality of His own knowledge, He is still not the ground of ours, because for us He is an object, which presupposes some reason in the chain of our knowledge that could determine His necessity for our knowledge.

The object as such never determines its own necessity, simply because and insofar as it is an object. For it is object only inasmuch as it is determined by something else. Indeed, inasmuch as it is an object it presupposes something in regard to which it is an object, that is, a subject.

For the time being, I call subject that which is determinable only by contrast with but also in relation to a previously posited object. Object is that which is determinable only in contrast with but also in relation to a subject. Thus, in the first place, the object as such cannot be the unconditional at all, because it necessarily presupposes a subject which determines the object's existence by going beyond the sphere of merely thinking the object. The next thought is to look for the unconditional in the object insofar as it is determined by the subject and is conceivable only in regard to the latter. Or, in the third place, since object necessarily presupposes subject, and subject object, the unconditional could be looked for in the subject, which is conditioned by the object and can be conceived only in relation to the object. Still, this kind of endeavor to realize the unconditional carries a contradiction within itself, which is obvious at first glance. Since the subject is thinkable only in regard to an object, and the object only in regard to a subject, neither of them can contain the unconditional because both are conditioned reciprocally, both are equally unserviceable. Furthermore, in order to determine the relationship of the two, an ulterior reason for the determination must be presupposed, owing to which both are determined. For one cannot say that the subject alone determines the object because the subject is conceiveable only in relationship to the object, and vice versa, and it would amount to the same if I were to treat as unconditional a subject determined by an object or an object determined by a subject. What is more, this kind of a subject as such is also determinable as an object, and for this reason the endeavor to turn the subject into an unconditional fails, as does the endeavor with an absolute object.

The question as to where the unconditional must be looked for becomes slowly clearer, owing to its inherent logic. At the outset I asked only in which specific object we could look for the unconditional, within the whole sphere of objects. Now it becomes clear that we must not look for it in the sphere of objects at all, nor even within the sphere of that subject which is also determinable as an object.

§3

The philosophically revealing formation of the languages, especially manifest in languages still well aware of their roots, is a veritable miracle worked by the mechanism of the human mind. Thus the word I have used casually thus far, the word *bedingen*, is an eminently striking term of which one can say that it contains almost the entire treasure of philosophical truth. *Bedingen* means the action by which anything becomes a *thing* [*Ding*]. *Bedingt* (determined) is what has been turned into a thing. Thus it is clear at once that nothing can posit itself as a thing, and that an unconditional thing is a contradiction in terms. *Unbedingt* (unconditional) is what has not been turned into a thing, and what cannot at all become a thing.

The problem, therefore, which we must solve now changes into something more precise: *to find something that cannot be thought of as a thing at all.*

Consequently, the unconditional can lie neither in a thing as such, nor in anything that can become a thing, that is, not in the subject. It can lie only in that which cannot become a thing at all; that is, if there is an absolute *I*, it can lie only in the *absolute I*. Thus, for the time being, the absolute *I* is ascertained as *that which can never become an object at all.* For the moment no further determination is being made.

That there is an absolute *I* can never be proved objectively, that is, it cannot be proved with regard to that *I* which can exist as an object, because we are supposed to prove precisely that the absolute *I* can never become an object. The *I*, if it is to be unconditional, must be outside the sphere of objective proof. To *prove* objectively that the *I* is unconditional would mean to prove that it was conditional. In the case of the unconditional the principle of its being and the principle of its being thought must coincide. It is, only *because* it is; it is thought only *because* it is thought. The absolute can be given only by the absolute; indeed, if it is to be absolute, it must precede all thinking and imagining. Therefore it must be realized through itself (§1), not through objective proofs, which go beyond the mere concept of the entity to be proved. If the *I* were not realized through itself, then the sentence which expresses its existence would be, 'if I am, then I am'. But in the case of the *I*, the condition 'if I am' already contains the conditioned 'then I'. The condition is not thinkable without the conditioned. I cannot think of myself as a merely conditional existence without knowing myself as already existing. Therefore, in that conditional sentence, the condition does not condition the conditioned but, vice versa, the conditioned conditions the condition, that is, *as* a conditional sentence it cancels itself and becomes unconditional: '*I am because I am*'.[2]

I am! My I contains a being which precedes all thinking and imagining. It *is* by being thought, and it is being thought because it *is*; and all for only one reason –

---

[2] Additional sentence in the first edition: '*I am!*' is the unique form by which it announces itself with unconditional authority [*Selbstmacht*].

that is *is* only and is being thought only inasmuch as its thinking is its *own*. Thus it *is* because it alone is what does the thinking, and it thinks only itself because it is. It produces itself by its own thinking – out of absolute *causality*.

'I *am*, because I am!' That takes possession of everyone instantaneously. Say to him: 'the I *is* because it is;' he will not grasp it quite so quickly because the I is only *by itself* and *unconditioned* inasmuch as it is at the same time *unconditionable*, that is, it can never become a thing, an object. An object receives its existence from something outside the sphere of its mere conceivability. In contrast, the I is not even conceivable unless it first exists as an I. If it does not so exist it is nothing at all. And it is *not at all thinkable except insofar as it thinks itself*, that is, *insofar as it is*. Therefore we must not even say: Everything that thinks is, because that kind of statement talks about the thinking as if it were an object. We can only say: *I* think, *I* am. (Therefore it is clear that, as soon as we turn that which can never become an object into a *logical* object to be investigated, such investigations would labor under a peculiar *incomprehensibility*. We cannot at all confine it as an object, and we could not even talk about it nor understand each other with regard to it, if it were not for the assistance of the [intellectual] intuition [we have of our selves]. However, insofar as our knowledge is tied to an object, that intuition is as alien to us as the I which never can become an object.)

Thus the I is determined as unconditional only through itself.[3] Yet, if it is determined at the same time as that which furnishes validity in the entire system of my knowledge, then a regress must be possible; that is, I must be able to *ascend* from the lowest conditioned proposition to the unconditional, just as I can *descend* from the unconditional principle to the lowest proposition in the conditional sequence.

You may therefore pick from any series of conditional propositions whichever one you want and, in the regress, it must lead back to the absolute I. Hence, to come back to a previous example, the concept of subject must lead to the absolute I. For if there were no absolute I, then the concept of subject, that is, the concept of the I which is conditioned by an object, would be the ultimate. But since the concept of an object contains an antithesis, the basic determination of this concept cannot stop at a mere contrast with a subject which in turn is conceivable only in

---

[3] Perhaps I can make this matter clearer if I return to the above-mentioned example. For me, God cannot be the ground of the reality of knowledge if He is determined as an object because, if so determined, He would fall into the sphere of conditional knowledge. However, if I should determine God not as an object at all but as = I, then indeed He would be the real ground of my knowledge. Still, that determination is impossible in the theoretical [i.e., objectivistic] philosophy. Nevertheless, even in theoretical philosophy, which determines God as an object, a determination of God's essence as = I is necessary and then I must indeed assume that for Himself God is the absolute and real ground of His own knowledge, but not for me. For me, in theoretical philosophy, He is determined not only as I but also as object. Yet if He is an I, then, *for Himself*, he is not object at all but only I. Incidentally, it follows that one falsely depicts the ontological proof of God's existence as deceptive artifice; the deception is quite natural. For, whatever can say *I* to itself, also says *I am*! The pity is that, in theoretical philosophy, God is not determined as identical with *my* I but, in relation to my I, is determined as an object, and an ontological proof for the existence of an object is a contradictory concept.

relation to an object. The determination is possible only in contrast to something which flatly excludes the concept of an object as such. Therefore both the concept of an object and the concept of a subject which is conceivable only in contrast to some object must lead to an absolute which excludes every object and thus is in absolute contrast to any object. For if you suppose that the original position is that of an object which would not require the antecedent position of an absolute I as basis for all positing, then that original object cannot be determined *as* object, that is, as opposed to the I since, as long as the latter is not posited, nothing can be in opposition to it. Therefore any object posited as antecedent to any I would be *no* object at all; the very supposition cancels itself. Or again, suppose that there is an I, but only an I conceptually contrasted (*aufgehoben*) by the object, that is, an original subject; then this supposition likewise cancels itself for, where no absolute I is posited, none can be set aside (*aufgehoben*) by contrast. If there is no I antecedent to any object, neither can there be an object whose concept would set aside the I by contrast. (I have in mind a chain of knowledge that is conditioned throughout and attains stability only in one supreme, unconditional point. Now, whatever is conditional in that chain can be conceived only by presupposing the absolute condition, that is, the unconditional. Thus the conditional cannot be posited as conditional antecedent to the unconditional and unconditionable, but only owing to the latter, by contrast to it. Therefore, whatever is posited as only a conditional thing is conceivable only through that [logically antecedent entity] which is no thing at all but is unconditional. The object itself then is originally determinable only in contrast to the absolute I, that is, only as the antithesis to the I or as not-I. Thus the very concepts of subject and object are guarantors of the absolute, unconditionable I.)

§4

Once the I is determined as the unconditional in human knowledge, then the whole content of all knowledge must be determinable through the I itself and through its antithesis, and thus one must also be able to sketch a priori every possible theory regarding the unconditional.

Inasmuch as the I is the absolute I, that which is not = I can be determined only in contrast to the I and by presupposing the I. Any not-I posited absolutely, as if it were in no contrast to anything, is a contradiction in terms. If, on the other hand, the I is not presupposed as the absolute I, then the not-I can be posited either as antecedent to any I or as on a par with the I. A third alternative is not possible.

The two extremes are dogmatism and criticism. The principle of dogmatism is a not-I posited as antecedent to any I; the principle of criticism, an I posited as antecedent to all [that is] not-I and as exclusive of any not-I. Halfway between the two lies the principle of an I conditioned by a not-I or, what amounts to the same, of a not-I conditioned by an I.

(1) The principle of dogmatism contradicts itself (§2), because it presupposes an unconditional thing [*ein unbedingtes Ding*] that is, a thing that is not a thing. In dogmatism therefore, consistency (which is the first requirement for any true philosophy) attains nothing other than that which is not-I should become I, and that that which is I should become not-I, as is the case with Spinoza. But as yet no dogmatist has proved that a not-I could give itself reality and that it could have any meaning except that of standing in contrast to an absolute I. Even Spinoza has not proved anywhere that the unconditional could and should lie in the not-I. Rather, led only by his concept of the absolute, he straightway posits it in an absolute object, and he does so as if he presupposed that everybody who conceded him his concept of the unconditional would follow him automatically in believing that, of necessity, it had to be posited in a not-I. Once having assumed though not proved it, he fulfills the duty of consistency more strictly than any single one of his enemies. For it suddenly becomes clear that – as if against his own will – through the sheer force of his consistency, which did not shun any conclusion based on his supposition, he elevated the not-I to the I, and demeaned the I to a not-I. For him, the world is no longer world, the absolute object no longer object. No sense perception, no concept reaches his One Substance whose nonfinitude is present only to the intellectual intuition. As everywhere, so also in this present investigation, his system can take the place of perfect dogmatism. No philosopher was so worthy as he to recognize his own great misunderstanding; to do so and to arrive at his goal would have been one and the same for him. No recrimination is more unbearable than the one made against him so often, that he arbitrarily presupposed the idea of absolute substance, or even that the idea sprang from an arbitrary explanation of words. To be sure, it seems easier to overthrow a whole system by means of a small grammatical remark, rather than to insist on the discovery of its final fundamentals which, no matter how erroneous, must be detectable somewhere in the human mind. The first one to see that Spinoza's error was not in the idea [of the unconditional] but in the fact that Spinoza posited it outside the I, had understood him and thus had found the way to [philosophy as a] science.

§5

(2) Any system that takes its start from the subject, that is, from the I which is thinkable only in respect to an object, and that is supposed to be neither dogmatism nor criticism, is like dogmatism in that it contradicts itself in its own principle, insofar as the latter is supposed to be the supreme principle. However, it is worth while to trace the origin of this principle.

It was customary to presuppose – to be sure, rashly – that the supreme principle of all philosophy must express a *fact*. If, in line with linguistic usage, one understood fact to mean something that was outside the sphere of the pure, absolute I (and therefore inside the sphere of the conditional) then, of necessity, the question had to arise: What could be the conditioning principle of this fact? A phenomenon, or else a thing in itself? That was the next question, once one found oneself in the world of objects. A phenomenon? And what could the principle of this phenomenon be? (Especially if, for instance, imagination [*Vorstellung*], which is itself a phenomenon, was postulated as the principle of all philosophy. Is it in turn a phenomenon, and so on, ad infinitum? Or was it the intention that that phenomenon which was to furnish the principle of fact should not presuppose any other phenomenon? Or was the principle to be a thing in itself? Let us examine this matter more closely.

The *thing in itself* is the not-I posited as antecedent to any I. (Speculation demands the unconditional. Once the question as to where the unconditional lies is settled, by some in favor of the I, by others of the not-I, then both systems must proceed in the same manner. What the one asserts about the I, the other must assert about the not-I, and vice versa. In short, we must be able to use their theorems interchangeably, simply by substituting in one system a not-I for the I, in the other an I for the not-I. If one could not do that without damage to the system, one of the two would have to be inconsistent.) The *phenomenon* is the not-I conditioned by the I.

If the principle of all philosophy is to be a fact, and if the principle of the fact is to be a *thing in itself*, then every I is done away with, there is no longer any pure I, any freedom, and there is no reality in any I but instead only negation. For the I is cancelled in its very origin when a not-I is posited absolutely. In reverse, when the I is posited absolutely, all not-I is canceled as original and posited as a mere negation. (A system which takes its start from the subject, that is, from the conditioned I, must necessarily presuppose a thing in itself which, however, can occur in the imagination [*Vorstellung*], that is, as an object, only in relation to the subject, that is, only as phenomenon [*Erscheinung*]. In short, this system turns out to be the *kind* of realism that is most incomprehensible and most inconsistent.)

If the last principle of that ultimate fact is to be a phenomenon, it cancels itself immediately as the supreme principle, because an unconditional phenomenon is a contradiction. This is why all philosophers who took a not-I for the principle of their philosophy, at the same time elevated it to an absolute not-I, posited as independent of every I, that is, to a thing in itself.

The consequence is that it would be odd indeed to hear from the mouths of philosophers who affirm the freedom of the I any simultaneous assertion that the principle of all philosophy must be a fact, provided that one could really assume that they were aware of the consequence of that latter assertion, which is that the principle of all philosophy must be a not-I.

(This consequence follows necessarily for, in that case, the I is posited only as subject, that is, as conditional, and therefore cannot be the ultimate principle. Thus, either *all* philosophy is nullified as an unconditional science, since its merely conditional principle cannot be the highest possible one, or else the object must be taken as original and therefore as independent of every I, and the I itself must be determined as something that can be posited only in contrast to an absolute something, that is, determined as an absolute nothing.)

Nevertheless those philosophers really wanted the I, and not the not-I, as the principle of philosophy, but they did not want to abandon the concept of fact. In order to extricate themselves from the dilemma which confronted them, they had to choose the I, though not the absolute I, but the empirically conditioned I as the principle of all philosophy. And what could have been closer at hand than that? Now they had an I as the principle of philosophy. [It looked as if] their philosophy could not be dubbed dogmatism. At the same time they had a fact, since nobody could deny that the empirical I is the principle of a fact.

True, this was satisfactory only for a time. For, when the matter was inspected more closely, it turned out that either nothing at all was gained, or only this much, that again one had a not-I as principle of philosophy. It is evident that it makes no difference whether I start from the I conditioned by the not-I, or from the not-I conditioned by the I. Also, the I conditioned by the not-I is precisely the point at which dogmatism must arrive, though belatedly; in fact, all philosophy must arrive at it. Furthermore, all philosophers would necessarily have to explain in the same manner what the I conditioned by the not-I is, if they did not tacitly assume something superior to this fact (this conditionality of the I) about which they are secretly in disagreement – that is, assume some superior entity as ground of explanation of the conditioned I and not-I. That ground can be nothing other than either an absolute not-I, not conditioned by the I, or else an absolute I, not conditioned by a not-I. But the latter was already nullified by the establishment of the subject as the principle of philosophy. From there on consistency would demand either that one refrain from any further determination of that principle, that is, from all philosophy, or else that one assume an absolute not-I, that is, the principle of dogmatism which, in turn, is a principle that contradicts itself (§4). In short, the subject as ultimate principle would lead into contradictions no matter which way it might turn, and these contradictions could be hidden, after a fashion, only behind inconsistencies and precarious proofs. True enough, if the philosophers had agreed that the subject was the ultimate principle, peace could have been established in the philosophical world, because they could readily have agreed on the mere analysis of that principle, and as soon as anyone had gone beyond the mere analysis of it and (seeing that analysis could lead no farther) had tried by synthesis to explain the analytical fact of the determination of the I by the not-I and of the not-I by the I, he would have broken the agreement and presupposed a superior principle.

ANNOTATION. As is well known, it was Reinhold who tried to elevate the empirically conditioned I (which exists in consciousness) to the principle of philosophy. One would show very little insight into the necessity found in the progress of science if one were to mention Reinhold's attempt without due deference. He deserves the highest esteem, though meanwhile philosophy progressed farther. It was not his destiny to *solve* the intrinsic problem of philosophy, but to bring it into the clearest focus. Who is not aware of the great impact such a decisive presentation of the problem will have, precisely in philosophy where, as a rule, an intrinsic presentation is possible only owing to a fortuitous glimpse of the truth which is yet to be discovered? Even the author of the *Critique of Pure Reason*, in his attempt not only to arbitrate the dispute among philosophers but to resolve the antinomy in philosophy itself, did not know what else to do than to state the point at issue in an all-encompassing question, which he expressed as follows: How are synthetic judgements a priori possible? As will be shown in the course of this investigation, this question in its highest abstraction is none other than: How is it possible for the absolute I to step out of itself and oppose to itself a not-I? It was quite natural that this question (as long as it was not introduced in its highest abstraction) be misunderstood, along with its answer. The next merit, then, that a thinking man could earn was obviously to present the question in a higher abstraction and thus securely prepare the way for an answer. This merit was earned by the author of the *Theory of the Faculty of Imagination* by stating his principle of consciousness. In it he reached the last point of abstraction, where one had to stand before one could reach that which is higher than all abstraction.

§6

The perfect system of [philosophical] science proceeds from the absolute I, excluding everything that stands in contrast to it. This, as the One Unconditionable, conditions the whole chain of knowledge, circumscribes the sphere of all that is thinkable and, as the absolute all-comprehending reality, rules the whole system of our knowledge. Only through an absolute I, only through the fact that it is posited absolutely (*schlechthin gesetzt*) does it become possible that a not-I appears in contrast to it, indeed that philosophy itself becomes possible. For the whole task of theoretical and practical philosophy is nothing else than the solution of the contradiction between the pure and the empirically conditioned I.[4]

Theoretical philosophy, in order to solve the contradiction, proceeds from synthesis to synthesis, to the highest possible one in which I and not-I are identified (*gleich gesetzt*), where, because theoretical reasoning ends in contradictions, practical reason enters in order to cut the knot by means of absolute demands.

If, therefore, the principle of all philosophy were to lie in the empirically conditioned I (about which dogmatism and the unfinished criticism basically agree), then all spontaneity of the I, theoretical as well as practical, would be quite unexplainable. For the theoretical I strives to posit the I and the not-I as identical and, therefore, to elevate the not-I itself to the form of the I; the practical strives for pure unity by exclusion of all that is not-I. Both of them can do what they do only inasmuch as the absolute I has absolute causality and pure identity. Thus the

---

[4] The word *empirical* is usually taken in a much too narrow sense. Empirical is everything that is in contrast to the pure I, everything essentially related to a not-I, even the original positing of any contrast (*Entgegensetzen*) as posited in some not-I, a positing which is an act that has its source in the I itself, the very act by which any contrasting becomes possible. *Pure* is what exists without relation to objects. *Experienced* is what is possible only through objects. *A priori* is what is possible only in relation to objects but not through them. *Empirical* is that which makes objects possible.

ultimate principle of philosophy cannot be anything that lies outside the absolute I; it can be neither a phenomenon nor a thing in itself.

The absolute I is not a phenomenon. Even the very concept of absoluteness forbids it. It is neither a phenomenon nor a thing in itself, because it is no thing at all, but simply and purely I, which excludes all that is not-I.

The last point on which all our knowledge and the entire series of the conditional depend, cannot be conditioned by anything ulterior at all. The entirety of our knowledge has no stability if it has nothing to stabilize it, if it does not rest on that which is carried by its own strength. And that is nothing else than that which is real through freedom. The beginning and the end of all philosophy is *freedom*.

§7

So far we have determined the I as only that which can in no way be an object for itself, and which, for anything outside of it, can be neither object nor not-object, that is, cannot be anything at all. Therefore it does not receive its own reality, as objects do, through something lying outside its sphere, but exclusively through itself alone. This concept of the I is the only one by which the I is designated as absolute and my whole further investigation is now nothing but a plain development of this.

If the I were not identical with itself, if its original form were not the form of pure identity, then all we seem to have won so far would be lost again. For the I is only because it is. If it were not pure identity, that is, only that which it is then it could not be posited by itself, that is, it could also be like that which it is not. But the I is either not at all, or else only through itself. Therefore the original form [*Urform*] of the I must be pure identity.

Only that which is through itself gives itself the form of identity, because only that which is because it is, is determined in its own being by nothing but identity, that is, is determined by itself. The existence of everything else that exists is determined not only by its own identity but also by something outside of it. But if there were not something that is through itself, whose identity is the sole condition of its being, then there would be nothing at all identical with itself, because only that which is through its own identity can bestow identity on everything else that is. Only in an absolute, posited by its own being as identical, can everything that is achieve the unity of its own essence [*Wesen*]. How could anything be posited at all if everything that can be posited were mutable, and if nothing unconditional, nothing immutable, could be acknowledged, in which and through which everything that can be posited would receive stability and immutability? What would it mean to posit something if all positing, all existence [*Dasein*], all reality were dispersed constantly, lost ceaselessly, and if there were no common point of unity and stability that receives absolute identity, not through something else, but through itself, by its own being, in order to gather all rays of existence in the center of its identity, and to keep together in the sphere of its power all that is posited?

Thus it is the I alone that bestows unity and stability on everything that is. All identity pertains only to that which is posited in the I, and pertains to it only insofar as it is posited in the I.

Therefore it is the absolute I that furnishes the basis for all form of identity (A = A). If this form (A = A) preceded the I, then A could not express what is posited *in* the I but only that which is *outside* the I; therefore that form would become the form of objects as such, and even the I would be subordinated to it, as just another object determined by it. The I would not be absolute but conditional and, as a specific subform, would be subordinated to the generic concept of objects, that is, it would be one of the modifications of the absolute not-I, which alone would be self-identical.

Since the I, in its very nature [*Wesen*] is posited by its sheer being as absolute identity, there is no difference between the two expressions of it, either *I am I*, or *I am*!

§8

The I can be determined in no way except by being *unconditional*, for it *is* I owing to its sheer unconditionality, since it cannot become a thing at all. Thus it is exhaustively expressed when its unconditionality is expressed. Since it *is* only through its unconditionality, it would be nullified if any conceivable predicate of it could be conceived in any way other than through its unconditionality; a different way would either contradict its unconditionality or else presuppose something even higher in which could be found a unity of both the unconditional and the presumed predicate.

The essence [Wesen] of the I is freedom, that is, it is not thinkable except inasmuch as it posits itself by its own absolute power [*Selbstmacht*], not, indeed, as any kind of *something*, but as sheer I. This freedom can be determined *positively*, because we want to attribute freedom not to a thing in itself but to the pure I as posited by itself, present to itself alone, and excluding all that is not-I. No objective freedom belongs to the *I* because it is not an object at all. As soon as we try to determine the I as an object, it withdraws into the most confined sphere, under the conditions of the interdependence of objects – its freedom and independence disappear. An object is possible only through some other object, and only inasmuch as it is bound to conditions. Freedom *is* only through itself and it encompasses the nonfinite.

With regard to objective freedom we are not less knowledgeable than with regard to any other concept which contradicts itself. And our inability to think a contradiction is not ignorance. The freedom of the I, however, can be determined *positively*. For the I, its freedom is neither more nor less than unconditional positing of reality in itself through its own absolute power [*Selbstmacht*]. It can be determined

negatively as complete independence, even as complete incompatibility with all that
is not-I.

You insist that you should be conscious of this freedom? But are you bearing
in mind that all your consciousness is possible only through this freedom, and that
the condition cannot be contained in the conditioned? Are you considering in any
way that the I is no longer the pure, absolute I once it occurs in consciousness; that
there can be no object at all for the absolute I; and, moreover, that the absolute I
never can become an object? Self-awareness implies the danger of losing the I. It
is not a free act of the immutable but an unfree urge that induces the mutable I,
conditioned by the not-I, to strive to maintain its identity and to reassert itself in the
undertow of endless change.[5] (Or do you really feel free in your self-awareness?)
But that striving of the empirical I, and the consciousness stemming from it,
would itself not be possible without the freedom of the absolute I, and absolute
freedom is equally necessary as a condition for both imagination and action. For
your empirical I would never strive to save its identity if the absolute I were not
originally posited by itself, as pure identity, and out of its absolute power.

If you want to attain this freedom as something objective, whether you want
to comprehend it or deny it, you will always fail, because freedom consists in the
very fact that it excludes all that is not-I absolutely.

The I cannot be given by a mere *concept*. Concepts are possible only in the sphere
of the conditional; concepts of objects only are possible. If the I were a concept
then there would have to be something higher in which it could find its unity, and
something lower which would furnish its multiplicity. In short, the I would then be
conditioned throughout. Therefore the I can be determined only in an intuition
[*Anschauung*]. But since the I is I only because it can never become an object, it
cannot occur in an intuition of sense, but only in an intuition which grasps no
object at all and is in no way a sensation, in short, in an *intellectual* intuition. Where
there is an object there is sensuous intuition, and vice versa. Where there is no

---

[5] It is the character of finiteness to be unable to posit anything without at the same time positing something in
contrast. The form of this contrast is originally determined by the contrast of the not-I. For, while absolutely
positing itself as identical with itself, the finite I must necessarily posit itself in contrast to every not-I. And
that is not possible without positing the not-I itself. The nonfinite I would exlude all contrasting entities but
without letting the exclusion set them up in contrast to itself. It would simply equate everything with itself
and, therefore, wherever it posits anything it would posit it as *its own* reality. It could not strive to save its
own identity and, therefore, could not contain any synthesis of a manifold, any unity of consciousness, etc.
The empirical I, however, is determined by the original contrast and is nothing at all without it. Therefore
it owes its reality, as *empirical* I, not to itself but only to the restriction by the not-I. It manifests itself not by
a mere *I am*, but by *I think*, which means that it *is*, not by its own sheer being, but by thinking *something,
thinking objects*. In order to save the original identity of the I, the image [*Vorstellung*] of the identical I must
accompany all other images so that their manifoldness can be thought at all, in its inherent relation to unity.
Therefore the empirical I exists only *through* and *in relation* to the unity of images and, outside of that unity,
has no reality in itself at all but disappears as soon as one eliminates objects altogether along with the unity
of its synthesis. Thus its reality as *empirical* I is determined for it by something posited *outside* of it, by *objects*.
Its being is not determined absolutely, but by objective forms, and it is determined as an *existence* [*Dasein*].
Yet it is only *in* the nonfinite I, and through it; for mere objects could never bring about the image of I as
a principle of their unity.

object, that is, in the absolute I, there is no sense intuition, therefore either no intuition at all or else intellectual intuition. Therefore *the I is determined for itself as mere I in intellectual intuition.*

I know very well that Kant denied all intellectual intuition, but I also know the context in which he denied it. It was in an investigation which only *presupposes* the *absolute* I at every step and which, on the basis of presupposed higher principles, determines only the empirically conditioned I and the not-I in its synthesis with that I. I also know that the intellectual intuition must be completely incomprehensible as soon as one tries to liken it to sensuous intuition. Furthermore, it can occur in consciousness just as little as can absolute freedom, since consciousness presupposes an object, and since intellectual intuition is possible only inasmuch as it has no object. The attempt to refute it from the standpoint of consciousness must fail just as surely as the attempt to give it objective reality through consciousness, which would mean to do away with it altogether.

The I is determined only by its freedom, hence everything we say of the pure I must be determined by its freedom.

§9

The I is simply unity. For if it were multiplicity it would not *be* through its own being but through the reality of its parts. It would not be conditioned by itself alone, by its sheer being (that is, it would not be at all) but would be conditioned by all single parts of the multiplicity for, if any one part were canceled, the completeness of the I itself would be canceled. But that would contradict the concept of its freedom, therefore (§8) the I cannot contain any multiplicity; it must be simply unity – nothing but simply I.

Wherever there is unconditionality determined by freedom, there is I. Therefore *the I is absolutely one.* If there were to be several I's, if there were to be an I beside the I, these different I's would have to be differentiated by something. But since the I is conditioned only by itself and is determinable only in intellectual intuition, it must be identical with itself (not at all determinable by number). Accordingly, the I and the I-outside-the-I would coincide and would be indistinguishable. Thus the I can be naught but one. (If the I were not one, the reason why there should be several I's would not lie in the I itself, in the nature [*Wesen*] of it, for the I is not determinable as an object (§7); it would lie outside the I and thus have no meaning other than the canceling of the I.) The pure I is the same everywhere, I is everywhere = I. Wherever there is an attribute of I, there is I. The attributes of the I cannot differ from each other, since they are all determined by the same unconditionality (all are nonfinite). They would be determined as different from each other either by their mere concept, which is impossible since the I is an absolute oneness, or by something outside of them, whereby they would lose their unconditionality, which again makes no sense. The I is I everywhere; it fills, as it were, the entire infinity, if it would make sense to use such an expression.

Those who know no other I than the empirical one (which, however, is quite incomprehensible without the presupposition of the pure I), those who have never elevated themselves to the intellectual intuition of their own selves, can find only nonsense in the theorem that the I is only one. For only the completed science itself can prove that the empirical I is multiplicity. (Imagine an infinite sphere – of which by necessity there is only one – and inside this sphere imagine as many finite spheres as you wish. These, however, are possible only inside the one which is infinite. Thus, even if you do away with the finite ones, you still have [their locus or condition] the infinite sphere.) Those who have the habit of thinking only of the empirical I find it necessary to assume a plurality of I's, each of which is I for itself and not-I for the others, and they do not consider that a pure I is thinkable only through the unity of its being.

These adherents of the empirical I will be equally unable to think the concept of pure, absolute unity (*unitas*) because, whenever the absolute unity is mentioned, they can think only of an empirical, derivative unity (which is a concept symbolized by the number scheme).

The [pure] I has as little unity in the empirical sense (*unicitas*) as it has multiplicity. It is completely outside the sphere of determination by this concept; it is neither one nor many in the empirical sense, for both alternatives contradict its concept. The concept of a pure I not only lies outside the domain of whatever can be determined by the two concepts of empirical unity and multiplicity, but lies in an entirely opposite sphere. Whenever the talk is about a numerical unity, something is presupposed in regard to which one can speak of numerical oneness as such. What is presupposed is a generic concept under which the numerical one is comprehended as the unique member of its kind. However the (real and logical) possibility still remains that it might not be the only one; that is, it is one only in regard to its existence, not in regard to its essence. In contrast, the I is one precisely in regard to its simple, pure being, and not in regard to its existence (*Dasein*), which is no essential attribute of it at all. Also, it cannot be thought of at all in regard to something higher; it cannot fall under a generic concept. *Concept* as such is something that comprehends multiplicity in oneness. The I therefore cannot be a concept, neither a pure nor an abstracted one, because it is neither a comprehending nor a comprehended, but an absolute unity. It is neither genus nor species nor individual, because genus, species, and individual are thinkable only in regard to multiplicity. Whoever can take the I for a concept or can predicate numerical unity or multiplicity of it, knows nothing of the I. Whoever wants to turn it into a demonstrable concept, can no longer take it as unconditioned. For the absolute cannot be mediated at all, hence it can never fall into the domain of demonstrable concepts. Everything demonstrable presupposes either something already demonstrated, or else the ultimate, which cannot be further demonstrated. The very desire to demonstrate the absolute does away with it, and also with all freedom, all absolute identity, etcetera.

ANNOTATION. Someone might reverse this matter: 'Just because the I is not something general, it cannot become the principle of philosophy'.

If, as we shall now presuppose, philosophy must start from the unconditional, then it cannot start from something general. For the general is conditioned by the singular and is possible only in regard to conditional (empirical) knowledge. Therefore the most consistent system of dogmatism, the Spinozistic, declares itself most emphatically against the opinion that conceives of the one absolute substance as of an *ens rationis*, an abstract concept. Spinoza sees the unconditional in the absolute not-I, but not in an abstract concept nor in the idea of the world, nor of course in any single existing thing. On the contrary he inveighs vehemently – if one may use this word in speaking of a Spinoza – against it[6] and declares that he who calls God one, in an empirical sense, or thinks of Him as a mere abstraction, has not even an inkling of the nature [*Wesen*] of God. To be sure, one cannot understand how the not-I is supposed to lie outside of all numerical determination, but one must realize that Spinoza did not truly posit the unconditional in the not-I; rather he turned the not-I into the I by elevating it to the absolute.

Leibniz supposedly started from the generic concept of things as such. That would be a matter to investigate more closely, but this is not the place for it. It is certain, however, that his disciples started from that concept and thus founded one of the systems of incomplete dogmatism.

(*Question:* How, in that system, can one explain the monads and the preestablished harmony? As, in criticism, theoretical reason ends with the result that the I

[6] See several passages in Jacobi's book about the doctrine of Spinoza, pp. 179 ff. [*Über die Lehre des Spinoza, in Briefen an Herrn Moses Mendelssohn.* (Breslau, 1785); now *Werke*, vol. 4, pt. 1 (Darmstadt: Wissenschaftliche Buchgesellschaft, 1968)]. See other passages also, especially *Eth.* 2. prop. XL, schol. 1. Furthermore, in one of his letters he says Cum multa sint, quae nequaquam in *imaginatione*, sed solo *intellectu* assequi possumus, qualia sunt *Substantia, Aeternitas* el al. si quis talia eiusmodi notionibus, quae duntaxat auxilia *imaginationis* sunt, explicare conatur, nihilo plus agit, quam si det operam, ut sua imaginatione insaniat. [Since there are many things that we can grasp by no kind of imagination but only by the intellect, such as substance, eternity, and others, if anyone tries to explain them by means of the kind of notions which are mere auxiliaries to the imagination, then, although it seems expedient to such a one, he attains nothing but unsoundness of mind, owing to his imagination (Letter of April 20. 1663, to Ludovicus Meyer. Cf. the translation by A. Wolf in his *The Correspondence of Spinoza* (New York: Russell and Russell, 1966), letter 12, p. 1663). In order to understand this passage, one must know that Spinoza thought that abstract concepts were pure products of the power of imagination. He says that the transcendental expressions (which is what he calls expressions like *ens, res*, etc. [schol. 1]) arise from the fact that the body is capable of absorbing only a limited quantity of impressions, and when it is over-saturated the soul cannot imagine them except in a confused manner, without any differentiation, all under one attribute. He explains the general concepts in the same manner, e.g., man, animal, etc. Compare the passage in the *Ethics* referred to above, and especially his treatise *De Intellectus Emendatione*. For Spinoza the lowest level of knowledge is the imagining of single things; the highest is pure intellectual intuition of the infinite attributes of the absolute substance, and the resulting adequte knowledge of the essence of things. This is the highest point of his system. For him, mere confused imagination is the source of all error, but the intellectual intuition of God is the source of all truth and perfection in the broadest sense of the word. In the second part of his *Ethics*, in the scholion to proposition XLIII, he says [with regard to the idea of mind of which the scholion to proposition XXI said: the idea of the mind and the mind itself are one-and-the-same thing, which is considered under one-and-the-same-attribute, that of thought. For indeed the idea of the mind, that is to say, the idea of the idea, is nothing but the form of the idea insofar as this is considered as mode of thought without relation to any object]: 'What can be more clear and certain than this idea, as a norm of truth? Indeed, as light makes manifest both itself and darkness, so is truth the norm of itself and of falsehood'. What can surpass the quiet bliss of these words, the One and All (Εν χαì πᾶν) of our better life?

becomes not-I, so, in dogmatism, it must end with the opposite, that the not-I becomes I. In criticism, practical reason must reestablish the absolute I; in dogmatism
it must end with the reestablishment of the absolute not-I. It would be interesting
to devise a consistent system of dogmatism. Maybe that will yet be done).

"The greatest merit of the philosophical scholar is not to establish abstract concepts nor to spin systems of them. His ultimate aim is pure absolute being; his
greatest merit is to unveil and reveal that which can never be conceptualized, explained, deduced, in short, to reveal the undissectable, the immediate, the simple'.

§10

The I contains *all being, all reality*. If there were a reality outside of the I, either it
would coincide with the reality posited in the I or it would not. Now, all reality
of the I is determined by its unconditionality; it has no reality except by being
posited unconditionally. If there were a reality outside of the I that would *correspond*
to the reality of the I, then that outside reality would have to be unconditional also.
Yet, it is only through unconditionality that the I receives *all* its reality, therefore
any *one* reality of the I, if posited outside of it, would also have to contain all its
reality, that is, there would be an I outside of the I, which does not make sense
(§9). On the other hand, if that reality outside the I differed from the reality of
the I [instead of corresponding to it], then, owing to the absolute unity of the
I, the positing of the outside reality would at the same time cancel the I itself,
which makes no sense. (We are talking about the *absolute* I, whose function is to
be the generic concept of all reality. All reality must coincide with it, that is, must
be *its* reality. The absolute I must contain the data, the absolute content [*Materie*]
that determines all being, all possible reality.) If we want to anticipate objections,
then we must also anticipate answers. Of course my theorem [that the I contains all
being, all reality] could be readily refuted if either a not-I postulated as *antecedent* to
all that is I were conceivable, or else if that not-I which is originally and absolutely
opposed to the I were conceivable as an absolute not-I — if, in short, the reality of
the things in themselves could be proved in the philosophy hitherto prevailing for
then all original reality would be found in the absolute not-I.
[...]

Translated by Fritz Marti

G. W. F. Hegel, Phenomenology of Spirit (Phänomenologie des Geistes): *Introduction (1807)*

Although Hegel was born five years earlier than Schelling, he was for a certain period publicly under the latter's influence. In 1801 he published his first book, *The Difference between Fichte's and Schelling's Systems of Philosophy*, which staunchly defended Schelling's transcendental post-Fichtean phase. Inevitably Hegel was perceived by most to be an adherent of Schelling, and not a philosopher in his own right. But that all changed in 1807 when his *Phenomenology of Spirit* appeared.

Legend surrounds the publication of this book. As Hegel was completing the manuscript in the middle of 1806, French troops, accompanied by Napoleon himself, entered the town of Jena where Hegel was at work. Hegel perceived in Napoleon the glorious spirit of the French Revolution and was enraptured by Napoleon's very presence. He famously wrote at the time: 'I saw the Emperor – this world-soul – riding out of the city on reconnaissance'. Hegel's final version of the text was completed on the eve of the Battle of Jena and was delivered to the Jena publisher by a courier who, rather colourfully, must have had to make his way through all of the security complications of a town effectively under martial law.

The *Phenomenology of Spirit* is one of the most demanding texts in the history of philosophy. Few readers who make the effort to come to terms with it doubt the quality of its insights and arguments, yet there is a continuing lack of consensus about what exactly the *Phenomenology* is all about. The book, we are told, was originally to be known as *The Science of the Experience of Consciousness*. In some respects this is a more revealing title in that the book examines phenomenologically – that is, from the point of view of experience – the development of modern consciousness in its various forms. We are guided by Hegel through an examination of consciousness as it has increased in sophistication, both as the agent of modern rational society and as an agent capable, at last, of understanding the conditions of its own knowledge. For Hegel the goal of his study is to explain modern consciousness through the various rationally necessitated evolutionary stages of its development. The attainment of this goal is nothing less than what Hegel calls 'absolute knowledge' in the sense of making totally transparent to ourselves all of the conditions in which our knowledge arises and the rationality that underpins our social forms.

The complex narrative offered by Hegel entails a dialectical exploration of the conditions of knowledge, and amongst these is the social dimension. For Hegel recognition of this social dimension is tied in with a treatment of history in that different social contexts mark off the conditions of knowledge of one society or historical epoch from others. Each epoch has its own 'spirit' (or 'mind' as 'Geist', the word Hegel uses, is sometimes translated) which defines its key moral religious and intellectual values. The question of how we are to fit together these difficult and overlapping narratives is the major challenge facing Hegel's readers. One may doubt J. N. Findlay's contention that there was once a 'social and cultural group that could read the *Phenomenology* with ease and pleasure'.[1]

In the Introduction to the *Phenomenology* Hegel sets out his views of why absolute knowledge can be plausibly proposed as the goal of philosophy. The goal can be achieved if we reconceive what is involved in the process of knowledge. This leads Hegel to a consideration of some of the main presuppositions of modern epistemology, which, in his view, sets the subject (the knower) at odds with the object, and assumes in various ways that the subject and object cannot be reconciled in knowledge (assumes, that is, that there is an ineradicable non-identity between subject and object). Scepticism, according to Hegel, is the product of this assumption.

To know absolutely is to know without qualification. Such knowing, Hegel tells us, cannot be characterised as provisional or partial. To attain 'absolute knowledge' we must necessarily proceed through a process of provisionality or partiality: we begin with knowledge which is hugely qualified, that is to say. For Hegel absolute knowledge is an achievement gained after on-going revisions of earlier efforts: successful knowledge is therefore never a spontaneous intuition. Hegel believes that knowledge can eventually culminate in a system where all of the earlier judgements can be seen to be elements in a total body of knowledge.

In the Introduction to the *Phenomenology,* *experience* is the term Hegel gives to this process. The process through which the elements of experience are put together is judgement. Judgement typically involves placing elements of experience together under the categories of concept and object. Since it is Hegel's view that in experience concepts and objects are in a more or less satisfactory relationship at any given point it follows that experience is a judicative process. In other words, concept and object will at any given point be united in a judgement which expresses either partial or conclusive knowledge. Hegel argues further that experience has a discernible rational structure. This means, in effect, that the process of moving from partial to conclusive knowledge is neither haphazard nor random. Each phase of

[1] J. H. Findlay, *Hegel: A Re-Examination* (London: George Allen and Unwin, 1958), p. 83.

experience is produced by a rational compulsion: thought does not simply settle at any point which falls short of rationally acceptable knowledge. Rather, thought adjusts itself until it is satisfied that it has grasped the object it is attempting to understand. And in so doing thought must often abandon the preconceptions that in various ways hindered its attainment of knowledge. In contrast to scepticism, Hegel proposes that we can reflect productively on, and thereby advance beyond, the negative or apparently problematic moments of knowledge. This is a process of revealing, as Hegel puts it, the 'untrue consciousness in its untruth'.

It is clear that the *Phenomenology* offers a quite different account of the relationship between self and world to that proposed most strikingly in Fichte and the early Schelling in which subjectivity – the 'I' – is given pre-eminence, and the object explained as a determination of the 'I'. (Schelling, though, had already moved beyond the subjective approach before Hegel published the *Phenomenology*, a fact which Hegel, Schelling felt, had failed to communicate in his writings.) In the *Phenomenology* Hegel, by contrast, offers an account of experience in which subject and object are explained as engaged in a reciprocal relationship.

INTRODUCTION TO THE
PHENOMENOLOGY OF SPIRIT[†]

It is a natural assumption that in philosophy, before we start to deal with its proper subject–matter, viz. the actual cognition of what truly is, one must first of all come to an understanding about cognition, which is regarded either as the instrument to get hold of the Absolute, or as the medium through which one discovers it. A certain uneasiness seems justified, partly because there are different types of cognition, and one of them might be more appropriate than another for the attainment of this goal, so that we could make a bad choice of means; and partly because cognition is a faculty of a definite kind and scope, and thus, without a more precise definition of its nature and limits, we might grasp clouds of error instead of the heaven of truth. This feeling of uneasiness is surely bound to be transformed into the conviction that the whole project of securing for consciousness through cognition what exists in itself is absurd, and that there is a boundary between cognition and the Absolute that completely separates them. For, if cognition is the instrument for getting hold of absolute being, it is obvious that the use of an instrument on a thing certainly does not let it be what it is for itself, but rather sets out to reshape and alter it. If, on the other hand, cognition is not an instrument

---

[†]*HW* III, 68–81. *Phenomenology of Spirit* (Oxford: Oxford University Press, 1977).

of our activity but a more or less passive medium through which the light of truth reaches us, then again we do not receive the truth as it is in itself, but only as it exists through and in this medium. Either way we employ a means which immediately brings about the opposite of its own end; or rather, what is really absurd is that we should make use of a means at all.

It would seem, to be sure, that this evil could be remedied through an acquaintance with the way in which the *instrument* works; for this would enable us to eliminate from the representation of the Absolute which we have gained through it whatever is due to the instrument, and thus get the truth in its purity. But this 'improvement' would in fact only bring us back to where we were before. If we remove from a reshaped thing what the instrument has done to it, then the thing – here the Absolute – becomes for us exactly what it was before this [accordingly] superfluous effort. On the other hand, if the Absolute is supposed merely to be brought nearer to us through this instrument, without anything in it being altered, like a bird caught by a lime-twig, it would surely laugh our little ruse to scorn, if it were not with us, in and for itself, all along, and of its own volition. For a ruse is just what cognition would be in such a case, since it would, with its manifold exertions, be giving itself the air of doing something quite different from creating a merely immediate and therefore effortless relationship. Or, if by testing cognition, which we conceive of as a *medium,* we get to know the law of its refraction, it is again useless to subtract this from the end result. For it is not the refraction of the ray, but the ray itself whereby truth reaches us, that is cognition; and if this were removed, all that would be indicated would be a pure direction or a blank space.

Meanwhile, if the fear of falling into error sets up a mistrust of Science, which in the absence of such scruples gets on with the work itself, and actually cognizes something, it is hard to see why we should not turn round and mistrust this very mistrust. Should we not be concerned as to whether this fear of error is not just the error itself? Indeed, this fear takes something – a great deal in fact – for granted as truth, supporting its scruples and inferences on what is itself in need of prior scrutiny to see if it is true. To be specific, it takes for granted certain ideas about cognition as an *instrument* and as a *medium*, and assumes that there is a *difference between ourselves and this cognition*. Above all, it presupposes that the Absolute stands on one side and cognition on the other, independent and separated from it, and yet is something real; or in other words, it presupposes that cognition which, since it is excluded from the Absolute, is surely outside of the truth as well, is nevertheless true, an assumption whereby what calls itself fear of error reveals itself rather as fear of the truth.

This conclusion stems from the fact that the Absolute alone is true, or the truth alone is absolute. One may set this aside on the grounds that there is a type of cognition which, though it does not cognize the Absolute as Science aims to, is still true, and that cognition in general, though it be incapable of grasping the Absolute, is still capable of grasping other kinds of truth. But we gradually come to see that this kind of talk which goes back and forth only leads to a hazy distinction between an absolute truth and some other kind of truth, and that words like 'absolute', 'cognition', etc. presuppose a meaning which has yet to be ascertained.

Instead of troubling ourselves with such useless ideas and locutions about cognition as 'an instrument for getting hold of the Absolute', or as 'a medium through which we view the truth' (relationships which surely, in the end, are what all these ideas of a cognition cut off from the Absolute, and an Absolute separated from cognition, amount to); instead of putting up with excuses which create the incapacity of Science by assuming relationships of this kind in order to be exempt from the hard work of Science, while at the same time giving the impression of working seriously and zealously; instead of bothering to refute all these ideas, we could reject them out of hand as adventitious and arbitrary, and the words associated with them like 'absolute', 'cognition', 'objective' and 'subjective', and countless others whose meaning is assumed to be generally familiar, could even be regarded as so much deception. For to give the impression that their meaning is generally well known, or that their Notion (*Begriff*) is comprehended, looks more like an attempt to avoid the main problem, which is precisely to provide this Notion. We could, with better justification, simply spare ourselves the trouble of paying any attention whatever to such ideas and locutions; for they are intended to ward off Science itself, and constitute merely an empty appearance of knowing, which vanishes immediately as soon as Science comes on the scene. But Science, just because it comes on the scene, is itself an appearance: in coming on the scene it is not yet Science in its developed and unfolded truth. In this connection it makes no difference whether we think of Science as the appearance because it comes on the scene alongside another mode of knowledge, or whether we call that other untrue knowledge its manifestation. In any case Science must liberate itself from this semblance, and it can do so only by turning against it. For, when confronted with a knowledge that is without truth, Science can neither merely reject it as an ordinary way of looking at things, while assuring us that its Science is a quite different sort of cognition for which that ordinary knowledge is of no account whatever; nor can it appeal to the vulgar view for the intimations it gives us of something better to come. By the former *assurance*, Science would be declaring its power to lie simply in its *being*; but the untrue knowledge likewise appeals to the fact that *it is*, and *assures* us that for it Science is of no account. *One* bare assurance is worth just as much as another. Still less can Science appeal to whatever intimations of something better it may detect in the cognition that is without truth, to the signs which point in the direction of Science. For one thing, it would only be appealing again to what merely *is*; and for another, it would only be appealing to itself, and to itself in the mode in which it exists in the cognition that is without truth. In other words, it would be appealing to an inferior form of its being, to the way it appears, rather than to what it is in and for itself. It is for this reason that an exposition of how knowledge makes its appearance will here be undertaken.

Now, because it has only phenomenal knowledge for its object, this exposition seems not to be Science, free and self-moving in its own peculiar shape; yet from this standpoint it can be regarded as the path of the natural consciousness which presses forward to true knowledge; or as the way of the Soul which journeys through the series of its own configurations as though they were the stations appointed for it by its own nature, so that it may purify itself for the life of the Spirit, and achieve finally, through a completed experience of itself, the awareness of what it really is in itself.

Natural consciousness will show itself to be only the Notion of knowledge, or in other words, not to be real knowledge. But since it directly takes itself to be real knowledge, this path has a negative significance for it, and what is in fact the realization of the Notion, counts for it rather as the loss of its own self; for it does lose its truth on this path. The road can therefore be regarded as the pathway of *doubt*, or more precisely as the way of despair. For what happens on it is not what is ordinarily understood when the word 'doubt' is used: shilly-shallying about this or that presumed truth, followed by a return to that truth again, after the doubt has been appropriately dispelled – so that at the end of the process the matter is taken to be what it was in the first place. On the contrary, this path is the conscious insight into the untruth of phenomenal knowledge, for which the supreme reality is what is in truth only the unrealized Notion. Therefore this thoroughgoing scepticism is also not the scepticism with which an earnest zeal for truth and Science fancies it has prepared and equipped itself in their service: the *resolve*, in Science, not to give oneself over to the thoughts of others, upon mere authority, but to examine everything for oneself and follow only one's own conviction, or better still, to produce everything oneself, and accept only one's own deed as what is true.

The series of configurations which consciousness goes through along this road is, in reality, the detailed history of the *education* of consciousness itself to the standpoint of Science. That zealous resolve represents this education simplistically as something directly over and done with in the making of the resolution; but the way of the Soul is the actual fulfilment of the resolution, in contrast to the untruth of that view. Now, following one's own conviction is, of course, more than giving oneself over to authority; but changing an opinion accepted on authority into an opinion held out of personal conviction, does not necessarily alter the content of the opinion, or replace error with truth. The only difference between being caught up in a system of opinions and prejudices based on personal conviction, and being caught up in one based on the authority of others, lies in the added conceit that is innate in the former position. The scepticism that is directed against the whole range of phenomenal consciousness, on the other hand, renders the Spirit for the first time competent to examine what truth is. For it brings about a state of despair about all the so-called natural ideas, thoughts, and opinions, regardless of whether they are called one's own or someone else's, ideas with which the consciousness that sets about the examination [of truth] *straight away* is still filled and hampered, so that it is, in fact, incapable of carrying out what it wants to undertake.

The necessary progression and interconnection of the forms of the unreal consciousness will by itself bring to pass the *completion* of the series. To make this more intelligible, it may be remarked, in a preliminary and general way, that the exposition of the untrue consciousness in its untruth is not a merely *negative* procedure. The natural consciousness itself normally takes this one-sided view of it; and a knowledge which makes this one-sidedness its very essence is itself one of the patterns of incomplete consciousness which occurs on the road itself, and will manifest itself in due course. This is just the scepticism which only ever sees pure nothingness in its result and abstracts from the fact that this nothingness is specifically the nothingness of that *from which it results.* For it is only when it is taken as the result of that from which it emerges, that it is, in fact, the true result; in that case it is itself a *determinate* nothingness, one which has a *content.* The scepticism that ends up with the bare abstraction of nothingness or emptiness cannot get any further from there, but must wait to see whether something new comes along and what it is, in order to throw it too into the same empty abyss. But when, on the other hand, the result is conceived as it is in truth, namely, as a *determinate* negation, a new form has thereby immediately arisen, and in the negation the transition is made through which the progress through the complete series of forms comes about of itself.

But the *goal* is as necessarily fixed for knowledge as the serial progression; it is the point where knowledge no longer needs to go beyond itself, where knowledge finds itself, where Notion corresponds to object and object to Notion. Hence the progress towards this goal is also unhalting, and short of it no satisfaction is to be found at any of the stations on the way. Whatever is confined within the limits of a natural life cannot by its own efforts go beyond its immediate existence; but it is driven beyond it by something else, and this uprooting entails its death. Consciousness, however, is explicitly the *Notion* of itself. Hence it is something that goes beyond limits, and since these limits are its own, it is something that goes beyond itself. With the positing of a single particular the beyond is also established for consciousness, even if it is only *alongside* the limited object as in the case of spatial intuition. Thus consciousness suffers this violence at its own hands: it spoils its own limited satisfaction. When consciousness feels this violence, its anxiety may well make it retreat from the truth, and strive to hold on to what it is in danger of losing. But it can find no peace. If it wishes to remain in a state of unthinking inertia, then thought troubles its thoughtlessness, and its own unrest disturbs its inertia. Or, if it entrenches itself in sentimentality, which assures us that it finds everything to be *good in its kind,* then this assurance likewise suffers violence at the hands of Reason, for, precisely in so far as something is merely a kind, Reason finds it *not* to be good. Or, again, its fear of the truth may lead consciousness to hide, from itself and others, behind the pretension that its burning zeal for truth makes it difficult or even impossible to find any other truth but the unique truth of vanity – that of being at any rate cleverer than any thoughts that one gets by oneself or from others. This conceit which understands how to belittle every truth, in order to turn back into itself and gloat over its own understanding, which knows how to dissolve every thought and always find the same barren Ego instead of any content – this is a satisfaction which we must leave to itself, for it flees from the universal, and seeks only to be for itself.

In addition to these preliminary general remarks about the manner and the necessity of the progression, it may be useful to say something about the *method of carrying out the inquiry*. If this exposition is viewed as a way of *relating Science to phenomenal* knowledge, and as an investigation and *examination of the reality of cognition*, it would seem that it cannot take place without some presupposition which can serve as its underlying *criterion*. For an examination consists in applying an accepted standard, and in determining whether something is right or wrong on the basis of the resulting agreement or disagreement of the thing examined; thus the standard as such (and Science likewise if it were the criterion) is accepted as the *essence* or as the *in-itself*. But here, where Science has just begun to come on the scene, neither Science nor anything else has yet justified itself as the essence or the in–itself; and without something of the sort it seems that no examination can take place.

This contradiction and its removal will become more definite if we call to mind the abstract determinations of truth and knowledge as they occur in consciousness. Consciousness simultaneously *distinguishes* itself from something, and at the same time *relates* itself to it, or, as it is said, this something exists *for* consciousness; and the determinate aspect of this *relating*, or of the *being* of something for a consciousness, is *knowing*. But we distinguish this being-for-another from *being-in-itself*; whatever is related to knowledge or knowing is also distinguished from it, and posited as existing outside of this relationship; this *being-in-itself* is called *truth*. Just what might be involved in these determinations is of no further concern to us here. Since our object is phenomenal knowledge, its determinations too will at first be taken directly as they present themselves; and they do present themselves very much as we have already apprehended them.

Now, if we inquire into the truth of knowledge, it seems that we are asking what knowledge is *in itself*. Yet in this inquiry knowledge is *our* object, something that exists *for us*; and the *in-itself* that would supposedly result from it would rather be the being of knowledge *for us*. What we asserted to be its essence would be not so much its truth but rather just our knowledge of it. The essence or criterion would lie within ourselves, and that which was to be compared with it and about which a decision would be reached through this comparison would not necessarily have to recognize the validity of such a standard.

But the dissociation, or this semblance of dissociation and presupposition, is overcome by the nature of the object we are investigating. Consciousness provides its own criterion from within itself, so that the investigation becomes a comparison of consciousness with itself; for the distinction made above falls within it. In consciousness one thing exists *for* another, i.e. consciousness regularly contains the determinateness of the moment of knowledge; at the same time, this other is to consciousness not merely *for it*, but is also outside of this relationship, or exists *in itself*: the moment of truth. Thus in what consciousness affirms from within itself as *being-in-itself* or the *True* we have the standard which consciousness itself sets up by which to measure what it knows. If we designate *knowledge* as the Notion, but the essence or the *True* as what exists, or the *object*, then the examination consists in seeing whether the Notion corresponds to the object. But if we call the *essence* or in–itself of the *object* the *Notion*, and on the other hand understand by the *object* the Notion itself as *object*, viz. as it exists *for an other*, then the examination consists in seeing whether the object corresponds to its Notion. It is evident, of course, that the two procedures are the same. But the essential point to bear in mind throughout the whole investigation is that these two moments, 'Notion' and 'object', 'being-for-another' and 'being-in-itself', both fall *within* that knowledge which we are investigating. Consequently, we do not need to import criteria, or to make use of our own bright ideas and thoughts during the course of the inquiry; it is precisely when we leave these aside that we succeed in contemplating the matter in hand as it is *in and for itself.*

But not only is a contribution by us superfluous, since Notion and object, the criterion and what is to be tested, are present in consciousness itself, but we are also spared the trouble of comparing the two and really *testing* them, so that, since what consciousness examines is its own self, all that is left for us to do is simply to look on. For consciousness is, on the one hand, consciousness of the object, and on the other, consciousness of itself; consciousness of what for it is the True, and consciousness of its knowledge of the truth. Since both are *for* the same consciousness, this consciousness is itself their comparison; it is for this same consciousness to know whether its knowledge of the object corresponds to the object or not. The object, it is true, seems only to be for consciousness in the way that consciousness knows it; it seems that consciousness cannot, as it were, get behind the object as it exists for consciousness so as to examine what the object is *in itself*, and hence, too, cannot test its own knowledge by that standard. But the distinction between the in–itself and knowledge is already present in the very fact that consciousness knows an object at all. Something is *for it* the in-itself; and knowledge, or the being of the object for consciousness, is, *for it*, another moment. Upon this distinction, which is present as a fact, the examination rests. If the comparison shows that these two moments do not correspond to one another, it would seem that consciousness must alter its knowledge to make it conform to the object. But, in fact, in the alteration of the knowledge, the object itself alters for it too, for the knowledge that was present was essentially a knowledge of the object: as the knowledge changes, so too does the object, for it essentially belonged to this knowledge. Hence it comes to pass for consciousness that what it previously took to be the *in-itself* is not an *in-itself*, or that it was only an in-itself *for consciousness*. Since consciousness thus finds that its knowledge does not correspond to its object, the object itself does not stand the test; in other words, the criterion for testing is altered when that for which it was to have been the criterion fails to pass the test; and the testing is not only a testing of what we know, but also a testing of the criterion of what knowing is.

Inasmuch as the new true object issues from it, this *dialectical* movement which consciousness exercises on itself and which affects both its knowledge and its object, is precisely what is called *experience* [*Erfahrung*]. In this connection there is a moment in the process just mentioned which must be brought out more clearly, for through it a new light will be thrown on the exposition which follows. Consciousness knows *something*; this object is the essence or the *in–itself*; but it is also for consciousness the in–itself. This is where the ambiguity of this truth enters. We see that consciousness now has two objects: one is the first *in–itself*, the second is the *being-for-consciousness of this in–itself*. The latter appears at first sight to be merely the reflection of consciousness into itself, i.e. what consciousness has in mind is not an object, but only its knowledge of that first object. But, as was shown previously, the first object, in being known, is altered for consciousness; it ceases to be the in–itself, and becomes something that is the *in–itself* only *for consciousness*. And this then is the True: the being-for-consciousness of this in–itself. Or, in other words, this is the *essence*, or the *object* of consciousness. This new object contains the nothingness of the first, it is what experience has made of it.

This exposition of the course of experience contains a moment in virtue of which it does not seem to agree with what is ordinarily understood by experience. This is the moment of transition from the first object and the knowledge of it, to the other object, which experience is said to be about. Our account implied that our knowledge of the first object, or the being-*for*-consciousness of the first in–itself, itself becomes the second object. It usually seems to be the case, on the contrary, that our experience of the untruth of our first notion comes by way of a second object which we come upon by chance and externally, so that our part in all this is simply the pure *apprehension* of what is in and for itself. From the present viewpoint, however, the new object shows itself to have come about through a *reversal of consciousness itself*. This way of looking at the matter is something contributed by *us*, by means of which the succession of experiences through which consciousness passes is raised into a scientific progression – but it is not known to the consciousness that we are observing. But, as a matter of fact, we have here the same situation as the one discussed in regard to the relation between our exposition and scepticism, viz. that in every case the result of an untrue mode of knowledge must not be allowed to run away into an empty nothing, but must necessarily be grasped as the nothing *of that from which it results* – a result which contains what was true in the preceding knowledge. It shows up here like this: since what first appeared as the object sinks for consciousness to the level of its way of knowing it, and since the in–itself becomes a *being-for-consciousness* of the in–itself, the latter is now the new object. Herewith a new pattern of consciousness comes on the scene as well, for which the essence is something different from what it was at the preceding stage. It is this fact that guides the entire series of the patterns of consciousness in their necessary sequence. But it is just this necessity itself, or the *origination* of the new object, that presents itself to consciousness without its understanding how this happens, which proceeds for us, as it were, behind the back of consciousness. Thus in the movement of consciousness there occurs a moment of *being-in-itself* or *being-for-us* which is not present to the consciousness comprehended in the experience itself. The *content*, however, of what presents itself to us does exist *for it*; we comprehend only the formal aspect of that content, or its pure origination. *For it*, what has thus arisen exists only as an object; *for us*, it appears at the same time as movement and a process of becoming.

Because of this necessity, the way to Science is itself already *Science,* and hence, in virtue of its content, is the Science of the *experience of consciousness.*

The experience of itself which consciousness goes through can, in accordance with its Notion, comprehend nothing less than the entire system of consciousness, or the entire realm of the truth of Spirit. For this reason, the moments of this truth are exhibited in their own proper determinateness, viz. as being not abstract moments, but as they are for consciousness, or as consciousness itself stands forth in its relation to them. Thus the moments of the whole are *patterns of consciousness.* In pressing forward to its true existence, consciousness will arrive at a point at which it gets rid of its semblance of being burdened with something alien, with what is only for it, and some sort of 'other', at a point where appearance becomes identical with essence, so that its exposition will coincide at just this point with the authentic Science of Spirit. And finally, when consciousness itself grasps this its own essence, it will signify the nature of absolute knowledge itself.

Translated by A. V. Miller

Freedom and Morality

5

Immanuel Kant, Critique of Practical Reason
(Kritik der Praktischen Vernunft): *Of the Principles
of Pure Practical Reason (1788)*

The *Critique of Practical Reason*, the second of Kant's three *Critiques*, is arguably the most influential of all of Kant's writings. Of particular importance, even amongst readers with no interest in the kind of questions that concerned German Idealism, is its rigorous intellectualist theory of morality. When studied alongside the *Groundwork of the Metaphysic of Morals* the *Critique of Practical Reason* provides us with Kant's well worked-out notions of the categorical imperative and of duty. However, there is a metaphysical component to the second *Critique* that the philosophers of Kant's time found additionally significant, and that is the metaphysics of freedom that underpins his theory of moral agency.

The *Critique of Practical Reason* can be seen as Kant's attempt to demonstrate the reality of practical reason, that aspect of human reason that deals with issues of morality. The most fundamental concept of practical reason is freedom: without freedom, after all, morality would be an illusory exercise. A further task of the second *Critique*, therefore, is to provide some way of substantiating the belief in freedom.

In the section, 'Of the Principles of Pure Practical Reason', Kant emphasises what he sees as the rationality, universality and law-like character of morality. However, the characteristics of morality are not considered in abstraction. They are discussed in the context of Kant's efforts to establish the 'determining grounds of the will', that is, whether the will is determined by reason itself (freedom) or by some other cause, such as inclination (determinism). He argues that it is only when the will is determined by reason that it is free (rational determination being, for Kant, self-determination).

Kant insists that freedom is a practical matter. The *Critique of Pure Reason* had argued that freedom cannot be conclusively affirmed or rejected when considered in a purely theoretical discourse. As the unresolved debate throughout the history of philosophy on whether human beings are free or determined suggests there is what Kant sees as an irresolvable antinomy between the theoretical defences of freedom and determinism. It is the theoretical consideration of freedom itself that is the source of this antinomy. In the *Critique of Practical Reason* Kant goes on to argue that we reach an awareness of freedom instead only through the practice of morality. The activity of morality is a realisation of freedom, but freedom in morality can take place only when we act under reason. To act any other way is to act in a merely subjective way, that is, in a way motivated not by reason but by desire. The faculty of desire cannot provide practical laws because it is directed towards objects, particular things. Because desires are grounded in empirical objects they do not possess the required quality of law-likeness which is, for Kant, fundamental to the very notion of morality. Neither can pleasure nor happiness serve as the ground of determination of morality since they are contingent responses to given objects. The only form of determination consistent with moral agency is that which occurs through reason. Moral action can be a purely autonomous matter only when the (rational) will is not motivated by anything outside it, by anything heteronomous, that is.

The requirements of rationality are powerfully specified by Kant. For him rationality in morality entails acting under the rules of universalisability (that such and such a moral maxim can be recommended for all) and self-consistency. The self-consistency issue leads to a radical account of a moral reason (by name, the categorical imperative): certain propositions have moral efficacy not because of what they actually hold, but rather because of their form. The key measure of their form is that they cannot be self-refuting. For example, the proposition that one may lie whenever it is expedient to do so is self-refuting when considered rationally: to make expedient lying a universal law of morality is actually to deprive oneself of the conditions of truth-telling upon which lying is a parasitic practice.

Kant rejects the idea that we can ever reach the idea of freedom through 'intellectual intuition'. 'Intellectual intuition' would be the awareness of some inner object which corresponds with freedom. But freedom is known only in practical reason, by moral thinking. (This rejection of 'intellectual intuition' is particularly significant in the context of German Idealism given that Fichte and Schelling attempt to offer a reconstructed version of the concept in support of their ideas of freedom.)

In the 'Deduction of the Fundamental Principles of Pure Practical Reason' Kant offers the metaphysical thesis that the possibility for the realisation of freedom must lie outside the world which we experience through sense perception. He posits what he terms 'supersensible nature' as that aspect of the moral agent which is not subject to the laws of empirical causality. (In this regard Kant makes use of some of the thinking of the *Critique of Pure Reason* in that he claims that the subject has determinative force in its *a priori* capacities: subjectivity has the capacity to determine experience.) The moral agent, he argues, is in fact subject to its own laws: it is self-causing in so far as it operates under the laws of rationality as opposed to the empirical laws of desire.

It is important to see that Kant does not hold that the 'I think' of the 'Transcendental Deduction' is an epistemological relative of the supersensible self of the 'Deduction of the Fundamental Principles of Pure Practical Reason'.

The former is a theoretically demonstrable condition of perceptual experience: the latter must be assumed in order to make sense of the idea of
morality. However, the parallels between the two tempted German Idealism
in a certain direction: both selves, so to speak – the self of the Transcendental Deduction and the self of Practical Reason – are characterised by
spontaneity, that is, as not being subject to the laws of causality. Little ingenuity was required, therefore, to see in Kant a fully idealistic conception
of the self in which experience in its practical and moral characteristics is
effectively constituted by the self.

OF THE PRINCIPLES OF PURE PRACTICAL REASON
BOOK I. THE ANALYTIC OF PURE PRACTICAL REASON†

Chapter I
Of The Principles of Pure Practical Reason

§I. – Definition

Practical *Principles* are propositions which contain a general determination of the
will, having under it several practical rules. They are subjective, or *Maxims*, when
the condition is regarded by the subject as valid only for his own will, but are
objective, or practical *laws*, when the condition is recognized as objective, that is,
valid for the will of every rational being.

Remark

Supposing that *pure* reason contains in itself a practical motive, that is, one adequate
to determine the will, then there are practical laws; otherwise all practical principles
will be mere maxims. In case the will of a rational being is pathologically affected,
there may occur a conflict of the maxims with the practical laws recognized by
itself. For example, one may make it his maxim to let no injury pass unrevenged,
and yet he may see that this is not a practical law, but only his own maxim; that,
on the contrary, regarded as being in one and the same maxim a rule for the
will of every rational being, it must contradict itself. In natural philosophy the

---

†*KAA* V, 19–32. In *Critique of Practical Reason and Other Works on the Theory of Ethics* (London: Longmans,
6th edition 1909).

principles of what happens (e.g. the principle of equality of action and reaction in the communication of motion) are at the same time laws of nature; for the use of reason there is theoretical, and determined by the nature of the object. In practical philosophy, i.e. that which has to do only with the grounds of determination of the will, the principles which a man makes for himself are not laws by which one is inevitably bound; because reason in practical matters has to do with the subject, namely, with the faculty of desire, the special character of which may occasion variety in the rule. The practical rule is always a product of reason, because it prescribes action as a means to the effect. But in the case of a being with whom reason does not of itself determine the will, this rule is an *imperative*, i.e. a rule characterized by 'shall', which expresses the objective necessitation of the action, and signifies that if reason completely determined the will, the action would inevitably take place according to this rule. Imperatives, therefore, are objectively valid, and are quite distinct from maxims, which are subjective principles. The former either determine the conditions of the causality of the rational being as an efficient cause, i.e. merely in reference to the effect and the means of attaining it; or they determine the will only, whether it is adequate to the effect or not. The former would be hypothetical imperatives, and contain mere precepts of skill; the latter, on the contrary, would be categorical, and would alone be practical laws. Thus maxims are *principles*, but not *imperatives*. Imperatives themselves, however, when they are conditional (i.e. do not determine the will simply as will, but only in respect to a desired effect, that is, when they are hypothetical imperatives), are practical *precepts*, but not *laws*. Laws must be sufficient to determine the will as will, even before I ask whether I have power sufficient for a desired effect, or the means necessary to produce it; hence they are categorical: otherwise they are not laws at all, because the necessity is wanting, which, if it is to be practical, must be independent of conditions which are pathological, and are therefore only contingently connected with the will. Tell a man, for example, that he must be industrious and thrifty in youth, in order that he may not want in old age; this is a correct and important practical precept of the will. But it is easy to see that in this case the will is directed to something *else* which it is presupposed that it desires, and as to this desire, we must leave it to the actor himself whether he looks forward to other resources than those of his own acquisition, or does not expect to be old, or thinks that in case of future necessity he will be able to make shift with little. Reason, from which alone can spring a rule involving necessity, does, indeed, give necessity to this precept (else it would not be an imperative), but this is a necessity dependent on subjective conditions, and cannot be supposed in the same degree in all subjects. But that reason may give laws it is necessary that it should only need to presuppose *itself*, because rules are objectively and universally valid only when they hold without any contingent subjective conditions, which distinguish one rational being from another. Now tell a man that he should never make a deceitful promise, this is a rule which only concerns his will, whether the purposes he may have can be attained thereby or not; it is the volition only which is to be determined *a priori* by that rule. If now it is found that this rule is practically right, then it is a law, because it is a categorical imperative. Thus, practical laws refer to the will only, without considering what is attained by its causality, and we may disregard this latter (as belonging to the world of sense) in order to have them quite pure.

§II. – Theorem I

All practical principles which presuppose an object (matter) of the faculty of desire as the ground of determination of the will are empirical, and can furnish no practical laws.

By the matter of the faculty of desire I mean an object the realization of which is desired. Now, if the desire for this object *precedes* the practical rule, and is the condition of our making it a principle, then I say (*in the first place*) this principle is in that case wholly empirical, for then what determines the choice is the idea of an object, and that relation of this idea to the subject by which its faculty of desire is determined to its realization. Such a relation to the subject is called the *pleasure* in the realization of an object. This, then, must be presupposed as a condition of the possibility of determination of the will. But it is impossible to know *a priori* of any idea of an object whether it will be connected with *pleasure or pain*, or be indifferent. In such cases, therefore, the determining principle of the choice must be empirical, and, therefore, also the practical material principle which presupposes it as a condition.

In the second place, since susceptibility to a pleasure or pain can be known only empirically, and cannot hold in the same degree for all rational beings, a principle which is based on this subjective condition may serve indeed as a *maxim* for the subject which possesses this susceptibility, but not as a *law* even to him (because it is wanting in objective necessity, which must be recognized *a priori*); it follows, therefore, that such a principle can never furnish a practical law.

§III. – Theorem II

All material practical principles as such are of one and the same kind, and come under the general principle of self-love or private happiness.

Pleasure arising from the idea of the existence of a thing, in so far as it is to determine the desire of this thing, is founded on the *susceptibility* of the subject, since it *depends* on the presence of an object; hence it belongs to sense (feeling), and not to understanding, which expresses a relation of the idea *to an object* according to concepts, not to the subject according to feelings. It is, then, practical only in so far as the faculty of desire is determined by the sensation of agreeableness which the subject expects from the actual existence of the object. Now, a rational being's consciousness of the pleasantness of life uninterruptedly accompanying his whole existence is happiness; and the principle which makes this the supreme ground of determination of the will is the principle of self-love. All material principles, then, which place the determining ground of the will in the pleasure or pain to be received from the existence of any object are all of the same kind, inasmuch as they all belong to the principle of self-love or private happiness.

Corollary

All *material* practical rules place the determining principle of the will in the *lower desires*, and if there were no *purely formal* laws of the will adequate to determine it, then we could not admit *any higher desire* at all.

Remark I

It is surprising that men, otherwise acute, can think it possible to distinguish between *higher* and *lower desires*, according as the ideas which are connected with the feeling of pleasure have their origin in the *senses* or in the *understanding*; for when we inquire what are the determining grounds of desire, and place them in some expected pleasantness, it is of no consequence whence the *idea* of this pleasing object is derived, but only how much it *pleases*. Whether an idea has its seat and source in the understanding or not, if it can only determine the choice by presupposing a feeling of pleasure in the subject, it follows that its capability of determining the choice depends altogether on the nature of the inner sense, namely, that this can be agreeably affected by it. However dissimilar ideas of objects may be, though they be ideas of the understanding, or even of the reason in contrast to ideas of sense, yet the feeling of pleasure, by means of which they constitute the determining principle of the will (the expected satisfaction which impels the activity to the production of the object), is of one and the same kind, not only inasmuch as it can only be known empirically, but also inasmuch as it affects one and the same vital force which manifests itself in the faculty of desire, and in this respect can only differ in degree from every other ground of determination. Otherwise, how could we compare in respect of *magnitude* two principles of determination, the ideas of which depend upon different faculties, so as to prefer that which affects the faculty of desire in the highest degree. The same man may return unread an instructive book which he cannot again obtain, in order not to miss a hunt; he may depart in the midst of a fine speech, in order not to be late for dinner; he may leave a rational conversation, such as he otherwise values highly, to take his place at the gaming-table; he may even repulse a poor man whom he at other times takes pleasure in benefiting, because he has only just enough money in his pocket to pay for his admission to the theatre. If the determination of his will rests on the feeling of the agreeableness or disagreeableness that he expects from any cause, it is all the same to him by what sort of ideas he will be affected. The only thing that concerns him, in order to decide his choice, is, how great, how long continued, how easily obtained, and how often repeated, this agreeableness is. Just as to the man who wants money to spend, it is all the same whether the gold was dug out of the mountain or washed out of the sand, provided it is everywhere accepted at the same value; so the man who cares only for the enjoyment of life does not ask whether the ideas are of the understanding or the senses, but only *how much* and *how great pleasure* they will give for the longest time. It is only those that would gladly deny to pure reason the power of determining the will, without the presupposition of any feeling, who could deviate so far from their own exposition as to describe as quite heterogeneous what they have themselves previously brought under one and the same principle. Thus, for example, it is observed that we can find pleasure in the mere *exercise of power*, in the consciousness of our strength of mind in overcoming obstacles which are opposed to our designs, in the culture of our mental talents, etc.; and we justly call these more refined pleasures and enjoyments, because they are more in our power than others; they do not wear out, but rather increase the capacity for further enjoyment of them, and while they delight they at the same time cultivate. But to say on this account that they determine the will in a different way, and not through sense, whereas the possibility of the pleasure presupposes a feeling for it implanted in us, which is the first condition of this satisfaction; this is just as when ignorant persons that like to dabble in metaphysics imagine matter so subtle, so super-subtle, that they almost make themselves giddy with it, and then think that in this way they have conceived it as a *spiritual* and yet extended being. If with *Epicurus* we make virtue determine the will only by means of the pleasure it promises, we cannot afterwards blame him for holding that this pleasure is of the same kind as those of the coarsest senses. For we have no reason whatever to charge him with holding that the ideas by which this feeling is excited in us belong merely to the bodily senses. As far as can be conjectured, he sought the source of many of them in the use of the higher cognitive faculty; but this did not prevent him, and could not prevent him, from holding on the principle above stated, that the pleasure itself which those intellectual ideas give us, and by which alone they can determine the will, is just of the same kind. *Consistency* is the highest obligation of a philosopher, and yet the most rarely found. The ancient Greek schools give us more examples of it than we find in our *syncretistic* age, in which a certain shallow and dishonest *system of compromise* of contradictory principles is devised, because it commends itself better to a public which is content to know something of everything and nothing thoroughly, so as to please every party.

The principle of private happiness, however much understanding and reason may be used in it, cannot contain any other determining principles for the will than those which belong to the *lower* desires; and either there are no [higher] desires at all, or *pure* reason must of itself alone be practical: that is, it must be able to determine the will by the mere form of the practical rule without supposing any feeling, and consequently without any idea of the pleasant or unpleasant, which is the matter of the desire, and which is always an empirical condition of the principles. Then only, when reason of itself determines the will (not as the servant of the inclination), it is really a *higher* desire to which that which is pathologically determined is subordinate, and is really, and even specifically, distinct from the latter, so that even the slightest admixture of the motives of the latter impairs its strength and superiority; just as in a mathematical demonstration the least empirical condition would degrade and destroy its force and value. Reason, with its practical law, determines the will immediately, not by means of an intervening feeling of pleasure or pain, not even of pleasure in the law itself, and it is only because it can, as pure reason, be practical, that it is possible for it to be *legislative.*

Remark II

To be happy is necessarily the wish of every finite rational being, and this, therefore, is inevitably a determining principle of its faculty of desire. For we are not in possession originally of satisfaction with our whole existence – a bliss which would imply a consciousness of our own independent self-sufficiency – this is a problem imposed upon us by our own finite nature, because we have wants, and these wants regard the matter of our desires, that is, something that is relative to a subjective feeling of pleasure or pain, which determines what we need in order to be satisfied with our condition. But just because this material principle of determination can only be empirically known by the subject, it is impossible to regard this problem as a law; for a law being objective must contain the *very same principle of determination* of the will in all cases and for all rational beings. For, although the notion of happiness is *in every case* the foundation of the practical relation of the *objects* to the desires, yet it is only a general name for the subjective determining principles, and determines nothing specifically; whereas this is what alone we are concerned with in this practical problem, which cannot be solved at all without such specific determination. For it is every man's own special feeling of pleasure and pain that decides in what he is to place his happiness, and even in the same subject this will vary with the difference of his wants according as this feeling changes, and thus a law which is *subjectively necessary* (as a law of nature) is *objectively* a very contingent practical principle, which can and must be very different in different subjects, and therefore can never furnish a law; since, in the desire for happiness it is not the form (of conformity to law) that is decisive, but simply the matter, namely, whether I am to expect pleasure in following the law, and how much. Principles of self-love may, indeed, contain universal precepts of skill (how to find means to accomplish one's purposes), but in that case they are merely theoretical principles;[1] as, for example, how he who would like to eat bread should contrive a mill; but practical precepts founded on them can never be universal, for the determining principle of the desire is based on the feeling of pleasure and pain, which can never be supposed to be universally directed to the same objects.

Even supposing, however, that all finite rational beings were thoroughly agreed as to what were the objects of their feelings of pleasure and pain, and also as to the means which they must employ to attain the one and avoid the other; still, they could *by no means* set up the *principle of self-love* as a *practical law,* for this unanimity

---

[1] Propositions which in mathematics or physics are called *practical* ought properly to be called *technical.* For they have nothing to do with the determination of the will; they only point out how a certain effect is to be produced, and are therefore just as theoretical as any propositions which express the connexion of a cause with an effect. Now whoever chooses the effect must also choose the cause.

itself would be only contingent. The principle of determination would still be only subjectively valid and merely empirical, and would not possess the necessity which is conceived in every law, namely, an objective necessity arising from *a priori* grounds; unless, indeed, we hold this necessity to be not at all practical, but merely physical, viz. that our action is as inevitably determined by our inclination, as yawning when we see others yawn. It would be better to maintain that there are no practical laws at all, but only *counsels* for the service of our desires, than to raise merely subjective principles to the rank of practical laws, which have objective necessity, and not merely subjective, and which must be known by reason *a priori*, not by experience (however empirically universal this may be). Even the rules of corresponding phenomena are only called laws of nature (e.g. the mechanical laws), when we either know them really *a priori*, or (as in the case of chemical laws) suppose that they would be known *a priori* from objective grounds if our insight reached further. But in the case of merely subjective practical principles, it is expressly made a condition that they rest not on objective but on subjective conditions of choice, and hence that they must always be represented as mere maxims; never as practical laws. This second remark seems at first sight to be mere verbal refinement, but it defines the terms of the most important distinction which can come into consideration in practical investigations.

§IV. – Theorem III

A rational being cannot regard his maxims as practical universal laws, unless he conceives them as principles which determine the will, not by their matter, but by their form only.

By the matter of a practical principle I mean the object of the will. This object is either the determining ground of the will or it is not. In the former case the rule of the will is subjected to an empirical condition (viz. the relation of the determining idea to the feeling of pleasure and pain); consequently it cannot be a practical law. Now, when we abstract from a law all matter, i.e. every object of the will (as a determining principle), nothing is left but the mere *form* of a universal legislation. Therefore, either a rational being cannot conceive his subjective practical principles, that is, his maxims, as being at the same time universal laws, or he must suppose that their mere form, by which they are fitted for universal legislation, is alone what makes them practical laws.

Remark

The commonest understanding can distinguish without instruction what form of maxim is adapted for universal legislation, and what is not. Suppose, for example, that I have made it my maxim to increase my fortune by every safe means. Now, I have a deposit in my hands, the owner of which is dead and has left no writing about it. This is just the case for my maxim. I desire, then, to know whether that maxim can also hold good as a universal practical law. I apply it, therefore, to the present case, and ask whether it could take the form of a law, and consequently whether I can by my maxim at the same time give such a law as this, that everyone may deny a deposit of which no one can produce a proof. I at once become aware that such a principle, viewed as a law, would annihilate itself, because the result would be that there would be no deposits. A practical law which I recognize as such must be qualified for universal legislation; this is an identical proposition, and therefore self-evident. Now, if I say that my will is subject to a practical law, I cannot adduce my inclination (e.g. in the present case my avarice) as a principle of determination fitted to be a universal practical law; for this is so far from being fitted for a universal legislation that, if put in the form of a universal law, it would destroy itself.

It is, therefore, surprising that intelligent men could have thought of calling the desire of happiness a universal *practical law* on the ground that the desire is universal, and, therefore, also the *maxim* by which everyone makes this desire determine his will. For whereas in other cases a universal law of nature makes everything harmonious; here, on the contrary, if we attribute to the maxim the universality of a law, the extreme opposite of harmony will follow, the greatest opposition, and the complete destruction of the maxim itself, and its purpose. For, in that case, the will of all has not one and the same object, but everyone has his own (his private welfare), which may accidentally accord with the purposes of others which are equally selfish, but it is far from sufficing for a law; because the occasional exceptions which one is permitted to make are endless, and cannot be definitely embraced in one universal rule. In this manner, then, results a harmony like that which a certain satirical poem depicts as existing between a married couple bent on going to ruin, 'O, marvellous harmony, what he wishes, she wishes also'; or like what is said of the pledge of Francis I to the Emperor Charles V, 'What my brother Charles wishes that I wish also' (viz. Milan). Empirical principles of determination are not fit for any universal external legislation, but just as little for internal; for each man makes his own subject the foundation of his inclination, and in the same subject sometimes one inclination, sometimes another, has the preponderance. To discover a law which would govern them all under this condition, namely, bringing them all into harmony, is quite impossible.

§V. – Problem I

Supposing that the mere legislative form of maxims is alone the sufficient determining principle of a will, to find the nature of the will which can be determined by it alone.

Since the bare form of the law can only be conceived by reason, and is, therefore, not an object of the senses, and consequently does not belong to the class of phenomena, it follows that the idea of it, which determines the will, is distinct from all the principles that determine events in nature according to the law of causality, because in their case the determining principles must themselves be phenomena. Now, if no other determining principle can serve as a law for the will except that universal legislative form, such a will must be conceived as quite independent of the natural law of phenomena in their mutual relation, namely, the law of causality; such independence is called *freedom* in the strictest, that is in the transcendental sense; consequently, a will which can have its law in nothing but the mere legislative form of the maxim is a free will.

§VI. – Problem II

Supposing that a will is free, to find the law which alone is competent to determine it necessarily.

Since the matter of the practical law, i.e. an object of the maxim, can never be given otherwise than empirically, and the free will is independent of empirical conditions (that is, conditions belonging to the world of sense), and yet is determinable, consequently a free will must find its principle of determination in the law, and yet independently of the matter of the law. But, beside the matter of the law, nothing is contained in it except the legislative form. It is the legislative form, then, contained in the maxim, which can alone constitute a principle of determination of the [free] will.

Remarks

Thus freedom and an unconditional practical law reciprocally imply each other. Now I do not ask here whether they are in fact distinct, or whether an unconditional law is not rather merely the consciousness of a pure practical reason, and the latter identical with the positive concept of freedom; I only ask, whence *begins* our *knowledge* of the unconditionally practical, whether it is from freedom or from the practical law? Now it cannot begin from freedom, for of this we cannot be immediately conscious, since the first concept of it is negative; nor can we infer it from experience, for experience gives us the knowledge only of the law of phenomena, and hence of the mechanism of nature, the direct opposite of freedom. It is therefore the moral law, of which we become directly conscious (as soon as we trace for ourselves maxims of the will), that *first* presents itself to us, and leads directly to the concept of freedom, inasmuch as reason presents it as a principle of determination not to be outweighed by any sensible conditions, nay, wholly independent of them. But how is the consciousness of that moral law possible? We can become conscious of pure practical laws just as we are conscious of pure theoretical principles, by attending to the necessity with which reason prescribes them, and to the elimination of all empirical conditions, which it directs. The concept of a pure will arises out of the former, as that of a pure understanding arises out of the latter. That this is the true subordination of our concepts, and that it is morality that first discovers to us the notion of freedom, hence that it is *practical reason* which, with this concept, first proposes to speculative reason the most insoluble problem, thereby placing it in the greatest perplexity, is evident from the following consideration: – Since nothing in phenomena can be explained by the concept of freedom, but the mechanism of nature must constitute the only clue; moreover, when pure reason tries to ascend in the series of causes to the unconditioned, it falls into an antinomy which is entangled in incomprehensibilities on the one side as much as the other; whilst the latter (namely, mechanism) is at least useful in the explanation of phenomena, therefore no one would ever have been so rash as to introduce freedom into science, had not the moral law, and with it practical reason, come in and forced this notion upon us. Experience, however, confirms this order of notions. Suppose some one asserts of his lustful appetite that, when the desired object and the opportunity are present, it is quite irresistible. [Ask him] – if a gallows were erected before the house where he finds this opportunity, in order that he should be hanged thereon immediately after the gratification of his lust, whether he could not then control his passion; we need not be long in doubt what he would reply. Ask him, however – if his sovereign ordered him, on pain of the same immediate execution, to bear false witness against an honourable man, whom the prince might wish to destroy under a plausible pretext, would he consider it possible in that case to overcome his love of life, however great it may be. He would perhaps not venture to affirm whether he would do so or not, but he must unhesitatingly admit that it is possible to do so. He judges, therefore, that he can do a certain thing because he is conscious that he ought, and he recognizes that he is free – a fact which but for the moral law he would never have known.

§VII. – Fundamental Law of the Pure Practical Reason

Act so that the maxim of thy will can always at the same time hold good as a principle of universal legislation.

Remark

Pure geometry has postulates which are practical propositions, but contain nothing further than the assumption that we *can* do something if it is required that we *should* do it, and these are the only geometrical propositions that concern actual existence. They are, then, practical rules under a problematical condition of the will; but here the rule says: – We absolutely must proceed in a certain manner. The practical rule is, therefore, unconditional, and hence it is conceived *a priori* as a categorically practical proposition by which the will is objectively determined absolutely and immediately (by the practical rule itself, which thus is in this case a law); for *pure reason practical of itself* is here directly legislative. The will is thought as independent of empirical conditions, and, therefore, as pure will determined by *the mere form of the law,* and this principle of determination is regarded as the supreme condition of all maxims. The thing is strange enough, and has no parallel in all the rest of our practical knowledge. For the *a priori* thought of a possible universal legislation which is therefore merely problematical, is unconditionally commanded as a law without borrowing anything from experience or from any external will. This, however, is not a precept to do something by which some desired effect can be attained (for then the will would depend on physical conditions), but a rule that determines the will *a priori* only so far as regards the forms of its maxims; and thus it is at least not impossible to conceive that a law, which only applies to the *subjective* form of principles, yet serves as a principle of determination by means of the *objective* form of law in general. We may call the consciousness of this fundamental law a fact of reason, because we cannot reason it out from antecedent data of reason, e.g. the consciousness of freedom (for this is not antecedently given), but it forces itself on us as a synthetic *a priori* proposition, which is not based on any intuition, either pure or empirical. It would, indeed, be analytical if the freedom of the will were presupposed, but to presuppose freedom as a positive *concept* would require an intellectual intuition, which cannot here be assumed; however, when we regard this law as *given,* it must be observed, in order not to fall into any misconception, that it is not an empirical fact, but the sole fact of the pure reason, which thereby announces itself as originally legislative (*sic volo sic jubeo*).

[. . .]

I. – Of the Deduction of the Fundamental Principles of the Pure Practical Reason[†]

This Analytic shows that pure reason can be practical, that is, can of itself determine the will independently of anything empirical; and this it proves by a fact in which pure reason in us proves itself actually practical, namely, the autonomy shown in the fundamental principle of morality, by which reason determines the will to action.

It shows at the same time that this fact is inseparably connected with the consciousness of freedom of the will; nay, is identical with it; and by this the will of a rational being, although as belonging to the world of sense it recognizes itself as necessarily subject to the laws of causality like other efficient causes; yet, at the same time, on another side, namely, as a being in itself, is conscious of existing in and being determined by an intelligible order of things; conscious not by virtue of a special intuition of itself, but by virtue of certain dynamical laws which determine its causality in the sensible world; for it has been elsewhere proved that if freedom is predicated of us, it transports us into an intelligible order of things.

Now, if we compare with this the analytical part of the critique of pure speculative reason, we shall see a remarkable contrast. There it was not fundamental principles, but pure, sensible *intuition* (space and time), that was the first *datum* that made *a priori* knowledge possible, though only of objects of the senses. Synthetical principles could not be derived from mere concepts without intuition; on the contrary, they could only exist with reference to this intuition, and therefore to objects of possible experience, since it is the concepts of the understanding,

[†]*KAA* V, 42–50.

united with this intuition, which alone make that knowledge possible which we call experience. Beyond objects of experience, and therefore with regard to things as noumena, all positive knowledge was rightly disclaimed for speculative reason. This reason, however, went so far as to establish with certainty the concept of noumena; that is, the possibility, nay, the necessity, of thinking them; for example, it showed against all objections that the supposition of freedom, negatively considered, was quite consistent with those principles and limitations of pure theoretic reason. But it could not give us any definite enlargement of our knowledge with respect to such objects, but, on the contrary, cut off all view of them altogether.

On the other hand, the moral law, although it gives no *view,* yet gives us a fact absolutely inexplicable from any data of the sensible world, and the whole compass of our theoretical use of reason, a fact which points to a pure world of the understanding, nay, even defines it *positively,* and enables us to know something of it, namely, a law.

This law (as far as rational beings are concerned) gives to the world of sense, which is a sensible system of nature, the form of a world of the understanding, that is, of a *supersensible system of nature,* without interfering with its mechanism. Now, a system of nature, in the most general sense, is the existence of things under laws. The sensible nature of rational beings in general is their existence under laws empirically conditioned, which, from the point of view of reason, is *heteronomy.* The supersensible nature of the same beings, on the other hand, is their existence according to laws which are independent of every empirical condition, and therefore belong to the *autonomy* of pure reason. And, since the laws by which the existence of things depends on cognition are practical, supersensible nature, so far as we can form any notion of it, is nothing else than a *system of nature under the autonomy of pure practical reason.* Now, the law of this autonomy is the moral law, which, therefore, is the fundamental law of a supersensible nature, and of a pure world of understanding, whose counterpart must exist in the world of sense, but without interfering with its laws. We might call the former the *archetypal* world (*natura archetypa*), which we only know in the reason; and the latter the *ectypal* world (*natura ectypa*), because it contains the possible effect of the idea of the former which is the determining principle of the will. For the moral law, in fact, transfers us ideally into a system in which pure reason, if it were accompanied with adequate physical power, would produce the *summum bonum,* and it determines our will to give the sensible world the form of a system of rational beings.

The least attention to oneself proves that this idea really serves as a model for the determinations of our will.

When the maxim which I am disposed to follow in giving testimony is tested by the practical reason, I always consider what it would be if it were to hold as a universal law of nature. It is manifest that in this view it would oblige everyone to speak the truth. For it cannot hold as a universal law of nature that statements should be allowed to have the force of proof, and yet to be purposely untrue. Similarly, the maxim which I adopt with respect to disposing freely of my life is at once determined, when I ask myself what it should be, in order that a system, of which it is the law, should maintain itself. It is obvious that in such a system no one could *arbitrarily* put an end to his own life, for such an arrangement would not be a permanent order of things. And so in all similar cases. Now, in nature, as it actually is an object of experience, the free will is not of itself determined to maxims which could of themselves be the foundation of a natural system of universal laws, or which could even be adapted to a system so constituted; on the contrary, its maxims are private inclinations which constitute, indeed, a natural whole in conformity with pathological (physical) laws, but could not form part of a system of nature, which would only be possible through our will acting in accordance with pure practical laws. Yet we are, through reason, conscious of a law to which all our maxims are subject, as though a natural order must be originated from our will. This law, therefore, must be the idea of a natural system not given in experience, and yet possible through freedom; a system, therefore, which is supersensible, and to which we give objective reality, at least in a practical point of view, since we look on it as an object of our will as pure rational beings.

Hence the distinction between the laws of a natural system to which the *will is subject,* and of a natural system which is *subject to a will* (as far as its relation to its free actions is concerned), rests on this, that in the former the objects must be causes of the ideas which determine the will; whereas in the latter the will is the cause of the objects; so that its causality has its determining principle solely in the pure faculty of reason, which may therefore be called a pure practical reason.

There are therefore two very distinct problems: how, on *the one side,* pure reason can *cognise* objects *a priori,* and how *on the other side* it can be an immediate determining principle of the will, that is, of the causality of the rational being with respect to the reality of objects (through the mere thought of the universal validity of its own maxims as laws).

The former, which belongs to the critique of the pure speculative reason, requires a previous explanation, how intuitions without which no object can be given, and, therefore, none known synthetically, are possible *a priori*; and its solution turns out to be that these are all only sensible, and therefore do not render possible any speculative knowledge which goes further than possible experience reaches; and that therefore all the principles of that pure speculative reason avail only to make experience possible; either experience of given objects or of those that may be given *ad infinitum,* but never are completely given.

The latter, which belongs to the critique of practical reason, requires no explanation how the objects of the faculty of desire are possible, for that being a problem of the theoretical knowledge of nature is left to the critique of the speculative reason, but only how reason can determine the maxims of the will; whether this takes place only by means of empirical ideas as principles of determination, or whether pure reason can be practical and be the law of a possible order of nature, which is not empirically knowable. The possibility of such a supersensible system of nature, the conception of which can also be the ground of its reality through our own free will, does not require any *a priori* intuition (of an intelligible world) which, being in this case supersensible, would be impossible for us. For the question is only as to the determining principle of volition in its maxims, namely, whether it is empirical, or is a conception of the pure reason (having the legal character belonging to it in general), and how it can be the latter. It is left to the theoretic principles of reason to decide whether the causality of the will suffices for the realization of the objects or not, this being an inquiry into the possibility of the objects of the volition. Intuition of these objects is therefore of no importance to the practical problem. We are here concerned only with the determination of the will and the determining principles of its maxims as a free will, not at all with the result. For, provided only that the *will* conforms to the law of pure reason, then let its *power* in execution be what it may, whether according to these maxims of legislation of a possible system of nature any such system really results or not, this is no concern of the critique, which only inquires whether, and in what way, pure reason can be practical, that is directly determine the will.

In this inquiry criticism may and must begin with pure practical laws and their reality. But instead of intuition it takes as their foundation the conception of their existence in the intelligible world, namely, the concept of freedom. For this concept has no other meaning, and these laws are only possible in relation to freedom of the will; but freedom being supposed, they are necessary; or conversely freedom is necessary because those laws are necessary, being practical postulates. It cannot be further explained how this consciousness of the moral law, or, what is the same thing, of freedom, is possible; but that it is admissible is well established in the theoretical critique.

The *Exposition* of the supreme principle of practical reason is now finished; that is to say, it has been shown first, what it contains, that it subsists for itself quite *a priori* and independent of empirical principles; and next in what it is distinguished from all other practical principles. With the *deduction*, that is, the justification of its objective and universal validity, and the discernment of the possibility of such a synthetical proposition *a priori*, we cannot expect to succeed so well as in the case of the principles of pure theoretical reason. For these referred to objects of possible experience, namely, to phenomena; and we could prove that these phenomena could be *known* as objects of experience only by being brought under the categories in accordance with these laws; and consequently that all possible experience must conform to these laws. But I could not proceed in this way with the deduction of the moral law. For this does not concern the knowledge of the properties of objects, which may be given to the reason from some other source; but a knowledge which can itself be the ground of the existence of the objects, and by which reason in a rational being has causality, i.e. pure reason, which can be regarded as a faculty immediately determining the will.

Now all our human insight is at an end as soon as we have arrived at fundamental powers or faculties; for the possibility of these cannot be understood by any means, and just as little should it be arbitrarily invented and assumed. Therefore, in the theoretic use of reason, it is experience alone that can justify us in assuming them. But this expedient of adducing empirical proofs, instead of a deduction from *a priori* sources of knowledge, is denied us here in respect to the pure practical faculty of reason. For whatever requires to draw the proof of its reality from experience must depend for the grounds of its possibility on principles of experience; and pure, yet practical, reason by its very notion cannot be regarded as such. Further, the moral law is given as a fact of pure reason of which we are *a priori* conscious, and which is apodictically certain, though it be granted that in experience no example of its exact fulfilment can be found. Hence the objective reality of the moral law cannot be proved by any deduction by any efforts of theoretical reason, whether speculative or empirically supported, and therefore, even if we renounced its apodictic certainty, it could not be proved *a posteriori* by experience, and yet it is firmly established of itself.

But instead of this vainly sought deduction of the moral principle, something else is found which was quite unexpected, namely, that this moral principle serves conversely as the principle of the deduction of an inscrutable faculty which no experience could prove, but of which speculative reason was compelled at least to assume the possibility (in order to find amongst its cosmological ideas the unconditioned in the chain of causality, so as not to contradict itself) – I mean the faculty of freedom. The moral law, which itself does not require a justification, proves not merely the possibility of freedom, but that it really belongs to beings who recognize this law as binding on themselves. The moral law is in fact a law of the causality of free agents, and therefore of the possibility of a supersensible system of nature, just as the metaphysical law of events in the world of sense was a law of causality of the sensible system of nature; and it therefore determines what speculative philosophy was compelled to leave undetermined, namely, the law for a causality, the concept of which in the latter was only negative; and therefore for the first time gives this concept objective reality.

This sort of credential of the moral law, viz. that it is set forth as a principle of the deduction of freedom, which is a causality of pure reason, is a sufficient substitute for all *a priori* justification, since theoretic reason was compelled to assume *at least* the possibility of freedom, in order to satisfy a want of its own. For the moral law proves its reality, so as even to satisfy the critique of the speculative reason, by the fact that it adds a positive definition to a causality previously conceived only negatively, the possibility of which was incomprehensible to speculative reason, which yet was compelled to suppose it. For it adds the notion of a reason that directly determines the will (by imposing on its maxims the condition of a universal legislative form); and thus it is able for the first time to give objective, though only practical, reality to reason, which always became transcendent when it sought to proceed speculatively with its ideas. It thus changes the *transcendent* use of reason into an *immanent* use (so that reason is itself, by means of ideas, an efficient cause in the field of experience).

The determination of the causality of beings in the world of sense, as such, can never be unconditioned; and yet for every series of conditions there must be something unconditioned, and therefore there must be a causality which is determined wholly by itself. Hence, the idea of freedom as a faculty of absolute spontaneity was not found to be a want, but *as far as its possibility is concerned*, an analytic principle of pure speculative reason. But as it is absolutely impossible to find in experience any example in accordance with this idea, because amongst the causes of things as phenomena, it would be impossible to meet with any absolutely unconditioned determination of causality, we were only able to *defend our supposition* that a freely acting cause might be a being in the world of sense, in so far as it is considered in the other point of view as a *noumenon*, showing that there is no contradiction in regarding all its actions as subject to physical conditions so far as they are phenomena, and yet regarding its causality as physically unconditioned, in so far as the acting being belongs to the world of understanding, and in thus making the concept of freedom the regulative principle of reason. By this principle I do not indeed learn what the object is to which that sort of causality is attributed; but I remove the difficulty; for, on the one side, in the explanation of events in the world, and consequently also of the actions of rational beings, I leave to the mechanism of physical necessity the right of ascending from conditioned to condition *ad infinitum*, while on the other side I keep open for speculative reason the place which for it is vacant, namely, the intelligible, in order to transfer the unconditioned thither. But I was not able to *verify* this *supposition*; that is, to change it into the *knowledge* of a being so acting, not even into the knowledge of the possibility of such a being. This vacant place is now filled by pure practical reason with a definite law of causality in an intelligible world (causality with freedom), namely, the moral law. Speculative reason does not hereby gain anything as regards its insight, but only as regards the *certainty* of its problematical notion of freedom, which here obtains *objective reality*, which, though only practical, is nevertheless undoubted. Even the notion of causality – the application, and consequently the signification, of which holds properly only in relation to phenomena, so as to connect them into experiences (as is shown by the critique of pure reason) – is not so enlarged as to extend its use beyond these limits. For if reason sought to do this, it would have to show how the logical relation of principle and consequence can be used synthetically in a different sort of intuition from the sensible; that is how a *causa noumenon* is possible. This it can never do; and, as practical reason, it does not even concern itself with it, since it only places the *determining principle* of causality of man as a sensible creature (which is given) in *pure reason* (which is therefore called practical); and therefore it employs the notion of cause, not in order to know objects, but to determine causality in relation to objects in general. It can abstract altogether from the application of this notion to objects with a view to theoretical knowledge (since this concept is always found *a priori* in the understanding, even independently of any intuition). Reason, then, employs it only for a practical purpose, and hence we can transfer the determining principle of the will into the intelligible order of things, admitting, at the same time, that we cannot understand how the notion of cause can determine the knowledge of these things. But reason must cognise causality with respect to the actions of the will in the sensible world in a definite manner; otherwise, practical reason could not really produce any action. But as to the notion which it forms of its own causality as noumenon, it need not determine it theoretically with a view to the cognition of its supersensible existence, so as to give it significance in this way. For it acquires significance apart from this, though only for practical use, namely, through the moral law. Theoretically viewed, it remains always a pure *a priori* concept of the understanding, which can be applied to objects whether they have been given sensibly or not, although in the latter case it has no definite theoretical significance or application, but is only a formal, though essential, conception of the understanding relating to an object in general. The significance which reason gives it through the moral law is merely practical, inasmuch as the idea of the law of causality (of the will) has itself causality, or is its determining principle.

[...]

Translated by Thomas Kingsmill Abbott

6.

Johann Gottlieb Fichte, System of the Science of Ethics (Das System der Sittenlehre nach den Principien der Wissenschaftslehre): *First Part — Deduction of the Principle of Ethics (1798)*

In a letter of April 1795, that is, shortly after the completion of the *Science of Knowledge*, Fichte writes: 'My system is the first system of freedom. Just as France has freed man from external shackles, so my system frees him from the fetters of things in themselves, which is to say from those external influences with which all previous systems–including the Kantian– have more or less fettered man. Indeed the first principle of my system presents man as an independent being'.[1] Fichte's philosophy, from its very inception and throughout every stage of its development, is driven by the conviction that human beings are free and that freedom is our fundamental determination. He holds that all reason, all consciousness, is grounded in freedom, a contention which it is the task of philosophy to demonstrate. Fichte's philosophy should therefore be understood as a rational expression and justification of the pre-philosophical faith in freedom. Fichte himself characterises his philosophy as an 'idealism of freedom', claiming that his 'system, from beginning to end, is nothing other than an analysis of the concept of freedom'.[2] This claim holds true for the *Science of Knowledge*, and even more obviously so for Fichte's moral theory in the System *of the Science of Ethics* and his philosophy of law in the *Foundations of Natural Right.*

It was after reading Kant's *Critique of Practical Reason* that Fichte's notion of freedom took the shape of a life-long philosophical commitment to recognition of the profound dignity of the freedom of man. As early as 1790, he writes in a letter: 'I live now in a new world ever since reading the *Critique of Practical Reason.* Propositions which I believed to be irrefutable are revoked; things which I believed could never be proven to me, e.g. the concepts of an absolute freedom, of duty, etc. are proven to me, and I am

---

[1] Fichte, Letter to Baggesen (April or May 1795), letter no. 13, of *Selected Correspondence* in Fichte, *Early Philosophical Writings*, translated and edited by Daniel Breazeale (London / Ithaca, NY: Cornell University Press, 1988), p. 385.

[2] Fichte, *Briefwechsel*, II, p. 206; quoted in Peter Baumanns, *Fichtes ursprüngliches System. Sein Standort zwischen Kant und Hegel* (Stuttgart-Bad Cannstatt: Frommann Holzboog, 1972), p. 31.

all the happier for it. It is inconceivable what reverence for humanity, what power this system gives us'.[3] This view is manifest in the *System of the Science of Ethics*, published 1798, in which his moral philosophy bears the influence, in particular, of Kant's thesis of the primacy of practical reason. Even Kant's theoretical philosophy gives the concept of action a central role (Kant's theory of the synthesis as an act of understanding is an essential aspect of the 'transcendental analytic' in the *Critique of Pure Reason*), and Fichte develops his entire philosophy by starting from an analysis of the acts of the 'I'. The *Tathandlung* ('deed-action'), in fact, with its immanent dialectic of positing and counter-positing, 'I' and 'not-I' comes to be the principle of reason. The 'I' is self-activity, which, however, includes self-constraint as one of its necessary moments.

Chronologically, the *System of the Science of Ethics* (1798) follows the *Science of Knowledge* (1794) and the *Foundations of Natural Right* (1796/97) as the third part of Fichte's Jena 'original system'. And with the order of material Fichte proceeds as Kant had, where the latter's *Doctrine of Right* constitutes the first part and the *Doctrine of Virtue* the second part of the *Metaphysics of Morals*. Explicit references to Kant's theory of virtue are not, however, found in Fichte's theory of ethics, but an intensive, generally affirmative, yet in important respects also critical discussion and modification of Kant's categorical imperative can be.

Fichte's *System of the Science of Ethics* is linked to the *Science of Knowledge* (indeed, its full title is *System of the Science of Ethics following the Principles of the Science of Knowledge*), particularly to the third part of that book, the 'Foundation of Knowledge of the Practical', which develops the theses of 'striving' and of 'instincts'. And it is divided into three main parts. In the first main part the 'Principle of Morality' is 'transcendentally deduced' from self-consciousness. And in the second of them the 'Reality and Applicability of the Principle of Morality' is also deduced. The third and most extensive part is a 'Systematic Application of the Principle of Morality' (which, for Fichte, is synonymous with 'the theory of morality in the strict sense'). Here, Fichte develops – making reference to, amongst other concepts, the doctrine of interpersonality – a concrete catalogue of duties regarding how we are to behave towards our own body, other human beings, and nature as well as professional and family-specific duties.

The central idea of the deduction of the principle of morality is that the 'essential character of the I' consists in a 'tendency toward self-action for the sake of self-action',[4] and that we are 'to determine ourselves ... according to the concept of absolute self-action'.[5] To think oneself as free, according to Fichte, means to think one's freedom as under a law, and *vice versa*.

[3] Letter to F. A. Weisshuhn, Summer 1790, in Johann Gottlieb Fichte, *Gesamtausgabe der Bayerischen Akademie der Wissenschaften* (Stuttgart-Bad Canstatt: Frommann–Holzboog, 1962), ed. Reinhard Lauth, Erich Fuchs and H. Gliwitzky, volume III, p. 167.
[4] *FW* IV, 29.
[5] *FW* IV, 49.

This law is the moral law (*Sittengesetz*): Kant's categorical imperative. For Fichte freedom and the moral law are, as he puts it, 'one and the same thought; . . . a complete synthesis (according to the law of interaction)'.[6] It is interesting to see that Fichte modifies the formulation Kant had given to the categorical imperative: 'Always act after the best conviction of your duty; or, act according to your conscience'.[7]

And Fichte reconceives Kant's categorical imperative in one further respect. He takes Kant's theory of the purposiveness of nature, which Kant understood as a mediation between concepts of nature and concepts of freedom, and gives to the categorical imperative a teleological formulation connected to the purposes of nature: 'Act according to your knowledge of the original determinations (the end-purposes) of things outside you'.[8]

The *System of the Science of Ethics* has continued to stand in the shadow of the other two parts of the Jena system, the *Science of Knowledge* and *Foundations of Natural Right*. Schleiermacher's extensive review from the time indicates that this work was received with high expectations. However the critic might ask whether this book possesses Fichte's most original insights, especially when compared with Kant and with the other two parts of Fichte's Jena system. The conceptual foundations of the *System of the Science of Ethics* – including the doctrine of striving and of instinct – are for the most part laid down in the *Science of Knowledge*. And the theory of interpersonality is already introduced by Fichte in the *Foundations of Natural Right*.

[6] *FW* IV, 53.
[7] *FW* IV, 156.
[8] *FW* IV, 69.

FIRST PART – DEDUCTION OF THE PRINCIPLE OF ETHICS

Preamble to this Deduction[†]

It is asserted that a constraint[1] expresses itself in the soul of man to do certain things entirely independent of external aims, merely for the sake of doing them; furthermore, and likewise independent of external aims, to refrain from doing certain other things simply for the sake of leaving them undone. We term the

[†] *FW* IV, 13–18. New translation by David W. Wood.
[1] *Zunöthigung*. Many thanks to Daniel Breazeale for the suggestion to translate this technical term as 'constraint'.

constitution of man, in so far as such a constraint is necessarily expressed in him and as surely as he is a man, his *moral or ethical nature* in general.

Man's *knowledge* may relate to his moral nature in two different ways: On the one hand, if the asserted inner constraint is discovered as a fact in the observation of his self – which must in any case be assumed, since it will be uncovered by careful self-observation – he may simply accept this fact. He is content for it to *be so*, and does not ask *in what manner* and for *what reasons* it is so. Out of the inclination to freedom, he may also decide to submit this inner constraint to the claims of unconditional *belief*, to really *conceive* it as his supreme determination and to *act* inviolably in accordance with this belief. Consequently, there arises for him both *ordinary* knowledge and his moral nature as such, as well as his own particular duties – if at this stage of life he is acutely attentive to the claims of his conscience. This knowledge first becomes possible at the *standpoint of ordinary consciousness*, and suffices for engendering an attitude and conduct that accords with duty.

On the other hand, man may not be content simply to accept this fact conceptually, to remain at the immediate perception. Instead, he may desire to know the grounds for what is perceived. He ceases to be satisfied with factual knowledge, and demands genetic knowledge; he does not merely want to be aware that such a constraint is present within himself, but to possess insight into how it arises. If he were to acquire this sought-after knowledge, it would be an *intellectual* knowledge, and in order to obtain it he must pass from the standpoint of ordinary consciousness to a higher one. How can we solve this problem, how can we uncover *the grounds* of man's moral nature or his ethical principles? The only thing ultimately excluding any question of a higher ground is this: that we are this *we*; this *selfhood*, or our rational nature, is within ourselves (the latter term is not nearly as expressive as the former). Everything else which is either *within* us, as for instance the aforementioned constraint, or that exists *for* us, like the world we assume to be external to us, is precisely within and for us because we are the above, something easily proved in general. However, definite insight into the way in which something within us or for us is related to this rationality, and must necessarily proceed from it, is an intellectual and scientific knowledge of the grounds in question. An exposition of these grounds derived from the highest and absolute principle, from the selfhood, and shown as necessarily following from it, is a derivation or a deduction. Thus our task is to furnish a deduction of man's moral nature or of the ethical principle in him. Instead of giving a detailed account of the advantages of such a deduction, it will suffice to note that a science of morality arises through it, or indeed science on the whole, only if this is a possibility or an aim in itself.

With respect to scientific philosophy in general, the particular science of ethics proposed here is related to the *Foundation of the Entire Wissenschaftslehre* through this deduction. The deduction is carried out using the propositions of the latter, and shows how any particular science taking its starting point from the general science becomes a particular philosophical science. In order to appreciate this deduction correctly the following must be borne in mind. If our moral nature follows from our rationality in accordance with necessary laws, as has been asserted, then the aforementioned constraint is something primary and immediate for perception; it expresses itself without our assistance, and through our freedom we cannot change the slightest thing about its manifestation. Although we attain insight into its grounds through a deduction, we are not able to alter anything of it, since our knowledge is sufficient but not our power, and the entire relation is necessarily our own invariable nature itself. Hence, the deduction does not produce anything additional, and we should not expect anything more from it than theoretical knowledge. Just as after obtaining insight into the grounds of this procedure objects are not placed any differently in space and time than they were before this insight, so likewise the morality in man is not expressed any differently after the deduction than it was before. Furthermore, the theory of ethics is not a *theory of wisdom* (something altogether impossible, since wisdom tends to be more of an art than a science), rather, as with philosophy as a whole, it is a *Wissenschaftslehre* [theory of science]; and above all a *theory of the consciousness* of our moral nature, especially of our particular duties.

This shall suffice for the significance and aim of the above deduction. However, on account of the widespread ignorance of the nature of transcendental philosophy, it is necessary to make a few preliminary remarks concerning the correct understanding of this deduction.

The course of the deduction is as follows: To begin with, we should imagine ourselves under a certain prescribed condition, and then observe *how* we are forced to think of ourselves under this condition. Hence the above moral constraint is necessarily deduced from a state that we ourselves have determined. To begin with, the fact that we imagine ourselves precisely under this specific condition may appear arbitrary. Yet anyone possessing an overview of the whole of philosophy and the relationship between the individual philosophical sciences within this system requires this very condition. Someone else may initially view this procedure as an attempt to establish the theory of ethics as a science, which might either fail or succeed. For him, the correctness of this procedure is not proved until the required science is really established in this way. Therefore, such an objection will be of little value.

Notwithstanding, a more important objection, and because of its result more instructive, is the following. – Someone might say, you are going to *think* yourself. However, as critical philosophers you must surely be aware, and this indeed may be easily ascertained, that all your thinking proceeds according to certain inner laws; so that whatever is thought becomes modified by your manner of thinking, and that in your hands something becomes as it is for you, simply because you think it. Doubtless it is no different in the present case; by directing your thinking upon yourself, you yourself become modified in this thinking; and therefore you cannot say: *I am like this in and for myself.* This you can never know, since you have no other way of knowing yourself than through thinking; rather you can only say: *I must necessarily think myself in this manner.*

Now, if you keep in mind the true significance of your result and limit yourself to it, then no one can object to your procedure, and you yourself may see its value. Yet you do not seem to limit yourself to this significant result. You want to use it to explain the above constraint which is expressed in all of us. Hence you want to derive something real from out of thought; you want to pass from the region of thinking into the utterly different region of actual being.

Here we can reply: but we do not do this at all, we remain in the region of thinking; and the persistent misunderstandings of transcendental philosophy are entirely due to the fact that such a transition is still considered possible, one still seeks to discover a being in itself that is thinkable. However, what is this constraint in all of us, if none other than a forceful thinking, a necessary consciousness? Hence, can we here pass from the consciousness of mere consciousness to the object itself? Do we know anything more about this requirement than that we must necessarily think it so that it occurs within us? – What is inferred in the deduction through our conclusion is thinking; and what is independent of every conclusion as something primary and immediate within us is also thinking. The difference is merely this: in the latter thinking we are not conscious of grounds; rather, this thinking intrudes upon us with immediate necessity and *thereby* receives the predicate of reality, of perceptibility. On the other hand, in the former thinking we are conscious of a series of grounds. This is precisely the purpose of all philosophy, to uncover during the course of reasoning whatever remains unconsciousness at the standpoint of ordinary consciousness. Philosophy is not and may never be a discussion about being, about a being in itself; for reason can never go beyond itself. There is no being for the intelligence, and since there is only a being for it, there is no being as such, apart from a necessary consciousness. At the ordinary standpoint, this necessity of consciousness forces itself *directly* upon us; whereas at the transcendental standpoint, we investigate its *grounds*. Both the following deduction, as well as the entire system of morals that is to be built upon it, only furnish a part of this necessary consciousness; and it would be incorrect to understand it in any other way.

[...]

§ 3†

Strictly speaking our deduction is now at an end. Its actual aim, as is well known, was to necessarily deduce from the general system of reason the thought that we should act in a certain manner; to demonstrate that the assumption of a rational being also involves the assumption that this being thinks this thought. In any event, this is required for the science of a system of reason that has itself as its own goal.

However, a number of other advantages are gained by means of this deduction. And since nothing is understood entirely and correctly unless we see it arise from its grounds, the most complete insight into our morality can only be obtained through a deduction like this. Moreover, it sheds light upon the so-called categorical imperative, divesting it of that hidden quality (*qualitas occulta*) that it bore up

†*FW* IV, 49–62.

until now (admittedly, this is not the *positive* fault of the author of the *Critique of Reason*), and most surely destroys that obscure region which harboured a number of fanciful notions (such as a moral law vividly occasioned by the divinity, etc.). Hence, by means of freer and more diverse opinions it is thoroughly important to remove any obscurity lying at the base of our deduction; this is difficult to achieve as long as we are confined within a systematic exposition.

The main content of our deduction may also be understood in the following manner. A rational being, *considered by itself*, is absolute, independent and completely the ground of its own self. Originally, i.e. without its own agency, it *is* absolutely nothing. Whatever it shall *become*, it must become of its own accord, through its own activity. – This proposition will not be proved, for it is incapable of being proved. Every rational being is simply encouraged to discover and accept itself to be like this.

Thus, I ask the reader to conceive himself just as I have outlined. What is the actual content of your thought when you reflect upon what has been described? I ask you not to depart from the above given concept but simply to make it clear to yourself through pure analysis.

The rational being *itself* should produce whatever it might possibly become. Hence, we must attribute to it a kind of existence prior to all real (objective) being and existence, just as we saw above. This cannot be anything other than an existence as an intelligence in and with concepts. Thus, in your present concept you considered a rational being as an intelligence. You must also ascribe to this intelligence the faculty of producing an existence through its mere concept. You presuppose it as an intelligence, in order to discover a ground of existence. In a word: in your concept of a rational being you have exactly conceived what we have deduced in chapter § 2 under the 'name of freedom'.

Now, how much have you gained, and everything depends on this consideration, by trying to make your concept of a rational being comprehensible? By means of these characteristics did you conceive independence as the essence of reason? Not at all; rather you only conceived an empty undetermined faculty of independence. This merely makes the thought of an independent existence possible for you, but not a reality as you first imagined it. A faculty is something with which you *can* merely connect to a real existence, as onto its ground, whenever you are given something apart from this, yet *not deduced from it*. This concept does not contain the slightest indication *that* there is a reality, or *the kind of reality* that is to be thought. This faculty of independence might not even be employed, or might only be employed occasionally. Hence you either receive no independence, or simply an interrupted independence, yet never a permanent independence (that constitutes the *essence*).

Thus you did not conceive the independence of the rational being in the analysed concept; and you did not simply posit this independence problematically, but categorically, as the *essence* of reason. What it means to essentially posit something is sufficiently explained above; it means, positing it as necessarily and inseparably contained in the concept, as something already co-posited and predestined in it. Consequently, you have posited *independence* and *freedom* as *necessity*; however, this is surely contradictory, and therefore you could not have possibly thought it. Hence, you must have conceived this firmly posited existence in such a way that the thought of freedom might also be possible. Your determinacy was a determinacy of free intelligence; however, such a determinacy is a *necessary thought* of independence (on the part of the intelligence), a norm in which it resolves to freely determine itself. – As a result, this concept of independence contains both the faculty and the law to exercise this faculty uninterruptedly. So you cannot think this concept without conceiving them both as united. – Now that you have freely decided to philosophise with us, you have philosophised in accordance with the universal laws of reason. This is a necessity for every rational being, in particular for that representative of reason, which we have here termed the original I, and whose system of thought we are attempting to establish. If the I conceives itself as independent – and we start from this presupposition – then it necessarily thinks itself as free. And this is precisely our concern: that it thinks its freedom under the law of independence. This is the significance of our deduction.

We now return to our main point. One can be convinced in yet another way of the necessity of our deduced thought. – Let the rational being conceive itself as free in the above formal sense of the word. Yet it is finite, and every object of its reflection is either limited or determined through mere reflection. Hence its freedom is also something determined. But what is a specific determination of freedom as such? Precisely the above.

Or again, drawing it from the depths of the entire system of transcendental philosophy, and expressing it in the most comprehensive and decisive manner: – I am the identity of subject and object = X. Since I am only capable of conceiving objects, and then separate the subjective from them, it therefore follows that I cannot conceive myself like this. Consequently, I conceive myself as subject *and* object. I thereby join both when I reciprocally determine each of them (in accordance with the law of causality). Determining my objective through my subjective results in the concept of freedom as a faculty of independence. Determining my subjective through my objective results in the thought of necessity in the subjective, and determining myself through my freedom solely according to the concept of independence, is an immediate, primary and absolute thought, since it is the thought of my original determination. – Now my objective should neither be conceived as dependent on the subjective, as in the first case, nor my subjective as dependence on the objective, as in the second case, rather both should be conceived as absolutely one. I think of them as one when I reciprocally determine each of them in the specified determination (according to the law of interaction), and think freedom as determining the law, and the law as determining freedom. One cannot be thought without the other, and if one is thought, the other is also thought. When you think yourself as free, you are forced to think your freedom under a law; and when you think this law, you are forced to think yourself as free, for it presupposes your freedom and proclaims itself as a law for freedom.

Let us re-examine the latter part of the preposition established above. Freedom does not follow from the law, as little as the law follows from freedom. They are not two thoughts, each conceived as dependent on the other, but they are one and the same thought. As we have seen above, there is a complete synthesis (in accordance with the law of interaction). In various passages Kant derives the conviction of our freedom from the consciousness of the moral law. This should be understood in the following manner. The appearance of freedom is an immediate fact of consciousness, and not an inference from any other thought. None the less, as mentioned above, someone might want to further explain this appearance, thereby turning it into mere illusion. Yet the fact that we cannot explain it any further is not due to a theoretical reason, but surely to a practical reason. It is the firm resolve to recognise the primacy of practical reason and to cherish the moral law as the ultimate true determination of man's being, and not to turn it further into illusion by all manner of rationalising, which is of course thoroughly possible with the free imagination. However, if we do not proceed beyond this, then we also do not proceed beyond the appearance of freedom, and thus it becomes a truth for us. Namely the proposition: I *am* free, freedom is the only true being, and the ground of all other being. This is altogether different to the proposition: *I appear* to myself to be free. Belief *in the objective validity* of this appearance is to be deduced from the consciousness of the moral law. The first article of faith is this: *I am genuinely free*; for it paves a path into the intelligible world, and secures for us there a sure footing. This belief is at once the point of intersection between both these worlds, and our system starts from this belief and should embrace the two. Doing should not be deduced from being, otherwise it is turned into illusion, and I *must not* take it to be illusion; instead, being should be deduced from doing. Through the kind of reality now bestowed upon the former, nothing is lost of our true determination, but we gain a great deal more. The I is not to be deduced from the not-I, and life is not to be deduced from death, but rather the opposite, the not-I is to be deduced from the I. For this reason all philosophy must start from the latter.

This deduced thought is termed *a law*, a *categorical imperative*; the manner in which something is conceived in it is designated as an *ought*, in contrast to being, and common sense finds itself surprisingly well expressed in these terms. We shall show how these views can arise from our deduction.

As we have seen, freedom should not be conceived under a law, rather, the foundation of its determinacy is solely and merely contained in itself, i.e. the determinacy of a thinking conceived as the ground of being. Therefore, to conceive freedom correctly we have to think it in this way, since its essence consists in the concept; however the concept is utterly indeterminable through anything external to itself. Thus, because freedom can be determined in countless possible ways, we can also think it under a fixed rule, but its concept can only be produced by the free intelligence, and it can only freely determine itself according to this rule. Hence our intelligence can make vastly different rules or maxims for itself, for example, that of self-interest, laziness, the oppression of others, etc., and follow them unceasingly and without exception, although always with freedom. Yet now assume that the concept of such a rule forces itself upon the intelligence, that is to say, that it is required by a certain condition of thinking, by a certain rule, and that only through freedom can it be conceived as a determining rule. Here something may be rightfully assumed, that although the thinking of the intelligence is absolutely free as a mere act, it is still subject to certain laws in its nature and manner.

In this way the intelligence can conceive a certain acting as agreeing with this rule, and another as conflicting with this rule. Indeed, real acting is always dependent upon absolute freedom, and the acting of the free intelligence is not determined in the real world, and is not mechanically necessary, for this would abolish the freedom of self-determination, but it is only determined in the necessary concept of acting. Yet how can this mere conceptual necessity be conveniently described, since it is not a necessity in the real world? The best way to describe it is as follows: acting such as this is *fitting* and *appropriate*, it *ought* to be: whereas the opposite is not appropriate and ought not to be.

Now, as shown above, the concept of such a rule is an absolute, first, and unconditioned concept, with no external ground; rather, it is a concept absolutely grounded in itself. Consequently, this acting should not occur due to this or that reason, or because something else is willed or ought to be, but it ought to be simply because it ought to be. Hence this 'ought' is an absolute and categorical ought; and that rule is a law valid without exception, since its validity as such is not subject to any other condition.

If one also thinks that this absolute ought involves an imperative ought that suppresses every other inclination, then this characteristic cannot be explained here, since we solely relate this law to absolute freedom, which does not involve the thought of any kind of inclination.

One has rather appropriately termed this legislation '*autonomy*', or self-legislation. It may be called this in a threefold sense. – First, if this thought of a law is already presupposed, and the I is merely considered a free intelligence, then the law only becomes a *general* law when the I reflects upon it, and freely subjugates itself to it, i.e., when it is actively made into an irrevocable maxim of all its willing. And again, it becomes a law *in any particular case*, when the intelligence finds the required concept through judgement and freely realises the concept in question (though this is self-evident, it is not generally understood, so it will be rigorously proved below). Hence, our entire moral existence is nothing else than an uninterrupted legislation of the rational being to itself; and wherever this legislation ceases, immorality begins. – Secondly, as far as the content of the law is concerned, nothing is required but absolute independence, absolute indeterminacy through something or other external to the I. Consequently, the material determination of the will according to the law is solely derived from ourselves; and all *heteronomy*, or borrowing of the determining grounds from something or other external to us, is directly contrary to the law. – Thirdly, the entire concept of our necessary subjugation to a law solely arises through an absolutely free reflection of the I upon itself in its true essence, i.e. in its independence. As has been shown, the deduced thought neither forces itself upon us as something unconditioned, which would be completely incomprehensible and abolish the concept of an intelligence, nor mediates a feeling or the like; rather it is the condition, the necessary *manner* of a thinking that is free. Hence it is the I itself that brings a lawfulness to this whole relation, and reason remains in every respect its own law.

I think we can clearly see here how reason may be *practical*, and that practical reason is not the miraculous and incomprehensible thing it is sometimes made out to be; indeed, it is not at all a second reason, but the very same reason we all recognise as theoretical reason.

Reason is not a thing that *is there* and that *exists*, rather it is a doing – doing pure and simple. Reason intuits itself: it can and does so precisely because it is reason; however it cannot find itself to be anything other than what it is: a doing. Moreover, reason is *finite*, and everything that reason represents becomes finite and determined for itself, in so far it represents it. And consequently, its doing also becomes something determined for it, solely through self-intuition and the law of finitude to which it is bound. Yet the determinacy of a pure doing as such does not yield being, but rather an 'ought'. Thus reason *determines its activity through itself*; however – *determining an activity*, and *being practical*, are wholly identical. – In a certain sense it has always been conceded that reason is practical; in the sense that it must provide the *means* for some kind of given external purpose, whether through our natural needs or through our free arbitrary will. In this sense it is called *technical practical*. We claim that reason establishes a *purpose* absolutely from itself and through itself; and to this extent it is *absolutely* practical. The practical dignity of reason is its own *absoluteness*; a determinacy completely through itself and through nothing external to itself. Whoever does not recognise this absoluteness – and it can only be found in oneself by means of intuition – will instead take reason to be a mere faculty of rationalising that first needs to be given external objects before it can be set into motion. Such a person will always find it incomprehensible as to how reason may be absolutely practical, since he persists in believing that the conditions for the realisation of a law must be first recognised before the law may be accepted.

(The considerations now offered here for viewing philosophy as a whole are many and varied. I cannot refrain from mentioning at least one. – Reason determines itself through its own acting, because it intuits itself and is finite. This proposition has a double significance, since the acting of reason is viewed from two sides. In a theory of ethics it is chiefly related to the so-called acting that accompanies the consciousness of freedom, and it is therefore recognised as an action from the ordinary standpoint: *willing and working*. However, the proposition also holds for an action that one only finds at the transcendental standpoint, i.e. acting *in the representation*. Reason does not necessarily observe the law that it initially gives to itself, the moral law, because it is directed upon freedom.

However, the law that reason ultimately gives to itself, the thought law, is necessarily observed, because although the intelligence is active when applying it, it is not yet freely active. Consequently, the entire system of reason is necessarily predetermined through reason itself. This occurs both with respect to what *ought* to exist and is simply postulated as existing as a result of this 'ought', according to the initial legislation, as well as with respect to a directly given existence, according to the final legislation. Yet whatever reason itself has combined in accordance with its own laws, it should certainly dissolve again according to these same laws. In other words, reason necessarily knows itself completely, and an analysis of its entire procedure or a system of reason is possible. – Thus in our theory everything is interrelated with everything else, and this necessary presupposition is only possible under the condition of this result and under no other. Either all philosophy must be renounced, or the absolute autonomy of reason must be admitted. The idea of philosophy only makes sense under this presupposition. All doubt or denial of the possibility of a system of reason is based on the presupposition of a *heteronomy*; on the presupposition that reason could be determined by something external to itself. Yet such a presupposition is thoroughly contrary to reason; – and conflicts with reason itself.)

Description of the Principle of Ethics in Accordance with this Deduction

The principle of ethics is the necessary thought of the intelligence, that it should determine its freedom without exception in accordance with the concept of independence.

> It is a *thought*, and not a feeling or an intuition, although this thought is based on the intellectual intuition of the intelligence's absolute activity: it is a *pure* thought, devoid of even the slightest trace of feeling or sensible intuition, since it is the immediate concept of the pure intelligence itself; it is a *necessary* thought, because it is the form in which the freedom of the intelligence is conceived; it is the *first* and *absolute* thought, since it is the concept of the thinking self, and as a result of its ground, is neither founded on nor conditioned by any other thought.
>
> The content of this thought is that the free being *ought*; for *ought* is just an expression for the determinacy of freedom; that it ought to place its freedom under a *law*; and that this law is none other than *the concept of absolute independence* (absolute indeterminacy through something external to it); finally, that this law is valid *without exception*, since it contains the original determination of the free being.

Transcendental View of this Deduction

In our deliberations we proceeded from the presupposition that the essence of the I is its independence, or, since this independence can only be thought of as something real under certain as yet unproved conditions, it consists in the I's tendency to independence. By means of this presupposition we have examined how the self-thinking I must conceive itself. Therefore, our starting-point was the objective existence of the I. However, is the I something objective in itself, without any relation to a consciousness? For instance, does what is described in chapter § 1 have any relation to a consciousness? It is surely related to our own philosophising consciousness. We can now relate it to the consciousness of the original I; and only as a result of this relation can we view our deduction from the correct standpoint. It is not dogmatic, rather it is transcendental-idealistic. Our aim was not to infer thinking from an existence in itself; for the I only exists in and for its knowledge. We are much more concerned with an original system of thinking, with an original linking of the assertions of reason among and with each other. – The rational being posits itself as absolutely independent because it is independent, and it is independent because it posits itself thus; in this relation it is subject-object = X. By positing itself like this, it posits itself as partly free, in the above sense of the word, and partly subordinates its freedom to the law of independence. These concepts are the concept of its independence, and the concept of independence involves these concepts: both are completely one and the same.

Certain misunderstandings and objections render the following necessary. – It is not asserted that at the ordinary standpoint we are conscious of this relationship between the deduced thought and its grounds. It is well known that any insight into the grounds of the facts of consciousness belongs solely to philosophy, and is only possible from the transcendental standpoint. – Likewise, it is not asserted that this thought occurs among the facts of ordinary consciousness in the generality and abstraction with which we have deduced it; or that without the further agency of free reflection we become conscious of this law for our *freedom in general*. This generality is only reached through philosophical abstraction; and this abstraction is undertaken in order to specifically establish this problem. Within ordinary consciousness there only occurs as a fact a particular kind of thinking, and never an abstract thinking – for all abstraction presupposes a free acting of the intelligence. Thus, only this is asserted: if we consider *certain* acts to be free – here we mean real not merely ideal acts – then at the same time we feel compelled to think that they *ought* to be established in a certain manner. It is also granted that one is never in the position of having this experience when thinking about one's *own* acts, since one is always driven by passions and desires, and is scarcely aware of one's freedom; yet we can discover the truth of this principle by judging the actions of others we consider to be free. If someone therefore denies for his own person the consciousness of the moral law as a fact of his inner experience, then he may be much more justified compared with someone who defends this fact without sufficiently understanding it. If a universally expressed moral law is understood by these facts, then according to its nature it cannot be an immediate fact of consciousness. However, if someone denies what we have asserted, i.e. the specific application of this law to free individual acts, then he will easily find a contradiction between his procedure and his assertion when contemplating the judgements of others, yet only if he remains open-minded and is not influenced by his own philosophical system. For example, no one gets angry and upset at the flames consuming his house, but surely at the person who caused the fire or was negligent. Would he not be foolish to get angry at him, if he did not assume that this person could have acted differently, and ought to have acted differently?

Translated by David W. Wood

7.

G. W. F. Hegel, Phenomenology of Spirit (Phänomenologie des Geistes): *Lordship and Bondage (1807)*

Hegel's contribution to the question of freedom is worked out in a context of the notion of the reconciliation of subject with others, individual with society. He takes account of both the subjective conditions of freedom and also the intersubjective conditions which give it substance, that is, concrete social reality. Freedom, Hegel suggests, is achievable only when the subject is engaged in some kind of reciprocal recognition of another person. Clearly, this implies a radical critique of the idealistic accounts prevalent in early German idealism in which the 'I' was understood as the sufficient condition of freedom.

In the *Phenomenology of Spirit* Hegel's discussion of the possibility of freedom takes the form of an analysis of the development of 'self-consciousness'. Self-consciousness is intended in a very specific way: it is awareness of one's active agency as a free being, a thesis which carries on the basic conviction of the German Idealist movement that freedom is non-existent without a sense of one's agency. However, Hegel offers an intersubjective version of this thesis which adds innovative new dimensions to the notion of freedom. He discusses what we might at first regard as the paradox of self-consciousness, namely, that in order to be self-conscious one has to be conscious of another self-consciousness who is aware of you as a self-consciousness. The mechanism of this mutuality is recognition. To realise what one is and how one has become so is self-consciousness. Since the possibility of self-consciousness arises only in the process of the consciousness of another person – and a reciprocity between the two – Hegel argues that an examination of self-consciousness involves an examination of the process of recognition.

For Hegel the problem with the process of self-consciousness through recognition is that if I am to receive the sort of recognition which affirms me I have to be able to respect that person who recognises me, for otherwise their recognition is worthless. But mutuality is not granted by nature; it is an achievement of human history as it proceeds towards ever more rational forms of social life.

And this is where the master–slave dialectic (or dialectic of Lord and Bondsman, as Baillie's and Miller's translations render it) begins: it is a

parable of the development of selfhood. In the course of his presentation Hegel uses the term *Aufhebung* (noun) and its verb form *aufheben*.
Aufhebung is normally translated as 'sublation'. However, the original term
carries a complexity of meanings which the English translation cannot quite
capture. Michael Inwood points out that *aufheben* (to sublate) can entail
the following senses: (1) to raise, hold, lift up; (2) to annul, abolish, destroy, cancel, suspend; (3) to keep, save, preserve.[1] The analysis of master
and slave is dialectical in that we see a concept emerge, and deepen in
sophistication, as rational responses to difficulties or contradictions as they
arise. (In Hegel's system a 'sublation' is the positive outcome of a dialectical step or 'determinate negation', as discussed in the Introduction to the
Phenomenology.)

Reaching self-consciousness will involve a series of sublations: passing
through phases and yet retaining those phases as part of some final
understanding. These phases are, as mentioned, set out in the parable
of the development of selfhood, the sort of selfhood which can realise
freedom through full self-consciousness (in Hegel's sense): it is not a
requirement of any one of us, Hegel's readers, that we undertake the
ordeals set out by Hegel. The point is, though, that the development of
our modern concept of freedom has taken something like this course. As
a parable too the individuals referred to by Hegel may stand for various
elements of the institutional arrangements in society at earlier points in
history.

The dialectic of master and slave is extremely complex, but it can nevertheless be broken down into a number of demarcated phases. (*i*) At the
beginning, the most primitive stage, one consciousness sees for the first
time another consciousness and takes it as a threat to its own independence: the I cannot allow its own absoluteness – its previous total identity
with being – to be challenged or qualified by another I. (*ii*) In affirming
the self – by making it independent of an other – the other thereby also
becomes independent, since no relationship now exists between the two.
The self is independent of an other and sees other selves merely as though
they were objects.

(*iii*) Because each consciousness can only recognise the other as an object – and not as a potential agent of its recognition – it believes that it
can affirm itself only through the destruction of that other. Needless to say,
both consciousnesses – when they are at this phase – feel much the same
about each other. This attempt to dominate the other involves putting one's
own self at risk. Hegel's rather strong point is that one is a fully constituted
self-consciousness only if one has undergone (or even, it sometimes seems,
if one's society has historically undergone) *a struggle for freedom*. Why is
the struggle with another – this life and death struggle – bound up with the
idea of freedom? Because the status of the other, as something external to

---

[1] Michael Inwood, *A Hegel Dictionary* (Oxford: Blackwell, 1992), p. 283.

consciousness, represents something which is in opposition to one's own consciousness. It is thus a threat to freedom.

(*iv*) If one should die in this struggle the conditions of recognition are thereby denied. And this indicates to us the particular character and forward momentum of dialectical thinking: awareness of another has been achieved, and an original state of innocence before a sense of self emerged can never be restored. Hence, far from achieving an affirmation of the self it deprives itself of that by which it affirms itself. (*v*) The death of the other consciousness brings awareness of one crucial condition for self-consciousness: namely, life. What Hegel suggests here is that the struggle will not result in death, but be nevertheless a result which is consistent with the aim of self-affirmation. A consciousness affirms itself by enslaving another. This relationship is the inevitable product of the primitive phases of the development of self-consciousness.

(*vi*) The relationship between master and slave is ultimately unstable. As ever, the source of instability is the inability of the arrangement to produce the conditions for self-consciousness. The master controls the existence of the slave – the master is the independent element of the relationship. But the master is related to the world of things – to nature, we might say – 'mediately' through the slave: his desires are delivered through the labours of the slave. (And Hegel's dialectic of master and slave has been influentially read, by Kojève, as, amongst other things, an analysis of the transformative capacity of desire.[2]) The slave's attitude to nature is also negative in that s/he sees it as in opposition to the his/her consciousness. But as a slave, however, he/she is obliged to work on nature. (*vii*) And in this differentiation of activities different consciousnesses are produced (master consciousness and slave consciousness – two different ways of apprehending nature). What that leads to, ultimately, is the lack of mutuality which is required for recognition. (*viii*) Since the master is affirmed merely by the slave the master does not have the full conditions for the achievement of self-consciousness. He is dependent for recognition on an inessential (the slave) consciousness.

The conclusion must eventually be the achievement of mutual recognition which incorporates both the interdependence and freedom of self-consciousness through another self-consciousness. However, that mutuality is not reached in the text of the master–slave. Hegel's further analysis of historically specific institutions in the *Phenomenology*, and also later in the *Philosophy of Right*, bring the account of the modern concept of freedom to its conception.

[2]Alexandre Kojève, trans. James Nicholls, *Introduction to the Reading of Hegel* (New York: Basic Books, 1969).

INDEPENDENCE AND DEPENDENCE OF SELF-CONSCIOUSNESS: LORDSHIP AND BONDAGE†

Self-consciousness exists in and for itself when, and by the fact that, it so exists for another; that is, it exists only in being acknowledged. The Notion of this its unity in its duplication embraces many and varied meanings. Its moments, then, must on the one hand be held strictly apart, and on the other hand must in this differentiation at the same time also be taken and known as not distinct, or in their opposite significance. The twofold significance of the distinct moments has in the nature of self-consciousness to be infinite, or directly the opposite of the determinateness in which it is posited. The detailed exposition of the Notion of this spiritual unity in its duplication will present us with the process of Recognition.

Self-consciousness is faced by another self-consciousness; it has come *out of itself.* This has a twofold significance: first, it has lost itself, for it finds itself as an *other* being; secondly, in doing so it has superseded the other, for it does not see the other as an essential being, but in the other sees its own self.

It must supersede this otherness of itself. This is the supersession of the first ambiguity, and is therefore itself a second ambiguity. First, it must proceed to supersede the *other* independent being in order thereby to become certain of *itself* as the essential being; secondly, in so doing it proceeds to supersede its *own* self, for this other is itself.

This ambiguous supersession of its ambiguous otherness is equally an ambiguous return *into itself.* For first, through the supersession, it receives back its own self, because, by superseding *its* otherness, it again becomes equal to itself; but secondly, the other self-consciousness equally gives it back again to itself, for it saw itself in the other, but supersedes this being of itself in the other and thus lets the other again go free.

Now, this movement of self-consciousness in relation to another self-consciousness has in this way been represented as the action of *one* self-consciousness, but this action of the one has itself the double significance of being both its own action and the action of the other as well. For the other is equally independent and self-contained, and there is nothing in it of which it is not itself the origin. The first does not have the object before it merely as it exists primarily for desire, but as something that has an independent existence of its own, which, therefore, it cannot utilize for its own purposes, if that object does not of its own accord do what the first does to it. Thus the movement is simply the double movement of the two self-consciousnesses. Each sees the *other* do the same as it does; each does itself what it demands of the other, and therefore also does what it does

---

†*HW* III, 145–155. *Phenomenology of Spirit* (Oxford: Oxford University Press, 1977).

only in so far as the other does the same. Action by one side only would be useless because what is to happen can only be brought about by both.

Thus the action has a double significance not only because it is directed against itself as well as against the other, but also because it is indivisibly the action of one as well as of the other.

In this movement we see repeated the process which presented itself as the play of Forces, but repeated now in consciousness. What in that process was *for us*, is true here of the extremes themselves. The middle term is self-consciousness which splits into the extremes; and each extreme is this exchanging of its own determinateness and an absolute transition into the opposite. Although, as consciousness, it does indeed come *out of itself*, yet, though out of itself, it is at the same time kept back within itself, is *for itself*, and the self outside it, is for *it*. It is aware that it at once is, and is not, another consciousness, and equally that this other is *for itself* only when it supersedes itself as being for itself, and is for itself only in the being-for-self of the other. Each is for the other the middle term, through which each mediates itself with itself and unites with itself; and each is for itself, and for the other, an immediate being on its own account, which at the same time is such only through this mediation. They *recognize* themselves as *mutually recognizing* one another.

We have now to see how the process of this pure Notion of recognition, of the duplicating of self-consciousness in its oneness, appears to self-consciousness. At first, it will exhibit the side of the inequality of the two, or the splitting-up of the middle term into the extremes which, as extremes, are opposed to one another, one being only *recognized* the other only *recognizing*.

Self-consciousness is, to begin with, simple being-for-self, self-equal through the exclusion from itself of everything else. For it, its essence and absolute object is 'I'; and in this immediacy, or in this [mere] being, of its being-for-self, it is an *individual*. What is 'other' for it is an unessential, negatively characterized object. But the 'other' is also a self-consciousness; one individual is confronted by another individual. Appearing thus immediately on the scene, they are for one another like ordinary objects, *independent* shapes, individuals submerged in the being [or immediacy] of *Life* – for the object in its immediacy is here determined as Life. They are, *for each other*, shapes of consciousness which have not yet accomplished the movement of absolute abstraction, of rooting-out all immediate being, and of being merely the purely negative being of self-identical consciousness; in other words, they have not as yet exposed themselves to each other in the form of pure being-for-self, or as self-consciousnesses. Each is indeed certain of its own self, but not of the other, and therefore its own self-certainty still has no truth. For it would have truth only if its own being-for-self had confronted it as an independent object, or, what is the same thing, if the object had presented itself as this pure self-certainty. But according to the Notion of recognition this is possible only when each is for the other what the other is for it, only when each in its own self through its own action, and again through the action of the other, achieves this pure abstraction of being-for-self.

The presentation of itself, however, as the pure abstraction of self-consciousness consists in showing itself as the pure negation of its objective mode, or in showing that it is not attached to any specific *existence*, not to the individuality common to existence as such, that it is not attached to life. This presentation is a twofold action: action on the part of the other, and action on its own part. In so far as it is the action of the *other*, each seeks the death of the other. But in doing so, the second kind of action, action on its own part, is also involved; for the former involves the staking of its own life. Thus the relation of the two self-conscious individuals is such that they prove themselves and each other through a life-and–death struggle. They must engage in this struggle, for they must raise their certainty of being *for themselves* to truth, both in the case of the other and in their own case. And it is only through staking one's life that freedom is won; only thus is it proved that for self-consciousness, its essential being is not [just] being, not the *immediate* form in which it appears, not its submergence in the expanse of life, but rather that there is nothing present in it which could not be regarded as a vanishing moment, that it is only pure *being-for-self.* The individual who has not risked his life may well be recognized as a *person*, but he has not attained to the truth of this recognition as an independent self-consciousness. Similarly, just as each stakes his own life, so each must seek the other's death, for it values the other no more than itself; its essential being is present to it in the form of an 'other', it is outside of itself and must rid itself of its self-externality. The other is an *immediate* consciousness entangled in a variety of relationships, and it must regard its otherness as a pure being-for-self or as an absolute negation.

This trial by death, however, does away with the truth which was supposed to issue from it, and so, too, with the certainty of self generally. For just as life is the *natural* setting of consciousness, independence without absolute negativity, so death is the *natural* negation of consciousness, negation without independence, which thus remains without the required significance of recognition. Death certainly shows that each staked his life and held it of no account, both in himself and in the other; but that is not for those who survived this struggle. They put an end to their consciousness in its alien setting of natural existence, that is to say, they put an end to themselves, and are done away with as *extremes* wanting to be *for themselves*, or to have an existence of their own. But with this there vanishes from their interplay the essential moment of splitting into extremes with opposite characteristics; and the middle term collapses into a lifeless unity which is split into lifeless, merely immediate, unopposed extremes; and the two do not reciprocally give and receive one another back from each other consciously, but leave each other free only indifferently, like things. Their act is an abstract negation, not the negation coming from consciousness, which supersedes in such a way as to preserve and maintain what is superseded, and consequently survives its own supersession.

In this experience, self-consciousness learns that life is as essential to it as pure self-consciousness. In immediate self-consciousness the simple 'I' is absolute mediation, and has as its essential moment lasting independence. The dissolution of that simple unity is the result of the first experience; through this there is posited a pure self-consciousness, and a consciousness which is not purely for itself but for another, i.e. is a merely *immediate* consciousness, or consciousness in the form of *thinghood*. Both moments are essential. Since to begin with they are unequal and opposed, and their reflection into a unity has not yet been achieved, they exist as two opposed shapes of consciousness; one is the independent consciousness whose essential nature is to be for itself, the other is the dependent consciousness whose essential nature is simply to live or to be for another. The former is lord, the other is bondsman.

The lord is the consciousness that exists *for itself*, but no longer merely the Notion of such a consciousness. Rather, it is a consciousness existing *for itself* which is mediated with itself through another consciousness, i.e. through a consciousness whose nature it is to be bound up with an existence that is independent, or thinghood in general. The lord puts himself into relation with both of these moments, to a *thing* as such, the object of desire, and to the consciousness for which thinghood is the essential characteristic. And since he is (a) *qua* the Notion of self-consciousness an immediate relation of *being-for-self*, but (b) is now at the same time mediation, or a being-for-self which is for itself only through another, he is related (a) immediately to both, and (b) mediately to each through the other. The lord relates himself mediately to the bondsman through a being [a thing] that is independent, for it is just this which holds the bondsman in bondage; it is his chain from which he could not break free in the struggle, thus proving himself to be dependent, to possess his independence in thinghood. But the lord is the power over this thing, for he proved in the struggle that it is something merely negative; since he is the power over this thing and this again is the power over the other [the bondsman], it follows that he holds the other in subjection. Equally, the lord relates himself mediately to the thing through the bondsman; the bondsman, *qua* self-consciousness in general, also relates himself negatively to the thing, and takes away its independence; but at the same time the thing is independent *vis-à-vis* the bondsman, whose negating of it, therefore, cannot go the length of being altogether done with it to the point of annihilation; in other words, he only *works* on it. For the lord, on the other hand, the *immediate* relation becomes through this mediation the sheer negation of the thing, or the enjoyment of it. What desire failed to achieve, he succeeds in doing, viz. to have done with the thing altogether, and to achieve satisfaction in the enjoyment of it. Desire failed to do this because of the thing's independence; but the lord, who has interposed the bondsman between it and himself, takes to himself only the dependent aspect of the thing and has the pure enjoyment of it. The aspect of its independence he leaves to the bondsman, who works on it.

In both of these moments the lord achieves his recognition through another consciousness; for in them, that other consciousness is expressly something unessential, both by its working on the thing, and by its dependence on a specific existence. In neither case can it be lord over the being of the thing and achieve absolute negation of it. Here, therefore, is present this moment of recognition, viz. that the other consciousness sets aside its own being-for-self, and in so doing itself does what the first does to it. Similarly, the other moment too is present, that this action of the second is the first's own action; for what the bondsman does is really the action of the lord. The latter's essential nature is to exist only for himself; he is the sheer negative power for whom the thing is nothing. Thus he is the pure, essential action in this relationship, while the action of the bondsman is impure and unessential. But for recognition proper the moment is lacking, that what the lord does to the other he also does to himself, and what the bondsman does to himself he should also do to the other. The outcome is a recognition that is one-sided and unequal.

In this recognition the unessential consciousness is for the lord the object, which constitutes the *truth* of his certainty of himself. But it is clear that this object does not correspond to its Notion, but rather that the object in which the lord has achieved his lordship has in reality turned out to be something quite different from an independent consciousness. What now really confronts him is not an independent consciousness, but a dependent one. He is, therefore, not certain of *being-for-self* as the truth of himself. On the contrary, his truth is in reality the unessential consciousness and its unessential action.

The *truth* of the independent consciousness is accordingly the servile consciousness of the bondsman. This, it is true, appears at first *outside* of itself and not as the truth of self-consciousness. But just as lordship showed that its essential nature is the reverse of what it wants to be, so too servitude in its consummation will really turn into the opposite of what it immediately is; as a consciousness forced back into itself, it will withdraw into itself and be transformed into a truly independent consciousness.

We have seen what servitude is only in relation to lordship. But it is a self-consciousness, and we have now to consider what as such it is in and for itself. To begin with, servitude has the lord for its essential reality; hence the *truth* for it is the independent consciousness that is *for itself*. However, servitude is not yet aware that this truth is implicit in it. But it does in fact contain within itself this truth of pure negativity and being-for-self, for it has experienced this its own essential nature. For this consciousness has been fearful, not of this or that particular thing or just at odd moments, but its whole being has been seized with dread; for it has experienced the fear of death, the absolute Lord. In that experience it has been quite unmanned, has trembled in every fibre of its being, and everything solid and stable has been shaken to its foundations. But this pure universal movement, the absolute melting-away of everything stable, is the simple, essential nature of self-consciousness, absolute negativity, *pure being-for-self*, which consequently is *implicit* in this consciousness. This moment of pure being-for-self is also *explicit* for the bondsman, for in the lord it exists for him as his *object*. Furthermore, his consciousness is not this dissolution of everything stable merely in principle; in his service he *actually* brings this about. Through his service he rids himself of his attachment to natural existence in every single detail; and gets rid of it by working on it.

However, the feeling of absolute power both in general, and in the particular form of service, is only implicitly this dissolution, and although the fear of the lord is indeed the beginning of wisdom, consciousness is not therein aware that it is a being-for-self. Through work, however, the bondsman becomes conscious of what he truly is. In the moment which corresponds to desire in the lord's consciousness, it did seem that the aspect of unessential relation to the thing fell to the lot of the bondsman, since in that relation the thing retained its independence. Desire has reserved to itself the pure negating of the object and thereby its unalloyed feeling of self. But that is the reason why this satisfaction is itself only a fleeting one, for it lacks the side of objectivity and permanence. Work, on the other hand, is desire held in check, fleetingness staved off; in other words, work forms and shapes the thing. The negative relation to the object becomes its *form* and something *permanent*, because it is precisely for the worker that the object has independence. This *negative* middle term or the formative *activity* is at the same time the individuality or pure being-for-self of consciousness which now, in the work outside of it, acquires an element of permanence. It is in this way, therefore, that consciousness, *qua* worker, comes to see in the independent being [of the object] its *own* independence.

But the formative activity has not only this positive significance that in it the pure being-for-self of the servile consciousness acquires an existence; it also has, in contrast with its first moment, the negative significance of *fear*. For, in fashioning the thing, the bondsman's own negativity, his being-for-self, becomes an object for him only through his setting at nought the existing *shape* confronting him. But this objective *negative* moment is none other than the alien being before which it has trembled. Now, however, he destroys this alien negative moment, posits *himself* as a negative in the permanent order of things, and thereby becomes *for himself*, someone existing on his own account. In the lord, the being-for-self is an 'other' for the bondsman, or is only *for* him [i.e. is not his own]; in fear, the being-for-self is present in the bondsman himself; in fashioning the thing, he becomes aware that being-for-self belongs to *him*, that he himself exists essentially and actually in his own right. The shape does not become something other than himself through being made external to him; for it is precisely this shape that is his pure being-for-self, which in this externality is seen by him to be the truth. Through this rediscovery of himself by himself, the bondsman realizes that it is precisely in his work wherein he seemed to have only an alienated existence that he acquires a mind of his own. For this reflection, the two moments of fear and service as such, as also that of formative activity, are necessary, both being at the same time in a universal mode. Without the discipline of service and obedience, fear remains at the formal stage, and does not extend to the known real world of existence. Without the formative activity, fear remains inward and mute, and consciousness does not become explicitly *for itself*. If consciousness fashions the thing without that initial absolute fear, it is only an empty self-centred attitude; for its form or negativity is not negativity *per se*, and therefore its formative activity cannot give it a consciousness of itself as essential being. If it has not experienced absolute fear but only some lesser dread, the negative being has remained for it something external, its substance has not been infected by it through and through. Since the entire contents of its natural consciousness have not been jeopardized, determinate being still *in principle* attaches to it; having a 'mind of one's own' is self-will, a freedom which is still enmeshed in servitude. Just as little as the pure form can become essential being for it, just as little is that form, regarded as extended to the particular, a universal formative activity, an absolute Notion; rather it is a skill which is master over some things, but not over the universal power and the whole of objective being.

Translated by A. V. Miller

8

F. W. J. Schelling, Philosophical Investigations into the Essence of Human Freedom (Philosophische Untersuchungen über das Wesen der menschlichen Freiheit und die damit zusammenhängenden Gegenstände): *The Concept of Freedom (1809)*

Given that Schelling had already undertaken an avowedly subjective idealist approach in the first phase of his career, it is interesting that it was not until 1809 that he published his first systematic thoughts on the nature of freedom. After all, much of the motivation of subjective idealism – in Fichte as well as in Schelling – was to give philosophical foundation to the notion that the essence of human beings is freedom. But by 1809 Schelling, with a prickliness that the German Idealists had in common, decided that it was time to clear up the misconstructions of a 'Schellingian' account of freedom put forward by critics and self-constituted followers. The *Philosophical Investigations into the Essence of Human Freedom* is in certain respects a middle-period text: it draws on some of the ideas found in 'On the "I" as the Principle of Philosophy', but it points forward too to the speculative, philosophical-theological later writings.

Schelling sets out to understand the place of individual freedom in the context of a systematic understanding of the world. Since, for Schelling and most others of his time, philosophy was virtually synonymous with such a systematic understanding, or 'a total worldview', to use his phrase, and individual freedom apparently stands outside systematic encapsulation, it seems that either philosophy must be abandoned in the name of freedom, or vice versa. Schelling's reflection on this question took the form of a critique of Spinoza's philosophy, given that the latter's pantheism had come to seem to be the basis of a 'fatalism' or total determinism. (Schelling, it has to be noted, is entirely committed to God's existence and to the belief that God exercises those powers which are traditionally attributed to him.) However, it is not, as it turns out, pantheism *per se* which specifically leads to determinism, according to Schelling. He argues that freedom is not actually undermined by the dependence of the world on God. On the contrary, 'it would indeed be contradictory', he writes, 'if that which is dependent or consequent were not autonomous. There would be dependence without something being dependent, a result without a resultant'.[1] Schelling thinks of creatures as God's 'self-revelation', a process through which these creatures achieve 'life'. He argues that as God's thoughts, creatures are independent, just as thoughts are independent – have an existence of their own – otherwise, indeed, they would not be thoughts. He confidently concludes that '[i]mmanence in God is so little a contradiction of freedom that freedom alone, and insofar as it is free, exists in God, whereas all that lacks freedom, and insofar as it lacks freedom, is necessarily outside God'.[2]

Schelling pours scorn, in fact, on Spinoza's particular pantheistic construction of the relation between an absolute and independent God and dependent finite beings. It is not Spinoza's claim that all things are in God that is unreasonable, in Schelling's view. Rather, the problem is the mechanistic account of things in Spinoza, and that certainly does produce determinism. What Schelling is offering here, he believes, is a distinctly idealistic account of the very relations that Spinoza had misrepresented.

It is in the context of this idealism that Schelling wants to address the question of evil and freedom: how can evil be conceived within a world which is, effectively, an emanation of the Absolute, God? Schelling develops a breathtakingly speculative answer to this problem. He denies that 'evil' in created being is some sort of 'privation' or absence of God – a traditional orthodox theory – arguing that evil is something like an original darkness which pre-existed creation, creation being the 'light that could be raised out of it'. Evil emerged, he suggests, 'through the arousing of the dark natural basis – that is the *disunion* of light and darkness', which arose necessarily through the creative act of God.[3] This 'dark ground' – as a somehow co-existent property of created being – 'operates incessantly in individual man too'.[4] The moral struggle in individuals is characterised by Schelling as that of the divine light and universality against the 'will of the deep' and particularity. In the section reprinted here we can see how Schelling attempts to offer a description of the mechanisms of choice which allows for a decision between good and evil: this is Schelling's account, in effect, of the moral will.

Schelling develops a theory of freedom which, he believes, can take account of a number of seemingly irreconcilable elements. He wants to argue that freedom is consistent with the idea of a motivating reason (others claiming that motivating reason is insufficiently spontaneous to allow the possibility of freedom). What motivates action is not an external reason, but, in fact, the essence of the active agent. Schelling aligns himself at this point with what he understands as the Kantian and Fichtean accounts of

---

[1] F. W. J. Schelling, translated by James Gutmann, *Of Human Freedom* [*Philosophical Investigations into the Essence of Human Freedom*] (Chicago: Open Court, 1936), pp. 18–19 (*SSW* VII, 346).
[2] Ibid., p. 20 (*SSW* VII, 347).
[3] Ibid., p. 54 (*SSW* VII, 377).
[4] Ibid., p. 58 (*SSW* VII, 381).

freedom which connects freedom with reason, our intelligible nature. Our intelligible nature represents that part of us which cannot be attributed to our phenomenal characteristics, those aspects which arise from experience and personal history. But our intelligible character is not simply empty. If it were – indeed, if any choice were made by an agent without a determinate perspective or reason, as other philosophical accounts of free will point out – then our choices would be arbitrary. Schelling thinks it necessary, therefore, to show that the agent has some 'determination', that is, is an agent with a particular nature. Immense difficulties arise from this claim, as Schelling goes on to say that this nature must be the self-determined essence of the agent (otherwise it would be determined from outside and hence be acting out of motivations it has not given itself). Again Schelling takes a speculative route to explain how this self-determining essence could have come about. The intelligible part of any individual is supposedly constituted at the beginning of creation: what a person is – e.g. the treacherous side of Judas Iscariot's character – is set out at that point. Remarkably, Schelling thinks that this can explain both the possibility of moral culpability as well as the seemingly fixed character of individuals. Schelling wants to deny that he is proposing a 'predestination theory', in which one's character is condemned *ab initio*, in that he thinks that actions are freely performed within the character which one has from the beginning of creation. And as noted above, creation in some way produces the coexistence of dark and light, qualities which themselves characterise the essence of the individual. The struggle within human beings is between these forces. Schelling finally explains this struggle as one which is expressed by religion.

It is clear enough that the extraordinary metaphysics which Schelling claims informs our moral lives had some influence on the development of Schopenhauer's account of the will (even if Schopenhauer liked to see Schelling's philosophy – publicly at least – as 'humbug'). We know, in fact, from Schopenhauer's writings that he was acquainted with the *Philosophical Investigations into the Essence of Human Freedom*. Schopenhauer using similar concepts, however, drew conclusions which were in many respects supportive of Spinoza's determinism.

THE CONCEPT OF FREEDOM[†]

For the usual conception of freedom, according to which it consists of a completely undetermined power to will either one of two contradictory opposites without determining reasons, simply because it is desired, – this usual conception has indeed

†*SSW* VII, 382–394. *Of Human Freedom* (Chicago: Open Court, 1936).

in its favor the original indecision of essential human nature, but when applied to individual actions it leads to the greatest inconsistencies. To be able to decide for A or −A without any motivating reasons would, to tell the truth, only be a privilege to act entirely unreasonably, and would not indeed distinguish man in any worthy way from the well known beast of Buridan which, in the opinion of the advocates of this conception of free will, had to starve between two equally distant, equally large and altogether similar stacks of hay just because it did not have the privilege of arbitrary choice. The only proof of this conception consists in an appeal to the fact that, for instance, it is in everyone's power to draw back or extend his arm without further reason. For if one declares that he extends it just to prove his freedom to choose, he could, after all, do this just as well by drawing it back; his interest in proving the proposition could only determine him to do one of the two; thus an equilibrium is here manifest, etc. This is a thoroughly bad method of proof because it deduces the non-existence of a determining cause from ignorance about it. But this argument could here be applied in just the opposite way − for precisely where ignorance enters, determination all the more certainly takes place. The chief thing is that this conception makes individual actions completely accidental, and in this respect it has very rightly been compared to the accidental swerving of the atoms which Epicurus invented for the same purpose in physics, namely in order to escape Fate. But accident is impossible and contradicts reason as well as the necessary unity of the whole; and if freedom cannot be saved except by making actions totally accidental, then it cannot be saved at all. To this system of the equilibrium of choice, determinism (or, according to Kant, predeterminism) is opposed, indeed quite justly, in asserting the empirical necessity of all actions on the ground that each of them was determined by motives or other causes which lay in the past and which are no longer in our control at the time of the action. Both systems adopt essentially the same standpoint, except that if there were no higher position the second would undeniably deserve preference. Both are alike ignorant of that higher necessity which is equally far removed from accident and from compulsion or external determination but which is, rather, an inner necessity which springs from the essence of the active agent itself. Incidentally, nothing in the least is gained by all the improvements which have been appended to determinism, such as Leibniz's amendment that motivating causes might dispose but not determine the will.

It was, indeed, Idealism which first raised the doctrine of freedom into that realm in which it alone can be understood. In consequence of it the intelligible essence of everything, and particularly of man, is outside of all causal connections as it is outside or beyond all time. Therefore it can never be determined by anything which preceded, since it itself rather takes precedence over all else which is or develops within it, not in time but in terms of its concept as an absolute unity whose totality and completeness must ever be actual in order that a specific act or determination may be possible in it. For we are expressing the Kantian conception not exactly in his words but in just such a way as, we believe, it must be expressed in order to be understood. But if this conception is accepted then the following too seems to have been correctly inferred. Free activity follows immediately from the intelligible nature of man. But it is necessarily an activity of determinate character; for instance – to refer to what is nearest at hand – it must be a good or bad activity. However there is no transition from the absolutely undetermined to the determined. The notion that an intelligible being could determine itself from sheer and utter indetermination without any reason, leads back to the above mentioned system of the equilibrium of choice. In order to be able to determine itself it would have to be already determined in itself; not indeed from the outside, since this would be in contradiction to its nature, nor from within by any merely accidental or empirical necessity, since all this (psychological as well as physical) is subordinate to it. But it would have to be determined by its own essence, that is by its own nature. This essence is no indefinite generality but definitely the intelligible essence of this specific human being. The saying, *determinatio est negatio*, does not in any way apply to this sort of determination, since this is itself one with the reality and concept of this essence, thus really being the essential element in the essence. The intelligible being, therefore, insofar as it acts absolutely and with full freedom, can as certainly only act according to its own inner nature. Or the activity can follow from its inner nature only in accordance with the law of identity, and with absolute necessity which is also the only absolute freedom. For only that is free which acts according to the laws of its own inner being and is not determined by anything else either within it or outside it.

This view of the matter yields at least one advantage in that it removes the inconsistent notion of the contingency of individual acts. This must be established in every higher view as well: that an individual act is the consequence of an inner necessity of the free being and accordingly is itself necessary. But this necessity must not be confused, as still happens, with an empirical necessity based on compulsion (which is itself only a veiled contingency). But what is this inner necessity of the Being itself? This is the point at which necessity and freedom must be united if they can be united at all. If this Being were a dead being and, for man, a mere datum, then since its activity would only ensue from necessity, imputability and all freedom would be vitiated. But just this inner necessity is itself freedom; man's being is essentially *his own deed*. Necessity and freedom interpenetrate as one being which appears as the one or the other only as regarded from various aspects; in itself it is freedom, but formally regarded, necessity. The Ego, said Fichte, is its own deed; consciousness posits itself – but the Ego is nothing other than this, nothing but the positing itself. However this consciousness, insofar as it is thought of as mere self-apprehension or knowledge of the Ego, is not even the primary position, and like all mere knowledge it presupposes the actual 'Being'. But this Being which is assumed as prior to knowledge is no being, even if it is not knowledge either; it is real self-positing, it is a primal and basic willing which makes itself into something and is the basis and foundation of all essence.

But in a way far more definite than this general sense, these truths have an immediate relation to man. In original creation, as has been shown, man is an undetermined entity (which may be mythologically presented as a condition antecedent to this life, a state of innocence and of initial bliss). He alone can determine himself. But this determination cannot occur in time; it occurs outside of time altogether and hence it coincides with the first creation even though as an act differentiated from it. Man, even though born in time, is nonetheless a creature of creation's beginning (the centrum). The act which determines man's life in time does not itself belong in time but in eternity. Moreover it does not precede life in time but occurs throughout time (untouched by it) as an act eternal by its own nature. Through it man's life extends to the beginning of creation, since by means of it he is also more than creature, free and himself eternal beginning. Though this idea may seem beyond the grasp of common ways of thought, there is in every man a feeling which is in accord with it, as if each man felt that he had been what he is from all eternity, and had in no sense only come to be so in time. Thus, the undeniable necessity of all actions notwithstanding, and though everyone must admit, if he observes himself, that he is in no wise good or bad by accident or choice, yet a bad person, for instance, seems to himself anything but compelled (since compulsion can only be felt in becoming, not in being) but performs his acts wilfully, not against his will. That Judas became a traitor to Christ, neither he nor any creature could alter; nonetheless he betrayed Christ not under compulsion but willingly and with full freedom.[1] The same thing is true of a good man – namely that he is not good by accident or choice, but nonetheless is so little under compulsion that no coercion, indeed not even the very gates of hell, would be capable of overpowering his disposition. To be sure, this free act which becomes necessity cannot occur in consciousness, insofar as it is mere self-awareness and only ideal consciousness, since the act precedes it as it precedes being and indeed produces it. But, nevertheless, it is not at all an act of which no consciousness remains to man. Thus someone, who perhaps to excuse a wrong act, says: 'Well, that's the way I am' – is himself well aware that he is so because of his own fault, however correct he may be in thinking that it would have been impossible for him to act differently. How often does it not happen that a man shows a tendency to evil from childhood on, from a time when, empirically viewed, we can scarcely attribute freedom and deliberation to him, so that we can anticipate that neither punishment nor teaching will move him, and who subsequently really turns out to be the twisted limb which we anticipated in the bent twig. But no one questions his responsibility, and all are as convinced of the guilt of this person as one could be if every single act had been in his control. This common judgment of a tendency to do evil (a tendency which in its origin is entirely unconscious and even irresistible) as being a free deed, points to an act and thus to a life before this life. Only it must not just be thought of as prior in time, since what is intelligible is altogether outside time. In creation there is the greatest harmony, and nothing is so separate and sequent as we must represent it, but the subsequent cooperates in what precedes it and everything occurs at the

---

[1] Luther correctly writes to this effect in the tract, *De servo arbitrio*, even if he did not comprehend in the right way the union of such unavoidable necessity with freedom of action.

same time in one magic stroke. Therefore man, who here appears as fixed and determined, took on a specific form in first creation and is born as that which he is from eternity, since this primal act determined even the nature and condition of his corporealization. The greatest obstacle to the doctrine of freedom has ever been the relation of the assumed accidental nature of human conduct to the unity of the world-whole as previously planned in divine reason. Thus there came the assumption of predestination, since neither God's prescience nor actual providence could be relinquished. The authors of the doctrine of predestination felt that human conduct must have been determined from eternity. However they did not seek this determination in the eternal act contemporaneous with creation, which constitutes the being of man itself, but in an absolute (i.e. wholly unfounded) decision of God through which one individual was predetermined to damnation, the other to blessedness; and thus they destroyed the root of freedom. We, too, declare a predestination, but in an entirely different sense, namely thus: as man acts here so he has acted since eternity and already in the beginning of creation. His conduct does not *come to be*, as he himself, as a moral being, does not *come to be*; but it is eternal in its nature. In this, that oft heard distressing question also disappears: why is just this man determined to act wickedly and viciously while another acts, by contrast, piously and righteously? For this question assumes that man was from the very beginning not act and deed, and that as a spiritual being he has an existence prior to and independent of his will, – which, as has been shown, is impossible.

When, through the reaction of the depths to revelation, evil in general had once been aroused in creation, man from eternity took his stand in egotism and selfishness; and all who are born are born with the dark principle of evil attached to them, even though this evil is raised to self-consciousness only through the entrance of its opposite. As man now is, the good, the light as it were, can be produced only out of this dark principle through divine transmutation. Only he could gainsay this original evil in man who has but superficially come to know man in himself and in others. This evil, though it is entirely independent of freedom with respect to present empirical life, was at its source man's own deed, and hence the only original sin. The same cannot be said of that equally undeniable disorder of forces which spread as a contagion after the initial corruption. For it is not the passions which are in themselves evil, nor are we battling merely with flesh and blood, but with an evil within us and outside us, which is spirit. Only an evil which attaches to us by our own act, but does so from birth, can therefore be designated as radical evil. And it is noteworthy that Kant, who did not in theory rise to a transcendental act determining all human existence, was led in later investigations by sheer faithful observation of the phenomena of moral judgment, to the recognition of a subjective basis of human conduct (as he expressed it) which preceded every act within the range of the senses, but which, in turn, had itself to be an act of freedom. On the other hand Fichte, who had speculatively grasped the concept of such an act, reverted in his theory of morals, to the current humanitarianism and was content to find this evil (which precedes all empirical action) only in the inertia of human nature.

There seems to be only one reason that could be raised in objection to this view: namely that it cuts out all conversions from good to evil and *vice versa* for man, at least in this life. However if it happens that human or divine aid – for some aid man always needs – determines him to change his conduct to the good, the fact that man accepts this influence of the good, and does not positively shut it out from him, – this fact is also to be found in that initial act because of which he is this individual and not another. In the man in whom this transmutation has not yet taken place but in whom, too, the good principle has not completely died, there is that inner voice of his own better self (better in respect to himself as he now is). It never ceases to urge him to accomplish this transmutation, and as he only finds peace in his inner self through a real and decisive change, he becomes reconciled with his guardian spirit as though the original idea had only now been satisfied. In the strictest sense it is true that, however man be constituted, it is not he himself but either the good or the evil spirit which acts in him, and nevertheless this does no violence to freedom. For this very letting-act-in-him of the good or evil principle is the consequence of the intelligible deed, through which man's being and life are determined.

Having thus presented the origin and development of evil up to its realization in the individual human being, nothing then seems to remain except to describe its manifestation in man.

The general possibility of evil, as has been shown, consists in the fact that, instead of keeping his selfhood as the basis or the instrument, man can strive to elevate it to be the ruling and universal will, and, on the contrary, try to make what is spiritual in him into a means. If in a man the dark principle of selfhood and self-will is completely penetrated by light and is one with it, then God, as eternal love or as really existent, is the nexus of the forces in him. But if the two principles are at strife, then another spirit occupies the place where God should be. This, namely, is the reverse of God, a being which was roused to actualization by God's revelation but which can never attain to actuality from potentiality, a being which indeed never exists but always wishes to be, and which, like the 'matter' of the ancients, can thus never be grasped as real (actualized) by perfect reason but only by false imagination (λογισμῷ νόθῳ)[2] which is exactly what sin is. Wherefore, since it itself is not real, it takes on the appearance of true being in mirrored images, as the serpent borrows colors from light, and strives to lead man to folly in which alone it can be accepted and grasped by him. It is therefore rightly represented not only as the enemy of all creation (because this can only endure through the nexus of love) and especially as the enemy of man, but also as man's tempter who entices him into false pleasures and to the reception of non-being into his imagination. In this it is supported by man's own evil inclinations, for his eye, which is incapable of looking constantly at the glamor of divinity and

[2] The Platonic expression in the *Timaeus*.

truth, always gazes at non-being. So the beginning of sin consists in man's going over from actual being to non-being, from truth to falsehood, from light into darkness, in order himself to become the creative basis and to rule over all things with the power of the center which he contains. For even he who has moved out of the center retains the feeling that he has been all things when in and with God. Therefore he strives to return to this condition, but he does so for himself and not in the way he could, that is, in God. Hence there springs the hunger of selfishness which, in the measure that it deserts totality and unity becomes ever needier and poorer, but just on that account more ravenous, hungrier, more poisonous. In evil there is that contradiction which devours and always negates itself, which just while striving to become creature destroys the nexus of creation and, in its ambition to be everything, falls into non-being. Moreover, manifest sin, unlike mere weakness or impotence, does not fill us with pity but with fear and horror, a feeling which can only be explained by the fact that sin strives to break the Word, to touch the basis of creation and profane the mystery. But even sin should become manifest, for only in contrast to sin is there revealed the innermost tie of dependence of all things, and the essence of God which, as it were, was there *before* all existence (not yet mitigated by it) and therefore terrible. For God himself clothes this principle in creation and covers it with love, in that he makes it the basis and, as it were, the bearer of creatures. Now if someone rouses it through the abuse of self-will which has been raised to self-sufficiency, it becomes actual for him and works against him. For since God cannot, after all, be disturbed in his existence, and, still less, dismissed, therefore in accordance with the necessary correspondence which pertains between God and his basis, the very light of life which shines in the depths of darkness in every single man is fanned in the sinner into a consuming fire. It is the same as when, in a living organism, as soon as a single member organ or system is out of accord with the whole, it feels the very unity and collaboration to which it has opposed itself as fire (= fever) and is inflamed by inner heat.

We have seen how the spirit of man lays itself open to the spirit of lies and falsehood through false imagination and learning oriented towards non-being, and soon fascinated by it, is deprived of its initial freedom. From this it follows that, by contrast, the truly good can only be affected by a divine magic, that is by the immediate presence of being in consciousness and reason. Arbitrary good is as impossible as arbitrary evil. True freedom is in accord with a holy necessity, of a sort which we feel in essential knowledge when heart and spirit, bound only by their own law, freely affirm that which is necessary. If evil consists in strife between the two principles, then the good can only consist in their complete accord. And the tic which unites the two must be divine, since they are one not in a conditional way but completely and unconditionally. The relation of the two is not to be conceived as optional morality or one derived from self-determination. The last concept presupposed that they were not, in themselves, one; but how can they become one if they are not? Besides it leads back to the inconsistent system of the equilibrium of choices. The relation of the two principles is that the dark principle (selfhood) is bound to the light. We may be permitted to express this as religiosity, in the original sense of the word. By this we do not mean what an ailing age calls religiosity – idle brooding, pietistic intimations, or will-to-feel divinity. For God is in us clear knowledge and spiritual light itself. In this alone, far from its being unclear itself, all else becomes clear. And this knowledge does not permit him who has it to be idle or sanctimonious. Wherever it is real, religiosity is something far more substantial than our philosophers-of-feeling opine. We understand religiosity in the original, practical meaning of the word. It is conscientiousness, or acting in accordance with one's knowledge, and not acting contrary to the light of understanding. A man to whom this latter is impossible, not in a human, physical or psychological way but in a divine way, one calls religious, conscientious in the highest sense of the word. He is not conscientious who, in a given case, must first hold the command of duty before himself in order to decide to do right because of his respect for it. By the very meaning of the word, religiosity allows no choice between alternatives, no *aequilibrium arbitrii* (the bane of all morality) but only the highest commitment to the right, without any choice. Conscientiousness does not necessarily and always appear as enthusiasm or extraordinary elevation, although when the illusion of an optional morality has been laid low, another and even worse spirit of pride would like to have it so. Conscientiousness may appear quite formally, in strict performance of duty, in which case the qualities even of severity and harshness are mixed with it. Thus it was in the soul of Cato, to whom an ancient writer ascribes such an inward and almost divine necessity of action, in saying that he was most like virtue, in that he never did what was right in order to do so (out of respect for the command of duty) but because he simply could not have done otherwise. This severity of attitude, like the severity of life in nature, is the seed out of which alone true comeliness and godlikeness blossom; but the supposedly superior morality, which thinks that it can despise this kernel, is like a sterile blossom, incapable of bringing forth fruit.[3] The highest, just because it is the highest, does not always and everywhere obtain. And anyone will hesitate to declare it to be so who has come to know the breed of spiritual libertines who use just what is highest in science and in sentiment for the crassest spiritual improprieties and superciliousness toward the so-called common sense of duty. It can already be anticipated that on the road on which everyone would rather be a precious spirit than a reasonable one, and would rather be called noble than be just, we will arrive at a point at which ethics will be grounded on the general concept of 'taste', and wickedness, accordingly, will only consist of a poor or corrupt taste.[4] If the divine principle of morality itself pulses through a serious disposition, then virtue appears as enthusiasm – as heroism (in the battle against

[3] Very correct comments on this morality of the superior soul in this age are contained in the review I have frequently cited; by Mr. Friedrich Schlegel in the *Heidelberg Annuals*, p. 154.

[4] A young man who, like many other contemporaries, is probably too proud to walk along the honest path of Kant, and who is nonetheless incapable of raising himself to a better view, talks aesthetic nonsense and has already announced such an Ethics based on aesthetics. With such progress, the Kantian jest that Euclid might be considered a somewhat ponderous approach to the art of drawing, may perhaps still become serious too.

evil), as the splendid, free courage of a man to act as the god bids him and not to be inferior in action to that which he has recognized in knowledge. It would appear as faith, not in the sense of an ostensibly commendable assuming of something to be true, or as something less than certainty – a meaning which has been attached to this word, by its being used for common things – but in its original meaning, as trust, confidence in what is divine, which excludes all choice. If, finally, a ray of divine love is cast into the inviolable seriousness of purpose which is always presupposed, then the highest transfiguration of the moral life occurs in loveliness and divine beauty.

Translated by James Gutmann

III

Law and State

9.

Immanuel Kant, Metaphysics of Morals
(Die Metaphysik der Sitten): *Introduction to the
Doctrine of Right; The Right of a State (1797)*

Kant's *Critique of Practical Reason* is an analysis of the capacity of the rational agent to self-legislate through pure practical reason. This striking account of morality places reason at the centre of moral motivation, in contrast to the traditional idea that moral motivations may have an external or heteronomous source. The implications of this are radical enough for moral philosophy. But Kant went on to employ his rationalistic thesis as a foundational principle of a political theory. Holding to the notion of the individual as a rational, autonomous agent, the question was what sort of structure would be appropriate to the protection and co-ordination of such agents. The answer to this task took the form of a systematic integration of morality and politics.

The book in which Kant developed this integration is *The Metaphysics of Morals*. It appeared in 1797, that is, nine years after the *Critique of Practical Reason*. It might be said that whereas the *Critique of Practical Reason* dealt with the formal properties of moral willing, the *Metaphysics of Morals* sets out to account for the specific duties of moral beings. In the section reprinted here the pertinence of these duties to social obligation is outlined. The *Metaphysics of Morals* is a systematic consideration of social and political duties, ranging across such topics as private property, marriage (a notoriously dispassionate account of its basis), punishment, international relations and, of course, freedom. The book falls into two main parts: first, the 'Metaphysical First Principles of the Doctrine of Right' (part of the Introduction to which is reprinted here), which covers the sphere of 'private right' and 'public right'. Considered under private right are the network of individual rights (property, contract, marriage, parental, familial) and public right covers the rights of the state. The second main part, 'Metaphysical First Principles of the Doctrine of Virtue', deals with the concept of virtue both in the ways in which the individual treats him- or herself and the ways others are to be treated.

In the *Groundwork of the Metaphysics of Morals* (1785) Kant set out a distinction between what he calls 'perfect' and 'imperfect duties': perfect duties are those which one cannot violate without condemnation, whilst imperfect duties are those which it is praiseworthy to fulfil. *The Metaphysics of Morals* develops the range and amplification of these forms of duties. However, because the *Metaphysics of Morals* also reflects on the social life of the individual it leads to questions of politics. In that context there are certain duties whose violation it is not sufficient simply to condemn. These are duties which relate to the freedom of others, and in such cases the state is granted the right to coerce and punish violators of the law. These duties come under the sphere of 'right'.

The 'Doctrine of Right' – the *Rechtslehre* – concerns the concept of right. (The text is unfinished, unfortunately, as is evident from the rather fragmentary presentation, leaving the reader with a little more work than usual.) As is often noted the word *Recht* is not simply translatable as 'right': it means justice, law (as a principle) and a right. So the doctrine or theory of 'right', in *The Metaphysics of Morals*, considers, in effect, what system of justice or form of rights is appropriate to the particular conception of rational persons offered by Kant. What Kant attempts to develop is a distinctly liberal philosophy in that he supposes that the basic elements of right – of a system of justice – must be the mutuality of individuals and their choices, that is, that one person's choice can be compatible with the freedom of others.

In the Introduction to the 'Doctrine of Right' Kant employs a procedure familiar from his epistemological and ethical writings: he makes clear the need for an *a priori* principle – or at least a non-empirical one – which can ground the 'universal law' of right. A consequence that Kant also discusses is the justification of 'coercion': coercion is an inevitable element of the protection of the freedom that is consistent with the equality of freedom.

In some respects Kant's views of what a theory of right must achieve contain strong echoes of John Locke's seminal account of the individual as sovereign and related only externally to others. But for Kant the system which co-ordinates or unites 'the choice of one...with the choice of another' is not simply procedural: it is not just a convenient way of organising disparate individuals. Rather it reflects the voluntary commitments of rational agents to live with other rational agents in such arrangements. It is from these commitments that the state – or at least the rational justification for the state – emerges. In the section on the 'Right of the State' Kant's portrait of the state is that of 'a union of a multitude'. He emphasises that what creates this union is 'their common interest in being in a rightful condition': lawfulness is central. Unlike Hegel, Kant does not see that state as in any respect constitutive of the individual. Indeed he sees the transition from the state of nature to the state of justice as effectively a change in arrangements. Some of the key claims made by Kant will seem familiar to some of today's readers in that they have formed some of the central concepts of the liberal political theory set out in John Rawls' highly influential *A Theory of Justice* (1970).

INTRODUCTION TO THE DOCTRINE OF RIGHT†

§A.
What the Doctrine of Right is

The sum of those laws for which an external lawgiving is possible is called the *Doctrine of Right (Ius)*. If there has actually been such lawgiving, it is the doctrine of *positive Right*, and one versed in this, a jurist (*Iurisconsultus*), is said to be *experienced in the law (Iurisperitus)* when he not only knows external laws but also knows them externally, that is, in their application to cases that come up in experience. Such knowledge can also be called *legal expertise (Iurisprudentia)*, but without both together it remains mere *juridical science (Iurisscientia)*. The last title belongs to *systematic* knowledge of the doctrine of natural Right (*Ius naturae*), although one versed in this must supply the immutable principles for any giving of positive law.

§B.
What is Right?

Like the much-cited query 'what is truth?' put to the logician, the question 'what is Right?' might well embarrass the *jurist* if he does not want to lapse into a tautology or, instead of giving a universal solution, refer to what the laws in some country at some time prescribe. He can indeed state what is laid down as right (*quid sit iuris*), that is, what the laws in a certain place and at a certain time say or have said. But whether what these laws prescribed is also right, and what the universal criterion is by which one could recognize right as well as wrong (*iustum et iniustum*) – this would remain hidden from him unless he leaves those empirical principles behind for a while and seeks the sources of such judgments in reason alone, so as to establish the basis for any possible giving of positive laws (although positive laws can serve as excellent guides to this). Like the wooden head in Phaedrus' fable, a merely empirical doctrine of Right is a head that may be beautiful but unfortunately it has no brain.

The concept of Right, insofar as it is related to an obligation corresponding to it (i.e., the moral concept of Right), has to do, *first*, only with the external and indeed practical relation of one person to another, insofar as their actions, as facts, can have (direct or indirect) influence on each other. But, *second*, it does not signify the relation of one's choice to the mere wish (hence also to the mere need) of the other, as in actions of beneficence or callousness, but only a relation to the other's *choice*. *Third*, in this reciprocal relation of choice no account at all is taken of the

†*KAA* VI, 229–236. *Metaphysics of Morals* (Cambridge: Cambridge University Press, 1991).

matter of choice, that is, of the end each has in mind with the object he wants; it is not asked, for example, whether someone who buys goods from me for his own commercial use will gain by the transaction or not. All that is in question is the *form* in the relation of choice on the part of both, insofar as choice is regarded merely as *free*, and whether the action of one can be united with the freedom of the other in accordance with a universal law.

Right is therefore the sum of the conditions under which the choice of one can be united with the choice of another in accordance with a universal law of freedom.

§C.
The Universal Principle [*Prinzip*] of Right

'Any action is *right* if it can coexist with everyone's freedom in accordance with a universal law, or if on its maxim the freedom of choice of each can coexist with everyone's freedom in accordance with a universal law'.

If then my action or my condition generally can coexist with the freedom of everyone in accordance with a universal law, whoever hinders me in it does me *wrong*; for this hindrance (resistance) cannot coexist with freedom in accordance with a universal law.

It also follows from this that it cannot be required that this principle of all maxims be itself in turn my maxim, that is, it cannot be required that *I make it the maxim* of my action; for anyone can be free as long as I do not impair his freedom by my *external action*, even though I am quite indifferent to his freedom or would like in my heart to infringe upon it. That I make it my maxim to act rightly is a demand that ethics makes on me.

Thus the universal law of Right [*Rechtsgesetz*], so act externally that the free use of your choice can coexist with the freedom of everyone in accordance with a universal law, is indeed a law [*Gesetz*], which lays an obligation on me, but it does not at all expect, far less demand, that I *myself should* limit my freedom to those conditions just for the sake of this obligation; instead, reason says only that freedom *is* limited to those conditions in conformity with the Idea of it and that it may also be actively [*tätlich*] limited by others; and it says this as a postulate that is incapable of further proof. When one's aim is not to teach virtue but only to set forth what is *right*, one may not and should not represent that law of Right as itself the incentive to action.

§D.
Right is Connected with an Authorization to Use Coercion

Resistance that counteracts the hindering of an effect promotes this effect and is consistent with it. Now whatever is wrong is a hindrance to freedom in accordance with universal laws. But coercion is a hindrance or resistance to freedom. Therefore, if a certain use of freedom is itself a hindrance to freedom in accordance with universal laws (i.e., wrong), coercion that is opposed to this (as a *hindering of a hindrance to freedom*) is consistent with freedom in accordance with universal laws, that is, it is right. Hence there is connected with Right by the principle of contradiction an authorization to coerce someone who infringes upon it.

§E.
A Strict Right Can Also be Represented as the Possibility of a Fully Reciprocal Use of Coercion that is Consistent with Everyone's Freedom in Accordance with Universal Laws

This proposition says, in effect, that Right should not be conceived as made up of two elements, namely an obligation in accordance with a law and an authorization of him who by his choice puts another under obligation to coerce him to fulfill it. Instead one can locate the concept of Right directly in the possibility of connecting universal reciprocal coercion with the freedom of everyone. That is to say, just as Right generally has as its object only what is external in actions, so strict Right, namely that which is not mingled with anything ethical, requires only external grounds for determining choice; for only then is it pure and not mixed with any precepts of virtue. Only a completely external Right can therefore be called *strict* (Right in the narrow sense). This is indeed based on everyone's consciousness of obligation in accordance with a law; but if it is to remain pure, this consciousness may not and cannot be appealed to as an incentive to determine his choice in accordance with this law. Strict Right rests instead on the principle of its being possible to use external constraint that can coexist with the freedom of everyone in accordance with universal laws. Thus, when it is said that a creditor has a right to require his debtor to pay his debt, this does not mean that he can remind the debtor that his reason itself puts him under obligation to perform this; it means instead that coercion which constrains everyone to pay his debts can coexist with the freedom of everyone, including that of debtors, in accordance with a universal external law. Right and authorization to use coercion therefore mean one and the same thing.

The law of a reciprocal coercion necessarily in accord with the freedom of everyone under the principle of universal freedom is, as it were, the *construction* of that concept, that is, the presentation of it in pure intuition a priori, by analogy with presenting the possibility of bodies moving freely under the law of the *equality of action and reaction*. In pure mathematics we cannot derive the properties of its objects immediately from concepts but can discover them only by constructing concepts. Similarly, it is not so much the *concept* of Right as rather a fully reciprocal and equal coercion brought under a universal law and consistent with it, that makes the presentation of that concept possible. Moreover, just as a purely formal concept of pure mathematics (e.g., of geometry) underlies the dynamical concept [of the equality of action and reaction], reason has taken care to furnish the understanding as far as possible with a priori intuitions for constructing the concept of Right. A right line (*rectum*), one that is straight, is opposed to one that is *curved* on the one hand and to one that is *oblique* on the other hand. As opposed to one that is curved, straightness is that *inner property* of a line such that there is only *one* line between two given points. As opposed to one that is oblique, straightness is that *position* of a *line* toward another intersecting or touching it such that there can be only *one* line (the perpendicular) that does not incline more to one side than to the other and that divides the space on both sides equally. Analogously to this, the doctrine of Right wants to be sure that *what belongs* to each has been determined (with mathematical exactitude). Such exactitude cannot be expected in the doctrine of virtue, which cannot refuse some room for exceptions (*latitudinem*). But without making incursions into the province of ethics, one finds two cases that lay claim to a decision about rights, although no one can be found to decide them, and that belong as it were within the *intermundia* of Epicurus. We must first separate these two cases from the doctrine of Right proper, to which we are about to proceed, so that their wavering principles will not affect the firm basic principles of the doctrine of Right.

Appendix to the Introduction to the Doctrine of Right

On Equivocal Rights (Ius aequivocum)

An authorization to use coercion is connected with any right in the *narrow* sense (*ius strictum*). But people also think of a right in a *wider* sense (*ius latium*), in which there is no law by which an authorization to use coercion can be determined. There are two such true or alleged rights, *equity* and the *right of necessity*. The first admits a right without coercion, the second, coercion without a right. It can easily be seen that this equivocation really arises from the fact that there are cases in which a right is in question but for which no judge can be appointed to render a decision.

I.
Equity (*Aequitas*)

Equity (considered objectively) is in no way a basis for merely calling upon another to fulfill an ethical duty (to be benevolent and kind). One who demands something on this basis stands instead upon his *right*, except that he does not have the conditions that a judge needs in order to determine by how much or in what way his claim could be satisfied. Suppose that the terms on which a trading company was formed were that the partners should share equally in the profits, but that one partner nevertheless *did* more than the others and so *lost* more when the company met with reverses. By *equity* he can demand more from the company than merely an equal share with the others. In accordance with proper (strict) Right, however, his demand would be refused; for if one thinks of a judge in this case, he would have no definite particulars (*data*) to enable him to decide how much is due by the contract. Or suppose that a domestic servant is paid his wages at the end of a year in money that has depreciated in the interval, so that he cannot buy with it what he could have bought with it when he concluded the contract. The servant cannot appeal to his right to be compensated when he gets the same amount of money but it is of unequal value. He can appeal only on grounds of equity (a mute divinity who cannot be heard); for nothing was specified about this in the contract, and a judge cannot pronounce in accordance with indefinite conditions.

It also follows from this that a *court of equity* (in a conflict with others about their rights) involves a contradiction. Only where the judge's own rights are concerned, and he can dispose of the case for his own person, may and should he listen to equity, as, for example, when the crown itself bears the damages that others have incurred in its service and for which they petition it to indemnify them, even though it could reject their claim by strict Right on the pretext that they undertook this service at their own risk.

The *motto (dictum)* of *equity* is, 'the strictest Right is the greatest wrong' (*summum ius summa iniuria*). But this evil cannot be remedied by way of what is laid down as right, even though it concerns a claim to a right; for this claim belongs only to the *court of conscience (forum poli)* whereas every question of what is laid down as right must be brought before *civil Right (forum soli)*.

II.
The Right of Necessity (*Ius Necessitatis*)

This alleged right is supposed to be an authorization to take the life of another who is doing nothing to harm me, when I am in danger of losing my own life. It is evident that were there such a right the doctrine of Right would have to be in contradiction with itself. For the issue here is not that of a *wrongful* assailant upon my life whom I forestall by depriving him of his life (*ius inculpatae tutelae*), in which case a recommendation to show moderation (*moderamen*) belongs not to Right but only to ethics. It is instead a matter of violence being permitted against someone who has used no violence against me.

It is clear that this assertion is not to be understood objectively, in terms of what a law prescribes, but only subjectively, as the verdict that would be given by a court. In other words, there can be no *penal law* that would assign the death penalty to someone in a shipwreck who, in order to save his own life, shoves another, whose life is equally in danger, off a plank on which he had saved himself. For the punishment threatened by the law could not be greater than the loss of his own life. A penal law of this sort could not have the effect intended, since a threat of an evil that is still *uncertain* (death by a judicial verdict) cannot outweigh the fear of an evil that is *certain* (drowning). Hence the deed of saving one's life by violence is not to be judged *inculpable* (*inculpabile*) but only *unpunishable* (*impunibile*), and by a strange confusion jurists take this *subjective* impunity to be *objective* impunity (conformity with law).

The motto of the right of necessity says: 'Necessity has no law' (*necessitas non habet legem*). Yet there could be no necessity that would make what is wrong conform with law.

One sees that in both appraisals of what is right (in terms of a right of equity and a right of necessity) the *equivocation (aequivocatio)* arises from confusing the objective with the subjective basis of exercising the right (before reason and before a court). What someone by himself recognizes on good grounds as right will not be confirmed by a court, and what he must judge to be of itself wrong is treated with indulgence by a court; for the concept of Right, in these two cases, is not taken in the same sense.

[...]

Part 2: Public Right[†]
Section I
The Right of a State

§43.

The sum of the laws that need to be promulgated generally in order to bring about a rightful condition is *public Right*. Public Right is therefore a system of laws for a people, that is, a multitude of men, or for a multitude of peoples, that, because they affect one another, need a rightful condition under a will uniting them, a *constitution (constitutio)*, so that they may enjoy what is laid down as right. This condition of the individuals within a people in relation to one another is called a *civil* condition (*status civilis*), and the whole of individuals in a rightful condition, in relation to its own members is called a *state (civitas)*. Because of its form, by which all are united through their common interest in being in a rightful condition, a state is called a *commonwealth (res publica latius sic dicta)*. In relation to other peoples, however, a state is called simply a *power (potentia)* (hence the word *potentate*). Because the union of the members is (presumed to be) one they inherited, a state is also called a nation (*gens*). Hence, under the general concept of public Right we are led to think not only of the Right of a state but also of a *Right of nations (ius gentium)*. Since the earth's surface is not unlimited but closed, the concepts of the Right of a state and of a Right of nations lead inevitably to the Idea of a *Right for all nations (ius gentium)* or *cosmopolitan Right (ius cosmopoliticum)*. So if the principle of outer freedom limited by law is lacking in any one of these three possible forms of rightful condition, the framework of all the others is unavoidably undermined and must finally collapse.

§44.

It is not experience from which we learn of men's maxim of violence and of their malevolent tendency to attack one another before external legislation endowed with power appears. It is therefore not some fact that makes coercion through

[†]*KAA* VI, 311–315.

public law necessary. On the contrary, however well disposed and law-abiding men might be, it still lies a priori in the rational Idea of such a condition (one that is not rightful) that before a public lawful condition is established, individual men, peoples, and states can never be secure against violence from one another, since each has its own right to do *what seems right and good to it* and not to be dependent upon another's opinion about this. So, unless it wants to renounce any concepts of Right, the first thing it has to resolve upon is the principle that it must leave the state of nature, in which each follows its own judgment, unite itself with all others (with which it cannot avoid interacting), subject itself to a public lawful external coercion, and so enter into a condition in which what is to be recognized as belonging to it is determined *by law* and is allotted to it by adequate *power* (not its own but an external power); that is to say, it ought above all else to enter a civil condition.

It is true that the state of nature need not, just because it is natural, be a state of *injustice (iniustus)*, of dealing with one another only in terms of the degree of force each has. But it would still be a state *devoid of justice (status iustitia vacuus)*, in which, when rights are *in dispute (ius controversum)*, there would be no judge competent to render a verdict having rightful force. Hence each may impel the other by force to leave this state and enter into a rightful condition; for although each can acquire something external by taking control of it or by contract in accordance with its *concepts of Right*, this acquisition is still only *provisional* as long as it does not yet have the sanction of public law, since it is not determined by public (distributive) justice and secured by an authority putting this right into effect.

> If no acquisition were recognized as rightful even in a provisional way prior to entering the civil condition, the civil condition itself would be impossible. For in terms of their form, laws concerning what is mine or yours in the state of nature contain the same thing that they prescribe in the civil condition, insofar as the civil condition is thought of by pure rational concepts alone. The difference is only that the civil condition provides the conditions under which these laws are put into effect (in keeping with distributive justice). So if external objects were not even *provisionally* mine or yours in the state of nature, there would also be no duties of Right with regard to them and therefore no command to leave the state of nature.

§45.

A *state (civitas)* is a union of a multitude of men under laws of Right. Insofar as these are a priori necessary as laws, that is, insofar as they follow of themselves from concepts of external Right as such (are not statutory), its form is the form of a state as such, that is, of *the state as Idea*, as it ought to be in accordance with pure principles of Right. This Idea serves as a norm (*norma*) for every actual union into a commonwealth (hence serves as a norm for its internal constitution).

Every state contains three *authorities* within it, that is, the general united will consists of three persons (*trias politica*): the *sovereign authority* [*Herrschergewalt*] (sovereignty) in the person of the legislator; *the executive authority* in the person of the ruler (in conformity to law); and the *judicial authority* (to award to each what is his in accordance with the law) in the person of the judge (*potestas legislatoria, rectoria et iudiciaria*). These are like the three propositions in a practical syllogism: the major premise, which contains the *law* of that will; the minor premise, which contains the *command* to behave in accordance with the law, i.e. the principle of subsumption under the law; and the conclusion, which contains the *verdict* (sentence), what is laid down as right in the case at hand.

§46.

The legislative authority can belong only to the united will of the people. For since all Right is to proceed from it, it *cannot* do anyone wrong by its law. Now, when someone makes arrangements about *another*, it is always possible for him to do the other wrong; but he can never do wrong in what he decides upon with regard to himself (for *volenti non fit iniuria*).[1] Therefore only the concurring and united will of all, insofar as each decides the same thing for all and all for each, and so only the general united will of the people, can be legislative.

The members of such a society who are united for giving law (*societas civilis*), that is, the members of a state, are called *citizens of a state* (*cives*). In terms of rights, the attributes of a citizen, inseparable from his essence (as a citizen), are: lawful *freedom*, the attribute of obeying no other law than that to which he has given his consent; civil *equality*, that of not recognizing among the *people* any superior with the moral capacity to bind him as a matter of Right in a way that he could not in turn bind the other; and third, the attribute of civil *independence*, of owing his existence and preservation to his own rights and powers as a member of the commonwealth, not to the choice of another among the people. From his independence follows his civil personality, his attribute of not needing to be represented by another where rights are concerned.

The only qualification for being a citizen is being fit to vote. But being fit to vote presupposes the independence of someone who, as one of the people, wants to be not just a part of the commonwealth but also a member of it, that is, a part of the common-wealth acting from his own choice in community with others. This quality of being independent, however, requires a distinction between *active* and *passive* citizens, though the concept of a passive citizen seems to contradict the concept of a citizen as such. The following examples can serve to remove this difficulty: an apprentice in the service of a merchant or artisan; a domestic servant (as distinguished from a civil servant); a minor (*naturaliter vel civiliter*); all women and, in general, anyone whose preservation in existence (his being fed and protected) depends not on his management of his own business but on arrangements made by another (except the state). All these people lack civil personality and their existence is, as it were, only inherence. The woodcutter I hire to work in my yard; the blacksmith in India, who goes into people's houses to work on iron with his hammer, anvil, and bellows, as compared with the European carpenter or blacksmith who can put the products of his work up as goods for sale to the public; the private tutor, as compared with the schoolteacher; the tenant farmer

---

[1] 'No wrong is done to someone who consents.'

as compared with the leasehold farmer, and so forth; these are mere underlings [*Handlanger*] of the commonwealth because they have to be under the direction or protection of other individuals, and so do not possess civil independence.

This dependence upon the will of others and this inequality is, however, in no way opposed to their freedom and equality *as men*, who together make up a people; on the contrary, it is only in conformity with the conditions of freedom and equality that this people can become a state and enter into a civil constitution. But not all persons qualify with equal right to vote within this constitution, that is, to be citizens and not mere associates in the state. For from their capacity to demand that all others treat them in accordance with the laws of natural freedom and equality as *passive* parts of the state it does not follow that they also have the right to manage the state itself as *active* members of it, the right to organize it or to cooperate for introducing certain laws. It follows only that, whatever sort of positive laws the citizens might vote for, these laws must still not be contrary to the natural laws of freedom and of the equality of everyone in the people corresponding to this freedom, namely that anyone can work his way up from this passive condition to an active one. [...]

Translated by Mary Gregor

10.

Johann Gottlieb Fichte, Foundations of Natural Right (Grundlage des Naturrechts nach Principien der Wissenschaftslehre): *Selections (1796/97)*

Fichte's central text on the philosophy of right or law (*Recht*) and state is the *Foundations of Natural Right* of 1796/97. Chronologically it lies between the *Science of Knowledge* (1794) and the *System of the Science of Ethics* (1798), the three works which make up 'Fichte's original system'. There is, however, a later book dealing with questions of law and ethics – the *Doctrine of Right* (*Rechtslehre*) of 1812 – but it adds nothing substantially new to the earlier reflections. Of historical interest, perhaps, is the 1813 *Doctrine of State* (*Staatslehre*). Fichte's other significant political writings are *The Closed Commercial State* (1800) and the *Addresses to the German Nation* (1808). The sort of state-socialism and nationalism advocated in these two latter books proved, in the history of European politics in the century after Fichte's death, to lead to totalitarianism, an outcome with which Fichte is sometimes anachronistically associated. This troubling association perhaps explains why the more promising directions that lie within Fichte's philosophy – in the *Foundations of Natural Right* in particular – have not, at least until recently, received as much attention as they deserve.

In the *Foundations of Natural Right* Fichte's familiar deductive procedure can be found in application to the definition of the systematic status of right or law and state. As the full title of the book indicates – *Foundations of Natural Right According to the Principles of the Science of Knowledge* – Fichte develops his philosophy of right from the starting point of the science of knowledge. His division of practical philosophy into 'natural right' and the 'theory of morality' corresponds with Kant's division of the *Metaphysics of Morals* (1797) into a 'Doctrine of Right' and a 'Doctrine of Virtue', though Fichte had neither this division in mind when he wrote the *Foundations of Natural Right*, and nor was he aware of Kant's division of material. The basic thoughts behind Kant's philosophies of law and political philosophy can be found, however, in some writings published shortly earlier. In Kant's text of 1793, 'On the Common Saying: "This may be true in Theory, but it does not apply in Practice"' there is a definition of law as the reconciliation of the freedom of each 'within a general workable law'.[1] Also discussed

[1] Immanuel Kant, 'On the Common Saying: "This may be true in theory, but it does not apply in Practice,"' p. 74, in *Kant: Political Writings* (Cambridge: Cambridge University Press, 1991), ed. Hans Reiss (*KAA* VIII, 290).

in this text is the principle of self-determination of sovereign peoples, a principle firmly established as a precept of contemporary political theory: 'Whatever a people cannot impose upon itself cannot be imposed upon it by the legislator either'.[2]

Fichte develops this principle as a form of contractualism which, in ways other than those of his predecessors – Hobbes, Locke, Rousseau and Kant – grounds all areas of law in specific contracts. The enduring thesis of this position might be summarised as follows: right secured within the state is the sphere of the mutual recognition of persons (free, yet finite rational beings), which is institutionalised in mutual legal claims on external spheres of freedom on the basis of free agreement. Right is the quintessence of coercive institutions equipped with force agreed upon by persons with the common objective of a reciprocal protection of freedom.

This fundamental thesis is developed in the first two main divisions of the first part of the *Foundations of Natural Law*, that is, in the 'Deduction of the Concept of Right' and in the 'Deduction of the Applicability of the Concept of Right' (§§1–7). In the third main division, the 'Doctrine of Right', we find the theory of 'Original Right' (§§9–12), of the 'Right of Coercion' (§§13–15) and of 'Political Right' (§16). The developed 'doctrine of political right' is found in the second part of the book (published in 1797), which Fichte entitles 'applied natural law'. The doctrine of political right outlines the notion of the 'civil contract' (§17) and introduces basic definitions of the 'civil and property law' (§§18–19), as well as criminal law (§20). In the appendices to the book Fichte sketches an 'outline of family right' and an 'outline of the right of nations and cosmopolitan right'. The passages selected below trace the most important logical steps from the 'Introduction' up to the end of the 'Doctrine of Right' (that is, up to §16).

In the 'theorems' preceding the 'Doctrine of Right', Fichte introduces, amongst other things, his theory of corporeality and interpersonality, thereby anticipating in certain respects some of the claims of phenomenology and analytical philosophy. A person according to Fichte, is a 'material I', who (a) experiences itself as a freely effecting individual, by (b) assuming an outer sensory world, (c) ascribing free effectiveness also to *other rational beings*, (d) ascribing to itself a *body*, and (e) experiencing itself as standing under the possible influence of *other persons*. Legal relations are, according to Fichte, the only 'modus' in which persons mutually recognise each other as free finite rational beings. In the paragraphs leading from the 'Theorems' to the 'Doctrine of Right' Fichte summarises this train of thought and applies it to the basic question of the philosophy of right: 'Persons as such are to be absolutely free and dependent solely on their will. Persons, as surely as they are persons, are to stand with one another in a state of mutual influence, and thus not be dependent solely on themselves. The task of the science of right is to discover how both of these statements can

[2] Ibid., p. 85 (*KAA* VIII, 304).

exist together: the question that lies at the basis of this science is: how is a community of free beings, *qua* free beings, possible?'[3] This question is answered in the excerpts from §§8–16 printed here.

The key concept on which Fichte builds the corresponding theory of state is the concept of *contract*. In the theory of political right we can find his contractarian interpretation of the *civil* contract. The latter contains several partial contracts. The *property* contract (§17; in §18 Fichte also calls it a 'civil contract') is an *omission* contract, in which there is mutual agreement to refrain from interference by any contracting party in the property of any other contracting party. Another element of the civil contract is the *protection* contract. Here the contracting parties are positively committed to mutual protection. Finally, the contracting parties enter into a *unification* contract, 'by means of which alone the two previous contracts are protected and secured, and which makes all three contracts in their unity into a civil contract'.[4] Fichte understands the state (the 'whole') as a property-owner-community: 'The whole is the *owner* of all the possessions and rights of every individual, in so far as it regards and must regard any injury to such property or rights *as an injury to itself*. But in so far as the whole regards something as *subject to its free use*, the state's property is limited to what each individual is obligated to contribute towards shouldering the state's burdens'.[5]

The validity of the civil contract depends on the citizen contributing in this way. (The contract is 'cancelled as soon as the citizen does not contribute'.[6]) The civil contract is also 'hypothetically' a *subjection* contract. I become a subject only in not meeting my 'civic duties'. In meeting them, however, I am a 'participant in sovereignty' and a 'free individual'.[7] The civil contract contains a corresponding excluding principle, excluding those not meeting its demands from the legal relation. 'Anyone who does not fulfil this contract is not a part of it, and anyone who is a part of it necessarily fulfils it entirely. If someone exists apart from this contract, then he stands outside every rightful relation whatsoever and is rightfully excluded altogether from any reciprocity with other beings of his kind in the sensible world'.[8] Failure to fulfil the civil contract is thus equivalent to the loss of interpersonal recognition, which is only secured within the sphere of legal relations, and an attendant loss of freedom.

The primary purpose and end of the state is 'mutual security' and the common securing of conditions for the maintenance of one's future life through one's current activity. The right to life from one's own work is,

---

[3] J. G. Fichte. trans. Michael Baur, *Foundations of Natural Right, According to the Principles of the Wissenschaftslehre* (Cambridge: Cambridge University Press, 2000), p. 79 (*FW* III, 85).
[4] Ibid., p. 177 (*FW* III, 204).
[5] Ibid., p. 178 (*FW* III, 205–6).
[6] Ibid., p. 179 (*FW* III, 206).
[7] Ibid., p. 179 (*FW* III, 206)
[8] Ibid., p. 180 (*FW* III, 207).

Fichte tells us, immediately contained in the civil contract: 'everyone ought to be able to live from his labor'.[9] Persons who cannot live from their own work are 'no longer obligated by right to recognize anyone else's property'.[10] Aside from the distress to the person concerned, this creates a general destabilisation of property. Fichte stipulates, however, that in order to counteract this, 'all others must ... relinquish a portion of their own property, until he is able to live'.[11]

---

[9]Ibid., p. 185 (*FW* III, 212).
[10]Ibid., p. 186 (*FW* III, 213).
[11]Ibid., p. 186 (*FW* III, 213).

INTRODUCTION

II What the Doctrine of Natural Right, as a Real Philosophical Science, Has to Achieve in Particular[†]

(1) According to what has been said above, that a certain determinate concept is originally contained in reason and given through it, can mean nothing other than that the rational being, just as certainly as it is a rational being, acts necessarily in a certain determinate way. The philosopher's task is to show that this determinate action is a condition of self-consciousness, and showing this constitutes the deduction of that concept. The philosopher has to describe this determinate action itself with respect to its form, as well as to describe what emerges for reflection in this acting. By doing this, the philosopher simultaneously provides proof of the concept's necessity, determines the concept itself, and shows its application. None of these elements can be separated from the others, otherwise even the individually treated pieces will be treated incorrectly, and then one will be philosophizing in a merely formal manner. The concept of right should be an original concept of pure reason; therefore, this concept is to be treated in the manner indicated.

(2) This concept acquires necessity through the fact that the rational being cannot posit itself as a rational being with self-consciousness without positing itself as an *individual*, as one among several rational beings that it assumes to exist outside itself, just as it takes itself to exist.

[†]*FW* III, 1–16. *Foundations of Natural Right, According to the Principles of Wissenschaftslehre* (Cambridge: Cambridge University Press, 2000).

It is even possible to present in a sensory manner what one's mode of acting in this positing of the concept of right is like. I posit myself as rational, i.e. as free. In doing so, the representation of freedom is in me. In the same undivided action, I simultaneously posit other free beings. Thus, through my imagination I describe a sphere for freedom that several beings share. I do not ascribe to myself all the freedom I have posited, because I posit other free beings as well, and must ascribe to them a part of this freedom. In appropriating freedom for myself, I limit myself by leaving some freedom for others as well. Thus the concept of right is the concept of the necessary relation of free beings to one another.

(3) What is contained first and foremost in the concept of freedom is nothing but the capacity to construct [*entwerfen*], through absolute spontaneity, concepts of our possible efficacy [*Wirksamkeit*]; and the only thing that rational beings ascribe to one another with necessity is this bare capacity. But if a rational individual, or a person, is to find himself as free, then something more is required, namely, that the object in experience that is thought of through the concept of the person's efficacy actually correspond to that concept; what is required, therefore, is that something in the world outside the rational individual follow from the thought of his activity. Now if, as is certainly the case, the effects of rational beings are to belong within the same world, and thus be capable of influencing, mutually disturbing, and impeding one another, then freedom in this sense would be possible for persons who stand with one another in this state of mutual influence only on the condition that all their efficacy be contained within certain limits, and the world, as the sphere of their freedom, be, as it were, divided among them. But since these beings are posited as free, such a limit could not lie outside freedom, for freedom would thereby be nullified rather than limited *as freedom*; rather, all would have to posit this limit for themselves through freedom itself, i.e. all would have to have made it a law for themselves not to disturb the freedom of those with whom they stand in mutual interaction. –

(4) And so we would then have the *complete object* of the concept of right; namely, *a community among free beings as such*. It is necessary that every free being assume the existence of others of its kind outside itself; but it is not necessary that they all continue to exist alongside one another *as free beings*; thus the thought of such a community and its realization is something arbitrary or optional [*willkürliches*]. But *if* it is to be thought, how – through what concept, through what determinate mode of acting – is it thought? It turns out that, in thought, each member of the community lets his own external freedom be limited through inner freedom, so that all others beside him can also be externally free. This is the concept of right. Because the thought and task of such a community is arbitrary, this concept, if thought as a practical concept, is merely technical–practical: i.e. if one asks, in accordance with what principles could a community among free beings as such be established if someone wanted to establish one, the answer would have to be: in accordance with the concept of right. But this answer by no means asserts *that* such a community ought to be established.

(5) This entire presentation of the concept of right has refrained from refuting in detail those who attempt to derive the doctrine of right from the moral law; this is because, as soon as the correct deduction is given, every unbiased mind will accept it of its own accord, even if the incorrectness of the other deductions has not been shown; but as for biased minds and those who have their own axes to grind, every word uttered for the purpose of refuting them is wasted.

The rule of right, 'limit your freedom through the concept of the freedom of all other persons with whom you come in contact', does indeed receive a new sanction for conscience through the law of absolute agreement with oneself (the moral law); and then the philosophical treatment of conscience constitutes a chapter of morality; but this is not part of the philosophical doctrine of right, which ought to be a separate science standing on its own. One might say that several learned men who have put forth systems of natural right would have dealt with that chapter of morality without knowing it, had they not forgotten to state why compliance with the moral law (which they must always have had in mind regardless of the formula they used to express it) conditions the agreement of the rational being with itself. Similarly – I mention this in passing – the teachers of morality have generally not considered that the moral law is merely formal and therefore empty, and that a content cannot be obtained for it through sleight of hand, but must be rigorously deduced. It is possible to indicate briefly how the matter stands in our case. I must think of myself as necessarily in community with other human beings with whom nature has united me, but I cannot do this without thinking of my freedom as limited through their freedom; now I must also act in accordance with this necessary thought, otherwise my acting stands in contradiction with my thinking,[1] – and thus I stand in contradiction with myself; I am bound in conscience, by my knowledge of how things ought to be, to limit my freedom. Now in the doctrine of right there is no talk of moral obligation; each is bound only by the free, arbitrary [*willkürlichen*] decision to live in community with others, and if someone does not at all want to limit his free choice [*Willkür*], then within the field of the doctrine of right, one can say nothing further against him, other than that he must then remove himself from all human community.

(6) In the present text, the concept of right has been deduced as a condition of self-consciousness, along with the object of right; this concept has been derived and determined, and its application guaranteed, as is required of a real science. This has been done in the first and second sections of this investigation. The concept of right is further determined, and the way it must be realized in the sensible world is demonstrated, in the doctrine of civil rights [*Staatsbürgerrechte*]. The investigations

---

[1] I have read somewhere that the principle of moral theory is: 'The manifold actions of the free will ought to agree with themselves'. This is a very unfortunate application of the postulate of the absolute agreement of the rational being with itself, a postulate that I proposed in the *Lectures concerning the Scholar's Vocation*. In response, one only has to think of becoming a thoroughly consistent villain, as J. B. Erhard (Niethammer's *Philosophisches Journal*, 1795) portrays the devil in his 'Devil's Apology'; then the actions of the free will agree perfectly with themselves, for they all contradict a conviction concerning what ought to be, and [the criterion of] such a moral doctrine has been satisfied.

into original right [*Urrecht*] and the right of coercion [*Zwangsrecht*] serve as preparation for the doctrine of civil right. The three chapters necessary for the complete
determination of civil right (those listed in the book as covering the civil contract,
civil legislation, and the constitution) have already been worked out and presented
in lectures to my listeners;[2] they will appear at the next book fair, along with the
doctrines of the right of nations, cosmopolitan right, and family right, under the
title, *Applied Natural Right*.

III Concerning the Relation of the Present Theory of Right to the Kantian Theory

Apart from some excellent hints by Dr. *Erhard* in several of his most recent writings, and by *Maimon* in an essay on natural right in Prof. Niethammer's *Philosophical
Journal*, the author of the present work had found no trace of any philosopher having questioned the usual way of dealing with natural right, until, after completing
the foundations of his theory of right according to the principles of the *Wissenschaftslehre*, he was most pleasantly surprised by Kant's extremely important[3]
work, *Perpetual Peace*.

A comparison of the Kantian principles concerning right (insofar as these principles emerge from the work just cited) and the system presented here, may perhaps
be useful to some readers.

On the basis of the work just cited, it is not possible to see clearly whether Kant
derives the law of right from the moral law (in accordance with the usual way of
doing things) or whether he adopts another deduction of the law of right. But
Kant's remark concerning the concept of a permissive law [*Erlaubnisgesetz*] makes
it at least highly probable that his deduction agrees with the deduction given here.

A right is clearly something that one can avail oneself of or not. Thus a right
follows from a merely permissive law, and it is a permissive law because it is limited
only to a certain sphere, from which it can be inferred that outside the sphere of
the law one is free from it, and if there is no other law concerning this object, one

---

[2] It was not possible to print these chapters along with the present text; therefore, they remained behind,
and this gave me the opportunity to add to them the other parts of the general doctrine of right. – As
a result, there arises just one difficulty for the present book. Based on previous experience I am justified
in assuming that not all critics who read my principles will simultaneously acquire a competence to apply
them. Thus I ask anyone who does not have a sure self-consciousness of this competence already confirmed
by experience not to rush into applying them further, but to await my text.

[3] What is one to think of the acumen of part of the public, when one hears this work placed in the same
class with the ideas of the Abbé St.-Pierre, or with Rousseau's ideas on the same topic? These two said only
that the realization of this idea [of perpetual peace] would be desirable, to which every sensible person no
doubt responds that the idea would not be impossible, if human beings were different from how they still
presently are. *Kant* shows that this idea is a *necessary* task of reason and that the presentation of this idea is an
end of nature that nature will achieve sooner or later, since she works endlessly towards it and has actually
already reached so much that lies on the way to the goal: thus Kant's position is undoubtedly a very different
view of the same topic.

is generally left solely to one's own arbitrary choice [*Willkür*]. This permission is not explicitly contained in the law; it is merely inferred from an interpretation of the law, from its limited character. The limited character of a law manifests itself in the fact that it is conditioned. It is absolutely impossible to see how a permissive law should be derivable from the moral law, which commands unconditionally and thereby extends its reach to everything.

Our theory fully agrees with Kant's claims that the state of peace or lawfulness among human beings is not a natural state, but must be instituted; that one has the right to coerce even someone who has not yet attacked us, so that, by submitting to the authority of the government, the coerced person might afford us the requisite security; and in our theory these propositions have been proved in the same way in which they are proved by Kant.

Our theory is just as much in agreement with the Kantian argument for the propositions that the association of the state can be constructed only on the basis of a contract that is original, but necessarily entered into; further, that the people itself does not exercise executive power, but rather must transfer it, and that therefore democracy, in the proper sense of the word, is a constitution fully contrary to right.

But I have been led to different thoughts regarding the claim that, for the purpose of maintaining the security of right in the state, it is sufficient to separate the legislative and executive powers, as Kant seems to assume (merely *seems*, for in this work it was evidently not Kant's intention to given an exhaustive treatment of the subject). Here I shall briefly summarize the main points of the present treatise.

The law of right includes the idea that, when human beings are to live alongside one another, each must limit his freedom, so that the freedom of others can also exist alongside that freedom. But the law of right says nothing to the effect that a particular person should limit his freedom specifically through the freedom of a particular second, third, or fourth person. That I must restrict myself specifically in relation to these particular human beings derives from the fact that I live in community specifically with them; but I live in community specifically with them as a result of my free decision, not through any obligation. Applied to the civil contract, this means it is originally up to the free and arbitrary choice of every individual to determine whether he wants to live in this particular state or not, although if he wants to live among other human beings at all, then it is not up to his arbitrary choice to determine whether he enters into a state, or whether he wants to remain his own judge; but, just as he expresses his will to enter into a particular state and just as he is accepted into such a state, so he is, by virtue of this simple, reciprocal declaration, subjected without further ado to all the limitations that the law of right requires for this group of human beings; by virtue of the words, 'I want to live in this state', he has accepted all the laws of that state. The law of the state, with regard to its *form*, becomes his law by virtue of his consent, but the law of the state, with regard to its *content*, is determined without any consent by him by the law of right and the circumstances of this state.

Furthermore, the law, 'limit your freedom through the freedom of all others', is merely formal and, as set forth thus far, is not capable of being applied; for just how far should the sphere of each individual extend within which no one may disturb him and beyond which he, for his part, may not go without being regarded as someone who disturbs the freedom of others? On this, the parties must reach some agreement in good faith. Applied to the state, this means: on entering the state, each must come to an understanding with it concerning a certain range for his free actions (property, civil rights, etc.). What then limits him to precisely this sphere? Evidently, his own free decision; for without this decision, he would have just as much right as others to everything that remains left over and available to them. But then what determines how much can be granted to each individual for himself? Evidently the common will, in accordance with the rule: this particular number of human beings should be free alongside one another in this particular sphere for [the sake of] freedom in general; thus, so much belongs to each individual.

Now the citizens must be kept within these limits by coercion, and a certain, impending harm (in case they overstep them) must deter their will from deciding to overstep them. It is clear that this punishment, which is determined by criminal law, must be known to them if it is to have an effect on their will; furthermore, it is clear that, by entering into the state, they have made themselves subject to this harm, in case they overstep the law.

But then who is to *proclaim* the common will (which is, of course, completely *determined* by *the nature of the matter*) concerning both the rights of individuals and the punishment of those who overstep their rights? Who, then, is to *clarify and interpret* that necessary decree of nature and of the law of right? No one would be more ill-suited than the masses, and by aggregating individual votes one is likely to obtain a very impure version of the true common will. This task can belong to no one other than he who constantly oversees the whole and all of its needs, and who is responsible for the uninterrupted rule of the strictest right; in other words, it can belong to no one other than the administrator of the executive power. He provides the content of the law, which is given to him by reason and by the circumstances of the state; but the law gets its form, its binding power for the individual, only through the individual's consent, not specifically to this determinate law, but to be united with this state. For these reasons and in this sense, our theory claims that the legislative power in civil legislation and the executive power are not to be separated, but must remain necessarily united. Civil legislation is itself a branch of the executive power, insofar as it is only right in general that is being executed. The administrator of the executive power is the natural interpreter of the common will concerning the relationship of individuals to one another within the state; he is the interpreter, not exactly of the will that the individuals actually have, but rather of the will that they must have if they are to exist alongside one another; and this is so, even if not a single person should, in fact, have such a will (as one might well assume to be the case from time to time).

The law concerning how the law is to be executed, or the *constitution*, is of a completely different kind. Every citizen of the state must vote in favor of the constitution, which can be established only through absolute unanimity; for the constitution is the guarantee that each receives from all the others, for the sake of securing all his rights within the society. The most essential component of every constitution is the ephorate as it is established in the present theory. I leave it to the judgment of unbiased experts to determine whether the ephorate is sufficient to secure the rights of all without the separation of the legislative and executive powers, a suggestion that has been made by others but seems impracticable to me. (*The extent to which Kant* approves of this separation, which is quite correct *in part*, is not apparent from his essay.)

[…]

[*FW* III, 17] First Main Division
Deduction of the Concept of Right

§I First Theorem
A Finite Rational Being Cannot Posit Itself without Ascribing a
Free Efficacy to Itself [. . .]

[*FW* III, 23] *§2 Inference*
By thus Positing its Capacity of Exercise Free Efficacy, the
Rational Being Posits and Determines a Sensible World Outside
of Itself [. . .]

[*FW* III, 30] *§3 Second Theorem*
The Finite Rational Being Cannot Ascribe to Itself a Free Efficacy
in the Sensible World without also Ascribing Such Efficacy to
Others, and thus without also Presupposing the Existence of
Other Finite Rational Beings Outside of Itself

Proof

(I) (a) According to the proof conducted above (§ 1), the rational being cannot posit (perceive and comprehend) an object without simultaneously – in the same, undivided synthesis – ascribing an efficacy to itself.

(b) But it cannot ascribe an efficacy to itself without having posited an object upon which such efficacy is supposed to be exercised. The positing of the object as something that is determined through itself, and thus as something that constrains the rational being's free activity, must be posited in a prior moment in time; it is only through this prior moment that the moment in which one grasps the concept of efficacy becomes the present moment.

(c) Any act of comprehension is conditioned by a positing of the rational being's own efficacy; and all efficacy is conditioned by some prior act of comprehension by the rational being. Therefore, every possible moment of consciousness is conditioned by a prior moment of consciousness, and so the explanation of the possibility of consciousness.

[…]

[FW III, 41] §4 Third Theorem
The Finite Rational Being Cannot Assume the Existence of Other
Finite Rational Beings Outside it without Positing Itself as
Standing with Those Beings in a Particular Relation, Called a
Relation of Right [Rechtsverhältniß] [. . .]

[*FW* III, 51–53] (I posit myself as an individual in opposition to another particular individual, insofar as *I* ascribe to *myself* a sphere for my freedom from which I exclude the other, and ascribe a sphere *to the other* from which I exclude myself – obviously, this occurs merely in the thinking of a fact and in consequence of this fact. Thus I have posited myself as *free* alongside him and without harming the possibility of his freedom. Through this positing of my freedom, I have *determined* myself; being free constitutes my essential character. But what does *being free* mean? Evidently, it means being able to carry out the concepts of one's actions. But this carrying out always *follows* the concept, and the perception of what one takes to be the product of one's efficacy is always – relative to the formation of the concept of such a product – *in the future*. Thus freedom is always posited into the future; and if freedom is supposed to constitute a being's character, then it is posited for *all* of the individual's future; freedom is posited in the future to the extent that the *individual himself* is posited in the future.

But now my freedom is possible only through the fact that the other remains within his sphere; therefore, just as I demand my freedom for all the future, so too I also demand that the other be limited, and – since he is to be free – limited by himself for all the future: and I demand all this immediately, insofar as I posit myself as an individual.

This demand upon the other is contained in the act of positing myself as an individual.

But the other can limit himself only in consequence of a concept of me as a free being. Nevertheless, I demand this limitation absolutely; thus, I demand *consistency* from him, i.e. I demand that all of his future concepts be determined by a certain prior concept, by the knowledge of me as a rational being.

Now he can recognize me as a rational being only under the condition that I treat him as one, in accordance with my concept of him as a rational being. Thus, I impose the same consistency upon myself, and his action is conditioned by mine. We stand in reciprocal interaction with regard to the consistency of our thinking and our acting: our thinking is consistent with our acting, and my thinking and acting are consistent with his.)

(III) The conclusion to all of this has already emerged. – *I must in all cases recognize the free being outside me as a free being, i.e. I must limit my freedom through the concept of the possibility of his freedom.*

The relation between free beings that we have deduced (i.e. that each is to limit his freedom through the concept of the possibility of the other's freedom, under the condition that the latter likewise limit his freedom through the freedom of the former) is called the *relation of right*; and the formula that has now been established is the *principle of right*.

This relation is deduced from the concept of the individual. Thus what was to be proved has now been proved.

Furthermore, the concept of the individual was previously proved to be a condition of self-consciousness; thus the concept of right is itself a condition of self-consciousness. Therefore, the concept of right has been properly deduced *a priori*, i.e. from the pure form of reason, from the I.

[...]

[*FW* III, 56] Second Main Division
Deduction of the Applicability of the Concept of Right

§5 Fourth Theorem
The Rational Being Cannot Posit Itself as an Individual that has Efficacy without Ascribing to Itself, and Thereby Determining, a Material Body [...]

[*FW* III, 61] *§6 Fifth Theorem*
The Person Cannot Ascribe a Body to Himself without Positing it as Standing under the Influence of a Person Outside Him, and without Thereby Further Determining it [...]

[*FW* III, 92–97] Third Main Division
Systematic Application of the Concept of Right;
or the Doctrine of Right

§8
Deduction of the Subdivisions within a Doctrine of Right

(I) If reason is to be realized at all in the sensible world, it must be possible for several rational beings to exist alongside one another as such, i.e. as free beings.

But the postulated coexistence of the freedom of several beings – and this obviously means *enduring* coexistence in accordance with a rule, not merely coexistence here and there by chance – is possible only insofar as *each free being makes it a law for himself to limit his freedom through the concept of the freedom of all others.* For:

(a) the free being *can*, and has the physical capacity to, interfere with the freedom of other rational beings, or to annihilate it completely; but

(b) with respect to choosing from among all the things he can do, the free being is dependent only on his free will; thus if he does not interfere with the freedom of others, this would have to be the result of a *free decision*; and

(c) if within a community of rational beings such interference *never* occurs and *never* can occur, the only possible explanation for this is that all the free beings have freely made this way of acting into a *law* for themselves.

(The proposition just set forth is nothing more than the judgment of the philosopher who reflects on the possibility of a community of free beings, and should neither be nor mean anything more. *If* free beings as such are to coexist, then their coexistence can be thought only in the manner indicated; this can be proved, and has been proved satisfactorily. The issue is not whether they are to coexist or whether the condition of the possibility of such co-existence (the law) occurs. Nor is it a question of who wills one thing or the other. – For now we can say only this much about the law-giver: It is nature that willed a plurality of rational and free beings to exist alongside one another in the sensible world, insofar as she produced a plurality of bodies that can be cultivated to possess reason and freedom. This does not mean that nature has understanding and a will; about that we are resigned to ignorance. Rather, it simply means: *if* one were to ascribe an understanding and a will to nature in her various operations, her plan could be none other than that free beings should exist alongside one another. Thus it would be nature that willed that the freedom of each individual should be limited by the possibility of the freedom of all others. But since nature wills that everyone should be completely free, she also wills that they freely impose this law upon themselves – that is, she wills that it be a law for freedom, not one of her mechanical laws. What kind of measures nature may have hit upon in order to achieve her end without harming the freedom of such individuals, will become apparent.)

First, we shall once again analyze the law that has been set forth.

(a) It is to be a *law*, i.e. no exceptions to it are to be possible; once it has been accepted, it is to command universally and categorically.

(b) In consequence of this law, everyone is to limit his *freedom*, i.e. the sphere of his freely chosen actions and expressions in the sensible world. Accordingly, the concept of freedom here is *quantitative* and *material*.

(c) One is supposed to limit one's freedom by the possibility of the *freedom* of others. Here, the same word (freedom) has another meaning, one that is merely *qualitative* and *formal*. Each is said only to be able to be free in general, to be a person: but the law, at first, says nothing about *how far* the sphere of each person's possible free actions is supposed to extend. No one has a right to an action that makes the freedom and personality of another impossible; but everyone has a right to all other free actions.

Therefore, the first question is: what is entailed by the idea that someone is free in general, or is a person? Since here we are considering the content of this idea as a condition of the possibility of the co-existence of free beings, such content is to be called *a right*; and for the same reason, the conditions of freedom and personality will be set forth here only insofar as they can be violated by physical force.

This right, or these rights, are contained in the mere concept of the person as such and are therefore called *original rights*. The doctrine of original rights arises through the mere analysis of the concept of personality insofar as the content of this concept *could* be, but – in accordance with the law of right – *ought* not to be, violated by the free action of others.

The doctrine of original right will constitute the first chapter of our doctrine of right.

(II) The judgment that has just been established is *hypothetical*. If free beings as such are to exist alongside one another, then each of them must impose upon himself the law we have described. The antecedent (which we do not know to be posited or not) is conditioned by the consequent: *if* they are to co-exist, then each must give this law to himself, and if they do not give it to themselves, then they cannot exist with one another. – Thus the only reason the philosopher has for assuming that there is such a law is the presupposition that these free beings are to co-exist.

From this, we can draw the following conclusions. The law is conditioned, and a possible being that might want to give the law to himself can – so far as we know, at least up to this point – give it to himself only as a conditioned law. Such a being adopts this law in order to attain the end that the law presupposes. Thus the rational being can subject itself to the law only insofar as this end is attainable; or stated otherwise, the law holds for the rational being only insofar as the end is attainable.

But now the end of existing with another person in a community of freedom is attainable only under the condition that this other person has also imposed upon himself the law of respecting the first person's freedom, or his original rights. This law is completely inapplicable to my behavior with respect to someone who has not given this law to himself, since the end for the sake of which I was supposed to respect the other person's original rights no longer exists. Thus although I have subjected myself to the law in general, I am nevertheless not bound – in consequence of the law itself – to respect the freedom of this particular person. –

I think of myself as both subject to the law and not subject to it: I *think of myself* as subject to the law *in general* but as not subject to it in this particular case. In consequence of the former, I act *in accordance with right*, under the command of the law, and thus I possess a *right*; in consequence of the latter, I may violate the other person's freedom and personality, and my right is thus a *right of coercion*.

(a) Because the law is *conditioned*, and can be adopted only as conditioned, each person has the right to *judge* [*urteilen*] whether or not the law applies to a particular case. Here such judging – since it occurs with a view to the law of right – is *judging in a legal sense* [*ein Richten*]. Each is necessarily his own *judge* [*Richter*], and here – wherever a right of coercion exists – the one who has this right is at the same time the judge of the other against whom he has it; for the *right of coercion* is possible only on the basis of such a knowledge of right. But apart from this condition, no one is originally the judge of another, nor can he be. – The result of these inferences is: *there is no right of coercion without the right of passing legal judgment.*

(b) The person who is supposed to have the right of coercion must himself stand under the law and be thought of as having subjected himself to it; and as being someone about whom it cannot be proved – at least from his actions – that he does not obey the law. Otherwise, he may very well have the power to coerce another person, but never the right to do so, since such a right flows only from the law. Furthermore, one should pay attention to *the* character of the right of coercion, namely, that this right flows only from the law's silence, from its general non-applicability to a particular case, and not in any way from a *command* of the law. This is why there is only a *right* to coerce, a right a person may or may not avail himself of, but by no means a *duty* to coerce.

From this deduction of the *right of coercion*, it is clear when such a right can exist: namely, when a person has violated the original rights of another. Therefore, once original rights have been set forth in the first chapter, it will become clear when they are violated. Nevertheless, for the sake of a systematic overview, it will not be superfluous to enumerate and clarify the cases in which the right of coercion exists; this will be done in the second chapter of the doctrine of right.

(III) The right of coercion in general, including every particular instance of it, has its ground; but everything that is grounded is necessarily finite and extends no further than its ground. Thus, if one can determine the limit of the applicability of the ground, one can also indicate the limit of what is grounded. The ground of my right of coercion is the fact that the other person does not subject himself to the law of right. By appealing to this ground, I simultaneously posit that I would have no right of coercion if the other person subjected himself to the law, and – expressed quantitatively – that I have such a right only to the extent that he does not subject himself to the law and that I have no such right at all if he does subject himself to it. – The right of coercion has its limit in the other's voluntary subjection to the law of right; any coercion beyond this limit is contrary to right. This general proposition is obvious at once. The only question (since we are propounding a real and not merely formal doctrine of natural right) is whether and how this limit can be found and determined in applying the law. A right of coercion does not exist unless an *original right* has been violated; but when there has been a violation, such a right surely does exist, and in this way the right of coercion can be demonstrated in every particular case. Furthermore, it is immediately clear that anyone who wills that the right of coercion exist does not will the violation of an original right and, if such a violation does occur, he wills that it be undone and annulled. In view of this, the law's quantity would then also be *demonstrable every time*. In each case, the limit of the rightful use of coercion could be determined: it would extend to the point of complete restitution and complete compensation for the violation; it would extend to the point where both parties were returned to the condition in which they found themselves prior to the unjust violation. Thus the right of coercion, with respect to both its quality and quantity, would be precisely determined by reference to the damage suffered and would not depend on any further condition.

But – and this is a circumstance that recent treatments of the doctrine of right have for the most part overlooked – the right of coercion is by no means grounded simply on the fact that the other person fails to respect the law only in the present, particular case. Rather it is grounded first and foremost on the fact that – by his present violation – he makes it known that he has not made that rule into a universal law for himself. *One* action contrary to right, even after a series of rightful ones, proves that the rule of right is not an inviolable law for this person, and that until now he has refrained from unjust actions for quite different reasons. Now from this it becomes clear that no free being can live securely alongside him, since security can be grounded only on a law, and becomes possible only by being thus grounded; and thus the person who has suffered the violation acquires the right to annihilate completely the violator's freedom, to cancel altogether the possibility of ever again entering into community with him in the sensible world. Thus the right of coercion is *infinite* and has no limit whatsoever (a proposition that theorists of right have one-sidedly maintained at one moment, and one-sidedly denied the next), unless the violator accepts the law as such in his heart and subjects himself to it. But as soon as he accepts the law, the right of coercion ceases, for its duration was grounded solely on the duration of the other person's lawlessness; and from now on, any further coercion is contrary to right. In this respect the limit of the coercion is *conditioned*. [. . .]

[*FW* III, 99–107] A right of coercion in general, as a universal concept, can easily be derived from the law of right; but as soon as one attempts to demonstrate how this right is applied, one gets entangled in an irresolvable contradiction. This is because the ground for deciding how to apply it cannot be given in the sensible world, but resides instead in each person's conscience. The right of coercion, as a concept that can be applied, stands in clear contradiction to itself, in that it is impossible to decide in any particular case whether the coercion is rightful or not.

Whether or not the wronged party himself can exercise the right of coercion depends on nothing less than an answer to the question of whether a genuine doctrine of natural right is possible, by which we mean a science of the relation of right between persons outside the state and without positive law. Since most theorists of right are content to philosophize formally about the concept of right, and – as long as their concept is merely thinkable – care very little about how the concept can be applied, they very easily get around the question just posed. Here we have answered the first question – and thereby also the second – in the negative; and in order to be convinced of the undeniability of the present doctrine of right, one must come to see clearly that it is impossible for the wronged party himself to exercise the right of coercion (an impossibility that we have demonstrated here). Therefore, the proposition just established is of supreme importance for our entire doctrine of right.

The circle was this: the possibility of the mutual restoration of freedom between the two parties is conditioned by the entirety of future experience; but the possibility of future experience is conditioned by this mutual restoration of freedom. In order to eliminate the contradiction, these two elements will be synthetically united in accordance with the method demonstrated in the *Wissenschaftslehre*. *The mutual restoration of freedom and the entirety of future experience must be one and the same*, or more clearly stated: the entirety of future experience that both parties desire must already lie within and be guaranteed by the mutual restoration of freedom.

There is no doubt that this proposition had to be introduced; the only question is: how is what it requires possible?

First, it is immediately clear that, in consequence of what the proposition requires, the entirety of future experience – that is, the desired experience of the complete security of both – is to be made present in a single moment, the moment of their mutual restoration of freedom; and it is to be made present in a way that can be validated by external evidence, since neither party can know the inner dispositions of the other. Therefore, both would have to make it impossible, physically impossible, for themselves to violate one another further, and in such a way that the other party would have to see this impossibility and be convinced of it. Security for the future is called *a warranty, a guarantee*.

Thus the proposition above says: the parties must mutually guarantee security to one another; otherwise, they could no longer exist alongside one another, in which case one of them would necessarily have to be destroyed.

The further question is: how is this guarantee possible? – The two parties were not able simply to lay down their weapons, because neither was able to trust the other. Therefore, they would have to place their weapons, i.e. their entire power, into the hands of a *third* party they both trust. They would have to commission this third party to repel whoever among them would violate the other. The third party would have to be capable of doing this, and therefore would have to *have superior power*. Thus this third party would exercise the right of coercion on behalf of both of them. – If the third party is to do this, they must give this party the authority to decide their present dispute as well as any dispute that could possibly arise between them in the future; that is, they would have to surrender to this party their *right to pass legal judgment* [*Recht des Gerichts*]. They must surrender this right to the third party without reservation, and with no right of appeal. For if one of them could guide the decision of their now common judge, then he would still be taking right into his own hands; but the other party does not trust him, and therefore cannot consent to such an arrangement. *Thus, both must unconditionally subordinate their physical power and their right to pass a judgment, i.e. all their rights, to that third party.*

(IV) *Thesis.* According to the law of right, the person's freedom is limited by nothing but the possibility that others alongside him can also be free and have rights. According to that law, a person is supposed to be permitted to do anything that does not infringe the rights of another, for the person's right consists precisely in this permission. Each person has the right to pass his own judgment on the limit of his free actions, and to defend this limit.

Antithesis. The same law of right implies that each person must completely and without reservation alienate his power and his capacity to pass judgments of right, if a rightful condition is ever to be possible among free beings. Through this, each person fully loses both the right to pass judgment on the scope of his rights and the right to defend them; each person thereby becomes dependent on the knowledge and good will of the one to whom he has subjected himself, and thus ceases to be free.

This latter proposition contradicts the former. The former is the law of right itself; the latter is a correct inference drawn from that law. Thus, the law of right is in contradiction with itself. This contradiction must be canceled. The heart of the contradiction is this: within the province of the law of right, I can give up only so much of my freedom as is necessary in order that the rights of those with whom I enter into community in the sensible world can also exist. But now I am supposed to lay down all my rights and subject them to the opinion and authority of a stranger. This is impossible and contradictory, unless – in and through such subjection – all the freedom that properly belongs to me in my sphere, in accordance with the law of right, is secured.

Unless this condition is met, I cannot rationally subject myself to such an authority, and the law of right gives no one a right to demand that I do so. Thus I must be able to judge for myself whether this condition is met. My subjection of myself to the authority is conditional on the possibility of this judgment; such subjection is impossible and contrary to right if such a judgment is not made. Therefore, above all else, *I must subject myself with complete freedom.*

After having subjected myself, I no longer have a right to pass judgment on the scope of my rights (as has been expressly stated and proved); therefore, the requisite judgment must be possible and must actually be made *before* I subject myself. I am supposed to make the following judgment: 'In being subjected, my rightful freedom will never be infringed; I will never have to sacrifice any more of that freedom than I would have had to sacrifice pursuant to the law of right and according to my own judgment'. Thus before I subject myself, I am to imagine the entirety of my future experience in the state of being subjected, i.e. I am to receive a guarantee that I will be completely secure within the limits of my rights.

First of all: *what* is supposed to be guaranteed to me? – The complete security of all my rights over against the one to whom I have subjected myself and – through his protection – over against all individuals with whom I might possibly enter into community. I ought to be able to see for myself that all possible future judgments of right that might be pronounced upon matters relating to me can turn out only as I myself would have to pronounce upon them in accordance with the law of right. Therefore, *norms* concerning these future judgments of right must be submitted for my inspection; it is in accordance with these norms that the law of right is applied to all cases that might possibly arise. Such norms are called *positive laws*; the system of such laws in general is called (positive) *law*.

(a) All positive laws stand, either more or less directly, under the rule of right. These laws do not and cannot contain anything arbitrary. They must exist precisely as every intelligent, informed person would necessarily have to prescribe them.

(b) In positive laws, the rule of right in general is applied to the particular objects governed by that rule. Positive law hovers midway between the law of right and a judgment of right. In positive law, the rule of right is applied to particular objects; in a judgment of right, positive law is applied to particular persons. – The civil judge has nothing to do other than to decide what happened and to invoke the law. If legislation is clear and complete, as it should be, then the judge's verdict must already be contained in the law.

The contradiction presented above has been canceled in part. When I subject myself to the law, a law that has been inspected and approved by me (which inspection is – as has been proved – the exclusive condition of the possibility of my being rightfully subjected to it), I am not subjecting myself to the changeable, arbitrary will of a human being, but rather to a will that is immutable and fixed. In fact, since the law is exactly as I myself would have to prescribe it, in accordance with the rule of right, I am subjecting myself to my own immutable will, a will I would necessarily have to possess if I am acting rightfully and therefore if I am to have any rights at all. I am subjecting myself to *my* will, a will that is the condition of my capacity for having rights at all; for if my will were different from this, it would be contrary to right, since the law is the only rightful will; and thus I would be entirely without rights, since only he who has subjected himself to the law of right can possess rights. Therefore, far from losing my rights through such subjection, I first acquire them through it, since only through such subjection do I show that I fulfill the exclusive condition under which someone has rights. Although I am subjected, I remain always subjected only to my will. I actually did exercise my right to be my own judge this one time, and I exercised it as applying to my entire life and to all possible cases; and the only thing that has been taken from me is the trouble of carrying out my judgments of right by my own physical power.

Result. One can rationally alienate one's power and ability to pass judgments of right only to the necessary and unbending will of the law, but by no means to the free and changeable will of a human being. The law of right requires only the former; only this kind of alienation is the condition of all rights. The latter alienation is not exactly contrary to the law, because right is not the same as duty, and so a person may in fact give up his rights; but this alienation does not follow from the law of right either.

(V) The contradiction presented above has been canceled in part, but only in part. The person who subjects himself was supposed to have been given a guarantee by the *law* for the future security of all his rights. But what is the law? A concept. How, then, is the law supposed to be brought to life, how is this bare concept to be realized in the sensible world? – We shall present the question from yet another angle.

To guarantee somebody the security of his rights means: to make it impossible for those rights to be violated, and in such a way that the person must be convinced of that impossibility. Now through the subjection described above, the security of the subjected person is to be guaranteed, not only over against the one to whom he has subjected himself, but also over against all persons with whom he can ever enter into community; therefore, it is supposed to be completely impossible for the person's rights to be violated, and before he subjects himself, he is supposed to be able to convince himself of this complete impossibility. Now of course, this impossibility is contained in the will of the law; but the much larger question is: how, then, is the person supposed to be given *the* guarantee that the law, and only the law, will prevail?

The person is supposed to be secure before the law itself; therefore, it must never happen that the power of the law is used against him, except in those cases provided for by the law. Through the law, the person is supposed to be secure before all others: therefore, the law must constantly act where it is supposed to act. It must never rest once it has been awakened.

In short: *the law must be a power*: the concept of the *law* (from the preceding section of our investigation) and the concept of a *supreme power* (from the section immediately preceding that one) must be synthetically united. The law itself must be the supreme power, and the supreme power must be the law, both one and the same: and in subjecting myself I must be able to convince myself that this is so, that it is completely impossible for any force other than that of the law to be directed against me.

Our task is precisely defined. The question to be answered is: *how does the law become a power?* The power we are seeking does not exist immediately in nature; it is not a mechanical power (as was shown above), and human beings certainly have the physical power to perpetrate injustices. Thus, the power we are seeking must be one that depends on a will. But now this will is not supposed to be free, but necessarily and immutably determined by the law. There can be no such will belonging to an individual – that is, a will on whose rightfulness every other person could always securely rely. Therefore, it must be that the will we are seeking would have power only in cases where it willed the law, and would have no power where it did not will the law; and so our task, defined more narrowly, is: *to find a will that is a power only when it wills the law, and is an infallible power when it does so.*

A supreme power over a free being could come about only if several free beings
were to unite, for there is nothing in the sensible world more powerful than a free
being (precisely because it is free and can reflectively and purposefully direct its
power); and there is nothing more powerful than an individual free being except
for several free beings. Their strength therefore would consist solely in their being
united. Now their power is supposed to depend on the fact that they will the law,
or right. Therefore, their *union* (upon which their power depends) would have to
depend on the fact that they will the law, or right: their willing of right would
have to constitute the only bond of their union. As soon as they willed what was
contrary to right, their union and – along with that – their entire power would
have to dissolve.

Now in every union of free beings it is necessarily the case that willing what
is not rightful breaks the agreement. To say that a number of free beings become
united means: they will to live with one another. But they cannot coexist unless
each limits his freedom through the freedom of all the others. If a million human
beings exist alongside one another, each individual may very well will for himself
as much freedom as possible. But if the will of all were to be united into one
concept as in one will, this will would divide the sum of possible freedom into
equal parts, with the aim that all would be free together, and that therefore the
freedom of each would be limited by the freedom of all the others.[4] Thus right
is the only possible basis for the unity of their wills; and since a specific number
of human beings with specific inclinations, involvements, etc. exist together here,
this means right as *applied to them*, i.e. their *positive law*. They will the law just as
surely as they are all united. If even only one of them were to be oppressed, this
one person would certainly not give his consent, in which case they would no
longer all be united. [...]

[*FW* III, 111–113] First Chapter of the Doctrine of Right: Deduction of Original Right

§9
How can an Original Right be Thought?

It is possible to talk about rights only under the condition that a person is thought
of as a person, that is, as an individual, and thus as standing in relation to other

---

[4] This is Rousseau's *volonté générale*, whose distinction from the *volonté de tous* is by no means unintelligible.
All individuals will to keep as much as possible for themselves and to leave as little as possible for everyone
else; but precisely because of this conflict in their will, the parts in conflict cancel each other out, and what
remains as the final result is that each should have what belongs to him. If two people are involved in dealings
with each other, it can always be assumed that each wants to gain an advantage over the other; but since
neither of the two wants to be the disadvantaged one, this part of their will is mutually annihilated and their
common will is that each receive what is right.

individuals; only under the condition that there is a community between this person and others, a community that – if not posited as real – is at least imagined as possible. What initially, and from a merely speculative perspective, are the conditions of personality become rights simply by thinking of other beings who – in accordance with the law of right – may not violate the conditions of personality. Now it is not possible to think of free beings as existing together unless their rights mutually limit each other, and therefore unless the sphere of their original rights is transformed into the sphere of their rights within a commonwealth. Therefore, it would be utterly impossible to reflect on rights merely as original rights, i.e. without considering the necessary limitations imposed by the rights of others. Nevertheless, an investigation into original rights must precede an investigation of rights within a commonwealth and must ground the latter investigation. Accordingly, one must abstract from the limitations imposed by the rights of others, an abstraction that free speculation so readily engages in that it does so without even thinking, and only needs to be reminded of having done so. There is no difficulty, then, regarding the possibility of such abstraction.

What speculation needs to be reminded of and to have brought into focus is only *that* this abstraction has been made, and that therefore the concept it generates possesses ideal possibility (for thought), but no real meaning. If one disregards this point, one will arrive at a merely formal theory of right. – There is no condition in which original rights exist; and no original rights of human beings. The human being has actual rights only in community with others, just as – according to the higher principles noted above – the human being can be thought of only in community with others. An original right, therefore, is a mere *fiction*, but one that must necessarily be created for the sake of a science of right. Furthermore, it is clear – and this must be repeated once again, though it has already been emphasized many times before – that the conditions of personality are to be thought of as rights only insofar as they appear in the sensible world and can be violated by other free beings (as forces in the sensible world). Thus there can be, for example, a right to self-preservation in the sensible world, to the preservation of my body as such, but by no means a right to *think* or to *will* freely. Moreover, it is clear that we do indeed have a right of coercion against someone who attacks our body, but definitely not against someone who disturbs us in our comforting beliefs or who offends us with his immoral behavior.

§10
Definition of Original Right

The principle of any judgment of right is that each is to limit his freedom, the sphere of his free actions, through the concept of the freedom of the other (so that the other, as free in general, can exist as well). The concept of freedom at issue here (which, as already stated above, has only formal meaning) yields the concept of original right, that is, of that right that should belong absolutely to every person as such. We shall now discuss this concept more precisely.

With respect to *quality*, this concept is a concept of the capacity to be an absolutely first cause; with respect to *quantity*, what is comprehended under this concept has no limits at all, but is by its nature infinite, because what is at issue is only that the person is to be free in general, but not the extent to which he is to be free. Quantity stands in conflict with this concept as it has been put forth here as a merely formal concept. With respect to *relation*, the freedom of the person is at issue only insofar as the sphere of the free actions of others is to be limited in accordance with the law of right, because these others could make the required formal freedom impossible. This consideration determines the quantity [the scope] of the investigation. We are concerned here only with *causality* in the sensible world, as the only realm within which freedom can be limited by freedom. Finally, with respect to *modality*, this concept has apodeictic validity. Each person is to be free without qualification.

Original right is thus the absolute right of the person to be *only a cause* in the sensible world (and purely and simply never something caused).

[...]

[FW III, 145–154] §15
On Establishing a Law of Coercion

The law of coercion is supposed to function so that any violation of rights will result inevitably and with mechanical necessity (so that the violator can foresee it with complete certainty) in the same violation of the violator's own rights. The question is, how can such an order of things be brought about?

As the matter itself shows, what is needed is an irresistible coercive power that will punish the violator. Who is supposed to establish such a power?

This power is posited as a means for establishing mutual security when honesty and trust do not exist (and under no other circumstances). Thus one can will such a power, only if he wills this end (mutual security in the absence of honesty and trust), but he must also will this end necessarily. Now it is the contracting parties we have posited who will this end; therefore, they and only they can be the ones who will the means. In willing this end (and in this alone) their wills are united: thus their wills must also be united in their willing of the means, i.e. they must make a contract among themselves to establish a law of coercion and a coercive power.

Now what kind of power is this supposed to be? – This coercive power is guided by a concept and aims at the realization of a concept (indeed a concept that is constructed through absolute freedom), namely the concept of the limits posited by the two contracting parties in their contract concerning their efficacy in the sensible world; therefore, this power cannot be a mechanical power but must be a free one. Now such a power (one that would unite all these requirements within itself) is not posited apart from their own power, as determined by their common will. Thus the content of the contract they make to establish a right of coercion between themselves is this: *both will to deal with the one of them who has wronged the other by applying the law of coercion to him with their united power.*

Now if a case arises where there exists a right of coercion, the violator must be one of the two parties. It is contradictory to think that the violator might counter his own violation with his own powers; for in that case he would have refrained from perpetrating the violation, there would have been no violation, and the right of coercion would not have arisen. Thus the violator could promise only that he would not resist the other's coercion, but voluntarily submit to it.

But this, too, is contradictory, for – in accordance with our presupposition – the violator (regardless of whether he wronged the other intentionally or out of negligence) has a steadfast will to keep what is his. Indeed, the law of coercion aims exclusively at such a will. In the first case (i.e. if the wrong is intentional) it is directed even at the will to take possession of what belongs to the other; and it is precisely this will that the coercion is supposed to thwart. If the violator were to submit voluntarily to the coercive force, there would be no need to use such force against him; he would have voluntarily abandoned his wrongful act, and thus would not have the kind of will that the law of coercion presupposes. (A duty *to allow* oneself *to be coerced* is contradictory. Whoever allows himself to be coerced is not coerced, and whoever is coerced does not allow himself to be.)

But nevertheless it would have to be this way; from what other source could a superior power for enforcing rights come (since we must ascribe equal physical strength to the two persons)? Therefore, the same person whose promise not to interfere with others' property could not be trusted and who then actually failed to keep his word, would have to be trusted to keep the contract regarding coercion and to submit voluntarily to the penalty affecting his own property. –

Then, if the transgressed party enforces his own rights and if the transgressor must fully submit, his hands bound, to the transgressed party's judgment and its implementation, who will guarantee to the transgressor that the transgressed party will not either intentionally exceed the limits of the law of coercion or make a mistake in applying it to the present case? Therefore, even the party being penalized would have to place an unheard of and impossible trust in the other's rightfulness, impartiality, and wisdom, at a time when he no longer trusts the other at all. This is, without a doubt, contradictory.

Therefore, such a contract, as we have presented it here, is contradictory and simply unrealizable.

Such a contract could be realized only if the injured party were always the more powerful one – but only up to the limit dictated by the law of coercion deduced here – and then were to lose all power when he reached that limit; or – in accordance with the formula presented above – only if *each party were to have exactly as much power as right.* Now as we have also seen above, this occurs only within a commonwealth. Thus, the right of coercion can have absolutely no application apart from a commonwealth: otherwise, coercion is always only problematically rightful, and for this very reason it is always unjust actually to apply coercion, as if one had a categorical right to it.

(Accordingly, there is no *natural right* at all in the sense often given to that term, i.e. there can be no rightful relation between human beings except within a commonwealth and under positive laws. – *Either* there is thoroughgoing morality and a universal belief in such morality; and furthermore, the greatest of all co-incidences takes place (something that could hardly occur, even if everyone had the best intentions), namely, the claims made by different human beings are all compatible with one another. In this case the law of right is completely impotent and would have nothing at all to say, for what ought to happen in accordance with the law happens without it, and what the law forbids is never willed by anyone. – For a species of perfected moral beings, there is no law of right. It is already clear that humankind cannot be such a species, from the fact that the human being must *be educated* and must *educate himself* [*sich erziehen*] to the status of morality; for he is not moral by nature, but must make himself so through his own labor.

Or – the second possibility – there is no thoroughgoing morality, or at least no universal belief in it. In this case the external law of right exists, but can be applied only within a commonwealth. Thus, natural right disappears.

But what we lose on the one side, we recover on the other, and at a profit; for the state itself becomes the human being's natural condition, and its laws ought to be nothing other than natural right realized.)

Third Chapter of the Doctrine of Right: on Political Right [*Staatsrecht*], or Right within a Commonwealth

§16
Deduction of the Concept of a Commonwealth

The problem that we were left with, that we could not solve, and that we hope to solve through the concept of a commonwealth, was this: how to bring about a power that can enforce right (or what all persons necessarily will) amongst persons who live together.

(I) The object of their common will is *mutual security*; but since, as we have assumed, persons are motivated only by self-love and not morality, each individual wills the security of the other only because he wills his own, willing the other's security is subordinate to willing one's own; no one is concerned whether the other is secure against oneself, except to the extent that the other's security is the condition of one's own security against the other. We can express this briefly in the following formula: *Each person subordinates the common end to his private end.* (This is what the law of coercion reckons with; by linking the welfare of each in reality to the security of the welfare of all others, the law of coercion is meant to produce this reciprocity, this necessary conjunction of the two ends, in the will of each individual.)

The will of a power that exercises the right of coercion cannot be constituted in this way; for, since the private will is subordinated to the common will only through coercive power, and since this coercive power is supposed to be superior to all other power, the private will of the coercive power could be subordinated to the common will only by its own power, which is absurd. Therefore, the coercive power's private will must already be subordinated to and in harmony with the common will, and there must be no need to bring about such subordination and harmony, i.e. the private will of the coercive power and the common will must be one and the same; the common will itself, and nothing else, must be the private will of the coercive power, and this power must have no other particular and private will at all.

(II) Thus, the problem of political right and (according to our proof) of the entire philosophy of right is *to find a will that cannot possibly be other than the common will.*

Or, in accordance with the formula presented earlier (one that is more in keeping with the course of our investigation), the problem is: *to find a will in which the private and the common will are synthetically united.*

We shall solve this problem in accordance with a strict method. Let us call the will we are seeking X.

(a) Every will has itself (in the future) as an object. Everything that wills has self-preservation as its final end. The same goes for X; and so self-preservation would be *the private will* of X. – Now this private will is supposed to be one with the common will, which wills the security of the rights of all. Therefore, X, just as it wills *itself*, wills *the security of the rights of all.*

(b) *The security of the rights of all* is willed only through the harmonious will of all, through the concurrence of their wills. *It is only in this regard* that *all* agree; for in all other matters their will is particular and directed to their individual ends. In accordance with our assumption of universal egoism (which the law of coercion presupposes), no individual, no single part of the commonwealth, makes this an end for himself; rather, only *all* of them, taken as a whole, do.

(c) Thus X would itself be this *concurrence* of all. This concurrence, as surely as it willed *itself*, would also have to will the security of the rights of all; for it is one and the same as that security.

(III) But such *concurrence* is a mere concept; now it should not remain so, but ought rather to be realized in the sensible world, i.e. it ought to be brought forth in some particular external expression and have effect as a physical force.

For us, the only beings in the sensible world that have wills are human beings. Therefore, this concept would have to be realized in and through human beings. This requires:

(a) That the will of a certain number of human beings, at some point in time, actually becomes harmonious, and expresses itself or gets declared as such. – The task here is to show that the required concurrence does not take place of itself, but rather is based on an *express act* of all, an *act that takes place in the sensible world and is perceptible at some point in time and is made possible only through free self-determination.* Such an act is implied by a proof already presented above. That is, the law of right says only that each person should limit the use of his freedom through the rights of the other, but it does not determine how far and to which objects the rights of each ought to extend. These latter determinations must be expressly declared, and declared in such a way that the declarations of all are harmonious. Each person must have said to all: I want to live in this place, and to possess this or that thing as my own; and all must have responded by saying: yes, you may live here and possess that thing.

Our further investigation of this act will yield the first section of the doctrine of political right, *on the civil contract* [*vom Staatsbürgervertrage*].

(b) That this will be established as the steadfast and enduring will of all, a will that each person – just as certainly as he has expressed this will in the present moment – will recognize as his own so long as he lives in this place. In every previous investigation it was always necessary to assume that such willing for the entire future is present in a single moment, that such willing for all future life occurs all at once. Here, for the first time, this proposition is asserted with justification.

Because the present will is established as valid for all time, the common will that is expressed now becomes *law*.

(c) This common will determines both how far the rights of each person ought to extend, in which case the legislation is *civil* (*legislatio civilis*); and how a person who violates these rights in one way or another ought to be punished, in which case the legislation is criminal or penal (*legislatio criminalis, jus criminale, poenale*). Our investigation of this will yield the second section of the doctrine of political right, on *legislation*.

(d) This common will must be equipped with a power – and indeed a superior power, in the face of which any individual's power would be infinitely small – that will enable it to look after itself and its preservation by means of coercive force: *the state authority*. This authority includes two elements: the right to judge, and the right to execute the judgments it has made (*potestas judicialis et potestas executiva in sensu strictiori*, both of which belong to the *potestas executiva in sensu latiori*).

(IV) The common will has actually expressed itself at some point in time, and – by virtue of the civil contract that has been reached concerning it – has become universally valid as law.

In accordance with the principles established thus far, there can be no difficulty at all in seeing what this universal will will be, with regard both to the determination of each individual's rights, and to the penal laws [*Strafgesetze*]. But this will is still open-ended and has not yet been set down anywhere, nor has it been equipped with any power. The latter must occur if this will is to endure and if the previous insecurity and war of all against all are to be prevented from returning again soon. The common will, as a mere will, is realized, but not yet as a power that can preserve itself: and therefore the final part of our problem remains to be solved.

The question seems to answer itself.

That is, those who are thus joined together, as physical persons in the sensible world, necessarily possess power of their own. Now since a person can be judged only by his actions, so long as no one transgresses the law, it can be assumed that each person's private will concurs with the common will, and thus that his power is part of the power of the state. Each person, even if he were privately to develop an unjust will, must always fear the power of all, just as they all must also fear his power, because they can know nothing of the unjustness of his will, which has not yet shown itself in actions. The power of all (which is to be assumed to have been declared in favor of the law) keeps each individual's power within its boundaries; and therefore there exists the most perfect equilibrium of right. [. . .]

Translated by Michael Baur

11

G. W. F. Hegel, Elements of the Philosophy of Right (Grundlinien der Philosophie des Rechts): Civil Society, §§ 182–188; The State, §§ 257–269 (1821)

Hegel's *Philosophy of Right* – his seminal work on political philosophy – has fascinated and infuriated readers since its publication in 1821. To many liberals and radicals it seemed that Hegel was simply a reactionary who had attempted to defend an overbearing state in which individuals had somehow to acknowledge the norms of the state in order to be considered as individuals. And indeed much of the purchase of Hegel's position seemed to be gained by means of a critique of Kant, the philosopher with impeccable liberal and enlightenment credentials. Kant's political position – expressed in, amongst other places, the Doctrine of Right – might be regarded as the quintessence of a philosophical liberalism (operating with the foundational principle of individual autonomy), but Hegel, it could seem, attempted to roll back Kant's achievement, seeing Kant's position, at best, as rather 'empty'. Indeed, Hegel makes a series of striking contrasts through which he significantly distinguishes himself from Kant: he places the notion of the good or general welfare at the centre of the life of society (making him arguably a communitarian, in today's terminology), whereas Kant appears to emphasise the priority of the individual; unlike Kant he sees values as irreducible to processes of individual moral self-legislation; and he regards himself as the exponent of a 'concrete' programme of moral agency which takes consequences and not simply formal consistency as relevant to the consideration of the moral content of an action. The contrast between Kant's and Hegel's positions is designated by Hegel himself as the contrast between abstract 'morality' and concrete 'ethics'. But these contrasts have left him open to being misunderstood. In particular, it can seem that a reactionary conformism lurks in his political philosophy when he argues that we must supersede the notion that individuals may self-legislate with his alternative account which claims that values are, in a sense, quasi-heteronomous – not reducible to the individual – and have overriding normative value. Furthermore these heteronomous values, the concern goes, are somehow constitutive of what a society can be allowed to be.

This portrait of Hegel, however, emerges from a misapprehension of the nature of his actual project: it is far from the working out of the conservative thesis that individualism is somehow destructive of the common good. Rather, Hegel believes that individuals are inseparable from society in the sense that the classical characteristics of the individual can be expressed only within a society or a community. For Hegel community is the concrete condition of existence and it is therefore the context in which actions and the justification of those actions have to be understood: only in a society or community is one ideally free *to*, or free *from* something. In essence Hegel's political philosophy strives to demonstrate the necessity of a version of society – what he terms 'the ethical society' – in which the individual can be concretely realised. He believes, too, that concepts such as freedom and individuality are, in fact, historical: they are products of a social life in progress, and cannot be divorced therefore from social life.

The *Philosophy of Right* is intended as a system in which Hegel's views on morality, politics and history are set out together. It was written as a textbook around which Hegel would base his lecture material, and in the various versions of the text available to us today we find the addition of some of Hegel's notes as well as the transcriptions by those at the lectures of Hegel's spoken words. The book is divided into three very substantial sections. After a lengthy introduction, in which Hegel sets out his general principles of right and freedom, Part One, entitled 'Abstract Right', deals with the principles of property, contract and wrong (including systems of coercion and punishment). Because the book is designed systematically Part Two leads from Part One by way of 'transition' into a consideration of the principle of 'Morality' (rational self-governance as opposed to governance through coercion) under which the principles of the moral consciousness (such as responsibility, intention, conscience and duty) are examined. Part Three (again a transition from the previous part) is called 'Ethical Life', and here Hegel brings together his complex ideas of family, civil society and the state. Ethical Life sets out an account of the individual as placed within a rational social order which can be understood as a historical achievement, and Hegel also advances a form of political constitution (defending at one point, as Kant also had, a form of monarchy).

Many of the themes of the *Philosophy of Right* can be found in some of Hegel's other substantial texts. The relationship between history and forms of social life appear in various sections of the *Phenomenology of Spirit* (1807), and the later *Lectures on the Philosophy of World History* (1830–1) develop many of the ideas discussed in the final sub-section of the *Philosophy of Right*. Part Three of the *Encyclopaedia of the Philosophical Sciences* (1830), *Philosophy of Sprit*, compresses the notions of Objective Spirit already announced in the three parts of the *Philosophy of Right*.

In the sections reprinted here we see Hegel's account of what he understands as the connection between the individual and the community or state. Definitively, Hegel does not reduce individuality to a mere aspect of society, a moment at the service of the greater good: he argues that civil society has as its two principles the concrete particular person and relations between these particulars. In a way we can see civil society as the fulfilment of what had been started in the dialectic of master and slave. The reality of civil society is interdependence and mutuality. The achievement of civil society is that it can accommodate the individual whilst also managing to be cohesive: for Hegel this is a potent contrast with the Kantian notion of individuals bound only by contract. (In the Kantian picture society is effectively the aggregate of individuals.) Hegel holds that the property of the unity of a society or community is irreducible to individuality. Hegel's discussion of the state carries this idea forward, holding that the state is the 'actuality of the ethical idea'. Again the notion of the 'ethical' expresses the view that there are certain (rationally defensible) values which in some respect unite the individuals who share them. The contrast is with morality which, for Hegel (at least as he ascribed to Kant), could be achieved by purely individualist reflection. A further aspect of this is that Hegel, in certain respects, is expressing the thought that individuals will grant legitimacy to a state if they feel themselves to belong to it. His discussion can be considered as an analysis of what conditions can bring about the possibility of this belonging.

SECTION 2[†]

Civil Society

§182

The concrete person who, as a *particular* person, as a totality of needs and a mixture of natural necessity and arbitrariness, is his own end, is *one principle* of civil society. But this particular person stands essentially in *relation* [*Beziehung*] to other similar particulars, and their relation is such that each asserts itself and gains satisfaction through the others, and thus at the same time through the exclusive *mediation* of the form of *universality*, which is *the second principle*.

Addition. Civil society is the [stage of] difference [*Differenz*] which intervenes between the family and the state, even if its full development [*Ausbildung*] occurs later than that of the state; for as difference, it presupposes the state, which it must have

---

[†]*HW* VII, 339–346. *Elements of the Philosophy of Right* (Cambridge: Cambridge University Press, 1991).

before it as a self-sufficient entity in order to subsist [*bestehen*] itself. Besides, the creation of civil society belongs to the modern world, which for the first time allows all determinations of the Idea to attain their rights. If the state is represented as a unity of different persons, as a unity which is merely a community [of interests], this applies only to the determination of civil society. Many modern exponents of constitutional law have been unable to offer any view of the state but this. In civil society, each individual is his own end, and all else means nothing to him. But he cannot accomplish the full extent of his ends without reference to others; these others are therefore means to the end of the particular [person]. But through its reference to others, the particular end takes on the form of universality, and gains satisfaction by simultaneously satisfying the welfare of others. Since particularity is tied to the condition of universality, the whole [of civil society] is the sphere [*Boden*] of mediation in which all individual characteristics [*Einzelheiten*], all aptitudes, and all accidents of birth and fortune are liberated, and where the waves of all passions surge forth, governed only by the reason which shines through them. Particularity, limited by universality, is the only standard by which each particular [*person*] promotes his welfare.

§183

The selfish end in its actualization, conditioned in this way by universality, establishes a system of all-round interdependence, so that the subsistence [*Subsistenz*] and welfare of the individual [*des Einzelnen*] and his rightful existence [*Dasein*] are interwoven with, and grounded on, the subsistence, welfare, and rights of all, and have actuality and security only in this context. – One may regard this system in the first instance as the *external state*, the *state of necessity* and *of the understanding*.

§184

When it is divided in this way, the Idea gives a *distinct existence* [*Dasein*] to its *moments* – to *particularity* it gives the right to develop and express itself in all directions, and to universality the right to prove itself both as the ground and necessary form of particularity, and as the power behind it and its ultimate end. – It is the system of ethical life, lost in its extremes, which constitutes the abstract moment of the *reality* of the Idea, which is present here only as the *relative totality* and *inner necessity* of this external *appearance*.

Addition. Here, the ethical is lost in its extremes, and the immediate unity of the family has disintegrated into a plurality. Reality here is externality, the dissolution of the concept, the self-sufficiency of its liberated and existent moments. Although particularity and universality have become separated in civil society, they are nevertheless bound up with and conditioned by each other. Although each appears to do precisely the opposite of the other and imagines that it can exist only by keeping the other at a distance, each nevertheless has the other as its condition. Thus, most people regard the payment of taxes, for example, as an infringement of their particularity, as a hostile element prejudicial to their own ends; but however true this may *appear*, the particularity of their own ends cannot be satisfied without the universal, and a country in which no taxes were paid could scarcely distinguish itself in strengthening its particular interests [*Besonderheit*]. It might likewise appear that the universal would do better to absorb the strength of the particular, as described, for example, in Plato's *Republic*; but this again is only apparent, for the two exist solely through and for one another and are transformed into one another. In furthering my end, I further the universal, and this in turn furthers my end.

§185

Particularity in itself [*für sich*], on the one hand indulging itself in all directions as it satisfies its needs, contingent arbitrariness, and subjective caprice, destroys itself and its substantial concept in the act of enjoyment; on the other hand, as infinitely agitated and continually dependent on external contingency and arbitrariness and at the same time limited by the power of universality, the satisfaction of both necessary and contingent needs is itself contingent. In these opposites and their complexity, civil society affords a spectacle of extravagance and misery as well as of the physical and ethical corruption common to both.

The self-sufficient development of particularity (cf. Remarks to §124) is the moment which appears in the states of the ancient world as an influx of ethical corruption and as the ultimate reason [*Grund*] for their downfall. These states, some of which were based on the patriarchal and religious principle and others on the principle of a more spiritual, though simpler, ethical life, but all of which were based on *original* natural intuition, could not withstand the division which arose within the latter as self-consciousness became infinitely reflected into itself. As this reflection began to emerge, first as a disposition and then in actuality, they succumbed to it, because the simple principle on which they were still based lacked the truly infinite power which resides solely in that unity which allows the *opposition* within reason [*Vernunft*] *to develop to its full strength*, and has overcome it so as to preserve itself within it and *wholly contain it within itself*. – Plato, in his *Republic*, presents the substance of ethical life in its ideal *beauty* and *truth*; but he cannot come to terms with the principle of self-sufficient particularity, which had suddenly overtaken Greek ethical life in his time, except by setting up his purely substantial state in opposition to it and completely excluding it [*from this state*], from its very beginnings in *private property* (see Remarks to §46) and the *family* to its subsequent development [*Ausbildung*] as the arbitrary will of individuals and their choice of social position [*des Standes*], etc. This deficiency also explains why the great *substantial* truth of his *Republic* is imperfectly understood, and why it is usually regarded as a dream of abstract thought, as what is indeed often called an *ideal*. The principle of the *self-sufficient and inherently infinite personality* of the individual [*des Einzelnen*], the principle of subjective freedom, which arose in an inward form in the *Christian* religion and in an external form (which was therefore linked with abstract universality) in the *Roman* world, is denied its right in that merely substantial form of the actual spirit [in Plato's *Republic*]. This principle is historically later than the Greek world, and the philosophical reflection which can fathom these depths is likewise later than the substantial Idea of Greek philosophy.

Addition. Particularity in itself [*für sich*] is boundless [*maßlos*] extravagance, and the forms of this extravagance are themselves boundless. Through their representations [*Vorstellungen*] and reflections, human beings expand their desires, which do not form a closed circle like animal instinct, and extend them to false [*schlechte*] infinity. But on the other hand, deprivation and want are likewise boundless, and this confused situation can be restored to harmony only through the forcible intervention of the state. Although Plato's state sought to exclude particularity, this is of no help, because such help would contradict the infinite right of the Idea to allow particularity its freedom. It was primarily in the Christian religion that the right of subjectivity arose, along with the infinity of being-for-itself; and in this situation, the totality must also be endowed with sufficient strength to bring particularity into harmony with the ethical unity.

§186

But in the very act of developing itself independently [*für sich*] to totality, the principle of particularity passes over into *universality*, and only in the latter does it have its truth and its right to positive actuality. This unity is not that of ethical identity, because at this level of division (see § 184), the two principles are self-sufficient; and for the same reason, it is present not as *freedom*, but as the *necessity* whereby the *particular* must rise to the *form of universality* and seek and find its subsistence in this form.

§187

Individuals, as citizens of this state, are *private persons* who have their own interest as their end. Since this end is mediated through the universal, which thus *appears* to the individuals as a *means*, they can attain their end only in so far as they themselves determine their knowledge, volition, and action in a universal way and make themselves *links* in the chain of this *continuum* [*Zusammenhang*]. In this situation, the interest of the Idea, which is not present in the consciousness of these members of civil society as such, is the *process* whereby their individuality [*Einzelheit*] and naturalness are raised, both by natural necessity and by their arbitrary needs, *to formal freedom* and formal *universality of knowledge and volition*, and subjectivity is *educated* in its particularity.

> The ideas [*Vorstellungen*] of the *innocence* of the state of nature and of the ethical simplicity of uncultured [*ungebildeter*] peoples imply that *education* [*Bildung*] will be regarded as something purely *external* and associated with corruption. On the other hand, if one believes that needs, their satisfaction, the pleasures and comforts of individual [*partikularen*] life, etc. are *absolute*

ends, education will be regarded as merely a *means* to these ends. Both of these views show a lack of familiarity with the nature of spirit and with the end of reason. Spirit attains its actuality only through internal division, by imposing this limitation and finitude upon itself in [the shape of] natural needs and the continuum [*Zusammenhang*] of this external necessity, and, *in the very process of adapting itself to these* limitations, by overcoming them and gaining its *objective* existence [*Dasein*] within them. The end of reason is consequently neither the natural ethical simplicity referred to above, nor, as particularity develops, the pleasures as such which are attained through education. Its end is rather to work to eliminate *natural simplicity*, whether as passive selflessness or as barbarism of knowledge and volition – i.e. to eliminate the *immediacy* and *individuality* [*Einzelheit*] in which spirit is immersed, so that this externality may take on the rationality *of which it is capable*, namely the *form of universality or of the understanding*. Only in this way is the spirit *at home* and *with itself* in this *externality* as such. Its freedom thus has an existence [*Dasein*] within the latter; and, in this element which, *in itself*, is alien to its determination of freedom, the spirit becomes *for itself*, and has to do only with what it has impressed its seal upon and *produced* itself. – By this very means, the *form of universality* comes into existence [*Existenz*] for itself in thought, the only form which is a worthy element for the existence [*Existenz*] of the Idea. *Education*, in its absolute determination, is therefore *liberation* and *work* towards a higher liberation; it is the absolute transition to the infinitely subjective substantiality of ethical life, which is no longer immediate and natural, but spiritual and at the same time raised to the shape of universality. Within the subject, this liberation is the *hard work* of opposing mere subjectivity of conduct, of opposing the immediacy of desire as well as the subjective vanity of feeling [*Empfindung*] and the arbitrariness of caprice. The fact that it is such hard work accounts for some of the disfavour which it incurs. But it is through this work of education that the subjective will attains *objectivity* even within itself, that objectivity in which alone it is for its part worthy and capable of being the *actuality* of the Idea. – Furthermore, this form of universality to which particularity has worked its way upwards and cultivated [*heraufgebildet*] itself, i.e. the form of the understanding, ensures at the same time that particularity *becomes* the genuine *being-for-itself* of individuality [*Einzelheit*]; and, since it is from particularity that universality receives both the content which fills it and its infinite self-determination, particularity is itself present in ethical life as free subjectivity which has infinite being-for-itself. This is the level at which it becomes plain that *education* is an immanent moment of the absolute, and that it has infinite value.

Addition. By educated people, we may understand in the first place those who do everything as others do it and who do not flaunt their particular characteristics [*Partikularität*], whereas it is precisely these characteristics which the uneducated display, since their behaviour is not guided by the universal aspects of its object [*Gegenstand*]. Similarly, in his relations with others, the uneducated man can easily cause offence, for he simply lets himself go and does not reflect on the feelings [*Empfindungen*] of others. He does not wish to hurt others, but his conduct is not in harmony with his will. Thus, education irons out particularity to make it act in accordance with the nature of the thing [*Sache*]. True originality, by which the [universal] thing is produced, requires true education, whereas false originality assumes tasteless forms which occur only to the uneducated.

§188

Civil society contains the following three moments:

A. The mediation of *need* and the satisfaction of the *individual* [*des Einzelnen*] through his work and through the work and satisfaction of the needs of *all the others* – the system of *needs*.
B. The actuality of the universal of *freedom* contained therein, the protection of property through the *administration of justice*.
C. Provisions against the contingency which remains present in the above systems, and care for the particular interest as a *common* interest, by means of the *police* and the *corporation*.

Section 3†
The State

§257

The state is the actuality of the ethical Idea – the ethical spirit as substantial will, *manifest* and clear to itself, which thinks and knows itself and implements what it knows in so far as it knows it. It has its immediate existence [*Existenz*] in *custom* and its mediate existence in the *self-consciousness* of the individual [*des Einzelnen*], in the individual's knowledge and activity, just as self-consciousness, by virtue of its disposition, has its *substantial freedom* in the state as its essence, its end, and the product of its activity.

> The *Penates* are the inner and *lower* gods, and the *spirit of the nation* (Athene) is the divine which *knows* and *wills* itself. *Piety* is feeling [*Empfindung*] and ethical life governed by feeling, and *political virtue* is the willing of that thought end which has being in and for itself.

§258

The state is the actuality of the substantial *will*, an actuality which it possesses in the particular *self-consciousness* when this has been raised to its universality; as such, it is the *rational* in and for itself. This substantial unity is an absolute and unmoved end in itself, and in it, freedom enters into its highest right, just as this ultimate end possesses the highest right in relation to individuals [*die Einzelnen*], whose *highest duty* is to be members of the state.

> If the state is confused with civil society and its determination is equated with the security and protection of property and personal freedom, *the interest of individuals* [*der Einzelnen*] *as such* becomes the ultimate end for which they are united; it also follows from this that membership of the state is an optional matter. – But the relationship of the state to the individual [*Individuum*] is of quite a different kind. Since the state is objective spirit, it is only through being a member of the state that the individual [*Individuum*] himself has objectivity,

†*HW* VII, 398–415.

truth, and ethical life. *Union* as such is itself the true content and end, and the destiny [*Bestimmung*] of individuals [*Individuen*] is to lead a universal life; their further particular satisfaction, activity, and mode of conduct have this substantial and universally valid basis as their point of departure and result. – Considered in the abstract, rationality consists in general in the unity and interpenetration of universality and individuality [*Einzelheit*]. Here, in a concrete sense and in terms of its content, it consists in the unity of objective freedom (i.e. of the universal substantial will) and subjective freedom (as the freedom of individual [*individuellen*] knowledge and of the will in its pursuit of particular ends). And in terms of its form, it therefore consists in self-determining action in accordance with laws and principles based on *thought* and hence *universal*. – This Idea is the being of spirit as necessary and eternal in and for itself. – As far as the Idea of the state itself is concerned, it makes no difference what is or was the *historical* origin of the state in general (or rather of any particular state with its rights and determinations) – whether it first arose out of patriarchal conditions, out of fear or trust, out of corporations etc., or how the basis of its rights has been understood and fixed in the consciousness as divine and positive right or contract, habit, etc. In relation to scientific cognition, which is our sole concern here, these are questions of appearance, and consequently a matter [*Sache*] for history. In so far as the authority of any actual state concerns itself with the question of reasons, these will be derived from the forms of right which are valid within that state. – The philosophical approach deals only with the internal aspect of all this, with the *concept as thought* [*mit dem gedachten Begriffe*]. As far as the search for this concept is concerned, it was the achievement of Rousseau to put forward the *will* as the principle of the state, a principle which has *thought* not only as its form (as with the social instinct, for example, or divine authority) but also as its content, and which is in fact *thinking* itself. But Rousseau considered the will only in the determinate form of the *individual* [*einzelnen*] will (as Fichte subsequently also did) and regarded the universal will not as the will's rationality in and for itself, but only as the *common element* arising out of this individual [*einzelnen*] will *as a conscious will*. The union of individuals [*der Einzelnen*] within the state thus becomes a *contract*, which is accordingly based on their arbitrary will and opinions, and on their express consent given at their own discretion; and the further consequences which follow from this, and which relate merely to the understanding, destroy the divine [element] which has being in and for itself and its absolute authority and majesty. Consequently, when these abstractions were invested with power, they afforded the tremendous spectacle, for the first time we know of in human history, of the overthrow of all existing and given conditions within an actual major state and the revision of its constitution from first principles and purely in terms of *thought*; the *intention* behind this was to give it what was *supposed* to be a purely *rational* basis. On the other hand, since these were only abstractions divorced from the Idea, they turned the attempt into the most terrible and drastic event. – In opposition to the principle of the individual will, we should remember the fundamental concept according to which the objective will is rational in itself, i.e. in its *concept*, whether or not it is recognized by individuals [*Einzelnen*] and willed by them at their discretion – and that its opposite, knowledge and volition, the subjectivity of freedom (which is the *sole* content of the principle of the individual will) embodies only *one* (consequently one-sided) moment of the *Idea of the rational* will, which is rational solely because it has being both *in itself* and *for itself*. – Also at variance with the thought that the state may be apprehended by cognition as something rational for itself is [the practice of] taking the *externality* of appearance and the contingencies of want, need of protection, strength, wealth, etc. not as moments of historical development, but as the *substance* of the state. Here, the principle of cognition is once again that of separate individuality [*die Einzelheit der Individuen*], but not so much the *thought* of this individuality as the converse of this, namely empirical individuality with all its contingent qualities of strength and weakness, wealth and poverty, etc. This notion [*Einfall*] of ignoring the state's *infinity* and *rationality* in and for itself and of *banishing thought* from the apprehension of its inner nature has probably never appeared in so unadulterated a form as in Herr von Haller's *Restoration of Political Science*. It is *unadulterated*, because in all other attempts to grasp the essence of the state, however onesided or superficial their principles may be, this very intention of *comprehending* the state brings with it thoughts or universal determinations. Here, however, Herr von Haller not only consciously dispenses with the rational content of the state and with the form of thought, but fulminates with passionate zeal against them both. This *Restoration* doubtless owes part of what Herr von Haller assures us is the widespread influence of its principles to the fact that it has managed, in its presentation, to dispense with *all thoughts*, and has thereby managed to make the whole work as of *one* piece in its thoughtlessness. For in this way, it avoids the confusion and discontinuity which diminish the impact of a presentation in which references to the substantial are mixed in with the contingent, and reminders of the universal and rational are intermingled with the merely empirical and external, with the result that, in the sphere of the empty and insignificant, we are reminded of the higher realm of the infinite. – This presentation is equally *consistent* in one further respect. For since the sphere of contingency, rather than the substantial, is taken to be the essence of the state, the content of such a work is consistent precisely in the utter inconsistency of its thoughtlessness, in that it heedlessly goes its way and is soon just as much at home with the opposite of what it had approved a moment earlier.[1]

[1] *Hegel's note:* In view of the characteristics specified above, the book in question is of an original kind. In itself [*für sich*], the author's indignation could well have something noble about it, for it was sparked off by the false theories referred to above (which originated largely with Rousseau), and above all by attempts to put these theories into practice. But in order to escape from these, Herr von Haller has withdrawn to the opposite extreme, which is totally devoid of thought and therefore cannot claim to have any substance [*Gehalt*] – that is, the most virulent hatred of all *laws and legislation*, and of *all formally and legally determined right*. Hatred of *law*, of *legally* determined *right*, is the shibboleth whereby fanaticism, imbecility, and hypocritical good intentions manifestly and infallibly reveal themselves for what they are, no matter what disguise they may adopt. – Originality like that of Herr von Haller is always a remarkable phenomenon [*Erscheinung*], and I will cite some examples of it for those of my readers who are as yet unfamiliar with his book. Herr von Haller first puts forward his basic principle (Vol. I, pp. 342ff.), namely 'that just as, in the *inanimate* world, the larger displaces the smaller, the powerful the weak, etc., so also among the *animals*, and likewise among human beings, does the same law reappear in nobler (often surely also in ignoble?) [The words in parentheses are Hegel's own interjection.] forms [*Gestalten*]', and 'that this is *accordingly the eternal and unalterable ordinance of God*, that the *more powerful* rules, must rule, and always shall rule'. It is evident even from this, as well as from what follows, what is meant by *power* in this context: it is not the power of justice and ethics, but the contingent power of nature. In support of this, Herr von Haller further cites, among other reasons (pp. 365f.), the fact that nature, with admirable wisdom, has ordained that the very sense of one's *own superiority* irresistibly ennobles the character and favours the development of precisely those virtues which are most necessary to one's subordinates. He asks, with elaborate formal rhetoric, 'whether it is the strong or the weak in the realm of the sciences who more often abuse their authority and trust for base and selfish ends and to the detriment of credulous people, whether among jurists the masters of their science are the pettifoggers and cavilling lawyers who deceive the hopes of credulous clients, who call white black and black white, who misuse the laws as a vehicle of wrongdoing, who make beggars out of those who need their protection and who, like hungry *vultures*, tear the innocent *lamb* to pieces, etc.' Herr von Haller forgets at this point that he is employing such rhetoric precisely in order to defend the proposition that the *rule of the more powerful* is an eternal ordinance of God, the very ordinance whereby the vulture tears the innocent lamb to pieces, and that those whose knowledge [*Kenntnis*] of the law gives them greater power are therefore quite

Addition. The state in and for itself is the ethical whole, the actualization of free-dom, and it is the absolute end of reason that freedom should be actual. The state is the spirit which is present in the world and which *consciously* realizes itself therein, whereas in nature, it actualizes itself only as the other of itself, as dormant spirit. Only when it is present in consciousness, knowing itself as an existent object [*Gegenstand*], is it the state. Any discussion of freedom must begin not with individ-uality [*Einzelheit*] or the individual self-consciousness, but only with the essence of self-consciousness; for whether human beings know it or not, this essence realizes itself as a self-sufficient power of which single individuals [*die einzelnen Individuen*] are only moments. The state consists in the march of God in the world, and its basis is the power of reason actualizing itself as will. In considering the Idea of the state, we must not have any particular states or particular institutions in mind; instead, we should consider the Idea, this actual God, in its own right [*für sich*].

right to plunder the credulous people who need their protection, since they are the weak. But it would be expecting too much for two thoughts to be brought together where not a single thought is present. – It goes without saying that Herr von Haller is an enemy of *legal codes*. Civil laws, in his opinion, are on the one hand completely 'unnecessary, in that they follow *self-evidently from the law of nature*'. It would have saved much of the effort that has been expended on legislation and legal codes since states first began, and that is still expended on such matters and on the study of jurisprudence [*des gesetzlichen Rechts*], if people had always been content with the sound principle *that all this is self-evident.* 'On the other hand, laws are not in fact made for private persons, but as *instructions* for lesser magistrates to acquaint them with the will of the chief justice. *Jurisdiction* is not in any case a duty on the part of the state (Vol. I, pp. 297f. and *passim*), but a charitable act, a service provided by those with greater power and purely as an accessory. It is not the most perfect means of guaranteeing right, but is in fact *insecure* and *uncertain*. It is the only means with which our modern jurists have left us, for they have robbed us of the *other three means*, the very ones which *lead most quickly and reliably* to the *goal* and which, apart from the legal system, *friendly* nature has given to human beings in order to *secure their rightful freedom*'. And these three means are – what do you think? – '(1) *personal obedience* to, and *inculcation* of, the natural law; (2) *resistance* to injustice [*Unrecht*]; and (3) *flight*, when no other help is available'. (How unfriendly the jurists are in comparison with friendly nature!) 'The *natural* and *divine* law, however, which all-bountiful nature has given to everyone (Vol. I, p. 292), is: honour everyone as your equal' (on the author's own principles, this ought to read: 'honour him who is *not* your equal, but is more powerful than yourself'); 'give offence to no one *who gives no offence to you*; demand nothing but what he *owes* to you' (but what does he owe?); 'but more than this: love your neighbour and serve him where you can.' – The *implantation of this law* is supposed to render a legislation and constitution superfluous. It would be interesting to see how Herr von Haller interprets the fact that, despite the implantation of this law, legislations and constitutions have made their appearance in the world! In Volume III, pp. 362f., the author comes to the 'so-called national liberties', i.e. the juridical and constitutional laws of nations. (In this wider sense, every legally determined right may be described as a *liberty*.) He says of these laws, among other things, 'that their content is usually *very insignificant*, even if great value may be placed in *books* on such *documentary* liberties'. When we see then that the author is here referring to the national liberties of the German Imperial Estates, of the English nation (such as the Magna Charta '*which is little read, however, and even less understood* on account of its *archaic expressions*', the Bill of Rights etc.), of the Hungarian nation, etc., we are amazed to discover that these once so highly prized possessions are of no significance, and that it is *only in books* that these nations place any value on their laws, which have had an effect on every garment the individual wears and every morsel of bread he eats, and whose effects are daily and hourly present in everything. – If we may also mention the *General Legal Code of Prussia*, Herr von Haller speaks of it with particular disfavour (Vol. I, pp. 185ff.) because unphilosophical errors [Haller's text reads *neuphilosophischen Irrtümer* ('errors of modern philosophy').] (though not, at least, the Kantian philosophy, to which Herr von Haller reacts with particular bitterness) have exerted an *incredible* influence on it, and above all because it refers, among other things, to the *state*, the resources of the state, the end of the state, the head of state, the

Any state, even if we pronounce it bad in the light of our own principles, and even if we discover this or that defect in it, invariably has the essential moments of its existence [*Existenz*] within itself (provided it is one of the more advanced states of our time). But since it is easier to discover deficiencies than to comprehend the affirmative, one may easily fall into the mistake of overlooking the inner organism of the state in favour of individual [*einzelne*] aspects. The state is not a work of art; it exists in the world, and hence in the sphere of arbitrariness, contingency, and error, and bad behaviour may disfigure it in many respects. But the ugliest man, the criminal, the invalid, or the cripple is still a living human being; the affirmative aspect – life – survives [*besteht*] in spite of such deficiencies, and it is with this affirmative aspect that we are here concerned.

§259

The Idea of the state

(a) has *immediate* actuality and is the individual state as a self-related organism – the *constitution* or *constitutional law* [*inneres Staatsrecht*];

(b) passes over into the *relationship* of the individual state to other states – *international law* [*äußeres Staatsrecht*];

(c) is the universal Idea as a *genus* [*Gattung*] and as an absolute power in relation to individual states – the spirit which gives itself its actuality in the process of *world history*.

Addition. The state as actual is essentially an individual state, and beyond that a particular state. Individuality should be distinguished from particularity; it is a moment within the very Idea of the state, whereas particularity belongs to history. States as such are independent of one another, and their relationship can consequently only be an external one, so that there must be a third factor above

---

duties of the head of state, servants of the state, etc. Worst of all, in Herr von Haller's opinion, is 'the right to impose *taxes* on the private resources of individuals, their trade, their production, or their consumption in order *to pay for the needs of the state*; for this means that both the *king* himself (since the resources of the state are not the private property of the sovereign, but the resources of the state itself) and the *Prussian citizens have nothing of their own*, neither their persons nor their assets, and all subjects are *serfs in the eyes of the law*, because *they may not withdraw from the service of the state*'.

On top of all this incredible crudity, perhaps the most amusing touch is the emotion [*Rührung*] with which Herr von Haller describes his inexpressible pleasure at his discoveries (Vol. I, Preface [pp. xxiii–xxiv]) – 'a joy such as only the friend of truth can feel when, after honest enquiry, he attains the certainty that . . . he has, *so to speak* (yes, 'so to speak' indeed!), found the utterance of *nature*, the word of *God himself*. (On the contrary, the word of God quite expressly distinguishes its revelations from the utterances of nature and of natural man.) He tells us 'how he could have fallen on his knees in sheer wonderment, how a flood of joyful tears poured from his eyes, and living religiosity arose from that moment within him'. – Herr von Haller's religiosity ought rather to have bemoaned it as the harshest punishment imposed by God (for it is the harshest judgement human beings can experience) that he had strayed so far from thought and rationality, from respect for the laws, and from the knowledge [*Erkenntnis*] of how infinitely important and divine it is for the duties of the state and the rights of the citizens to be determined *by law* – that he had strayed so far from all this that absurdity was able to pass itself off in his eyes as the *word of God*.

them to link them together. This third factor is in fact the spirit which gives itself actuality in world history and is the absolute judge of states. Admittedly, several states may form a league and sit in judgement, as it were, on other states, or they may enter into alliances (like the Holy Alliance, for example), but these are always purely relative and limited, like [the ideal of] perpetual peace. The one and only absolute judge which always asserts its authority over the particular is the spirit which has being in and for itself, and which reveals itself as the universal and as the active genus in world history.

A. Constitutional Law

§260

The state is the actuality of concrete freedom. But *concrete freedom* requires that personal individuality [*Einzelheit*] and its particular interests should reach their full *development* and gain *recognition of their right* for itself (within the system of the family and of civil society), and also that they should, on the one hand, *pass over* of their own accord into the interest of the universal, and on the other, knowingly and willingly acknowledge this universal interest even as their own *substantial spirit*, and *actively pursue it* as their *ultimate end*. The effect of this is that the universal does not attain validity or fulfilment without the interest, knowledge, and volition of the particular, and that individuals do not live as private persons merely for these particular interests without at the same time directing their will to a universal end [*in und für das Allgemeine wollen*] and acting in conscious awareness of this end. The principle of modern states has enormous strength and depth because it allows the principle of subjectivity to attain fulfilment in the *self-sufficient extreme* of personal particularity, while at the same time *bringing it back to substantial unity* and so preserving this unity in the principle of subjectivity itself.

Addition. The Idea of the state in modern times has the distinctive characteristic that the state is the actualization of freedom not in accordance with subjective caprice, but in accordance with the concept of the will, i.e. in accordance with its universality and divinity. Imperfect states are those in which the Idea of the state is still invisible [*eingehüllt*] and where the particular determinations of this Idea have not yet reached free self-sufficiency. In the states of classical antiquity, universality was indeed already present, but particularity [*Partikularität*] had not yet been released and set at liberty and brought back to universality, i.e. to the universal end of the whole. The essence of the modern state is that the universal should be linked with the complete freedom of particularity [*Besonderheit*] and the well-being of individuals, and hence that the interest of the family and of civil society must become focused on the state; but the universality of the end cannot make further progress without the personal [*eigene*] knowledge and volition of the particular individuals [*der Besonderheit*], who must retain their rights. Thus, the universal must be activated, but subjectivity on the other hand must be developed as a living whole. Only when both moments are present [*bestehen*] in full measure can the state be regarded as articulated and truly organized.

§261

In relation to the spheres of civil law [*Privatrecht*] and private welfare, the spheres of the family and civil society, the state is on the one hand an *external* necessity and the higher power to whose nature their laws and interests are subordinate and on which they depend. But on the other hand, it is their *immanent* end, and its strength consists in the unity of its universal and ultimate end with the particular interest of individuals, in the fact that they have *duties* towards the state to the same extent as they also have rights (see § 155).

As has already been noted (in the Remarks to § 3 above), it was above all Montesquieu who, in his celebrated work *L'Esprit des Lois*, focused on and attempted to expound in detail both the thought that laws, including those of civil law in particular, are dependent on the specific character of the state, and the philosophical view that the part should be considered only with reference to the whole. – *Duty* is primarily an attitude *towards* something which, for me, is *substantial* and universal in and for itself. Right, on the other hand, is in general the *existence* [*Dasein*] of this substantial element, and is consequently the latter's *particular* aspect and that of my own *particular* freedom. Thus, on a formal level, right and duty appear to belong to different aspects or persons. In the state, as an ethical entity and as the interpenetration of the substantial and the particular, my obligation towards the substantial is at the same time the existence of my particular freedom; that is, duty and right are *united* within the state *in one and the same relation* [*Beziehung*]. But further, since the distinct moments also attain their *characteristic* shape and reality within the state, so that the distinction between right and duty again arises at this point, these moments, although identical *in themselves* (i.e. in a formal sense) are at the same time *different in content*. In the realms of civil law and morality, the relation [between right and duty] lacks *actual* necessity, so that only an *abstract* equality of content is present; in these abstract spheres, *what* is right for one person ought also to be right for another, and *what* is one person's duty ought also to be another person's duty. That absolute identity of duty and right [referred to above] occurs here only as an equivalent identity of *content*, in that the determination of the content is itself wholly universal; that is, there is a single principle for both duty and right, namely the personal freedom of human beings. Consequently, slaves have no duties because they have no rights, and vice versa. (Religious duties do not concern us here.) – But in the internal development of the concrete Idea, its moments become differentiated, and their determinacy becomes at the same time a different content: in the family, the rights of the son are not *the same in content* as the son's duties towards his father, and the rights of the citizen are not *the same in content* as the citizen's duties towards the sovereign and government. – The above concept of the union of duty and right is a factor [*Bestimmung*] of the greatest importance, and the inner strength of states is embodied in it. – The abstract aspect of duty consists simply in disregarding and excluding particular interests as an inessential and even unworthy moment. But if we consider the concrete aspect, i.e. the Idea, we can see that the moment of particularity is also essential, and that its satisfaction is therefore entirely necessary; in the process of fulfilling his duty, the individual must somehow attain his own interest and satisfaction or settle his own account, and from his situation within the state, a right must accrue to him whereby the universal cause [*Sache*] becomes *his own particular* cause. Particular interests should certainly not be set aside, let alone suppressed; on the contrary, they should be harmonized with the universal, so that both they themselves and the universal are preserved. The individual, whose duties give him the status of a subject [*Untertan*], finds that, in fulfilling his duties as a citizen, he gains protection for his person and property, consideration for his particular welfare, satisfaction of his substantial essence, and the consciousness and self-awareness of being a member of a whole. And through his performance of his duties as services and tasks undertaken on behalf of the state, the state itself is preserved and secured. Viewed in the abstract, the sole interest of the universal would be [to ensure] that the tasks and services which it requires are performed as duties.

Addition. Everything depends on the unity of the universal and the particular within the state. In the states of antiquity, the subjective end was entirely identical with the will of the state; in modern times, however, we expect to have our own views, our own volition, and our own conscience. The ancients had none of these in the present sense; for them, the ultimate factor was the will of the state. Whereas, under the despotic regimes of Asia, the individual has no inner life and no justification within himself, in the modern world human beings expect their inner life to be respected. The association of duty and right has a dual aspect, in that what the state requires as a duty should also in an immediate sense be the right of individuals, for it is nothing more than the organization of the concept of freedom. The determinations of the will of the individual acquire an objective existence through the state, and it is only through the state that they attain their truth and actualization. The state is the sole precondition of the attainment of particular ends and welfare.

§262

The actual Idea is the spirit which divides itself up into the two ideal spheres of its concept – the family and civil society – as its finite mode, and thereby emerges from its ideality to become infinite and actual spirit for itself. In so doing, it allocates the material of its finite actuality, i.e. individuals as a *mass*, to these two spheres, and in such a way that, in each individual case [*am Einzelnen*], this allocation appears to be *mediated* by circumstances, by the individual's arbitrary will and personal [*eigene*] choice of vocation [*Bestimmung*] (see § 185 and the appended Remarks).

Addition. In Plato's republic, subjective freedom is not yet recognized, because individuals still have their tasks assigned to them by the authorities [*Obrigkeit*]. In many oriental states, this assignment is governed by birth. But subjective freedom, which must be respected, requires freedom of choice on the part of individuals.

§263

In these spheres in which its moments, individuality [*Einzelheit*] and particularity, have their immediate and reflected reality, spirit is present as their objective universality which *manifests itself in them* [*als ihre in sie scheinende objektive Allgemeinheit*] as the power of the rational in necessity (see § 184), i.e. as the *institutions* considered above.

Addition. The state, as spirit, is divided up into the particular determinations of its concept or mode of being. If we take an example from nature, the nervous system is, properly speaking, the system of sensation: it is the abstract moment of being with oneself [*bei sich*] and of thereby having one's own identity. But the analysis of sensation reveals two aspects, and these are divided in such a way that both of them appear as complete systems: the first is abstract feeling or self-containment, dull internal movement, reproduction, inner self-nutrition, growth [*Produzieren*], and digestion. The second moment is that this being-with-oneself stands in opposition to the moment of difference [*Differenz*] or outward movement. This is irritability, the outward movement of sensation, which constitutes a system of its own, and there are lower classes of animals which have developed this system exclusively as distinct from the soul-governed unity of inner sensation. If we compare these natural relations [*Naturbeziehungen*] with those of spirit, we must liken the family to sensibility and civil society to irritability. Then the third factor is the state, the nervous system itself [*für sich*], with its internal organization; but it is alive only in so far as both moments – in this case, the family and civil society – are developed within it. The laws which govern them are the institutions of that rationality which manifests itself within them [*des in sie scheinenden Vernünftigen*]. But the ground and ultimate truth of these institutions is the spirit, which is their universal end and known object [*Gegenstand*]. The family, too, is ethical, but its end is not a known end; in civil society, however, separation is the determining factor.

§264

Individuals as a mass are themselves spiritual natures, and they therefore embody a dual moment, namely the extreme of *individuality* [*Einzelheit*] which knows and wills *for itself*, and the extreme of *universality* which knows and wills the substantial. They can therefore attain their right in both of these respects only in so far as they have actuality both as private and as substantial persons. In the spheres in question [i.e. family and civil society], they attain their right in the first respect directly; and in the second respect, they attain it by discovering their essential self-consciousness in [social] institutions as that *universal* aspect of their particular interests which has being in itself, and by obtaining through these institutions an occupation and activity directed towards a universal end within a corporation.

§265

These institutions together form the *constitution* – that is, developed and actualized rationality – in the realm of *particularity*, and they are therefore the firm foundation of the state and of the trust and disposition of individuals towards it. They are the pillars on which public freedom rests, for it is within them that particular freedom is realized and rational; hence the union of freedom and necessity is present *in itself* within these institutions.

Addition. It has already been noted that the sanctity of marriage and the institutions in which civil society takes on an ethical appearance constitute the stability of the whole – that is, the universal is simultaneously the concern [*Sache*] of each [individual] as a particular [entity]. What matters most is that the law of reason should merge with the law of particular freedom, and that my particular end should become identical with the universal; otherwise, the state must hang in the air. It is the self-awareness of individuals which constitutes the actuality of the state, and its stability consists in the identity of the two aspects in question. It has often been said that the end of the state is the happiness of its citizens. This is certainly true, for if their welfare is deficient, if their subjective ends are not satisfied, and if they do not find that the state as such is the means to this satisfaction, the state itself stands on an insecure footing.

§266

But the spirit is objective and actual to itself not only as this necessity and as a realm of appearance, but also as the *ideality* and inner dimension of these. Thus, this substantial universality becomes *its own object* [*Gegenstand*] and end, with the result that the necessity in question similarly becomes its own object and end in the *shape* of freedom.

§267

The *necessity* in ideality is the *development* of the Idea within itself; as *subjective* substantiality, it is the [individual's] political *disposition*, and as *objective* substantiality – in contrast with the former – it is the *organism* of the state, the *political* state proper and *its constitution*.

Addition. The unity of freedom which wills and knows itself is present in the first instance as necessity. Here, the substantial is present as the subjective existence [*Existenz*] of individuals; but the other mode of necessity is the organism, i.e. the spirit is a process within itself which is internally articulated, and which posits differences within itself through which it completes its cycle.

§268

The political *disposition*, i.e. *patriotism* in general, is certainty based on *truth* (whereas merely subjective certainty does not originate in *truth*, but is only opinion) and a volition which has become *habitual*. As such, it is merely a consequence of the institutions within the state, a consequence in which rationality is *actually* present, just as rationality receives its practical application through action in conformity with the state's institutions. – This disposition is in general one of *trust* (which may pass over into more or less educated insight), or the consciousness that my substantial and particular interest is preserved and contained in the interest and end of an other (in this case, the state), and in the latter's relation to me as an individual [*als Einzelnem*]. As a result, this other immediately ceases to be an other for me, and in my consciousness of this, I am free.

> Patriotism is frequently understood to mean only a willingness to perform *extraordinary* sacrifices and actions. But in essence, it is that disposition which, in the normal conditions and circumstances of life, habitually knows that the community is the substantial basis and end. It is this same consciousness, tried and tested in all circumstances of ordinary life, which underlies the willingness to make extraordinary efforts. But just as human beings often prefer to be guided by magnanimity instead of by right, so also do they readily convince themselves that they possess this extraordinary patriotism in order to exempt themselves from the genuine disposition, or to excuse their lack of it. – Furthermore, if we take this *disposition* to be something which can originate independently [*für sich*] and arise out of subjective representations [*Vorstellungen*] and thoughts, we are confusing it with opinion; for in this interpretation, it is deprived of its true ground, i.e. objective reality.

Addition. Uneducated people delight in argument [*Räsonieren*] and fault-finding, for it is easy to find fault, but difficult to recognize the good and its inner necessity. Education in its early stages always begins with fault-finding, but when it is complete, it sees the positive element in everything. In religion, it is equally easy to say that this or that is superstition, but it is infinitely more difficult to comprehend the truth which it contains. Thus people's apparent political disposition should be distinguished from what they genuinely will; for inwardly, they in fact will the thing [*Sache*], but they fasten on to details and delight in the vanity of claiming superior insight. They trust that the state will continue to exist [*bestehen*] and that particular interests can be fulfilled within it alone; but habit blinds us to the basis of our entire existence [*Existenz*]. It does not occur to someone who walks the streets in safety at night that this might be otherwise, for this habit of [living in] safety has become second nature, and we scarcely stop to think that it is solely the effect of particular institutions. Representational thought often imagines that the state is held together by force; but what holds it together is simply the basic sense of order which everyone possesses.

§269

The [*political*] disposition takes its particularly determined *content* from the various aspects of the organism of the state. This *organism* is the development of the Idea in its differences and their objective actuality. These different aspects are accordingly the *various powers* [within the state] with their corresponding tasks and functions, through which the universal continually *produces* itself. It does so in a *necessary* way, because these various powers are determined by the *nature of the concept*; and it *preserves* itself in so doing, because it is itself the presupposition of its own production. This organism is the *political constitution*.

Addition. The state is an organism, i.e. the development of the Idea in its differences. These different aspects are accordingly the various powers with their corresponding tasks and functions, through which the universal continually produces itself in a necessary way and thereby preserves itself, because it is itself the presupposition of its own production. This organism is the political constitution; it proceeds perpetually from the state, just as it is the means by which the state preserves itself. If the two diverge and the different aspects break free, the unity which the constitution produces is no longer established. The fable of the belly and the other members is relevant here. It is in the nature of an organism that all its parts must perish if they do not achieve identity and if one of them seeks independence. Predicates, principles, and the like get us nowhere in assessing the state, which must be apprehended as an organism, just as predicates are of no help in comprehending the nature of God, whose life must instead be intuited as it is in itself.

Translated by H. B. Nisbet

IV

Beauty and Art

12

Immanuel Kant, Critique of Judgement (Kritik der Urteilskraft): *Analytic of the Beautiful, §§ 1–11, §§ 18–22 (1790)*

For Kant, aesthetic experience is not some formless, deeply personal reverie. Rather, Kant wants to show that aesthetic experience takes the form of judgements – judgements of taste – which have a determinate structure and specifiable characteristics. In the *Critique of Judgement* – the section entitled 'Analytic of the Beautiful' – Kant, amongst other things, outlines the essential components of these judgements.

Judgement is understood as the most basic expression of experience across all of Kant's philosophy: theoretical judgement, moral judgement and aesthetic judgement. The nature of what is expressed by each of the three forms of judgement differs, of course. Epistemic judgements (*Critique of Pure Reason*) may be judgements about some objective feature of our perceptual experience. Moral judgements (*Critique of Practical Reason*) posit universally binding maxims of action for a rational being. Aesthetic judgements (*Critique of Judgement*, first part, *Critique of Aesthetic Judgement*) – judgements of taste – however deal with a different order of 'objects', namely the sense that expressions of aesthetic appreciation convey an assumption of possible universal assent, or that they 'impute' such assent.

Aesthetic judgements – judgements of taste – are designated 'judgements of reflection' in that they pertain to a state of the person who makes the judgements, as opposed to some intrinsic property of the object judged. In the *Critique of Pure Reason* Kant had used the term 'aesthetic' as a designation for two basic human capacities which ground our capacity to be affected by objects outside us: spatial and temporal intuition. Aesthetic experience is also a matter of being affected, but our affectedness is not explicable by reference to the nature of an object outside us. Clearly this is a highly attenuated version of valid experience. Nevertheless, Kant sets out to show that it is supported by the very structure of judgement itself.

Kant argues that a judgement of taste contains four dimensions. The *Critique of Pure Reason* outlined the four dimensions that are constitutive of any judgement: quality, quantity, relation and modality. Typical of Kant's architectonic of thought is the translation of these dimensions from their epistemological context into that of aesthetic experience. The *quality* of a judgement pertains to what it describes: in a logical judgement – such as we make, for example, in our perceptual experience – we designate the property of an object. But a judgement of taste, being a judgement of reflection, has as its qualitative dimension its reference to a particular way in which the subject feels herself affected by the representations of an object. A further part of this attitude is that the subject experiences the object with disinterest as opposed to desire.

The *quantity* of a judgement (for Kant) refers to the extension of its assent to validity, that is, whether it attains to single or universal assent. Kant argues that the aesthetic judgement always implies that the object of delight is regarded as an object of delight for all similarly formed human beings. It is, as he claims, *as if* the object contained an objective property of beauty. The 'universal' quality of aesthetic judgements distinguishes them from what Kant calls, 'judgements of sense', in which a person may express delight in an object – their favourite beverages, for example – without implying that the preference will be shared by all.

Kant claims that the *relational* element of judgements of taste is that they involve some notion of the purposiveness of the object. This is not purposiveness in the sense we have for non-beautiful objects – that is, questions of what they are for – but purposiveness in the sense that we cannot appreciate a beautiful object without assuming that it is somehow the product of a will, even though we might know that it is not (in the case of natural beauty): 'purpose without purposiveness' (*Zweckmäßigkeit ohne Zweck*). Beautiful objects of nature stand out from amongst other objects, and that suggests that they have been endowed, somehow, with the extra property of beauty. Indeed their purpose seems to be that of being beautiful.

With regards to *modality* Kant claims that aesthetic judgements contain necessity. He does not mean by necessity that one must judge the object beautiful. Nevertheless aesthetic judgements appear to contain an assumption that others will in fact find an object compellingly beautiful. The source of this assumption is what Kant terms *Gemeinsinn, sensus communis*, common sense. *Gemeinsinn* is what one understands as public sensibility – the background of certain beliefs – which is expressive of an aesthetic norm. In a later section of the *Critique of Judgement* (§40) Kant explains it as follows: 'by the name *sensus communis* is to be understood the idea of a *public* sense, i.e. a critical faculty which in its reflective act takes account (*a priori*) of the mode of representation of everyone else, in order, *as it were*, to weigh its judgement with the collective reason of mankind, and thereby avoid the illusion arising from subjective and personal conditions which could readily be taken for objective, an illusion that would exert a prejudicial influence upon its judgement.' Of course this norm does not exist in the manner of moral norms which compel the assent of rational beings: if it did than all would assent. But it is an ideal which is presupposed in the judgement itself.

One of the striking features of Kant's account of aesthetic experience is that it deals with beauty as such, and therefore makes no important distinction between beautiful natural objects and beautiful artefacts. This approach has a marked effect on his analysis of aesthetic judgement: it allows him to focus on the state of subjectivity occasioned in aesthetic judgements, and leaves aside entirely whether the object deemed to be beautiful contains any meaning (the latter idea being inapplicable to natural objects). It would however be mistaken to think that Kant has nothing to say about art. In sections 43–53 of the *Critique of Judgement* he describes the nature of the fine arts, and the process of production. Nevertheless, the idea of aesthetic experience remains applicable identically to artefacts and natural objects.

ANALYTIC OF THE BEAUTIFUL[†]

First Moment of the Judgment of Taste[1] According to Quality

§1. The Judgment of Taste is Aesthetic

In order to distinguish whether anything is beautiful or not, we refer the representation not by the Understanding to the Object for cognition, but by the Imagination (perhaps in conjunction with the Understanding) to the subject, and its feeling of pleasure or pain. The judgment of taste is therefore not a judgment of cognition, and is consequently not logical but aesthetic, by which we understand that whose determining ground can be *no other than subjective*. Every reference of representations, even that of sensations, may be objective (and then it signifies the real [element] of an empirical representation); save only the reference to the feeling of pleasure and pain, by which nothing in the Object is signified, but through which there is a feeling in the subject, as it is affected by the representation.

To apprehend a regular, purposive building by means of one's cognitive faculty (whether in a clear or a confused way of representation) is something quite different from being conscious of this representation as connected with the sensation of satisfaction. Here the representation is altogether referred to the subject and to its feeling of life, under the name of the feeling of pleasure or pain. This establishes a quite separate faculty of distinction and of judgment, adding nothing to cognition, but only comparing the given representation in the subject with the whole faculty

---

[1] The definition of taste which is laid down here is that it is the faculty of judging of the beautiful. But the analysis of judgments of taste must show what is required in order to call an object beautiful. The moments, to which this Judgment has regard in its reflection, I have sought in accordance with the guidance of the logical functions of judgment (for in a judgment of taste a reference to the Understanding is always involved). I have considered the moment of quality first, because the aesthetic judgment upon the beautiful first pays attention to it.

[†] *KAA* V, 203–221, *Kant's Kritik of Judgment* (London: Macmillan and Co; 1892).

of representations, of which the mind is conscious in the feeling of its state. Given representations in a judgment can be empirical (consequently, aesthetic); but the judgment which is formed by means of them is logical, provided they are referred in the judgment to the Object. Conversely, if the given representations are rational, but are referred in a judgment simply to the subject (to its feeling), the judgment is so far always aesthetic.

§2. The Satisfaction which Determines the Judgment of Taste is Disinterested

The satisfaction which we combine with the representation of the existence of an object is called interest. Such satisfaction always has reference to the faculty of desire, either as its determining ground or as necessarily connected with its determining ground. Now when the question is if a thing is beautiful, we do not want to know whether anything depends or can depend on the existence of the thing either for myself or for any one else, but how we judge it by mere observation (intuition or reflection). If any one asks me if I find that palace beautiful which I see before me, I may answer: I do not like things of that kind which are made merely to be stared at. Or I can answer like that Iroquois *Sachem* who was pleased in Paris by nothing more than by the cook-shops. Or again after the manner of *Rousseau* I may rebuke the vanity of the great who waste the sweat of the people on such superfluous things. In fine I could easily convince myself that if I found myself on an uninhabited island without the hope of ever again coming among men, and could conjure up just such a splendid building by my mere wish, I should not even give myself the trouble if I had a sufficiently comfortable hut. This may all be admitted and approved; but we are not now talking of this. We wish only to know if this mere representation of the object is accompanied in me with satisfaction, however indifferent I may be as regards the existence of the object of this representation. We easily see that in saying it is *beautiful* and in showing that I have taste, I am concerned, not with that in which I depend on the existence of the object, but with that which I make out of this representation in myself. Every one must admit that a judgment about beauty, in which the least interest mingles, is very partial and is not a pure judgment of taste. We must not be in the least prejudiced in favour of the existence of the things, but be quite indifferent in this respect, in order to play the judge in things of taste.

We cannot, however, better elucidate this proposition, which is of capital importance, than by contrasting the pure disinterested[2] satisfaction in judgments of taste, with that which is bound up with an interest, especially if we can at the same

[2] A judgment upon an object of satisfaction may be quite *disinterested*, but yet very *interesting*, i.e. not based upon an interest, but bringing an interest with it; of this kind are all pure moral judgments. Judgments of taste, however, do not in themselves establish any interest. Only in society is it *interesting* to have taste: the reason of this will be shown in the sequel.

time be certain that there are no other kinds of interest than those which are to be now specified.

§3. The Satisfaction in the P*LEASENT* is Bound up with Interest

That which pleases the senses in sensation is PLEASANT. Here the opportunity presents itself of censuring a very common confusion of the double sense which the word sensation can have, and of calling attention to it. All satisfaction (it is said or thought) is itself sensation (of a pleasure). Consequently everything that pleases is pleasant because it pleases (and according to its different degrees or its relations to other pleasant sensations it is *agreeable, lovely, delightful, enjoyable*, etc.) But if this be admitted, then impressions of Sense which determine the inclination, fundamental propositions of Reason which determine the Will, mere reflective forms of intuition which determine the Judgment, are quite the same, as regards the effect upon the feeling of pleasure. For this would be pleasantness in the sensation of one's state, and since in the end all the operations of our faculties must issue in the practical and unite in it as their goal, we could suppose no other way of estimating things and their worth than that which consists in the gratification that they promise. It is of no consequence at all how this is attained, and since then the choice of means alone could make a difference, men could indeed blame one another for stupidity and indiscretion, but never for baseness and wickedness. For thus they all, each according to his own way of seeing things, seek one goal, that is, gratification.

If a determination of the feeling of pleasure or pain is called sensation, this expression signifies something quite different from what I mean when I call the representation of a thing (by sense, as a receptivity belonging to the cognitive faculty) sensation. For in the latter case the representation is referred to the Object, in the former simply to the subject, and is available for no cognition whatever, not even for that by which the subject *cognises* itself.

In the above elucidation we understand by the word sensation, an objective representation of sense; and in order to avoid misinterpretation, we shall call that, which must always remain merely subjective and can constitute absolutely no representation of an object, by the ordinary term 'feeling.' The green colour of the meadows belongs to *objective* sensation, as a perception of an object of sense; the pleasantness of this belongs to *subjective* sensation by which no object is represented, i.e. to feeling, by which the object is considered as an Object of satisfaction (which does not furnish a cognition of it).

Now that a judgment about an object, by which I describe it as pleasant, ex-presses an interest in it, is plain from the fact that by sensation it excites a desire for objects of that kind; consequently the satisfaction presupposes not the mere judgment about it, but the relation of its existence to my state, so far as this is affected by such an Object. Hence we do not merely say of the pleasant, *it pleases*; but, *it gratifies*. I give to it no mere assent, but inclination is aroused by it; and in the case of what is pleasant in the most lively fashion, there is no judgment at all upon the character of the Object, for those [persons] who always lay themselves out for enjoyment (for that is the word describing intense gratification) would fain dispense with all judgment.

§4. The Satisfaction in the GOOD is Bound up with Interest

Whatever by means of Reason pleases through the mere concept is GOOD. That which pleases only as a means we call *good for something* (the useful); but that which pleases for itself is *good in itself.* In both there is always involved the concept of a purpose, and consequently the relation of Reason to the (at least possible) volition, and thus a satisfaction in the *presence* of an Object or an action, *i.e.* some kind of interest.

In order to find anything good, I must always know what sort of a thing the object ought to be, i.e. I must have a concept of it. But there is no need of this, to find a thing beautiful. Flowers, free delineations, outlines intertwined with one another without design and called [conventional] foliage, have no meaning, depend on no definite concept, and yet they please. The satisfaction in the beautiful must depend on the reflection upon an object, leading to any concept (however indefinite); and it is thus distinguished from the pleasant which rests entirely upon sensation.

It is true, the Pleasant seems in many cases to be the same as the Good. Thus people are accustomed to say that all gratification (especially if it lasts) is good in itself; which is very much the same as to say that lasting pleasure and the good are the same. But we can soon see that this is merely a confusion of words; for the concepts which properly belong to these expressions can in no way be interchanged. The pleasant, which, as such, represents the object simply in relation to Sense, must first be brought by the concept of a purpose under principles of Reason, in order to call it good, as an object of the Will. But that there is [involved] a quite different relation to satisfaction in calling that which gratifies at the same time *good,* may be seen from the fact that in the case of the good the question always is, whether it is mediately or immediately good (useful or good in itself); but on the contrary in the case of the pleasant there can be no question about this at all, for the word always signifies something which pleases immediately. (The same is applicable to what I call beautiful.)

Even in common speech men distinguish the Pleasant from the Good. Of a dish which stimulates the taste by spices and other condiments we say unhesitatingly that it is pleasant, though it is at the same time admitted not to be good; for though it immediately *delights* the senses, yet mediately, i.e. considered by Reason which looks to the after results, it displeases. Even in the judging of health we may notice this distinction. It is immediately pleasant to every one possessing it (at least negatively, i.e. as the absence of all bodily pains). But in order to say that it is good, it must be considered by Reason with reference to purposes; viz., that it is a state which makes us fit for all our business. Finally in respect of happiness every one believes himself entitled to describe the greatest sum of the pleasantness of life (as regards both their number and their duration) as a true, even as the highest, good. However Reason is opposed to this. Pleasantness is enjoyment. And if we were concerned with this alone, it would be foolish to be scrupulous as regards the means which procure it for us, or [to care] whether it is obtained passively by the bounty of nature or by our own activity and work. But Reason can never be persuaded that the existence of a man who merely lives for *enjoyment* (however busy he may be in this point of view), has a worth in itself; even if he at the same time is conducive as a means to the best enjoyment of others, and shares in all their gratifications by sympathy. Only what he does, without reference to enjoyment, in full freedom and independently of what nature can procure for him passively, gives an [absolute] worth to his presence [in the world] as the existence of a person; and happiness, with the whole abundance of its pleasures, is far from being an unconditioned good.[3]

However, notwithstanding all this difference between the pleasant and the good, they both agree in this that they are always bound up with an interest in their object; so are not only the pleasant (§ 3), and the mediate good (the useful) which is pleasing as a means towards pleasantness somewhere, but also that which is good absolutely and in every aspect, viz., moral good, which brings with it the highest interest. For the good is the Object of will (i.e. of a faculty of desire determined by Reason). But to wish for something, and to have a satisfaction in its existence, i.e. to take an interest in it, are identical.

§5. Comparison of the Three Specifically Different Kinds of Satisfaction

The pleasant and the good have both a reference to the faculty of desire; and they bring with them – the former a satisfaction pathologically conditioned (by impulses, *stimuli*) – the latter a pure practical satisfaction, which is determined not merely by the representation of the object, but also by the represented connection of the subject with the existence of the object. [It is not merely the object that pleases, but also its existence.] On the other hand, the judgment of taste is merely *contemplative*; i.e. it is a judgment which, indifferent as regards the existence of an object, compares its character with the feeling of pleasure and pain. But this contemplation itself is not directed to concepts; for the judgment of taste is not a cognitive judgment (either theoretical or practical), and thus is not *based* on concepts, nor has it concepts as its *purpose.*

The Pleasant, the Beautiful, and the Good, designate then, three different relations of representations to the feeling of pleasure and pain, in reference to which we distinguish from each other objects or methods of representing them. And the expressions corresponding to each, by which we mark our complacency in them,

[3] An obligation to enjoyment is a manifest absurdity. Thus the obligation to all actions which have merely enjoyment for their aim can only be a pretended one; however spiritually it may be conceived (or decked out), even if it is a mystical, or so-called heavenly, enjoyment.

are not the same. That which GRATIFIES a man is called *pleasant*; that which merely PLEASES him is *beautiful*; that which is ESTEEMED [or *approved*] by him, i.e. that to which he accords an objective worth, is *good*. Pleasantness concerns irrational animals also; but Beauty only concerns men, *i.e.* animal, but still rational, beings – not merely *qua* rational (*e.g.* spirits), but *qua* animal also; and the Good concerns every rational being in general. This is a proposition which can only be completely established and explained in the sequel. We may say that of all these three kinds of satisfaction, that of taste in the Beautiful is alone a disinterested and *free* satisfaction; for no interest, either of Sense or of Reason, here forces our assent. Hence we may say of satisfaction that it is related in the three aforesaid cases to *inclination*, to *favour*, or to *respect*. Now *favour* is the only free satisfaction. An object of inclination, and one that is proposed to our desire by a law of Reason, leaves us no freedom in forming for ourselves anywhere an object of pleasure. All interest presupposes or generates a want; and, as the determining ground of assent, it leaves the judgment about the object no longer free.

As regards the interest of inclination in the case of the Pleasant, every one says that hunger is the best sauce, and everything that is eatable is relished by people with a healthy appetite; and thus a satisfaction of this sort shows no choice directed by taste. It is only when the want is appeased that we can distinguish which of many men has or has not taste. In the same way there may be manners (conduct) without virtue, politeness without goodwill, decorum without modesty, etc. For where the moral law speaks there is no longer, objectively, a free choice as regards what is to be done; and to display taste in its fulfilment (or in judging of another's fulfilment of it) is something quite different from manifesting the moral attitude of thought. For this involves a command and generates a want, whilst moral taste only plays with the objects of satisfaction, without attaching itself to one of them.

Explanation of the Beautiful Resulting from the First Moment

Taste is the faculty of judging of an object or a method of representing it by an *entirely disinterested* satisfaction or dissatisfaction. The object of such satisfaction is called *beautiful*.

Second Moment of the Judgment of Taste, viz., According to Quantity

§6. The Beautiful is that which Apart from Concepts is Represented as the Object of a Universal Satisfaction

This explanation of the beautiful can be derived from the preceding explanation of it as the object of an entirely disinterested satisfaction. For the fact of which every one is conscious, that the satisfaction is for him quite disinterested, implies in his judgment a ground of satisfaction for all men. For since it does not rest on any inclination of the subject (nor upon any other premeditated interest), but since the person who judges feels himself quite *free* as regards the satisfaction which he attaches to the object, he cannot find the ground of this satisfaction in any private conditions connected with his own subject; and hence it must be regarded as grounded on what he can presuppose in every other person. Consequently he must believe that he has reason for attributing a similar satisfaction to every one. He will therefore speak of the beautiful, as if beauty were a characteristic of the object and the judgment logical (constituting a cognition of the Object by means of concepts of it); although it is only aesthetic and involves merely a reference of the representation of the object to the subject. For it has this similarity to a logical judgment that we can presuppose its validity for all men. But this universality cannot arise from concepts; for from concepts there is no transition to the feeling of pleasure or pain (except in pure practical laws, which bring an interest with them such as is not bound up with the pure judgment of taste). Consequently the judgment of taste, accompanied with the consciousness of separation from all interest, must claim validity for every man, without this universality depending on Objects. That is, there must be bound up with it a title to subjective universality.

§7. Comparison of the Beautiful with the Pleasant and the Good by Means of the above Characteristic

As regards the Pleasant every one is content that his judgment, which he bases upon private feeling, and by which he says of an object that it pleases him, should be limited merely to his own person. Thus he is quite contented that if he says 'Canary wine is pleasant,' another man may correct his expression and remind him that he ought to say 'It is pleasant *to me*.' And this is the case not only as regards the taste of the tongue, the palate, and the throat, but for whatever is pleasant to any one's eyes and ears. To one violet colour is soft and lovely, to another it is washed out and dead. One man likes the tone of wind instruments, another that of strings. To strive here with the design of reproving as incorrect another man's judgment which is different from our own, as if the judgments were logically opposed, would be folly. As regards the pleasant therefore the fundamental proposition is valid, *every one has his own taste* (the taste of Sense).

The case is quite different with the Beautiful. It would (on the contrary) be laughable if a man who imagined anything to his own taste, thought to justify himself by saying: 'This object (the house we see, the coat that person wears, the concert we hear, the poem submitted to our judgment) is beautiful *for me*.' For he must not call it *beautiful* if it merely pleases him. Many things may have for him charm and pleasantness; no one troubles himself at that; but if he gives out anything as beautiful, he supposes in others the same satisfaction — he judges not merely for himself, but for every one, and speaks of beauty as if it were a property of things. Hence he says 'the *thing* is beautiful'; and he does not count on the agreement of others with this his judgment of satisfaction, because he has found this agreement several times before, but he *demands* it of them. He blames them if they judge otherwise and he denies them taste, which he nevertheless requires from them. Here then we cannot say that each man has his own particular taste. For this would be as much as to say that there is no taste whatever; i.e. no aesthetic judgment, which can make a rightful claim upon every one's assent.

At the same time we find as regards the Pleasant that there is an agreement among men in their judgments upon it, in regard to which we deny Taste to some and attribute it to others; by this not meaning one of our organic senses, but a faculty of judging in respect of the pleasant generally. Thus we say of a man who knows how to entertain his guests with pleasures (of enjoyment for all the senses), so that they are all pleased, 'he has taste.' But here the universality is only taken comparatively; and there emerge rules which are only *general* (like all empirical ones), and not *universal*; which latter the judgment of Taste upon the beautiful undertakes or lays claim to. It is a judgment in reference to sociability, so far as this rests on empirical rules. In respect of the Good it is true that judgments make rightful claim to validity for every one; but the Good is represented only *by means of a concept* as the Object of a universal satisfaction, which is the case neither with the Pleasant nor with the Beautiful.

§8. The Universality of the Satisfaction is Represented in a Judgment of Taste only as Subjective

This particular determination of the universality of an aesthetic judgment, which is to be met with in a judgment of taste, is noteworthy, not indeed for the logician, but for the transcendental philosopher. It requires no small trouble to discover its origin, but we thus detect a property of our cognitive faculty which without this analysis would remain unknown.

First, we must be fully convinced of the fact that in a judgment of taste (about the Beautiful) the satisfaction in the object is imputed to *every one*, without being based on a concept (for then it would be the Good). Further, this claim to universal validity so essentially belongs to a judgment by which we describe anything as *beautiful*, that if this were not thought in it, it would never come into our thoughts to use the expression at all, but everything which pleases without a concept would be counted as pleasant. In respect of the latter every one has his own opinion; and no one assumes in another, agreement with his judgment of taste, which is always the case in a judgment of taste about beauty. I may call the first the taste of Sense, the second the taste of Reflection; so far as the first lays down mere private judgments, and the second judgments supposed to be generally valid (public), but in both cases aesthetic (not practical) judgments about an object merely in respect of the relation of its representation to the feeling of pleasure and pain. Now here is something strange. As regards the taste of Sense not only does experience show that its judgment (of pleasure or pain connected with anything) is not valid universally, but every one is content not to impute agreement with it to others (although actually there is often found a very extended concurrence in these judgments).

On the other hand, the taste of Reflection has its claim to the universal validity of its judgments (about the beautiful) rejected often enough, as experience teaches; although it may find it possible (as it actually does) to represent judgments which can demand this universal agreement. In fact it imputes this to every one for each of its judgments of taste, without the persons that judge disputing as to the possibility of such a claim; although in particular cases they cannot agree as to the correct application of this faculty.

Here we must, in the first place, remark that a universality which does not rest on concepts of Objects (not even on empirical ones) is not logical but aesthetic, i.e. it involves no objective quantity of the judgment but only that which is subjective. For this I use the expression *general validity* which signifies the validity of the reference of a representation not to the cognitive faculty, but to the feeling of pleasure and pain for every subject. (We can avail ourselves also of the same expression for the logical quantity of the judgment, if only we prefix *objective* to 'universal validity,' to distinguish it from that which is merely subjective and aesthetic.)

A judgment with *objective universal validity* is also always valid subjectively; i.e. if the judgment holds for everything contained under a given concept, it holds also for every one who represents an object by means of this concept. But from a *subjective universal validity*, i.e. aesthetic and resting on no concept, we cannot infer that which is logical; because that kind of judgment does not extend to the Object. But therefore the aesthetic universality which is ascribed to a judgment must be of a particular kind, because it does not unite the predicate of beauty with the concept of the *Object*, considered in its whole logical sphere, and yet extends it to the whole sphere of judging persons.

In respect of logical quantity all judgments of taste are *singular* judgments. For because I must refer the object immediately to my feeling of pleasure and pain, and that not by means of concepts, they cannot have the quantity of objective generally valid judgments. Nevertheless if the singular representation of the Object of the judgment of taste in accordance with the conditions determining the latter, were transformed by comparison into a concept, a logically universal judgment could result therefrom. E.g. I describe by a judgment of taste the rose, that I see, as beautiful. But the judgment which results from the comparison of several singular judgments, 'Roses in general are beautiful' is no longer described simply as aesthetic, but as a logical judgment based on an aesthetic one. Again the judgment 'The rose is pleasant' (to use) is, although aesthetic and singular, not a judgment of Taste but of Sense. It is distinguished from the former by the fact that the judgment of Taste carries with it an *aesthetic quantity* of universality i.e. of validity for every one; which cannot be found in a judgment about the Pleasant. It is only judgments about the Good which – although they also determine satisfaction in an object, – have logical and not merely aesthetic universality; for they are valid of the Object, as cognitive of it, and thus are valid for every one.

If we judge Objects merely according to concepts, then all representation of beauty is lost. Thus there can be no rule according to which any one is to be forced to recognise anything as beautiful. We cannot press [upon others] by the aid of any reasons or fundamental propositions our judgment that a coat, a house, or a flower is beautiful. People wish to submit the Object to their own eyes, as if the satisfaction in it depended on sensation; and yet if we then call the object beautiful, we believe that we speak with a universal voice, and we claim the assent of every one, although on the contrary all private sensation can only decide for the observer himself and his satisfaction.

We may see now that in the judgment of taste nothing is postulated but such a *universal voice*, in respect of the satisfaction without the intervention of concepts; and thus the *possibility* of an aesthetic judgment that can, at the same time, be regarded as valid for every one. The judgment of taste itself does not *postulate* the agreement of every one (for that can only be done by a logically universal judgment because it can adduce reasons); it only *imputes* this agreement to every one, as a case of the rule in respect of which it expects, not confirmation by concepts, but assent from others. The universal voice is, therefore, only an Idea (we do not yet inquire upon what it rests). It may be uncertain whether or not the man, who believes that he is laying down a judgment of taste, is, as a matter of fact, judging in conformity with that Idea; but that he refers his judgment thereto, and, consequently, that it is intended to be a judgment of taste, he announces by the expression 'beauty.' He can be quite certain of this for himself by the mere consciousness of the separating off everything belonging to the Pleasant and the Good from the satisfaction which is left; and this is all for which he promises himself the agreement of every one – a claim which would be justifiable under these conditions, provided only he did not often make mistakes, and thus lay down an erroneous judgment of taste.

§9. Investigation of the Question Whether in the Judgment of Taste the Feeling of Pleasure Precedes or Follows the Judging of the Object

The solution of this question is the key to the Critique of Taste, and so is worthy of all attention.

If the pleasure in the given object precedes, and it is only its universal communicability that is to be acknowledged in the judgment of taste about the representation of the object, there would be a contradiction. For such pleasure would be nothing different from the mere pleasantness in the sensation, and so in accordance with its nature could have only private validity, because it is immediately dependent on the representation through which the object *is given*.

Hence, it is the universal capability of communication of the mental state in the given representation which, as the subjective condition of the judgment of taste, must be fundamental, and must have the pleasure in the object as its consequent. But nothing can be universally communicated except cognition and representation, so far as it belongs to cognition. For it is only thus that this latter can be objective; and only through this has it a universal point of reference, with which the representative power of every one is compelled to harmonise. If the determining ground of our judgment as to this universal communicability of the representation is to be merely subjective, i.e. is conceived independently of any concept of the object, it can be nothing else than the state of mind, which is to be met with in the relation of our representative powers to each other, so far as they refer a given representation to *cognition in general.*

The cognitive powers, which are involved by this representation, are here in free play, because no definite concept limits them to a definite rule of cognition. Hence, the state of mind in this representation must be a feeling of the free play of the representative powers in a given representation with reference to a cognition in general. Now a representation by which an object is given, that is to become a cognition in general, requires *Imagination*, for the gathering together the manifold of intuition, and *Understanding*, for the unity of the concept uniting the representations. This state of *free play* of the cognitive faculties in a representation by which an object is given, must be universally communicable; because cognition, as the determination of the Object with which given representations (in whatever subject) are to agree, is the only kind of representation which is valid for every one.

The subjective universal communicability of the mode of representation in a judgment of taste, since it is to be possible without presupposing a definite concept, can refer to nothing else than the state of mind in the free play of the Imagination and the Understanding (so far as they agree with each other, as is requisite for *cognition in general*). We are conscious that this subjective relation, suitable for cognition in general, must be valid for every one, and thus must be universally communicable, just as if it were a definite cognition, resting always on that relation as its subjective condition.

This merely subjective (aesthetic) judging of the object, or of the representation by which it is given, precedes the pleasure in the same, and is the ground of this pleasure in the harmony of the cognitive faculties; but on that universality of the subjective conditions for judging of objects is alone based the universal subjective validity of the satisfaction bound up by us with the representation of the object that we call beautiful.

That the power of communicating one's state of mind, even though only in respect of the cognitive faculties, carries a pleasure with it; this we can easily show from the natural propension of man towards sociability (empirical and psychological). But this is not enough for our design. The pleasure that we feel is, in a judgment of taste, necessarily imputed by us to every one else; as if, when we call a thing beautiful, it is to be regarded as a characteristic of the object which is determined in it according to concepts; though beauty, without a reference to the feeling of the subject, is nothing by itself. But we must reserve the examination of this question until we have answered that other: 'If and how aesthetic judgments are possible *a priori?*'

We now occupy ourselves with the easier question, in what way we are conscious of a mutual subjective harmony of the cognitive powers with one another in the judgment of taste; is it aesthetically by mere internal sense and sensation? or is it intellectually by the consciousness of our designed activity, by which we bring them into play?

If the given representation, which occasions the judgment of taste, were a concept uniting Understanding and Imagination in the judging of the object, into a cognition of the Object, the consciousness of this relation would be intellectual (as in the objective schematism of the Judgment of which the Critique treats). But then the judgment would not be laid down in reference to pleasure and pain, and consequently would not be a judgment of taste. But the judgment of taste, independently of concepts, determines the Object in respect of satisfaction and of the predicate of beauty. Therefore that subjective unity of relation can only make itself known by means of sensation. The excitement of both faculties (Imagination and Understanding) to indeterminate, but yet, through the stimulus of the given sensation, harmonious activity, viz., that which belongs to cognition in general, is the sensation whose universal communicability is postulated by the judgment of taste. An objective relation can only be thought, but yet, so far as it is subjective according to its conditions, can be felt in its effect on the mind; and, of a relation based on no concept (like the relation of the representative powers to a cognitive faculty in general), no other consciousness is possible than that through the sensation of the effect, which consists in the more lively play of both mental powers (the Imagination and the Understanding) when animated by mutual agreement. A representation which, as individual and apart from comparison with others, yet has an agreement with the conditions of universality which it is the business of the Understanding to supply, brings the cognitive faculties into that proportionate accord which we require for all cognition, and so regard as holding for every one who is determined to judge by means of Understanding and Sense in combination (i.e. for every man).

Explanation of the Beautiful Resulting from the Second Moment

The *beautiful* is that which pleases universally without [requiring] a concept.

Third Moment of Judgments of Taste, According to the Relation of the Purposes which are Brought into Consideration in Them

§10. Of Purposiveness in General

If we wish to explain what a purpose is according to its transcendental determinations (without presupposing anything empirical like the feeling of pleasure) [we say that] the purpose is the object of a concept, in so far as the concept is regarded as the cause of the object (the real ground of its possibility); and the causality of a *concept* in respect of its *Object* is its purposiveness (*forma finalis*). Where then not merely the cognition of an object, but the object itself (its form and existence) is thought as an effect only possible by means of the concept of this latter, there we think a purpose. The representation of the effect is here the determining ground of its cause and precedes it. The consciousness of the causality of a representation, for *maintaining* the subject in the same state, may here generally denote what we call pleasure; while on the other hand pain is that representation which contains the ground of the determination of the state of representations into their opposite [of restraining or removing them].

The faculty of desire, so far as it is determinable to act only through concepts, i.e. in conformity with the representation of a purpose, would be the Will. But an Object, or a state of mind, or even an action, is called purposive, although its possibility does not necessarily presuppose the representation of a purpose, merely because its possibility can be explained and conceived by us only so far as we assume for its ground a causality according to purposes, i.e. in accordance with a will which has regulated it according to the representation of a certain rule. There can be, then, purposiveness without purpose, so far as we do not place the causes of this form in a Will, but yet can only make the explanation of its possibility intelligible to ourselves by deriving it from a Will. Again, we are not always forced to regard what we observe (in respect of its possibility) from the point of view of Reason. Thus we can at least observe a purposiveness according to form, without basing it on a purpose (as the material of the *nexus finalis*), and remark it in objects, although only by reflection.

§11. The Judgment of Taste has Nothing at its Basis but the Form of the Purposiveness of an Object (or of its Mode of Representation)

Every purpose, if it be regarded as a ground of satisfaction, always carries with it an interest — as the determining ground of the judgment — about the object of pleasure. Therefore no subjective purpose can lie at the basis of the judgment of taste. But also the judgment of taste can be determined by no representation of an objective purpose, i.e. of the possibility of the object itself in accordance with principles of purposive combination, and consequently by no concept of the good; because it is an aesthetic and not a cognitive judgment. It therefore has to do with no *concept* of the character and internal or external possibility of the object by means of this or that cause, but merely with the relation of the representative powers to one another, so far as they are determined by a representation.

Now this relation in the determination of an object as beautiful is bound up with the feeling of pleasure, which is declared by the judgment of taste to be valid for every one; hence a pleasantness, [merely] accompanying the representation, can as little contain the determining ground [of the judgment] as the representation of the perfection of the object and the concept of the good can. Therefore it can be nothing else than the subjective purposiveness in the representation of an object without any purpose (either objective or subjective); and thus it is the mere form of purposiveness in the representation by which an object is *given* to us, so far as we are conscious of it, which constitutes the satisfaction that we without a concept judge to be universally communicable; and, consequently, this is the determining ground of the judgment of taste.

[···]

Explanation of the Beautiful Derived from this Third Moment[†]

Beauty is the form of the *purposiveness* of an object, so far as this is perceived in it *without any representation of a purpose.*[4]

Fourth Moment of the Judgment of Taste, According to the Modality of the Satisfaction in the Object

§18. What the Modality in a Judgment of Taste is

I can say of every representation that it is at least *possible* that (as a cognition) it should be bound up with a pleasure. Of a representation that I call *pleasant* I say that it *actually* excites pleasure in me. But the *beautiful* we think as having a *necessary* reference to satisfaction. Now this necessity is of a peculiar kind. It is not a theoretical objective necessity; in which case it would be cognised a *priori* that every one *will feel* this satisfaction in the object called beautiful by me. It is not a practical necessity; in which case, by concepts of a pure rational will serving as a rule for freely acting beings, the satisfaction is the necessary result of an objective law and only indicates that we absolutely (without any further design) ought to act in a certain way. But the necessity which is thought in an aesthetic judgment can only be called *exemplary; i.e.* a necessity of the assent of *all* to a judgment which is regarded as the example of a universal rule that we cannot state. Since an aesthetic judgment is not an objective cognitive judgment, this necessity cannot be derived from definite concepts, and is therefore not apodictic. Still less can it be inferred from the universality of experience (of a complete agreement of judgments as to the beauty of a certain object). For not only would experience hardly furnish sufficiently numerous vouchers for this; but also, on empirical judgments we can base no concept of the necessity of these judgments.

[†] *KAA* V, 236–240.

[4] It might be objected to this explanation that there are things, in which we see a purposive form without cognising any purpose in them, like the stone implements often got from old sepulchral tumuli with a hole in them as if for a handle. These, although they plainly indicate by their shape a purposiveness of which we do not know the purpose, are nevertheless not described as beautiful. But if we regard a thing as a work of art, that is enough to make us admit that its shape has reference to some design and definite purpose. And hence there is no immediate satisfaction in the contemplation of it. On the other hand a flower, e.g. a tulip, is regarded as beautiful; because in perceiving it we find a certain purposiveness which, in our judgment, is referred to no purpose at all.

§19. The Subjective Necessity, which we Ascribe to the Judgment of Taste, is Conditioned

The judgment of taste requires the agreement of every one; and he who describes anything as beautiful claims that every one *ought* to give his approval to the object in question and also describe it as beautiful. The *ought* in the aesthetic judgment is therefore pronounced in accordance with all the data which are required for judging and yet is only conditioned. We ask for the agreement of every one else, because we have for it a ground that is common to all; and we could count on this agreement, provided we were always sure that the case was correctly subsumed under that ground as rule of assent.

§20. The Condition of Necessity which a Judgment of Taste Asserts is the Idea of a Common Sense

If judgments of taste (like cognitive judgments) had a definite objective principle, then the person who lays them down in accordance with this latter would claim an unconditioned necessity for his judgment. If they were devoid of all principle, like those of the mere taste of sense, we would not allow them in thought any necessity whatever. Hence they must have a subjective principle which determines what pleases or displeases only by feeling and not by concepts, but yet with universal validity. But such a principle could only be regarded as a *common sense*, which is essentially different from common Understanding which people sometimes call common Sense (*sensus communis*); for the latter does not judge by feeling but always by concepts, although ordinarily only as by obscurely represented principles.

Hence it is only under the presupposition that there is a common sense (by which we do not understand an external sense, but the effect resulting from the free play of our cognitive powers) – it is only under this presupposition, I say, that the judgment of taste can be laid down.

§21. Have We Ground for Presupposing a Common Sense?

Cognitions and judgments must, along with the conviction that accompanies them, admit of universal communicability; for otherwise there would be no harmony between them and the Object, and they would be collectively a mere subjective play of the representative powers, exactly as scepticism desires. But if cognitions are to admit of communicability, so must also the state of mind, – i.e. the accordance of the cognitive powers with a cognition generally, and that proportion of them which is suitable for a representation (by which an object is given to us) in order that a cognition may be made out of it – admit of universal communicability. For without this as the subjective condition of cognition, cognition as an effect could not arise. This actually always takes place when a given object by means of Sense excites the Imagination to collect the manifold, and the Imagination in its turn excites the Understanding to bring about a unity of this collective process in concepts. But this accordance of the cognitive powers has a different proportion according to the variety of the Objects which are given. However, it must be such that this internal relation, by which one mental faculty is excited by another, shall be generally the most beneficial for both faculties in respect of cognition (of given objects); and this accordance can only be determined by feeling (not according to concepts). Since now this accordance itself must admit of universal communicability, and consequently also our feeling of it (in a given representation), and since the universal communicability of a feeling presupposes a common sense, we have grounds for assuming this latter. And this common sense is assumed without relying on psychological observations, but simply as the necessary condition of the universal communicability of our knowledge, which is presupposed in every Logic and in every principle of knowledge that is not sceptical.

§22. The Necessity of the Universal Agreement that is Thought in a Judgment of Taste is a Subjective Necessity, which is Represented as Objective under the Presupposition of a Common Sense

In all judgments by which we describe anything as beautiful, we allow no one to be of another opinion; without however grounding our judgment on concepts but only on our feeling, which we therefore place at its basis not as a private, but as a common, feeling. Now this common sense cannot be grounded on experience; for it aims at justifying judgments which contain an *ought*. It does not say that every one *will* agree with my judgment, but that he *ought*. And so common sense, as an example of whose judgment I here put forward my judgment of taste and on account of which I attribute to the latter an *exemplary* validity, is a mere ideal norm, under the supposition of which I have a right to make into a rule for every one a judgment that accords therewith, as well as the satisfaction in an Object expressed in such judgment. For the principle, which concerns the agreement of different judging persons, although only subjective, is yet assumed as subjectively universal (an Idea necessary for every one); and thus can claim universal assent (as if it were objective) provided we are sure that we have correctly subsumed [the particulars] under it.

This indeterminate norm of a common sense is actually presupposed by us; as is shown by our claim to lay down judgments of taste. Whether there is in fact such a common sense, as a constitutive principle of the possibility of experience, or whether a yet higher principle of Reason makes it only into a regulative principle for producing in us a common sense for higher purposes: whether therefore Taste is an original and natural faculty, or only the Idea of an artificial one yet to be acquired, so that a judgment of taste with its assumption of a universal assent in fact, is only a requirement of Reason for producing such harmony of sentiment; whether the ought, i.e. the objective necessity of the confluence of the feeling of any one man with that of every other, only signifies the possibility of arriving at this accord, and the judgment of taste only affords an example of the application of this principle: these questions we have neither the wish nor the power to investigate as yet; we have now only to resolve the faculty of taste into its elements in order to unite them at last in the Idea of a common sense.

Explanation of the Beautiful Resulting from the Fourth Moment

The *beautiful* is that which without any concept is cognised as the object of a *necessary* satisfaction.

Translated by J. H. Bernard

13

Friedrich Schiller, On the Aesthetic Education of Man, in a Series of Letters (Über die ästhetische Erziehung des Menschen): *Letters 3, 4, 5, 6, 12, 14, 15 (1795)*

The relationship of Friedrich Schiller (1759–1805) to the broader movement that was to become known as German Idealism is a complex one. If one characterises German Idealism as a project that, in its various manifestations, attempts to reconstruct human experience systematically in order to reveal the rationality of its inner workings, then Schiller is to be excluded. Nor does his main philosophical work cover anything like the ambitious scope of issues considered by Kant, Fichte, Schelling or Hegel. And a further way of differentiating him from this group is to point to certain doubts in Schiller's philosophy that reason is yet achievable amongst human beings. Nevertheless Schiller's *On the Aesthetic Education of Man* should be regarded as playing an important part in the general movement. Schiller's commitment to the possibility of political freedom and his belief that a rational society might eventually be achieved are characteristic themes in the works of the idealists. The fact too that a great deal of Schiller's philosophical framework – as Schiller freely admitted – was a Fichtean version of Kant was immediately apparent to his readers. Indeed, at times aspects of *On the Aesthetic Education of Man* are unintelligible without some acquaintance with the commitments of certain parts of Kant's theory of freedom and beauty.

The text of the *Aesthetic Education of Man* began as a set of letters written by Schiller to his patron, the Danish prince Friedrich Christian. They contained reflections on freedom, politics; and aesthetics. However, Schiller carefully reworked these letters to prepare them for general publication, and hence the original letters to the prince are simply drafts of the finished book. But before the letters were to appear as a book they were published during 1795 in three instalments in the journal, *Die Horen*, of which Schiller himself was editor. A few years later Schiller assembled the 'letters' and, with some minor emendations, published them (in 1801) in book form.

On the Aesthetic Education of Man argues that culture has generative effects: the right sort of culture will, as it were, cultivate reasonable or liberty-minded human beings. When by contrast human beings are subject to nature they are led away from freedom. For Schiller – as for Kant and Fichte – nature represents our regressive tendencies. In fact, it is on these grounds that Schiller famously champions the Greeks. He compares our 'present state' with that of the Greeks: they had simplicity, refinement, culture, wisdom, unified character. Their arts – unlike those of contemporary society – exhibited a culture unified in body and spirit. This claim brings into question the very idea that modern culture represents an advance in sophistication.

Schiller offers an account of what a balanced humanity would look like, and – in the present – how it has been distorted by the mechanistic forms of social organisation. The state in its current form suffices for individuals who operate not at the level of intellect, but of physical reality. Such individuals see as the only value of the state its capacity to control violence (it has no higher aims); that is, 'the physical man', to use Schiller's phrase, sees as valuable in the state only that it overcomes the dangers of a state of nature. Schiller then goes on to describe the existence of the moral agent – one for whom the state as it exists would not suffice – as a 'problematic' existence: the rational moral agent is posited as one who would require a state of reason. In the *Critique of Pure Reason* Kant had explained problematical judgements as 'those in which affirmation or negation is taken as merely possible' (A74/B100). There seems, then, to be duality between the two competing conceptions of society, i.e. as enforcer or as liberating.

Schiller suggests that 'if man is ever to solve the problem of politics in practice he will have to approach it through the problem of the aesthetic, because it is only through beauty that man makes his way to Freedom' (Second Letter), thereby drawing an influential connection between aesthetics and politics. This seems to be a quite oblique approach to the fundamental and practical question of liberty. However, liberty can be achieved only where there is reason, and reason is not obtainable by individuals who are given to purely 'physical' reality. Only when reason and physicality or nature are unified can freedom become a possibility. And their unity can be achieved in, what Schiller calls, a 'play drive (*Spieltrieb*)', our capacity for aesthetic pleasure. The play drive is an essential mediation point between the sensuous and the formal or rational drives (Fichte's terms) – and, in political terms, between physical and reasonable society – which he describes as follows: 'If the [sensuous] drive only furnishes *cases*, this [formal drive] gives *laws*, laws for every judgement, where it is a question of knowledge, laws for every will, where it is a question of action' (Twelfth Letter). In aesthetic experience both drives, then, are involved.

Schiller's strategy is a cautious one in that he believes that to insist that human beings immediately transform their natures from sensuousness to rationality is too dramatic: it would involve a sudden move from sensuous particularism to lawful universalism. Furthermore, a proposal to extinguish 'physical society' instantly in order to start again is excluded by Schiller as this would jeopardise the operations of society: it would be a loss of what, however meagre, has been achieved by physical society. Hence the transitional point must be able to prop up physical society as it moves forward. The prop will have some of the character of the 'physical' – since it must be based on the human character as it is now – and something of the 'formal', which Schiller, following Kant, sees as synonymous with morality, since that is where humanity needs to go. This third way, which contains an element of both, is, again, the aesthetic. Through the aesthetic we can generate a consciousness of the formal or lawful through our capacity to be 'aesthetic' – to enjoy the beautiful (beauty is a formal property) – whilst also engaging our sensuous dimension. Schiller is not foolish about the contentful implications of this: being 'aesthetic' does not entail anything about the determinate content of our opinions. However, it is a necessary state, it seems, for having the right kind of opinions. (It is not definitively clear whether Schiller really saw the aesthetic as a transition to reason or as a terminus which might recapture the synthetic experiences enjoyed by the Greeks.)

It is obvious that Schiller's notion of the mediational play drive influenced Hegel's later idea that the advances of historical epochs are characterised by changes of 'consciousness', and that we cannot move from one form of life to another without such changes. Schiller's position also provided Nietzsche with a framework for a critique of culture as, for him, directly antagonistic to human sensuousness.

ON THE AESTHETIC EDUCATION OF MAN, IN A SERIES OF LETTERS[†]

Third Letter

1. Nature deals no better with Man than with the rest of her works: she acts for him as long as he is as yet incapable of acting for himself as a free intelligence. But what makes him Man is precisely this: that he does not stop short at what Nature herself made of him, but has the power of retracing by means of Reason the steps she took on his behalf, of transforming the work of blind compulsion into a work of free choice, and of elevating physical necessity into moral necessity.

2. Out of the long slumber of the senses he awakens to consciousness and knows himself for a human being; he looks about him, and finds himself – in the State. The force of his needs threw him into this situation before he was as yet capable of exercising his freedom to choose it; compulsion organized it according to purely natural laws before he could do so according to the laws of Reason. But with

[†] *On the Aesthetic Education of Man, in a Series of Letters* (Oxford: Clarendon Press, 1967).

this State of compulsion, born of what Nature destined him to be, and designed to this end alone, he neither could nor can rest content as a Moral Being. And woe to him if he could! With that same right, therefore, by virtue of which he is Man, he withdraws from the dominion of blind necessity, even as in so many other respects he parts company from it by means of his freedom; even as, to take but one example, he obliterates by means of morality, and ennobles by means of beauty, the crude character imposed by physical need upon sexual love. And even thus does he, in his maturity, retrieve by means of a fiction the childhood of the race: he conceives, as idea, a *state of nature*, a state not indeed given him by any experience, but a necessary result of what Reason destined him to be; attributes to himself in this idealized natural state a purpose of which in his actual natural state he was entirely ignorant, and a power of free choice of which he was at that time wholly incapable; and now proceeds exactly as if he were starting from scratch, and were, from sheer insight and free resolve, exchanging a state of complete independence for a state of social contracts. However skilfully, and however firmly, blind caprice may have laid the foundations of her work, however arrogantly she may maintain it, and with whatever appearance of venerability she may surround it – Man is fully entitled in the course of these operations to treat it all as though it had never happened. For the work of blind forces possesses no authority before which Freedom need bow, and everything must accommodate itself to the highest end which Reason now decrees in him as Person. This is the origin and justification of any attempt on the part of a people grown to maturity to transform its Natural State into a Moral one.

3. This Natural State (as we may term any political body whose organization derives originally from forces and not from laws) is, it is true, at variance with man as moral being, for whom the only Law should be to act in conformity with law. But it will just suffice for man as physical being; for he only gives himself laws in order to come to terms with forces. But physical man does in fact exist, whereas the existence of moral man is as yet *problematic*. If, then, Reason does away with the Natural State (as she of necessity must if she would put her own in its place), she jeopardizes the physical man who actually exists for the sake of a moral man who is as yet problematic, risks the very existence of society for a merely hypothetical (even though morally necessary) ideal of society. She takes from man something he actually possesses, and without which he possesses nothing, and refers him instead to something which he could and should possess. And if in so doing she should have counted on him for more than he can perform, then she would, for the sake of a humanity which he still lacks – and can without prejudice to his mere existence go on lacking – have deprived him of the means of that animal existence which is the very condition of his being human at all. Before he has had time to cleave unto the Law with the full force of his moral will, she would have drawn from under his feet the ladder of Nature.

4. What we must chiefly bear in mind, then, is that physical society *in time* must never for a moment cease to exist while moral society *as idea* is in the process of

being formed; that for the sake of man's moral dignity his actual existence must never be jeopardized. When the craftsman has a timepiece to repair, he can let its wheels run down; but the living clockwork of the State must be repaired while it is still striking, and it is a question of changing the revolving wheel while it still revolves. For this reason a support must be looked for which will ensure the continuance of society, and make it independent of the Natural State which is to be abolished.

5. This support is not to be found in the natural character of man which, selfish and violent as it is, aims at the destruction of society rather than at its preservation. Neither is it to be found in his moral character which has, *ex hypothesi*, first to be fashioned, and upon which, just because it is free, and *because it never becomes manifest*, the lawgiver could never exert influence, nor with any certainty depend. It would, therefore, be a question of abstracting from man's physical character its arbitrariness, and from his moral character its freedom; of making the first conformable to laws, and the second dependent upon sense-impressions; of removing the former somewhat further from matter, and bringing the latter somewhat closer to it; and all this with the aim of bringing into being a third character which, kin to both the others, might prepare the way for a transition from the rule of mere force to the rule of law, and which, without in any way impeding the development of moral character, might on the contrary serve as a pledge in the sensible world of a morality as yet unseen.

Fourth Letter

1. This much is certain: Only the predominance of such a character among a people makes it safe to undertake the transformation of a State in accordance with moral principles. And only such a character can guarantee that this transformation will endure. The setting up of a moral State involves being able to count on the moral law as an effective force, and free will is thereby drawn into the realm of cause and effect, where everything follows from everything else in a chain of strict necessity. But we know that the modes of determination of the human will must always remain contingent, and that it is only in Absolute Being that physical necessity coincides with moral necessity. If, therefore, we are to be able to count on man's moral behaviour with as much certainty as we do on *natural* effects, it will itself have to be nature, and he will have to be led by his very impulses to the kind of conduct which is bound to proceed from a moral character. But the will of man stands completely free between duty and inclination, and no physical compulsion can, or should, encroach upon this sovereign right of his personality. If, then, man is to retain his power of choice and yet, at the same time, be a reliable link in the chain of causality, this can only be brought about through both these motive forces, inclination and duty, producing completely identical results in the world of

phenomena; through the content of his volition remaining the same whatever the difference in form; that is to say, through impulse being sufficiently in harmony with reason to qualify as universal legislator.

2. Every individual human being, one may say, carries within him, potentially and prescriptively, an ideal man, the archetype of a human being, and it is his life's task to be, through all his changing manifestations, in harmony with the unchanging unity of this ideal.[1] This archetype, which is to be discerned more or less clearly in every individual, is represented by the *State*, the objective and, as it were, canonical form in which all the diversity of individual subjects strive to unite. One can, however, imagine two different ways in which man existing in time can coincide with man as Idea, and, in consequence, just as many ways in which the State can assert itself in individuals: either by the ideal man suppressing empirical man, and the State annulling individuals; or else by the individual himself *becoming* the State, and man in time being *ennobled to the stature* of man as Idea.

3. It is true that from a one-sided moral point of view this difference disappears. For Reason is satisfied as long as her law obtains unconditionally. But in the complete anthropological view, where content counts no less than form, and living feeling too has a voice, the difference becomes all the more relevant. Reason does indeed demand unity; but Nature demands multiplicity; and both these kinds of law make their claim upon man. The law of Reason is imprinted upon him by an incorruptible consciousness; the law of Nature by an ineradicable feeling. Hence it will always argue a still defective education if the moral character is able to assert itself only by sacrificing the natural. And a political constitution will still be very imperfect if it is able to achieve unity only by suppressing variety. The State should not only respect the objective and generic character in its individual subjects; it should also honour their subjective and specific character, and in extending the invisible realm of morals take care not to depopulate the sensible realm of appearance.

4. When the artisan lays hands upon the formless mass in order to shape it to his ends, he has no scruple in doing it violence; for the natural material he is working merits no respect for itself, and his concern is not with the whole for the sake of the parts, but with the parts for the sake of the whole. When the artist lays hands upon the same mass, he has just as little scruple in doing it violence; but he avoids showing it. For the material he is handling he has not a whit more respect than has the artisan; but the eye which would seek to protect the freedom of the material he will endeavour to deceive by a show of yielding to this latter. With the pedagogic or the political artist things are very different indeed. For him Man is at once the material on which he works and the goal towards which he strives. In this case the end turns back upon itself and becomes identical with the medium; and it is

---

[1] I refer to a recent publication of my friend Fichte, *Lectures on the Vocation of a Scholar*, in which illuminating deductions are drawn from this proposition in a way not hitherto attempted.

only inasmuch as the whole serves the parts that the parts are in any way bound to submit to the whole. The statesman–artist must approach his material with a quite different kind of respect from that which the maker of Beauty feigns towards his. The consideration he must accord to its uniqueness and individuality is not merely subjective, and aimed at creating an illusion for the senses, but objective and directed to its innermost being.

5. But just because the State is to be an organization formed by itself and for itself, it can only become a reality inasmuch as its parts have been tuned up to the idea of the whole. Because the State serves to represent that ideal and objective humanity which exists in the heart of each of its citizens, it will have to observe toward those citizens the same relationship as each has to himself, and will be able to honour their subjective humanity only *to the extent* that this has been ennobled in the direction of objective humanity. Once man is inwardly at one with himself, he will be able to preserve his individuality however much he may universalize his conduct, and the State will be merely the interpreter of his own finest instinct, a clearer formulation of his own sense of what is right. If, on the other hand, in the character of a whole people, subjective man sets his face against objective man with such vehemence of contradiction that the victory of the latter can only be ensured by the suppression of the former, then the State too will have to adopt towards its citizens the solemn rigour of the law, and ruthlessly trample underfoot such powerfully seditious individualism in order not to fall a victim to it.

6. But man can be at odds with himself in two ways: either as savage, when feeling predominates over principle; or as barbarian, when principle destroys feeling. The savage despises Civilization, and acknowledges Nature as his sovereign mistress. The barbarian derides and dishonours Nature, but, more contemptible than the savage, as often as not continues to be the slave of his slave. The man of Culture makes a friend of Nature, and honours her freedom whilst curbing only her caprice.

7. Consequently, whenever Reason starts to introduce the unity of the moral law into any actually existing society, she must beware of damaging the variety of Nature. And whenever Nature endeavours to maintain her variety within the moral framework of society, moral unity must not suffer any infringement thereby. Removed alike from uniformity and from confusion, there abides the triumph of form. *Wholeness* of character must therefore be present in any people capable, and worthy, of exchanging a State of compulsion for a State of freedom.

Fifth Letter

1. Is this the character which the present age, which contemporary events present to us? Let me turn my attention at once to the object most in evidence on this enormous canvas.

2. True, the authority of received opinion has declined, arbitrary rule is unmasked and, though still armed with power, can no longer, even by devious means, maintain the appearance of dignity. Man has roused himself from his long indolence and self-deception and, by an impressive majority, is demanding restitution of his inalienable rights. But he is not just demanding this; over there, and over here, he is rising up to seize by force what, in his opinion, has been wrongfully denied him. The fabric of the natural State is tottering, its rotting foundations giving way, and there seems to be a *physical* possibility of setting law upon the throne, of honouring man at last as an end in himself, and making true freedom the basis of political associations. Vain hope! The *moral* possibility is lacking, and a moment so prodigal of opportunity finds a generation unprepared to receive it.

3. Man portrays himself in his actions. And what a figure he cuts in the drama of the present time! On the one hand, a return to the savage state; on the other, to complete lethargy: in other words, to the two extremes of human depravity, and both united in a *single* epoch!

4. Among the lower and more numerous classes we are confronted with crude, lawless instincts, unleashed with the loosening of the bonds of civil order, and hastening with ungovernable fury to their animal satisfactions. It may well be that objective humanity had cause for complaint against the State; subjective humanity must respect its institutions. Can the State be blamed for having disregarded the dignity of human beings as long as it was still a question of ensuring their very existence? Or for having hastened to divide and unite by the [mechanical] forces of gravity and cohesion, while there could as yet be no thought of any [organic] formative principle from within? Its very dissolution provides the justification of its existence. For society, released from its controls, is falling back into the kingdom of the elements, instead of hastening upwards into the realm of organic life.

5. The cultivated classes, on the other hand, offer the even more repugnant spectacle of lethargy, and of a depravation of character which offends the more because culture itself is its source. I no longer recall which of the ancient or modern philosophers it was who remarked that the nobler a thing is, the more repulsive it is when it decays; but we shall find that this is no less true in the moral sphere. The child of Nature, when he breaks loose, turns into a madman; the creature of Civilization into a knave. That Enlightenment of the mind, which is the not altogether groundless boast of our refined classes, has had on the whole so little of an ennobling influence on feeling and character that it has tended rather to bolster up depravity by providing it with the support of precepts. We disown Nature in her rightful sphere only to submit to her tyranny in the moral, and while resisting the impact she makes upon our senses are content to take over her principles. The sham propriety of our manners refuses her the *first* say — which would be pardonable — only to concede to her in our materialistic ethics the final and decisive one. In the very bosom of the most exquisitely developed social life egotism has founded its system, and without ever acquiring therefrom a heart that is truly

sociable, we suffer all the contagions and afflictions of society. We subject our free judgement to its despotic opinion, our feeling to its fantastic customs, our will to its seductions; only our caprice do we uphold against its sacred rights. Proud self-sufficiency contracts the heart of the man of the world, a heart which in natural man still often beats in sympathy; and as from a city in flames each man seeks only to save from the general destruction his own wretched belongings. Only by completely abjuring sensibility can we, so it is thought, be safe from its aberrations; and the ridicule which often acts as a salutary chastener of the enthusiast is equally unsparing in its desecration of the noblest feeling. Civilization, far from setting us free, in fact creates some new need with every new power it develops in us. The fetters of the physical tighten ever more alarmingly, so that fear of losing what we have stifles even the most burning impulse towards improvement, and the maxim of passive obedience passes for the supreme wisdom of life. Thus do we see the spirit of the age wavering between perversity and brutality, between unnaturalness and mere nature, between superstition and moral unbelief; and it is only through an equilibrium of evils that it is still sometimes kept within bounds.

Sixth Letter

1. Have I not perhaps been too hard on our age in the picture I have just drawn? That is scarcely the reproach I anticipate. Rather a different one: that I have tried to make it prove too much. Such a portrait, you will tell me, does indeed resemble mankind as it is today; but does it not also resemble any people caught up in the process of civilization, since all of them, without exception, must fall away from Nature by the abuse of Reason before they can return to her by the use of Reason?

2. Closer attention to the character of our age will, however, reveal an astonishing contrast between contemporary forms of humanity and earlier ones, especially the Greek. The reputation for culture and refinement, on which we otherwise rightly pride ourselves *vis-à-vis* humanity in its *merely* natural state, can avail us nothing against the natural humanity of the Greeks. For they were wedded to all the delights of art and all the dignity of wisdom, without however, like us, falling a prey to their seduction. The Greeks put us to shame not only by a simplicity to which our age is a stranger; they are at the same time our rivals, indeed often our models, in those very excellences with which we are wont to console ourselves for the unnaturalness of our manners. In fullness of form no less than of content, at once philosophic and creative, sensitive and energetic, the Greeks combined the first youth of imagination with the manhood of reason in a glorious manifestation of humanity.

3. At that first fair awakening of the powers of the mind, sense and intellect did not as yet rule over strictly separate domains; for no dissension had as yet provoked them

into hostile partition and mutual demarcation of their frontiers. Poetry had not as yet coquetted with wit, nor speculation prostituted itself to sophistry. Both of them could, when need arose, exchange functions, since each in its own fashion paid honour to truth. However high the mind might soar, it always drew matter lovingly along with it; and however fine and sharp the distinctions it might make, it never proceeded to mutilate. It did indeed divide human nature into its several aspects, and project these in magnified form into the divinities of its glorious pantheon; but not by tearing it to pieces; rather by combining its aspects in different proportions, for in no single one of their deities was humanity in its entirety ever lacking. How different with us Moderns! With us too the image of the human species is projected in magnified form into separate individuals – but as fragments, not in different combinations, with the result that one has to go the rounds from one individual to another in order to be able to piece together a complete image of the species. With us, one might almost be tempted to assert, the various faculties appear as separate in practice as they are distinguished by the psychologist in theory, and we see not merely individuals, but whole classes of men, developing but one part of their potentialities, while of the rest, as in stunted growths, only vestigial traces remain.

4. I do not underrate the advantages which the human race today, considered as a whole and weighed in the balance of intellect, can boast in the face of what is best in the ancient world. But it has to take up the challenge in serried ranks, and let whole measure itself against whole. What individual Modern could sally forth and engage, man against man, with an individual Athenian for the prize of humanity?

5. Whence this disadvantage among individuals when the species as a whole is at such an advantage? Why was the individual Greek qualified to be the representative of his age, and why can no single Modern venture as much? Because it was from all-unifying Nature that the former, and from the all-dividing Intellect that the latter, received their respective forms.

6. It was civilization itself which inflicted this wound upon modern man. Once the increase of empirical knowledge, and more exact modes of thought, made sharper divisions between the sciences inevitable, and once the increasingly complex ma-chinery of State necessitated a more rigorous separation of ranks and occupations, then the inner unity of human nature was severed too, and a disastrous conflict set its harmonious powers at variance. The intuitive and the speculative understand-ing now withdrew in hostility to take up positions in their respective fields, whose frontiers they now began to guard with jealous mistrust; and with this confining of our activity to a particular sphere we have given ourselves a master within, who not infrequently ends by suppressing the rest of our potentialities. While in the one a riotous imagination ravages the hard-won fruits of the intellect, in another the spirit of abstraction stifles the fire at which the heart should have warmed itself and the imagination been kindled.

[...]

Twelfth Letter

1. Towards the accomplishment of this twofold task — of giving reality to the necessity *within*, and subjecting to the law of necessity the reality *without* — we are impelled by two opposing forces which, since they drive us to the realization of their object, may aptly be termed drives. The first of these, which I will call the *sensuous* drive, proceeds from the physical existence of man, or his sensuous nature. Its business is to set him within the limits of time, and to turn him into matter — not to provide him with matter, since that, of course, would presuppose a free activity of the Person capable of receiving such matter, and distinguishing it from the Self as from that which persists. By matter in this context we understand nothing more than change, or reality which occupies time. Consequently this drive demands that there shall be change, that time shall have a content. This state, which is nothing but time occupied by content, is called sensation, and it is through this alone that physical existence makes itself known.

2. Since everything that exists in time exists as a *succession*, the very fact of something existing at all means that everything else is excluded. When we strike a note on an instrument, only this single note, of all those it is capable of emitting, is actually realized; when man is sensible of the present, the whole infinitude of his possible determinations is confined to this single mode of his being. Wherever, therefore, this drive functions exclusively, we inevitably find the highest degree of limitation. Man in this state is nothing but a unit of quantity, an occupied moment of time — or rather, *he* is not at all, for his Personality is suspended as long as he is ruled by sensation, and swept along by the flux of time.[2]

3. The domain of this drive embraces the whole extent of man's finite being. And since form is never made manifest except in some material, nor the Absolute except through the medium of limitation, it is indeed to this sensuous drive that the whole of man's phenomenal existence is ultimately tied. But although it is this drive alone which awakens and develops the potentialities of man, it is also this drive alone which makes their complete fulfilment impossible. With indestructible chains it binds the ever-soaring spirit to the world of sense, and summons abstraction from its most unfettered excursions into the Infinite back to the limitations of the Present. Thought may indeed escape it for the moment, and a firm will triumphantly resist its demands; but suppressed nature soon resumes her rights, and presses for

---

[2] For this condition of self-loss under the dominion of feeling linguistic usage has the very appropriate expression: *to be beside oneself*, i.e., to be outside of one's own Self. Although this turn of phrase is only used when sensation is intensified into passion, and the condition becomes more marked by being prolonged, it can nevertheless be said that every one is beside himself as long as he does nothing but feel. To return from this condition to self-possession is termed, equally aptly: *to be oneself again*, i.e., to return into one's own Self, to restore one's Person. Of someone who has fainted, by contrast, we do not say that he is beside himself, but that he is *away from himself*, i.e., he has been rapt away from his Self, whereas in the former case he is merely not in his Self. Consequently, someone who has come out of a faint has merely *come to himself*, which state is perfectly compatible with being beside oneself.

reality of existence, for some content to our knowing and some purpose for our doing.

4. The second of the two drives, which we may call the *formal drive*, proceeds from the absolute existence of man, or from his rational nature, and is intent on giving him the freedom to bring harmony into the diversity of his manifestations, and to affirm his Person among all his changes of Condition. Since this Person, being an absolute and indivisible unity, can never be at variance with itself, *since we are to all eternity we ourselves*, that drive which insists on affirming the Personality can never demand anything but that which is binding upon it to all eternity; hence it decides for ever as it decides for this moment, and commands for this moment what it commands for ever. Consequently it embraces the whole sequence of time, which is as much as to say: it annuls time and annuls change. It wants the real to be necessary and eternal, and the eternal and the necessary to be real. In other words, it insists on truth and on the right.

5. If the first drive only furnishes *cases*, this second one gives *laws* – laws for every judgement, where it is a question of knowledge, laws for every will, where it is a question of action. Whether it is a case of knowing an object, i.e., of attributing objective validity to a condition of our subject, or of acting upon knowledge, i.e., of making an objective principle the determining motive of our condition – in both cases we wrest this our condition from the jurisdiction of time, and endow it with reality for all men and all times, that is with universality and necessity. Feeling can only say: this is true *for this individual* and *at this moment*, and another moment, another individual, can come along and revoke assertions made thus under the impact of momentary sensation. But once thought pronounces: that is, it decides for ever and aye, and the validity of its verdict is guaranteed by the Personality itself, which defies all change. Inclination can only say: this is good for *you as an individual* and *for your present need*; but your individuality and your present need will be swept away by change, and what you now so ardently desire will one day become the object of your aversion. But once the moral feeling says: *this shall be*, it decides for ever and aye – once you confess truth because it is truth, and practise justice because it is justice, then you have made an individual case into a law for all cases, and treated one moment of your life as if it were eternity.

6. Where, then, the formal drive holds sway, and the pure object acts within us, we experience the greatest enlargement of being: all limitations disappear, and from the mere unit of quantity to which the poverty of his senses reduced him, man has raised himself to *a unity of ideas* embracing the whole realm of phenomena. During this operation we are no longer in time; time, with its whole never-ending succession, is in us. We are no longer individuals; we are species. The judgement of all minds is expressed through our own, the choice of all hearts is represented by our action.

[...]

Fourteenth Letter

1. We have now been led to the notion of a reciprocal action between the two drives, reciprocal action of such a kind that the activity of the one both gives rise to, and sets limits to, the activity of the other, and in which each in itself achieves its highest manifestation precisely by reason of the other being active.

2. Such reciprocal relation between the two drives is, admittedly, but a task enjoined upon us by Reason, a problem which man is only capable of solving completely in the perfect consummation of his existence. It is, in the most precise sense of the word, *the Idea of his Human Nature*, hence something Infinite, to which in the course of time he can approximate ever more closely, but without ever being able to reach it. 'He is not to strive for form at the cost of reality, nor for reality at the cost of form; rather is he to seek absolute being by means of a determinate being, and a determinate being by means of infinite being. He is to set up a world over against himself because he is Person, and he is to be Person because a world stands over against him. He is to feel because he is conscious of himself, and be conscious of himself because he feels'. – That he does actually conform to this Idea, that he is consequently, in the fullest sense of the word, a human being, is never brought home to him as long as he satisfies only one of these two drives to the exclusion of the other, or only satisfies them one after the other. For as long as he only feels, his Person, or his absolute existence, remains a mystery to him; and as long as he only thinks, his existence in time, or his Condition, does likewise. Should there, however, be cases in which he were to have this twofold experience *simultaneously*, in which he were to be at once conscious of his freedom and sensible of his existence, were, at one and the same time, to feel himself matter and come to know himself as mind, then he would in such cases, and in such cases only, have a complete intuition of his human nature, and the object which afforded him this vision would become for him a symbol of his *accomplished destiny* and, in consequence (since that is only to be attained in the totality of time), serve him as a manifestation of the Infinite.

3. Assuming that cases of this sort could actually occur in experience, they would awaken in him a new drive which, precisely because the other two drives co-operate within it, would be opposed to each of them considered separately and could justifiably count as a new drive. The sense-drive demands that there shall be change and that time shall have a content; the form-drive demands that time shall be annulled and that there shall be no change. That drive, therefore, in which both the others work in concert (permit me for the time being, until I have justified the term, to call it the *play-drive*), the play-drive, therefore, would be directed towards annulling time *within time*, reconciling becoming with absolute being and change with identity.

4. The sense-drive wants to *be* determined, wants to receive its object; the form-drive wants *itself* to determine, wants to bring forth its object. The play-drive,

therefore, will endeavour so to receive as if it had itself brought forth, and so to bring forth as the intuitive sense aspires to receive.

5. The sense-drive excludes from its subject all autonomy and freedom; the form-drive excludes from its subject all dependence, all passivity. Exclusion of freedom, however, implies physical necessity, exclusion of passivity moral necessity. Both drives, therefore, exert constraint upon the psyche; the former through the laws of nature, the latter through the laws of reason. The play-drive, in consequence, as the one in which both the others act in concert, will exert upon the psyche at once a moral and a physical constraint; it will, therefore, since it annuls all contingency, annul all constraint too, and set man free both physically and morally. When we embrace with passion someone who deserves our contempt, we are painfully aware of the *compulsion of nature*. When we feel hostile towards another who compels our esteem, we are painfully aware of the *compulsion of reason*. But once he has at the same time engaged our affection and won our esteem, then both the compulsion of feeling and the compulsion of reason disappear and we begin to love him, i.e., we begin to play with both our affection and our esteem.

6. Since, moreover, the sense-drive exerts a physical, the form-drive a moral constraint, the first will leave our formal, the second our material disposition at the mercy of the contingent; that is to say, it is a matter of chance whether our happiness will coincide with our perfection or our perfection with our happiness. The play-drive, in consequence, in which both work in concert, will make our formal as well as our material disposition, our perfection as well as our happiness, contingent. It will therefore, just because it makes *both* contingent and because with all constraint all contingency too disappears, abolish contingency in both, and, as a result, introduce form into matter and reality into form. To the extent that it deprives feelings and passions of their dynamic power, it will bring them into harmony with the ideas of reason; and to the extent that it deprives the laws of reason of their moral compulsion, it will reconcile them with the interests of the senses.

Fifteenth Letter

1. I am drawing ever nearer the goal towards which I have been leading you by a not exactly encouraging path. If you will consent to follow me a few steps further along it, horizons all the wider will unfold and a pleasing prospect perhaps requite you for the labour of the journey.

2. The object of the sense-drive, expressed in a general concept, we call *life*, in the widest sense of this term: a concept designating all material being and all that is immediately present to the senses. The object of the form-drive, expressed in a general concept, we call *form*, both in the figurative and in the literal sense of this word: a concept which includes all the formal qualities of things and all the relations

of these to our thinking faculties. The object of the play-drive, represented in a general schema, may therefore be called *living form*: a concept serving to designate all the aesthetic qualities of phenomena and, in a word, what in the widest sense of the term we call *beauty*.

3. According to this explanation, if such it be, the term beauty is neither extended to cover the whole realm of living things nor is it merely confined to this realm. A block of marble, though it is and remains lifeless, can nevertheless, thanks to the architect or the sculptor, become living form; and a human being, though he may live and have form, is far from being on that account a living form. In order to be so, his form would have to be life, and his life form. As long as we merely think about his form, it is lifeless, a mere abstraction; as long as we merely feel his life, it is formless, a mere impression. Only when his form lives in our feeling and his life takes on form in our understanding, does he become living form; and this will always be the case whenever we adjudge him beautiful.

4. But because we know how to specify the elements which when combined produce beauty, this does not mean that its genesis has as yet in any way been explained; for that would require us to understand *the actual manner of their combining*, and this, like all reciprocal action between finite and infinite, remains for ever inaccessible to our probing. Reason, on transcendental grounds, makes the following demand: Let there be a bond of union between the form-drive and the material drive; that is to say, let there be a play-drive, since only the union of reality with form, contingency with necessity, passivity with freedom, makes the concept of human nature complete. Reason must make this demand because it is reason – because it is its nature to insist on perfection and on the abolition of all limitation, and because any exclusive activity on the part of either the one drive or the other leaves human nature incomplete and gives rise to some limitation within it. Consequently, as soon as reason utters the pronouncement: Let humanity exist, it has by that very pronouncement also promulgated the law: Let there be beauty. Experience can provide an answer to the question *whether* there is such a thing as beauty, and we shall know the answer once experience has taught us whether there is such a thing as humanity. But *how* there can be beauty, and how humanity is possible, neither reason nor experience can tell us.

5. Man, as we know, is neither exclusively matter nor exclusively mind. Beauty, as the consummation of his humanity, can therefore be neither exclusively life nor exclusively form. Not mere life, as acute observers, adhering too closely to the testimony of experience, have maintained, and to which the taste of our age would fain degrade it; not mere form, as it has been adjudged by philosophers whose speculations led them too far away from experience, or by artists who, philosophizing on beauty, let themselves be too exclusively guided by the needs of their craft.[3] It is the object common to both drives, that is to say, the object of the

[3] *Burke*, in his *Philosophical Enquiry into the Origin of our Ideas of the Sublime and the Beautiful*, makes beauty into mere life. As far as I know, every adherent of *dogmatic* philosophy, who has ever confessed his belief

play-drive. This term is fully justified by linguistic usage, which is wont to designate as 'play' everything which is neither subjectively nor objectively contingent, and yet imposes no kind of constraint either from within or from without. Since, in contemplation of the beautiful, the psyche finds itself in a happy medium between the realm of law and the sphere of physical exigency, it is, precisely because it is divided between the two, removed from the constraint of the one as of the other. The material drive, like the formal drive, is wholly *earnest* in its demands; for, in the sphere of knowledge, the former is concerned with the reality, the latter with the necessity of things; while in the sphere of action, the first is directed towards the preservation of life, the second towards the maintenance of dignity: both, therefore, towards truth and towards perfection. But life becomes of less consequence once human dignity enters in, and duty ceases to be a constraint once inclination exerts its pull; similarly our psyche accepts the reality of things, or material truth, with greater freedom and serenity once this latter encounters formal truth, or the law of necessity, and no longer feels constrained by abstraction once this can be accompanied by the immediacy of intuition. In a word: by entering into association with ideas all reality loses its earnestness because it then becomes of *small account*; and by coinciding with feeling necessity divests itself of its earnestness because it then becomes of *light weight*.

6. But, you may long have been tempted to object, is beauty not degraded by being made to consist of mere play and reduced to the level of those frivolous things which have always borne this name? Does it not belie the rational concept as well as the dignity of beauty – which is, after all, here being considered as an instrument of culture – if we limit it to *mere play*? And does it not belie the empirical concept of play – a concept which is, after all, entirely compatible with the exclusion of all taste – if we limit it merely to beauty?

7. But how can we speak of *mere* play, when we know that it is precisely play and play *alone*, which of all man's states and conditions is the one which makes him whole and unfolds both sides of his nature at once? What you, according to your idea of the matter, call *limitation*. I, according to mine – which I have justified by proof – call *expansion*. I, therefore, would prefer to put it exactly the opposite way round and say: the agreeable, the good, the perfect, with these man is *merely* in earnest; but with beauty he plays. True, we must not think here of the various forms of play which are in vogue in actual life, and are usually directed to very material objects. But then in actual life we should also seek in vain for the kind of beauty with which we are here concerned. The beauty we find in actual existence is precisely what the play-drive we find in actual existence deserves; but with the ideal of Beauty that is set up by Reason, an ideal of the play-drive, too, is enjoined upon man, which he must keep before his eyes in all his forms of play.

on this subject, makes it into mere form: among artists, *Raphael Mengs*, in his *Reflections on Taste in Painting*, not to speak of others. In this, as in everything else, *critical* philosophy has opened up the way whereby empiricism can be led back to principles, and speculation back to experience.

8. We shall not go far wrong when trying to discover a man's ideal of beauty if we inquire how he satisfies his play-drive. If at the Olympic Games the peoples of Greece delighted in the bloodless combats of strength, speed, and agility, and in the nobler rivalry of talents, and if the Roman people regaled themselves with the death throes of a vanquished gladiator or of his Libyan opponent, we can, from this single trait, understand why we have to seek the ideal forms of a Venus, a Juno, an Apollo, not in Rome, but in Greece.[4] Reason, however, declares: The beautiful is to be neither mere life, nor mere form, but living form, i.e., Beauty; for it imposes upon man the double law of absolute formality and absolute reality. Consequently Reason also makes the pronouncement: With beauty man shall *only play*, and it is *with beauty only* that he shall play.

9. For, to mince matters no longer, man only plays when he is in the fullest sense of the word a human being, and *he is only fully a human being when he plays*. This proposition, which at the moment may sound like a paradox, will take on both weight and depth of meaning once we have got as far as applying it to the two-fold earnestness of duty and of destiny. It will, I promise you, prove capable of bearing the whole edifice of the art of the beautiful, and of the still more difficult art of living. But it is, after all, only in philosophy that the proposition is unexpected; it was long ago alive and operative in the art and in the feeling of the Greeks, the most distinguished exponents of both; only they transferred to Olympus what was meant to be realized on earth. Guided by the truth of that same proposition, they banished from the brow of the blessed gods all the earnestness and effort which furrow the cheeks of mortals, no less than the empty pleasures which preserve the smoothness of a vacuous face; freed those ever-contented beings from the bonds inseparable from every purpose, every duty, every care, and made *idleness* and *indifferency* the enviable portion of divinity – merely a more human name for the freest, most sublime state of being. Both the material constraint of natural laws and the spiritual constraint of moral laws were resolved in their higher concept of Necessity, which embraced both worlds at once; and it was only out of the perfect union of those two necessities that for them true Freedom could proceed. Inspired by this spirit, the Greeks effaced from the features of their ideal physiognomy, together with *inclination*, every trace of *volition* too; or rather they made both indiscernible, for they knew how to fuse them in the most intimate union. It is not Grace, nor is it yet Dignity, which speaks to us from the superb countenance of a *Juno Ludovisi*; it is neither the one nor the other because it is both at once. While the woman-god demands our veneration, the god-like woman kindles our love; but even as we abandon ourselves in ecstasy to her heavenly grace, her celestial self-sufficiency makes us recoil in terror. The whole figure reposes and dwells

---

[4] If (to confine ourselves to the modern world) we compare horse-racing in London, bull-fights in Madrid, *spectacles* in the Paris of former days, the gondola races in Venice, animal-baiting in Vienna, and the gay attractive life of the Corso in Rome, it will not be difficult to determine the different nuances of taste among these different peoples. However, there is far less uniformity among the amusements of the common people in these different countries than there is among those of the refined classes in those same countries, a fact which it is easy to account for.

in itself, a creation completely self-contained, and, as if existing beyond space, neither yielding nor resisting; here is no force to contend with force, no frailty where temporality might break in. Irresistibly moved and drawn by those former qualities, kept at a distance by these latter, we find ourselves at one and the same time in a state of utter repose and supreme agitation, and there results that wondrous stirring of the heart for which mind has no concept nor speech any name.

Translated by Elizabeth M. Wilkinson
and L. A. Willoughby

14

F. W. J. Schelling, System of Transcendental Idealism
(System des transcendentalen Idealismus): *Part VI*
(Essentials of the Philosophy of Art) (1800)

The analysis of the nature of art plays a fundamental role in Schelling's work. In an effort to provide the solution to the deepest and most troubling question of his earlier philosophy he daringly posited a metaphysical theory of art. Schelling's main discussion of the metaphysical dimensions of art is found in the *System of Transcendental Idealism* (1800).

This work comes after his 1797 and 1799 books dealing with the so-called philosophy of nature. The philosophy of nature explored the problem of 'intelligence' in nature: we start with an analysis of the world of independent objects and forces – nature – and we discover the operations of intelligence and purpose. In the *System of Transcendental Idealism* we take an opposite line: we start with the intelligence – our rationality – and see how it manifests itself in nature. There is a progressive story – one that Hegel found remarkably useful – about the emergence of this 'intelligence' in a series of 'epochs'. The philosophy of nature moves from object to 'ego', whereas the philosophy of transcendental idealism moves from ego to object. For Fichte the latter move was the only defensible one and he was, on these grounds, a subjective idealist. But Schelling does not stop at that in that in the *System of Transcendental Idealism* he attempts to go beyond Fichte's as well as his own earlier subjective idealism, and he thereby initiates the development of German Idealism, known as objective idealism, in that he sees both approaches as necessary for a comprehensive understanding of reality.

The problem, for Schelling, is that of how the respective explanations of the philosophies of nature and transcendental idealism can be united: the former exhibits a world of ready-made objects, the latter the processes of production. What is the connection? In the *System of Transcendental Idealism* Schelling seeks that connection in art. In his own introduction to the book he writes: 'The objective world is simply the original, as yet unconscious, poetry of the spirit; the universal organon of philosophy – and the keystone of its entire arch – *is the philosophy of art.*'[1] This claim is

---

[1] F. W. J. Schelling, trans. Peter Heath, *System of Transcendental Idealism* (Charlottesville, VA: University Press of Virginia, 1978), p. 12 (*SSW* III, 349).

substantiated only in the latter sections of the book after certain key ideas – sketched below – have been set out.

Schelling attempts to find the moment which unifies nature and freedom through a theory of intuition. He explains that 'intellectual intuition' is the activity of the philosopher who takes the standpoint of transcendental idealism. He calls it 'inner sense'. It is distinguished from empirical self-awareness in that it is essentially untranslatable into third party perceptions. Taking the attitude of transcendental idealism towards one's thoughts means accepting them only in so far as one can validate them as one's own production: 'the objects of the transcendental philosopher exist not at all, save in so far as they are freely produced.'[2] Inner intuition entails a dual function: the production of concepts and intuition of these concepts: 'Two conditions are therefore required for the understanding of philosophy, *first* that one be engaged in a constant inner activity, a constant producing of these original acts of the intellect; and *second*, that one be constantly reflecting upon this production . . .'[3] Schelling argues that this dual activity likens the activity of philosophy to that of art: 'all philosophy is *productive* [it produces concepts]. Thus philosophy depends as much as art does on the productive capacity, and the difference between them rests merely on the different direction taken by the productive force.'[4] He believes that this likeness entitles him to think of the very activity of philosophy as in a certain respect aesthetic: 'The proper sense by which this type of philosophy must be apprehended is thus the *aesthetic* sense, and that is why the philosophy of art is the true organon of philosophy.'[5] But there is an intuition which unites this experience of productive freedom with that of necessity or compulsion, and it can be found only in the artist. Schelling, then, has three accounts of intuition: outer intuition (of unconscious objects); inner intuition (of my own conscious producing); aesthetic intuition (a synthesis of the other two). This latter will encompass both the conscious and unconscious products (the latter being nature).

Schelling's argument for the existence of aesthetic intuition is curious in that it takes its starting point from a quite non-transcendental premise. He claims that it is 'well known' that the artist experiences the contradiction of forces – conscious and unconscious forces – in the creative process: all artists, he claims are compelled by a mysterious force to create, a unique experience in which 'free activity becomes involuntary'. Genius is the capacity to be so motivated. This tension in the productive activity is resolved, however, is the execution of the artwork where the artist experiences 'the feeling of an *infinite* harmony'.

Schelling goes on to use this metaphysical schema to explain the unique essence of artworks: the artwork is irreducible to the intentions of its maker

[2] Ibid., p. 13 (*SSW* III, 350).
[3] Ibid., p. 13 (*SSW* III, 350).
[4] Ibid., pp. 13–14 (*SSW* III, 351).
[5] Ibid., p. 14 (*SSW* III, 351).

as it contains 'an infinity of purposes', produced through the 'infinite op-position' of the artist's 'conscious and unconscious activities'; the artwork represents itself as a 'silent grandeur' precisely because it is the resolution in infinite tranquillity of the competing tensions within the artistic process; beauty in art is the product of 'an infinite finitely displayed.'

Schelling makes a few sharp distinctions between his own position and those of his immediate predecessors. Against Kant he allows for the idea of sublimity in art, and in distinction from Schiller he holds that the motivations of the artist are purely aesthetic, excluding even moral considerations of the artwork's contents.

The *System of Transcendental Idealism* did not mark the end of Schelling's considerations of art. Further elaborations of some the ideas presented within the metaphysical framework are found in the *Philosophy of Art*, published a few years later (1802–3).

PART SIX†
DEDUCTION OF A UNIVERSAL ORGAN OF PHILOSOPHY, OR: ESSENTIALS OF THE PHILOSOPHY OF ART ACCORDING TO THE PRINCIPLES OF TRANSCENDENTAL IDEALISM

§1 Deduction of the Art-Product as Such

The intuition we have postulated is to bring together that which exists in separation in the appearance of freedom and in the intuition of the natural product; namely *identity of the conscious* and the *unconscious* in the *self*, and *consciousness of this identity*. The product of this intuition will therefore verge on the one side upon the product of nature, and on the other upon the product of freedom, and must unite in itself the characteristics of both. If we know the product of the intuition, we are also acquainted with the intuition itself, and hence we need only derive the product, in order to derive the intuition.

With the product of freedom, our product will have this in common, that it is consciously brought about; and with the product of nature, that it is unconsciously brought about. In the former respect it will thus be the reverse of the organic natural product. Whereas the unconscious (blind) activity is reflected out of the organic product as a conscious one, the conscious activity will conversely be reflected out of the product here under consideration as an unconscious (objective) one;

---

†*SSW* III, 612–629. *System of Transcendental Idealism* (Charlottesville, VA: University Press of Virginia, 1978).

whereas the organic product reflects its unconscious activity to me as determined by conscious activity, the product here being derived will conversely reflect conscious activity as determined by unconscious. To put it more briefly: nature begins as unconscious and ends as conscious; the process of production is not purposive, but the product certainly is so. In the activity at present under discussion, the self must begin (subjectively) with consciousness, and end without consciousness, or *objectively*; the self is conscious in respect of production, unconscious in regard to the product.

But now how are *we* to explain transcendentally to *ourselves* an intuition such as this, in which the unconscious activity operates as it were, through the conscious, to the point of attaining complete identity therewith? – Let us first give thought to the fact that the activity is to be a conscious one. But now it is utterly impossible for anything objective to be brought forth with consciousness, although that is being demanded here. The objective is simply that which arises without consciousness, and hence what is properly objective in this intuition must likewise be incapable of being brought forth *with consciousness*. On this point we may appeal directly to the arguments already brought forward in regard to free action, namely that the objective factor therein is supplied by something independent of freedom. The difference is merely this, [a)] that in the free act the identity of the two activities must be abolished, precisely in order that the act may thereby appear as free, [whereas here, the two are to appear as one in *consciousness* itself, without negation thereof]. Moreover, [b)] in the free act the two activities can *never* become absolutely identical, whence even the object of the free act is necessarily an *infinite* one, never completely realized, for if it was, the conscious and the objective activities would merge into one, that is, the appearance of freedom would cease. Now that which was utterly impossible through freedom is to become possible through the act here postulated, though as the price of this the latter must cease to be a free act, and becomes one in which freedom and necessity are absolutely united. But now the production was still supposed to take place with consciousness, which is impossible unless the two [activities] are separated. So here is a manifest contradiction. [I present it once again.] Conscious and unconscious activities are to be absolutely one in the product, just as they also are in the organic product, but they are to be one in a different manner; the two are to be one *for the self itself*. This is impossible, however, unless the self is conscious of the production. But if it is so, the two activities must be separated, for this is a necessary condition for being conscious of the production. So the two activities must be one, since otherwise there is no identity, and yet must both be separated, since otherwise there is identity, but not for the self. How is this contradiction to be resolved?

The two activities must be separated for purposes of the appearing, the becoming–objective of the production, just as in the free act they had to be separated in order that the intuition might become objective. But they cannot be separated *ad infinitum*, as in the free act, since otherwise the objective element would never be a complete manifestation of this identity.[1] The identity of the two was to be abolished only for the sake of consciousness, but the production is to end in unconsciousness; so there must be a point at which the two merge into one; and conversely, where the two merge into one, the production must cease to appear as a free one.[2]

If this point in production is reached, the producing must absolutely stop, and it must be impossible for the producer to go on producing; for the condition of all producing is precisely the opposition between conscious and unconscious activity; but here they have absolutely to coincide, and thus within the intelligence all conflict has to be eliminated, all contradiction reconciled.[3]

The intelligence will therefore end with a complete recognition of the identity expressed in the product as an identity whose principle lies in the intelligence itself; it will end, that is, in a complete intuiting of itself.[4] Now since it was the free tendency to self-intuition in that identity which originally divided the intelligence from itself, the feeling accompanying this intuition will be that of an infinite tranquillity. With the completion of the product, all urge to produce is halted, all contradictions are eliminated, all riddles resolved. Since production set out from freedom, that is, from an unceasing opposition of the two activities, the intelligence will be unable to attribute this absolute union of the two, in which production ends, to *freedom*; so as soon as the product is completed, all appearance of freedom is removed. The intelligence will feel itself astonished and *blessed* by this union, will regard it, that is, in the light of a bounty freely granted by a higher nature, by whose aid the impossible has been made possible.

This unknown, however, whereby the objective and the conscious activities are here brought into unexpected harmony, is none other than that absolute[5] which contains the common ground of the preestablished harmony between the conscious and the unconscious. Hence, if this absolute is reflected from out of the product, it will appear to the intelligence as something lying above the latter, and which, in contrast to freedom, brings an element of the unintended to that which was begun with consciousness and intention.

This unchanging identity, which can never attain to consciousness, and merely radiates back from the product, is for the producer precisely what destiny is for the agent, namely a dark unknown force which supplies the element of completeness or objectivity to the piecework of freedom; and as that power is called destiny, which through our free action realizes, without our knowledge and even against our will, goals *that we did not envisage*, so likewise that incomprehensible agency

---

[1] That which lies, for the free act, in an infinite progress, is to be, in the current engendering, a *thing present*, is to become actual, objective, in something finite.

[2] At that point the free activity has wholly gone over into the objective, the necessary aspect. Hence production is free at the outset, whereas the product appears as an absolute identity of the free activity with the necessary one.

[3] *Translator's note:* This paragraph cancelled in the author's copy.

[4] For it (the intelligence) is itself the producer; but at the same time this identity has wholly broken loose therefrom, and become totally objective to the intelligence, i.e., totally objective *to itself.*

[5] The primordial self.

which supplies objectivity to the conscious, without the cooperation of freedom, and to some extent in opposition to freedom (wherein is eternally dispersed what in this production is united), is denominated by means of the obscure concept of *genius.*

The product we postulate is none other than the product of genius, or, since genius is possible only in the arts, the *product of art.*

The deduction is concluded, and our next task is simply to show by thorough-going analysis that all the features of the production we have postulated come together in the aesthetic.

The fact that all aesthetic production rests upon a conflict of activities can be justifiably inferred already from the testimony of all artists, that they are involuntarily driven to create their works, and that in producing them they merely satisfy an irresistible urge of their own nature; for if every urge proceeds from a contradiction in such wise that, given the contradiction, free activity becomes involuntary, the artistic urge also must proceed from such a feeling of inner contradiction. But since this contradiction sets in motion the whole man with all his forces, it is undoubtedly one which strikes at *the ultimate in him*, the root of his whole being.[6] It is as if, in the exceptional man (which artists above all are, in the highest sense of the word), that unalterable identity, on which all existence is founded, had laid aside the veil wherewith it shrouds itself in others, and, just as it is directly affected by things, so also works directly back upon everything. Thus it can only be the contradiction between conscious and unconscious in the free act which sets the artistic urge in motion; just as, conversely, it can be given to art alone to pacify our endless striving, and likewise to resolve the final and uttermost contradiction within us. Just as aesthetic production proceeds from the feeling of a seemingly irresoluble contradiction, so it ends likewise, by the testimony of all artists, and of all who share their inspiration, in the feeling of an *infinite* harmony; and that this feeling which accompanies completion is at the same time a *deep emotion*, is itself enough to show that the artist attributes that total resolution of his conflict which he finds achieved in his work of art, not to himself [alone], but to a bounty freely granted by his own nature, which, however unrelentingly it set him in conflict with himself, is no less gracious in relieving him of the pain of this contradiction.[7] For just as the artist is driven into production involuntarily and even in spite of himself (whence the ancient expressions *pati deum*, etc., and above all the idea of being inspired by an afflatus from without), so likewise is his production endowed with objectivity as if by no help of his own, that is, itself in a purely objective manner. Just as the man of destiny does not execute what he wishes or intends, but rather what he is obliged to execute by an inscrutable fate which governs him, so the artist, however deliberate he may be, seems nonetheless to be governed, in regard to what is truly objective in his creation, by a power which separates him from all other men, and compels him to say or depict things which he does not

---

[6] The true in-itself.

[7] Attributes . . . to a bounty freely granted by his own nature, and thus to a coincidence of the unconscious with the conscious activity [Author's copy].

fully understand himself, and whose meaning is infinite. Now every absolute con-currence of the two antithetical activities is utterly unaccountable, being simply a *phenomenon* which although incomprehensible,[8] yet cannot be denied; and art, therefore, is the one everlasting revelation which yields that concurrence, and the marvel which, had it existed but once only, would necessarily have convinced us of the absolute reality of that supreme event.

Now again if art comes about through two activities totally distinct from one another, genius is neither one nor the other, but that which presides over both. If we are to seek in one of the two activities, namely the conscious, for what is ordinarily called *art*, though it is only one part thereof, namely that aspect of it which is exercised with consciousness, thought and reflection, and can be taught and learnt and achieved through tradition and practice, we shall have, on the other hand, to seek in the unconscious factor which enters into art for that about it which cannot be learned, nor attained by practice, nor in any other way, but can only be inborn through the free bounty of nature; and this is what we may call, in a word, the element of *poetry* in art.

It is self-evident from this, however, that it would be utterly futile to ask which of the two constituents should have preference over the other, since each of them, in fact, is valueless without the other, and it is only in conjunction that they bring forth the highest. For although what is not attained by practice, but is born in us, is commonly regarded as the nobler, the gods have in fact tied the very exercise of that innate power so closely to a man's serious application, his industry and thought, that even where it is inborn, poetry without art engenders, as it were, only dead products, which can give no pleasure to any man's mind, and repel all judgment and even intuition, owing to the wholly blind force which operates therein. It is, on the contrary, far more to be expected that art without poetry should be able to achieve something, than poetry without art; partly because it is not easy for a man to be by nature wholly without poetry, though many are wholly without art; and partly because a persistent study of the thoughts of great masters is able in some degree to make up for the initial want of objective power. All that can ever arise from this, however, is merely a semblance of poetry, which, by its superficiality and by many other indications, *e.g.*, the high value it attaches to the mere mechanics of art, the poverty of form in which it operates, etc., is easily distinguishable in contrast to the unfathomable depth which the true artist, though he labors with the greatest diligence, involuntarily imparts to his work, and which neither he nor anyone else is wholly able to penetrate.

But now it is also self-evident that just as poetry and art are each individually incapable of engendering perfection, so a divided existence of both is equally inadequate to the task.[9] It is therefore clear that, since the identity of the two can only be innate, and is utterly impossible and unattainable through freedom, perfection is possible only through genius, which, for that very reason, is for the

---

[8] From the standpoint of mere reflection.

[9] Neither has priority over the other. It is, indeed, simply the equipoise of the two (art and poetry) which is reflected in the work of art.

aesthetic what the self is for philosophy, namely the supreme absolute reality, which never itself becomes objective, but is the cause of everything that is so.

§2 Character of the Art-Product

a) The work of art reflects to us the identity of the conscious and unconscious activities. But the opposition between them is an infinite one, and its removal is effected without any assistance from freedom. Hence the basic character of the work of art is that of an *unconscious infinity* [synthesis of nature and freedom]. Besides what he has put into his work with manifest intention, the artist seems instinctively, as it were, to have depicted therein an infinity, which no finite understanding is capable of developing to the full. To explain what we mean by a single example: the mythology of the Greeks, which undeniably contains an infinite meaning and a symbolism for all ideas, arose among a people, and in a fashion, which both make it impossible to suppose any comprehensive forethought in devising it, or in the harmony whereby everything is united into one great whole. So it is with every true work of art, in that every one of them is capable of being expounded *ad infinitum*, as though it contained an infinity of purposes, while yet one is never able to say whether this infinity has lain within the artist himself, or resides only in the work of art. By contrast, in the product which merely apes the character of a work of art, purpose and rule lie on the surface, and seem so restricted and circumscribed, that the product is no more than a faithful replica of the artist's conscious activity, and is in every respect an object for reflection only, not for intuition, which loves to sink itself in what it contemplates, and finds no resting place short of the infinite.

b) Every aesthetic production proceeds from the feeling of an infinite contradiction, and hence also the feeling which accompanies completion of the art-product must be one of an infinite tranquillity; and this latter, in turn, must also pass over into the work of art itself. Hence the outward expression of the work of art is one of calm, and silent grandeur, even where the aim is to give expression to the utmost intensity of pain or joy.

c) Every aesthetic production proceeds from an intrinsically infinite separation of the two activities, which in every free act of producing are divided. But now since these two activities are to be depicted in the product as united, what this latter presents is an infinite finitely displayed. But the infinite finitely displayed is beauty. The basic feature of every work of art, in which both the preceding are comprehended, is therefore *beauty*, and without beauty there is no work of art. There are, admittedly, sublime works of art, and beauty and sublimity in a certain respect are opposed to each other, in that a landscape, for example, can be beautiful without therefore being sublime, and *vice versa*. However, the opposition between beauty and sublimity is one which occurs only in regard to the object, not in regard to the subject of intuition. For the difference between the beautiful and the sublime work of art consists simply in this, that where beauty is present, the infinite contradiction is eliminated in the object itself; whereas when sublimity is present, the conflict is not reconciled in the object itself, but merely uplifted to a point at which it is involuntarily eliminated in the intuition; and this, then, is much as if it were to be eliminated in the object.[10] It can also be shown very easily that sublimity rests upon the same contradiction as that on which beauty rests. For whenever an object is spoken of as sublime, a magnitude is admitted by the unconscious activity which it is impossible to accept into the conscious one: whereupon the self is thrown into a conflict with itself which can end only in an aesthetic intuition, whereby both activities are brought into unexpected harmony; save only that the intuition, which here lies not in the artist, but in the intuiting subject himself, is a wholly involuntary one, in that the sublime (quite unlike the merely strange, which similarly confronts the imagination with a contradiction, though one that is not worth the trouble of resolving) sets all the forces of the mind in motion, in order to resolve a contradiction which threatens our whole intellectual existence.

Now that the characteristics of the work of art have been derived, its difference from all other products has simultaneously been brought to light.

For the art-product differs from the organic product of nature primarily in these respects: [a) that the organic being still exhibits unseparated what the aesthetic production displays after separation, though united; b)] that the organic production does not proceed from consciousness, or therefore from the infinite contradiction, which is the condition of aesthetic production. Hence [if beauty is essentially the resolution of an infinite conflict] the organic product of nature will likewise not necessarily be *beautiful*, and if it is so, its beauty will appear as altogether contingent, since the condition thereof cannot be thought of as existing in nature. From this we may explain the quite peculiar interest in natural beauty, not insofar as it is beauty as such, but insofar as it is specifically *natural beauty*. Whence it is self-evident what we are to think of the imitation of nature as a principle of art; for so far from the merely contingent beauty of nature providing the rule to art, the fact is, rather, that what art creates in its perfection is the principle and norm for the judgment of natural beauty.

It is easy to conceive how the aesthetic product is to be distinguished from the *common artifact*, since all aesthetic creation is absolutely free in regard to its principle, in that the artist can be driven to create by a contradiction, indeed, but only by one which lies in the highest regions of his own nature; whereas every other sort of creation is occasioned by a contradiction which lies outside the actual producer, and thus has in every case a goal outside itself.[11] This independence of external goals is the source of that holiness and purity of art, which goes so far that it not

---

[10] This passage replaced in the author's copy by the following: For although there are sublime works of art, and sublimity is customarily contrasted with beauty, there is actually no true objective opposition between beauty and sublimity; the truly and absolutely beautiful is invariably also sublime, and the sublime (if it truly is so) is beautiful as well.

[11] (Absolute transition into the objective).

only rules out relationship with all mere sensory pleasure, to demand which of art is the true nature of barbarism; or with the useful, to require which of art is possible only in an age which supposes the highest efforts of the human spirit to consist in economic discoveries.[12] It actually excludes relation with everything pertaining to morality, and even leaves far beneath it the sciences (which in point of disinterestedness stand closest to art), simply because they are always directed to a goal outside themselves, and must ultimately themselves serve merely as a means for the highest (namely art).

So far as particularly concerns the relation of art to science, the two are so utterly opposed in tendency, that if science were ever to have discharged its whole task, as art has always discharged it, they would both have to coincide and merge into one – which is proof of directions that they are radically opposed. For though science at its highest level has one and the same business as art, this business, owing to the manner of effecting it, is an endless one for science, so that one may say that art constitutes the ideal of science, and where art is, science has yet to attain to. From this, too, it is apparent why and to what extent there is no genius in science; not indeed that it would be impossible for a scientific problem to be solved by means of genius, but because this same problem whose solution can be found by genius, is also soluble mechanically. Such, for example, is the Newtonian system of gravitation, which could have been a discovery of genius, and in its first discoverer, Kepler, really was so, but could equally also have been a wholly scientific discovery, which it actually became in the hands of Newton. Only what art brings forth is simply and *solely* possible through genius, since in every task that art has discharged, an infinite contradiction is reconciled. What science brings forth, *can* be brought forth through genius, but it is not necessarily engendered through this. It therefore is and remains problematic in science, i.e., one can, indeed, always say definitely where it is not present, but never where it is. There are but few indications which allow us to infer genius in the sciences; (that one has to infer it is already evidence of the peculiarity of the matter). It is, for example, assuredly not present, where a whole, such as a system, arises piecemeal and as though by putting together. One would thus have to suppose, conversely, that genius is present, where the idea of the whole has manifestly preceded the individual parts. For since the idea of the whole cannot in fact become clear save through its development in the individual parts, while those parts, on the other hand, are possible only through the idea of the whole, there seems to be a contradiction here which is possible only through an act of genius, i.e., an unexpected concurrence of the unconscious with the conscious activity. Another ground for the presumption of genius in the sciences would be if someone were to say and maintain things whose meaning he could not possibly have understood entirely, either owing to the period at which he lived, or by reason of his other utterances; so that he has thus asserted something apparently with consciousness, which he could in fact only have asserted unconsciously. It

---

[12] Beetroots.

could, however be readily shown in a number of ways, that even these grounds for the presumption may be delusive in the extreme.

Genius is thus marked off from everything that consists in mere talent or skill by the fact that through it a contradiction is resolved, which is soluble absolutely and otherwise by nothing else. In all producing, even of the most ordinary and commonplace sort, an unconscious activity operates along with the conscious one; but only a producing whose condition was an infinite opposition of the two activities is an aesthetic producing, and one that is *only* possible through genius.

§3 Corollaries
Relation of Art to Philosophy

Now that we have deduced the nature and character of the art-product as completely as was necessary for purposes of the present enquiry, there is nothing more we need do except to set forth the relation which the philosophy of art bears to the whole system of philosophy.

1. The whole of philosophy starts, and must start, from a principle which, *qua* absolutely identical, is utterly nonobjective. But now how is this absolutely nonobjective to be called up to consciousness and understood – a thing needful, if it is the condition for understanding the whole of philosophy? That it can no more be apprehended through concepts than it is capable of being set forth by means of them, stands in no need of proof. Nothing remains, therefore, but for it to be set forth in an immediate intuition, though this is itself in turn inconceivable, and, since its object is to be something utterly nonobjective, seems, indeed, to be self-contradictory. But now were such an intuition in fact to exist, having as its object the absolutely identical, in itself neither subjective nor objective, and were we, in respect of this intuition, which can only be an intellectual one, to appeal to immediate experience, then how, in that case, could even this intuition be in turn posited objectively? How, that is, can it be established beyond doubt, that such an intuition does not rest upon a purely subjective deception, if it possesses no objectivity that is universal and acknowledged by all men? This universally acknowledged and altogether incontestable objectivity of intellectual intuition is art itself. For the aesthetic intuition simply is the intellectual intuition become objective.[13] The work of art merely reflects to me what is otherwise not reflected by anything, namely that absolutely identical which has already divided itself even

---

[13] The preceding is replaced in the author's copy by: The whole of philosophy starts, and must start, from a principle which, as the absolute principle, is also at the same time the absolutely identical. An absolutely simple and identical cannot be grasped or communicated through description, nor through concepts at all. It can only be intuited. Such an intuition is the organ of all philosophy. – But this intuition, which is an intellectual rather than a sensory one, and has as its object neither the objective nor the subjective, but the absolutely identical, in itself neither subjective nor objective, is itself merely an internal one, which cannot in turn become objective for itself: it can become objective only through a second intuition. This second intuition is the aesthetic.

in the self. Hence, that which the philosopher allows to be divided even in the primary act of consciousness, and which would otherwise be inaccessible to any intuition, comes, through the miracle of art, to be radiated back from the products thereof.

It is not, however, the first principle of philosophy, merely, and the first intuition that philosophy proceeds from, which initially become objective through aesthetic production; the same is true of the entire mechanism which philosophy deduces, and on which in turn it rests.

Philosophy sets out from an infinite dichotomy of opposed activities;[14] but the same dichotomy is also the basis of every aesthetic production, and by each individual manifestation of art it is wholly resolved.[15] Now what is this wonderful power whereby, in productive intuition (so the philosopher claims), an infinite opposition is removed? So far we have not been able to render this mechanism entirely intelligible, since it is only the power of art which can unveil it completely. This productive power is the same whereby art also achieves the impossible, namely to resolve an infinite opposition in a finite product. It is the poetic gift, which in its primary potentiality constitutes the primordial intuition, and conversely.[16] What we speak of as the poetic gift is merely productive intuition, reiterated to its highest power. It is one and the same capacity that is active in both, the only one whereby we are able to think and to couple together even what is contradictory – and its name is imagination. Hence, that which appears to us outside the sphere of consciousness, as real, and that which appears within it, as ideal, or as the world of art, are also products of one and the same activity. But this very fact, that where the conditions of emergence are otherwise entirely similar, the one takes its origin from outside consciousness, the other from within it, constitutes the eternal difference between them which can never be removed.

To be sure, then, the real world evolves entirely from the same original opposition as must also give rise to the world of art, which has equally to be viewed as one great whole, and which in all its individual products depicts only the one infinite. But outside consciousness this opposition is only infinite inasmuch as an infinity is exhibited by the objective world as a *whole*, and never by any individual object; whereas for art this opposition is an infinite one in regard to *every single object*, and infinity is exhibited in every one of its products. For if aesthetic production proceeds from freedom, and if it is precisely for freedom that this opposition of conscious and unconscious activities is an absolute one, there is properly speaking but one absolute work of art, which may indeed exist in altogether different versions, yet is still only one, even though it should not yet exist in its most ultimate

---

[14] Philosophy makes all production of intuition proceed from a separation of activities that were previously not opposed.

[15] The final words, 'and . . . resolved,' struck out in the author's copy.

[16] Replaced in the author's copy by: That productive power whereby the object arises is likewise the source from which an object also springs forth to art, save only that in the first case the activity is dull and limited, while in the latter it is clear and boundless. The poetic gift, regarded in its primary potentiality, is the soul's most primitive capacity for production, insofar as the latter declares itself in finite and actual things, and conversely . . . .

form. It can be no objection to this view, that if so, the very liberal use now made of the predicate 'work of art' will no longer do. Nothing is a work of art which does not exhibit an infinite, either directly, or at least by reflection. Are we to call works of art, for example, even such compositions as by nature depict only the individual and subjective? In that case we shall have to bestow this title also upon every epigram, which preserves merely a momentary sensation or current impression; though indeed the great masters who have practiced in such genres were seeking to bring forth objectivity itself only through the totality of their creations, and used them simply as a means to depict a whole infinite life, and to project it back from a many-faceted mirror.

2. If aesthetic intuition is merely transcendental[17] intuition become objective, it is self-evident that art is at once the only true and eternal organ and document of philosophy, which ever and again continues to speak to us of what philosophy cannot depict in external form, namely the unconscious element in acting and producing, and its original identity with the conscious. Art is paramount to the philosopher, precisely because it opens to him, as it were, the holy of holies, where burns in eternal and original unity, as if in a single flame, that which in nature and history is rent asunder, and in life and action, no less than in thought, must forever fly apart. The view of nature, which the philosopher frames artificially, is for art the original and natural one. What we speak of as nature is a poem lying pent in a mysterious and wonderful script. Yet the riddle could reveal itself, were we to recognize in it the odyssey of the spirit, which, marvelously deluded, seeks itself, and in seeking flies from itself; for through the world of sense there glimmers, as if through words the meaning, as if through dissolving mists the land of fantasy, of which we are in search. Each splendid painting owes, as it were, its genesis to a removal of the invisible barrier dividing the real from the ideal world, and is no more than the gateway, through which come forth completely the shapes and scenes of that world of fantasy which gleams but imperfectly through the real. Nature, to the artist, is nothing more than it is to the philosopher, being simply the ideal world appearing under permanent restrictions, or merely the imperfect reflection of a world existing, not outside him, but within.

But now what may be the source of this kinship of philosophy and art, despite the opposition between them, is a question already sufficiently answered in what has gone before.

We therefore close with the following observation. – A system is completed when it is led back to its starting point. But this is precisely the case with our own. The ultimate ground of all harmony between subjective and objective could be exhibited in its original identity only through intellectual intuition; and it is precisely this ground which, by means of the work of art, has been brought forth entirely from the subjective, and rendered wholly objective, in such wise, that we have gradually led our object, the self itself, up to the very point where we ourselves were standing when we began to philosophize.

[17] Intellectual (author's correction).

But now if it is art alone which can succeed in objectifying with universal validity what the philosopher is able to present in a merely subjective fashion, there is one more conclusion yet to be drawn. Philosophy was born and nourished by poetry in the infancy of knowledge, and with it all those sciences it has guided toward perfection; we may thus expect them, on completion, to flow back like so many individual streams into the universal ocean of poetry from which they took their source. Nor is it in general difficult to say what the medium for this return of science to poetry will be; for in mythology such a medium existed, before the occurrence of a breach now seemingly beyond repair.[18] But how a new mythology is itself to arise, which shall be the creation, not of some individual author, but of a new race, personifying, as it were, one single poet – that is a problem whose solution can be looked for only in the future destinies of the world, and in the course of history to come.

Translated by Peter Heath

---

[18] The further development of this idea is contained in a treatise *On Mythology*, already sketched out a number of years ago.

15.

G. W. F. Hegel, Lectures on Aesthetics (Vorlesungen über die Ästhetik): *Introduction (1835)*

In the *Phenomenology of Spirit* (1807) Hegel devotes a substantial section to the spiritual – cultural-historical – content of art, and in the later *Encyclopaedia of the Philosophical Sciences* (1830) he examines art, in a shorter section, under the category of 'Objective Spirit'. But the lectures on aesthetics, where Hegel's views are most comprehensively set out, are on an altogether different scale (taking up three volumes of the *Werke* edition of his philosophy, as edited by Eva Moldenhauer and Karl Markus Michel). Indeed, it is evidence of the remarkable productivity of Hegel's mind that the lecture courses on aesthetics were never prepared by him for publication.

Hegel's central thesis is that art is essentially beautiful, and its beauty consists in its sensuous revelation of truth. Its truthfulness lies in its manifestation of the spiritual condition of the society in which it is produced. In this respect Hegel's philosophy of art is embedded within his wider philosophical system in that he identifies it alongside religion and philosophy as containing a truth-revealing capacity. However, art does this it in its own way, namely, by means of sensuous images. Religion, by contrast, operates with mental images as its material, whereas philosophy functions with pure concepts. Hegel describes the artwork as a 'free reconciled totality', that is, as a mediation of sensuous image with its content, its idea.

The primary motivation of the artist is the creation of beauty, a process that entails the revelation of truth. These two elements are fundamentally connected in the appearance of any artwork. Were art to be subservient to some other purpose – deliberately employed for extra-aesthetic proposes – it would be attempting to achieve by means of beauty something that is supposedly more fundamental than beauty (the extra-aesthetic purpose). Hegel suggests that in its 'freedom alone is fine art truly art'.[1] When it is free it follows its own distinctive medium. But – and this is the revolutionary insight – in its freedom it actually becomes what Hegel describes as a deposit for the 'richest inner intuitions and ideas' that a nation possesses.[2] The insight is that the more free or autonomous art is the more it

[1] G. W. F. Hegel, trans. T. M. Knox, *Aesthetics: Lectures on Fine Art*, volume I (Oxford: Clarendon Press, 1975), p. 7 (*HW* XIII, 20).
[2] Ibid., p. 7 (*HW* XIII, 21).

reveals to us about the society in which it is produced: it reveals its 'spirit' (*Geist*). This view places him completely at odds with Kant, whose theory of aesthetic judgements he criticises as 'directed only to the external surface on which feelings play', in contrast to his own view, which holds that art has a meaning-bearing content that is irreducible to appearances and subjective delight. Given this identification of beauty with the revelation of truth (appropriately understood), it is clear why Hegel rejects the philosophical significance of natural beauty: it is not a manifestation of 'spirit'.

Hegel argues that art's expressive revelatory capacity is superior to 'historical writing'. Historical writing contains information about contingent events, unlike art which reveals to us 'the eternal powers that govern history'.[3] Art thus points beyond itself to what Hegel calls 'a higher reality'.[4] The philosophical interpreter can decipher the artwork to learn the 'higher reality' conveyed by its essentially expressive-revelatory character. This approach might be characterised generally as an analysis of form. The form of each work of art is both its possibility and its limitation. It is the case with romantic art, for instance, that its failure is the failure of its form to encompass the 'actuality' in which it is situated (the complex modern Christian conception of the relation of the divine and humanity). And this is instructive: it reveals to us something about the truth which art is failing to represent. It is in this context that Hegel introduces his first thoughts on the famous discussion of the death of art. The death of art may be a loss in one sense, but it is indicative of progress in the life of the spirit in that the traditional forms of classical art can no longer encompass the truth about human beings' conceptions of their spiritual lives. Hegel elsewhere suggests that art has been superseded by religion and philosophy, particularly the latter, in terms of its truth-expressing capacity.

Over the course of the many pages of the lectures Hegel gives greater precision to the expressive-revelatory function of art. In the following selection, he outlines the idea of the expressive-revelatoriness of art. He differentiates between the different aesthetic media and between the historical epochs in terms of their capacity to express the 'Idea' or truth. Ultimately, poetry is the highest art. But Hegel's historical approach opens up a truly profound understanding of the motivations behind various historical epochs in a way that does justice to the artworks themselves. The different periods of art are not primarily determined by levels of technical competence, but rather by the spiritual state in which the artist produces.

---

[3] Ibid., p. 9 (*HW* XIII, 23).
[4] Ibid., p. 9 (*HW* XIII, 22).

DIVISION OF THE SUBJECT[†]

1. After the above introductory remarks, it is now time to pass to the study of our object-matter. But we are still in the introduction, and an introduction cannot do more than lay down, for the sake of explanation, the general sketch of the entire course which will be followed by our subsequent scientific considerations. As, however, we have spoken of art as proceeding from the absolute Idea, and have even assigned as its end the sensuous representation of the absolute itself, we shall have to conduct this review in a way to show, at least in general, how the particular divisions of the subject spring from the conception of artistic beauty as the representation of the absolute. Therefore we must attempt to awaken a very general idea of this conception itself.

It has already been said that the content of art is the Idea, and that its form lies in the plastic use of images accessible to sense. These two sides art has to reconcile into a full and united totality. The *first* attribution which this involves is the requirement that the content, which is to be offered to artistic representation, shall show itself to be in its nature worthy of such representation. Otherwise we only obtain a bad combination, whereby a content that will not submit to plasticity and to external presentation, is forced into that form, and a matter which is in its nature prosaic is expected to find an appropriate mode of manifestation in the form antagonistic to its nature.

The *second* requirement, which is derivable from this first, demands of the content of art that it should not be anything abstract in itself. This does not mean that it must be concrete as the sensuous is concrete in contrast to everything spiritual and intellectual, these being taken as in themselves simple and abstract. For everything that has genuine truth in spirit (*Geist*) as well as in nature is concrete in itself, and has, in spite of its universality, nevertheless, both subjectivity and particularity within it. If we say, e.g., of God that he is simply *One*, the supreme Being as such, we have only enunciated a lifeless abstraction of the irrational understanding. Such a God, as he himself is not apprehended in his concrete truth, can afford no material for art, least of all for plastic art. Hence the Jews and the Turks have not been able to represent their God, who does not even amount to such an abstraction of the understanding, in the positive way in which Christians have done so. For God in Christianity is conceived in His truth, and therefore, as in Himself thoroughly concrete, as a person, as a subject, and more closely determined, as spirit. What He is as spirit unfolds itself to the religious apprehension as the Trinity of Persons, which at the same time in relation with itself is *One*. Here is essentiality, universality, and particularity, together with their reconciled unity; and it is only such unity that constitutes the concrete. Now, as a content

---

[†]*HW* XIII, 100–124. *The Introduction to Hegel's Philosophy of Fine Art* (London: Kegan Paul, Trench, Trübner and Co., 1905).

in order to possess truth at all must be of this concrete nature, art demands the same concreteness, because a mere abstract universal has not in itself the vocation to advance to particularity and phenomenal manifestation and to unity with itself therein.

If a true and therefore concrete content is to have corresponding to it a sensuous form and modelling, this sensuous form must, in the third place, be no less emphatically something individual, wholly concrete in itself, and one. The character of concreteness as belonging to both elements of art, to the content as to the representation, is precisely the point in which both may coincide and correspond to one another; as, for instance, the natural shape of the human body is such a sensuous concrete as is capable of representing spirit, which is concrete in itself, and of displaying itself in conformity therewith. Therefore we ought to abandon the idea that it is a mere matter of accident than an actual phenomenon of the external world is chosen to furnish a shape thus conformable to truth. Art does not appropriate this form either because it simply finds it existing or because there is no other. The concrete content itself involves the element of external and actual, we may say indeed of sensible manifestation. But in compensation this sensuous concrete, in which a content essentially belonging to spirit expresses itself, is in its own nature addressed to the inward being; its external element of shape, whereby the content is made perceptible and imaginable, has the aim of existing purely for the heart and spirit. This is the only reason for which content and artistic shape are fashioned in conformity with each other. The *mere* sensuous concrete, external nature as such, has not this purpose for its exclusive ground of origin. The birds' variegated plumage shines unseen, and their song dies away unheard, the *Cereus* which blossoms only for a night withers without having been admired in the wilds of southern forests, and these forests, jungles of the most beautiful and luxuriant vegetation, with the most odorous and aromatic perfumes, perish and decay no less unenjoyed. The work of art has not such a naïve self-centred being, but is essentially a question, an address to the responsive heart, an appeal to affections and to spirits.

Although the artistic bestowal of sensuous form is in this respect not accidental, yet on the other hand it is not the highest mode of apprehending the spiritually concrete. Thought is a higher mode than representation by means of the sensuous concrete. Although in a relative sense abstract, yet it must not be one-sided but concrete thinking, in order to be true and rational. Whether a given content has sensuous artistic representation for its adequate form, or in virtue of its nature essentially demands a higher and more spiritual embodiment, is a distinction that displays itself at once, if, for instance, we compare the Greek gods with God as conceived according to Christian ideas. The Greek god is not abstract but individual, and is closely akin to the natural human shape; the Christian God is equally a concrete personality, but in the mode of pure spiritual existence, and is to be known as spirit and in spirit. His medium of existence is therefore essentially inward knowledge and not external natural form, by means of which He can only be represented imperfectly, and not in the whole depth of His idea.

But inasmuch as the task of art is to represent the idea to direct perception in sensuous shape, and not in the form of thought or of pure spirituality as such, and seeing that this work of representation has its value and dignity in the correspondence and the unity of the two sides, i.e. of the Idea and its plastic embodiment, it follows that the level and excellency of art in attaining a realization adequate to its idea, must depend upon the grade of inwardness and unity with which Idea and Shape display themselves as fused into one.

Thus the higher truth is spiritual being that has attained a shape adequate to the conception of spirit. This is what furnishes the principle of division for the science of art. For before the spirit can attain the true notion of its absolute essence, it has to traverse a course of stages whose ground is in this idea itself; and to this evolution of the content with which it supplies itself, there corresponds an evolution, immediately connected therewith, of the plastic forms of art, under the shape of which the spirit as artist presents to itself the consciousness of itself.

This evolution within the art-spirit has again in its own nature two sides. In the *first* place the development itself is a spiritual and universal one, in so far as the graduated series of definite *conceptions of the world* as the definite but comprehensive consciousness of nature, man and God, gives itself artistic shape; and, in the *second* place, this *universal* development of art is obliged to provide itself with external existence and sensuous form, and the definite modes of the sensuous art-existence are themselves a totality of necessary distinctions in the realm of art – which are *the several arts.* It is true, indeed, that the necessary kinds of artistic representation are on the one hand *qua* spiritual of a very general nature, and not restricted to any one material; while sensuous existence contains manifold varieties of matter. But as this latter, like spirit, has the Idea potentially for its inner soul, it follows from this that particular sensuous materials have a close affinity and secret accord with the spiritual distinctions and types of art presentation.

In its completeness, however, our science divides itself into three principal portions.

First, we obtain a *general part.* It has for its content and object the universal Idea of artistic beauty – this beauty being conceived as the Ideal – together with the nearer relation of the latter both to nature and to subjective artistic production.

Secondly, there develops itself out of the idea of artistic beauty a *particular* part, in as far as the essential differences which this idea contains in itself evolve themselves into a scale of *particular* plastic forms.

In the *third* place there results a *final* part, which has for its subject the individualization of artistic beauty, that consists in the advance of art to the sensuous realization of its shapes and its self-completion as a system of the several arts and their genera and species.

2. With respect to the first part, we must begin by recalling to mind, in order to make the sequel intelligible, that the Idea *qua* the beautiful in art is not the Idea as such, in the mode in which a metaphysical logic apprehends it as the absolute,

but the Idea as developed into concrete form fit for reality, and as having entered into immediate and adequate unity with this reality. For the *Idea as such*, although it is the essentially and actually true, is yet the truth only in its generality which has not yet taken objective shape; but the *Idea* as the *beautiful in art* is at once the Idea when specially determined as in its essence individual reality, and also an individual shape of reality essentially destined to embody and reveal the Idea. This amounts to enunciating the requirement that the Idea, and its plastic mould as concrete reality, are to be made completely adequate to one another. When reduced to such form the Idea, as a reality moulded in conformity with the conception of the Idea, is the *Ideal*. The problem of this conformity might, to begin with, be understood in the sense that any Idea would serve, so long as the actual shape, it did not matter what shape, represented this particular Idea and no other. But if so, the required truth of he Ideal is confounded with mere correctness, which consists in the expression of any meaning whatever in appropriate fashion so that its import may be readily recognized in the shape created. The Ideal is not to be thus understood. Any content whatever may attain to being represented quite adequately, judged by the standard of its own nature, but it does not therefore gain the right to claim the artistic beauty of the Ideal. Compared indeed with ideal beauty, even the presentation will in such a case appear defective. From this point of view we must remark to begin with, what cannot be proved till later, that the defects of a work of art are not to be regarded simply as always due, for instance, to individual unskilfulness. *Defectiveness of form* arises from *defectiveness of content*. So, for example, the Chinese, Indians, and Egyptians in their artistic shapes, their forms of deities, and their idols, never got beyond a formless phase, or one of a vicious and false definiteness of form, and were unable to attain genuine beauty; because their mythological ideas, the content and thought of their works of art, were as yet indeterminate in themselves, or of a vicious determinateness, and did not consist in the content that is absolute in itself. The more that works of art excel in true beauty of presentation, the more profound is the inner truth of their content and thought. And in dealing with this point, we have not to think merely perhaps of the greater or lesser skill with which the natural forms as given in external reality are apprehended and imitated. For in certain stages of art-consciousness and of representation, the distortion and disfigurement of natural structures is not unintentional technical inexpertness and want of skill, but intentional alteration, which emanates from the content that is in consciousness, and is required thereby. Thus, from this point of view, there is such a thing as imperfect art, which may be quite perfect, both technically and in other respects, *in its determinate* sphere, yet reveals itself to be defective when compared with the conception of art as such, and with the Ideal. Only in the highest art are the Idea and the representation genuinely adequate to one another, in the sense that the outward shape given to the Idea is in itself essentially and actually the true shape, because the content of the Idea, which that shape expresses, is itself the true and real content. It is a corollary from this, as we indicated above, that the Idea must be defined in and through itself as concrete totality, and thereby possess in itself the principle and standard of its particularization and determination in external appearance. For example, the Christian imagination will be able to represent God only in human form and with man's spiritual expression, because it is herein that God Himself is completely known in Himself as spirit. Determinateness is, as it were, the bridge to phenomenal existence. Where this determinateness is not totality derived from the Idea itself, where the Idea is not conceived as self-determining and self-particularizing, the Idea remains abstract and has its determinateness, and therefore the principle that dictates its particular and exclusively appropriate mode of presentation, not in itself but external to it. Therefore, the Idea when still abstract has even its shape external, and not dictated by itself. The Idea, however, which is concrete in itself bears the principle of its mode of manifestation within itself, and is by that means the free process of giving shape to itself. Thus it is only the truly concrete Idea that can generate the true shape, and this correspondence of the two is the Ideal.

3. Now because the Idea is in this fashion concrete unity, it follows that this unity can enter into the art-consciousness only by the expansion and reconciliation of the particularities of the Idea, and it is through this evolution that artistic beauty comes to possess a *totality of particular stages and forms*. Therefore, after we have studied the beauty of art in itself and on its own merits, we must see how beauty as a whole breaks up into its particular determinations. This gives, as our *second part, the doctrine of the types of art*. These forms find their genesis in the different modes of grasping the Idea as artistic content, whereby is conditioned a difference of the form in which it manifests itself. Hence the types of art are nothing but the different relations of content and shape, relations which emanate from the Idea itself, and furnish thereby the true basis of division for this sphere. For the principle of division must always be contained in *that* conception whose particularization and division is in question.

We have here to consider *three* relations of the Idea to its outward shaping.

(α) First, the Idea gives rise to the beginning of Art when, being itself still in its indistinctness and obscurity, or in vicious untrue determinateness, it is made the import of artistic creations. As indeterminate it does not yet possess in itself that individuality which the Ideal demands; its abstractness and one-sidedness leave its shape to be outwardly bizarre and defective. The first form of art is therefore rather a mere search after plastic portrayal than a capacity of genuine representation. The Idea has not yet found the true form even within itself, and therefore continues to be merely the struggle and aspiration thereafter. In general terms we may call this form the *Symbolic* form of art. In it the abstract Idea has its outward shape external to itself in natural sensuous matter, with which the process of shaping begins, and from which, *qua* outward expression, it is inseparable.

Natural objects are thus primarily left unaltered, and yet at the same time invested with the substantial Idea as their significance, so that they receive the vocation of expressing it, and claim to be interpreted as though the Idea itself were present in them. At the root of this is the fact that natural objects have in them an aspect in which they are capable of representing a universal meaning. But as an adequate correspondence is not yet possible, this reference can only concern *an abstract attribute*, as when a lion is used to mean strength.

On the other hand, this abstractness of the relation brings to consciousness no less strongly the foreignness of the Idea to natural phenomena; and the Idea, having no other reality to express it, expatiates in all these shapes, seeks itself in them in all their unrest and disproportion, but nevertheless does not find them adequate to itself. Then it proceeds to exaggerate the natural shapes and the phenomena of reality into indefiniteness and disproportion, to intoxicate itself in them, to seethe and ferment in them, to do violence to them, to distort and explode them into unnatural shapes, and strives by the variety, hugeness, and splendour of the forms employed to exalt the phenomenon to the level of the Idea. For the Idea is here still more or less indeterminate and non–plastic, but the natural objects are in their shape thoroughly determinate.

Hence, in view of the unsuitability of the two elements to each other, the relation of the Idea to objective reality becomes a *negative* one, for the former, as in its nature inward, is unsatisfied with such an externality, and as being its inner universal substance persists in exaltation or *Sublimity* beyond and above all this inadequate abundance of shapes. In virtue of this sublimity the natural phenomena and the human shapes and incidents are accepted, and left as they were, though at the same time understood to be inadequate to their significance, which is exalted far above every earthly content.

These aspects may be pronounced in general terms to constitute the character of the primitive artistic pantheism of the East, which either charges even the meanest objects with the absolute import, or again coerces nature with violence into the expression of its view. By this means it becomes bizarre, grotesque, and tasteless, or turns the infinite but abstract freedom of the substantive Idea disdainfully against all phenomenal being as null and evanescent. By such means the import cannot be completely embodied in the expression, and in spite of all aspiration and endeavour the reciprocal inadequacy of shape and Idea remains insuperable. This may be taken as the first form of art, – Symbolic art with its aspiration, its disquiet, its mystery and its sublimity.

(β) In the second form of art, which we propose to call '*Classical*,' the double defect of symbolic art is cancelled. The plastic shape of symbolic art is imperfect, because, in the first place, the Idea in it only enters into consciousness in *abstract* determinateness or indeterminateness, and, in the second place, this must always make the conformity of shape to import defective, and in its turn merely abstract. The classical form of art is the solution of this double difficulty; it is the free and adequate embodiment of the Idea in the shape that, according to its conception, is peculiarly appropriate to the Idea itself. With it, therefore, the Idea is capable of entering into free and complete accord. Hence, the classical type of art is the first to afford the production and intuition of the completed Ideal, and to establish it as a realized fact.

The conformity, however, of notion and reality in classical art must not be taken in the purely *formal* sense of the agreement of a content with the external shape given to it, any more than this could be the case with the Ideal itself. Otherwise every copy from nature, and every type of countenance, every landscape, flower, or scene, etc., which forms the purport of any representation, would be at once made classical by the agreement which it displays between form and content. On the contrary, in classical art the peculiarity of the content consists in being itself concrete idea, and, as such, the concrete spiritual; for only the spiritual is the truly inner self. To suit such a content, then, we must search out that in Nature which on its own merits belongs to the essence and actuality of the spirit. It must be the absolute notion that *invented* the shape appropriate to concrete spirit, so that the *subjective* notion – in this case the spirit of art – has merely *found* it, and brought it, as an existence possessing natural shape, into accord with free individual spirituality. This shape, with which the Idea as spiritual – as individually determinate spirituality – invests itself when manifested as a temporal phenomenon, is *the human form*. Personification and anthropomorphism have often been decried as a degradation of the spiritual; but art, in as far as its end is to bring before perception the spiritual in sensuous form, must advance to such anthropomorphism, as it is only in its proper body that spirit is adequately revealed to sense. The migration of souls is in this respect a false abstraction, and physiology ought to have made it one of its axioms that life had necessarily in its evolution to attain to the human shape, as the sole sensuous phenomenon that is appropriate to spirit. The human form is employed in the classical type of art not as mere sensuous existence, but exclusively as the existence and physical form corresponding to spirit, and is therefore exempt from all the deficiencies of what is merely sensuous, and from the contingent finiteness of phenomenal existence. The outer shape must be thus purified in order to express in itself a content adequate to itself; and again, if the conformity of import and content is to be complete, the spiritual meaning which is the content must be of a particular kind. It must, that is to say, be qualified to express itself completely in the physical form of man, without projecting into another world beyond the scope of such an expression in sensuous and bodily terms. This condition has the effect that spirit is by it at once specified as a particular case of spirit, as human spirit, and not as simply absolute and eternal, inasmuch as spirit in this latter sense is incapable of proclaiming and expressing itself otherwise than as spiritual being.

Out of this latter point arises, in its turn, the defect which brings about the dissolution of classical art, and demands a transition into a third and higher form, viz. into the *romantic* form of art.

(γ) The romantic form of art destroys the completed union of the Idea and its reality, and recurs, though in a higher phase, to that difference and antagonism of two aspects which was left unvanquished by symbolic art. The classical type attained the highest excellence, of which the sensuous embodiment of art is capable; and if it is in any way defective, the defect is in art as a whole, i.e. in the limitation of its sphere. This limitation consists in the fact that art as such takes for its object spirit – the conception of which is *infinite* concrete universality – in the shape of *sensuous* concreteness, and in the classical phase sets up the perfect amalgamation of spiritual and sensuous existence as a Conformity of the two. Now, as a matter of fact, in such an amalgamation spirit cannot be represented according to its true notion. For spirit is the infinite subjectivity of the Idea, which, as absolute inwardness, is not capable of finding free expansion in its true nature on condition of remaining transposed into a bodily medium as the existence appropriate to it.

As *an escape from such a condition* the romantic form of art in its turn dissolves the inseparable unity of the classical phase, because it has won a significance which goes beyond the classical form of art and its mode of expression. This significance – if we may recall familiar ideas – coincides with what Christianity declares to be true of God as Spirit, in contradistinction to the Greek faith in gods which forms the essential and appropriate content for classical art. In Greek art the concrete import is potentially, but not explicitly, the unity of the human and divine nature; a unity which, just because it is purely *immediate* and *not explicit*, is capable of adequate manifestation in an immediate and sensuous mode. The Greek god is the object of naïve intuition and sensuous imagination. His shape is, therefore, the bodily shape of man. The circle of his power and of his being is individual and individually limited. In relation with the subject, he is, therefore, an essence and a power with which the subject's inner being is merely in latent unity, not itself possessing this unity as inward subjective knowledge. Now the higher stage is the *knowledge* of this *latent* unity, which as latent is the import of the classical form of art, and capable of perfect representation in bodily shape. The elevation of the latent or potential into self-conscious knowledge produces an enormous difference. It is the infinite difference which, e.g., separates man as such from the animals. Man is animal, but even in his animal functions he is not confined within the latent and potential as the animal is, but becomes conscious of them, learns to know them, and raises them – as, for instance, the process of diges-tion – into self-conscious science. By this means Man breaks the boundary of merely potential and immediate consciousness, so that just for the reason that he knows himself to be animal, he ceases to be animal, and, as *spirit*, attains to self-knowledge.

If in the above fashion the unity of the human and divine nature, which in the former phase was potential, is raised from an *immediate* to a *conscious* unity, it follows that the true medium for the reality of this content is no longer the sensuous immediate existence of the spiritual, the human bodily shape, but *self-conscious inward intelligence*. Now, Christianity brings God before our intelligence *as spirit*, or mind – not as particularized individual spirit, but as absolute, in *spirit* and in truth. And for this reason Christianity retires from the sensuousness of imagination into spiritual inwardness, and makes this, not bodily shape, the medium and actual existence of its significance. So, too, the unity of the human and divine nature is a conscious unity, only to be realized by *spiritual* knowledge and in *spirit*. Thus the new content, won by this unity, is not inseparable from sensuous representation, as if that were adequate to it, but is freed from this immediate existence, which has to be posited as negative, absorbed, and reflected into the spiritual unity. In this way, romantic art must be considered as art transcending itself, while remaining within the artistic sphere and in artistic form.

Therefore, in short, we may abide by the statement that in this third stage the object (of art) is *free*, concrete spiritual being, which has the function of revealing itself as spiritual existence for the inward world of spirit. In conformity with such an object-matter, art cannot work for sensuous perception. It must address itself to the inward spirit, which coalesces with its object simply and as though this were itself, to the subjective inwardness, to the heart, the feeling, which, being spiritual, aspires to freedom within itself, and seeks and finds its reconciliation only in the spirit within. It is this *inner* world that forms the content of the romantic, and must therefore find its representation as such inward feeling, and in the show or presentation of such feeling. The world of inwardness celebrates its triumph over the outer world, and actually in the sphere of the outer and in its medium manifests this its victory, owing to which the sensuous appearance sinks into worthlessness.

But, on the other hand, this type of Art, like every other, needs an external vehicle of expression. Now the spiritual has withdrawn into itself out of the external and its immediate oneness therewith. For this reason, the sensuous externality of concrete form is accepted and represented, as in Symbolic art, as something transient and fugitive. And the same measure is dealt to the subjective finite spirit and will, even including the peculiarity or caprice of the individual, of character, action, etc., or of incident and plot. The aspect of external existence is committed to contingency, and left at the mercy of freaks of imagination, whose caprice is no more likely to mirror what is given *as* it is given, than to throw the shapes of the outer world into chance medley, or distort them into grotesqueness. For this external element no longer has its notion and significance, as in classical art, in its own sphere, and in its own medium. It has come to find them in the feelings, the display of which is *in themselves* instead of being in the external and *its* form of reality, and which have the power to preserve or to regain their state of reconciliation with themselves, in every accident, in every unessential circumstance that takes independent shape, in all misfortune and grief, and even in crime.

Owing to this, the characteristics of symbolic art, in difference, discrepancy, and severance of Idea and plastic shape, are here reproduced, but with an essential difference. In the sphere of the romantic, the Idea, whose defectiveness in the case of the symbol produced the defect of external shape, has to reveal itself in the medium of spirit and feelings as perfected in itself. And it is because of this higher perfection that it withdraws itself from any adequate union with the external element, inasmuch as it can seek and achieve its true reality and revelation nowhere but in itself.

This we may take as in the abstract the character of the symbolic, classical, and romantic forms of art, which represent the three relations of the Idea to its embodiment in the sphere of art. They consist in the aspiration after, and the attainment and transcendence of the Ideal as the true Idea of beauty.

4. The third part of our subject, in. contradistinction to the two just described, presupposes the conception of the Ideal, and the general types of art, inasmuch as it simply consists of their realization in particular sensuous media. Hence we have no longer to do with the inner development of artistic beauty in conformity with

its general fundamental principles. What we have to study is how these principles pass into actual existence, how they distinguish themselves in their external aspect, and how they give actuality to every element contained in the idea of beauty, separately and by itself *as a work of art*, and not merely as a general type. Now, what art transfers into external existence are the differences proper to the idea of beauty and immanent therein. Therefore, the general types of art must reveal themselves in this third part, as before, in the character of the fundamental principle that determines the arrangement and definition of the *several arts*; in other words, the species of art contain in themselves the same essential modifications as those with which we become acquainted as the general types of art. External objectivity, however, to which these forms are introduced through the medium of a sensuous and therefore *particular* material, affects these types in the way of making them *separate* into independent and so particular forms embodying their realization. For each type finds its definite character in some one definite external material, and its adequate actuality in the mode of portrayal which that prescribes. But, moreover, these types of art, being for all their determinateness, its *universal* forms, break the bounds of *particular* realization by a determinate form of art, and achieve existence in other arts as well, although in subordinate fashion. Therefore, the particular arts belong each of them specifically to *one* of the general types of art, and constitute *its adequate* external actuality; and also they represent, each of them after its own mode of external plasticity, the totality of the types of art.

Then, speaking generally, we are dealing in this third principal division with the beautiful of art, as it unfolds itself in the several arts and in their creations into a *world* of actualized beauty. The content of this world is the beautiful, and the true beautiful, as we saw, is spiritual being in concrete shape, the Ideal; or, more closely looked at, the absolute spirit, and the truth itself. This region, that of divine truth artistically represented to perception and to feeling, forms the centre of the whole world of art. It is the independent, free, and divine plasticity, which has thoroughly mastered the external elements of form and of medium, and wears them simply as a means to manifestation of itself. Still, as the beautiful unfolds itself in this region in the character of *objective* reality, and in so doing distinguishes within itself its individual aspects and elements, permitting them independent particularity, it follows that this centre erects its extremes, realized in their peculiar actuality, into its own antitheses. Thus one of these extremes comes to consist in an objectivity as yet devoid of spirit, in the merely natural vesture of God. At this point the external element takes plastic shape as something that has its spiritual aim and content, not in itself, but in another.

The other extreme is the divine as inward, as something known, as the variously particularized *subjective* existence of the Deity; it is the truth as operative and vital in sense, heart, and spirit of individual subjects, not persisting in the mould of its external shapes, but as having returned into subjective, individual inwardness. In such a mode, the Divine is at the same time distinguished from its first manifestation as Deity, and passes thereby into the diversity of particulars which belongs to all subjective knowledge – emotion, perception, and feeling. In the analogous province of religion, with which art at its highest stage is immediately connected, we conceive this same difference as follows. *First*, we think of the earthly natural life in its finiteness as standing on one side; but, then, *secondly*, consciousness makes God its object, in which the distinction of objectivity and subjectivity is done away. And at last, *thirdly*, we advance from God as such to the devotion of the community, that is, to God as living and present in the subjective consciousness. Just so these three chief modifications present themselves in the world of art in independent development.

(α) The *first* of the particular arts with which, according to their fundamental principle, we have to begin, is architecture considered as a fine art. Its task lies in so manipulating external inorganic nature that it becomes cognate to spirit, as an artistic outer world. The material of architecture is matter itself in its immediate externality as a heavy mass subject to mechanical laws, and its forms do not depart from the forms of inorganic nature, but are merely set in order in conformity with relations of the abstract understanding, i.e. with relations of symmetry. In this material and in such forms, the ideal as concrete spirituality does not admit of being realized. Hence the reality which is represented in them remains contrasted with the Idea, as something external which it has not penetrated, or has penetrated only to establish an abstract relation. For these reasons, the fundamental type of the fine art of building is the *symbolical* form of art. It is architecture that pioneers the way for the adequate realization of the God, and in this its service bestows hard toil upon existing nature, in order to disentangle it from the jungle of finitude and the abortiveness of chance. By this means it levels a space for the God, gives form to his external surroundings, and builds him his temple as a fit place for concentration of spirit, and for its direction to the absolute objects of spirit. It raises an enclosure round the assembly of those gathered together, as a defence against the threatening of the storm, against rain, the hurricane, and wild beasts, and reveals the will to assemble, although externally, yet in conformity with principles of art. With such import as this it has power to inspire its material and its forms more or less effectively, as the determinate character of the content on behalf of which it sets to work is more or less significant, more concrete or more abstract, more profound in sounding its own depths, or more dim and more superficial. So much, indeed, may architecture attempt in this respect as even to create an adequate artistic existence for such an import in its shapes and in its material. But in such a case it has already overstepped its own boundary, and is leaning to sculpture, the phase above it. For the limit of architecture lies precisely in this point, that it retains the spiritual as an inward existence over against the external forms of the art, and consequently must refer to what has soul only as to something other than its own creations.

(β) Architecture, however, as we have seen, has purified the external world, and endowed it with symmetrical order and with affinity to spirit; and the temple of the God, the house of his community, stands ready. Into this temple, then, in the *second* place, the God enters in the lightning–flash of individuality, which strikes and permeates the inert mass, while the infinite and no longer merely symmetrical form belonging to spirit itself concentrates and gives shape to the corresponding bodily existence. This is the task of *Sculpture*. In as far as in this art the spiritual inward being which architecture can but indicate makes itself at home in the sensuous shape and its external matter, and in as far as these two sides are so adapted to one another that neither is predominant, sculpture must be assigned the *classical form of art* as its fundamental type. For this reason the sensuous element itself has here no expression which could not be that of the spiritual element, just as, conversely, sculpture can represent no spiritual content which does not admit throughout of being adequately presented to perception in bodily form. Sculpture should place the spirit before us in its bodily form and in immediate unity therewith at rest and in peace; and the form should be animated by the content of spiritual individuality. And so the external sensuous matter is here no longer manipulated, either in conformity with its mechanical quality alone, as a mass possessing weight, nor in shapes belonging to the inorganic world, nor as indifferent to colour, etc.; but it is wrought in ideal forms of the human figure, and, it must be remarked, in all three spatial dimensions.

In this last respect we must claim for sculpture, that it is in it that the inward and spiritual are first revealed in their eternal repose and essential self-completeness. To such repose and unity with itself there can correspond only that external shape which itself maintains its unity and repose. And this is fulfilled by shape in its abstract spatiality.* The spirit which sculpture represents is that which is solid in itself, not broken up in the play of trivialities and of passions; and hence its external form too is not abandoned to any manifold phases of appearance, but appears under this one aspect only, as the abstraction of space in the whole of its dimensions.

(γ) Now, after architecture has erected the temple, and the hand of sculpture has supplied it with the statue of the God, then, in the third place, this god present to sense is confronted in the spacious halls of his house by the *community*. The community is the spiritual reflection into itself of such sensuous existence, and is the animating subjectivity and inner life which brings about the result that the determining principle for the content of art, as well as for the medium which represents it in outward form, comes to be particularization [dispersion into various shapes, attributes, incidents, etc.], individualization, and the subjectivity which they require. The solid unity which the God has in sculpture breaks up into the multitudinous inner lives of individuals, whose unity is not sensuous, but purely ideal.

It is only in this stage that God Himself comes to be really and truly spirit – the spirit in His (God's) community; for He here begins to be a to-and-fro, an alternation between His unity within himself and his realization in the individual's knowledge and in its separate being, as also in the common nature and union of the multitude. In the community, God is released from the abstractness of unexpanded self-identity, as well as from the simple absorption in a bodily medium, by which sculpture represents Him. And He is thus exalted into spiritual existence and into knowledge, into the reflected appearance which essentially displays itself as inward

---

*i.e. shape taken simply as an object filling space.

and as subjectivity. Therefore the higher content is now the spiritual nature, and that in its absolute shape. But the dispersion of which we have spoken reveals this at the same time as particular spiritual being, and as individual character. Now, what manifests itself in this phase as the main thing is not the serene quiescence of the God in Himself, but appearance as such, being which is *for* another, self-manifestation. And hence, in the phase we have reached, all the most manifold subjectivity in its living movement and operation – as human passion, action, and incident, and, in general, the wide realm of human feeling, will, and its negation – is for its own sake the object of artistic representation. In conformity with this content, the sensuous element of art has at once to show itself as made particular in itself and as adapted to subjective inwardness. Media that fulfil this requirement we have in colour, in musical sound, and finally in sound as the mere indication of inward perceptions and ideas; and as modes of realizing the import in question by help of these media we obtain painting, music, and poetry. In this region the sensuous medium displays itself as subdivided in its own being and universally set down as ideal. Thus it has the highest degree of conformity with the content of art, which, as such, is spiritual, and the connection of intelligible import and sensuous medium develops into closer intimacy than was possible in the case of architecture and sculpture. The unity attained, however, is a more inward unity, the weight of which is thrown wholly on the subjective side, and which, in as far as form and content are compelled to particularize themselves and give themselves merely ideal existence, can only come to pass at the expense of the objective universality of the content and also of its amalgamation with the immediately sensuous element.

The arts, then, of which form and content exalt themselves to ideality, abandon the character of symbolic architecture and the classical ideal of sculpture, and therefore borrow their type from the romantic form of art, whose mode of plasticity they are most adequately adapted to express. And they constitute a *totality* of arts, because the romantic type is the most concrete in itself.

i. The articulation of this *third sphere* of the individual arts may be determined as follows. The *first* art in it, which comes next to sculpture, is painting. It employs as a medium for its content and for the plastic embodiment of that content visibility as such in as far as it is specialized in its own nature, i.e. as developed into colour. It is true that the material employed in architecture and sculpture is also visible and coloured; but it is not, as in painting, visibility as such, not the simple light which, differentiating itself in virtue of its contrast with darkness, and in combination with the latter, gives rise to colour. This quality of visibility, made subjective in itself and treated as ideal, needs neither, like architecture, the abstractly mechanical attribute of mass as operative in the properties of heavy matter, nor, like sculpture, the complete sensuous attributes of space, even though concentrated into organic shapes. The visibility and the rendering visible which belong to painting have their differences in a more ideal form, in the several kinds of colour, and they liberate art from the sensuous completeness in space which attaches to material things, by restricting themselves to a plane surface.

On the other hand, the content also attains the most comprehensive specification. Whatever can find room in the human heart, as feeling, idea, and purpose; whatever it is capable of shaping into act – all this diversity of material is capable of entering into the varied content of painting. The whole realm of particular existence, from the highest embodiment of spirit down to the most isolated object of nature, finds a place here. For it is possible even for finite nature, in its particular scenes and phenomena, to make its appearance in the realm of art, if only some allusion to an element of spirit endows it with affinity to thought and feeling.

ii. The *second* art in which the romantic type realizes itself is contrasted with painting, and is music. Its medium, though still sensuous, yet develops into still more thorough subjectivity and particularization. Music, too, treats the sensuous as ideal, and does so by negating [*Aufheben*], and idealizing into the individual isolation of a single point, the indifferent externality of space, whose complete semblance is accepted and imitated by painting. The single point, *qua* such a negativity (excluding space) is in itself a concrete and active process of positive negation [*Aufheben*] within the attributes of matter, in the shape of a motion and tremor of the material body within itself and in its relation to itself. Such an inchoate ideality of matter, which appears no longer as under the form of space, but as temporal ideality, is sound, the sensuous set down as negated, with its abstract visibility converted into audibility, inasmuch as sound, so to speak, liberates the ideal content from its immersion in matter. This earliest inwardness of matter and inspiration of soul into it furnishes the medium for the mental inwardness – itself as yet indefinite – and for the soul into which spirit concentrates itself; and finds utterance in its tones for the heart with its whole gamut of feelings and passions. Thus music forms the centre of the romantic arts, just as sculpture represents the central point between architecture and the arts of romantic subjectivity. Thus, too, it forms the point of transition between abstract spatial sensuousness, such as painting employs, and the abstract spirituality of poetry. Music has within itself, like architecture, a relation of quantity comformable to the understanding, as the antithesis to emotion and inwardness; and has also as its basis a solid conformity to law on the part of the tones, of their conjunction, and of their succession.

iii. As regards the *third* and most spiritual mode of representation of the romantic art-type, we must look for it in *poetry*. Its characteristic peculiarity lies in the power with which it subjects to the spirit and to its ideas the sensuous element from which music and painting in their degree began to liberate art. For sound, the only external matter which poetry retains, is in it no longer the feeling of the sonorous itself, but is a *sign*, which by itself is void of import. And it is a sign of the idea which has become concrete in itself, and not merely of indefinite feeling and of its *nuances* and grades. This is how sound develops into the *Word*, as voice articulate in itself, whose import it is to indicate ideas and notions. The merely negative point up to which music had developed now makes its appearance as the completely concrete point, the point which is spirit, the self-conscious individual, which, producing out of itself the infinite space of its ideas, unites it with the temporal character of sound. Yet this sensuous element, which in music was still immediately one with inward feeling, is in poetry separated from the content of consciousness. In poetry the spirit determines this content for its own sake, and apart from all else, into the shape of ideas, and though it employs sound to express them, yet treats it solely as a symbol without value or import. Thus considered, sound may just as well be reduced to a mere letter, for the audible, like the visible, is thus depressed into a mere indication of spirit. For this reason the proper medium of poetical representation is the poetical imagination and spiritual portrayal itself. And as this element is common to all types of art, it follows that poetry runs through them all and develops itself independently in each. Poetry is the universal art of the spirit which has become free in its own nature, and which is not tied to find its realization in external sensuous matter, but expatiates exclusively in the inner space and inner time of the ideas and feelings. Yet just in this its highest phase art ends by transcending itself, inasmuch as it abandons the medium of a harmonious embodiment of spirit in sensuous form, and passes from the poetry of imagination into the prose of thought.

5. Such we may take to be the articulated totality of the particular arts, viz. the external art of architecture, the objective art of sculpture, and the subjective art of painting, music and poetry. Many other classifications have been attempted, for a work of art presents so many aspects, that, as has often been the case, first one and then another is made the basis of classification. For instance, one might take the sensuous medium. Thus architecture is treated as crystallization; sculpture, as the organic modelling of the material in its sensuous and spatial totality; painting, as the coloured surface and line; while in music, space, as such, passes into the point of time possessed of content within itself, until finally the external medium is in poetry depressed into complete insignificance. Or, again, these differences have been considered with reference to their purely abstract attributes of space and time. Such abstract peculiarities of works of art may, like their material medium, be consistently explored in their characteristic traits; but they cannot be worked out as the ultimate and fundamental law, because any such aspect itself derives its origin from a higher principle, and must therefore be subordinate thereto.

This higher principle we have found in the types of art – symbolic, classical, and romantic – which are the universal stages or elements of the Idea of beauty itself. For *symbolic art* attains its most adequate reality and most complete application in *architecture*, in which it holds sway in the full import of its notion, and is not yet degraded to be, as it were, the inorganic nature dealt with by another art. The *classical* type of art, on the other hand, finds adequate realization in sculpture, while it treats architecture only as furnishing an enclosure in which it is to operate, and has not acquired the power of developing painting and music as absolute forms for its content. The *romantic* type of art, finally, takes possession of painting and music, and in like manner of poetic representation, as substantive and unconditionally adequate modes of utterance. Poetry, however, is conformable to all types of the beautiful, and extends over them all, because the artistic imagination is its proper medium, and imagination is essential to every product that belongs to the beautiful, whatever its type may be.

And, therefore, what the particular arts realize in individual works of art, are according to their abstract conception simply the universal types which constitute the self-unfolding Idea of beauty. It is as the external realization of this Idea that the wide Pantheon of art is being erected, whose architect and builder is the spirit of beauty as it awakens to self-knowledge, and to complete which the history of the world will need its evolution of ages.

Translated by Bernard Bosanquet
(with minor changes)

V

History and Reason

16

Immanuel Kant, 'Idea for a Universal History from a Cosmopolitan Point of View' ('Idee zu einer allgemeinen Geschichte in weltbürgerlicher Absicht') (1784)

It may seem surprising to some that Kant had a philosophy of history. After all, he is synonymous in philosophy with universalism and atemporalism: what holds as valid for one case holds for all and forever. However, that misperception is likely to be caused by two fundamental prejudices: first, our view of history as nothing but the collection of random events, and second our convenient categorisation of Kant as committed only to the realm of the *a priori*, and disinterested in the contingencies of *a posteriori* experience. Yet he wrote extensively on the subject of history. (Two English language collections, *On History*, edited by Lewis White Beck, and *Political Writings*, edited by Hans Reiss, contain the main writings.[1])

To think that Kant can have no interest in the philosophy of history is to forget his seriousness about the idea of Enlightenment. We might broadly think of the so-called Age of Enlightenment as that period in which human beings began to move away from the allegedly natural order and towards arrangements compatible with the notion of autonomy. The old world of 'created being' and all the institutions supposedly based on it (the authority of monarchs and theologians in particular) was brought into question by an attitude of critical evaluation. Conservatives, of course, saw this as a destruction of cohesive order, but Enlightenment intellectuals saw it as a vital step in the progress of humanity. It is this optimistic thought which infused many of the notions of history prevalent at this period, including Kant's. Although aware of what he referred to as the 'crooked wood as man is made of' Kant nevertheless believed that history could be reasonably construed as progressive, that is, that there is something more than coincidental about the ascent of human beings from barbarism to civilised human society. 'Enlightenment is man's release from his self-incurred tutelage', Kant boldly announced in the first line of 'What is Enlightenment?'[2] Enlightenment, however, remained to be achieved, as Voltaire's parody of the theodicy of Leibniz no doubt reminded him.

---

[1] Immanuel Kant, *On History* (Indianapolis, IN: Bobbs-Merrill, 1963), edited by Lewis White Beck; Immanuel Kant, *Political Writings* (Cambridge: Cambridge University Press, 1991), edited by Hans Reiss.
[2] Kant, 'What is Enlightenment?' p. 3, in *On History* (also in *Political Writings*, p. 54) (*KAA* VIII, 35).

Kant posits history as lawful progress, or at least as a coherent narrative of progress. Now, it is essential to understand that this notion of progress is in no way grounded in a metaphysical theory: there are no predetermined or causal laws which entail that humanity will necessarily move to enlightenment, as, say, biological organisms inevitably and unknowingly reach maturity, given certain favourable environmental factors. But we can attempt to understand history through the 'idea' of its progress. For Kant an 'idea' in this sense is a hypothesis which operates heuristically as an aid to interpretation, and can be no more than this. Kant's reticence is typical of his general reluctance to make claims for metaphysical hypotheses that are not verifiable through the constraints of critical philosophy. Indeed in the 1798 piece, 'An Old Question Raised Again: Is the Human Race Constantly Progressing?' he immediately dismisses the idea that the method of his critical philosophy – the validation of synthetic *a priori* propositions – is applicable to notions of history and progress. And this distinguishes Kant also from providential theories of history which hold that history and progress are ways in which God has provided for the well-being of humanity (and thus that history is always, in some sense, good), as this would require a kind of knowledge which lies beyond the limits of understanding.

The essay 'Idea for a Universal History from a Cosmopolitan Point of View' appeared in 1794 (the same year as the influential and polemical 'What is Enlightenment?'). In this essay Kant sets out a number of theses that show the coherence of history. This standpoint, in fact, led him to write a famously polemical review of the philosophy of history of his former student J. G. Herder. Herder argued that history is the totality of the diversity of cultures and their non-linear relations with each other. Against this Kant wrote that 'what philosophy of the history of humanity means to [Herder] may very well be something quite different from what is normally understood under that name. His is not a logical precision in the definition of concepts or careful adherence to principles, but rather a fleeting, sweeping view, an adroitness in unearthing analogies in the wielding of which he shows a bold imagination', allegations which clearly reflect Kant's impatience with a philosophy of history not sufficiently cognisant of the 'idea' or hypothetical structure of history.[3]

Kant's position is this: The possibility of historical progress lies in the potential of human beings for rationality. The vastness of this potential, however, is such that it could never be realised by a single individual, but only across the species, as Kant puts it. Human rationality means that we, unlike the animals, make decisions about how our lives are to be organised. He posits the selfishness of human beings combined with a desire to live among other human beings – 'unsocial sociability' – as the source of progress: human beings must curb their selfishness to find means of coexistence, but at the same time they will remain selfish, or competitively related

---

[3] Kant, Reviews of Herder's 'Ideas for a Philosophy of the History of Mankind', p. 27, in *On History* (also in *Political Writings*, p. 201) (*KAA* VIII, 45).

to others: competition constrained within peaceful coexistence brings out the superior capacities of human beings. No system of coexistence can be perfect, however, given that it is composed of human beings who, because of their selfish tendencies, need governance, but who must, of course, be governed by human beings with the same tendencies. The same forces which give rise to states – the inevitable co-operation of individuals – lie behind the development of international relations: the destructiveness of war eventually alerts nations to the need for co-operation. If the vastness of human potential can be realised only across the species, and individuals must develop means of co-operation which then produce the conditions for human development, it seems that the realisation of human potential ultimately points towards the need for a stable political and democratic environment: a constitution. Kant rounds off these propositions with the notion that history thus conceived is not simply descriptive of what human beings have thus far achieved: it is educational in that it can encourage those of us who know it to carry forward the project which is consistent with the realisation of our nature.

Some of Kant's remarks seem, at times, to construe nature as some sort of agent ('nature has willed', 'nature's secret plan', etc.). Does Kant really think that nature is subject, rather than object? Nothing in the critical philosophy could permit this interpretation, and it is clear that Kant is speaking non-technically in an essay designed to engage a wide audience. Attaching an intentional stance to nature is a device that serves the purpose of telling us a story of what human beings are capable of and what they might become. The narrative of that process is history.

IDEA FOR A UNIVERSAL HISTORY FROM A COSMOPOLITAN POINT OF VIEW[†1]

Whatever concept one may hold, from a metaphysical point of view, concerning the freedom of the will, certainly its appearances, which are human actions, like every other natural event are determined by universal laws. However obscure their causes, history, which is concerned with narrating these appearances, permits us

---

[†] *KAA* VIII, 17–31. *On History* (Indianapolis, IN: Bobbs-Merrill, 1963).

[1] A statement in the 'Short Notices' or the twelfth number of the *Gothaische Gelehrte Zeitung* of this year [1784], which no doubt was based on my conversation with a scholar who was traveling through, occasions this essay, without which that statement could not be understood.

[The notice said: 'A favorite idea of Professor Kant's is that the ultimate purpose of the human race is to achieve the most perfect civic constitution, and he wishes that a philosophical historian might undertake to give us a history of humanity from this point of view, and to show to what extent humanity in various ages has approached or drawn away from this final purpose and what remains to be done in order to reach it.']

to hope that if we attend to the play of freedom of the human will in the large, we may be able to discern a regular movement in it, and that what seems complex and chaotic in the single individual may be seen from the standpoint of the human race as a whole to be a steady and progressive though slow evolution of its original endowment. Since the free will of man has obvious influence upon marriages, births, and deaths, they seem to be subject to no rule by which the number of them could be reckoned in advance. Yet the annual tables of them in the major countries prove that they occur according to laws as stable as [those of] the unstable weather, which we likewise cannot determine in advance, but which, in the large, maintain the growth of plants, the flow of rivers, and other natural events in an unbroken, uniform course. Individuals and even whole peoples think little on this. Each, according to his own inclination, follows his own purpose, often in opposition to others; yet each individual and people, as if following some guiding thread, go toward a natural but to each of them unknown goal; all work toward furthering it, even if they would set little store by it if they did know it.

Since men in their endeavors behave, on the whole, not just instinctively, like the brutes, nor yet like rational citizens of the world according to some agreed-on plan, no history of man conceived according to a plan seems to be possible, as it might be possible to have such a history of bees or beavers. One cannot suppress a certain indignation when one sees men's actions on the great world-stage and finds, beside the wisdom that appears here and there among individuals, everything in the large woven together from folly, childish vanity, even from childish malice and destructiveness. In the end, one does not know what to think of the human race, so conceited in its gifts. Since the philosopher cannot presuppose any [conscious] individual purpose among men in their great drama, there is no other expedient for him except to try to see if he can discover a natural purpose in this idiotic course of things human. In keeping with this purpose, it might be possible to have a history with a definite natural plan for creatures who have no plan of their own.

We wish to see if we can succeed in finding a clue to such a history; we leave it to Nature to produce the man capable of composing it. Thus Nature produced Kepler, who subjected, in an unexpected way, the eccentric paths of the planets to definite laws; and she produced Newton, who explained these laws by a universal natural cause.

First Thesis

All natural capacities of a creature are destined to evolve completely to their natural end.

Observation of both the outward form and inward structure of all animals confirms this of them. An organ that is of no use, an arrangement that does not achieve its purpose, are contradictions in the teleological theory of nature. If we give up this fundamental principle, we no longer have a lawful but an aimless course of nature, and blind chance takes the place of the guiding thread of reason.

Second Thesis

In man (as the only rational creature on earth) those natural capacities which are directed to the use of his reason are to be fully developed only in the race, not in the individual.

Reason in a creature is a faculty of widening the rules and purposes of the use of all its powers far beyond natural instinct; it acknowledges no limits to its projects. Reason itself does not work instinctively, but requires trial, practice, and instruction in order gradually to progress from one level of insight to another. Therefore a single man would have to live excessively long in order to learn to make full use of all his natural capacities. Since Nature has set only a short period for his life, she needs a perhaps unreckonable series of generations, each of which passes its own enlightenment to its successor in order finally to bring the seeds of enlightenment to that degree of development in our race which is completely suitable to Nature's purpose. This point of time must be, at least as an ideal, the goal of man's efforts, for otherwise his natural capacities would have to be counted as for the most part vain and aimless. This would destroy all practical principles, and Nature, whose wisdom must serve as the fundamental principle in judging all her other offspring, would thereby make man alone a contemptible plaything.

Third Thesis

Nature has willed that man should, by himself, produce everything that goes beyond the mechanical ordering of his animal existence, and that he should partake of no other happiness or perfection than that which he himself, independently of instinct, has created by his own reason.

Nature does nothing in vain, and in the use of means to her goals she is not prodigal. Her giving to man reason and the freedom of the will which depends upon it is clear indication of her purpose. Man accordingly was not to be guided by instinct, not nurtured and instructed with ready-made knowledge; rather, he should bring forth everything out of his own resources. Securing his own food, shelter, safety and defense (for which Nature gave him neither the horns of the bull, nor the claws of the lion, nor the fangs of the dog, but hands only), all amusement which can make life pleasant, insight and intelligence, finally even goodness of heart – all this should be wholly his own work. In this, Nature seems to have moved with the strictest parsimony, and to have measured her animal gifts precisely to the most stringent needs of a beginning existence, just as if she had willed that, if man ever did advance from the lowest barbarity to the highest skill and mental perfection and thereby worked himself up to happiness (so far as it is possible on earth), he alone should have the credit and should have only himself to thank – exactly as if she aimed more at his rational self-esteem than at his well-being. For along this march of human affairs, there was a host of troubles awaiting him. But it seems not to have concerned Nature that he should live well, but only that he should work himself upward so as to make himself, through his own actions, worthy of life and of well-being.

It remains strange that the earlier generations appear to carry through their toilsome labor only for the sake of the later, to prepare for them a foundation on which the later generations could erect the higher edifice which was Nature's goal, and yet that only the latest of the generations should have the good fortune to inhabit the building on which a long line of their ancestors had (unintentionally) labored without being permitted to partake of the fortune they had prepared. However puzzling this may be, it is necessary if one assumes that a species of animals should have reason, and, as a class of rational beings each of whom dies while the species is immortal, should develop their capacities to perfection.

Fourth Thesis

The means employed by Nature to bring about the development of all the capacities of men is their antagonism in society, so far as this is, in the end, the cause of a lawful order among men.

By 'antagonism' I mean the unsocial sociability of men, i.e., their propensity to enter into society, bound together with a mutual opposition which constantly threatens to break up the society. Man has an inclination to associate with others, because in society he feels himself to be more than man, i.e., as more than the developed form of his natural capacities. But he also has a strong propensity to isolate himself from others, because he finds in himself at the same time the unsocial characteristic of wishing to have everything go according to his own wish. Thus he expects opposition on all sides because, in knowing himself, he knows that he, on his own part, is inclined to oppose others. This opposition it is which awakens all his powers, brings him to conquer his inclination to laziness and, propelled by vainglory, lust for power, and avarice, to achieve a rank among his fellows whom he cannot tolerate but from whom he cannot withdraw. Thus are taken the first true steps from barbarism to culture, which consists in the social worth of man; thence gradually develop all talents, and taste is refined; through continued enlightenment the beginnings are laid for a way of thought which can in time convert the coarse, natural disposition for moral discrimination into definite practical principles, and thereby change a society of men driven together by their natural feelings into a moral whole. Without those in themselves unamiable characteristics of unsociability from whence opposition springs – characteristics each man must find in his own selfish pretensions – all talents would remain hidden, unborn in an Arcadian shepherd's life, with all its concord, contentment, and mutual affection. Men, good-natured as the sheep they herd, would hardly reach a higher worth than their beasts; they would not fill the empty place in creation by achieving their end, which is rational nature. Thanks be to Nature, then, for the incompatibility, for heartless competitive vanity, for the insatiable desire to possess and to rule! Without them, all the excellent natural capacities of humanity would forever sleep, undeveloped. Man wishes concord; but Nature knows better what is good for the race; she wills discord. He wishes to live comfortably and pleasantly; Nature wills that he should be plunged from sloth and passive contentment into labor and trouble, in order that he may find means of extricating himself from them. The natural urges to this, the sources of unsociableness and mutual opposition from which so many evils arise, drive men to new exertions of their forces and thus to the manifold development of their capacities. They thereby perhaps show the ordering of a wise Creator and not the hand of an evil spirit, who bungled in his great work or spoiled it out of envy.

Fifth Thesis

The greatest problem for the human race, to the solution of which Nature drives man, is the achievement of a universal civic society which administers law among men.

The highest purpose of Nature, which is the development of all the capacities which can be achieved by mankind, is attainable only in society, and more specifically in the society with the greatest freedom. Such a society is one in which there is mutual opposition among the members, together with the most exact definition of freedom and fixing of its limits so that it may be consistent with the freedom of others. Nature demands that humankind should itself achieve this goal like all its other destined goals. Thus a society in which freedom under external laws is associated in the highest degree with irresistible power, i.e., a perfectly just civic constitution, is the highest problem Nature assigns to the human race; for Nature can achieve her other purposes for mankind only upon the solution and completion of this assignment. Need forces men, so enamored otherwise of their boundless freedom, into this state of constraint. They are forced to it by the greatest of all needs, a need they themselves occasion inasmuch as their passions keep them from living long together in wild freedom. Once in such a preserve as a civic union, these same passions subsequently do the most good. It is just the same with trees in a forest: each needs the others, since each in seeking to take the air and sunlight from others must strive upward, and thereby each realizes a beautiful, straight stature, while those that live in isolated freedom put out branches at random and grow stunted, crooked, and twisted. All culture, art which adorns mankind, and the finest social order are fruits of unsociableness, which forces itself to discipline itself and so, by a contrived art, to develop the natural seeds to perfection.

Sixth Thesis

This problem is the most difficult and the last to be solved by mankind.

The difficulty which the mere thought of this problem puts before our eyes is this. Man is an animal which, if it lives among others of its kind, requires a master. For he certainly abuses his freedom with respect to other men, and although as a reasonable being he wishes to have a law which limits the freedom of all, his selfish animal impulses tempt him, where possible, to exempt himself from them. He thus requires a master, who will break his will and force him to obey a will that is universally valid, under which each can be free. But whence does he get this master? Only from the human race. But then the master is himself an animal, and needs a master. Let him begin it as he will, it is not to be seen how he can procure a magistracy which can maintain public justice and which is itself just, whether it be a single person or a group of several elected persons. For each of them will always abuse his freedom if he has none above him to exercise force in accord with the laws. The highest master should be just in himself, and yet a man. This task is therefore the hardest of all; indeed, its complete solution is impossible, for from such crooked wood as man is made of, nothing perfectly straight can be built.[2] That it is the last problem to be solved follows also from this: it requires that there be a correct conception of a possible constitution, great experience gained in many paths of life, and – far beyond these – a good will ready to accept such a constitution. Three such things are very hard, and if they are ever to be found together, it will be very late and after many vain attempts.

Seventh Thesis

The problem of establishing a perfect civic constitution is dependent upon the problem of a lawful external relation among states and cannot be solved without a solution of the latter problem.

What is the use of working toward a lawful civic constitution among individuals, i.e., toward the creation of a commonwealth? The same unsociability which drives man to this causes any single commonwealth to stand in unrestricted freedom in relation to others; consequently, each of them must expect from another precisely the evil which oppressed the individuals and forced them to enter into a lawful civic state. The friction among men, the inevitable antagonism, which is a mark of even the largest societies and political bodies, is used by Nature as a means to establish a condition of quiet and security. Through war, through the taxing and never-ending accumulation of armament, through the want which any state, even in peacetime, must suffer internally, Nature forces them to make at first inadequate and tentative attempts; finally, after devastations, revolutions, and even complete exhaustion, she brings them to that which reason could have told them at the beginning and with

---

[2] The role of man is very artificial. How it may be with the dwellers on other planets and their nature we do not know. If, however, we carry out well the mandate given us by Nature, we can perhaps flatter ourselves that we may claim among our neighbors in the cosmos no mean rank. Maybe among them each individual can perfectly attain his destiny in his own life. Among us, it is different; only the race can hope to attain it.

far less sad experience, to wit, to step from the lawless condition of savages into a league of nations. In a league of nations, even the smallest state could expect security and justice, not from its own power and by its own decrees, but only from this great league of nations (*Foedus Amphictyonum*),[3] from a united power acting according to decisions reached under the laws of their united will. However fantastical this idea may seem – and it was laughed at as fantastical by the Abbé de St. Pierre[4] and by Rousseau,[5] perhaps because they believed it was too near to realization – the necessary outcome of the destitution to which each man is brought by his fellows is to force the states to the same decision (hard though it be for them) that savage man also was reluctantly forced to take, namely, to give up their brutish freedom and to seek quiet and security under a lawful constitution.

All wars are accordingly so many attempts (not in the intention of man, but in the intention of Nature) to establish new relations among states, and through the destruction or at least the dismemberment of all of them to create new political bodies, which, again, either internally or externally, cannot maintain themselves and which must thus suffer like revolutions; until finally, through the best possible civic constitution and common agreement and legislation in external affairs, a state is created which, like a civic commonwealth, can maintain itself automatically.

[There are three questions here, which really come to one.] Would it be expected from an Epicurean concourse of efficient causes that states, like minute particles of matter in their chance contacts, should form all sorts of unions which in their turn are destroyed by new impacts, until once, finally, by chance a structure should arise which could maintain its existence – a fortunate accident that could hardly occur? Or are we not rather to suppose that Nature here follows a lawful course in gradually lifting our race from the lower levels of animality to the highest level of humanity, doing this by her own secret art, and developing in accord with her law all the original gifts of man in this apparently chaotic disorder? Or perhaps we should prefer to conclude that, from all these actions and counteractions of men in the large, absolutely nothing, at least nothing wise, is to issue? That everything should remain as it always was, that we cannot therefore tell but that discord, natural to our race, may not prepare for us a hell of evils, however civilized we may now be, by annihilating civilization and all cultural progress through barbarous devastation? (This is the fate we may well have to suffer under the rule of blind chance – which is in fact identical with lawless freedom – if there is no secret wise guidance in Nature.) These three questions, I say, mean about the same as this: Is it reasonable to assume a purposiveness in all the parts of nature and to deny it to the whole?

---

[3] [An allusion to the Amphictyonic League, a league of Greek tribes originally for the protection of a religious shrine, which later gained considerable political power.]

[4] Charles-Irénée Castel, Abbé de Saint Pierre (1658–1743), in his *Projet de paix perpetuelle* (Utrecht, 1713). Trans. H. H. Bellot (London, 1927).]

[5] [In his *Extrait du projet de paix perpetuelle de M. l'Abbé de St. Pierre* (1760). Trans. C. E. Vaughn, *A Lasting Peace through the Federation of Europe* (London, 1917).]

Purposeless savagery held back the development of the capacities of our race; but finally, through the evil into which it plunged mankind, it forced our race to renounce this condition and to enter into a civic order in which those capacities could be developed. The same is done by the barbaric freedom of established states. Through wasting the powers of the commonwealths in armaments to be used against each other, through devastation brought on by war, and even more by the necessity of holding themselves in constant readiness for war, they stunt the full development of human nature. But because of the evils which thus arise, our race is forced to find, above the (in itself healthy) opposition of states which is a consequence of their freedom, a law of equilibrium and a united power to give it effect. Thus it is forced to institute a cosmopolitan condition to secure the external safety of each state.

Such a condition is not unattended by the danger that the vitality of mankind may fall asleep; but it is at least not without a principle of balance among men's actions and counteractions, without which they might be altogether destroyed. Until this last step to a union of states is taken, which is the halfway mark in the development of mankind, human nature must suffer the cruelest hardships under the guise of external well-being; and Rousseau was not far wrong in preferring the state of savages, so long, that is, as the last stage to which the human race must climb is not attained.

To a high degree we are, through art and science, *cultured*. We are *civilized* – perhaps too much for our own good – in all sorts of social grace and decorum. But to consider ourselves as having reached *morality* – for that, much is lacking. The ideal of morality belongs to culture; its use for some simulacrum of morality in the love of honor and outward decorum constitutes mere civilization. So long as states waste their forces in vain and violent self-expansion, and thereby constantly thwart the slow efforts to improve the minds of their citizens by even withdrawing all support from them, nothing in the way of a moral order is to be expected. For such an end, a long internal working of each political body toward the education of its citizens is required. Everything good that is not based on a morally good disposition, however, is nothing but pretense and glittering misery. In such a condition the human species will no doubt remain until, in the way I have described, it works its way out of the chaotic conditions of its international relations.

Eighth Thesis

The history of mankind can be seen, in the large, as the realization of Nature's secret plan to bring forth a perfectly constituted state as the only condition in which the capacities of mankind can be fully developed, and also bring forth that external relation among states which is perfectly adequate to this end.

This is a corollary to the preceding. Everyone can see that philosophy can have her belief in a millenium, but her millenarianism is not Utopian, since the

Idea can help, though only from afar, to bring the millenium to pass. The only question is: Does Nature reveal anything of a path to this end? And I say: She reveals something, but very little. This great revolution seems to require so long for its completion that the short period during which humanity has been following this course permits us to determine its path and the relation of the parts to the whole with as little certainty as we can determine, from all previous astronomical observation, the path of the sun and his host of satellites among the fixed stars. Yet, on the fundamental premise of the systematic structure of the cosmos and from the little that has been observed, we can confidently infer the reality of such a revolution.

Moreover, human nature is so constituted that we cannot be indifferent to the most remote epoch our race may come to, if only we may expect it with certainty. Such indifference is even less possible for us, since it seems that our own intelligent action may hasten this happy time for our posterity. For that reason, even faint indications of approach to it are very important to us. At present, states are in such an artificial relation to each other that none of them can neglect its internal cultural development without losing power and influence among the others. Therefore the preservation of this natural end [culture], if not progress in it, is fairly well assured by the ambitions of states. Furthermore, civic freedom can hardly be infringed without the evil consequences being felt in all walks of life, especially in commerce, where the effect is loss of power of the state in its foreign relations. But this freedom spreads by degrees. When the citizen is hindered in seeking his own welfare in his own way, so long as it is consistent with the freedom of others, the vitality of the entire enterprise is sapped, and therewith the powers of the whole are diminished. Therefore limitations on personal actions are step by step removed, and general religious freedom is permitted. Enlightenment comes gradually, with intermittent folly and caprice, as a great good which must finally save men from the selfish aggrandizement of their masters, always assuming that the latter know their own interest. This enlightenment, and with it a certain commitment of heart which the enlightened man cannot fail to make to the good he clearly understands, must step by step ascend the throne and influence the principles of government.

Although, for instance, our world rulers at present have no money left over for public education and for anything that concerns what is best in the world, since all they have is already committed to future wars, they will still find it to their own interest at least not to hinder the weak and slow, independent efforts of their peoples in this work. In the end, war itself will be seen as not only so artificial, in outcome so uncertain for both sides, in aftereffects so painful in the form of an ever-growing war debt (a new invention) that cannot be met, that it will be regarded as a most dubious undertaking. The impact of any revolution on all states on our continent, so closely knit together through commerce, will be so obvious that the other states, driven by their own danger but without any legal basis, will offer themselves as arbiters, and thus they will prepare the way for a distant international government for which there is no precedent in world history.

Although this government at present exists only as a rough outline, nevertheless in all the members there is rising a feeling which each has for the preservation of the whole. This gives hope finally that after many reformative revolutions, a universal cosmopolitan condition, which Nature has as her ultimate purpose, will come into being as the womb wherein all the original capacities of the human race can develop.

Ninth Thesis

A philosophical attempt to work out a universal history according to a natural plan directed to achieving the civic union of the human race must be regarded as possible and, indeed, as contributing to this end of Nature.

It is strange and apparently silly to wish to write a history in accordance with an Idea of how the course of the world must be if it is to lead to certain rational ends. It seems that with such an Idea only a romance could be written. Nevertheless, if one may assume that Nature, even in the play of human freedom, works not without plan or purpose, this Idea could still be of use. Even if we are too blind to see the secret mechanism of its workings, this Idea may still serve as a guiding thread for presenting as a system, at least in broad outlines, what would otherwise be a planless conglomeration of human actions. For if one starts with Greek history, through which every older or contemporaneous history has been handed down or at least certified;[6] if one follows the influence of Greek history on the construction and misconstruction of the Roman state which swallowed up the Greek, then the Roman influence on the barbarians who in turn destroyed it, and so on down to our times; if one adds episodes from the national histories of other peoples insofar as they are known from the history of the enlightened nations, one will discover a regular progress in the constitution of states on our continent (which will probably give law, eventually, to all the others). If, further, one concentrates on the civic constitutions and their laws and on the relations among states, insofar as through the good they contained they served over long periods of time to elevate and adorn nations and their arts and sciences, while through the evil they contained they destroyed them, if only a germ of enlightenment was left to be further developed by this overthrow and a higher level was thus prepared – if, I say, one carries through this study, a guiding thread will be revealed. It can serve

---

[6] Only a learned public, which has lasted from its beginning to our own day, can certify ancient history. Outside it, everything else is *terra incognita;* and the history of peoples outside it can only be begun when they come into contact with it. This happened with the Jews in the time of the Ptolemies through the translation of the Bible into Greek, without which we would give little credence to their isolated narratives. From this point, when once properly fixed, we can retrace their history. And so with all other peoples. The first page of Thucydides, says Hume ['Of the Populousness of Ancient Nations,' in *Essays Moral, Political, and Literary*, eds. Green and Grose, Vol. I, p. 414], is the only beginning of all real history.

not only for clarifying the confused play of things human, and not only for the art of prophesying later political changes (a use which has already been made of history even when seen as the disconnected effect of lawless freedom), but for giving a consoling view of the future (which could not be reasonably hoped for without the presupposition of a natural plan) in which there will be exhibited in the distance how the human race finally achieves the condition in which all the seeds planted in it by Nature can fully develop and in which the destiny of the race can be fulfilled here on earth.

Such a justification of Nature – or, better, of Providence – is no unimportant reason for choosing a standpoint toward world history. For what is the good of esteeming the majesty and wisdom of Creation in the realm of brute nature and of recommending that we contemplate it, if that part of the great stage of supreme wisdom which contains the purpose of all the others – the history of mankind – must remain an unceasing reproach to it? If we are forced to turn our eyes from it in disgust, doubting that we can ever find a perfectly rational purpose in it and hoping for that only in another world?

That I would want to displace the work of practicing empirical historians with this Idea of world history, which is to some extent based upon an a priori principle, would be a misinterpretation of my intention. It is only a suggestion of what a philosophical mind (which would have to be well versed in history) could essay from another point of view. Otherwise the notorious complexity of a history of our time must naturally lead to serious doubt as to how our descendants will begin to grasp the burden of the history we shall leave to them after a few centuries. They will naturally value the history of earlier times, from which the documents may long since have disappeared, only from the point of view of what interests them, i.e., in answer to the question of what the various nations and governments have contributed to the goal of world citizenship, and what they have done to damage it. To consider this, so as to direct the ambitions of sovereigns and their agents to the only means by which their fame can be spread to later ages: this can be a minor motive for attempting such a philosophical history.

Translated by Lewis White Beck

17

F. W. J. Schelling, System of Transcendental Idealism (System des transcendentalen Idealismus): *Part Four, Section Three – Deduction of the Concept of History (1800)*

Schelling's most systematic thoughts on the concept and meaning of history are set out in the idealist theory of his *System of Transcendental Idealism* (1800), a book which attempts to find a reconciliation between the freedom of the intellect and the apparent necessity of nature. For Schelling, history manifests these twin characteristics. Art (as can be seen in section 14 of this Anthology) ultimately provides the philosophical solution to the synthesis of these concepts.

Schelling's thoughts on history bear some similarities with Kant's, though differences of genre and philosophical framework must be noted. Kant's essayistic analysis of the idea of history lent itself to an ultimately hesitant conclusion about the *nature* of history. Schelling's views are presented within a work of systematic philosophy in which the notion of the deducibility of concepts is taken rather seriously. And again in so far as the notion of history is considered within the framework of objective idealism its grounds are to be sought within the systematic concepts relating to the reconciliation of freedom and necessity. Schelling's position has in essence a metaphysical structure.

Schelling's reflections on history, like Kant's, start out with the idea that human beings have reached the point at which an enlightened world at peace is possible. But how have we arrived at this condition? Schelling is quite certain that is not 'mere chance'. Instead, we must point to some kind of necessity in history. History is effectively the produce of a species attempting to attain an ideal. It bears certain necessary features: it has law-like structure, and historical actors are free in making decisions which contribute to progress – in that they do not work through a predetermined programme – and that this free activity can be carried out through reason. Schelling concludes that the very notion of history therefore entails both law-likeness and freedom. History, in the sense of interest to philosophy, is not a matter then of randomness or disconnected fact.

Despite Schelling's argued view that history is essentially progressive he offers a curiously agnostic view of our capacity to measure progress.

Nevertheless he is committed to the idea that human beings through their actions strive towards the 'perfect constitution', as Kant had also argued. The task of progress is always, as a phrase much used in this period by Schelling and others puts it, that of infinite approximation to perfection.

Schelling's considerations of the concept of history bear on the problem of action: individuals, as the agents of history, act freely, yet their actions conform to a law which underpins progress. This is also found in the acting out of tragedy, in which free actions conform to a higher order (though it is not clear in this analogy what sort of progress can be accommodated by tragedy). The contrast between freedom and necessity is characterized by Schelling as a contrast between conscious and unconscious results of our actions. A way of thinking about the notion of action entailed in Schelling's notion of history is to contrast it with Kant's. Kant's moral theory posits two standpoints: the perspective of the spontaneity of the will, and that of the necessity of nature. Schelling's theory, however, might be regarded as entailing three standpoints: there is necessity (nature), subjective freedom (the intellect), but also the point of view of 'the absolute' in which the other two are united.[1]

As in Schelling's discussion of art the idea of intuition is given a particular role in explaining our awareness of that which is not the produce of our conscious actions, in this case, namely, our sense of the 'hidden necessity' of history. He argues nevertheless that the awareness by historical actors of the identity of their actions with the lawfulness of history would endanger the very notion of freedom: it would come to seem that all actions were the mere working out of a preconceived plan. The synthesis of these two activities – that is the perspective which unites them, which perceives their identity – is ultimately found only in art.

The metaphysical framework of Schelling's theory is striking. History is, as he puts it, a 'progressive, gradually self-disclosing revelation of the absolute'. Interestingly, the notion of revelation was to become a central theme of Schelling's later work. This revelation falls, he argues, into three periods of history, and notably (given the later Hegelian philosophy) these three periods seem to be related as thesis, antithesis and synthesis. (The periods are, namely, destiny, natural law, providence.) Schelling's metaphysical account of history might seem to be quite gratuitous. However, if we contrast his position with Kant we can see that the very issues which Kant tentatively proposed and defended – history with a meaning, progress – can for Schelling be supported only by a metaphysics. Rejecting the notion that progress is chance comes with the requirement that we answer the question of what gives it its structure. Schelling's thoughts on history are an effort to answer that very question.

---

[1] Cf. 'Die Geschichte' (section 8: Schelling), pp. 230–233, in *Handbuch Deutscher Idealismus* (Stuttgart: Metzler Verlag, 2005), ed. Hans Jörg Sandkühler.

III CONCEPT OF HISTORY[†]

The emergence of the universal constitution cannot be consigned to mere chance, and is accordingly to be anticipated only from the free play of forces that we discern in history. The question arises, therefore, as to whether a series of circumstances without plan or purpose can deserve the name of history at all, and whether in the mere *concept* of history there is not already contained also the concept of a necessity which choice itself is compelled to serve.

Here it is primarily a question of our ascertaining the concept of history.

Not everything that happens is on that account an object of history; natural circumstances, for example, owe their historical character, if they attain it, merely to the influence which they have had upon human actions; still less by far, however, do we regard as a historical object that which takes place according to a known rule, periodically recurs, or is in general a consequence that can be calculated *a priori*. If we wanted to speak of a history of nature in the true sense of the word, we should have to picture nature as though, apparently free in its productions, it had gradually brought forth the whole multiplicity thereof through constant departures from a primordial original; which would then be a history, not of *natural objects* (which is properly the description of nature), but of generative *nature itself*. Now how would we view nature in a history of this sort? We would view her, so to speak, as ordering and managing in various ways with one and the same sum or proportion of forces, which she could never exceed; we should thus regard her, to be sure, as acting freely in this creation, but not on that account as working in utter lawlessness. Nature would thus become an object of history, on the one hand, through the appearance of freedom in her productions, since in fact we would be unable to determine *a priori* the directions of her productive activity, although there would be no doubt at all that these directions had their specific law; but she would also be an object, on the other hand, through the confinement and conformity to law inherent in her, owing to the proportion of the forces at her command; whence it is therefore apparent that history comes about neither with absolute lawfulness nor with absolute freedom either, but exists only where a single ideal is realized under an infinity of deviations, in such a way that, not the particular detail indeed, but assuredly the whole, is in conformity thereto.

But now such a successive realizing of an ideal, where only the progress as a whole, as it might be seen by an intellectual intuition, does justice to the ideal, can moreover be thought of as possible only through such beings as have the character of a species; for the individual, in fact, precisely because he is so, is incapable of attaining to the ideal, though the latter, which is necessarily determinate, has still got to be realized. We therefore see ourselves led on to a new feature of history, namely that there can only be a history of such beings as have

[†] *SSW* III, 587–604. *System of Transcendental Idealism* (Charlottesville, VA: University Press of Virginia, 1978).

an ideal before them, which can never be carried out by the individual, but only by the species. And for this it is needful that every succeeding individual should start in at the very point where the preceding one left off, and thus that continuity should be possible between succeeding individuals, and, if that which is to be realized in the progress of history is something attainable only through reason and freedom, that there should also be the possibility of tradition and transmission.

But now from the foregoing deduction of the concept of history it is self-evident that an absolutely lawless series of events is no more entitled to the name of history than an absolutely law-abiding one; whence it is apparent:

(a) that the idea of progress implicit in all history permits no conformity to law such as would limit free activity to a determinate and constantly recursive succession of acts;

(b) that nothing whatever can be an object of history which proceeds according to a determinate mechanism, or whose theory is *a priori*. Theory and history are totally opposed. Man has a history only because what he will do is incapable of being calculated in advance according to any theory. Choice is to that extent the goddess of history. Mythology has history begin with the first step out of the domain of instinct into the realm of freedom, with the loss of the Golden Age, or with the Fall, that is, with the first expression of choice. In the schemes of the philosophers, history ends with the reign of reason, that is, with the Golden Age of law, when all choice shall have vanished from the earth, and man shall have returned through freedom to the same point at which nature originally placed him, and which he forsook when history began;

(c) that neither absolute lawlessness, nor a series of events without aim or purpose, deserve the name of history, and that its true nature is constituted only by freedom and lawfulness in conjunction, or of by the gradual realization, on the part of a whole species of beings, of an ideal that they have never wholly lost.

After this derivation, now completed, of the main characteristics of history, we must now enquire more closely into the transcendental possibility thereof; and this will lead us to a philosophy of *history*, which latter is for the practical part of philosophy precisely what nature is for the theoretical part.

A

The first question which can justifiably be asked of a philosophy of history is, no doubt, how a history is conceivable at all, since if everything that exists is posited for each of us only through his own consciousness, the whole of past history can likewise be posited for each through his consciousness alone. Now we do in fact also maintain that no individual consciousness could be posited, with all the determinations it is posited with, and which necessarily belong to it, unless the whole of history had gone before; and if we needed to do the trick, this could very easily be shown by means of examples. Thus past history admittedly belongs merely to appearance, just as does the individuality of consciousness itself; it is therefore no more, but also no less real for each of us than his own individuality is. This particular individuality presupposes this particular period, of such and such a character, such and such a degree of culture, etc.; but such a period is impossible without the whole of past history. Historiography, which otherwise has no object save that of explaining the present state of the world, could thus equally set out from the current situation and infer to past history, and it would be no uninteresting endeavor to see how the whole of the past could be derived from this in a strictly necessary manner.

Now it might be objected to this account that past history is not posited with *each* individual consciousness, nor is the *whole* of the past posited with any, but only the main happenings thereof, which are indeed recognizable as such only through the fact that they have extended their influence up to the present time, and so far as the individuality of each single person; but to this we reply, in the first place, that a history exists only for those upon whom the past has operated, and even for these, only to the extent that it has worked upon them; and secondly, that all that has ever *been* in history is also truly connected, or will be, with the individual consciousness of each, not immediately, maybe, but certainly by means of innumerable linkages, of such a kind that if one could point them out it would also become obvious that the *whole* of the past was necessary in order to put this consciousness together. But now it is admittedly certain that, just as the great majority of men in every age have never had any existence in the world wherein history properly belongs, so also is this true of a multitude of happenings. For just as it is insufficient, for the remembrance of posterity, to have perpetuated oneself merely as a physical cause by means of physical effects, so likewise it is not enough to deserve even a place in history that one is a mere intellectual product or mere intermediary, whereby, as a mere medium, without having oneself been the cause of a new future, the culture acquired by the past is transmitted to later generations. Thus assuredly, with the consciousness of each individual, only so much is posited as has so far continued to exert an effect; but then this in turn is also the only thing that belongs in history and has existed therein.

But now so far as the transcendental *necessity* of history is concerned, it has already been deduced in the foregoing from the fact that the universal reign of law has been set before rational beings as a problem, realizable only by the species as a whole, that is, only by way of history. We content ourselves here, therefore, with merely drawing the conclusion, that the sole true object of the historian can only be the gradual emergence of a political world order, for this, indeed, is the sole ground for a history. All other history which is not universal can only be set forth *pragmatically*, that is, according to the notion already vouchsafed to the ancients, as being directed toward a particular empirical goal. Whereas, conversely, a pragmatic universal history is a self-contradictory conception. Everything else, however, which is otherwise commonly included in the writing of history, the progress of the arts and sciences etc., properly does not belong in history at all, or else serves therein merely as a document or a connecting link; because even discoveries in the arts and sciences, primarily through the fact that they multiply and enhance the means of mutual injury, and give rise to a plethora of other evils previously unknown, serve the purpose of accelerating man's progress toward the setting up of a universal legal order.

B

That the concept of history embodies the notion of an infinite *tendency to progress*, has been sufficiently shown above. But it cannot, indeed, be straightway concluded from this that the human race is infinitely perfectible. For those who deny it could equally well maintain that man is no more possessed of a history than the animal, being confined, on the contrary, to an eternal circuit of actions, in which, like Ixion upon his wheel, he revolves unceasingly, and despite continuous oscillations and at times even seeming deviations from the line of curvature, still constantly finds himself back at the point from which he started. There is all the less expectation, moreover, of arriving at a sensible answer to this question, in that those who purport to resolve it, either for or against, find themselves in the greatest perplexity as to the standard whereby progress is to be measured. Some address themselves to the *moral* advances of mankind, of which we should certainly be glad to possess the yardstick; others, to progress in the *arts* and *sciences*, although, seen from the historical (practical) standpoint, this represents a regress, or at best a movement against the course of history, on which point we could appeal to history itself, and to the judgment and example of those nations (such as the Romans), who may be termed classical in the historical sense. But if the sole object of history is the gradual realization of the rule of law, there remains to us, even as a historical measure of man's progress, only the gradual approximation to this goal, whose final attainment, however, can neither be inferred from experience, so far as it has hitherto unfolded, nor be theoretically demonstrated *a priori*, but will be only an eternal article of faith to man as he acts and works.

C

We now pass on, however, to the primary characteristic of history, namely that it should exhibit a union of freedom and necessity, and be possible through this union alone.

But now it is just this union of freedom and lawfulness in action which we have already deduced to be necessary, from an entirely different point of view, as following simply from the concept of history itself.

The universal rule of law is a condition of freedom, since without it there is no guarantee of the latter. For freedom that is not guaranteed by a universal order of nature exists only precariously, and – as in the majority of our contemporary states – is a plant that flourishes only parasitically, tolerated in general by way of a necessary inconsistency, but in such wise that the individual is never certain of his freedom. That is not how it should be. Freedom should not be a favor granted, or a good that may be enjoyed only as a forbidden fruit. It must be guaranteed by an order that is as open and unalterable as that of nature.

But now this order can in fact be realized only through freedom, and its establishment is entrusted wholly and solely to freedom. This is a contradiction. That which is the first condition of outward freedom is, for that very reason, no less necessary than freedom itself. And it is likewise to be realized only through freedom, that is, its emergence is consigned to chance. How can this contradiction be reconciled?

The only way of resolving it is that in freedom itself there should again be necessity; but how, then, can such a resolution be conceived of?

We arrive here at the supreme problem of transcendental philosophy, which has admittedly been set forth above (II), but has not been resolved.

Freedom is to be necessity, and necessity freedom. But now in contrast to freedom, necessity is nothing else but the unconscious. That which exists in me without consciousness is involuntary; that which exists with consciousness is in me through my willing.

To say that necessity is again to be present in freedom, amounts, therefore, to saying that through freedom itself, and in that I believe myself to act freely, something I do not intend is to come about unconsciously, i.e., without my consent; or, to put it otherwise, the conscious, or that freely determining activity which we deduced earlier on, is to be confronted with an unconscious, whereby out of the most uninhibited expression of freedom there arises unawares something wholly involuntary, and perhaps even contrary to the agent's will, which he himself could never have realized through his willing. This statement, however paradoxical it may seem, is yet nothing other than a mere transcendental expression of the generally accepted and assumed relationship between freedom and a hidden necessity, at times called fate and at times providence, though neither of these terms expresses any clear idea; a relationship whereby men through their own free action, and yet against their will, must become cause of something which they never wanted, or by which, conversely, something must go astray or come to naught which they have sought for freely and with the exertion of all their powers.

Such intervention of a hidden necessity into human freedom is presupposed, not only, say, in tragedy, whose whole existence rests on that presumption, but even in normal doing and acting. Without such a presumption one can will nothing aright; without it, the disposition to act quite regardless of consequences, as duty enjoins us, could never inspire a man's mind. For if no sacrifice is possible without the conviction that the species we belong to can never cease to progress, how is this conviction itself possible, if it is wholly and solely based upon freedom? There must be something here that is higher than human freedom, and on which alone we can reckon with assurance in doing and acting; something without which a man could never enture to undertake an act fraught with major consequences, since even the most perfect calculation thereof can be so completely upset by the incursion of other men's freedom, that an outcome may result from his action entirely different from what he intended. Duty itself cannot bid me, once my decision is made, to be wholly at ease over the consequences of my actions, unless, though my acting surely depends on me, that is, upon my freedom, the consequences of those actions, or that which will emerge from them for all mankind, depend not at all on my freedom, but rather upon something quite different and of a higher sort.

It is thus a presumption which itself is necessary for the sake of freedom, that though man is admittedly free in regard to the action itself, he is nonetheless dependent, in regard to the finite result of his actions, upon a necessity that stands over him, and itself takes a hand in the play of his freedom. Now this presumption requires a transcendental explanation. To account for it by providence or fate is not to explain it at all, for providence or fate are precisely what need to be explained. We are not in doubt about providence, any more than we are about what is called fate, for we sense its incursions into our own doings, in the success and failure of our own enterprises. But what, then, is this fate?

If we reduce our problem to transcendental terms, it amounts to this: how, when we act quite freely, that is, with consciousness, can something arise for us unconsciously, which we never intended, and which freedom, left to itself, could never have brought about?

That which arises for me unintended, arises as the objective world does; but now by means of my free action, something else objective, a second nature, the moral order, is also to arise for me. But by free action nothing objective can arise for me, for everything objective arises, as such, without consciousness. It would thus be unintelligible how this second objective order could arise through free action, did not an unconscious activity stand in contrast to the conscious activity.

But an objective arises for me without consciousness only in intuition, so this proposition says, in effect: the objective in my free acting must in fact be an intuition; by which we thereupon come back to an earlier principle, which is in part explained already, but in part can only here for the first time attain to its full clarity.

For here in fact the objective element in acting acquires a significance quite different from what it has hitherto possessed. All my actions, in fact, proceed, as to their final goal, toward something that can be realized, not by the individual alone, but only *by the entire species;* at least all my actions ought to proceed towards this. The success of my actions is thus dependent not upon myself, but upon the willing of everyone else, and I can accomplish nothing toward such a goal unless everyone wills that goal. But this is assuredly doubtful and uncertain, indeed impossible, since the vast majority do not even have this goal in mind. How then can we extricate ourselves from this uncertainty? One might here perhaps think oneself driven immediately toward a moral world-order, and postulate the latter as a condition of attaining this goal. But how is one to furnish the proof that this moral world-order can be thought of as objective, as existing in absolute independence of freedom? The moral world-order, one might say, exists as soon as we establish it, but where, then, is it established? It is the communal effect of all intelligences, so far, that is, as they all, directly or indirectly, will nothing else but an order of this very sort. So long as this is not the case, the order itself has no existence either. Every individual intelligence can be regarded as a constitutive part of God, or of the moral world-order. Every rational being can say to himself: I too am entrusted with the execution of the law, and the practice of righteousness within my sphere of influence; I too have assigned to me a portion of the moral government of the world; but what am I, against so many? That order exists only insofar as all others think as I do, and exercise, each of them, his divine right to see that righteousness prevails.

Thus either I appeal to a *moral* world-order, but then cannot conceive it as absolutely objective; or else I demand something absolutely objective, which shall assure and as it were guarantee, in a manner wholly independent of *freedom*, the success of actions in contributing to the highest goal, and then, since the only objective element in willing is the unconscious element, I find myself driven toward an *unconscious* factor, whereby the external success of all actions has got to be assured.

For only if an unconscious lawfulness again prevails in the arbitrary, that is, wholly lawless actions of men, can I conceive of a finite unification of all actions toward a communal goal. But lawfulness is to be found only in intuition, and so this lawfulness is not possible unless that which appears to us as a free action is, objectively or regarded in itself, an intuition.

But now we are here of course talking, not of the individual's action, but of the act of the entire species. This second objective element which is to arise for us can be realized only by the species, that is, in history. But history, objectively regarded, is nothing else but a series of data which appears only subjectively as a series of free actions. The objective factor in history is thus an intuition indeed, but not an intuition of the individual, for it is not the individual who acts in history, but rather the species; hence the intuitant, or the objective factor in history, will have to be *one* for the entire species.

But now although the objective element in all intelligences is the same, yet every distinct individual acts with absolute freedom, and thus the actions of different rational beings would not necessarily harmonize; on the contrary, the freer the individual, the more contradiction there would be in the whole, unless this objective factor common to all intelligences were an *absolute synthesis*, wherein all contradictions were resolved and eliminated beforehand. – From the wholly lawless play of freedom, in which every free being indulges on his own behalf, as though there were no other outside him (which must always be assumed as a rule), something rational and harmonious is still to emerge eventually, and this I am obliged to presuppose in every action. Such a thing is inconceivable unless the objective factor in all acting is something communal, whereby all the acts of men are guided to one harmonious goal; and are so guided, that however they may set about things, and however unbridled the exercise of their choice, they yet must go where they did not want to, without, and even against, their own will; and this owing to a necessity hidden from them, whereby it is determined in advance that by the very lawlessness of their act, and the more lawless it is, the more surely, they bring about a development of the drama which they themselves were powerless to have in view. But this necessity can itself be thought of only through an absolute synthesis of all actions, from which there develops everything that happens, and hence also the whole of history; and in which, because it is absolute, everything is so far weighed and calculated that everything that may happen, however contradictory and discordant it may seem, still has and discovers its ground of union therein. But this absolute synthesis must itself be posited in the absolute, which in all free action is the intuitant, and the eternally and universally objective.

But now this whole viewpoint still leads us only to a natural mechanism, whereby the final outcome of all actions is assured, and by which, without any contribution from freedom, they are all directed toward the highest goal of the entire species. For the eternally objective factor – and the only one – for all intelligences is simply the lawfulness of nature, or of intuition, which in willing becomes something utterly independent of the intelligence. But now this unity of the objective for all intelligences serves only to disclose to me a predetermination of all history for *intuition*, by means of an absolute synthesis, whose mere development in a variety of sequences is what constitutes history. It does not tell me how this objective predetermination of all actions accords with the freedom of action itself. So this unity also explains to us but one of the determinations in the concept of history, namely *conformity to law*, which, as can now be seen, comes about solely in regard to the objective factor in acting (for this does in fact really belong to nature, and thus *must* obey law just insofar as it is nature; whence it would also be wholly useless to wish to derive this objective lawfulness of acting from freedom, since it generates itself quite mechanically and by itself, so to speak). But this unity does not explain for me the other determination, namely the coexistence of lawlessness, i.e., of *freedom*, with conformity to law. In other words, it leaves us none the wiser as to how that harmony is effected between this *objective* element, which brings forth what it generates through its own lawfulness, in complete independence of freedom, and the *freely determining* element.

At the present stage of our reflection there stand confronted – on the one hand the intelligence in itself (the absolutely objective element common to all intelligences), and on the other the freely determinant, absolutely subjective. The *intelligence in itself* serves to predetermine once and for all the objective lawfulness of history, but the objective and the freely determining factors are wholly independent of each other, and dependent each on itself alone – so how am I to be sure that objective predetermination and the infinite possibilities open to freedom are mutually exhaustive, and that the objective element is thus really an *absolute* synthesis for the whole of all free acts? And how, in that case, since freedom is absolute and can in no wise be determined by the objective, is there assurance nonetheless of a continuing agreement between the two? If the objective is always the determined, how then does it come to be precisely so determined that it accords objectively to freedom, which vents itself solely in choice, that which cannot itself lie therein, namely conformity to law? Such a preestablished harmony of the objective (or law-governed) and the determinant (or free) is conceivable only through some higher thing, set *over* them both, and which is therefore neither intelligence nor free, but rather is the common source of the intelligent and likewise of the free.

Now if this higher thing be nothing else but the ground of identity between the absolutely subjective and the absolutely objective, the conscious and the unconscious, which part company precisely in order to appear in the free act, then this higher thing itself can be neither subject nor object, nor both at once, but only the *absolute identity*, in which is no duality at all, and which, precisely because duality is the condition of all consciousness, can never attain thereto. This eternal unknown, which, like the everlasting sun in the realm of spirits, conceals itself behind its own unclouded light, and though never becoming an object, impresses its identity upon all free actions, is simultaneously the same for all intelligences, the invisible root of which all intelligences are but powers, and the eternal mediator between the self-determining subjective within us, and the objective or intuitant; at once the ground of lawfulness in freedom, and of freedom in the lawfulness of the object.

But now it is easy to see that this *absolutely identical principle*, which is already divided in the first act of consciousness, and by this separation generates the entire system of finitude, cannot, in fact, have any predicates whatever; for it is the absolutely simple, and thus can have no predicates drawn either from intelligence or free agency, and hence, too, can never be an object of knowledge, being an object only that is eternally presupposed in action, that is, an object of belief.

But now if this absolute is the true ground of harmony between objective and subjective in the free action, not only of the individual, but of the entire species, we shall be likeliest to find traces of this eternal and unalterable identity in the lawfulness which runs, like the weaving of an unknown hand, through the free play of choice in history.

Now if our reflection be directed merely to the *unconscious* or *objective* aspect in all action, we are obliged to suppose all free acts, and thus the whole of history, to be absolutely predetermined, not by a conscious foreordaining, but by a wholly blind one, finding expression in the obscure concept of destiny; and this is the system of *fatalism*. If reflection be directed solely to the *subjective* in its arbitrary determining, we arrive at a system of absolute lawlessness, the true system of *irreligion* and *atheism*, namely the claim that in all doing and acting there is neither law nor necessity anywhere. But if reflection be elevated to that absolute which is the common ground of the harmony between freedom and intelligence, we reach the system of providence, that is, *religion* in the only true sense of the word.

But now if this absolute, which can everywhere only *reveal* itself, had actually and fully revealed itself in history, or were ever to do so, it would at once make an end of the appearance of freedom. This perfect revelation would come about if free action were to coincide completely with predetermination. But if there ever were such a coincidence, if the absolute synthesis, that is, were ever completely evolved, we should recognize that everything which has come about through freedom in the course of history, was governed in this whole by law, and that all actions, although they seemed to be free, were in fact necessary, precisely in order to bring this whole into being. The opposition between conscious and unconscious activity is necessarily in unending one, for were it ever to be done away with, the appearance of freedom, which rests entirely upon it, would be done away with too. We can therefore conceive of no point in time at which the absolute synthesis – or to put it in empirical terms, the design of providence – should have brought its development to completion.

If we think of history as a play in which everyone involved performs his part quite freely and as he pleases, a rational development of this muddled drama is conceivable only if there be a single spirit who speaks in everyone, and if the playwright, whose mere fragments (*disjecta membra poetae*) are the individual actors, has already so harmonized beforehand the objective outcome of the whole with the free play of every participant, that something rational must indeed emerge at the end of it. But now if the playwright *were to exist* independently of his drama, we should be merely the actors who speak the lines he has written. If he *does* not exist independently of us, but reveals and discloses himself successively only, through the very play of our own freedom, so that without this freedom even he himself *would not be*, then we are collaborators of the whole and have ourselves invented the particular roles we play. – The ultimate ground of the harmony between freedom and the objective (or lawful) can therefore never become wholly objectified, if the appearance of freedom is to remain. – The absolute acts through each single intelligence, whose action is thus *itself* absolute, and to that extent neither free nor unfree, but both at once, *absolutely* free, and for that very reason also necessary. But if now the intelligence steps out from the absolute point of view, that is, out of the universal identity in which nothing can be distinguished, and becomes conscious of (distinguishes) itself, which comes about in that its act becomes objective to it, or passes over into the objective world, the free and the necessary are then separated therein. It is free only as an inner appearance, and that is why we are and believe ourselves to be always inwardly free, although insofar as it passes into the objective world the appearance of our freedom, or our freedom itself, falls just as much under laws of nature as any other occurrence.

Now it can straightway be inferred from the foregoing, which view of history is the only true one. History as a whole is a progressive, gradually self-disclosing revelation of the absolute. Hence one can never point out in history the particular places where the mark of providence, or God Himself, is as it were visible. For God never *exists*, if the existent *is* that which presents itself in the objective world; if *He existed* thus, then *we* should not; but He continually *reveals* Himself. Man, through his history, provides a continuous demonstration of God's presence, a demonstration, however, which only the whole of history can render complete. Everything depends upon these alternatives being understood. *If* God exists, that is, if the objective world constitutes a perfect manifestation of God, or what comes to the same, of the total congruence of the free with the unconscious, then nothing can be *otherwise* than it is. But the objective world is assuredly not like this. Or is it, perhaps, really a complete revelation of God? – Now if the appearance of freedom is necessarily infinite, the total evolution of the absolute synthesis is also an infinite process, and history itself a never wholly completed revelation of that absolute which, for the sake of consciousness, and thus merely for the sake of appearance, separates itself into conscious and unconscious, the free and the intuitant; but which *itself*, however, in the light inaccessible wherein it dwells, is eternal identity and the everlasting ground of harmony between the two.

We can presume three periods of this revelation, and thus three periods of history. The ground for such a division is provided by the two opposites, destiny and providence, between which the middle ground is occupied by nature, which supplies the transition from one to the other.

The first period is that wherein the ruling power still operates as destiny, i.e., as a wholly blind force, which coldly and unwittingly destroys even what is greatest and most splendid; to this period of history, which we may call the tragic period, belongs the downfall of the glory and the wonder of the ancient world, the collapse of those great empires of which scarcely the memory has survived, and whose greatness we deduce only from their ruins; the downfall of the noblest race of men that ever flourished upon earth, and whose return there is simply a perennial wish.

The second period of history is that wherein what appeared in the first as destiny, or a wholly blind power, reveals itself as nature, and the dark decree which formerly prevailed at least appears transformed into a manifest *natural law*, compelling freedom and wholly unbridled choice to subserve a *natural plan*, and thus gradually importing into history at least a mechanical conformity to law. This period seems to start with the expansion of the mighty republic of Rome, from which point onwards the unruly will, expressing itself in a general urge to conquer and subdue, is brought under constraint. In first joining the nations generally together, and in bringing into mutual contact such customs and laws, such arts and sciences, as had hitherto been merely conserved in isolation among particular peoples, it was compelled unconsciously, and even against its will, to subserve a natural plan which, in its full development, is destined to lead to a general comity of nations and the universal state. All events which fall within this period are thus to be regarded also as mere natural consequences, so that even the fall of the Roman Empire has neither a tragic nor a moral aspect, being a necessary outcome of nature's laws, and indeed a mere tribute that was paid over to nature.

The third period of history will be that wherein the force which appeared in the earlier stages as destiny or nature has evolved itself as *providence*, and wherein it will become apparent that even what seemed to be simply the work of destiny or nature was already the beginning of a providence imperfectly revealing itself.

When this period will begin, we are unable to tell. But whenever it comes into existence, God also will then *exist*.

Translated by Peter Heath

18.

Johann Gottlieb Fichte, The Characteristics of the Present Age (Die Grundzüge des gegenwärtigen Zeitalters): *Lectures 1 and 2 (1806)*

The Characteristics of the Present Age is a lecture course which Fichte held in Berlin in 1804–5 and then published 1806. This was, in fact, slightly prior to the foundation of the University of Berlin, a project for which he presented, in 1807, a 'Deduced Scheme for an Academy to be Established in Berlin', and where from 1810 onwards he worked as professor, dean and rector. *The Characteristics of the Present Age* belongs amongst Fichte's popular-philosophical writings, writings that were not intended to serve as academic instruction, but addressed instead a wider public. Having finished his 'original system', which comprises the *Science of Knowledge*, *Foundations of Natural Right* and the *System of the Science of Ethics*, Fichte, between 1800 and 1808, published a whole series of such popular-philosophical writings, achieving, indeed, some influence: *The Vocation of Man* (1800), *The Characteristics of the Present Age* (1804–5), *On the Nature of the Scholar* (1805), *The Way towards the Blessed Life, or the Doctrine of Religion* (1806), *Addresses to the German Nation* (1807–8).

In the seventeen lectures of the *Characteristics* Fichte offers an analysis of the historical development of humanity, focusing on the idea of freedom. At the end, in the seventeenth lecture, Fichte proclaims that a religious stance is the essence of any philosophical contemplation of history. His view, influenced by Kant and Herder, is that 'empirical observation' of ongoing processes suffices merely to 'list' the phenomena, but it does not furnish an *understanding* of their connection. The substance of Fichte's lectures is to explore the significance of the present age rather than merely to have 'added to the number of its phenomena'.[1] Historical understanding requires *concepts* which refer 'back the multiform phenomena which lie before us to the unity of one common principle'. It is not 'chroniclers' but 'historiographers' who understand history. The philosophical conception of an age or epoch establishes the 'necessary' connection of each epoch with 'time as a whole'. Philosophy must be able to 'describe all possible

---

[1] J. G. Fichte, trans. William Smith, *Characteristics of the Present Age* [1806], in *The Popular Works of Johann Gottlieb Fichte* (London: Trübner and Co, 1889), volume II, p. 271 (*FW* VII, 248).

epochs *a priori* '. Fichte takes this methodological conception of an *a priori* philosophy of history – one based on concepts of reason – from Kant.

Fichte is a Kantian also in the way in which his philosophy of history concentrates on the concept of freedom: for him the history of human culture (of 'earthly life') is a history of freedom. He starts with this principle: 'the End of the Life of Mankind on Earth is this, – that in this life they may order all their relations with Freedom according to Reason'. And applying this principle Fichte divides the cultural history of mankind *a priori* into '*Five* Principal Epochs of Earthly Life'. At the beginning of these epochs, reason stands as a mere 'dark instinct', and at the end the laws of reason stand as realised freedom. Where Kant often (albeit non-explicitly) speaks in his philosophy of history of the ends of nature that manifest themselves in the progress of mankind Fichte uses the speculative assumption of a 'world plan' in the *Characteristics*. He considers the latter a historiographically necessary *a priori* precondition of understanding.

Fichte develops a series of epochs by means of a dialectic of intermediate elements. From the conceptual contrast between the epochs of (i) 'instinct' and (v) 'freedom' he derives (iii) a middle epoch. And from the opposition of (i: instinct) to (iii) he develops (ii) a second epoch, and from the opposition of (iii) to (v: freedom) we have (iv) a fourth epoch. In the second lecture Fichte summarises the 'five main epochs' as follows: 'that in which Reason governs in the form of blind Instinct; that in which this instinct is changed into an external ruling Authority; that in which the dominion of this Authority, and with it that of reason itself, is overthrown; that in which Reason and its laws are understood with clear consciousness; and finally, that in which all the relations of the [human] Race shall be directed and ordered by perfect Freedom according to Reason'.

Fichte characterises his epoch (i.e. that of 1804) as standing 'precisely in the middle of Earthly Time'. It stands between the 'the World of Darkness and that of Light, – the World of Constraint and that of Freedom' and as such shares the features of both of these crucial epochs. It is an epoch of the liberation from the blind instinct of reason and from external authority, as well as an epoch of 'absolute indifference towards all truth, and of entire and unrestrained licentiousness: – the State of completed Sinfulness'. Following a scientific, social and political-philosophical diagnosis of his time, Fichte's lectures on the philosophy of history lead to the somewhat sanctimonious recommendation of a religious attitude from which alone modern humanity can fulfil its historic-epochal mission: the turn from the 'thoughtlessness' and 'frivolity' to an understanding of the 'whole' and the 'noble in man',[2] from superficiality to 'the highest inward blessedness',[3] from egoist to a conscious species-being, from subject to free citizen. Only the 'light of religion' would be able to achieve this. It consists in 'regarding and recognizing all Earthly Life as a necessary development of the one, original,

[2] Ibid., p. 284 (*FW* VII, 250).
[3] Ibid., p. 285 (*FW* VII, 251).

perfectly good and perfectly blessed Divine Life'⁴ and in doing so, finding 'inward Peace'.⁵

Fichte's assumption of a 'world-plan', however, might be questioned by means of Kant's critique of Herder: 'What should we think of this hypothesis of invisible forces acting on the organism; and then, how should we regard the design which aims to explain that which does not comprehend by that which one comprehends even less?'⁶ And if philosophical argument rather than a form of existential taste is to count the religious message that eventually concludes the *Characteristics* is not likely to convince.

The Characteristics of the Present Age deserves continuing attention, nevertheless. In its methodology of an *a priori*-deductive and dialectical philosophy of history Fichte's lectures provide an often unnoticed but important step from Kant's reason based theory of history towards Hegel's dialectic of history. And what remains of philosophical significance in Fichte's philosophy of history is his freedom-teleology, which might be considered a necessary heuristic fiction of any philosophy of history which intends to have practical application.

---

⁴ Ibid., p. 273 (*FW* VII, 240).
⁵ Ibid., p. 287 (*FW* VII, 253).
⁶ Immanuel Kant, 'Reviews of Herder's *Idea for a Philosophy of the History of Mankind*', in *Kant on History* (Indianapolis, Ind.: Bobbs-Merrill, 1963), p. 37 (*KAA* VIII, 53), edited by Lewis White Beck.

LECTURE I.
(IDEA OF UNIVERSAL HISTORY)†

We now enter upon a series of meditations which, nevertheless, at bottom contains only a single thought, constituting of itself one organic whole. If I could at once communicate to you this single thought in the same clearness with which it must necessarily be present to my own mind before I begin my undertaking, and with which it must guide me in every word which I have now to address to you, then from the first step of our progress, perfect light would overspread the whole path which we have to pursue together. But I am compelled gradually, and in your own sight, to build up this single thought out of its several parts, disengaging it at the same time from various modifying elements: this is the necessary condition of every communication of thought, and only by this its fundamental law does that which in itself is but one single thought become expanded and broken up into a series of thoughts and meditations.

Such being the case, and especially as I am not here to repeat what has been already known of old, but to put forth new views of things, – I must request of

†*FW* VII, 3–18. *Characteristics of the Present Age*, in *The Popular Works of Johann Gottlieb Fichte* (London: Trübner and Co., 1889), volume II.

you at the outset not to be surprised if our subject does not at first manifest that clearness which, according to the laws of all communication of thought, it can acquire only through subsequent development; and I must entreat you to look for perfect light only at our conclusion, when a complete survey of the whole shall have become possible. Nevertheless it is the duty of every man who undertakes to propound any subject whatever, to take care that each separate thought shall assume its proper place in his arrangement, and be produced there with all the distinctness which it is possible to throw around it in that place, – at least for those who can appreciate distinct language, and are capable of following a connected discourse; and I shall use my most earnest efforts to fulfil this duty.

With this first and only premonition, let us now, without farther delay, proceed to our subject.

A philosophical picture of the Present Age is what we have promised in these lectures. But that view only can be called philosophical which refers back the multiform phenomena which lie before us in experience to the unity of one common principle, and, on the other hand, from that one principle can deduce and completely explain those phenomena. The mere Empiricist who should undertake a description of the Age would seize upon some of its most striking phenomena, just as they presented themselves to casual observation, and recount these, without having any assured conviction that he had understood them all, and without being able to point out any other connexion between them than their coexistence in one and the same time. The Philosopher who should propose to himself the task of such a description would, independently of all experience, seek out an Idea of the Age (which indeed in its own form, – *as Idea*, – cannot be apparent in experience), and exhibit the mode in which this Idea would reveal itself under the forms of the necessary phenomena of the Age; and in so doing he would distinctly exhaust the circle of these phenomena, and bring them forth in necessary connexion with each other, through the common Idea which lies at the bottom of them all. The first would be the *Chronicler* of the Age; the second would have made a *History* of it a possible thing.

In the first place, if the Philosopher must deduce from the unity of his presupposed principle all the possible phenomena of experience, it is obvious that in the fulfilment of this purpose he does not require the aid of experience; that in following it out he proceeds merely as a Philosopher, confining himself strictly within the limits which that character imposes upon him, paying no respect whatever to experience, and thus absolutely *a priori*, as this method is termed in scientific phraseology; – and in respect to our own subject it is clear that he must be able *a priori* to describe Time as a whole, and all its possible Epochs. It is an entirely different question whether the *present time* be actually characterized by the phenomena that are deduced from the principle which he may lay down, and thus whether the Age so pictured by the speaker be really the Present Age, – should he maintain such a position, as we, for example, shall maintain it. On this part of the subject every man must consult for himself the experience of his life, and compare it with the history of the Past, as well as with his anticipations of the Future; for here the business of the Philosopher is at an end, and that of the Observer of the world and of men begins. We, for our part, intend to be no more than philosophers in this place, and have bound ourselves to nothing more; and thus the final judgment, so soon as you are in a position to pass such a judgment, must devolve upon you. It is now our business, in the first place, strictly to settle and define our theme.

Thus then: Every particular Epoch of Time, as we have already hinted above, is the fundamental Idea of a particular Age. These Epochs and fundamental Ideas of particular Ages, however, can only be thoroughly understood by and through each other, and by means of their relation to Universal Time. Hence it is clear that the Philosopher, in order to be able rightly to characterize and individual Age – and, if he will, his own – must first have understood *a priori* and thoroughly penetrated into the signification of Universal Time and all its possible Epochs.

This comprehension of Universal Time, like all philosophical comprehension, again presupposes a fundamental Idea of Time; an Idea of a fore-ordered, although only gradually unfolding, accomplishment of Time, in which each successive period is determined by the preceding; – or, to express this more shortly and in more common phraseology, – it presupposes a *World-plan*, which, in its primitive unity, may be clearly comprehended, and from which may be correctly deduced all the great Epochs of human life on Earth, so that they may be distinctly understood both in their origin, and in their connexion with each other. The former, – the World-plan, – is the fundamental Idea of the entire life of Man on Earth; the latter, – the chief Epochs of this life, – are the fundamental Ideas of particular Ages of which we have spoken, from which again the phenomena of these Ages are to be deduced.

We have thus, in the first place, a fundamental Idea of the entire life of Man, dividing itself into different Epochs, which can only be understood by and through each other; each of which Epochs is again the fundamental Idea of a particular Age, and is revealed in manifold phenomena therein.

The life of Mankind *on this Earth* stands here in place of the *One Universal Life*, and *Earthly Time* in place of *Universal Time*; – such are the limits within which we are confined by the proposed popular character of our discourses, since it is impossible to speak at once profoundly and popularly of the Heavenly and Eternal. Here, I say, and in these discourses only, shall this be so; for, strictly speaking, and in the higher flights of speculation, Human Life on Earth, and Earthly Time itself, are but necessary Epochs of the OEN TIME and of the ONE ETERNAL LIFE; – and this Earthly Life with all its subordinate divisions may be deduced from the fundamental Idea of the ETERNAL LIFE already accessible to us here below. It is our present voluntary limitation alone which forbids us to undertake this strictly demonstrable deduction, and permits us here only to declare the fundamental Idea of the Earthly Life, requesting every hearer to bring this Idea to the test of his own sense of truth, and, if he can, to approve it thereby. Life of MANKIND on Earth, we have said, and Epochs of this Life. We speak here only of the progressive Life of the [human] *Race*, not of the *Individual*, which last in all these discourses shall remain untouched, – and I beg of you never to lose sight of this our proper point of view.

The Idea of a World-Plan is thus implied in our inquiry, which, however, I am not at this time to deduce from the fundamental Idea indicated above, but only to point out. I say therefore, – and so lay the foundation of our rising edifice, – *the End of the Life of Mankind on Earth is this, – that in this Life they may order all their relations with* FREEDOM *according to* REASON.

With FREEDOM, I have said; – their own Freedom, – the Freedom of Mankind in their collective capacity, – *as a Race*: – and this Freedom is the first accessory condition of our fundamental principle which I intend at present to pursue, leaving the other conditions, which may likewise need explanation, to the subsequent lectures. This Freedom becomes apparent in the collective consciousness of the Race, and it appears there as the proper and peculiar Freedom of the Race; – as a true and real fact; – the product of the Race during its Life and proceeding from its Life, so that the absolute existence of the Race itself is necessarily implied in the existence of the fact and product thus attributed to it. (If a certain person has done something, it is unquestionably implied in that fact that the person has been in existence prior to the deed, in order that he might form the resolution so to act; and also during the accomplishment of the deed, in order that he might carry his previous resolution into effect; and every one might justly accept the proof of *non-existence* at a particular time, as equivalent to the proof of *non-activity* at the same time. In the same way, – if Mankind, as a Race, has done something, and appeared as the actor in such deed, this act must necessarily imply the existence of the Race at a time when the act had not yet been accomplished.)

As an immediate consequence of this remark, the Life of Mankind on Earth divides itself, according to the fundamental Idea which we have laid down, into two principal Epochs or Ages: – the one in which the Race exists and lives without as yet having ordered its relations with FREEDOM according to REASON; and the other in which this voluntary and reasonable arrangement is brought about.

To begin our farther inquiry with the first Epoch; – it does not follow, because the Race has not yet, *by its own free act*, ordered its relations according to Reason, that therefore these relations are not ordered by Reason; and hence the one assertion is by no means to be confounded with the other. It is possible that Reason of itself, by its own power, and without the cooperation of human Freedom, may have determined and ordered the relations of Mankind. And so it is in reality. Reason is the FIRST LAW of the Life of a Race of Men, as of all Spiritual Life; and in this sense and in no other shall the word 'Reason' be used in these lectures. Without the living activity of this law a Race of Men could never have come into existence; or, even if it could be supposed to have attained to being, it could not, without this activity, maintain its existence for a single moment. Hence, where Reason cannot as yet work by Freedom, as in the first Epoch, it acts as a law or power of Nature; and thus may be present in consciousness and active there, only without insight into the grounds of its activity; or, in other words, may exist as mere feeling, for so we call consciousness without insight.

In short, to express this in common language: – Reason acts as *blind Instinct*, where it cannot as yet act through Free Will. It acts thus in the first Epoch of the Life of Mankind on Earth; and this first Epoch is thereby more closely characterized and more strictly defined.

By means of this stricter definition of the first Epoch, we are also enabled, by contrast, more strictly to define the second. Instinct is *blind*; – a consciousness without insight. Freedom, as the opposite of Instinct, is thus *seeing*, and clearly conscious of the grounds of its activity. But the sole ground of this free activity is Reason; – Freedom is thus conscious of Reason, of which Instinct was unconscious. Hence, between the dominion of Reason through mere Instinct, and the dominion of the same Reason through Freedom, there arises an intermediate condition, – *the Consciousness or Knowledge of Reason.*

But further: – Instinct as a blind impulse excludes Knowledge; hence the birth of Knowledge presupposes a liberation from the compulsive power of Instinct as already accomplished; and thus between the dominion of Reason as Instinct and that of Reason as Knowledge, there is interposed a third condition, – *that of Liberation from Reason as Instinct.*

But how could humanity free itself, or even wish to free itself, from that Instinct which is the law of its existence, and rules it with beloved and unobtrusive power? – or how could the *one* Reason which while it speaks in Instinct, is likewise active in the impulse towards Freedom, – how could this *same* Reason come into conflict and opposition with itself in human life? Clearly not directly; and hence a new medium must intervene between the dominion of Reason as Instinct, and the impulse to cast off that dominion. This medium arises in the following way: – the results of Reason as Instinct are seized upon by the more powerful individuals of the Race; – in whom, on this very account, that Instinct speaks in its loudest and fullest tones, as the natural but precipitate desire to elevate the whole race to the level of their own greatness, or rather to put themselves in the room and place of the Race; – and by them it is changed into an *external ruling Authority*, upheld through outward constraint; and then among other men Reason awakes in another form – *as the impulse towards Personal Freedom*, – which, although it never opposes the mild rule of the inward Instinct which it loves, yet rises in rebellion against the pressure of a foreign Instinct which has usurped its rights; and in this awakening it breaks the chains, – not of Reason as Instinct itself, – but of the Instinct of foreign natures clothed in the garb of external power. And thus the change of the individual Instinct into a compulsive Authority becomes the medium between the dominion of Reason as Instinct and the liberation from that dominion.

And finally, to complete this enumeration of the necessary divisions and Epochs of the Earthly Life of our Race: – We have said that through liberation from the dominion of Reason as *Instinct*, the *Knowledge* of Reason becomes possible. By the laws of this Knowledge, all the relations of Mankind must be ordered and directed by *their own free act*. But it is obvious that mere cognizance of the law, which nevertheless is all that Knowledge of itself can give us, is not sufficient for the attainment of this purpose, but that there is also needed a peculiar knowledge of action, which can only be thoroughly acquired by practice, – in a word, *Art*. This Art of ordering the whole relations of Mankind according to that Reason which has been already consciously apprehended, (for in this higher sense we shall always use the word Art when we employ it without explanatory remark) – this Art must be universally applied to all the relations of Mankind, and realized therein, – until the Race becomes a perfect image of its everlasting archetype in Reason; – and then shall the purpose of this Earthly Life be attained, its end become apparent, and Mankind enter upon the higher spheres of Eternity.

Thus have we endeavoured to pre-figure the whole Earthly Life of Man by a comprehension of its purpose; – to perceive *why* our Race had to begin its Existence here, and by this means to describe the whole present Life of humankind: – this is what we wished to do, – it was our first task. There are, according to this view, *Five* Principal Epochs of Earthly Life, each of which, although taking its rise in the life of the individual, must yet, in order to become an Epoch in the Life of the Race, gradually lay hold of and interpenetrate all Men; and to that end must endure throughout long periods of time, so that the great Whole of Life is spread out into Ages, which sometimes seem to cross, sometimes to run parallel with each other: – 1*st*, The Epoch of the unlimited dominion of Reason as Instinct: – *the State of Innocence of the Human Race.* 2*nd*, The Epoch in which Reason as Instinct is changed into an external ruling Authority; – the Age of positive Systems of life and doctrine, which never go back to their ultimate foundations, and hence have no power to convince but on the contrary merely desire to compel, and which demand blind faith and unconditional obedience: – *the State of progressive Sin.* 3*rd*, The Epoch of Liberation, – *directly* from the external ruling Authority – *indirectly* from the power of Reason as Instinct, and *generally* from Reason in any form; – the Age of absolute indifference towards all truth, and of entire and unrestrained licentiousness: – *the State of completed Sinfulness.* 4*th*, The Epoch of Reason as *Knowledge*; – the Age in which Truth is looked upon as the *highest*, and loved before all other things: – *the State of progressive Justification.* 5*th*, The Epoch of Reason as Art; – the Age in which Humanity with more sure and unerring hand builds itself up into a fitting image and representative of Reason: – *the State of completed Justification and Sanctification.* Thus, the whole progress which, upon this view. Humanity makes here below, is only a retrogression to the point on which it stood at first, and has nothing in view save that return to its original condition. But Humanity must make this journey on its own feet; by its own strength it must bring itself back to that state in which it was once before without its own cooperation, and which, for that very purpose, it must first of all leave. If Humanity could not of itself re-create its own true being, then would it possess no real Life; and then were there indeed no real Life at all, but all things would remain dead, rigid, immoveable. In Paradise, – to use a well-known picture, – in the Paradise of innocence and well-being, without knowledge, without labour, without art, Humanity awakes to life. Scarcely has it gathered courage to venture upon independent existence when the Angel comes with the fiery sword of compulsion to good and drives it forth from the seat of its innocence and its peace. Fugitive and irresolute it wanders through the empty waste, scarcely daring to plant its foot firmly anywhere lest the ground should sink beneath it. Grown bolder by necessity, it settles in some poor corner, and in the sweat of its brow roots out the thorns and thistles of barbarism from the soil on which it would rear the beloved fruit of knowledge. Enjoyment opens its eyes and strengthens its hands, and it builds a Paradise for itself after the image of that which it has lost; – the tree of Life arises; it stretches forth its hand to the fruit, and eats, and lives in Immortality.

This is the delineation of Earthly Life as a whole and in all its various Epochs, which is necessary for our present purpose. As surely as our present Age is a part of this Earthly Life, which no one can doubt; – and further, as surely as there are no other possible Epochs of the Earthly Life but the five which we have indicated, – so surely does our Present Age belong to one of these. It shall be my business to point out, according to my knowledge and experience of the world, to which of these five it belongs, and to unfold the necessary phenomena in which the principles above stated must manifest themselves; – and it will be yours to consider and observe whether you have not encountered these phenomena during your whole life both internal and external, and do not still encounter them; – and this shall be the business of our future lectures.

The Present Age considered *as a whole*, I mean; – for since, as I have remarked above, different Ages may, in perfect accordance with their spiritual principle, coëxist in one and the same chronological Time, and even cross or run parallel to each other in different individuals, – so it may be anticipated that such will be the case in our own Age, and hence that our application of the *a priori* principle to the present condition of the world and of humanity may not embrace all men alive in the present Time, but only those who are truly products of the Age and in whom it most completely reveals itself. One may be behind his Age, because in the course of his culture he has not come into contact with a sufficiently extensive mass of his fellow-men, but has been trained in some narrow circle which is only a remnant of a former Time. Another may be in advance of his Age, and bear in his breast the germs of a future Time, while that which has become old to him still rules around him in true, actual, present and efficient power. Finally, – Science raises itself above all Ages and all Times, embracing and apprehending the ONE UNCHANGING TIME as the higher source of all Ages and Epochs, and grasping that vast idea in its free, unbounded comprehension. None of these three can be included in the picture of *any* present Age.

The object of our lectures in this course, during the present winter, is now strictly defined, and, as it seems to me, clearly enough set forth and announced; – and such was the purpose of today's address. Allow me, further, a few words on the external form of these discourses.

Whatever may be our judgment upon the Present Age, and in whatever Epoch we may feel ourselves compelled to place it, you are not to expect here either the tone of lamentation or of satire, particularly of a personal description. Not of lamentation: – for it is the sweetest reward of Philosophy that, looking upon all things in their mutual dependence, and upon nothing as isolated and alone, she finds all to be necessary and therefore good, and accepts that which is, as it is, because it is subservient to a higher end. Besides, it is unmanly to waste in lamentation over existing evil the time which would be more wisely applied in striving, so far as in us lies, to create the Good and the Beautiful. Not of satire: – an infirmity which affects the whole race, is no proper object for the scorn of an individual who belongs to that race, and who, before he could depict it, must himself have known it and cast it off. But individuals disappear altogether from the view of the philosopher, and are lost in the one great commonwealth. His thought embraces all objects in a clear and consequential light, which they can never attain amid the endless fluctuations of reality; – hence it does not concern itself with individuals and, never descending to portraits, dwells in the higher sphere of idealized conception. As to the advantages derivable from considerations of this kind, it will be better to leave you to judge for yourselves after you have gone through some considerable portion of them, than to say much in praise of them beforehand. No one is further than the philosopher from the vain desire that his Age should be impelled forward to some obvious extent through his exertions. Every one, indeed, to whom God has given strength and opportunity, should exert all his powers for this end, were it only for his own sake, and in order to maintain the place which has been assigned to him in the ever-flowing current of existence. For the rest, Time rolls on in the steadfast course marked out for it from eternity, and individual effort can neither hasten nor retard its progress. Only the cooperation of all, and especially of the indwelling Eternal Spirit of Ages and of Worlds, may promote it.

As to my present labours, it will be to me a flattering reward, if a cultivated and intelligent audience shall pass a few hours of this half year in an agreeable and worthy manner, raised above the business and pleasures of everyday life into a freer and purer region, – a more spiritual atmosphere. Above all, should it happen that upon some young and powerful mind a spark may fall which shall dwell and live there, and perhaps develop my feeble thoughts into better and more perfect results, and kindle a vigorous determination to realize them, – then would my reward be complete.

In this spirit I have been induced to invite you to such lectures as the present; in this spirit I now take my leave of you, and leave it to your own judgment whether you desire to proceed further in my company.

LECTURE II.
(GENERAL DELINEATION OF THE THIRD AGE)

In the first place, let him who desires to be met with the same honest purpose which I presume leads him here, cast back a kindly glance upon our former lecture.

It appears that many of this assembly have not been able altogether to follow the greater part of that which I said at the beginning of my previous address. In so far as this may have any other cause than want of acquaintance with the style, voice, and manner of the lecturer, and the novelty of the whole situation, – all of which may be overcome by a few minutes' custom, – allow me, as some consolation should the like happen again, to add the following: – That which some of my hearers have been unable thoroughly to comprehend, does not so much belong to the subject itself, as to the practice of the art which we now employ, – the art of philosophizing. It is serviceable to us in finding an introduction and commencement in the circle of other knowledge from which to set forth our subject, and in strictly defining our point of separation from this system of knowledge; it is a part of the account which we teachers and masters must render of our manner of working. Every other art, – as poetry, music, painting, – may be practised without the process showing forth the rules according to which it is conducted; – but in the self-cognizant art of the philosopher no step can be taken without declaring the grounds upon which it proceeds; and in it theory and practice go hand in hand. It was necessary for me to proceed in this way on the former occasion, and in similar circumstances I must proceed in the same way again. But if any one chooses to admit beforehand, and without further proof, that I proceed correctly and according to the rules of my art, and will calmly and candidly test, by his own natural sense of truth, that which I have laid down as the foundation of the edifice, such an one will lose nothing essential by thus missing the scientific explanation; and it will be perfectly sufficient for our present purpose if, out of that which we laid down in our former lecture, he has thoroughly understood and accepted the following propositions, and has retained them in his memory, so that he may connect with them what we have further to lay before you.

He must, I say, thoroughly understand, accept, and keep in mind the following: – The life of the Human Race does not depend upon blind chance; nor is it, as is often superficially pretended, everywhere alike, so that it has always been as it is now and will always so remain; but it proceeds and moves onward according to a settled plan which *must* necessarily be fulfilled, and therefore *shall* certainly be fulfilled. This plan is – that the Race shall in this Life *and with freedom* mould and cultivate itself into a pure and express Image of Reason. The whole Life of Man is divided – I am now supposing that the strict derivation of this has not been thoroughly understood or has been forgotten, – the whole Life of Man is divided into *five* principal Epochs: – that in which Reason governs in the form of blind Instinct; that in which this Instinct is changed into an external ruling Authority; that in which the dominion of this Authority, and with it that of Reason itself, is overthrown; that in which Reason and its laws are understood with clear consciousness; and finally, that in which all the relations of the Race shall be directed and ordered by perfect Art and perfect Freedom according to Reason: – and, in order to impress these different Epochs firmly upon your memory by means of a sensuous representation, we made use of the universally known picture of Paradise. Further, he must understand that the Present Age, to which especially our present purpose refers, must fall within one or other of these five Epochs; that we have now to set forth the fundamental Idea of this Epoch, distinguishing it from the other four, which, except for the purposes of illustrating our own, we may here lay out of view; and that from this fundamental Idea we must deduce the peculiar phenomena of the Age as its necessary consequences. At this point our second lecture begins.

And so let us set forth with declaring at what point of the whole Earthly life of the Race we place our Present Age. I, for my part, hold that the Present Age stands precisely in the middle of Earthly Time; and as we may characterize the two first Epochs of our scheme (in which Reason rules first *directly* as Instinct, and then *indirectly* as Instinct through Authority) as the one Epoch of the dominion of *blind* or *unconscious Reason*; – and in like manner the two last Epochs in our scheme (in which Reason first appears as Knowledge, and then, by means of Art, enters upon the government of Life) as the one Epoch of the dominion of *seeing or conscious Reason*; – so the Present Age unites the ends of two essentially different Worlds, – the World of Darkness and that of Light, – the World of Constraint and that of Freedom, – without itself belonging to either of them. In other words, the Present Age, according to my view of it, stands in that Epoch which in my former lecture I named the THIRD, and which I characterized as *the Epoch of Liberation – directly from the external ruling Authority, – indirectly from the power of Reason as Instinct, and generally from Reason in any form; the Age of absolute indifference towards all truth, and of entire and unrestrained licentiousness: – the State of completed Sinfulness.* Our Age stands, I think, in this Epoch, taken with the limitations which I have already laid down, – namely, that I do not here include all men now living in our time, but only those who are truly products of the Age, and in whom it most completely reveals itself. [. . .]

Translated by William Smith

19

G. W. F. Hegel, Lectures on the Philosophy of World History (Vorlesungen über die Philosophie der Weltgeschichte): *Introduction (1840)*

Hegel's thoughts on the nature of history can be found throughout his works. However, it is in the *Lectures on the Philosophy of World History* that we find his ideas in their most systematic and accessible form. The lecture course of 1830–1 (posthumously published in 1840) was considered for many years the very centre of Hegel's philosophy. It seemed to set out issues which had been tortuously treated in the *Phenomenology of Spirit* (1807). It also provided historical background to some of the compressed views of the development of freedom explored in the *Philosophy of Right* (1821). The interest of scholars in the *Lectures on the Philosophy of World History* is rather limited these days, perhaps because it contains many speculative ideas that cannot easily be explained away by Hegel's many analytically-oriented interpreters.

The notion of *Geist* or *Spirit* plays a central role in Hegel's philosophy of history. It is clear that Hegel thinks of *Geist* as something more than the collective consciousness, or self-identity of a nation. *Geist* is not simply the distilled idea of what a group thinks: it is also intelligence. For Hegel progress in history is grounded in the efforts of *Geist* to realise itself, to come to completion. And its completion, according to Hegel, is the realisation of freedom. The element of intelligence or reason here is manifest by the apparent overcoming of obstacles and the growth beyond limitations which face *Geist* as it reaches toward its self-realisation.

The thesis that history might reach some kind of end-point – the self-realisation of *Geist* – has been the source of significant debate. It is a claim that can be made only from a point of view which can trace all of the steps or moments of this progression. Were we to posit that there might be future steps whose character, precisely as future events, we could not predict we might not know whether after all progress really was the case. But this leaves Hegel in a much criticised position: can he really be committed to the notion that his contemporaneous world is the culmination of history? And if so, is this a consequence of the logic of his philosophy of world history or a basic commitment of his political and allegedly dangerously conservative worldview (as the Young Hegelians feared)?

In the Introduction to the lectures (which we are considering here) Hegel carefully makes a number of distinctions which help define the specific task of a philosophical account of history. He distinguishes between original history, reflective history and philosophical history. It is worth paying some attention to the subdivisions within reflective history as they come closest to what today might be considered the proper domain of a philosophy of history. For instance, postmodern historiography understands history as what Hegel terms 'pragmatic', in that it alleges that historical narratives operate with an implicit though unacknowledged didactic agenda. And within more conventional philosophy of history we are likely to find issues surrounding what Hegel notes as 'critical history', that is, 'a History of History: a criticism of the historical narratives and an investigation of their truth and credibility'. It is clear that philosophical history, that kind of history which Hegel wants to discuss, is in no way akin to our contemporary sense of what a philosophy of history might be. (And the argument that Hegel has no philosophy of history as such deserves attention.[1]) Its task is not to understand specific events in themselves, but rather 'universal history'. Hegel sees philosophical history as a 'thoughtful consideration' (*denkende Betrachtung*) of history. This is further specified as the effort to find reason in history. In terms which remind us of his debt to Spinoza, Hegel sees reason as substance: it is the very material and form of the universe. Empirically the world and its history may appear arbitrary and structureless. Philosophically, or rather speculatively, however, it is substance. And as substance it can be understood as a process of unfolding, as – in Hegel's sense – a rational process. There is an interesting hermeneutic issue raised here: the rationality of history is to be assumed by the reader – with the promissory note that Hegel himself can reveal it to us – and yet rationality is to be discovered in history in so far as it is assumed to be there in the first place. The sceptical reader may not be willing to follow in that reason might be considered an arbitrary category by which to mould historical evidence. Indeed, this is a familiar problem in Hegel's systematic texts: if the truth of a proposition can only be demonstrated once we have traversed 'the whole' of which it is the truth why do we assume that proposition in the first place? Is there not the danger that the proposition assumed will prejudice the account we develop of 'the whole'?

Hegel sees history as the free – that is rationally guided – development of *Spirit* or *Geist*. This process is famously likened to an organic process in which a seed or germ contains implicitly its fully realised form as, say, a tree. However, it must, of course, undergo a process of development to be the actual realization of its potential, to self-actualise. The specific idea which lies behind the self-unfolding of *Geist* is, in fact, the modern notion of freedom. Here we find a classic thesis of German Idealism: the realisation of freedom is coextensive with the development of rationality

---

[1] Cf. George Dennis O'Brien, 'Does Hegel have a Philosophy of History?' in *Hegel* (Oxford: Oxford University Press, 1985), ed. Michael Inwood.

or reason. The forms of social life we are prepared to defend – differentiated as they are by the models of freedom under which they operate – depend ultimately on the forms of rationality we have available to us. In the *Lectures on the Philosophy of World History* Hegel traces this parallel development.

It is a matter of some controversy that Hegel both poignantly outlines the destructive and bloody tendencies of humanity whilst also seeking some sense of purpose behind them. A complaint against Hegel is that even the most gruesome events of history are for him simply moments in the self-development of *Geist*. The idea that history is the self-realisation of *Geist* raises the question: is not history enacted by human beings? And how do human beings with their selfish passions contribute to the crucial development of *Geist*? One of Hegel's most famous ideas is put forward as the answer: there are certain 'world historical individuals' – as examples, Alexander the Great, Julius Caesar, Napoleon – whose actions might be explained on a purely historical level as the result of their own selfish ambition. However, the changes made upon the world by their actions suggest something more: these were individuals whose actions were the result of 'the cunning of reason' which somehow made a neat agreement of personal ambition and the broader historical picture of 'what was ripe for development'.

Once Hegel's lectures move on from the Introduction, in which the main concepts are set out, he examines the development of history through a narrative of the progressive unfolding, passing-away and replacement of civilisations. This story begins with the 'Oriental World', concerning, amongst other things, China, India, Persia and Egypt. He then examines the 'Greek World', the 'Roman World', and, finally, what he calls the 'German World'. Despite its name the 'German World' includes key historical developments from outside the Nordic and Anglo-Saxon spheres, and it is united as that space which has evolved the modern notion of individual autonomy and rational statehood.

THE PHILOSOPHY OF HISTORY

Introduction†

The subject of this course of Lectures is the Philosophical History of the World. And by this must be understood, not a collection of general observations respecting it, suggested by the study of its records, and proposed to be illustrated by its facts,

---

† *HW* XII, 11–23. *The Philosophy of History* (New York: Collier, 1900).

but Universal History itself.[1] To gain a clear idea, at the outset, of the nature of our task, it seems necessary to begin with an examination of the other methods of treating History. The various methods may be ranged under three heads:

I. ORIGINAL HISTORY.
II. REFLECTIVE HISTORY.
III. PHILOSOPHICAL HISTORY.

I. Of the first kind, the mention of one or two distinguished names will furnish a definite type. To this category belong *Herodotus, Thucydides,* and other historians of the same order, whose descriptions are for the most part limited to deeds, events, and states of society, which they had before their eyes, and whose spirit they shared. They simply transferred what was passing in the world around them, to the realm of representative intellect. An external phenomenon is thus translated into an internal conception. In the same way the *poet* operates upon the material supplied him by his emotions, projecting it into an image for the conceptive faculty. These original historians did, it is true, find statements and narratives of other men ready to hand. One person cannot be an eye and ear witness of everything. But they make use of such aids only as the poet does of that heritage of an already-formed language, to which he owes so much, merely as an ingredient. Historiographers bind together the fleeting elements of story, and treasure them up for immortality in the Temple of Mnemosyne. Legends, Ballad-stories, Traditions must be excluded from such original history. These are but dim and hazy forms of historical apprehension, and therefore belong to nations whose intelligence is but half awakened. Here, on the contrary, we have to do with people fully conscious of what they were and what they were about. The domain of reality – actually seen, or capable of being so – affords a very different basis in point of firmness from that fugitive and shadowy element, in which were engendered those legends and poetic dreams whose historical prestige vanishes as soon as nations have attained a mature individuality.

Such original historians, then, change the events, the deeds and the states of society with which they are conversant, into an object for the conceptive faculty. The narratives they leave us cannot, therefore, be very comprehensive in their range. Herodotus, Thucydides, Guicciardini, may be taken as fair samples of the class in this respect. What is present and living in their environment, is their proper material. The influences that have formed the writer are identical with those which have molded the events that constitute the matter of his story. The author's spirit, and that of the actions he narrates, is one and the same. He describes scenes in which he himself has been an actor, or at any rate an interested spectator. It is short periods of time, individual shapes of persons and occurrences, single,

---

[1] I cannot mention any work that will serve as a compendium of the course, but I may remark that in my 'Outlines of the Philosophy of Law', §§ 341–360, I have already given a definition of such a Universal History as it is proposed to develop, and a syllabus of the chief elements or periods into which it naturally divides itself.

unreflected traits, of which he makes his picture. And his aim is nothing more than the presentation to posterity of an image of events as clear as that which he himself possessed in virtue of personal observation, or lifelike descriptions. Reflections are none of his business, for he lives in the spirit of his subject; he has not attained an elevation above it. If, as in Cæsar's case, he belongs to the exalted rank of generals or statesmen, it is the prosecution of *his own aims* that constitutes the history.

Such speeches as we find in Thucydides (for example) of which we can positively assert that they are not *bona fide* reports, would seem to make against our statement that a historian of his class presents us no reflected picture; that persons and people appear in his works *in propria persona*. Speeches, it must be allowed, are veritable transactions in the human commonwealth; in fact, very gravely influential transactions. It is, indeed, often said, 'Such and such things are only talk'; by way of demonstrating their harmlessness. That for which this excuse is brought may be mere 'talk', and talk enjoys the important privilege of being harmless. But addresses of peoples to peoples, or orations directed to nations and to princes, are integrant constituents of history. Granted that such orations as those of Pericles – that most profoundly accomplished, genuine, noble statesman – were elaborated by Thucydides; it must yet be maintained that they were not foreign to the character of the speaker. In the orations in question, these men proclaim the maxims adopted by their countrymen, and which formed their own character; they record their views of their political relations, and of their moral and spiritual nature, and the principles of their designs and conduct. What the historian puts into their mouths is no supposititious system of ideas, but an uncorrupted transcript of their intellectual and moral habitudes.

Of these historians, whom we must make thoroughly our own, with whom we must linger long, if we would live with their respective nations, and enter deeply into their spirit: of these historians, to whose pages we may turn not for the purpose of erudition merely, but with a view to deep and genuine enjoyment, there are fewer than might be imagined. Herodotus the *Father*, i.e. the *Founder* of History, and Thucydides have been already mentioned. Xenophon's *Retreat of the Ten Thousand*, is a work equally original. Cæsar's *Commentaries* are the simple masterpiece of a mighty spirit. Among the ancients, these annalists were necessarily great captains and statesmen. In the Middle Ages, if we except the Bishops, who were placed in the very centre of the political world, the Monks monopolize this category as naive chroniclers who were as decidedly *isolated* from active life as those elder annalists had been connected with it. In modern times the relations are entirely altered. Our culture is essentially comprehensive, and immediately changes all events into historical representations. Belonging to the class in question, we have vivid, simple, clear narrations – especially of military transactions – which might fairly take their place with those of Cæsar. In richness of matter and fulness of detail as regards strategic appliances, and attendant circumstances, they are even more instructive. The French 'Mémoires' also fall under this category. In many cases these are written by men of mark, though relating to affairs of little note.

They not infrequently contain a large proportion of anecdotal matter, so that the ground they occupy is narrow and trivial. Yet they are often veritable masterpieces in history, as those of Cardinal Retz, which in fact trench on a larger historical field. In Germany such masters are rare. Frederick the Great ('Histoire de mon temps') is an illustrious exception. Writers of this order must occupy an elevated position. Only from such a position is it possible to take an extensive view of affairs – to see everything. This is out of the question for him, who from below merely gets a glimpse of the great world through a miserable cranny.

II. The second kind of history we may call the *reflective*. It is history whose mode of representation is not really confined by the limits of the time to which it relates, but whose spirit transcends the present. In this second order a strongly marked variety of species may be distinguished.

1. It is the aim of the investigator to gain a view of the entire history of a people or a country, or of the world, in short, what we call *Universal History*. In this case the working up of the historical material is the main point. The workman approaches his task with *his own* spirit, a spirit distinct from that of the element he is to manipulate. Here a very important consideration will be the principles to which the author refers the bearing and motives of the actions and events which he describes, and those which determine the form of his narrative. Among us Germans this reflective treatment, and the display of ingenuity which it occasions, assume a manifold variety of phases. Every writer of history proposes to himself an original method. The English and French confess to general principles of historical composition. Their standpoint is more that of cosmopolitan or of national culture. Among us each labors to invent a purely individual point of view. Instead of writing history, we are always beating our brains to discover how history ought to be written. This first kind of Reflective History is most nearly akin to the preceding, when it has no further aim than to present the annals of a country complete. Such compilations (among which may be reckoned the works of Livy, Diodorus Siculus, Johannes von Müller's History of Switzerland) are, if well performed, highly meritorious. Among the best of the kind may be reckoned such annalists as approach those of the first class, who give so vivid a transcript of events that the reader may well fancy himself listening to contemporaries and eye-witnesses. But it often happens that the individuality of tone which must characterize a writer belonging to a different culture is not modified in accordance with the periods such a record must traverse. The spirit of the writer is quite other than that of the times of which he treats. Thus Livy puts into the mouths of the old Roman kings, consuls, and generals, such orations as would be delivered by an accomplished advocate of the Livian era, and which strikingly contrast with the genuine traditions of Roman antiquity (e.g. the fable of Menenius Agrippa). In the same way he gives us descriptions of battles, as if he had been an actual spectator, but whose features would serve well enough for battles in any period, and whose distinctness contrasts on the other hand with the want of connection, and the inconsistency that prevail elsewhere, even in his treatment of chief points of interest. The difference between such a compiler and an original historian may

be best seen by comparing Polybius himself with the style in which Livy uses, expands, and abridges his annals in those periods of which Polybius's account has been preserved. Johannes von Müller has given a stiff, formal, pedantic aspect to his history, in the endeavor to remain faithful in his portraiture to the times he describes. We much prefer the narratives we find in old Tschudy. All is more naive and natural than it appears in the garb of a fictitious and affected archaism.

A history which aspires to traverse long periods of time, or to be universal, must indeed forego the attempt to give individual representations of the past as it actually existed. It must foreshorten its pictures by abstractions, and this includes not merely the omission of events and deeds, but whatever is involved in the fact that Thought is, after all, the most trenchant epitomist. A battle, a great victory, a siege, no longer maintains its original proportions, but is put off with a bare mention. When Livy e.g. tells us of the wars with the Volsci, we sometimes have the brief announcement: 'This year war was carried on with the Volsci'.

2. A second species of Reflective History is what we may call the *Pragmatical*. When we have to deal with the Past, and occupy ourselves with a remote world, a Present rises into being for the mind – produced by its own activity, as the reward of its labor. The occurrences are, indeed, various, but the idea which pervades them – their deeper import and connection – is *one*. This takes the occurrence out of the category of the Past and makes it virtually Present. Pragmatical (didactic) reflections, though in their nature decidedly abstract, are truly and indefeasibly of the Present, and quicken the annals of the dead Past with the life of today. Whether, indeed, such reflections are truly interesting and enlivening, depends on the writer's own spirit. Moral reflections must here be specially noticed – the moral teaching expected from history, which latter has not infrequently been treated with a direct view to the former. It may be allowed that examples of virtue elevate the soul, and are applicable in the moral instruction of children for impressing excellence upon their minds. But the destinies of peoples and states, their interests, relations, and the complicated tissue of their affairs, present quite another field. Rulers, Statesmen, Nations, are wont to be emphatically commended to the teaching which experience offers in history. But what experience and history teach is this – that peoples and governments never have learned anything from history, or acted on principles deduced from it. Each period is involved in such peculiar circumstances, exhibits a condition of things so strictly idiosyncratic, that its conduct must be regulated by considerations connected with itself, and itself alone. Amid the pressure of great events, a general principle gives no help. It is useless to revert to similar circumstances in the Past. The pallid shades of memory struggle in vain with the life and freedom of the Present. Looked at in this light, nothing can be shallower than the oft-repeated appeal to Greek and Roman examples during the French Revolution. Nothing is more diverse than the genius of those nations and that of our times. Johannes v. Müller, in his Universal History as also in his History of Switzerland, had such moral aims in view. He designed to prepare a body of political doctrines for the instruction of princes, governments and peoples (he formed a special collection of doctrines and reflections – frequently giving us

in his correspondence the exact number of apothegms which he had compiled in a week), but he cannot reckon this part of his labor as among the best that he accomplished. It is only a thorough, liberal, comprehensive view of historical relations (such e.g. as we find in Montesquieu's 'Esprit des Loix'), that can give truth and interest to reflections of this order. One Reflective History, therefore, supersedes another. The materials are patent to every writer: each is likely enough to believe himself capable of arranging and manipulating them, and we may expect that each will insist upon his own spirit as that of the age in question. Disgusted by such reflective histories, readers have often returned with pleasure to a narrative adopting no particular point of view. These certainly have their value, but for the most part they offer only material for history. We Germans are content with such. The French, on the other hand, display great genius in reanimating bygone times, and in bringing the past to bear upon the present condition of things.

3. The third form of Reflective History is the *Critical*. This deserves mention as pre-eminently the mode of treating history now current in Germany. It is not history itself that is here presented. We might more properly designate it as a History of History, a criticism of historical narratives and an investigation of their truth and credibility. Its peculiarity in point of fact and of intention, consists in the acuteness with which the writer extorts something from the records which was not in the matters recorded. The French have given us much that is profound and judicious in this class of composition. But they have not endeavored to pass a merely critical procedure for substantial history. They have duly presented their judgments in the form of critical treatises. Among us, the so-called 'higher criticism', which reigns supreme in the domain of philology, has also taken possession of our historical literature. This 'higher criticism' has been the pretext for introducing all the anti-historical monstrosities that a vain imagination could suggest. Here we have the other method of making the past a living reality, putting subjective fancies in the place of historical data, fancies whose merit is measured by their boldness, that is, the scantiness of the particulars on which they are based, and the peremptoriness with which they contravene the best established facts of history.

4. The last species of Reflective History announces its fragmentary character on the very face of it. It adopts an abstract position, yet, since it takes general points of view (e.g. as the History of Art, of Law, of Religion), it forms a transition to the Philosophical History of the World. In our time this form of the history of ideas has been more developed and brought into notice. Such branches of national life stand in close relation to the entire complex of a people's annals, and the question of chief importance in relation to our subject is, whether the connection of the whole is exhibited in its truth and reality, or referred to merely external relations. In the latter case, these important phenomena (Art, Law, Religion, etc.) appear as purely accidental national peculiarities. It must be remarked that, when Reflective History has advanced to the adoption of general points of view, if the position taken is a true one, these are found to constitute – not a merely external thread, a superficial series – but are the inward guiding soul of the occurrences and actions that occupy a nation's annals. For, like the soul-conductor Mercury, the

Idea is, in truth, the leader of peoples and of the World, and Spirit, the rational and necessitated will of that conductor, is and has been the director of the events of the World's History. To become acquainted with Spirit in this its office of guidance is the object of our present undertaking. This brings us to

III. The third kind of history – the *Philosophical*. No explanation was needed of the two previous classes; their nature was self-evident. It is otherwise with this last, which certainly seems to require an exposition or justification. The most general definition that can be given, is, that the Philosophy of History means nothing but the *thoughtful consideration of it*. Thought is, indeed, essential to humanity. It is this that distinguishes us from the brutes. In sensation, cognition and intellection, in our instincts and volitions, as far as they are truly human, Thought is an invariable element. To insist upon Thought in this connection with history, may, however, appear unsatisfactory. In this science it would seem as if Thought must be subordinate to what is given, to the realities of fact, that this is its basis and guide: while Philosophy dwells in the region of self-produced ideas, without reference to actuality. Approaching history thus prepossessed, Speculation might be expected to treat it as a mere passive material, and, so far from leaving it in its native truth, to force it into conformity with a tyrannous idea, and to construe it, as the phrase is, '*a priori*'. But as it is the business of history simply to adopt into its records what is and has been, actual occurrences and transactions, and since it remains true to its character in proportion as it strictly adheres to its data, we seem to have in Philosophy a process diametrically opposed to that of the historiographer. This contradiction, and the charge consequently brought against speculation, shall be explained and confuted. We do not, however, propose to correct the innumerable special misrepresentations, trite or novel, that are current respecting the aims, the interests, and the modes of treating history, and its relation to Philosophy.

The only Thought which Philosophy brings with it to the contemplation of History, is the simple conception of *Reason*: that Reason is the Sovereign of the World; that the history of the world, therefore, presents us with a rational process. This conviction and intuition is a hypothesis in the domain of history as such. In that of Philosophy it is no hypothesis. It is there proved by speculative cognition, that Reason – and this term may here suffice us, without investigating the relation sustained by the Universe to the Divine Being – is *Substance*, as well as *Infinite Power*; its own *Infinite Material* underlying all the natural and spiritual life which it originates, as also the *Infinite Form* – that which sets this Material in motion. On the one hand, Reason is the *substance* of the Universe; viz. that by which and in which all reality has its being and subsistence. On the other hand, it is the *Infinite Energy* of the Universe, since Reason is not so powerless as to be incapable of producing anything but a mere ideal, a mere intention – having its place outside reality, nobody knows where, something separate and abstract, in the heads of certain human beings. It is *the infinite complex of things*, their entire Essence and Truth. It is its own material which it commits to its own Active Energy to work up; not needing, as finite action does, the conditions of an external material of given means from which it may obtain its support, and the objects of its activity.

It supplies its own nourishment, and is the object of its own operations. While it is exclusively its own basis of existence, and absolute final aim, it is also the energizing power realizing this aim, developing it not only in the phenomena of the Natural, but also of the Spiritual Universe – the History of the World. That this 'Idea' or 'Reason' is the *True*, the *Eternal*, the absolutely *powerful* essence, that it reveals itself in the World, and that in that World nothing else is revealed but this and its honor and glory – is the thesis which, as we have said, has been proved in Philosophy, and is here regarded as demonstrated.

In those of my hearers who are not acquainted with Philosophy, I may fairly presume, at least, the existence of a *belief* in Reason, a desire, a thirst for acquaintance with it, in entering upon this course of Lectures. It is, in fact, the wish for rational insight, not the ambition to amass a mere heap of requirements, that should be presupposed in every case as possessing the mind of the learner in the study of science. If the clear idea of Reason is not already developed in our minds, in beginning the study of Universal History, we should at least have the firm, unconquerable faith that Reason *does* exist there, and that the World of intelligence and conscious volition is not abandoned to chance, but must show itself in the light of the self-cognizant Idea. Yet I am not obliged to make any such preliminary demand upon your faith. What I have said thus provisionally, and what I shall have further to say, is, even in reference to *our* branch of science, not to be regarded as hypothetical, but as a summary view of the whole; the *result of the investigation* we are about to pursue, a result which happens to be known to *me*, because I have traversed the entire field. It is only an inference from the history of the World, that its development has been a rational process, that the history in question has constituted the rational necessary course of the World-Spirit – that Spirit whose nature is always one and the same, but which unfolds this its one nature in the phenomena of the World's existence. This must, as before stated, present itself as the ultimate *result* of History. But we have to take the latter as it is. We must proceed historically – empirically. Among other precautions we must take care not to be misled by professed historians who (especially among the Germans, and enjoying a considerable authority) are chargeable with the very procedure of which they accuse the Philosopher – introducing *a priori* inventions of their own into the records of the Past. It is, for example, a widely current fiction, that there was an original primeval people, taught immediately by God, endowed with perfect insight and wisdom, possessing a thorough knowledge of all natural laws and spiritual truth; that there have been such or such sacerdotal peoples; or, to mention a more specific averment, that there was a Roman Epos, from which the Roman historians derived the early annals of their city, etc. Authorities of this kind we leave to those talented historians by profession, among whom (in Germany at least) their use is not uncommon. – We might then announce it as the first condition to be observed, that we should faithfully adopt all that is historical. But in such general expressions themselves, as 'faithfully' and 'adopt', lies the ambiguity. Even the ordinary, the 'impartial' historiographer, who believes and professes that he maintains a simply receptive attitude, surrendering himself only to the data supplied him – is by no means passive as regards the exercise of his thinking powers. He brings his categories with him, and sees the phenomena presented to his mental vision, exclusively through these media. And, especially in all that pretends to the name of science, it is indispensable that Reason should not sleep – that reflection should be in full play. To him who looks upon the world rationally, the world in its turn presents a rational aspect. The relation is mutual. But the various exercises of reflection – the different points of view – the modes of deciding the simple question of the relative importance of events (the first category that occupies the attention of the historian), do not belong to this place. [. . .]

[*HW* XII, 29–47] II. The inquiry into the *essential destiny* of Reason – as far as it is considered in reference to the World – is identical with the question, *what is the ultimate design of the world?* And the expression implies that that design is destined to be realized. Two points of consideration suggest themselves: first, the *import* of this design – its abstract definition; and secondly, its *realization*.

It must be observed at the outset, that the phenomenon we investigate – Universal History – belongs to the realm of *Spirit*. The term 'World', includes both physical and psychical Nature. Physical Nature also plays its part in the World's History, and attention will have to be paid to the fundamental natural relations thus involved. But Spirit, and the course of its development, is our substantial object. Our task does not require us to contemplate Nature as a Rational System in itself – though in its own proper domain it proves itself such – but simply in its relation to *Spirit*. On the stage on which we are observing it – Universal History. – Spirit displays itself in its most concrete reality. Notwithstanding this (or rather for the very purpose of comprehending the *general* principles which this, its form of *concrete reality*, embodies) we must premise some abstract characteristics of the *nature of Spirit*. Such an explanation, however, cannot be given here under any other form than that of bare assertion. The present is not the occasion for unfolding the idea of Spirit speculatively, for whatever has a place in an Introduction, must, as already observed, be taken as simply historical; something assumed as having been explained and proved elsewhere, or whose demonstration awaits the sequel of the Science of History itself.

We have therefore to mention here:

(1) The abstract characteristics of the nature of Spirit.
(2) What means Spirit uses in order to realize its Idea.
(3) Lastly, we must consider the shape which the perfect embodiment of Spirit assumes – the State.

(1.) The nature of Spirit may be understood by a glance at its direct opposite – *Matter*. As the essence of Matter is Gravity, so, on the other hand, we may affirm that the substance, the essence of Spirit is Freedom. All will readily assent to the doctrine that Spirit, among other properties, is also endowed with Freedom, but philosophy teaches that all the qualities of Spirit exist only through Freedom, that all are but means for attaining freedom, that all seek and produce this and this alone. It is a result of speculative Philosophy, that Freedom is the sole truth of Spirit. Matter possesses gravity in virtue of its tendency toward a central point. It is essentially composite, consisting of parts that *exclude* each other. It seeks its Unity; and therefore exhibits itself as self-destructive, as verging toward its opposite [an indivisible point]. If it could attain this, it would be Matter no longer, it would have perished. It strives after the realization of its Idea, for in Unity it exists *ideally*. Spirit, on the contrary, may be defined as that which has its centre in itself. It has not a unity outside itself, but has already found it; it exists *in* and *with itself*. Matter has its essence out of itself; Spirit is *self-contained existence (Bei-sich-selbst-seyn)*. Now this is Freedom, exactly. For if I am dependent, my being is referred to something else which I am not; I cannot exist independently of something external. I am free, on the contrary, when my existence depends upon myself. This self-contained existence of Spirit is none other than self-consciousness — consciousness of one's own being. Two things must be distinguished in consciousness; first, the fact *that I know*; secondly, *what I know*. In *self* consciousness these are merged in one; for Spirit *knows itself*. It involves an appreciation of its own nature, as also an energy enabling it to realize itself, to make itself *actually* that which it is *potentially*. According to this abstract definition it may be said of Universal History, that it is the exhibition of Spirit in the process of working out the knowledge of that which it is potentially. And as the germ bears in itself the whole nature of the tree, and the taste and form of its fruits, so do the first traces of Spirit virtually contain the whole of that History. The Orientals have not attained the knowledge that Spirit — Man *as such* — is free, and because they do not know this, they are not free. They only know that *one is free*. But on this very account, the freedom of that one is only caprice, ferocity — brutal recklessness of passion, or a mildness and tameness of the desires, which is itself only an accident of Nature — mere caprice like the former. — That *one* is therefore only a Despot; not a *free man*. The consciousness of Freedom first arose among the Greeks, and therefore they were free; but they, and the Romans likewise, knew only that *some* are free — not man as such. Even Plato and Aristotle did not know this. The Greeks, therefore, had slaves, and their whole life and the maintenance of their splendid liberty, was implicated with the institution of slavery: a fact, moreover, which made that liberty on the one hand only an accidental, transient and limited growth, on the other hand, constituted it a rigorous thraldom of our common nature — of the Human. The German nations, under the influence of Christianity, were the first to attain the consciousness, that man, as man, is free: that it is the *freedom* of Spirit which constitutes its essence. This consciousness arose first in religion, the inmost region of Spirit, but to introduce the principle into the various relations of the actual world, involves a more extensive problem than its simple implantation, a problem whose solution and application require a severe and lengthened process of culture. In proof of this, we may note that slavery did not cease immediately on the reception of Christianity. Still less did liberty predominate in States, or Governments and Constitutions adopt a rational organization, or recognize freedom as their basis.

That application of the principle to political relations, the thorough molding and interpenetration of the constitution of society by it, is a process identical with history itself. I have already directed attention to the distinction here involved, between a principle as such, and its *application*; i.e. its introduction and carrying out in the actual phenomena of Spirit and Life. This is a point of fundamental importance in our science, and one which must be constantly respected as essential. And in the same way as this distinction has attracted attention in view of the *Christian* principle of self-consciousness — Freedom; it also shows itself as an essential one, in view of the principle of Freedom *generally*. The History of the world is none other than the progress of the consciousness of Freedom, a progress whose development according to the necessity of its nature it is our business to investigate.

The general statement given above, of the various grades in the consciousness of Freedom – and which we applied in the first instance to the fact that the Eastern nations knew only that *one* is free; the Greek and Roman world only that *some* are free; while *we* know that all men absolutely (man *as man*) are free – supplies us with the natural division of Universal History, and suggests the mode of its discussion. This is remarked, however, only incidentally and anticipatively; some other ideas must be first explained.

The destiny of the spiritual World, and – since this is the *substantial World*, while the physical remains subordinate to it, or, in the language of speculation, has no truth *as against* the spiritual – the *final cause of the World at large*, we allege to be the *consciousness* of its own freedom on the part of Spirit, and *ipso facto*, the *reality* of that freedom. But that this term 'Freedom', without further qualification, is an indefinite, and incalculable ambiguous term, and that while that which it represents is the *ne plus ultra* of attainment, it is liable to an infinity of misunderstandings, confusions and errors, and to become the occasion for all imaginable excesses – has never been more clearly known and felt than in modern times. Yet, for the present, we must content ourselves with the term itself without further definition. Attention was also directed to the importance of the infinite difference between a principle in the abstract, and its realization in the concrete. In the process before us, the essential nature of freedom – which involves in it absolute necessity – is to be displayed as coming to a consciousness of itself (for it is in its very nature self-consciousness) and thereby realizing its existence. Itself is its own object of attainment, and the sole aim of Spirit. This result it is, at which the process of the World's History has been continually aiming, and to which the sacrifices that have ever and anon been laid on the vast altar of the earth, through the long lapse of ages, have been offered. This is the only aim that sees itself realized and fulfilled, the only pole of repose amid the ceaseless change of events and conditions, and the sole efficient principle that pervades them. This final aim is God's purpose with the world, but God is the absolutely perfect Being, and can, therefore, will nothing other than himself – his own Will. The Nature of His Will – that is, His Nature itself – is what we here call the Idea of Freedom, translating the language of Religion into that of Thought. The question, then, which we may next put, is: What means does this principle of Freedom use for its realization? This is the second point we have to consider.

(2.) The question of the *means* by which Freedom develops itself to a World, conducts us to the phenomenon of History itself. Although Freedom is, primarily, an undeveloped idea, the means it uses are external and phenomenal, presenting themselves in History to our sensuous vision. The first glance at History convinces us that the actions of men proceed from their needs, their passions, their characters and talents, and impresses us with the belief that such needs, passions and interests are the sole springs of action – the efficient agents in this scene of activity. Among these may, perhaps, be found aims of a liberal or universal kind – benevolence it may be, or noble patriotism, but such virtues and general views are but insignificant as compared with the World and its doings. We may perhaps see the Ideal of Reason actualized in those who adopt such aims, and within the sphere of their influence, but they bear only a trifling proportion to the mass of the human race; and the extent of that influence is limited accordingly. Passions, private aims, and the satisfaction of selfish desires, are, on the other hand, most effective springs of action. Their power lies in the fact that they respect none of the limitations which justice and morality would impose on them, and that these natural impulses have a more direct influence over man than the artificial and tedious discipline that tends to order and self-restraint, law and morality. When we look at this display of passions, and the consequences of their violence, the Unreason which is associated not only with them, but even (rather we might say *especially*) with *good* designs and righteous aims; when we see the evil, the vice, the ruin that has befallen the most flourishing kingdoms which the mind of man ever created, we can scarce avoid being filled with sorrow at this universal taint of corruption, and, since this decay is not the work of mere Nature, but of the Human Will – a moral imbitterment – a revolt of the Good Spirit (if it have a place within us) may well be the result of our reflections. Without rhetorical exaggeration, a simply truthful combination of the miseries that have overwhelmed the noblest of nations and polities, and the finest exemplars of private virtue – forms a picture of most fearful aspect, and excites emotions of the profoundest and most hopeless sadness, counterbalanced by no consolatory result. We endure in beholding it a mental torture, allowing no defence or escape but the consideration that what has happened could not be otherwise; that it is a fatality which no intervention could alter. And at last we draw back from the intolerable disgust with which these sorrowful reflections threaten us into the more agreeable environment of our individual life – the Present formed by our private aims and interests. In short we retreat into the selfishness that stands on the quiet shore, and thence enjoys in safety the distant spectacle of 'wrecks confusedly hurled'. But even regarding History as the slaughter-bench at which the happiness of peoples, the wisdom of States, and the virtue of individuals have been victimized – the question involuntarily arises – to what principle, to what final aim these enormous sacrifices have been offered. From this point the investigation usually proceeds to that which we have made the general commencement of our inquiry. Starting from this we pointed out those phenomena which made up a picture so suggestive of gloomy emotions and thoughtful reflections – as *the very field* which we, for our part, regard as exhibiting only the means for realizing what we assert to be the essential destiny – the absolute aim, or – which comes to the same thing – the true *result* of the World's History. We have all along purposely eschewed 'moral reflections' as a method of rising from the scene of historical specialities to the general principles which they embody. Besides, it is not the interest of such sentimentalities really to rise above those depressing emotions, and to solve the enigmas of Providence which the considerations that occasioned them present. It is essential to their character to find a gloomy satisfaction in the empty and fruitless sublimities of that negative result. We return then to the point of view which we have adopted, observing that the successive steps (Momente) of the analysis to which it will lead us, will also evolve the conditions requisite for answering the inquiries suggested by the panorama of sin and suffering that history unfolds.

The *first* remark we have to make, and which – though already presented more than once – cannot be too often repeated when the occasion seems to call for it – is that what we call *principle, aim, destiny*, or the nature and idea of Spirit, is something merely general and abstract. Principle – Plan of Existence – Law – is a hidden, undeveloped essence, which *as such* – however true in itself – is not completely real. Aims, principles, etc., have a place in our thoughts, in our subjective design only, but not yet in the sphere of reality. That which exists for itself only, is a possibility, a potentiality; but has not yet emerged into Existence. A *second* element must be introduced in order to produce actuality – viz. actuation, realization, and whose motive power is the Will – the activity of man in the widest sense. It is only by this activity that that Idea as well as abstract characteristics generally, are realized, actualized, for of themselves they are powerless. The motive power that puts them in operation, and gives them determinate existence, is the need, instinct, inclination, and passion of man. That some conception of mine should be developed into act and existence, is my earnest desire: I wish to assert my personality in connection with it: I wish to be satisfied by its execution. If I am to exert myself for any object, it must in some way or other be *my* object. In the accomplishment of such or such designs I must at the same time find *my* satisfaction, although the purpose for which I exert myself includes a complication of results, many of which have no interest for me. This is the absolute right of personal existence – to find *itself* satisfied in its activity and labor. If men are to interest themselves for anything, they must (so to speak) have part of their existence involved in it, find their individuality gratified by its attainment. Here a mistake must be avoided. We intend blame, and justly impute it as a fault, when we say of an individual, that he is 'interested' (in taking part in such or such transactions), that is, seeks only his private advantage. In reprehending this we find fault with him for furthering his personal aims without any regard to a more comprehensive design, of which he takes advantage to promote his own interest, or which he even sacrifices with this view. But he who is active in *promoting an object*, is not simply 'interested', but interested in that object itself. Language faithfully expresses this distinction. – Nothing therefore happens, nothing is accomplished, unless the individuals concerned seek their own satisfaction in the issue. They are particular units of society; i.e. they have special needs, instincts, and interests generally, peculiar to themselves. Among these needs are not only such as we usually call necessities – the stimuli of individual desire and volition – but also those connected with individual views and convictions; or – to use a term expressing less decision – leanings of opinion, supposing the impulses of reflection, understanding, and reason to have been awakened. In these cases people demand, if they are to exert themselves in any direction, that the object should commend itself to them, that in point of opinion – whether as to its goodness, justice, advantage, profit – they should be able to 'enter into it' (*dabei seyn*). This is a consideration of especial importance in our age, when people are less than formerly influenced by reliance on others, and by authority; when, on the contrary, they devote their activities to a cause on the ground of their own understanding, their independent conviction and opinion.

We assert then that nothing has been accomplished without interest on the part of the actors, and – if interest be called passion, inasmuch as the whole individuality, to the neglect of all other actual or possible interests and claims, is devoted to an object with every fibre of volition, concentrating all its desires and powers upon it – we may affirm absolutely that *nothing great in the World* has been accomplished without *passion*. Two elements, therefore, enter into the object of our investigation; the first the Idea, the second the complex of human passions; the one the warp, the other the woof of the vast arras-web of Universal History. The concrete mean and union of the two is Liberty, under the conditions of morality in a State. We have spoken of the Idea of Freedom as the nature of Spirit, and the absolute goal of History. Passion is regarded as a thing of sinister aspect, as more or less immoral. Man is required to have no passions. Passion, it is true, is not quite the suitable word for what I wish to express. I mean here nothing more than human activity as resulting from private interests – special, or if you will, self-seeking designs – with this qualification, that the whole energy of will and character is devoted to their attainment, that other interests (which would in themselves constitute attractive aims), or rather all things else, are sacrificed to them. The object in question is so bound up with the man's will, that it entirely and alone determines the 'hue of resolution', and is inseparable from it. It has become the very essence of his volition. For a person is a specific existence, not man in general (a term to which no real existence corresponds), but a particular human being. The term 'character' likewise expresses this idiosyncrasy of Will and Intelligence. But *Character* comprehends all peculiarities whatever, the way in which a person conducts himself in private relations, etc., and is not limited to his idiosyncrasy in its practical and active phase. I shall, therefore, use the term 'passion', understanding thereby the particular bent of character, as far as the peculiarities of volition are not limited to private interest, but supply the impelling and actuating force for accomplishing deeds shared in by the community at large. Passion is in the first instance the *subjective*, and therefore the *formal* side of energy, will, and activity – leaving the object or aim still undetermined. And there is a similar relation of formality to reality in merely individual conviction, individual views, individual conscience. It is always a question of essential importance, what is the purport of my conviction, what the object of my passion, in deciding whether the one or the other is of a true and substantial nature. Conversely, if it is so, it will inevitably attain actual existence – be realized.

From this comment on the second essential element in the historical embodiment of an aim, we infer – glancing at the institution of the State in passing – that a State is then well constituted and internally powerful, when the private interest of its citizens is one with the common interest of the State; when the one finds its gratification and realization in the other – a proposition in itself very important. But in a State many institutions must be adopted, much political machinery invented, accompanied by appropriate political arrangements – necessitating long struggles of the understanding before what is really appropriate can be discovered – involving, moreover, contentions with private interest and passions, and a tedious discipline of these latter, in order to bring about the desired harmony. The epoch, when a State attains this harmonious condition, marks the period of its bloom, its virtue, its vigor, and its prosperity. But the history of mankind does not begin with a *conscious* aim of any kind, as it is the case with the particular circles into which men form themselves of set purpose. The mere social instinct implies a conscious purpose of security for life and property, and when society has been constituted, this purpose becomes more comprehensive. The History of the World begins with its general aim – the realization of the Idea of Spirit – only in an *implicit* form (*an sich*) that is, as Nature, a hidden, most profoundly hidden, unconscious instinct; and the whole process of History (as already observed) is directed to rendering this unconscious impulse a conscious one. Thus appearing in the form of merely natural existence, natural will – that which has been called the subjective side – physical craving, instinct, passion, private interest, as also opinion and subjective conception – spontaneously present themselves at the very commencement. This vast congeries of volitions, interests and activities constitute the instruments and means of the World-Spirit for attaining its object; bringing it to consciousness, and realizing it. And this aim is none other than finding itself – coming to itself – and contemplating itself in concrete actuality. But that those manifestations of vitality on the part of individuals and peoples, in which they seek and satisfy their own purposes, are, at the same time, the means and instruments of a higher and broader purpose of which they know nothing – which they realize unconsciously – might be made a matter of question; rather has been questioned, and in every variety of form negatived, decried and contemned as mere dreaming and 'Philosophy'. But on this point I announced my view at the very outset, and asserted our hypothesis – which, however, will appear in the sequel, in the form of a legitimate inference – and our belief, that Reason governs the world, and has consequently governed its history. In relation to this independently universal and substantial existence – all else is subordinate, subservient to it, and the means for its development. – The Union of Universal Abstract Existence generally with the

Individual – the Subjective – that this alone is Truth, belongs to the department of speculation, and is treated in this general form in Logic. – But in the process of the World's History itself – as still incomplete – the abstract final aim of history is not yet made the distinct object of desire and interest. While these limited sentiments are still unconscious of the purpose they are fulfilling, the universal principle is implicit in them, and is realizing itself through them. The question also assumes the form of the union of *Freedom* and *Necessity*; the latent abstract process of Spirit being regarded as *Necessity*, while that which exhibits itself in the conscious will of men, as their interest, belongs to the domain of *Freedom*. As the metaphysical connection (i.e. the connection in the Idea) of these forms of thought belongs to Logic, it would be out of place to analyze it here. The chief and cardinal points only shall be mentioned.

Philosophy shows that the Idea advances to an infinite antithesis; that, viz., between the Idea in its free, universal form – in which it exists for itself – and the contrasted form of abstract introversion, reflection on itself, which is formal existence-for-self, personality, formal freedom, such as belongs to Spirit only. The universal Idea exists thus as the substantial totality of things on the one side, and as the abstract essence of free volition on the other side. This reflection of the mind on itself is individual self-consciousness – the polar opposite of the Idea in its general form, and therefore existing in absolute Limitation. This polar opposite is consequently limitation, particularization, for the universal absolute being; it is the side of its *definite existence*, the sphere of its formal reality, the sphere of the reverence paid to God. – To comprehend the absolute connection of the antithesis, is the profound task of metaphysics. This Limitation originates all forms of particularity of whatever kind. The formal volition [of which we have spoken] wills itself, desires to make its own personality valid in all that it purposes and does: even the pious individual wishes to be saved and happy. This pole of the antithesis, existing for itself, is – in contrast with the Absolute Universal Being – a special separate existence, taking cognizance of speciality only, and willing that alone. In short it plays its part in the region of mere phenomena. This is the sphere of particular purposes, in effecting which individuals exert themselves on behalf of their individuality – give it full play and objective realization. This is also the sphere of happiness and its opposite. He is happy who finds his condition suited to his special character, will, and fancy, and so enjoys himself in that condition. The History of the World is not the theatre of happiness. Periods of happiness are blank pages in it, for they are periods of harmony – periods when the antithesis is in abeyance. Reflection on self – the Freedom above described – is abstractly defined as the formal element of the activity of the absolute Idea. The realizing *activity* of which we have spoken is the middle term of the Syllogism, one of whose extremes is the Universal essence, the *Idea*, which reposes in the penetralia of Spirit; and the other, the complex of external things – objective matter. That activity is the medium by which the universal latent principle is translated into the domain of objectivity.

I will endeavor to make what has been said more vivid and clear by examples.

The building of a house is, in the first instance, a subjective aim and design. On the other hand we have, as means, the several substances required for the work – Iron, Wood, Stones. The elements are made use of in working up this material: fire to melt the iron, wind to blow the fire, water to set wheels in motion, in order to cut the wood, etc. The result is, that the wind, which has helped to build the house, is shut out by the house; so also are the violence of rains and floods, and the destructive powers of fire, so far as the house is made fireproof. The stones and beams obey the law of gravity – press downward – and so high walls are carried up. Thus the elements are made use of in accordance with their nature, and yet to co-operate for a product, by which their operation is limited. Thus the passions of men are gratified; they develop themselves and their aims in accordance with their natural tendencies, and build up the edifice of human society, thus fortifying a position for Right and Order *against themselves.*

The connection of events above indicated involves also the fact, that in history an additional result is commonly produced by human actions beyond that which they aim at and obtain – that which they immediately recognize and desire. They gratify their own interest, but something further is thereby accomplished, latent in the actions in question, though not present to their consciousness, and not included in their design. An analogous example is offered in the case of a man who, from a feeling of revenge – perhaps not an unjust one, but produced by injury on the other's part – burns that other man's house. A connection is immediately established between the deed itself and a train of circumstances not directly included in it, taken abstractedly. In itself it consisted in merely presenting a small flame to a small portion of a beam. Events not involved in that simple act follow of themselves. The part of the beam which was set fire to is connected with its remote portions; the beam itself is united with the woodwork of the house generally, and this with other houses, so that a wide conflagration ensues, which destroys the goods and chattels of many other persons besides his against whom the act of revenge was first directed, perhaps even costs not a few men their lives. This lay neither in the deed abstractedly, nor in the design of the man who committed it. But the action has a further general bearing. In the design of the doer it was only revenge executed against an individual in the destruction of his property, but it is moreover a crime, and that involves punishment also. This may not have been present to the mind of the perpetrator, still less in his intention, but his deed itself, the general principles it calls into play, its substantial content entails it. By this example I wish only to impress on you the consideration that in a simple act, something further may be implicated than lies in the intention and consciousness of the agent. The example before us involves, however, this additional consideration, that the substance of the act, consequently we may say the act itself, recoils upon the perpetrator – reacts upon him with destructive tendency. This union of the two extremes – the embodiment of a general idea in the form of direct reality, and the elevation of a speciality into connection with universal truth – is brought to pass, at first sight, under the conditions of an utter diversity of nature between the two, and an indifference of the one extreme toward the other. The aims which the agents set before them are limited and special, but it must be remarked that the agents themselves are intelligent thinking beings. The purport of their desires is interwoven with *general, essential* considerations of justice, good, duty, etc.; for mere desire – volition in its rough and savage forms – falls not within the scene and sphere of Universal History. Those general considerations, which form at the same time a norm for directing aims and actions, have a determinate purport, for such an abstraction as 'good for its own sake', has no place in living reality. If men are to act, they must not only intend the Good, but must have decided for themselves whether this or that particular thing is a Good. What special course of action, however, is good or not, is determined, as regards the ordinary contingencies of private life, by the laws and customs of a State, and here no great difficulty is presented. Each individual has his position; he knows on the whole what a just, honorable course of conduct is. As to ordinary, private relations, the assertion that it is difficult to choose the right and good – the regarding it as the mark of an exalted morality to find difficulties and raise scruples on that score – may be set down to an evil or perverse will, which seeks to evade duties not in themselves of a perplexing nature; or, at any rate, to an idly reflective habit of mind – where a feeble will affords no sufficient exercise to the faculties – leaving them therefore to find occupation within themselves, and to expend themselves on moral self-adulation.

It is quite otherwise with the comprehensive relations that History has to do with. In this sphere are presented those momentous collisions between existing, acknowledged duties, laws, and rights, and those contingencies which are adverse to this fixed system, which assail and even destroy its foundations and existence, whose tenor may nevertheless seem good – on the large scale advantageous – yes, even indispensable and necessary. These contingencies realize themselves in History: they involve a general principle of a different order from that on which depends the *permanence* of a people or a State. This principle is an essential phase in the development of the *creating* Idea, of Truth, striving and urging toward [consciousness of] itself. Historical men – *World-Historical Individuals* – are those in whose aim such a general principle lies.

Cæsar, in danger of losing a position, not perhaps at that time of superiority, yet at least of equality with the others who were at the head of the State, and of succumbing to those who were just on the point of becoming his enemies – belongs essentially to this category. These enemies – who were at the same time pursuing *their* personal aims – had the form of the constitution, and the power conferred by an appearance of justice, on their side. Cæsar was contending for the maintenance of his position, honor, and safety; and, since the power of his opponents included the sovereignty over the provinces of the Roman Empire, his victory secured for him the conquest of that entire Empire, and he thus became (though leaving the form of the constitution) the Autocrat of the State. That which secured for him the execution of a design, which in the first instance was of negative import – the Autocracy of Rome – was, however, at the same time an independently necessary feature in the history of Rome and of the world. It was not then his private gain merely, but an unconscious impulse that occasioned the accomplishment of that for which the time was ripe. Such are all great historical men – whose own particular aims involve those large issues which are the will of the World-Spirit. They may be called Heroes, inasmuch as they have derived their purposes and their vocation, not from the calm, regular course of things, sanctioned by the existing order, but from a concealed fount – one which has not attained to phenomenal, present existence – from that inner Spirit, still hidden beneath the surface, which, impinging on the outer world as on a shell, bursts it in pieces, because it is another kernel than that which belonged to the shell in question. They are men, therefore, who appear to draw the impulse of their life from themselves, and whose deeds have produced a condition of things and a complex of historical relations which appear to be only *their* interest, and *their* work.

Such individuals had no consciousness of the general Idea they were unfolding, while prosecuting those aims of theirs; on the contrary, they were practical, political men. But at the same time they were thinking men, who had an insight into the requirements of the time – *what was ripe for development*. This was the very Truth for their age, for their world; the species next in order, so to speak, and which was already formed in the womb of time. It was theirs to know this nascent principle; the necessary, directly sequent step in progress, which their world was to take; to make this their aim, and to expend their energy in promoting it. World-historical men – the Heroes of an epoch – must, therefore, be recognized as its clear-sighted ones; *their* deeds, *their* words are the best of that time. Great men have formed purposes to satisfy themselves, not others. Whatever prudent designs and counsels they might have learned from others, would be the more limited and inconsistent features in their career, for it was they who best understood affairs, from whom *others* learned, and approved, or at least acquiesced in – their policy. For that Spirit which had taken this fresh step in history is the inmost soul of all individuals, but in a state of unconsciousness which the great men in question aroused. Their fellows, therefore, follow these soul-leaders, for they feel the irresistible power of their own inner Spirit thus embodied. If we go on to cast a look at the fate of these World-Historical persons, whose vocation it was to be the agents of the World-Spirit – we shall find it to have been no happy one. They attained no calm enjoyment; their whole life was labor and trouble; their whole nature was naught else but their master-passion. When their object is attained they fall off like empty hulls from the kernel. They die early, like Alexander; they are murdered, like Cæsar; transported to St. Helena, like Napoleon. This fearful consolation – that historical men have not enjoyed what is called happiness, and of which only private life (and this may be passed under very various external circumstances) is capable – this consolation those may draw from history, who stand in need of it, and it is craved by Envy – vexed at what is great and transcendent – striving, therefore, to depreciate it, and to find some flaw in it. Thus in modern times it has been demonstrated *ad nauseam* that princes are generally unhappy on their thrones, in consideration of which the possession of a throne is tolerated, and men acquiesce in the fact that not themselves but the personages in question are its occupants. The Free Man, we may observe, is not envious, but gladly recognizes what is great and exalted, and rejoices that it exists.

Translated by J. Sibree

VI

Nature and Science

20

Immanuel Kant, Critique of Judgement (Kritik der Urteilskraft): *Critique of Teleological Judgement, §§ 61–68 (1790)*

The central theses of transcendental idealism might be understood as Kant's effort to provide, through his arguments for the categories of the understanding and the forms of intuition, philosophical justification for our ordinary beliefs about the laws of nature and our experience of objects: namely, that we encounter objects as substantial (not as randomly changing bundles of attributes) and as causal (as affecting and capable of being affected). But does this imply that Kant thinks of nature itself – understood as the totality of objects that can be experienced – as reducible to the categories of the understanding as defined by transcendental idealism? To put this another way, is Kant satisfied with a purely formal account of nature? The *Critique of Judgement* plainly shows us that there is more to Kant's understanding of nature than this: he is no reductionist in that he is quite aware that our understanding of nature goes beyond a narrow satisfaction with the purely mechanical operations of cause and effect. He also wants to explain our interest in knowing nature and the objects of nature from the point of view of the ends or purposes towards which they operate. Furthermore, Kant sets out to explore reason's own legitimate though problematic demand for complete systematic unity in explanation, including in the explanation of nature.

At first, this further dimension of Kant's thoughts on nature may seem to lead to a dichotomy in his philosophy: namely, that nature, on the one hand, must be explained in terms of (blind) mechanical causality and, on the other, that nature must be understood as operating according to some ends. This is precisely the *antinomy of teleological judgement*, mentioned by Kant himself. This antinomy dissolves if we refer to a distinction utterly central to Kant's philosophy, that of understanding (*Verstand*) and reason (*Vernunft*). At the level of understanding, in which we determine objects through the categories, nature is experienced in and through the forms (as well as in the contingent empirical specifics of each object). However, human reason in its very structure is compelled to find order: amongst our ordering principles is that which seeks finality or purpose in nature. (Translations of Kant vary in the choice of 'finality' or 'purposiveness' for *Zweckmäßigkeit*.) When we judge nature or its objects as operating according to purpose or finality we judge it teleologically. The notion of teleological judgement is actually already discussed in the first part of the *Critique of Judgement* in relation to judgements of taste. When we judge objects of nature to be beautiful it is *as if* they were designed to produce pleasurable feelings in us. Teleological judgements with respect to the purpose of objects and nature as a system of ends is to be differentiated from judgements of taste (see Beauty and Art above for Kant's treatment of judgements of taste). Experience by itself gives us no reason to seek finality in objects, except in the sense, as Kant noted, that we 'find by experience' that certain things, namely organisms, cannot be explained mechanically and that prompts us to apply the regulative principle of teleology to them. For that reason the ordering principles are seen by Kant as *a priori*: as 'in us', not in nature itself.

The idea that we judge the objects of nature and nature as a whole as operating according to some purpose may seem to have dangerously loaded implications: the very notion of an object having a purpose seems to entail that it has been given a purpose, a thought which leads us soon enough to that of a supernatural creator. But this is an implication that Kant wants to avoid. As philosophers we must hesitate before deriving the existence of a creator from the apparent purposiveness of nature. Therefore teleological judgements are judgements which entitle us to say *only* that certain objects of nature really can be made intelligible only if they are judged *as though* they operate according to a purpose. For that reason Kant terms teleological judgements as judgements of reflection, not as determinative judgements. Determinative judgements – those that operate with the employment of the *a priori* categories of the understanding – decide the intrinsic structure and general mechanical lawfulness of the object: they are constitutive. Judgements of reflection, however, are regulative (not constitutive) in that they are ideas and principles which we bring to reality as it appears to us. And teleological judgements are regulative in the sense that they give us reason to think of all the data of experience as somehow more than the forms of our perception: we think of the objects of nature as conforming to ends or purposes, that is, as having finality or purposiveness. (It is the 'Transcendental Dialectic' section of the *Critique of Pure Reason*, in fact, that first introduces us to the importance of the distinction between regulative and constitutive ideas.) An influential implication of this position, which Kant later draws out, is the role it gives to human autonomy: it sees human reason as having the capacity to organise nature in accordance with its own principles, as it attempts to bring nature under its own principles of reason. The notions of reason and freedom in the realm of knowledge (and not simply morality) was to become one of the foundations for the further development of German Idealist philosophy.

Kant distinguishes between a number of conceptions of finality. Where one item of nature serves another (e.g. grass to feed grazing animals) that item has a relative or outer finality or purpose: its purpose lies in the needs of something else. In this respect the object is a means, and not, therefore, strictly an end in itself. Clearly such relations between things of nature are quite contingent and even arbitrary: the grass, in this instance, would have no purpose were there no grazing animals. Extrinsic or outer finality is therefore not, as Kant sees it, an 'absolute teleological judgement'. The latter is applicable only where a thing exists as a physical end or 'natural purpose', which Kant defines as a thing being 'both cause and effect of itself' (a definition which contrasts with the notion of purposiveness implicit in extrinsic purposiveness, in effect, an organism). It is 'cause and effect of itself' if (a) it reproduces another of its own genus, (b) if it reproduces itself through growth, and (c) its parts are reciprocally dependent (it is a whole). An organism is not then a 'blind mechanism of nature'. These definitions of an organism – of a physical end – distinguish it from a mechanism: although an engine, for instance, may function only through the harmonious inter-action of its various parts it cannot be considered a 'self-organised being' (whose parts determine each other).

Kant notes that there is no logical connection between the notion of an object as a physical end or organism and an object as 'an end of nature'. And yet we are naturally led, he thinks, from the notion of objects of na-ture to the idea of nature as a 'system of ends' in which nature as a whole operates according to purposes. That is, if we think of organisms as man-ifesting purpose we will also be justified methodologically, or heuristically, in a merely regulative manner, in seeking purpose in nature in general, un-derstood as the aggregate of purposive objects. The notion of nature as a system of ends is therefore a supersensible notion supplied as a product of the regulative function of reason.

CRITIQUE OF TELEOLOGICAL JUDGMENT†

§61. Of the Objective Purposiveness of Nature

We have on transcendental principles good ground to assume a subjective purpo-siveness in nature, in its particular laws, in reference to its comprehensibility by human Judgment and to the possibility of the connection of particular experiences in a system. This may be expected as possible in many products of nature, which, as if they were established quite specially for our Judgment, contain a specific form conformable thereto, which through their manifoldness and unity serve at once to strengthen and to sustain the mental powers (that come into play in the employment of this, faculty), and to these we therefore give the name of *beautiful* forms.

But that the things of nature serve one another as means to purposes, and that their possibility is only completely intelligible through this kind of causality – for

---

†*KAA* V, 359–384. *Kant's Krtik of Judgment* (London: Macmillan and Co., 1892).

this we have absolutely no ground in the universal Idea of nature, as the complex of the objects of sense. In the above-mentioned case, the representation of things, because it is something in ourselves, can be quite well thought *a priori* as suitable and useful for the internally purposive determination of our cognitive faculties; but that purposes, which neither are our own nor belong to nature (for we do not regard nature as an intelligent being), could or should constitute a particular kind of causality, at least a quite special conformity to law, – this we have absolutely no *a priori* reason for presuming. Yet more, experience itself cannot prove to us the actuality of this; there must then have preceded a rationalising subtlety which only sportively introduces the concept of purpose into the nature of things, but which does not derive it from Objects or from their empirical cognition. To this latter it is of more service to make nature comprehensible according to analogy with the subjective ground of the connection of our representations, than to cognise it from objective grounds.

Further, objective purposiveness, as a principle of the possibility of things of nature, is so far removed from *necessary* connection with the concept of nature, that it is much oftener precisely that upon which one relies to prove the contingency of nature and of its form. When, e.g., we adduce the structure of a bird, the hollowness of its bones, the disposition of its wings for motion and of its tail for steering, etc., we say that all this is contingent in the highest degree according to the mere *nexus effectivus* of nature, without calling in the aid of a particular kind of causality, namely that of purpose (*nexus finalis*). In other words, nature, considered as mere mechanism, can produce its forms in a thousand different ways without stumbling upon unity in accordance with such a principle. It is not in the concept of nature but quite apart from it that we can hope to find the least ground *a priori* for this.

Nevertheless the teleological act of judgment is rightly brought to bear, at least problematically, upon the investigation of nature; but only in order to bring it under principles of observation and inquiry according to the *analogy* with the causality of purpose, without any pretence to *explain* it thereby. It belongs therefore to the reflective and not to the determinant judgment. The concept of combinations and forms of nature in accordance with purposes is then at least *one principle more* for bringing its phenomena under rules where the laws of simply mechanical causality do not suffice. For we bring in a teleological ground, where we attribute causality in respect of an Object to the concept of an Object, as if it were to be found in nature (not in ourselves); or rather when we represent to ourselves the possibility of the Object after the analogy of that causality which we experience in ourselves, and consequently think nature technically as through a special faculty. If, on the other hand, we did not ascribe to it such a method of action, its causality would have to be represented as blind mechanism. If, on the contrary, we supply to nature causes acting *designedly*, and consequently place at its basis teleology, not merely as a *regulative* principle for the mere *judging* of phenomena, to which nature can be thought as subject in its particular laws, but as a *constitutive* principle of the *derivation* of its products from their causes; then would the concept of a natural purpose no longer belong to the reflective but to the determinant Judgment. Then, in fact, it would not belong specially to the Judgment (like the concept of beauty regarded as formal subjective purposiveness), but as a rational concept it would introduce into a natural science a new causality, which we only borrow from ourselves and ascribe to other beings, without meaning to assume them to be of the same kind with ourselves.

First Division: Analytic of the Teleological Judgment

§62. Of the Objective Purposiveness which is Merely Formal as Distinguished from that Which is Material

All geometrical figures drawn on a principle display a manifold, oft admired, objective purposiveness; i.e. in reference to their usefulness for the solution of several problems by a single principle, or of the same problem in an infinite variety of ways. The purposiveness is here obviously objective and intellectual, not merely subjective and aesthetic. For it expresses the suitability of the figure for the production of many intended figures, and is cognised through Reason. But this purposiveness does not make the concept of the object itself possible, i.e. it is not regarded as possible merely with reference to this use.

In so simple a figure as the circle lies the key to the solution of a multitude of problems, each of which would demand various appliances; whereas their solution results of itself, as it were, as one of the infinite number of excellent properties of this figure. Are we, for example, asked to construct a triangle, being given the base and vertical angle? The problem is indeterminate, i.e. it can be solved in an infinite number of ways. But the circle embraces them all together as the geometrical locus of the vertices of triangles satisfying the given conditions. Again, suppose that two lines are to cut one another so that the rectangle under the segments of the one should be equal to the rectangle under the segments of the other; the solution of the problem from this point of view presents much difficulty. But all chords intersecting inside a circle divide one another in this *proportion*. Other curved lines suggest other purposive solutions of which nothing was thought in the rule that furnished their construction. All conic sections in themselves and when compared with one another are fruitful in principles for the solution of a number of possible problems, however simple is the definition which determines their concept. – It is a true joy to see the zeal with which the old geometers investigated the properties of lines of this class, without allowing themselves to be led astray by the questions of narrow-minded persons, as to what use this knowledge would be. Thus they worked out the properties of the parabola without knowing the law of gravitation, which would have suggested to them its application to the trajectory of heavy bodies (for the motion of a heavy body can be seen to be parallel to the curve of a parabola). Again, they found out the properties of an ellipse without surmising that any of the heavenly bodies had weight, and without knowing the law of force at different distances from the point of attraction, which causes it to describe this curve in free motion. While they thus unconsciously worked for the science of the future, they delighted themselves with a purposiveness in the [essential] being of things which yet they were able to present completely *a priori* in its necessity. *Plato*, himself master of this science, hinted at such an original constitution of things in the discovery of which we can dispense with all experience, and at the power of the mind to produce from its supersensible principle the harmony of beings (where the properties of number come in, with which the mind plays in music). This [he touches upon] in the inspiration that raised him above the concepts of experience to Ideas, which seem to him to be explicable only through an intellectual affinity with the origin of all beings. No wonder that he banished from his school the man who was ignorant of geometry, since he thought he could derive from pure intuition, which has its home in the human spirit, that which *Anaxagoras* drew from empirical objects and their purposive combination. For in the very necessity of that which is purposive, and is constituted just as if it were designedly intended for our use, – but at the same time seems to belong originally to the being of things without any reference to our use – lies the ground of our great admiration of nature, and that not so much external as in our own Reason. It is surely excusable that this admiration should through misunderstanding gradually rise to the height of fanaticism.

But this intellectual purposiveness, although no doubt objective (not subjective like aesthetic purposiveness), is in reference to its possibility merely formal (not real). It can only be conceived as purposiveness in general without any [definite] purpose being assumed as its basis, and consequently without teleology being needed for it. The figure of a circle is an intuition which is determined by means of the Understanding according to a principle. The unity of this principle which I arbitrarily assume and use as fundamental concept, applied to a form of intuition (space) which is met with in myself as a representation and yet *a priori*, renders intelligible the unity of many rules resulting from the construction of that concept, which are purposive for many possible designs. But this purposiveness does not imply a *purpose* or any other ground whatever. It is quite different if I meet with order and regularity in complexes of *things*, external to myself, enclosed within certain boundaries; as, e.g., in a garden, the order and regularity of the trees, flower-beds, and walks. These I cannot expect to derive *a priori* from my bounding of space made after a rule of my own; for this order and regularity are existing things which must be given empirically in order to be known, and not a mere representation in myself determined *a priori* according to a principle. So then the latter (empirical) purposiveness, as *real*, is dependent on the concept of a purpose.

But the ground of admiration for a perceived purposiveness, although it be in the being of things (so far as their concepts can be constructed), may be very well involved and apprehended as rightful. The manifold rules whose unity (derived from a principle) excites admiration, are all synthetical and do not follow from the *concept* of the Object as in the case of the circle; but require this Object to be given in intuition. Hence this unity gets the appearance of having empirically an external basis of rules distinct from our representative faculty; as if therefore the correspondence of the Object to that need of rules which is proper to the Understanding were contingent in itself, and therefore only possible by means of a purpose expressly directed thereto. Now because this harmony, notwithstanding all this purposiveness, is not cognised empirically but *a priori*, it should bring us of itself to this point – that space, through whose determination (by means of the Imagination, in accordance with a concept) the Object is alone possible, is not a characteristic of things external to me, but a mere mode of representation in myself. Hence, in the figure which I draw *in conformity with a concept*, i.e. in my own mode of representing that which is given to me externally, whatever it may be in itself, *it is I that introduce the purposiveness*; I get no empirical instruction from the Object about the purposiveness, and so I require in it no particular purpose external to myself. But because this consideration already calls for a critical employment of Reason, and consequently cannot be involved in the judging of the Object according to its properties; so this latter [judging] suggests to me immediately nothing but the unification of heterogeneous rules (even according to their very diversity) in a principle. This principle, without requiring any particular *a priori* basis external to my concept, or indeed, generally speaking, to my representation, is yet cognised *a priori* by me as true. Now *wonder* is a shock of the mind arising from the incompatibility of a representation, and the rule given by its means, with the principles already lying at its basis; which provokes a doubt as to whether we have rightly seen or rightly judged. *Admiration*, however, is wonder which ever recurs, despite the disappearance of this doubt. Consequently the latter is a quite natural effect of that observed purposiveness in the being of things (as phenomena). It cannot indeed be censured, whilst the unification of the form of sensible intuition (space) – with the faculty of concepts (the Understanding) – is inexplicable to us; and that not only on account of the union being just of the kind that it is, but because it is enlarging for the mind to surmise [the existence of] something lying outside our sensible representations in which, although unknown to us, the ultimate ground of that agreement may be met with. We are, it is true, not necessitated to cognise this if we have only to do with the formal purposiveness of our representations; but the fact that we are compelled to look out beyond it inspires at the same time an admiration for the object that impels us thereto.

We are accustomed to speak of the already mentioned properties of geometrical figures or of numbers as *beautiful*, on account of a certain *a priori* purposiveness they have for all kinds of cognitive uses, this purposiveness being quite unexpected on account of the simplicity of the construction. We speak, e.g., of this or that *beautiful* property of the circle, which was discovered in this or that way. But there is no aesthetic act of judgment through which we find it purposive, no act of judgment without a concept which renders noticeable a mere *subjective* purposiveness in the free play of our cognitive faculties; but an intellectual act according to concepts which enables us clearly to cognise an objective purposiveness, i.e. availableness for all kinds of (infinitely manifold) purposes. We must rather call this *relative perfection* than a beauty of the mathematical figure. To speak thus of an *intellectual beauty* cannot in general be permissible; for otherwise the word beauty would lose all determinate significance or the intellectual satisfaction all superiority over the sensible. We should rather call a *demonstration* of such properties beautiful, because through it the Understanding as the faculty of concepts, and the Imagination as the faculty of presenting them, feel themselves strengthened *a priori*. (This, when viewed in connection with the precision introduced by Reason, is spoken of as elegant.) Here, however, the satisfaction, although it is based on concepts, is subjective; while perfection brings with itself an objective satisfaction.

§63. Of the Relative as Distinguished from the Inner Purposiveness of Nature

Experience leads our Judgment to the concept of an objective and material purposiveness, i.e. to the concept of a purpose of nature, only when[1] we have to judge of a relation of cause to effect which we find ourselves able to apprehend as legitimate only by presupposing the Idea of the effect of the causality of the cause as the fundamental condition, in the cause, of the possibility of the effect. This can take place in two ways. We may regard the effect directly as an art product, or only as material for the art of other possible natural beings; in other words, either as a purpose or as a means towards the purposive employment of other causes. This latter purposiveness is called utility (for man) or mere advantage (for other creatures), and is merely relative; while the former is an inner purposiveness of the natural being.

For example, rivers bring down with them all kinds of earth serviceable for the growth of plants which sometimes is deposited inland, often also at their mouths. The tide brings this mud to many coasts over the land or deposits it on the shore; and so, more especially if men give their aid so that the ebb shall not carry it back again, the fruit-bearing land increases in area, and the vegetable kingdom gains the place which formerly was the habitation of fish and shells. In this way has nature itself brought about most of the extensions of the land, and still continues to do so, although very slowly. – Now the question is whether this is to be judged a purpose of nature, because it contains profit for men. We cannot put it down to the account of the vegetable kingdom, because just as much is subtracted from sea-life as is added to land-life.

Or, to give an example of the advantageousness of certain natural things as means for other creatures (if we suppose them to be means), no soil is more suitable to pine trees than a sandy soil. Now the deep sea, before it withdrew from the land, left behind large tracts of sand in our northern regions, so that on this soil, so unfavourable for all cultivation, widely extended pine forests were enabled to grow, for the unreasoning destruction of which we frequently blame our ancestors.

---

[1] As in pure mathematics we can never talk of the existence, but only of the possibility of things, viz. of an intuition corresponding to a concept, and so never of cause and effect, it follows that all purposiveness observed there must be considered merely as formal and never as a natural purpose.

We may ask if this original deposit of tracts of sand was a purpose of nature for the benefit of the possible pine forests? So much is clear, that if we regard this as a purpose of nature, we must also regard the sand as a relative purpose, in reference to which the ocean strand and its withdrawal were means: for in the series of the mutually subordinated members of a purposive combination, every member must be regarded as a purpose (though not as a final purpose), to which its proximate cause is the means. So too if cattle, sheep, horses, etc., are to exist, there must be grass on the earth, but there must also be saline plants in the desert if camels are to thrive; and again these and other herbivorous animals must be met with in numbers if there are to be wolves, tigers, and lions. Consequently the objective purposiveness, which is based upon advantage, is not an objective purposiveness of things in themselves; as if the sand could not be conceived for itself as an effect of a cause, viz. the sea, without attributing to the latter a purpose, and regarding the effect, namely the sand, as a work of art. It is a merely relative purposiveness contingent upon the thing to which it is ascribed; and although in the examples we have cited, the different kinds of grass are to be judged as in themselves organised products of nature, and consequently as artificial, yet are they to be regarded, in reference to the beasts which feed upon them, as mere raw material.

But above all, though man, through the freedom of his causality, finds certain natural things of advantage for his designs – designs often foolish, such as using the variegated plumage of birds to adorn his clothes, or coloured earths and the juices of plants for painting his face; often again reasonable as when the horse is used for riding, the ox or (as in Minorca) the ass or pig for ploughing – yet we cannot even here assume a relative natural purpose. For his Reason knows how to give things a conformity with his own arbitrary fancies for which he was not at all predestined by nature. Only, *if* we assume that men are to live upon the earth, then the means must be there without which they could not exist as animals, and even as rational animals (in however low a degree of rationality); and thereupon those natural things, which are indispensable in this regard, must be considered as natural purposes.

We can hence easily see that external purposiveness (advantage of one thing in respect of others) can be regarded as an external natural purpose only under the condition, that the existence of that [being], to which it is immediately or distantly advantageous, is in itself a purpose of nature. Since that can never be completely determined by mere contemplation of nature, it follows that relative purposiveness, although it hypothetically gives indications of natural purposes, yet justifies no absolute teleological judgment.

Snow in cold countries protects the crops from the frost; it makes human intercourse easier (by means of sleighs). The Laplander finds in his country animals by whose aid this intercourse is brought about, i.e. reindeer, who find sufficient sustenance in a dry moss which they have to scratch out for themselves from under the snow, and who are easily tamed and readily permit themselves to be deprived of that freedom in which they could have remained if they chose. For other people in the same frozen regions marine animals afford rich stores; in addition to the food and clothing which are thus supplied, and the wood which is floated in by the sea to their dwellings, these marine animals provide material for fuel by which, their huts are warmed. Here is a wonderful concurrence of many references of nature to one purpose; and all this applies to the cases of the Greenlander, the Lapp, the Samoyede, the inhabitant of Yakutsk, etc. But then we do not see why, generally, men must live there at all. Therefore to say that vapour falls out of the atmosphere in the form of snow, that the sea has its currents which float down wood that has grown in warmer lands, and that there are in it great sea monsters filled with oil, *because* the idea of advantage for certain poor creatures is fundamental for the cause which collects all these natural products, would be a very venturesome and arbitrary judgment. For even if there were none of this natural utility, we should miss nothing as regards the adequateness of natural causes to [man's] constitution; much more even to desire such a tendency in, and to attribute such a purpose to, nature would be the part of a presumptuous and inconsiderate fancy. For indeed it might be observed that it could only have been the greatest want of harmony among men which thus scattered them into such inhospitable regions.

§64. Of the Peculiar Character of Things as Natural Purposes

In order to see that a thing is only possible as a purpose, that is to be forced to seek the causality of its origin not in the mechanism of nature but in a cause whose faculty of action is determined through concepts, it is requisite that its form be not possible according to mere natural laws, i.e. laws which can be cognised by us through the Understanding alone when applied to objects of Sense; but that even the empirical knowledge of it as regards its cause and effect presupposes concepts of Reason. This *contingency* of its form in all empirical natural laws in reference to Reason affords a ground for regarding its causality as possible only through Reason. For Reason, which must cognise the necessity of every form of a natural product in order to comprehend even the conditions of its genesis, cannot assume such [natural] necessity in that particular given form. The causality of its origin is then referred to the faculty of acting in accordance with purposes (a will); and the Object which can only thus be represented as possible is represented as a purpose.

If in a seemingly uninhabited country a man perceived a geometrical figure, say a regular hexagon, inscribed on the sand, his reflection busied with such a concept would attribute, although obscurely, the unity in the principle of its genesis to Reason, and consequently would not regard as a ground of the possibility of such a shape the sand, or the neighbouring sea, or the winds, or beasts with familiar footprints, or any other irrational cause. For the chance against meeting with such a concept, which is only possible through Reason, would seem so infinitely great, that it would be just as if there were no natural law, no cause in the mere mechanical working of nature capable of producing it; but as if only the concept of such an Object, as a concept which Reason alone can supply and with which it can compare the thing, could contain the causality for such an effect. This then would be regarded as a purpose, but as a product of *art*, not as a natural purpose (*vestigium hominis video*).[2]

But in order to regard a thing cognised as a natural product as a purpose also – consequently as a *natural purpose*, if this is not a contradiction – something more is required. I would say provisionally: a thing exists as a natural purpose, if it is [although in a double sense][3] both *cause and effect of itself.* For herein lies a causality the like of which cannot be combined with the mere concept of a nature without attributing to it a purpose; it can certainly be thought without contradiction, but cannot be comprehended. We shall elucidate the determination of this Idea of a natural purpose by an example, before we analyse it completely.

In the first place, a tree generates another tree according to a known natural law. But the tree produced is of the same genus; and so it produces itself *generically.* On the one hand, as effect it is continually self-produced; on the other hand, as cause it continually produces itself, and so perpetuates itself generically.

Secondly, a tree produces itself as an *individual.* This kind of effect no doubt we call growth; but it is quite different from any increase according to mechanical laws, and is to be reckoned as generation, though under another name. The matter that the tree incorporates it previously works up into a specifically peculiar quality, which natural mechanism external to it cannot supply; and thus it develops itself by aid of a material which, as compounded, is its own product. No doubt, as regards the constituents got from nature without, it must only be regarded as an educt; but yet in the separation and recombination of this raw material we see such an originality in the separating and formative faculty of this kind of natural being, as is infinitely beyond the reach of art, if the attempt is made to reconstruct such vegetable products out of elements obtained by their dissection or material supplied by nature for their sustenance.

Thirdly, each part of a tree generates itself in such a way that the maintenance of any one part depends reciprocally on the maintenance of the rest. A bud of one tree engrafted on the twig of another produces in the alien stock a plant of its own kind, and so also a scion engrafted on a foreign stem. Hence we may regard each twig or leaf of the same tree as merely engrafted or inoculated into it, and so as an independent tree attached to another and parasitically nourished by it. At the same time, while the leaves are products of the tree they also in turn give support to it; for the repeated defoliation of a tree kills it, and its growth thus depends on the action of the leaves upon the stem. The self-help of nature in case of injury in the vegetable creation, when the want of a part that is necessary for the maintenance of its neighbours is supplied by the remaining parts; and the abortions or malformations in growth, in which certain parts, on account of casual

---

[2] The allusion is to Vitruvius *de Architectura*, Bk. vi. Praef. 'Aristippus philosophus Socraticus, naufragio cum ejectus ad Rhodiensium litus animadvertisset geometrica schemata descripta, exclamavisse ad comites ita dicitur, Bene speremus, hominum enim vestigia video'.

[3] Second edition.

defects or hindrances, form themselves in a new way to maintain what exists, and so produce an anomalous creature, I shall only mention in passing, though they are among the most wonderful properties of organised creatures.

§65. Things Regarded as Natural Purposes are Organised Beings

According to the character alleged in the preceding section, a thing, which, though a natural product, is to be cognised as only possible as a natural purpose, must bear itself alternately as cause and as effect. This, however, is a somewhat inexact and indeterminate expression which needs derivation from a determinate concept.

Causal combination as thought merely by the Understanding is a connection constituting an ever-progressive series (of causes and effects); and things which as effects presuppose others as causes cannot be reciprocally at the same time causes of these. This sort of causal combination we call that of effective causes (*nexus effectivus*). But on the other hand, a causal combination according to a concept of Reason (of purposes) can also be thought, which regarded as a series would lead either forwards or backwards; in this the thing that has been called the effect may with equal propriety be termed the cause of that of which it is the effect. In the practical department of human art we easily find connections such as this; e.g. a house, no doubt, is the cause of the money received for rent, but also conversely the representation of this possible income was the cause of building the house. Such a causal connection we call that of final causes (*nexus finalis*). We may perhaps suitably name the first the connection of real causes, the second of those which are ideal; because from this nomenclature it is at once comprehended that there can be no more than these two kinds of causality.

For a thing to be a natural purpose in the *first* place it is requisite that its parts (as regards their presence and their form) are only possible through their reference to the whole. For the thing itself is a purpose and so is comprehended under a concept or an Idea which must determine *a priori* all that is to be contained in it. But so far as a thing is only thought as possible in this way, it is a mere work of art; i.e. a product of one rational cause distinct from the matter (of the parts), whose causality (in the collection and combination of the parts) is determined through its Idea of a whole possible by their means (and consequently not through external nature).

But if a thing as a natural product is to involve in itself and in its internal possibility a reference to purposes, – i.e. to be possible only as a natural purpose, and without the causality of the concepts of rational beings external to itself, – then it is requisite *secondly* that its parts should so combine in the unity of a whole that they are reciprocally cause and effect of each other's form. Only in this way can the Idea of the whole conversely (reciprocally) determine the form and combination of all the parts; not indeed as cause – for then it would be an artificial product – but as the ground of cognition, for him who is judging it, of the systematic unity and combination of all the manifold contained in the given material.

For a body then which is to be judged in itself and its internal possibility as a natural purpose, it is requisite that its parts mutually depend upon each other both as to their form and their combination, and so produce a whole by their own causality; while conversely the concept of the whole may be regarded as its cause according to a principle (in a being possessing a causality according to concepts adequate to such a product). In this case then the connection of *effective causes* may be judged as an *effect through final causes.*

In such a product of nature every part not only exists *by means of* the other parts, but is thought as existing *for the sake of* the others and the whole, that is as an (organic) instrument. Thus, however, it might be an artificial instrument, and so might be represented only as a purpose that is possible in general; but also its parts are all organs reciprocally *producing* each other. This can never be the case with artificial instruments, but only with nature which supplies all the material for instruments (even for those of art). Only a product of such a kind can be called a *natural purpose*, and this because it is an *organised* and *self-organising being.*

In a watch one part is the instrument for moving the other parts, but the wheel is not the effective cause of the production of the others; no doubt one part is for the sake of the others, but it does not exist by their means. In this case the producing cause of the parts and of their form is not contained in the nature (of the material), but is external to it in a being which can produce effects according to Ideas of a whole possible by means of its causality. Hence a watch wheel does not produce other wheels, still less does one watch produce other watches, utilising (organising) foreign material for that purpose; hence it does not replace of itself parts of which it has been deprived, nor does it make good what is lacking in a first formation by the addition of the missing parts, nor if it has gone out of order does it repair itself – all of which, on the contrary, we may expect from organised nature. – An organised being is then not a mere machine, for that has merely *moving* power, but it possesses in itself *formative* power of a self-propagating kind which it communicates to its materials though they have it not of themselves; it organises them, in fact, and this cannot be explained by the mere mechanical faculty of motion.

We say of nature and its faculty in organised products far too little if we describe it as an *analogon of art*; for this suggests an artificer (a rational being) external to it. Much rather does it organise itself and its organised products in every species, no doubt after one general pattern but yet with suitable deviations, which self-preservation demands according to circumstances. We perhaps approach nearer to this inscrutable property, if we describe it as an *analogon of life*; but then we must either endow matter, as mere matter, with a property which contradicts its very being (hylozoism), or associate therewith an alien principle *standing in communion* with it (a soul). But in the latter case we must, if such a product is to be a natural product, either presuppose organised matter as the instrument of that soul, which does not make the soul a whit more comprehensible; or regard the soul as artificer of this structure and so remove the product from (corporeal) nature. To speak strictly, then, the organisation of nature has in it nothing analogous to any causality we know.[4] Beauty in nature can be rightly described as an analogon of art, because it is ascribed to objects only in reference to reflection upon their *external* aspect, and consequently only on account of the form of their external surface. But *internal natural perfection*, as it belongs to those things which are only possible as *natural purposes*, and are therefore called organised beings, is not analogous to any physical, i.e. natural, faculty known to us; nay even, regarding ourselves as, in the widest sense, belonging to nature, it is not even thinkable or explicable by means of any exactly fitting analogy to human art.

The concept of a thing as in itself a natural purpose is therefore no constitutive concept of Understanding or of Reason, but it can serve as a regulative concept for the reflective Judgment, to guide our investigation about objects of this kind by a distant analogy with our own causality according to purposes generally, and in our meditations upon their ultimate ground. This latter use, however, is not in reference to the knowledge of nature or of its original ground, but rather to our own practical faculty of Reason, in analogy with which we considered the cause of that purposiveness.

Organised beings are then the only beings in nature which, considered in themselves and apart from any relation to other things, can be thought as possible only as purposes of nature. Hence they first afford objective reality to the concept of a *purpose of nature*, as distinguished from a practical purpose; and so they give to the science of nature the basis for a teleology, i.e. a mode of judgment about natural Objects according to a special principle which otherwise we should in no way be justified in introducing (because we cannot see *a priori* the possibility of this kind of causality).

§66. Of the Principle of Judging of Internal Purposiveness in Organised Beings

This principle, which is at the same time a definition, is as follows: *An organised product of nature is one in which every part is reciprocally purpose [end] and means.* In it nothing is vain, without purpose, or to be ascribed to a blind mechanism of nature.

The principle is no doubt, as regards its occasion, derived from experience, viz. from that methodised experience called observation; but on account of the universality and necessity which it ascribes to such purposiveness it cannot rest solely on empirical grounds, but must have at its basis an *a priori* principle, although it be merely regulative and these purposes lie only in the idea of the judging

---

[4] We can conversely throw light upon a certain combination, much more often met with in Idea than in actuality, by means of an analogy to the so-called immediate natural purposes. In a recent complete transformation of a great people into a state the word *organisation* for the regulation of magistracies, etc., and even of the whole body politic, has often been fitly used. For in such a whole every member should surely be purpose as well as means, and, whilst all work together towards the possibility of the whole, each should be determined as regards place and function by means of the Idea of the whole. [Kant probably alludes here to the organisation of the United States of America.]

[subject] and not in an effective cause. We may therefore describe the aforesaid principle as a *maxim* for judging of the internal purposiveness of organised beings.

It is an acknowledged fact that the dissectors of plants and animals, in order to investigate their structure and to find out the reasons, why and for what end such parts, such a disposition and combination of parts, and just such an internal form have been given them, assume as indisputably necessary the maxim that nothing in such a creature is *vain*; just as they lay down as the fundamental proposition of the universal science of nature, that *nothing* happens *by chance*. In fact, they can as little free themselves from this teleological proposition as from the universal physical proposition; for as without the latter we should have no experience at all, so without the former we should have no guiding thread for the observation of a species of natural things which we have conceived teleologically under the concept of natural purposes.

Now this concept brings the Reason into a quite different order of things from that of a mere mechanism of nature, which is no longer satisfying here. An Idea is to be the ground of the possibility of the natural product. But because this is an absolute unity of representation, instead of the material being a plurality of things that can supply by itself no definite unity of composition, – if that unity of the Idea is to serve at all as the *a priori* ground of determination of a natural law of the causality of such a form of composition, – the purpose of nature must be extended to *everything* included in its product. For if we once refer action of this sort *on the whole* to any supersensible ground of determination beyond the blind mechanism of nature, we must judge of it altogether according to this principle; and we have then no reason to regard the form of such a thing as partly dependent on mechanism – for by such mixing up of disparate principles no certain rule of judging would be left.

For example, it may be that in an animal body many parts can be conceived as concretions according to mere mechanical laws (as the hide, the bones, the hair). And yet the cause which brings together the required matter, modifies it, forms it, and puts it in its appropriate place, must always be judged of teleologically; so that here everything must be considered as organised, and everything again in a certain relation to the thing itself is an organ.

§67. Of the Principle of the Teleological Judging of Nature in General as a System of Purposes

We have already said above that the *external* purposiveness of natural things affords no sufficient warrant for using them as purposes of nature in order to explain their presence, and for regarding their contingently purposive effects as the grounds of their presence according to the principle of final causes. Thus we cannot take for natural purposes, *rivers* because they promote intercourse among inland peoples, *mountains* because they contain the sources of the rivers and for their *maintenance* in rainless seasons have a store of snow, or the *slope* of the land which carries away the water and leaves the country dry; because although this shape of the earth's surface be very necessary for the origin and maintenance of the vegetable and animal kingdoms, it has nothing in itself for the possibility of which we are forced to assume a causality according to purposes. The same is true of plants which man uses for his needs or his pleasures; of beasts, the camel, the ox, the horse, dog, etc., which are indispensable for him as well for food as because they are used in his service in many different ways. In the case of things which we have no reason for regarding in themselves as purposes, such external relation can only be hypothetically judged as purposive.

To judge of a thing as a natural purpose on account of its internal form is something very different from taking the existence of that thing to be a purpose of nature. For the latter assertion we require not merely the concept of a possible purpose, but the knowledge of the final purpose (*scopus*) of nature. But this requires a reference of such knowledge to something supersensible far transcending all our teleological knowledge of nature, for the purpose of the existence of nature must itself be sought beyond nature. The internal form of a mere blade of grass is sufficient to show that for our human faculty of judgment its origin is possible only according to the rule of purposes. But if we change our point of view and look to the use which other natural beings make of it, abandon the consideration of its internal organisation and only look to its externally purposive references, we shall arrive at no categorical purpose; all this purposive reference rests on an ever more distant condition, which, as unconditioned (the presence of a thing as final purpose), lies quite outside the physico-teleological view of the world. For example, grass is needful for the ox, which again is needful for man as a means of existence, but then we do not see why it is necessary that men should exist (a question this, which we shall not find so easy to answer if we sometimes cast our thoughts on the New Hollanders or the inhabitants of Tierra del Fuego). So conceived, the thing is not even a natural purpose, for neither it (nor its whole genus) is to be regarded as a natural product.

Hence it is only so far as matter is organised that it necessarily carries with it the concept of a natural purpose, because this its specific form is at the same time a product of nature. But this concept leads necessarily to the Idea of collective nature as a system in accordance with the rule of purposes, to which Idea all the mechanism of nature must be subordinated according to principles of Reason (at least in order to investigate natural phenomena in it). The principle of Reason belongs to it only as a subjective principle or a maxim: viz. everything in the world is some way good for something; nothing is vain in it. By the example that nature gives us in its organic products we are justified, nay called upon, to expect of it and of its laws nothing that is not purposive on the whole.

It is plain that this is not a principle for the determinant but only for the reflective judgment; that it is regulative and not constitutive; and that we derive from it a clue by which we consider natural things in reference to an already given ground of determination according to a new law-abiding order; and extend our natural science according to a different principle, viz. that of final causes, but yet without prejudice to the principle of mechanical causality. Furthermore, it is in no wise thus decided, whether anything of which we judge by this principle, is a *designed* purpose of nature; whether the grass is for the ox or the sheep, or whether these and the other things of nature are here for men. It is well also from this side to consider the things which are unpleasant to us and are contrary to purpose in particular references. Thus, for example, we can say: The vermin that torment men in their clothes, their hair, or their beds, may be, according to a wise appointment of nature, a motive to cleanliness which is in itself an important means for the preservation of health. Or again the mosquitoes and other stinging insects that make the wildernesses of America so oppressive to the savages, may be so many goads to activity for these primitive men, [inducing them] to drain the marshes and bring light into the forests which intercept every breath of air, and in this way, as well as by cultivating the soil, to make their habitations more healthy. The same thing, which appears to men contradictory to nature in its inner organisation, if viewed in this light gives an entertaining, sometimes an instructive, outlook into a teleological order of things, to which, without such a principle, mere physical observation would not lead us by itself. Thus some persons regard the tapeworm as given to the men or animals in whom it resides, as a kind of set-off for some defect in their vital organs; now I would ask if dreams (without which we never sleep, though we seldom remember them) may not be a purposive ordinance of nature? For during the relaxation of all the moving powers of the body, they serve to inwardly excite the vital organs by the medium of the Imagination and its great activity (which in this state generally rises to the height of affection). During sleep the Imagination commonly is more actively at play when the stomach is overloaded, in which case this excitement is the more necessary. Consequently, then, without this internal power of motion and this fatiguing unrest, on account of which we complain about our dreams (though in fact they are rather remedies), sleep even in a sound state of health would be a complete extinction of life.

Also the beauty of nature, i.e. its connection with the free play of our cognitive faculties in apprehending and judging of its appearance, can be regarded as a kind of objective purposiveness of nature in its whole [content] as a system of which man is a member; if once the teleological judging of the same by means of the natural purposes with which organised beings furnish us, has justified for us the Idea of a great system of purposes of nature. We can regard it as a favour[5] which nature has felt for us, that, in addition to what is useful it has so profusely dispensed beauty and charm; and we can therefore love it, as well as regard it with respect

---

[5] In the aesthetic part [§58] it was said: *We view beautiful nature with favour,* whilst we have a quite free (disinterested) satisfaction in its form. For in this mere judgment of taste no consideration is given to the purpose for which these natural beauties exist; whether to excite pleasure in us, or as purposes without any reference to us at all. But in a teleological judgment we pay attention to this reference, and here we can *regard it as a favour of nature* that it has been willing to minister to our culture by the exhibition of so many beautiful figures.

on account of its immensity, and feel ennobled ourselves by such regard; just as if nature had established and adorned its splendid theatre precisely with this view.

We shall say only one thing more in this paragraph. If we have once discovered in nature a faculty of bringing forth products that can only be thought by us in accordance with the concept of final causes, we go further still. We venture to judge that things belong to a system of purposes, which yet do not (either in themselves or in their purposive relations) necessitate our seeking for any principle of their possibility beyond the mechanism of causes working blindly. For the first Idea, as concerns its ground, already brings us beyond the world of sense; since the unity of the supersensible principle must be regarded as valid in this way not merely for certain species of natural beings, but for the whole of nature as a system.

§68. Of the Principle of Teleology as Internal Principle of Natural Science

The principles of a science are either internal to it and are then called domestic (*principia domestica*), or are based on concepts that can only find their place outside it and so are *foreign* principles (*peregrina*). Sciences that contain the latter, place at the basis of their doctrines auxiliary propositions (*lemmata*), i.e. they borrow some concept, and with it a ground of arrangement, from another science.

Every science is in itself a system, and it is not enough in it to build in accordance with principles and thus to employ a technical procedure, but we must go to work with it architectonically, as a building subsisting for itself; we must not treat it as an additional wing or part of another building, but as a whole in itself, although we may subsequently make a passage from it into that other or conversely.

If then we introduce into the context of natural science the concept of God in order to explain the purposiveness in nature, and subsequently use this purposiveness to prove that there is a God, there is no internal consistency in either science [i.e. either in natural science or theology]; and a delusive circle brings them both into uncertainty, because they have allowed their boundaries to overlap.

The expression, a purpose of nature, already sufficiently prevents the confusion of mixing up natural science and the occasion that it gives for judging *teleologically* of its objects, with the consideration of God, and so of a *theological* derivation of them. We must not regard it as insignificant, if one interchanges this expression with that of a divine purpose in the ordering of nature, or gives out the latter as more suitable and proper for a pious soul, because it must come in the end to deriving these purposive forms in nature from a wise author of the world. On the contrary, we must carefully and modestly limit ourselves to the expression, a purpose of nature, which asserts exactly as much as we know. Before we ask after the cause of nature itself, we find in nature, and in the course of its development, products of the same kind which are developed in it according to known empirical laws, in accordance with which natural science must judge of its objects, and, consequently, must seek in nature their causality according to the rule of purposes. So then it must not transgress its bounds in order to introduce into itself as a domestic principle that, to whose concept no experience can be commensurate, upon which we are only entitled to venture after the completion of natural science.

Natural characteristics which demonstrate themselves *a priori*, and consequently admit of insight into their possibility from universal principles without any admixture of experience, although they carry with them a technical purposiveness, yet cannot, because they are absolutely necessary, be referred to the Teleology of nature, as to a method belonging to Physics for solving its problems. Arithmetical or geometrical analogies, as well as universal mechanical laws, – however strange and admirable may seem to us the union of different rules, quite independent of one another according to all appearance, in a single principle, – possess on that account no claim to be teleological grounds of explanation in Physics. Even if they deserve to be brought into consideration in the universal theory of the purposiveness of things of nature, yet they belong to another [science], i.e. Metaphysics, and constitute no internal principle of natural science; as with the empirical laws of natural purposes in organised beings, it is not only permissible but unavoidable to use the teleological *mode of judging* as a principle of the doctrine of nature in regard to a particular class of its objects.

So to the end that Physics may keep within its own bounds, it abstracts itself entirely from the question, whether natural purposes are *designed* or *undesigned*; for that would be to meddle in an extraneous business, in Metaphysics. It is enough that there are objects, alone *explicable* according to natural laws which we can only think by means of the Idea of purposes as principle, and also alone internally *cognisable* as concerns their internal form, in this way. In order, therefore, to remove the suspicion of the slightest assumption, – as if we wished to mix with our grounds of cognition something not belonging to Physics at all, viz. a supernatural cause, – we speak, indeed, in Teleology of nature as if the purposiveness in it were designed, but in such a way that this design is ascribed to nature, i.e. to matter. Now in this way there can be no misunderstanding, because no design in the proper meaning of the word can possibly be ascribed to inanimate matter; we thus give notice that this word here only expresses a principle of the reflective not of the determinant Judgment, and so is to introduce no particular ground of causality; but only adds for the use of the Reason a different kind of investigation from that according to mechanical laws, in order to supplement the inadequacy of the latter even for empirical research into all particular laws of nature. Hence we speak quite correctly in Teleology, so far as it is referred to Physics, of the wisdom, the economy, the forethought, the beneficence of Nature, without either making an intelligent being of it, for that would be preposterous; or even without presuming to place another intelligent Being above it as its Architect, for that would be presumptuous.[6] But there should be only signified thereby a kind of causality of nature after the analogy

---

[6] The German word *vermessen* is a good word and full of meaning. A judgment in which we forget to consider the extent of our powers (our Understanding) may sometimes sound very humble, and yet make great pretensions, and so be very presumptuous. Of this kind are most of those by which we pretend to

of our own in the technical use of Reason, in order to have before us the rule according to which certain products of nature must be investigated.

But now why is it that Teleology usually forms no proper part of theoretical natural science, but is regarded as a propaedeutic or transition to Theology? This is done in order to restrict the study of nature mechanically considered to that which we can so subject to observation or experiment that we are able to produce it ourselves as nature does, or at least by similar laws. For we see into a thing completely only so far as we can make it in accordance with our concepts and bring it to completion. But organisation, as an inner purpose of nature, infinitely surpasses all our faculty of presenting the like by means of art. And as concerns the external contrivances of nature regarded as purposive (wind, rain, etc.), Physics, indeed, considers their mechanism, but it cannot at all present their reference to purposes, so far as this is a condition necessarily belonging to cause; for this necessity of connection has to do altogether with the combination of our concepts and not with the constitution of things.

Translated by J. H. Bernard

extol the divine wisdom by ascribing to it designs in the works of creation and preservation which are really meant to do honour to the private wisdom of the reasoner.

21

F. W. J. Schelling, Introduction to the Outline of a System of the Philosophy of Nature (Einleitung zu dem Entwurf eines Systems der Naturphilosophie) *(1799)*

A great deal of the recent discussions of the development of German Idealist philosophy interprets it as a selective reconstruction of Kant's critical philosophy. Certainly Fichte's *Science of Knowledge*, and the many further theses he derives from it, might be characterised in this way. So too might the transcendental idealism of Schelling's first period of philosophy. However, Schelling's philosophy of nature introduces a different dimension which owes considerably less to Kantianism. Indeed, it is clear that when we look at some of the most central claims of Schelling and Hegel we find them in many instances committed to principles which are fundamentally opposed not only to the spirit but also to the rationale of transcendental idealism. This can be explained as the direct influence of certain aspects of Spinoza's philosophy on Schelling, but not those aspects, however, which impinge on the possibility of human freedom.

In the intense period of philosophical innovation at the end of the eighteenth century the notion of an absolute 'I' developed by Fichte – and initially subscribed to by Schelling – came to seem one-sided (and in any case riddled with problems of coherence). The absolute 'I' required relations to objects, otherwise there would be no world of experience, and this introduced something other than the 'I': of course, Fichte attempted to explain the 'I' as the source of its own otherness. But once the notion of an other is conceded, the absoluteness of the 'I' is eroded. The 'absolute' – if there is such a thing – must instead be understood as the relationship of subject and object, of self and nature. Nature as part of a relationship could not be adequately understood were it to be conceived as composed of merely inanimate objects simply given. The notion of 'dead nature', synonymous with the mechanism and materialism condemned by Goethe and others of the time, had to be superseded by a notion of nature as dynamic and internally generated. And it is at this point precisely that Spinoza seemed to provide a useful model. The 'absolute' was not self, but self and nature. In the Introduction to *Ideas for a Philosophy of Nature* Schelling notes: 'The *first* who, with complete clarity, saw mind and matter as one, thought and extension simply as modifications of the same principle, was *Spinoza*.[1]

Schelling's view of nature took a number of forms, as his general philosophical position developed. The text we examine here is, as one study describes it, 'the crucial transition to the view that the philosophy of nature is a necessary part of philosophy'.[2] However, it is by no means Schelling's first effort: in 1797 *Ideas for a Philosophy of Nature* appeared (with a new edition in 1803). The analysis there still employs some of the transcendental idealist method developed by Fichte. (Indeed, in his early career Schelling, as section 3 of this Anthology shows, was initially interested in explaining experience by reference to a grounding subject: transcendental philosophy.) In the *Introduction to the Outline of a System of the Philosophy of Nature* we find the Spinozistic positive notion of nature as a self-developing totality. The Spinozistic position sees nature as a quasi-subject: and Schelling develops this claim by seeing it as a self-unfolding subject from which the various elements of nature emerge. Tellingly, Schelling refers to the position he is proposing – one specifically opposed to a transcendental deduction of reality from the self – as a 'Spinozism of physics'. In contrast to transcendental idealism the philosophy of nature aims to explain nature in terms of natural forces. The philosophy of nature is, according to Schelling, a 'realist' position. The transcendental attitude to nature is to see it as product, as *natura naturata*: the product of the absolute subject. The philosophy of nature, however, takes nature as productive, as *natura naturans*. The reason for this extraordinary claim is that objects are always conditioned – they can be explained as the effects of other objects – but being itself is unconditioned: it is not the effect of something else. Nature, as being, is unconditional and is productive in the sense that objects of nature emerge through it. The philosophy of nature is the effort to find the structures and procedures of this productivity: to see nature as cause. In so far as nature is also its products however nature contains an 'original duplicity': it is both cause and effect. Schelling explains the notion of pure productivity as indeterminate: what is determinate, however, is also within nature. For the productivity of nature to become determinate nature must 'cease to be pure identity', it must sunder itself and become subject-object to itself.

The relationship between what Schelling terms his 'speculative physics' (a challenging idea when placed alongside his realist claims) and empirical physics is characteristic of the philosophy of science of this time: empirical physics works on the surface of things, examining the mechanical forces of phenomena, whereas speculative physics seeks specifically 'what is not objective in it': that is, what is not a phenomenon but an 'inner' principle of phenomena. A common allegation against the German Idealist philosophies

---

[1] F. W. J. Schelling, trans Errol E. Harris and Peter Heath, *Ideas for a Philosophy of Nature* (Cambridge: Cambridge University Press, 1988), p. 15 (*SSW* II, 20).

[2] Dale E. Snow, *Schelling and the End of Idealism* (Albany, NY: State University of New York Press, 1996), p. 94.

of nature is that they place theories before facts: however, it is noteworthy that Schelling insists that we can only accept a theory of nature in so far as it is capable of accommodating all the relevant facts of nature.

Schelling's essay contains significant statements of some of the concepts of the later phase of German Idealism (which he must be understood to have initiated). For example, he defines knowledge as knowing the inner structure of an object, contrasting with knowledge of the appearance of things. Allied to this claim is the idea that we 'only *know* what we ourselves have produced'. But is this not a repetition of the constructivism of transcendental idealism? Schelling's point is rather that our understanding of anything is achieved only when we have grasped its process of development. This is the form of constructivism found here. Another interesting differentiation with Kant lies in Schelling's concept (later assumed by Hegel) of the meaning of the *a priori*. For Kant what is *a priori* is a rule necessary for the possibility of experience. However, for Schelling what we know as *a priori* are all the aspects of nature (inorganic and organic) understood as necessary: so it is necessity in this broader sense that defines apriority, contingency as the *a posteriori*. Nature is an *a priori* system which appears only as a system when we consider it from the speculative standpoint. And as an *a priori* system it can be investigated as a system of interrelated principles. Of course, the latter can be proven only in the exposition. Hence analysis is a process of reconstructing the stages of the construction of nature out of its original unity.

INTRODUCTION TO THE OUTLINE OF A SYSTEM OF THE PHILOSOPHY OF NATURE. OR, ON THE CONCEPT OF SPECULATIVE PHYSICS AND THE INTERNAL ORGANISATION OF A SYSTEM OF THIS SCIENCE[†]

§ 1
What We Call the Philosophy of Nature is a Necessary Science in the System of Knowledge.

The intelligence is productive in a two-fold manner: either blindly and unconsciously, or freely and consciously; it is unconsciously productive in intuiting the world, and consciously productive in the creation of an ideal world.

Philosophy cancels this antithesis by assuming the unconscious activity to be originally identical and springing from the same root, so to speak, as the conscious. This identity is *directly* demonstrated by philosophy in an activity that is at once distinctively conscious and unconscious, and that is expressed in the productions

[†] *SSW* III, 271–290. New translation by David W. Wood.

of *genius*; and *indirectly* and *external* to consciousness in the products of *nature*, in so far as one perceives in all of them the most perfect fusion of the ideal and the real.

When philosophy posits the unconscious activity, or, as it may also be termed, the real activity, as identical with the conscious or the ideal activity, then its original tendency is to trace the real back to the ideal, thus giving rise to what one calls transcendental philosophy. The regularity exhibited in all the movements of nature, for instance, in that sublime geometry exercised in the movements of the heavenly bodies, is not explained by saying that nature is the most perfect geometry, but rather the opposite, that the most perfect geometry is what is productive in nature. In this mode of explanation the real itself is placed in the ideal world, and the above movements become transformed into intuitions that only occur within ourselves and do not correspond to anything external to us. Again, when nature is entirely given over to itself it freely brings forth regular forms, as it were, in every transition from the fluid to the solid state (a regularity which even appears to have purpose in the crystallisations of a higher kind, the organic). Or within the animal kingdom, that product of blind natural forces, there are actions that are equally regular to those occurring in consciousness, or even arise in their way like perfected works of art – all this is explained by saying that it is an unconscious productivity, yet consciously related to the original productivity, whose mere reflection we behold in nature. From the natural standpoint it must appear as one and the same blind drive – and which is only effective in different stages, from crystallisation up until the highest organic formations (and, on the other hand, reverts back again to mere crystallisation by means of the artistic drive).

According to this view, since nature is merely the visible organism of our understanding it *can* do nothing else but produce what is regular and purposeful, and that it is *compelled* to produce it. However, if nature *can* do nothing else but produce what is regular and if it produces it from necessity, then it also follows that in a nature conceived as independent and real it must also be necessarily demonstrated, and again, with respect to nature's forces, be the origin of such regular and purposeful products. *Therefore, the ideal in turn must also originate from out of the real and be explained by means of it.*

If the task of transcendental philosophy is to order the real under the ideal, then conversely, the task of the philosophy of nature is to explain the ideal by means of the real. Hence, the two sciences form a unity, and differ only in the opposing orientations of their tasks. Furthermore, not only are the two directions equally possible, they are equally necessary, and hence both receive the same necessity in the system of knowledge.

§ 2
Scientific Character of the Philosophy of Nature

The philosophy of nature is opposed to transcendental philosophy, and primarily differs from the latter by positing nature as independent (indeed, not in so far as it is a product but to the extent that it is both productive and product), and so may be most briefly termed the *Spinozism of physics*. It then follows that in this science there do not occur any idealistic modes of explanation, ones of the type clearly favoured by transcendental philosophy, since for it nature is nothing else but the organ of self-consciousness, and thus everything in nature is necessary because self-consciousness can only be mediated through a nature of this kind. Yet for physics and the standpoint of our science this kind of explanation is just as meaningless as those earlier teleological modes of explanation and the introduction of general final causes in the resulting science of nature. Any idealistic type of explanation transplanted from its own domain into that of the explanation of nature degenerates into the most fanciful nonsense of which there are countless well-known examples. The first maxim of all genuine natural science is to explain everything by means of natural forces. This is broadly accepted by our science and has even been extended to a domain before which all explanations of nature have up to now had to stop short, e.g. the domain of organic phenomena, which seems to presuppose an analogy with reason. If we really grant that there is something in the actions of the animal that presupposes such an analogy, then nothing else follows from this apart from accepting realism as a principle, and thus what we call reason is merely a play of higher and necessarily unknown natural forces. If all thinking can ultimately be reduced to producing and reproducing, then there is nothing impossible in the thought that the same activity by which nature reproduces anew in every moment, is reproductive in thought only through the medium of the organism (just as through the influence and the play of light, independently existing nature is really *immaterial,* and becomes created for a second time, so to speak). Therefore, it is natural that what defines the limit of our intuitive faculty no longer falls within the sphere of our intuition itself.

§ 3
The Philosophy of Nature is Speculative Physics

As one can gather from the foregoing, our science is indeed entirely realistic, i.e. it is nothing other than physics, it is simply *speculative* physics. Its tendency is precisely the same as the systems of the ancient physicists, and what in modern times is the restoration of the Epicurean system of philosophy: *Le Sage's* mechanical physics, which after a long period of scientific slumber has reawakened the speculative spirit in physics. Here it cannot be proved in detail – for this proof falls within the sphere of our science – that the idea of speculative physics cannot be realised upon the mechanical or atomistic paths followed by Le Sage and his most successful predecessors. The ultimate goal of this science, which is to investigate the *absolute* cause of motion (and without which nature is not completed and whole), cannot be grasped or even solved mechanically, because mechanical motion can only result from motion *ad infinitum.* In order genuinely to establish speculative physics there merely remains one path open, the dynamic path, which states that motion arises not only from motion, but also even from rest. Therefore, there is even motion in the stasis of nature, and all mechanical motion is merely secondary and derivative of that sole primitive and original motion which only arises from the very first factors of the construction of nature in general (the fundamental forces).

By clearly indicating how our investigation differs from all previous investigations of a similar nature we have also shown how speculative physics differs from so-called empirical physics; this distinction boils down to the fact that the former is solely concerned with the original causes of motion in nature, i.e. solely with dynamic phenomena. The latter, in contrast, is only occupied with secondary motions and with the original motion as mechanical motion (and therefore capable of mathematical construction), since it never arrives at an ultimate source of motion in nature. The former is specifically directed to the inner workings of nature and to what is *non-objective* in it; the latter, on the contrary, only aims at the *surface* of nature, and to what is objective and, as it were, *external* in nature.

§ 4
On the Possibility of a Speculative Physics

Since our investigation is not so much directed to the phenomena of nature themselves as to their ultimate foundations, and is less concerned in deducing the latter from the former but more the former from the latter, then our goal is nothing else than this: to establish the *science of nature* in the strictest sense of the term. In order to gauge whether such a speculative physics is possible, we must know what belongs to the possibility of a theory of nature considered as science.

(*a*) The concept of knowledge is here taken in its most rigorous meaning; and it is then easy to see that in this sense of the word we can actually only *know* those objects for which we have insight into the principles of their possibility, since without this insight my entire knowledge of the object is a mere seeing. For example, I merely see a machine of whose construction I am ignorant, i.e. I am merely convinced of its existence. The machine's inventor, in contrast, possesses the most perfect knowledge of it, because he is its soul, so to speak, and it pre-existed in his mind before he presented it as a reality.

It would certainly be impossible to catch a glimpse of the internal construction of nature if an intervention in nature were not possible through freedom. Nature certainly acts openly and freely, yet never in isolation, but rather under the influence of a whole host of causes, which first have to be excluded in order to obtain a pure result. Hence, nature must be forced to act under certain conditions that either usually never exist in it or else only exist in a modified manner by means of others. – Such an intervention in nature is called an experiment. Every experiment is a question put to nature, to which it is forced to provide an answer. However, every question implicitly contains an *a priori* judgement; every experiment that is an experiment is a prophecy; experimenting itself is a production of phenomena. – Thus, the first stage of science, at least in physics, is when we begin to produce the objects of this science.

(*b*) We *know* only what we ourselves have produced; knowledge in the *strictest* sense of the word is therefore *pure* knowledge *a priori*. The construction mediated by experimentation is never an absolute self-production of the phenomena. There is no question that countless things in natural science can be known comparatively *a priori*, as for instance in the theory of electricity, magnetism and the phenomenon of light, where a simple recurring law is present in every appearance, such that the success of every experiment may be determined in advance. Here my knowledge is directly derived from a known law, without the mediation of any specific experience. Nevertheless, from where does the law itself spring? All phenomena relate to a single absolute and *contingent* law, from which they may all be deduced; in short, everything we know in natural science may be known absolutely *a priori*. However, it is patently clear that the experiment itself can never lead us to such knowledge; it can never go beyond the forces of nature, which it uses as a means.

Since the final *causes* of natural phenomena do not appear themselves, we either have to forego insight into them or we simply have to posit them within nature, situate them within nature itself. Yet, whatever we situate within nature does not possess any other value than that of a presupposition (hypothesis), and a science founded on this must also be hypothetical, just like the principle itself. This can only be avoided in one particular case, when the presupposition in question is as involuntary and contingent as nature itself. Assuming, for instance, what must be assumed, that the totality of appearances is not a mere world but of necessity a nature (that is to say, that this totality is not simply a product but furthermore productive), then it follows that within this whole we can never arrive at absolute identity, because this would entail an absolute transition of nature as productive into nature as a product, i.e. it would produce absolute rest. Thus, this alternation in nature between productivity and product must appear as a general duplicity of principles, in which nature maintains a constant activity and is prevented from exhausting itself in its product. And this general duality, as the principle of all natural explanation, would be just as necessary as the concept of nature itself.

This absolute presupposition must bear its necessity within itself, and moreover, it must be subjected to empirical tests *to see if one cannot derive all the phenomena of nature from it. If there exists within the entire nexus of nature a single phenomenon that fails to be necessary according to this principle or even contradicts it, then the presupposition is interpreted to be false*, and henceforth ceases to be valid as a principle.

By deriving all the phenomena of nature from an absolute presupposition, our knowledge is transformed into a construction of nature itself, i.e. into a science of nature *a priori*. If this derivation is possible, something which can only be proved by the fact itself, then the theory of nature is also possible as a science of nature, it is purely speculative physics, which was to be proved.

Note. This note would not be required if the prevailing confusion with regard to certain concepts was not itself in need of explanation.

The assertion that natural science must be able to derive all its propositions *a priori* has been partly understood as: natural science must dispense with all experience, and be able to spin its propositions from out of itself without the mediation of any experience, an assertion so absurd that even the objections to it deserve our sympathy. – *We not only know this or that through experience, but originally we do not have any knowledge except through experience and by means of experience, and to this extent our entire knowledge only consists of the propositions of experience.* These propositions only become propositions *a priori* in so far as we become conscious of them as contingent, and thus every proposition, whatever its content, can be raised to that dignity. The distinction between *a priori* and *a posteriori* propositions is not as many people imagine, as something originally bound to the propositions, rather, it is a distinction that we make with respect to our knowledge and our type of knowledge of the propositions. Therefore, every proposition that is merely historical for me, is a proposition of experience. However, as soon as I directly or indirectly attain insight into its internal necessity it becomes a proposition *a priori*. Yet it must now be possible to recognise every original natural phenomenon as thoroughly necessary; for if there is no such thing as chance in nature then likewise no original phenomenon of nature can be fortuitous. This is due to the fact that nature is a system, and everything occurring or emerging in nature has a necessary relation to one of the principles that connects the whole of nature. – This insight into the internal necessity of all natural phenomena will surely be even more complete as soon as we realise that there exists no true system that is not at the same time an organic system. If all things reciprocally carry and support each other in every organic whole, then this organisation must have existed as a whole prior its parts; the whole could not have arisen from the parts, but the parts must have emerged from out of the whole. *Thus, we do not know nature a priori, rather nature is itself a priori*, i.e. all its singularities are predetermined by the whole or by the idea of nature as such. Yet if nature is *a priori*, then it must also be possible to *recognise* it *as* something that is *a priori*, and this is really the meaning if our assertion.

Such a science as this is compatible with neither the hypothetical nor the merely probable; rather, it proceeds to what is evident and certain. Now we may indeed be quite sure that every natural phenomenon, even if it has to pass through countless intermediate links, relates to the final conditions of nature. However, the intermediate links themselves may still be unknown to us and lie hidden in the depths of nature. The task of experimental natural research is to uncover these intermediate links. Speculative physics has nothing to do but highlight the necessity of these intermediate links.[1] Yet since every new discovery casts us into fresh ignorance, and when one knot is untangled another one tightens, then it is conceivable that the complete discovery of every intermediate link in the nexus of nature renders our science of nature into a never-ending task. – However, nothing has more

---

[1] For example, it will become clear through the entire course of our inquiry that in order to reveal the dynamic organisation of the universe in all its parts we still lack that *central phenomenon* already alluded to by *Francis Bacon*, which is certainly present in nature but not yet extracted from it by experiment.

impeded the infinite progress of this science than the arbitrariness of the fictions, whereby a lack of reliable insight has remained concealed for so long. This fragmentary aspect of our knowledge only becomes apparent when we separate the merely hypothetical from the pure products of science, and thereby proceed to gather together again into a system all the fragments of the great whole of nature. It is therefore conceivable that *speculative physics* (the soul of true experimentation) has always been the mother of all the greatest discoveries in nature.

§ 5
On the System of Speculative Physics as Such

Hitherto we have derived and developed the idea of speculative physics; another task would be to show how this idea must be realised and actually carried out. In this regard the author would refer to his *Outline of a System of the Philosophy of Nature*, if he did not have reason to suspect that many who might bestow their attention upon this *Outline* would also approach it with certain preconceived ideas, which he himself has not presupposed, and does not wish to be presupposed.

What might complicate insight into the tendency of this *Outline* (apart from the deficiencies of the presentation), are mainly the following:

(1) Misled, perhaps, by the words 'philosophy of nature', many people may expect to find transcendental deductions of natural phenomena which similarly exist elsewhere in different fragments, and therefore regard the philosophy of nature as a part of transcendental philosophy, although it forms an entirely independent and distinct science.

(2) That the notions commonly current in dynamical physics greatly vary from the ones established by the author, and partly contradict them. I am not talking about those modes of representation which many people discuss whose area is really that of mere experiment. For example, many reject the dynamic explanation of galvanic fluids and assume instead certain vibrations in the metals; these people revert to their old habits of thought when they realise that they have not understood anything. I am speaking of those modes of representation that have gained currency in philosophical minds due to Kant, and for the most part can be reduced to this: that we perceive nothing more in matter than a space occupied to a certain degree, and that the difference in matter, therefore, is only a difference in the occupation of space (i.e. density). Furthermore, that all dynamic (qualitative) changes are simply changes in the relation between the forces of repulsion and attraction. According to this mode of representation, all the phenomena of nature can only be perceived at their lowest levels, and the dynamical physics of these philosophers begins precisely where it ought to cease. It is obvious that the final result of every dynamic process yields an altered degree in the occupation of space, i.e. an altered density. Since the dynamic process of nature is but a single process, and the various dynamic processes are merely different fragments of this single fundamental process, then viewed from this standpoint even the magnetic and electrical phenomena are not

effects of certain kinds of matter, but changes in the *constitution of matter itself*. And since this depends on the reciprocal action of the fundamental forces, there must ultimately be changes in the relation between the fundamental forces themselves. We certainly do not deny that at the most extreme limit of their appearance these phenomena are changes in the relation between the fundamental forces; we only deny that these changes *do not otherwise exist*. Moreover, we are convinced that this so-called dynamic principle, as the fundamental explanation of all natural phenomena, is much too superficial and impoverished to reach the actual depths and variety of natural phenomena, since it is in fact incapable of constructing a qualitative change in matter as such (because the change in density is only the external manifestation of a higher change). It is not our intention to furnish a proof of this assertion, unless, on the other hand, this explicative principle can in fact be shown to exhaust nature and bridge the giant chasm between the above kind of dynamic philosophy and the empirical knowledge of physics (yet with regard to the different types of effects in the basic substances, for example, we immediately wish to say that this is impossible).

We may therefore be permitted to replace the prevailing dynamic mode of representation with our own, which will doubtless clearly demonstrate how the latter differs from the former, and which of the two will most securely raise the theory of nature up to a science of nature.

§ 6
Internal Organisation of the System of Speculative Physics

I.

Any investigation into the *principle* of speculative physics must be preceded by investigations into the difference between the speculative and the empirical generally. Here it is chiefly a question of being convinced that there is such a perfect opposition between empiricism and theory that there exists no third element which might link the two. Hence, the idea of an *empirical science* is a hybrid concept, in which nothing is connected, or rather which cannot be conceived at all. What is purely empirical is not science, and conversely, what is science is not empirical. This is not said in order to disparage empiricism, but simply to place it in its true and proper light. Pure empiricism, whatever its object, is history (the absolute antithesis of theory), and vice versa, only history is empirical.[2]

As empiricism, physics is nothing more than a collection of facts and accounts of observations that have occurred in a natural or controlled environment. In the

[2] If only those warm eulogists of empiricism, who are faithful to the idea of empiricism and exalt it at the expense of science, did not try to sell us their own judgements as empiricism, and what they have placed within nature and imposed upon its objects. Though many people think they can talk about this – to purely extract what occurs in nature and faithfully reproduce what has been seen – is a great deal more difficult than many people imagine.

physics of today empiricism and science are thoroughly intermingled, and as a result it is neither the one nor the other.

In this respect our goal is simply to distinguish between science and empiricism, as one does between body and soul, and to strip empiricism of all theory and restore it again to its bare essentials by rejecting anything in science that is not capable of construction *a priori*.

The opposition between empiricism and science is due to the fact that the former views its object in *being*, as something finished and ready-made. Science, on the other hand, views its object in the process of *becoming*, as something that is yet to be brought into existence. And since science cannot proceed from anything that is a product, i.e. a thing, then it must proceed from the unconditioned. Thus the first investigation of speculative physics is into the unconditioned in natural science.

II.

Since this investigation in the *Outline* is derived from the highest principles, the following may be regarded as merely an illustration of our inquiry.

Because everything of which we say that it exists is of a conditioned nature, only *Being itself* can be unconditioned. However, as something unconditioned, individual Being can only be conceived as a definite limitation of the productive activity (of the one and only substrate of all reality), and therefore *Being itself* is merely this same productive activity *conceived without any limitations*. For the science of nature, therefore, nature is originally only productivity, and science must take its starting point from this principle.

As long as we only know the entirety of objects as the totality of Being, then this entirety is a mere *world* to us, i.e. a mere product. In the science of nature it would be clearly impossible to find a higher concept than that of Being, if all permanence (which is conceived in the concept of Being) were not deceptive and really a continuous and uniform reproduction.

By positing the entirety of objects as not merely a product, but necessarily at the same time as productive, we raise it up to *nature*, and *this identity of product and productivity*, and this alone, is designated in ordinary language using the concept of nature.

Nature as mere *product* (*natura naturata*) is termed nature as *object* (all empiricism is solely concerned with this). *Nature as productivity* (*natura naturans*) is termed *nature as subject* (all theory is solely concerned with this).

Since the object is never unconditioned, something entirely non-objective must be posited in nature, and this absolutely non-objective element is indeed the original productivity of nature. In the ordinary view productivity vanishes in the product; conversely, in the philosophical view, the product vanishes in the productivity.

This identity of productivity and product in the *original* conception of nature is expressed as a whole in the ordinary views of nature, and which is both cause and effect of itself, and is identical again in its duplicity (running through all the phenomena). Furthermore, the identity of the ideal and the real coincides in this concept, which is conceived in the concept of every product of nature, and in this respect alone are nature and art opposed. Whereas in art the concept precedes the act and execution, in nature concept and act are much more simultaneous and one, the concept merges directly with the product and cannot be separated from it.

The empirical view cancels this identity by only seeing the *effect* in nature (although due to the continual encroachment of empiricism into the field of science there now exist maxims in purely empirical physics which presuppose a concept of nature as subject; for instance: 'nature chooses the shortest route'; 'nature is sparing in causes but lavish in effects'); this is cancelled by speculation, which only sees the *cause* in nature.

III.

We can only say of nature as object that it *is*; we cannot say this about nature as subject, for this is Being or productivity itself.

This absolute productivity must merge into an empirical nature. The concept of an *ideal* infinity is contained in the concept of absolute productivity. This ideal infinity must become an empirical infinity.

However, empirical infinity is an infinite becoming. – Every infinite series is nothing but a presentation of an intellectual or ideal infinity. The original infinite series (the ideal of every infinite series) is *time*, i.e. the very thing within which our intellectual infinity evolves. The activity underpinning this series is the same as the one underpinning our consciousness; consciousness, however, is continuous. Therefore, as the evolution of this activity, time cannot arise by composition. Since all other infinite series are simply imitations of the original infinite series, of time itself, an infinite series cannot be anything other than continuous. What is restrictive in the original evolution (without which evolution would occur with infinite velocity) is none other than the *original reflection*; the necessity of reflection upon our acting in every moment (the constant duplicity in identity) is the secret device whereby our existence receives *permanence*. – Thus, absolute continuity only exists for intuition, not for *reflection*. Intuition and reflection are opposed to one another. The infinite series is continuous for the productive *intuition*; it is interrupted and composite for reflection. These sophisms are based on this *contradiction* between intuition and reflection. Here the possibility of all motion is disputed, but is resolved in every moment by the productive intuition. For example, for intuition the effects of gravity take place with perfect continuity; for reflection, they occur discretely. Hence all the laws of mechanics in which an object of the productive intuition becomes an object of reflection, are really only laws for reflection itself – i.e. those fictitious notions of mechanics, the atoms of time in which gravitation acts; the law stating that the moment of solicitation is infinitely small, because otherwise an infinity velocity would be produced in a finite time, and so on. And finally, that in mathematics we cannot really conceive an infinite series as continuous, but only one proceeding discretely.

This entire inquiry into the opposition between reflection and the productivity of intuition allows us to derive the general proposition: that there is absolute *continuity* in *all* productivity and only in productivity alone; it is a proposition that is important for the study of the whole of nature. For instance, the law stating there are no leaps in nature but only a continuity of forms, and so on, is restricted to the original productivity of nature, in which in any case there must be continuity. Whereas at the standpoint of reflection, everything in nature must appear as *disconnected* and *devoid* of continuity, as coexistent as it were. Thus we should accord both standpoints their due – the one asserting continuity within nature (e.g. in organic nature), as well as the other that denies it. Moreover, we deduce an opposition between dynamic and atomistic physics, for as will soon become apparent, the two are only distinguished by the fact that the one occupies the standpoint of *intuition*, the other the standpoint of *reflection*.

IV.

By taking into account these general fundamental principles we may now proceed more surely to our goal and analyse the internal organism of our system.

(a) The concept of becoming contains the concept of gradualness. However, absolute productivity presents itself empirically as a becoming with an infinite velocity, in which nothing real is engendered for intuition.

(As infinite productivity, nature must actually be conceived as engaged in an infinite evolution, and the permanence and repose of nature's products [e.g. the organic world] must not be thought of as at absolute rest, but only as an evolution proceeding with an infinitely small velocity or with infinite tardiness. Yet hitherto evolution has never been constructed with a finite velocity, let alone with an infinitely small velocity.)

(b) The fact that the evolution of nature occurs with a finite velocity and is therefore an object of intuition is inconceivable without an original limitation of the productivity.

(c) Yet if nature is absolute productivity, then the basis of this limitation cannot lie *outside* of it. Nature is originally *only* productivity, thus there cannot be anything determined in this productivity (since all determination is negation), i.e. it cannot arrive at products through it. – In order to arrive at products, the productivity must pass from being undetermined to being determined, i.e. the *pure* productivity must be cancelled. If the determining factor of the productivity lay outside of nature, then nature would not originally be absolute productivity. – In any case, nature should receive determination, i.e. negativity; however, from a higher standpoint this negativity must again be viewed as positivity.

(d) None the less, if the reason for this limitation lies *in nature itself*, then nature ceases to be *pure identity*. (Nature is pure identity *only* in so far as it is productivity, and nothing at all can be distinguished in it. If something is to be distinguished in it, its identity must be cancelled, hence nature must not be identity, but duplicity).

Nature must originally be an object to itself, and this transformation of a *pure subject* into a *subject-object* is inconceivable without an original sundering in nature itself. This duplicity, therefore, cannot be further deduced physically, for as the condition of all nature generally it is the principle of all physical explanation. All physical explanation traces every antithesis manifesting in nature back to that original antithesis in the interior of nature *which itself is no longer manifest.* – Why is there no original phenomenon of nature devoid of that duplicity, if everything in nature is not at once reciprocally subject and object *ad infinitum*, and if nature is not originally already product and productive? –

(e) If nature is originally duplicity, then there must already be opposing tendencies in the original productivity of nature. (The positive tendency must be opposed to another tendency, which is anti-productive, as it were, and restricts production; not something that rejects, but something negative, and the real antithesis of the former.) There is no passivity in nature if this limiting factor is also positive, and its original duplicity is a conflict of real opposing tendencies.

(f) To reach the product, these opposing tendencies must coincide. However, since they are *equally* posited (for there is not any reason to posit them as unequal) they will reciprocally destroy one another whenever they meet; the product is therefore $= 0$, and once again the product is not reached.

This unavoidable, but hitherto barely noticed contradiction (namely, that the product only arises through the concurrence of opposing tendencies, although these opposing tendencies reciprocally destroy one another) can only be solved in the following manner: We cannot conceive the *subsistence* of a product *without* a continual *process of being reproduced*. The product must be thought of as *destroyed at every moment*, and then *reproduced afresh at every moment*. We never actually behold the subsistence of the product, but only this continual process of being reproduced.

(It is rather easy to grasp that the series $1 - 1 + 1 \ldots$ *into infinity,* may neither be conceived as $= 1$ nor $= 0$. Yet the reason why this infinite series $= 1/2$ lies deeper. A single absolute quantity $(= 1)$ is continually destroyed and continually recurs in this series, and by means of this recurrence it does not produce itself but the mean between itself and nothing. – Nature as object is what comes into being in such an infinite series and $=$ a fraction of the original unity, in which the never cancelled duplicity supplies the numerator).

(g) If the subsistence of a product is a continual process of being reproduced, then in all nature as *object* there is only *permanence*, and in nature as *subject* there is only infinite *activity*.

Originally the product is nothing more than a mere point, a mere limit; only when nature begins to struggle against this point does it become raised to a filled sphere, to a product as it were. (Consider a stream, it is *pure identity*; when it encounters resistance it forms a whirlpool, but this whirlpool is nothing fixed, rather it can vanish and reappear at any moment. – Originally in nature nothing can be distinguished, all products are dissolved and invisible, so to speak, within the general productivity. Only when the limiting points are given do they gradually become disengaged, and emerge from out of the general identity. – The stream breaks against every point of this kind [the productivity is destroyed], however, a new wave may appear at any moment, filling the sphere.)

The philosophy of nature does not have to explain what is productive in nature, for if it does not originally posit it within nature, it would never bring it into nature. It has to explain what is permanent. Yet *the fact* that there is something permanent in nature can only be explained by nature's struggle against *all permanence*. Products would simply appear as mere points if nature did not give them extension and depth through its own pressure, and the products themselves would last but for an instance if nature did not struggle against them at every moment.

(h) This apparent product that is reproduced in every moment cannot really be an infinite product, for otherwise the productivity would be exhausted in it. Likewise, it cannot be a finite product, for the whole of nature's force would be poured into it. It must therefore be both finite and infinite; it must only be seemingly finite, but in infinite *development*. [...]

Translated by David W. Wood *

* *Translator's note*: This is a translation of the version of *Einleitung zu dem Entwurf eines Systems der Naturphiloso-phie* as it appears in *Natur und geschichtlicher Prozeß: Studien zur Naturphilosophie F. W. J. Schellings* (Frankfurt am Main: Suhrkamp Verlag, 1984), edited by Hans Jörg Sandkühler.

22

G. W. F. Hegel, Encyclopaedia: Philosophy of Nature (Enzyklopädie der philosophischen Wissenschaften im Grundrisse: *Zweiter Teil. Die Naturphilosophie): Introduction, §§ 245–252 (1817, 1830)*

Hegel's philosophy of nature is presented as the second part of the three-part *Encyclopaedia of the Philosophical Sciences* (placed between the Logic and the Philosophy of Spirit). It was published originally as the minimal framework for a lecture series (1817) during which further elucidations were to be delivered. (The text here is the third edition, 1830.) These elucidations appear in the text as additions – the *Zusätze* – transcribed by those who attended the lectures. Disputes naturally exist as to the reliability of these additions, given that they are correlated from Hegel's extemporised thoughts on the material that he prepared for publication. It is probably most sensible to regard them as aids to interpretation, rather than as containing claims independent of the main text.

The very project of the *Encyclopaedia of the Philosophical Sciences* might be viewed as the effort to bring to completion the post-Kantian phase of German Idealism in that it sets out to confirm the extensive and fundamental operations of reason in reality. The *Encyclopaedia* ranges across all of the concepts and principles discovered and developed by philosophers, scientists and other theorists. Hegel sees these concepts as standing in some sort of systematic relation ('organic totality'): they are all ultimately moments of the Idea, which Hegel understands as reality with all of its essential inner determinations. Within the Absolute Idea each concept, as a moment in a whole, stands in logical relation to all other concepts. The system of knowledge in which we apprehend the Absolute is then a self-standing whole, in which each concept is validated internally within this system. The validation is independent of the alleged demands of the given world. And the truths confirmed within this system turn out to be necessary truths since they are elements of a holistic system. In this regard Hegel claims that 'philosophy is a philosophical whole, a circle that closes upon itself'.[1] So as philosophy seeks to make sense of the 'fundamental concepts

---

[1] G. W. F. Hegel, trans. T. F. Geraets, W. A. Suchting and H. S. Harris, *The Encyclopaedia Logic* (Indianapolis, IN / Cambridge: Hackett, 1991), §15, p. 39 (*HW* VIII, §15, 60).

of the particular sciences' it proceeds in an inferentialist manner, identify-ing the implicit and rationally grounded relations of one concept to another until ultimately a holistic – for Hegel, systematic – relation emerges.[2] Hegel writes that a 'philosophizing *without system* cannot be scientific at all . . .'[3] But this systematicity cannot simply be assumed; it must be demonstrated. Hegel recommends that we work through a series of concepts, seeking a philosophical account of their relation, which becomes possible only when we have reached the end of the series. The *Encyclopaedia* is not then an assembly, even a peculiarly orderly assembly of the key concepts of West-ern intellectual culture: it can be seen at its conclusion as a philosophical reconstruction of the relationship between these concepts.

This holistic thinking informs Hegel's approach to nature. He tells us that we should see nature as, 'in itself, a living Whole'. Hegel terms his phi-losophy of nature 'rational physics' (Schelling used the term 'speculative physics' for his version). This may seem to imply that physics as practised by scientists lacks rationality. In a sense it does, but in Hegel's specific sense of what it would mean for a position to be fully rational. That is, the mark of reasonableness in a body of knowledge is that its basic claims must be able to stand within a system, within an organic relation of concepts. Only then, in Hegel's view, is the operation of reason in knowledge fully revealed. Science, obviously enough, does not consider its basic concepts and claims in this way.

An important part of Hegel's discussion is his account of the fundamental role played by what he calls the *Begriff* (notion or concept) in the foundation of any system of knowledge. The role it plays in the philosophy of nature is typical: the principles discovered and articulated by science cannot serve as the foundation of the very possibility of science: science is founded by the 'necessity of the Notion': 'experience is not its final warrant and base'. What nature really is – what it is as articulable through reason – is its 'notion'.

At no point does Hegel attempt to suggest that empirical knowledge can be gained or enhanced through his systematic, inferentialist, method. He is entirely convinced that science has delivered definite knowledge: the task of philosophy, which takes a broader perspective, is to show that that each of these intellectual achievements as an achievement of human reason stands within a system of human reason. As Hegel writes in the introduc-tion to the *Encyclopaedia*: 'philosophy does owe its development to the empirical sciences, but it gives to their content the fully essential shape of the freedom of thinking (or of what is a priori) as well as the *validation of necessity* (instead of the content being warranted because it is simply found to be present, and because it is a fact of experience)'.[4] By bringing to the content of science 'the freedom of thinking' Hegel thinks he can

---

[2] Hegel, *Encyclopaedia Logic*, §16, p. 39 (*HW* VIII, §16, 60).
[3] Hegel, *Encyclopaedia Logic*, §14, p. 39 (*HW* VIII, §14, 59).
[4] Hegel, *Encyclopaedia Logic*, §12, p. 37 (*HW* VIII, §12, 58).

show that reason is the organising principle of nature. From this account of the general aims of the *Encyclopaedia* we can see specifically that a philosophy of nature is not a substitute for empirical science. And nor is it, Hegel argues, to be characterised as the 'deduction' of nature and natural laws from thought, as many of its critics have alleged. The truths of science are taken as the material: the task of philosophy is to show the essential holistic relation of these truths. Nevertheless, readers of Hegel will be struck by a certain tension between Hegel's acknowledgement of the findings of science and his further notion that these findings are in need of systematicity. The idea that science is a disconnected series of claims that needs some kind of philosophical framework will seem high-handed. As indeed will the speculative perspective from which Hegel explains the emergence of nature. Indeed it is from this speculative perspective that Hegel sets out his most notorious rejection of the thesis of evolution (albeit pre-Darwinian articulations of evolution): he thinks of the development of nature as a development of our intellectual articulation of it. The priority of the philosophical claim to development leads him to conclude that the thesis of natural development expressed by evolution is simply false: for him it is the misapplication of the development of thought to a sensuous development. Although a complicated defence of Hegel's criticisms of the theory of evolution might be offered it is clear that for some Hegel is irretrievably committed to an aprioristic view of scientific knowledge, a commitment that undermines the scientific basis and relevance of his speculative philosophy of nature.[5]

[5]Cf. Errol E. Harris, 'How Final is Hegel's Rejection of Evolution', in *Hegel and the Philosophy of Nature* (Albany, NY: State University of New York Press, 1998), ed. Stephen Houlgate.

INTRODUCTION TO THE PHILOSOPHY OF NATURE[†]

Zusatz. It can be said perhaps that in our time, philosophy does not enjoy any special favour and liking. At least, it is no longer recognized, as it was formerly, that the study of philosophy must constitute the indispensable introduction and foundation for all further scientific education and professional study. But this much may be assumed *without hesitation* as correct, that the *Philosophy of Nature* in particular is in considerable disfavour. I do not intend to deal at length with the extent to which this prejudice against the Philosophy of Nature in particular, is justified; and yet I cannot altogether pass it over. What is seldom absent from a period of great intellectual ferment has, of course, happened in connection with the *idea of the*

[†]*HW* IX, 9–40. *Hegel's Philosophy of Nature* (Oxford: Clarendon Press, 1970).

Philosophy of Nature as recently expounded. It can be said that in the first satisfaction afforded by its discovery, this idea met with crude treatment at unskilled hands, instead of being cultivated by thinking Reason; and it has been brought low not so much by its opponents as by its friends. It has in many respects, in fact for the most part, been transformed into an external formalism and perverted into a thoughtless instrument for superficial thinking and fanciful imagination. I do not want to characterize in any further detail the eccentricities for which the Idea, or rather its lifeless forms, have been used. I said more about this some while ago in the preface to the *Phenomenology of Spirit*. It is, then, not to be wondered at that a more thoughtful examination of Nature, as well as crude empiricism, a knowing led by the Idea, as well as the external, abstract Understanding, alike turned their backs on a procedure which was as fantastic as it was pretentious, which itself made a chaotic mixture of crude empiricism and uncomprehended thoughts, of a purely capricious exercise of the imagination and the most commonplace way of reasoning by superficial analogy, and which passed off such a hotchpotch as the Idea, Reason, philosophical science, divine knowledge, and pretended that the complete lack of method and scientific procedure was the acme of scientific procedure. It is on account of such charlatanism that the Philosophy of Nature, especially Schelling's has become discredited.

It is quite another thing, however, to reject the Philosophy of Nature itself because of such aberration and misunderstanding of the Idea. It not infrequently happens that those who are obsessed by a hatred of philosophy, welcome abuses and perversions of it, because they use the perversion to disparage the science itself and they hope to make their reasoned rejection of the perversion a justification in some vague way for their claim to have hit philosophy itself.

It might seem appropriate first of all, in view of the existing misunderstandings and prejudices in regard to the Philosophy of Nature, to set forth the *true* Notion (*Begriff*) of this science. But this opposition which we encounter at the outset, is to be regarded as something contingent and external, and all such opposition we can straightway leave on one side. Such a treatment of the subject tends to become polemical and is not a procedure in which one can take any pleasure. What might be instructive in it falls partly within the science itself, but it would not be so instructive as to justify reducing still further the available space which is already restricted enough for the wealth of material contained in an *Encyclopaedia*. We shall therefore content ourselves with the observation made above; it can serve as a kind of protest against that style of philosophizing about Nature, as an assurance that such a style is not to be expected in this exposition. That style, it is true, often appears brilliant and entertaining, arousing astonishment at least; but it can only satisfy those who openly confess to seeing in the Philosophy of Nature simply a brilliant display of fireworks, thus sparing themselves the effort of thought. What we are engaged on here, is not an affair of imagination and fancy, but of the Notion, of Reason.

In keeping with this standpoint, we do not propose to discuss here the Notion, the task, the manner and method, of the Philosophy of Nature; but it is quite in place to preface a scientific work with a statement of the specific character of its subject-matter and purpose, and what is to be considered in it, and how it is to be considered. The opposition between the Philosophy of Nature and a perverted form of it, disappears of its own accord when we determine its Notion more precisely. The science of philosophy is a circle in which each member has an antecedent and a successor, but in the philosophical encyclopaedia, the Philosophy of Nature appears as only one circle in the whole, and therefore the procession of Nature from the eternal Idea, its creation, the proof that there necessarily is a Nature, lies in the preceding exposition (§ 244); here we have to presuppose it as known. If we do want to determine what the Philosophy of Nature is, our best method is to separate it off from the subject-matter with which it is contrasted; for all determining requires two terms. In the first place, we find the Philosophy of Nature in a peculiar relationship to natural science in general, to physics, natural history, and physiology; it is itself physics, but *rational physics*. It is at this point that we have to grasp what the Philosophy of Nature is and, in particular, to determine its relationship to physics. In so doing, one may imagine that this contrast between natural science and the Philosophy of Nature is something new. The Philosophy of Nature may perhaps be regarded prima facie as a new science; this is certainly correct in one sense, but in another sense it is not. For it is ancient, as ancient as any study of Nature at all; it is not distinct from the latter and it is, in fact, older than physics; Aristotelian physics, for example, is far more a Philosophy of Nature than it is physics. It is only in modern times that the two have been separated. We already see this separation in the science which, as cosmology, was distinguished in Wolff's philosophy from physics, and though supposed to be a metaphysics of the world or of Nature was confined to the wholly abstract categories of the Understanding. This metaphysics was, of course, further removed from physics than is the Philosophy of Nature as we now understand it. In connection with this distinction between physics and the Philosophy of Nature, and of the specific character of each as contrasted with the other, it must be noted, right from the start, that the two do not lie so far apart as is at first assumed. Physics and natural history are called empirical sciences *par excellence*, and they profess to belong entirely to the sphere of perception and experience, and in this way to be opposed to the Philosophy of Nature, i.e. to a knowledge of Nature from thought. The fact is, however, that the principal charge to be brought against physics is that it contains much more thought than it admits and is aware of, and that it is better than it supposes itself to be; or if, perhaps, all thought in physics is to be counted a defect, then it is worse than it supposes itself to be. Physics and the Philosophy of Nature, therefore, are not distinguished from each other as perception and thought, but only by *the kind and manner of their thought*; they are both a thinking apprehension of Nature.

It is this which we shall consider *first*, i.e. how thought is present in physics: then, *secondly*, we have to consider what Nature is: and, *thirdly*, to give the divisions of the philosophy of Nature.

A. Ways of Considering Nature

In order to find the *Notion of the Philosophy of Nature*, we must *first* of all indicate the Notion of the knowledge of Nature in general, and *secondly*, develop the *distinction between physics and the Philosophy of Nature*.

What is Nature? We propose to answer this general question by reference to the knowledge of Nature and the Philosophy of Nature. Nature confronts us as a riddle and a problem, whose solution both attracts and repels us: attracts us, because Spirit is presaged in Nature; repels us, because Nature seems an alien existence, in which Spirit does not find itself. That is why Aristotle said that philosophy started from wonder. We start to perceive, we collect facts about the manifold formations and laws of Nature; this procedure, on its own account, runs on into endless detail in all directions, and just because no end can be perceived in it, this method does not satisfy us. And in all this wealth of knowledge the question can again arise, or perhaps come to us for the first time: What is Nature? It remains a problem. When we see Nature's processes and transformations we want to grasp its simple essence, to compel this Proteus to cease its transformations and show itself to us and declare itself to us; so that it may not present us with a variety of ever new forms, but in simpler fashion bring to our consciousness in language what it *is*. This inquiry after the *being* of something has a number of meanings, and can often refer simply to its name, as in the question: What kind of a plant *is* this? or it can refer to perception if the name is given; if I do not know what a compass is, I get someone to show me the instrument, and I say, now I know what a compass is. 'Is' can also refer to status, as for example when we ask: What is this man? But this is not what we mean when we ask: What is Nature? It is the meaning to be attached to this question that we propose to examine here, remembering that we want to acquire a knowledge of the Philosophy of Nature.

We could straightway resort to the philosophical Idea and say that the Philosophy of Nature ought to give us the Idea of Nature. But to begin thus might be confusing. For we must grasp the Idea itself as concrete and thus apprehend its various specifications and then bring them together. In order therefore to possess the Idea, we must traverse a series of specifications through which it is first there for us. If we now take these up in forms which are familiar to us, and say that we want to approach Nature as thinkers, there are, in the first place, other ways of approaching Nature which I will mention, not for the sake of completeness, but because we shall find in them the elements or moments which are requisite for a knowledge of the Idea and which individually reach our consciousness earlier in other *ways of considering Nature*. In so doing, we shall come to the point where the characteristic feature of our inquiry becomes prominent. Our approach to Nature is partly practical and partly theoretical. An examination of the theoretical approach will reveal a contradiction which, thirdly, will lead us to our standpoint; to resolve the contradiction we must incorporate what is peculiar to the practical approach, and by this means practical and theoretical will be united and integrated into a totality.

§ 245

In man's *practical* approach to Nature, the latter is, for him, something immediate and external; and he himself is an external and therefore sensuous individual, although in relation to natural objects, he correctly regards himself as *end*. A consideration of Nature according to this relationship yields the standpoint of *finite* teleology (§ 205). In this, we find the correct presupposition that Nature does not itself contain the absolute, final end (§§ 207–11). But if this way of considering the matter starts from particular, *finite* ends, on the one hand it makes them into presuppositions whose contingent content may in itself be even insignificant and trivial. On the other hand, the end-relationship demands for itself a deeper mode of treatment than that appropriate to external and finite relationships, namely, the mode of treatment of the Notion, which in its own general nature is immanent and therefore is immanent in Nature as such.

Zusatz. The practical approach to Nature is, in general, determined by appetite, which is self-seeking; need impels us to use Nature for our own advantage, to wear her out, to wear her down, in short, to annihilate her. And here, two characteristics at once stand out. (α) The practical approach is concerned only with individual products of Nature, or with individual aspects of those products. The necessities and the wit of man have found an endless variety of ways of using and mastering Nature. Sophocles says:

ουδὲν ανθρώπου δεινότερον πελέι, –
άπορος επ ουδὲν ἔρχεται.

Whatever forces Nature develops and lets loose against man – cold, wild beasts, water, fire – he knows means to counter them; indeed, he takes these means from Nature and uses them against herself. The cunning of his reason enables him to preserve and maintain himself in face of the forces of Nature, by sheltering behind other products of Nature, and letting these suffer her destructive attacks. Nature herself, however, in her universal aspect, he cannot overcome in this way, nor can he turn her to his own purposes. (β) The other characteristic of the practical approach is that, since it is *our* end which is paramount, not natural things themselves, we convert the latter into means, the destiny of which is determined by us, not by the things themselves; an example of this is the conversion of food into blood. (γ) What is achieved is our satisfaction, our self-feeling, which had been disturbed by a lack of some kind or another. The negation of myself which I suffer within me in hunger, is at the same time present as an other than myself, as something to be consumed; my act is to annul this contradiction by making this other identical with myself, or by restoring my self-unity through sacrificing the thing.

The teleological standpoint which was formerly so popular, was based, it is true, on a reference to Spirit, but it was confined to external purposiveness only, and took Spirit in the sense of finite Spirit caught up in natural ends; but because the finite ends which natural objects were shown to subserve were so trivial, teleology has become discredited as an argument for the wisdom of God. The notion of end, however, is not merely external to Nature, as it is, for example, when I say that the wool of the sheep is there only to provide me with clothes; for this often results in trivial reflections, as in the *Xenia*,[1] where God's wisdom is admired in that He has provided cork-trees for bottle-stoppers, or herbs for curing disordered stomachs, and cinnabar for cosmetics. The notion of end as immanent in natural objects is their simple determinateness, e.g. the seed of a plant, which contains the real possibility of all that is to exist in the tree, and thus, as a purposive activity, is directed solely to self-preservation. This notion of end was already recognized by Aristotle, too, and he called this activity the *nature of a thing*; the true teleological method – and this is the highest – consists, therefore, in the method of regarding Nature as free in her own peculiar vital activity.

§ 246

What is now called *physics* was formerly called *natural philosophy*, and it is also a *theoretical*, and indeed a *thinking* consideration of Nature; but, on the one hand, it does not start from determinations which are external to Nature, like those ends already mentioned; and secondly, it is directed to a knowledge of the *universal* aspect of Nature, a universal which is also *determined* within itself – directed to a knowledge of forces, laws and genera, whose content must not be a simple aggregate, but arranged in orders and classes, must present itself as an organism. As the Philosophy of Nature is a *comprehending* (*begreifend*) treatment, it has as its object the same *universal*, but *explicitly*, and it considers this universal in its *own immanent necessity* in accordance with the self-determination of the Notion.

Remark

The relation of philosophy to the empirical sciences was discussed in the general introduction [to the *Encyclopaedia*]. Not only must philosophy be in agreement with our empirical knowledge of Nature, but the *origin* and *formation* of the Philosophy of Nature presupposes and is conditioned by empirical physics. However, the course of a science's origin and the preliminaries of its construction are one thing, while the science itself is another. In the latter, the former can no longer appear as the foundation of the science; here, the foundation must be the necessity of the Notion.

It has already been mentioned that, in the progress of philosophical knowledge, we must not only give an account of the object *as determined by its Notion*, but we must also name the *empirical* appearance corresponding to it, and we must show that the appearance does, in fact, correspond to its Notion. However, this

---

[1] Goethe – Schiller, *Xenien* (1796), No. 286.

is not an appeal to experience in regard to the necessity of the content. Even less admissible is an appeal to what is called *intuition (Anschauung)*, which is usually nothing but a fanciful and sometimes fantastic exercise of the imagination on the lines of *analogies*, which may be more or less significant, and which impress determinations and schemata on objects only *externally* (§231, Remark).

Zusatz. In the theoretical approach to Nature (α) the first point is that we stand back from natural objects, leaving them as they are and adjusting ourselves to them. Here, we start from our sense-knowledge of Nature. However, if physics were based solely on perceptions, and perceptions were nothing more than the evidence of the senses, then the physical act would consist only in seeing, hearing, smelling, etc., and animals, too, would in this way be physicists. But what sees, hears, etc., is a spirit, a thinker. Now if we said that, in our theoretical approach to Nature, we left things free, this applied only partly to the outer senses, for these are themselves partly theoretical and partly practical (§358); it is only our ideational faculty (*Vorstellen*), our intelligence, that has this free relationship to things. We can, of course, consider things practically, as means; but then knowing is itself only a means, not an end in itself. (β) The second bearing of things on us is that things acquire the character of universality for us or that we transform them into universals. The more thought enters into our representation of things, the less do they retain their naturalness, their singularity and immediacy. The wealth of natural forms, in all their infinitely manifold configuration, is impoverished by the all-pervading power of thought, their vernal life and glowing colours die and fade away. The rustle of Nature's life is silenced in the stillness of thought; her abundant life, wearing a thousand wonderful and delightful shapes, shrivels into arid forms and shapeless generalities resembling a murky northern fog. (γ) These two characteristics are not only opposed to the two practical ones, but we also find that the theoretical approach is self-contradictory, for it seems to bring about the direct opposite of what it intends; for we want to know the Nature that really is, not something that is not. But instead of leaving Nature as she is, and taking her as she is in truth, instead of simply perceiving her, we make her into something quite different. In thinking things, we transform them into something universal; but things are singular and the Lion as Such does not exist. We give them the form of something subjective, of something produced by us and belonging to us, and belonging to us in our specifically human character: for natural objects do not think, and are not presentations or thoughts. But according to the second characteristic of the theoretical approach referred to above, it is precisely this inversion which does take place; in fact, it might seem that what we are beginning is made impossible for us at the outset. The theoretical approach begins with the arrest of appetite, is disinterested, lets things exist and go on just as they are; with this attitude to Nature, we have straightway established a duality of object and subject and their separation, something here and something yonder. Our intention, however, is rather to grasp, to comprehend Nature, to make her ours, so that she is not something alien and yonder. Here, then, comes the difficulty: How do we, as subjects, come into contact with objects ? If we venture to bridge this gulf and mislead ourselves along that line and so think this Nature, we make Nature, which is an Other than we are, into an Other than she is. Both theoretical approaches are also directly opposed to each other: we transform things into universals, or make them our own, and yet as natural objects they are supposed to have a free, self-subsistent being. This, therefore, is the point with which we are concerned in regard to the nature of cognition – this is the interest of philosophy.

But the Philosophy of Nature is in the unfavourable position of having to demonstrate its existence, and, in order to justify it, we must trace it back to something familiar. Mention must be made here of a special solution of the contradiction between subjectivity and objectivity, a solution which has been made familiar both by science and religion – in the latter case in the past – and which makes short shrift of the whole difficulty. The union of the two determinations is, namely, what is called the *primal state of innocence*, where Spirit is identical with Nature, and the spiritual eye is placed directly in the centre of Nature; whereas the standpoint of the divided consciousness is the fall of man from the eternal, divine unity. This unity is represented as a primal intuition (*Anschauung*), a Reason, which is at the same time one with fantasy, i.e. it forms sensuous shapes, and in so doing gives them a rational significance. This intuitive Reason is the divine Reason; for God, we are entitled to say, is that Being in whom Spirit and Nature are united, in whom intelligence at the same time also has being and shape. The eccentricities of the Philosophy of Nature originate partly in such an idea, namely in the idea that, although nowadays we no longer dwell in this paradisal state, there still are favoured ones, seers to whom God imparts true knowledge and wisdom in sleep; or that man, even without being so favoured, can at least by faith in it, transport himself into a state where the inner side of Nature is immediately revealed to him, and where he need only let fancies occur to him, i.e. give free play to his fancy, in order to declare prophetically what is true. This visionary state, about the source of which nothing further can be said, has, in general, been regarded as the consummation of the scientific faculty; and it is, perhaps, added that such a state of perfect knowledge preceded the present history of the world, and that, since man's fall from his unity with Nature, there has remained for us in myths, traditions or in other vestiges, still some fragments and faint echoes of that spiritual, illuminated state. These fragments have formed the basis for the further religious education of humanity, and are the source of all scientific knowledge. If it had not been made so difficult to know the truth, but one needed only to sit on the tripod and utter oracles, then, of course, the labour of thought would not be needed.

In order to state briefly what is the defect of this conception, we must at once admit that there is something lofty in it which at first glance makes a strong appeal. But this unity of intelligence and intuition, of the inwardness of Spirit and its relation to externality, must be, not the beginning, but the goal, not an immediate, but a resultant unity. A natural unity of thought and intuition is that of the child and the animal, and this can at the most be called feeling, not spirituality. But man must have eaten of the tree of the knowledge of good and evil and must have gone through the labour and activity of thought in order to become what he is, having overcome this separation between himself and Nature. The immediate unity is thus only an abstract, implicit truth, not the actual truth; for not only must the content be true, but the form also. The healing of this breach must be in the form of the knowing Idea, and the moments of the solution must be sought in consciousness itself. It is not a question of betaking oneself to abstraction and vacuity, of taking refuge in the negation of knowing; on the contrary, consciousness must preserve itself in that we must use the ordinary consciousness itself to refute the assumptions which have given rise to the contradiction.

The difficulty arising from the one-sided assumption of the theoretical consciousness, that natural objects confront us as permanent and impenetrable objects, is directly negatived by the practical approach which acts on the absolutely idealistic belief that individual things are nothing in themselves. The defect of appetite, from the side of its relationship to things, is not that it is realistic towards them, but that it is all too idealistic. Philosophical, true idealism consists in nothing else but laying down that the truth about things is that as such immediately single, i.e. sensuous things, they are only a show, an appearance (*Schein*). Of a metaphysics prevalent today which maintains that we cannot know things because they are absolutely shut to us, it might be said that not even the animals are so stupid as these metaphysicians; for they go after things, seize and consume them. The same thing is laid down in the second aspect of the theoretical approach referred to above, namely, that we think natural objects. Intelligence familiarizes itself with things, not of course in their sensuous existence, but by thinking them and positing their content in itself; and in, so to speak, adding form, universality, to the practical ideality which, by itself, is only negativity, it gives an affirmative character to the negativity of the singular. This universal aspect of things is not something subjective, something belonging to us: rather is it, in contrast to the transient phenomenon, the noumenon, the true, objective, actual nature of things themselves, like the Platonic Ideas, which are not somewhere afar off in the beyond, but exist in individual things as their substantial genera. Not until one does violence to Proteus – that is not until one turns one's back on the sensuous appearance of Nature – is he compelled to speak the truth. The inscription on the veil of Isis, 'I am that which was, is, and will be, and my veil no mortal hath lifted', melts away before thought. 'Nature', Hamann therefore rightly says, 'is a Hebrew word written only with consonants and the understanding must point it'.

Now although the empirical treatment of Nature has this category of universality in common with the Philosophy of Nature, the empiricists are sometimes uncertain whether this universal is subjective or objective; one can often hear it said that these classes and orders are only made as aids to cognition. This uncertainty is still more apparent in the search for distinguishing marks, not in the belief that they are essential, objective characteristics of things, but that they only serve our convenience to help us to distinguish things. If nothing more than that were involved, we might, e.g., take the lobe of the ear as the sign of man, for no animal has it; but we feel at once that such a characteristic is not sufficient for a knowledge of the essential nature of man. When, however, the universal is characterized as law, force, matter, then we cannot allow that it counts only as an external form and a subjective addition; on the contrary, objective reality is attributed to laws, forces are immanent, and matter is the true nature of the thing itself. Something similar may be conceded in regard to genera too, namely that they are not just a grouping of similarities, an abstraction made by us, that they not only have common features but that they are the objects' own inner essence; the orders not only serve to give us a general view, but form a graduated scale of Nature itself. The distinguishing marks, too, should be the universal, substantial element of the genus. Physics looks on these universals as its triumph: one can say even that, unfortunately, it goes too far in its generalizations. Present-day philosophy is called the philosophy of identity: this name can be much more appropriately given to that physics which simply ignores specific differences (*Bestimmtheiten*), as occurs, for example, in the current theory of electro-chemistry in which magnetism, electricity, and chemistry are regarded as one and the same. It is the weakness of physics that it is too much dominated by the category of identity; for identity is the fundamental category of the Understanding.

The Philosophy of Nature takes up the material which physics has prepared for it empirically, at the point to which physics has brought it, and reconstitutes it, so that experience is not its final warrant and base. Physics must therefore work into the hands of philosophy, in order that the latter may translate into the Notion the abstract universal transmitted to it, by showing how this universal, as an intrinsically necessary whole, proceeds from the Notion. The philosophical way of putting the facts is no mere whim, once in a way to walk on one's head for a change, after having walked for a long while on one's legs, or once in a way to see our everyday face bedaubed with paint: no, it is because the method of physics does not satisfy the Notion, that we have to go further.

What distinguishes the Philosophy of Nature from physics is, more precisely, the kind of metaphysics used by them both; for metaphysics is nothing else but the entire range of the universal determinations of thought, as it were, the diamond net into which everything is brought and thereby first made intelligible. Every educated consciousness has its metaphysics, an instinctive way of thinking, the absolute power within us of which we become master only when we make it in turn the object of our knowledge. Philosophy in general has, as philosophy, other categories than those of the ordinary consciousness: all education (*Bildung*) reduces to the distinction of categories. All revolutions, in the sciences no less than in world history, originate solely from the fact that Spirit, in order to understand and comprehend itself with a view to possessing itself, has changed its categories, comprehending itself more truly, more deeply, more intimately, and more in unity with itself. Now the inadequacy of the thought-determinations used in physics can be traced to two points which are closely bound up with each other. (α) The universal of physics is abstract or only formal; its determination is not immanent in it and it does not pass over into particularity. (β) The determinate content falls for that very reason outside the universal; and so is split into fragments, into parts which are isolated and detached from each other, devoid of any necessary connection, and it is just this which stamps it as only finite. If we examine a flower, for example, our understanding notes its particular qualities; chemistry dismembers and analyses it. In this way, we separate colour, shape of the leaves, citric acid, etheric oil, carbon, hydrogen, etc.; and now we say that the plant consists of all these parts.

> If you want to describe life and gather its meaning,
> To drive out its spirit must be your beginning,
> Then though fast in your hand lie the parts one by one
> The spirit that linked them, alas is gone
> And 'Nature's Laboratory' is only a name
> That the chemist bestows on't to hide his own shame.[2]

as Goethe says. Spirit cannot remain at this stage of thinking in terms of detached, unrelated concepts (*Verstandesreflexion*) and there are two ways in which it can advance beyond it. (α) The naïve mind (*der unbefangene Geist*), when it vividly contemplates Nature, as in the suggestive examples we often come across in Goethe, feels the life and the universal relationship in Nature; it divines that the universe is an organic whole and a totality pervaded by Reason, and it also feels in single forms of life an intimate oneness with itself; but even if we put together all those ingredients of the flower the result is still not a flower. And so, in the Philosophy of Nature, people have fallen back on intuition (*Anschauung*) and set it above reflective thought; but this is a mistake, for one cannot philosophize out of intuition. (β) What is intuited must also be thought, the isolated parts must be brought back by thought to simple universality; this thought unity is the Notion, which contains the specific differences, but as an immanent self-moving unity. The determinations of philosophical universality are not indifferent; it is the universality which fulfils itself, and which, in its diamantine identity, also contains difference.

The true infinite is the unity of itself and the finite; and this, now, is the category of philosophy and so, too, of the Philosophy of Nature. If genera and forces are the inner side of Nature, the universal, in face of which the outer and individual is only transient, then still a third stage is demanded, namely, the inner side of the inner side, and this, according to what has been said, would be the unity of the universal and the particular.

> To Nature's heart there penetrates no mere created mind:
> Too happy if she but display the outside of her rind.
> *   *   *   *
> I swear – of course but to myself – as rings within my ears
> That same old warning o'er and o'er again for sixty years,
> And thus a thousand times I answer in my mind: –
> With gladsome and ungrudging hand metes Nature from her store:

[2] *Faust*, part I, sc. 4. (Wallace's rendering, but see his note on p. 398 of his translation of the *Encyclopaedia Logic*. Only the last four lines are quoted, though in a different order, by Hegel, and a prose version of them would run: 'Nature's laboratory' the chemist calls it, mocking himself and confessing his ignorance. The parts, certainly, he holds in his hand, but alas the spiritual link is missing.)

> She keeps not back the core,
> Nor separates the rind,
> But all in each both rind and core has evermore combined.[3]

In grasping this inner side, the one-sidedness of the theoretical and practical approaches is transcended, and at the same time each side receives its due. The former contains a universal without determinateness, the latter an individuality without a universal; the cognition which comprehends (*begreifendes Erkennen*) is the middle term in which universality does not remain on *this* side, in *me*, over against the individuality of the objects: on the contrary, while it stands in a negative relation to things and assimilates them to itself, it equally finds individuality in them and does not encroach upon their independence, or interfere with their free self-determination. The cognition which comprehends is thus the unity of the theoretical and practical approaches: the negation of individuality is, as negation of the negative, the affirmative universality which gives permanence to its determinations; for the true individuality is at the same time within itself a universality.

As regards the objections which can be raised against this standpoint, the first question which can be asked is: How does the universal determine itself? How does the infinite become finite? A more concrete form of the question is: How has God come to create the world? God is, of course, conceived to be a subject, a self-subsistent actuality far removed from the world; but such an abstract infinity, such a universality which had the particular outside it, would itself be only one side of the relation, and therefore itself only a particular and finite: it is characteristic of the Understanding that it unwittingly nullifies the very determination it posits, and thus does the very opposite of what it intends. The particular is supposed to be separate from the universal, but this very separateness, this independence, makes it a universal, and so what is present is only the unity of the universal and the particular. God reveals Himself in two different ways: as Nature and as Spirit. Both manifestations are temples of God which He fills, and in which He is present. God, as an abstraction, is not the true God, but only as the living process of positing His Other, the world, which, comprehended in its divine form is His Son; and it is only in unity with His Other, in Spirit, that God is Subject. This, now, is the specific character and the goal of the Philosophy of Nature, that Spirit finds in Nature its own essence, i.e. the Notion, finds its counterpart in her. The study of Nature is thus the liberation of Spirit in her, for Spirit is present in her in so far as it is in relation, not with an Other, but with itself. This is also the liberation of Nature; implicitly she is Reason, but it is through Spirit that Reason as such first emerges from Nature into existence. Spirit has the certainty which Adam had when he looked on Eve: 'This is flesh of my flesh, and bone of my bone'. Thus Nature is the bride which Spirit weds. But is this certainty also truth? Since the inner being of Nature is none other than the universal, then in our thoughts of this inner being we are at home with ourselves. Truth in its subjective meaning is the agreement of thought with the object: in its objective meaning, truth is the

---

[3] Goethe, *Zur Morphologie*, vol. i, part 3, 1820. (Wallace's rendering in the *Encyclopaedia Logic*, pp. 421–2.)

agreement of the object with its own self, the correspondence of its reality with its Notion. The Ego in its essence is the Notion, which is equal to itself and pervades all things, and which, because it retains the mastery over the particular differences, is the universal which returns into itself. This Notion is directly the true Idea, the divine Idea of the universe which alone is the Actual. Thus God alone is the Truth, in Plato's words, the immortal Being whose body and and soul are joined in a single nature. The first question here is: Why has God willed to create Nature?

B. The Notion of Nature

§ 247

Nature has presented itself as the Idea in the form of *otherness*. Since therefore the Idea is the negative of itself, or is *external to itself*, Nature is not merely external in relation to this Idea (and to its subjective existence Spirit); the truth is rather that *externality* constitutes the specific character in which Nature, as Nature, exists.

Zusatz. If God is all-sufficient and lacks nothing, why does He disclose Himself in a sheer Other of Himself? The divine Idea is just this: to disclose itself, to posit this Other outside itself and to take it back again into itself, in order to be subjectivity and Spirit. The Philosophy of Nature itself belongs to this path of return; for it is that which overcomes the division between Nature and Spirit and assures to Spirit the knowledge of its essence in Nature. This, now, is the place of Nature in the whole; its determinateness is this, that the Idea determines itself, posits difference within itself, an Other, but in such a way that in its indivisible nature it is infinite goodness, imparting to its otherness and sharing with it its entire fullness of content. God, therefore, in determining Himself, remains equal to Himself; each of these moments is itself the whole Idea and must be posited as the divine totality. The different moments can be grasped under three different forms: the universal, the particular, and the individual. First, the different moments remain preserved in the eternal unity of the Idea; this is the Logos, the eternal Son of God as Philo conceived it. The other to this extreme is individuality, the form of finite Spirit. As a return into itself individuality is, indeed, Spirit; but, as otherness with exclusion of all others, it is finite or human Spirit; for finite spirits other than human beings do not concern us here. The individual man grasped as also in unity with the divine essence is the object of the Christian religion; and this is the most tremendous demand that can be made on him. The third form which concerns us here, the Idea in the mode of particularity, is Nature, which lies between the two extremes. This form presents the least difficulty for the Understanding; Spirit is posited as the contradiction existing explicitly, for the Idea in its infinite freedom, and again in the form of individuality, are in objective contradiction; but in Nature, the contradiction is only implicit or for us, the otherness appearing in the Idea as a quiescent form. In Christ, the contradiction is posited and overcome, as His life, passion, and resurrection: Nature is the son of God, but not as the Son, but as abiding in otherness – the divine Idea as held fast for a moment outside the divine love. Nature is Spirit estranged from itself; in Nature, Spirit lets itself go (*ausgelassen*), a Bacchic god unrestrained and unmindful of itself; in Nature, the unity of the Notion is concealed.

A rational consideration of Nature must consider how Nature is in its own self this process of becoming Spirit, of sublating its otherness – and how the Idea is present in each grade or level of Nature itself; estranged from the Idea, Nature is only the corpse of the Understanding. Nature is, however, only implicitly the Idea, and Schelling therefore called her a petrified intelligence, others even a frozen intelligence; but God does not remain petrified and dead; the very stones cry out and raise themselves to Spirit. God is subjectivity, activity, infinite actuosity, in which otherness has only a transient being, remaining implicit within the unity of the Idea, because it is itself this totality of the Idea. Since Nature is the Idea in the form of otherness, the Idea, comformable to its Notion, is not present in Nature as it is in and for itself, although nevertheless, Nature is one of the ways in which the Idea manifests itself, and is a necessary mode of the Idea. However, the fact that this mode of the Idea is Nature, is the second question to be discussed and demonstrated; to this end we must compare our definition with the ordinary idea of Nature and see whether the two correspond; this will occur in the sequel. In other respects, however, philosophy need not trouble itself about ordinary ideas, nor is it bound to realize in every respect what such ideas demand, for ideas are arbitrary; but still, generally speaking, the two must agree.

In connection with this fundamental determination of Nature, attention must be drawn to the metaphysical aspect which has been dealt with in the form of the question of the *eternity of the world*. It might be thought that we need pay no attention to metaphysics here; but this is the very place to bring it to notice, and we need not hesitate to do so, for it does not lead to prolixity and is readily dealt with. Now the metaphysics of Nature, i.e. Nature's essential and distinctive characteristic, is to be the Idea in the form of otherness, and this implies that the being of Nature is essentially ideality, or that, as only relative, Nature is essentially related to a First. The question of the eternity of the world (this is confused with Nature, since it is a collection of both spiritual and natural objects) has, in the first place, the meaning of the conception of time, of an eternity as it is called, of an infinitely long time, so that the world had no beginning in time; secondly, the question implies that Nature is conceived as uncreated, eternal, as existing independently of God. As regards this second meaning, it is completely set aside and eliminated by the distinctive character of Nature to be the Idea in its otherness. As regards the first meaning, after removing the sense of the absoluteness of the world, we are left only with eternity in connection with the conception of time.

About this, the following is to be said: (α) eternity is not before or after time, not before the creation of the world, nor when it perishes; rather is eternity the absolute present, the Now, without before and after. The world is created, is now being created, and has eternally been created; this presents itself in the form of the preservation of the world. Creating is the activity of the absolute Idea; the Idea of Nature, like the Idea as such, is eternal. (β) In the question whether the world or Nature, in its finitude, has a beginning in time or not, one thinks of the world or Nature as such, i.e. as the universal; and the true universal is the Idea, which we have already said is eternal. The finite, however, is temporal, it has a before and an after; and when the finite is our object we are in time. It has a beginning but not an absolute one; its time begins with it, and time belongs only to the sphere of finitude. Philosophy is timeless comprehension, of time too and of all things generally in their eternal mode. Having rid oneself of the conception of the absolute beginning of time, one assumes the opposite conception of an infinite time; but infinite time, when it is still conceived as time, not as sublated time, is also to be distinguished from eternity. It is not this time but another time, and again another time, and so on (§ 258), if thought cannot resolve the finite into the eternal. Thus matter is infinitely divisible; that is, its nature is such that what is posited as a Whole, as a One, is completely self-external and within itself a Many. But matter is not in fact so divided, as if it consisted of atoms; on the contrary, this infinite divisibility of matter is a possibility and only a possibility: that is, this division *ad infinitum* is not something positive and actual, but is only a subjective idea. Similarly, infinite time is only an idea, a going into the beyond, which remains infected with the negative; a necessary idea so long as one is confined to a consideration of the finite as finite. However, if I pass on to the universal, to the non-finite, I leave behind the standpoint where singularity and its alternate variations have their place. In our ordinary way of thinking, the world is only an aggregate of finite existences, but when it is grasped as a universal, as a totality, the question of a beginning at once disappears. Where to make the beginning is therefore undetermined; a beginning is to be made, but it is only a relative one. We pass beyond it, but not to infinity, but only to another beginning which, of course, is also only a conditioned one; in short, it is only the nature of the relative which is expressed, because we are in the sphere of finitude.

This is the metaphysics which passes hither and thither from one abstract determination to another, taking them for absolute. A plain, positive answer cannot be given to the question whether the world has, or has not, a beginning in time. A plain answer is supposed to state that *either* the one *or* the other is true. But the plain answer is, rather, that the question itself, this 'either-or', is badly posed. If we are talking of the finite, then we have both a beginning and a non-beginning; these opposed determinations in their unresolved and unreconciled conflict with each other, belong to the finite: and so the finite, because it is this contradiction, perishes. The finite is preceded by an Other, and in tracing out the context of the finite, its antecedents must be sought, e.g., in the history of the earth or of man. There is no end to such an inquiry, even though we reach an end of each finite thing; time has its power over the manifoldness of the finite. The finite has a beginning, but this beginning is not the First; the finite has an independent existence, but its immediacy is also limited. When ordinary thinking forsakes this determinate finite, which is preceded and followed by other finites, and goes on to the empty thought of time as such, or the world as such, it flounders about in empty ideas, i.e. merely abstract thoughts.

§ 248

In this externality, the determinations of the Notion have the show of an *indifferent subsistence* and *isolation* (*Vereinzelung*) in regard to each other, and the Notion, therefore, is present only as something inward. Consequently, Nature exhibits no freedom in its existence, but only *necessity* and *contingency*.

Remark

For this reason, Nature in the determinate existence which makes it Nature, is not to be deified; nor are sun, moon, animals, plants, etc., to be regarded and cited as more excellent, as works of God, than human actions and events. *In itself*, in the Idea, Nature is divine: but as it *is*, the being of Nature does not accord with its Notion; rather is Nature the *unresolved contradiction*. Its characteristic is *positedness*, the negative, in the same way that the ancients grasped matter in general as the *non-ens*. Thus Nature has also been spoken of as the *self-degradation of the Idea*, in that the Idea, in this form of externality, is in a disparity with its own self. It is only to the external and immediate stage of consciousness, that is, to *sensuous* consciousness, that Nature appears as the First, the immediate, as mere being (*das Seiende*). But because, even in this element of externality, Nature is a representation of the *Idea*, one may, and indeed ought, to admire in it the wisdom of God. Vanini said that a stalk of straw suffices to demonstrate God's being: but every mental image, the slightest fancy of mind, the play of its most capricious whims, every word, affords a superior ground for a knowledge of God's being than any single object of Nature. In Nature, not only is the play of forms a prey to boundless and unchecked contingency, but each separate entity is without the Notion of itself. The highest level to which Nature attains is life; but this, as only a natural mode of the Idea, is at the mercy of the unreason of externality, and the living creature is throughout its whole life entangled with other alien existences, whereas in every expression of Spirit there is contained the moment of free, universal self-relation. It is equally an error to regard the products of mind as inferior to natural objects, and to regard the latter as superior to *human works of art*, on the ground that these must take their material from outside, and that they are not alive. As if the spiritual form did not contain a higher kind of life, and were not more worthy of the Spirit, than the natural form, and as though form generally were not superior to matter, and throughout the ethical sphere even what can be called matter did not belong to Spirit alone: as if in Nature the higher form, the living creature, did not also receive its matter from outside. It is put forward as a further superiority of Nature that throughout all the contingency of its manifold existence it remains obedient to eternal laws. But surely this is also true of the realm of self-consciousness, a fact which finds recognition in the belief that human affairs are governed by Providence; or are the laws of this Providence in the field of human affairs supposed to be only contingent and irrational? But if the contingency of Spirit, the free will (*Willkür*) does *evil*, this is still infinitely superior to the regular motions of the celestial bodies, or to the innocence of plant life; for what thus errs is still Spirit.

Zusatz. The infinite divisibility of matter simply means that matter is external to itself. The immeasurableness of Nature, which at first excites our wonder, is precisely this same externality. Because each material point seems to be entirely independent of all the others, a failure to hold fast to the Notion prevails in Nature which is unable to bring together its determinations. The sun, planets, comets, the Elements, plants, animals, exist separately by themselves. The sun is an individual other than the earth, connected with the planets only by gravity. It is only in *life* that we meet with subjectivity and the counter to externality. The heart, liver, eye, are not self-subsistent individualities on their own account, and the hand, when separated from the body, putrefies. The organic body is still a whole composed of many members external to each other; but each individual member exists only in the subject, and the Notion exists as the power over these members. Thus it is that the Notion, which at the stage of Notionlessness (*Begrifflosigkeit*) is only something inward, first comes into existence in life, as soul. The spatiality of the organism has no truth whatever for the soul; otherwise there would be as many souls as material points, for the soul feels in each point of the organism. One must not be deceived by the show of mutual externality, but must comprehend that mutually external points form only one unity. The celestial bodies only *appear* to be independent of each other, they are the guardians of *one* field. But because the unity in Nature is a relation between things which are apparently self-subsistent, Nature is not free, but is only necessary and contingent. For necessity is the inseparability of different terms which yet appear as indifferent towards each other; but because this abstract state of externality also receives its due, there is contingency in Nature, i.e. external necessity, not the inner necessity of the Notion. There has been a lot of talk in physics about polarity. This concept is a great advance in the metaphysics of the science; for the concept of polarity is simply nothing else but the specific relation of necessity between two different terms which are one, in that when one is given, the other is also given. But this polarity is restricted to the opposition. However, through the opposition there is also given the return of the opposition into unity, and this is the third term which the necessity of the Notion has over and above polarity. In Nature, as the otherness [of the Idea], there also occur the square or the tetrad, for example, the four Elements, the four colours, etc., and even the pentad, e.g. the fingers and the senses. In Spirit, the fundamental form of necessity is the triad. The totality of the disjunction of the Notion exists in Nature as a tetrad because the first term is the universal as such, and the second, or the difference, appears itself as a duality – in Nature, the Other must exist explicitly as Other; with the result that the subjective unity of the universal and the particular is the fourth term which then has a separate existence in face of the other three terms. Further, as the monad and the dyad themselves constitute the entire particularity, the totality of the Notion can go as far as the pentad.

Nature is the negative because it is the negative of the Idea. Jacob Boehme says that God's first-born is Lucifer; and this son of Light centred his imagination on himself and became evil: that is the moment of difference, of otherness held fast against the Son, who is otherness within the divine love. The ground and significance of such conceptions which occur wildly in an oriental style, is to be found in the negative nature of Nature. The other form of otherness is immediacy, which consists in the moment of difference existing abstractly on its own. This existence, however, is only momentary, not a true existence; the Idea alone exists eternally, because it is being in and for itself, i.e. being which has returned into itself. Nature is the first in point of time, but the absolute *prius* is the Idea; this absolute *prius* is the last, the true beginning, Alpha is Omega. What is unmediated is often held to be superior, the mediated being thought of as dependent. The Notion, however, has both aspects: it is mediation through the sublation of mediation, and so is immediacy. People speak, for example, of an immediate belief in God; but this is the inferior mode of being, not the higher; the primitive religions were religions of nature-worship. The affirmative element in Nature is the manifestation of the Notion in it; the nearest instance of the power of the Notion is the perishableness of this outer existence; all natural existences form but a single body in which dwells the soul [the Notion]. The Notion manifests itself in these giant members, but not *qua* Notion; this occurs only in Spirit where the Notion exists as it is.

§ 249

Nature is to be regarded as a *system of stages*, one arising necessarily from the other and being the proximate truth of the stage from which it results: but it is not generated *naturally* out of the other but only in the inner Idea which constitutes the ground of Nature. *Metamorphosis* pertains only to the Notion as such, since only *its* alteration is development. But in Nature, the Notion is partly only something inward, partly existent only as a living individual: *existent* metamorphosis, therefore, is limited to this individual alone.

Remark

It has been an inept conception of ancient and also recent Philosophy of Nature to regard the progression and transition of one natural form and sphere into a higher as an outwardly-actual production which, however, to be made *clearer*, is relegated to the *obscurity* of the past. It is precisely externality which is characteristic of Nature, that is, differences are allowed to fall apart and to appear as indifferent to each other: the dialectical Notion which leads forward the *stages*, is the inner side of them. A thinking consideration must reject such nebulous, at bottom, sensuous ideas, as in particular the so-called *origination*, for example, of plants and animals from water, and then the *origination* of the more highly developed animal organisms from the lower, and so on.

Zusatz. The consideration of the utility of natural objects contains this truth, that they are not an absolute end in and for themselves. This negative aspect, however, is not external to them but is the immanent moment of their Idea, which effects their perishability and transition into another existence, but at the same time into a higher Notion. The Notion timelessly and in a universal manner posits all particularity in existence. It is a completely empty thought to represent species as developing successively, one after the other, in time. Chronological difference has no interest whatever for thought. If it is only a question of enumerating the series of living species in order to show the mind how they are divided into classes, either by starting from the poorest and simplest terms, and rising to the more developed and richer in determinations and content, or by proceeding in the reverse fashion, this operation will always have a general interest. It will be a way of arranging things as in the division of Nature into three kingdoms; this is preferable to jumbling them together, a procedure which would be somewhat repellent to an intelligence which had an inkling of the Notion. But it must not be imagined that such a dry series is made dynamic or philosophical, or more intelligible, or whatever you like to say, by representing the terms as producing each other. Animal nature is the truth of vegetable nature, vegetable of mineral; the earth is the truth of the solar system. In a system, it is the most abstract term which is the first, and the truth of each sphere is the last; but this again is only the first of a higher sphere. It is the necessity of the Idea which causes each sphere to complete itself by passing into another higher one, and the variety of forms must be considered as necessary and determinate. The land animal did not develop *naturally* out of the aquatic animal, nor did it fly into the air on leaving the water, nor did perhaps the bird again fall back to earth. If we want to compare the different stages of Nature, it is quite proper to note that, for example, a certain animal has one ventricle and another has two; but we must not then talk of the fact as if we were dealing with parts which had been put together. Still less must the category of earlier spheres be used to explain others: for this is a formal error, as when it is said that the plant is a carbon pole and the animal a nitrogen pole.

The two forms under which the serial progression of Nature is conceived are *evolution* and *emanation*. The way of evolution, which starts from the imperfect and formless, is as follows: at first there was the liquid element and aqueous forms of life, and from the water there evolved plants, polyps, molluscs, and finally fishes; then from the fishes were evolved the land animals, and finally from the land animals came man. This gradual alteration is called an explanation and understanding; it is a conception which comes from the Philosophy of Nature, and it still flourishes. But though this quantitative difference is of all theories the easiest to understand, it does not really explain anything at all. The way of emanation is peculiar to the oriental world. It involves a series of degradations of being, starting from the perfect being, the absolute totality, God. God has created, and from Him have proceeded splendours, lightnings and likenesses in such fashion that the first likeness is that which most resembles God. This first likeness in its turn, is supposed to have generated another but less perfect one, and so on, so that each created being has become, in its turn, a creative being, down to the negative being, matter, the extreme of evil. Emanation thus ends with the absence of all form. Both ways are one-sided and superficial, and postulate an indeterminate goal. That which proceeds from the perfect to the imperfect has this advantage, that then we have before us the type of the complete organism; and this is the type which picture-thinking must have before it in order to understand the imperfect organisms. What appear in the latter as subordinate, for example, organs which have no functions, is first understood through the more developed organisms which enable one to see the place the organ fills. The perfect, if it is to have the advantage over the imperfect, must exist not only in picture-thinking but also in reality.

The basis of the idea of metamorphosis is also a single Idea which persists in the various genera and even in each particular organ, so that these genera and organs are only the diverse forms of a single, self-same type. Similarly, one speaks of the metamorphosis of an insect, in that the caterpillar, the pupa and the butterfly, are one and the same individual. In the case of individuals, the development certainly takes place in time, but it is otherwise with the genus. With the existence of the genus in a particular form, the other modes of its existence are necessarily postulated. Water being given, then air, fire, etc., too, are necessarily postulated. It is important to hold fast to identity; but to hold fast to difference is no less important, and this gets pushed into the background when a change is conceived only quantitatively. This makes the mere idea of metamorphosis inadequate.

Under the same heading, too, comes the idea of the *series* formed by things, and especially living things. The desire to know the necessity of this development leads to the search for a law of the series, a basic determination which, while positing difference, repeats itself in such difference and in so doing also produces a fresh difference. But to enlarge a series merely by the successive addition of elements similarly determined, and to see only the same relationship between all the members of the series, is not the way in which the Notion generates its determinations. It is this very fact of imagining a *series* of stages and the like, which has been such a hindrance to any progress in understanding the necessity of the various forms of Nature. To seek to arrange in serial form the planets, the metals or chemical substances in general, plants and animals, and then to ascertain the law of the series, is a fruitless task, because Nature does not arrange its forms in such articulate series: the Notion differentiates things according to their own specific qualitative character, and to that extent advances by leaps. The old saying, or so-called law, *non datur saltus in natura*, is altogether inadequate to the diremption of the Notion. The continuity of the Notion with itself is of an entirely different character.

§ 250

The *contradiction* of the Idea, arising from the fact that, as Nature, it is external to itself, is more precisely this: that on the one hand there is the *necessity* of its forms which is generated by the Notion, and their rational determination in the organic totality; while on the other hand, there is their indifferent *contingency* and indeterminable irregularity. In the sphere of Nature contingency and determination from without has its right, and this contingency is at its greatest in the realm of concrete individual forms, which however, as products of Nature, are concrete only in an *immediate* manner. The *immediately* concrete thing is a group of properties, external to one another and more or less indifferently related to each other; and for that very reason, the simple subjectivity which exists for itself is also indifferent and abandons them to contingent and external determination. This is the *impotence* of Nature, that it preserves the determinations of the Notion only *abstractly*, and leaves their detailed specification to external determination.

Remark

The infinite wealth and variety of forms and, what is most irrational, the contingency which enters into the external arrangement of natural things, have been extolled as the sublime freedom of Nature, even as the divinity *of Nature*, or at least the divinity present *in* it. This confusion of contingency, caprice, and disorder, with freedom and rationality is characteristic of sensuous and unphilosophical thinking. This impotence of Nature sets limits to philosophy and it is quite improper to expect the Notion to comprehend – or as it is said, construe or deduce – these contingent products of Nature. It is even imagined that the more trivial and isolated the object, the easier is the task of deducing it.[4] Undoubtedly, traces of determination by the Notion are to be found even in the most particularized object, although these traces do not exhaust its nature. Traces of this influence of the Notion and of this inner coherence of natural objects will often surprise the investigator, but especially will they seem startling, or rather incredible, to those who are accustomed to see only contingency in natural, as in human, history. One must, however, be careful to avoid taking such trace of the Notion for the total determination of the object, for that is the route to the analogies previously mentioned.

In the impotence of Nature to adhere strictly to the Notion in its realization, lies the difficulty and, in many cases, the impossibility of finding fixed distinctions for classes and orders from an empirical consideration of Nature. Nature everywhere blurs the essential limits of species and genera by intermediate and defective

---

[4] It was in this – and other respects too – quite naïve sense that Herr Krug once challenged the Philosophy of Nature to perform the feat of deducing *only* his pen. One could perhaps give him hope that *his* pen would have the glory of being deduced, if ever philosophy should advance so far and have such a clear insight into every great theme in heaven and on earth, past and present, that there was nothing more important to comprehend.

forms, which continually furnish counter examples to every fixed distinction; this even occurs within a specific genus, that of man, for example, where monstrous births, on the one hand, must be considered as belonging to the genus, while on the other hand, they lack certain essential determinations characteristic of the genus. In order to be able to consider such forms as defective, imperfect and deformed, one must presuppose a fixed, invariable type. This type, however, cannot be furnished by experience, for it is experience which also presents these so-called monstrosities, deformities, intermediate products, etc. The fixed type rather presupposes the self-subsistence and dignity of the determination stemming from the Notion.

§ 251

Nature is, in itself, a living Whole. The movement through its stages is more precisely this: that the Idea *posits* itself as that which it is *in itself*, or what is the same thing, that it returns *into itself* out of its immediacy and externality which is *death*, in order to be, first a *living creature*, but further, to sublate this determinateness also in which it is only Life, and to give itself an existence as Spirit, which is the truth and the final goal of Nature and the genuine actuality of the Idea.

Zusatz. The development of the Notion towards its destination, its end or, if you like, its purpose, is to be grasped as a positing of what it is in itself, so that these determinations of its content come into existence, are manifested, but at the same time not as independent and self-subsistent, but as moments which remain in the unity of the Notion, as ideal, i.e. posited moments. This positing can therefore be grasped as an utterance or expression, a coming forth, a setting forth, a coming-out-of-self, in so far as the subjectivity of the Notion is lost in the mutual outsideness of its determinations. But it preserves itself in them, as their unity and ideality; and this going out of the centre from itself to the periphery is therefore, looked at from the opposite side, equally a taking up again of this outer into the inner, an inwardizing or remembering (*Erinnern*) that it is it, the Notion, that exists in this externality. Starting therefore from the externality in which the Notion at first exists, its progress is a movement into itself, into the centre, i.e. a bringing of immediate and external existence which is inadequate to itself, to subjective unity, to being-within-self: not in such a way that the Notion withdraws itself from this externality, leaving it behind like a dead shell, but rather that existence as such is within self or conforms to the Notion, that the being-within-self itself exists, which is Life. The Notion strives to burst the shell of outer existence and to become for itself. Life is the Notion which has attained to the manifestation of itself, which has explicated, set forth, what it is in itself; but the Understanding finds this the most difficult of things to grasp because what it finds easiest to grasp is the most simple of things, i.e. the abstract and the dead.

C. Division

§ 252

The Idea as Nature is:

I.   in the determination of asunderness or mutual outsideness, of infinite sep-
     arateness, the unity of form being outside it; this unity, as *ideal*, is only *in
     itself* and is consequently a unity which is only *sought*. This is *matter* and its
     ideal system – Mechanics;

II. in the determination of *particularity*, so that reality is posited with an imma-
     nent determinateness of form and with an existent difference in it. This is
     a relationship of Reflection (*Reflexionsverhältnis*) whose being-within-self is
     natural *individuality* – Physics;

III. in the determination of *subjectivity*, in which the real differences of form are
     also brought back to the *ideal* unity which has found itself and is for itself –
     Organics.

Zusatz. The division is made from the standpoint of the Notion grasped in its
totality, and it indicates the diremption of the Notion into its determinations; and
since in this diremption the Notion explicates its determinations and gives them
a self-subsistence, though only as moments, the process is one of self-realization
in which the Notion posits itself as Idea. But the Notion not only sets forth its
moments, and not only articulates itself in its differences, but it also brings these
apparently self-subsistent stages back to their ideality and unity, to itself; and only
then, in fact, has it made itself the concrete Notion, the Idea and the Truth. It
seems, therefore, that there are two ways of presenting both the Division and the
scientific exposition: one way would start from the concrete Notion, and in Nature
this is Life, which would be considered on its own account. It would then be led
to consider the externalized forms of the Notion, the forms being thrown out by
the Notion to exist separately as spheres of Nature, the Notion being related to
them as to other – consequently more abstract – modes of its existence; this way
would close with the complete extinction of life. The other way is the reverse of
this. It starts with the, at first, only immediate mode of the Notion's existence,
with its uttermost self-externality, and it closes with the true existence of the
Notion, with the truth of the whole course of its exposition. The first way can be
compared to the process implied in the conception of emanation, the second, to
the process implied in the conception of evolution (§ 249, *Zusatz*). Each of these
forms taken separately is one-sided, but they exist together; the eternal divine
process is a flowing in two opposite directions which meet and permeate each
other in what is simply and solely *one*. The First, let it be called by the loftiest
name, is only an immediate, even though we mean by it something concrete.
Matter, for example, negates itself as an untrue existence and from this negation
emerges a higher existence. From one aspect, it is by an evolution that the earlier

stages are cancelled but from another aspect matter remains in the background and is produced anew by emanation. Evolution is thus also an involution, in that matter interiorizes itself to become life. In virtue of the urge of the Idea to become objective to itself, the self-subsistent becomes a moment: the senses of the animal, for example, made objective and external, are the Sun and the lunar and cometary bodies. Even in the sphere of Physics these bodies lose their independence although they still retain the same form with some modifications; they are the Elements [air, fire, and water]. The subjective sense of sight existing outwardly is the Sun, taste is water, and smell is the air. But as our task here is to posit the determinations of the Notion, we must not start from the most concrete, the true sphere, but from the most abstract.

Matter is the form in which the self-externality of Nature achieves its first being-within-self, an abstract being-for-self which is exclusive and therefore a plurality, which has its unity, as what brings the independent many into a universal being-for-self, at once within and outside itself: gravity. In the sphere of Mechanics, being-for-self is not yet an individual, stable unity having the power to subordinate plurality to itself. Heavy matter does not yet possess the individuality which preserves its determinations; and since in matter the determinations of the Notion are still external to each other, its differences are not qualitative but indifferent or purely quantitative, and matter, merely as mass, has no form. Form is acquired by individual bodies in Physics, and with this we have at once gravity revealed for the first time as the mastery of being-for-self over multiplicity, a being-for-self which is no longer merely a striving but which has come to rest, although at first only in the mode of appearance (*nur auf erscheinende Weise*). Each atom of gold, for example, contains all the determinations or properties of the whole lump of gold, and matter is immanently specified and particularized. The second determination is that here, still, particularity as qualitative determinateness, and being-for-self as the point of individuality, fall together in unity, and therefore body is finitely determined; individuality is still bound to definite exclusive specific properties, does not yet exist as totality. If such a body enters into a process in which it loses such properties, then it ceases to be what it is; the qualitative determinateness is therefore affirmatively posited, but not at the same time also negatively. The organic being is totality as found in Nature, an individuality which is for itself and which internally develops into its differences: but in such a way that first, these determinations are not only specific properties but also concrete totalities; secondly, they remain also qualitatively determined against each other, and, as thus finite, are posited as ideal moments by Life, which preserves itself in the process of these members. Thus we have a number of beings-for-self which, however, are brought back to the being-for-self which is for itself and which, as its own end (*Selbstzweck*), subdues the members and reduces them to means: this is the unity of qualitatively determined being and gravity, which finds itself in Life.

Each stage is a specific realm of Nature and all appear to have independent existence, But the last is the concrete unity of all the preceding ones, just as, in general, each successive stage embodies the lower stages, but equally posits these, as its non-organic nature, over against itself. One stage is the power of the other, and this relation is reciprocal. Here can be seen the true meaning of *powers* (*Potenzen*). The non-organic Elements are powers opposed to what is individual, subjective – the non-organic destroys the organic. But equally the organism, in its turn, is the power which subdues its universal powers, air, water; these are perpetually liberated and also perpetually subdued and assimilated. The eternal life of Nature consists in this: first, that the Idea displays itself in each sphere so far as it can within the finitude of that sphere, just as each drop of water provides an image of the sun, and secondly, that the Notion, through its dialectic, breaks through the limitation of this sphere, since it cannot rest content with an inadequate element, and necessarily passes over into a higher stage.

Translated by A. V. Miller

VII

God and Religion

23

Immanuel Kant, Critique of Practical Reason (Kritik der praktischen Vernunft): *The Existence of God as a Postulate of Pure Practical Reason (1788)*

In 1793 Kant, at almost seventy years of age, completed *Religion within the Limits of Reason Alone*. It proved to be the most controversial book of his career. This is largely explained by the newly promulgated Prussian censorship laws introduced by the recently enthroned and religiously orthodox Frederick William II. These laws were to create a prohibitive environment unlike anything Kant had had to negotiate for the publication of earlier works. The suspicions of the ever-vigilant censors would undoubtedly have been aroused by the very title of the book. And in order to satisfy the censors that he was not an enemy of religion, Kant was obliged to gain the imprimatur of a recognised Faculty of Theology (which, in fact, he received from Jena). *Religion within the Limits of Reason Alone* developed the idea that ethics and religion effectively imply each other. Although the exercise of duty for duty's sake is all that is required for the conduct of morality, we are driven, Kant believes, by a consideration in our moral lives of the 'end' of our actions: that is, considerations of *'what is to result from this right conduct of ours'*.[1] Religion, it seemed to Kant, had accurately captured the notion of a final end.

The rational notion of religion which Kant puts forward is not orthodox in any unqualified sense: to the worried observer Kant seems to make religion subordinate to the prior truths of morality, thereby postulating God's existence merely as a postulate of practical reason. In 1794 – that is, after the publication of *Religion within the Limits of Reason Alone* – the King himself sent Kant a stiff letter in which he insisted that Kant refrain from any further destructive philosophising on religion. He stated:

Our most high person has for a long time observed with great displeasure how you misuse your philosophy to undermine many of the most important and fundamental doctrines of the Holy Scriptures and Christianity . . . We demand of you immediately a most conscientious answer and expect that in the future, towards the avoidance of our highest disfavor, you will give no such cause for offence,

---

[1] Immanuel Kant, trans. Theodore M. Greene and Hoyt H. Hudson, *Religion within the Limits of Reason Alone* (New York: Harper and Row, 1960), p. 4 (*KAA* VI, 5).

but rather, in accordance with your duty, employ your talents and authority so that our paternal purpose may be more and more attained. If you continue to resist, you may certainly expect unpleasant consequences to yourself.[2]

For the remainder of the King's reign Kant imposed a moratorium on himself with regard to writings on religion, thereby putting in abeyance an important part of his Enlightenment project: that of making the major claims of the Christian life reasonable to people by demonstrating their centrality to our moral lives.

The controversy that surrounded the publication of *Religion within the Limits of Reason Alone* must have been somewhat unexpected as the views Kant expressed in this book on the relationship between faith and morality were entirely within the framework of some of his previous works. The *Critique of Pure Reason* had famously undermined traditional philosophical arguments for the existence of God. In the Preface to the first *Critique* Kant claimed that the philosophical assumption of intellectual accessibility to God's existence was motivated by unjustifiable 'pretensions to transcendent insight'.[3] The effect of this pretension was to misapply the cognitive faculty, which operated paradigmatically in the sphere of space/time objectivity, to alleged phenomena which by their definition lay outside our ordinary world of objects. Very significantly he went on to say that the demonstrable misconstructions of our cognitive faculty – our reduction of the transcendent to the phenomenal – showed 'all *practical extension* of pure reason impossible'. And famously he wrote, 'I have therefore found it necessary to deny *knowledge*, in order to make room *for faith*'.[4]

But it is the *Critique of Practical Reason*, published just one year after the second edition of the *Critique of Pure Reason*, that anticipates the central and most controversial thesis of *Religion within the Limits of Reason Alone*. In that text (in the section reprinted here) Kant stresses that one cannot be moral if one is motivated heteronomously: duty for duty's sake entails quite simply that religious motivations cannot be a reason for being moral. However, Kant develops the notion of a state of moral virtue that is not fulfilled simply by adherence to the moral law. The moral law entails only that it be obeyed unconditionally, whereas virtue in addition implies the notion, Kant claims, of being deserving of happiness. Clearly, happiness cannot be a motive for morality, nor will morality likely in all instances lead to happiness. Yet, Kant seems to think, these notions operate in some sort of harmony in our practical lives. But where does this sense of the necessary harmony come from, if in our empirical lives it occurs only irregularly? Kant believes that a postulate of our morality is the existence of a God who can guarantee the possibility of an appropriate harmony; that is, the basic assumption of morality that such a harmony is possible depends on the

[2] Cited by Theodore M. Greene, 'The Historical Context and Religious Significance of Kant's *Religion*', in *Religion within the Limits of Reason Alone*, p. xxxiv.
[3] Immanuel Kant, trans. Norman Kemp Smith, *Critique of Pure Reason* (London: Macmillan, 1929), Bxxx.
[4] Kant, *Critique of Pure Reason*, Bxxx.

notion that there is a God who somehow brings harmony to these two notions. As Kant notes: 'the existence of a cause of all nature, distinct from nature itself and containing the principle of this connection, namely, of the exact harmony of happiness with morality, is also postulated'. For Kant an important element of Christianity is precisely its notion of the highest good, 'the Kingdom of God', which facilitates the harmony of happiness and morality through its ideas of the holiness of morals and that of 'how we are to be worthy of happiness'. Christianity, then, just so happens to furnish the prerequisites of a moral life.

Kant's 'pietistic' upbringing would have predisposed him to consider religion a matter not of theological and speculative niceties, but one of practice, devotion and indeed individual conscience. That the religious life could never be delivered by 'proofs' of God's existence, by theoretical arguments, that is – as proposed, for example, by Scholastic Catholicism – was simply a misrepresentation of the Christian life. To add to the pietistic influence was the presence of rationalistic deism in the German philosophy of Kant's formative years. Rationalist deism (put forward most famously by Christian Wolff, the philosopher whose work in metaphysics had so strongly determined Kant's pre-critical writings) held that religion could be founded on reason, a claim that obviously excluded what seemed to be the dogmatic notion of revelation. Whilst pietism and deism were not immediately compatible Kant effectively developed a synthesis in which what was important in religion was its practical moral requirements, and that these requirements could be demonstrated to be rational.

V. – THE EXISTENCE OF GOD AS A POSTULATE OF PURE PRACTICAL REASON.[†]

In the foregoing analysis the moral law led to a practical problem which is prescribed by pure reason alone, without the aid of any sensible motives, namely, that of the necessary completeness of the first and principal element of the *summum bonum*, viz. Morality; and as this can be perfectly solved only in eternity, to the postulate of *immortality*. The same law must also lead us to affirm the possibility of the second element of the *summum bonum*, viz. Happiness proportioned to that morality, and this on grounds as disinterested as before, and solely from impartial reason; that is, it must lead to the supposition of the existence of a cause adequate to this effect; in other words, it must postulate the *existence of God* as the necessary condition of the possibility of the *summum bonum* (an object of the will which is

---

[†] *KAA* V, 124–32. *Critique of Practical Reason* in *Kant's Critique of Practical Reason and Other Works on the Theory of Ethics* (London: Longmans, 6th edition 1909).

necessarily connected with the moral legislation of pure reason). We proceed to exhibit this connexion in a convincing manner.

Happiness is the condition of a rational being in the world with whom *everything goes according to his wish and will*; it rests, therefore, on the harmony of physical nature with his whole end, and likewise with the essential determining principle of his will. Now the moral law as a law of freedom commands by determining principles, which ought to be quite independent of nature and of its harmony with our faculty of desire (as springs). But the acting rational being in the world is not the cause of the world and of nature itself. There is not the least ground, therefore, in the moral law for a necessary connexion between morality and proportionate happiness in a being that belongs to the world as part of it, and therefore dependent on it, and which for that reason cannot by his will be a cause of this nature, nor by his own power make it thoroughly harmonize, as far as his happiness is concerned, with his practical principles. Nevertheless, in the practical problem of pure reason, i.e. the necessary pursuit of the *summum bonum*, such a connexion is postulated as necessary: we ought to endeavour to promote the *summum bonum*, which, therefore, must be possible. Accordingly, the existence of a cause of all nature, distinct from nature itself, and containing the principle of this connexion, namely, of the exact harmony of happiness with morality, is also *postulated*. Now, this supreme cause must contain the principle of the harmony of nature, not merely with a law of the will of rational beings, but with the conception of this *law*, in so far as they make it the *supreme determining principle of the will*, and consequently not merely with the form of morals, but with their morality as their motive, that is, with their moral character. Therefore, the *summum bonum* is possible in the world only on the supposition of a Supreme Being having a causality corresponding to moral character. Now a being that is capable of acting on the conception of laws is an *intelligence* (a rational being), and the causality of such a being according to this conception of laws is his *will*; therefore the supreme cause of nature, which must be presupposed as a condition of the *summum bonum* is a being which is the cause of nature by *intelligence* and *will*, consequently its author, that is God. It follows that the postulate of the possibility of the *highest derived good* (the best world) is likewise the postulate of the reality of a *highest original good*, that is to say, of the existence of God. Now it was seen to be a duty for us to promote the *summum bonum*; consequently it is not merely allowable, but it is a necessity connected with duty as a requisite, that we should presuppose the possibility of this *summum bonum*; and as this is possible only on condition of the existence of God, it inseparably connects the supposition of this with duty; that is, it is morally necessary to assume the existence of God.

It must be remarked here that this moral necessity is *subjective*, that is, it is a want, and not *objective*, that is, itself a duty, for there cannot be a duty to suppose the existence of anything (since this concerns only the theoretical employment of reason). Moreover, it is not meant by this that it is necessary to suppose the existence of God *as a basis of all obligation in general* (for this rests, as has been sufficiently proved, simply on the autonomy of reason itself). What belongs to duty here is only the endeavour to realize and promote the *summum bonum* in the world, the possibility of which can therefore be postulated; and as our reason finds it not conceivable except on the supposition of a supreme intelligence, the admission of this existence is therefore connected with the consciousness of our duty, although the admission itself belongs to the domain of speculative reason. Considered in respect of this alone, as a principle of explanation, it may be called a *hypothesis*, but in reference to the intelligibility of an object given us by the moral law (the *summum bonum*), and consequently of a requirement for practical purposes, it may be called *faith*, that is to say a pure *rational faith*, since pure reason (both in its theoretical and its practical use) is the sole source from which it springs.

From this *deduction* it is now intelligible why the *Greek* schools could never attain the solution of their problem of the practical possibility of the *summum bonum*, because they made the rule of the use which the will of man makes of his freedom the sole and sufficient ground of this possibility, thinking that they had no need for that purpose of the existence of God. No doubt they were so far right that they established the principle of morals of itself independently of this postulate, from the relation of reason only to the will, and consequently made it the *supreme* practical condition of the *summum bonum*; but it was not therefore the *whole* condition of its possibility. The *Epicureans* had indeed assumed as the supreme principle of morality a wholly false one, namely, that of happiness, and had substituted for a law a maxim of arbitrary choice according to every man's inclination; they proceeded, however, *consistently* enough in this, that they degraded their *summum bonum* likewise just in proportion to the meanness of their fundamental principle, and looked for no greater happiness than can be attained by human prudence (including temperance and moderation of the inclinations), and this, as we know, would be scanty enough and would be very different according to circumstances; not to mention the exceptions that their maxims must perpetually admit and which make them incapable of being laws. The *Stoics*, on the contrary, had chosen their supreme practical principle quite rightly, making virtue the condition of the *summum bonum*; but when they represented the degree of virtue required by its pure law as fully attainable in this life, they not only strained the moral powers of the *man* whom they called *the wise* beyond all the limits of his nature, and assumed a thing that contradicts all our knowledge of men, but also and principally they would not allow the second *element* of the *summum bonum*, namely, happiness, to be properly a special object of human desire, but made their *wise man*, like a divinity in his consciousness of the excellence of his person, wholly independent of nature (as regards his own contentment); they exposed him indeed to the evils of life, but made him not subject to them (at the same time representing him also as free from moral evil). They thus, in fact, left out the second element of the *summum bonum*, namely, personal happiness, placing it solely in action and satisfaction with one's own personal worth, thus including it in the consciousness of being morally minded, in which they might have been sufficiently refuted by the voice of their own nature.

The doctrine of Christianity,[1] even if we do not yet consider it as a religious doctrine, gives, touching this point, a conception of the *summum bonum* (the kingdom of God), which alone satisfies the strictest demand of practical reason. The moral law is holy (unyielding) and demands holiness of morals, although all the moral perfection to which man can attain is still only virtue, that is, a rightful disposition arising from *respect* for the law, implying consciousness of a constant propensity to transgression, or at least a want of purity, that is, a mixture of many spurious (not moral) motives of obedience to the law, consequently a self-esteem combined with humility. In respect, then, of the holiness which the Christian law requires, this leaves the creature nothing but a progress *in infinitum*, but for that very reason it justifies him in hoping for an endless duration of his existence. The *worth* of a character *perfectly* accordant with the moral law is infinite, since the only restriction on all possible happiness in the judgment of a wise and all-powerful distributor of it is the absence of conformity of rational beings to their duty. But the moral law of itself does not *promise* any happiness, for according to our conceptions of an order of nature in general, this is not necessarily connected with obedience to the law. Now Christian morality supplies this defect (of the second indispensable element of the *summum bonum*) by representing the world, in which rational beings devote themselves with all their soul to the moral law, as a *kingdom of God*, in which nature and morality are brought into a harmony foreign to each of itself, by a holy Author who makes the derived *summum bonum* possible. *Holiness*

---

[1] It is commonly held that the Christian precept of morality has no advantage in respect of purity over the moral conceptions of the Stoics; the distinction between them is, however, very obvious. The Stoic system made the consciousness of strength of mind the pivot on which all moral dispositions should turn; and although its disciples spoke of duties and even defined them very well, yet they placed the spring and proper determining principle of the will in an elevation of the mind above the lower springs of the senses, which owe their power only to weakness of mind. With them, therefore, virtue was a sort of heroism in the *wise man* who, raising himself above the animal nature of man, is sufficient for himself, and while he prescribes duties to others is himself raised above them, and is not subject to any temptation to transgress the moral law. All this, however, they could not have done if they had conceived this law in all its purity and strictness, as the precept of the Gospel does. When I give the name *idea* to a perfection to which nothing adequate can be given in experience, it does not follow that the moral ideas are something transcendent, that is something of which we could not even determine the concept adequately, or of which it is uncertain whether there is any object corresponding to it at all, as is the case with the ideas of speculative reason; on the contrary, being types of practical perfection, they serve as the indispensable rule of conduct and likewise as the *standard of comparison*. Now if I consider *Christian morals* on their philosophical side, then compared with the ideas of the Greek schools they would appear as follows: the ideas of the *Cynics*, the *Epicureans*, the *Stoics*, and the *Christians* are: *simplicity of nature, prudence, wisdom,* and *holiness*. In respect of the way of attaining them, the Greek schools were distinguished from one another thus, that the Cynics only required *common sense*, the others the path of *science*, but both found the mere *use of natural powers* sufficient for the purpose. Christian morality, because its precept is framed (as a moral precept must be) so pure and unyielding, takes from man all confidence that he can be fully adequate to it, at least in this life, but again sets it up by enabling us to hope that if we act as well as it is in our *power* to do, then what is not in our power will come in to our aid from another source, whether we know how this may be or not. *Aristotle* and *Plato* differed only as to the *origin* of our moral conceptions.

of life is prescribed to them as a rule even in this life, while the welfare proportioned to it, namely, *bliss*, is represented as attainable only in an eternity; because the *former* must always be the pattern of their conduct in every state, and progress towards it is already possible and necessary in this life; while the *latter*, under the name of happiness, cannot be attained at all in this world (so far as our own power is concerned), and therefore is made simply an object of hope. Nevertheless, the Christian principle of *morality* itself is not theological (so as to be heteronomy), but is autonomy of pure practical reason, since it does not make the knowledge of God and His will the foundation of these laws, but only of the attainment of the *summum bonum*, on condition of following these laws, and it does not even place the proper *spring* of this obedience in the desired results, but solely in the conception of duty, as that of which the faithful observance alone constitutes the worthiness to obtain those happy consequences.

In this manner the moral laws lead through the conception of the *summum bonum* as the object and final end of pure practical reason to *religion*, that is, to the *recognition of all duties as divine commands, not as sanctions, that is to say, arbitrary ordinances of a foreign will and contingent in themselves*, but as essential *laws* of every free will in itself, which, nevertheless, must be regarded as commands of the Supreme Being, because it is only from a morally perfect (holy and good) and at the same time all-powerful will, and consequently only through harmony with this will, that we can hope to attain the *summum bonum* which the moral law makes it our duty to take as the object of our endeavours. Here again, then, all remains disinterested and founded merely on duty; neither fear nor hope being made the fundamental springs, which if taken as principles would destroy the whole moral worth of actions. The moral law commands me to make the highest possible good in a world the ultimate object of all my conduct. But I cannot hope to effect this otherwise than by the harmony of my will with that of a holy and good Author of the world; and although the conception of the *summum bonum* as a whole, in which the greatest happiness is conceived as combined in the most exact proportion with the highest degree of moral perfection (possible in creatures), includes *my own happiness*, yet it is not this that is the determining principle of the will which is enjoined to promote the *summum bonum*, but the moral law, which, on the contrary, limits by strict conditions my unbounded desire of happiness.

Hence also morality is not properly the doctrine how we should *make* ourselves happy, but how we should become *worthy* of happiness. It is only when religion is added that there also comes in the hope of participating some day in happiness in proportion as we have endeavoured to be not unworthy of it.

A man is *worthy* to possess a thing or a state when his possession of it is in harmony with the *summum bonum*. We can now easily see that all worthiness depends on moral conduct, since in the conception of the *summum bonum* this constitutes the condition of the rest (which belongs to one's state), namely, the participation of happiness. Now it follows from this that *morality* should never be treated as a *doctrine of happiness*, that is, an instruction how to become happy; for it has to do simply with the rational condition (*conditio sine qua non*) of happiness, not with the means of attaining it. But when morality has been completely expounded (which merely imposes duties instead of providing rules for selfish desires), then first, after the moral desire to promote the *summum bonum* (to bring the kingdom of God to us) has been awakened, a desire founded on a law, and which could not previously arise in any selfish mind, and when for the behoof of this desire the step to religion has been taken, then this ethical doctrine may be also called a doctrine of happiness because the *hope* of happiness first begins with religion only.

We can also see from this that, when we ask what is *God's ultimate end* in creating the world, we must not name the *happiness* of the rational beings in it, but the *summum bonum*, which adds a further condition to that wish of such beings, namely, the condition of being worthy of happiness, that is, the *morality* of these same rational beings, a condition which alone contains the rule by which only they can hope to share in the former at the hand of a *wise* Author. For as *wisdom* theoretically considered signifies *the knowledge of the summum bonum*, and practically *the accordance of the will with the summum bonum*, we cannot attribute to a supreme independent wisdom an end based merely on *goodness*.[2] For we cannot conceive the action of this goodness (in respect of the happiness of rational beings) as suitable to the highest original good, except under the restrictive conditions of harmony with the holiness of His will. Therefore those who placed the end of creation in the glory of God (provided that this is not conceived anthropomorphically as a desire to be praised) have perhaps hit upon the best expression. For nothing glorifies God more than that which is the most estimable thing in the world, respect for His command, the observance of the holy duty that His law imposes on us, when there is added thereto His glorious plan of crowning such a beautiful order of things with corresponding happiness. If the latter (to speak humanly) makes Him worthy of love, by the *former* He is an object of adoration. Even men can never acquire respect by benevolence alone, though they may gain love, so that the greatest beneficence only procures them honour when it is regulated by worthiness.

That in the order of ends, man (and with him every rational being) is *an end in himself*, that is, that he can never be used merely as a means by any (not even by God) without being at the same time an end also himself, that therefore *humanity*

---

[2] In order to make these characteristics of these conceptions clear, I add the remark that whilst we ascribe to God various attributes, the quality of which we also find applicable to creatures, only that in Him they are raised to the highest degree, *e.g.* power, knowledge, presence, goodness, etc., under the designations of omnipotence, omniscience, omnipresence, etc., there are three that are ascribed to God exclusively, and yet without the addition of greatness, and which are all moral. He is the *only holy*, the *only blessed*, the *only wise*, because these conceptions already imply the absence of limitation. In the order of these attributes He is also the *holy lawgiver* (and creator), the *good governor* (and preserver), and the *just judge*, three attributes which include everything by which God is the object of religion, and in conformity with which the metaphysical perfections are added of themselves in the reason.

in our person must be *holy* to ourselves, this follows now of itself because he is the *subject of the moral law*, in other words, of that which is holy in itself, and on account of which and in agreement with which alone can anything be termed holy. For this moral law is founded on the autonomy of his will, as a free will which by its universal laws must necessarily be able to agree with that to which it is to submit itself.

Translated by Thomas Kingsmill Abbott

24

Johann Gottlieb Fichte, 'On the Foundation of Our Belief in a Divine Government of the World'
('Ueber den Grund unseres Glaubens an eine göttliche Weltregierung') (1798)

Just five years after the publication of Kant's controversial *Religion within the Limits of Reason Alone*, Fichte's essay 'On the Foundation of our Belief in a Divine Government of the World' appeared. In its central claims it is a Kantian piece: following Kant, Fichte argues that the very end at which our moral actions aim, perfection, supports our belief in the existence of God, and we would not pursue moral actions, Fichte thinks, without the certainty that perfection is possible. But since perfection is not empirically realisable, its nature must be divine. Fichte also follows Kant in thinking of morality and freedom as two sides of the same coin (though his presentation is more dogmatic than that of his predecessor).

Typically, Fichte's position can be understood as his effort to systematise Kant: to introduce what he perceives as the need for logical order in the critical philosophy. That is, what Kant argues in *Religion within the Limits of Reason Alone* and in parts of the *Critique of Practical Reason* is given 'systematic form', in Fichte's sense. And Fichte's notion of system, as is evident from the *Science of Knowledge*, involves a series of deductions. His explanation of the validity of our belief in the Divine starts with the certainty of our self-awareness of freedom, which is equivalent to awareness of self and also, he thinks, equivalent to awareness of our moral vocation. Morality, he goes on, is a practical matter: it involves acting towards some end, an end which we know to be possible. In the case of morality that end is a morally perfect order, and the grounds of our belief in this certainty – without which, he claims we could not even begin to act morally – is the divine order. Fichte sees his own position as the elucidation of claims which lie implicit in certain self-evident elements of experience (matters of faith, in Fichte's sense, in that they do not come into being through argument).

In Fichte's view this argument is a compelling explanation of the validity of the concept of God. However, shockingly for Fichte, the article was to lead to his dismissal from the professorship of philosophy at the University of Jena on the charge that it supported atheism. This was an event of no small significance. It was also a very great irony as it was a Kantian treatment of religion and morality – in the book *Attempt at a Critique of All Revelation* (1792) – that had effectively gained Fichte the position at Jena. Fichte was considered among the major philosophers in the German world at the time of this controversy. When we examine Fichte's article the reasons for the dismissal seem rather unfortunate: the dismissal is not entirely to be traced back to what Fichte actually said. Context, carelessness and arrogance conjoined. The article appeared in the *Philosophisches Journal* of which Fichte (with Friedrich Niethammer) was co-editor. However, alongside it was published an article by Friedrich Forberg, a follower in certain respects of the critical philosophy (his article was entitled, 'On the Development of the Concept of Religion') which also contained the Kantian elements above, but it drew from Kant conclusions more radical than what Fichte himself could have conceded. Forberg considered that God as a practical postulate was nothing more than an idea, and it was not necessary to posit any reality behind this idea. The claim for atheism was made. Fichte following Kant should not have ostensibly accepted this (by not publicly repudiating it) because it contains the problem that were the idea of perfection merely a human convention it could not provide the motivations required for morality. In short, Fichte should have made it clear that on this specific point he diverged from the bold Forberg.

Fichte's carelessness was to prove costly. His official sanctionable mistake was to have published Forberg and to have responded to Forberg's article in 'On the Foundation of Our Belief in a Divine Government of the World' without criticism, indeed with considerable praise (referring to Forberg as 'an excellent Philosopher'). He saw Forberg's article as coinciding on many points with his own views, though he did not specify which points. The element of arrogance was Fichte's antagonising polemic against the metaphysical assumptions behind the orthodox scholastic view of God. He mockingly describes the notion of God the creator as 'an unintelligible pronouncement' and 'a few empty words'. All that we can say and defend, Fichte thinks, is that we believe in God as the reality that necessarily supports all of our endeavours at moral perfection. For him rejection of the scholastic metaphysics was rejection of a merely philosophical and existentially irrelevant idea of God, a rejection which he believed had no atheistic entailment. The context of these disputes was a reactionary attitude among orthodox theologians already troubled by the anti-metaphysical implications of the critical philosophy.

In Fichte's essay there is an implicit problematisation of the notion of transcendence, a metaphysical notion which he implicitly derides. (It is difficult to distinguish Fichte from Kant here: the *Critique of Pure Reason* also rules out the philosophical justification of the idea of God as substance. However Kant was the more cautious in his representation of this idea.) This problematisation turned out to have momentous significance for the subsequent development of post-Kantian German Idealism. Fichte's claim that God or the Divine is effectively bound up with certain interested actions of human beings was – as his accusers feared – the reduction of the divine to the course of human history, particularly rational history. From this thesis, thus expressed, the systematic philosophies of Schelling and Hegel would emerge.

ON THE FOUNDATION OF OUR BELIEF IN A DIVINE GOVERNMENT OF THE WORLD[†]

The author of the present essay has for some time recognized it as his duty to set before a larger public the results of his philosophical work on the above subject. Hitherto this has been made available only to the auditors of his academic lectures. He had intended to present his ideas on this subject with the definiteness and precision that is appropriate to the sanctity which it possesses for so many honorable persons. Unfortunately the author's time was occupied with other tasks and the execution of his plan had to be repeatedly postponed.

As coeditor of the present journal, the author is obliged to put before the public the following essay of an excellent philosopher[1] and this has facilitated the execution of the plan just mentioned. The [Forberg's] essay coincides on many points with the present author's own convictions and hence he can on several matters simply refer the reader to it as an exposition of his own position as well. In other respects, however, the [Forberg's] essay, although not exactly opposed to the present author's views, has not quite reached the latter's position; and this makes it imperative to make the present writer's position publicly known, especially since he believes that his special intellectual approach involves more basic issues than those usually raised by philosophers. However, for the time being nothing more is attempted than a sketch of this approach. A more elaborate treatment will have to wait for another occasion.

The tendency to treat the so-called moral proof or any of the other arguments for the existence of God as genuine proofs has been a source of almost universal confusion and is likely to remain so for a long time. The assumption is apparently made that belief in God was for the first time given to the human race by means of such argumentation. Poor philosophy! I should like to know how your representatives who, after all, are also only human beings obtain what they wish to give us by means of their proofs; or if these representatives are in fact beings of a higher nature, one wonders how they can count on obtaining acceptance and understanding in us others without presupposing something analogous to their belief. No, this is not how things stand. Philosophy can explain facts – it cannot

---

[†]*FW* V, 177–188. In *Nineteenth Century Philosophy* (New York, Free Press, 1969), ed. Patrick L. Gardiner.
[1] Fichte here refers to Forberg's 'Entwickelung des Begriffs der Religion' ('The Development of the Concept of Religion'), which was published in the same issue of the *Philosophisches Journal*.

bring them into existence except for the one fact of philosophy itself. As little as it will occur to the philosopher to persuade mankind to believe from now on in the existence of material objects in space or to treat the changes of these objects as successive events in time, so little should he be inclined to persuade mankind to believe in a divine government of the world. All of this happens without any persuasion on the philosopher's part and he accepts these facts without question. It is the business of the philosopher to deduce these facts as necessarily implied in the essence of rational beings as such. Hence our procedure must not be regarded as a conversion of the unbeliever but as a deduction of the believer's conviction. Our only task is to deal with the causal question, 'How does man arrive at his belief?'

In dealing with this question it is essential to realize that this belief must not be represented as an arbitrary assumption which a human being may make or not make as he sees fit – as a freely chosen decision to take as true what the heart desires and because the heart desires it and as a supplement or substitute for the insufficiency of the available logical arguments. What is founded in reason is absolutely necessary; and what is not necessary is therefore a violation of reason. A person who regards the latter as fact is a deluded dreamer, however pious his attitude may be.

Where now will the philosopher, who presupposes belief in God, search for the necessary ground which he is supposed to furnish? Should he base himself on the alleged necessity with which the existence or the nature of the world of the senses implies a rational author? The answer must be an emphatic 'no'. For he knows only too well that such an inference is totally unwarranted, although misguided thinkers have made such a claim in their embarrassment to explain something whose existence they cannot deny but whose true ground is hidden from them. The original understanding, which is placed under the guardianship of reason and the direction of its mechanism, is incapable of such a step. One may regard the world of the senses either from the point of view of commonsense which is also that of the natural sciences or else from the transcendental standpoint. In the former case reason is required to stop at the existence of the world as something absolute: the world exists simply because it does and it is the way it is simply because it is that way. From this point of view something absolute is accepted and this absolute being simply is the universe: the two are identical. The universe is regarded as a whole which is grounded in itself and complete by itself. From this point of view, the world is an organized and organizing whole containing the ground of all phenomena within itself and its immanent laws. If, while occupying the standpoint of the pure natural sciences, we demand an explanation of the existence and nature of the universe in terms of an intelligent cause, our demand is total nonsense. Moreover, the assertion that an intelligent being is the author of the world of the senses does not help us in the least – it is not really an intelligible pronouncement and what we get are a few empty words instead of a genuine answer to a question that should not have been raised in the first place. An intelligent being is unquestionably constituted by thoughts; and the first intelligible word has yet to be spoken on the subject of how, in the monstrous system of a creation out of nothing, thoughts can be transmuted into matter, or how, in a system that is hardly more rational, the world can become what it is as the result of the action of thoughts upon self-sufficient eternal matter.

It may be admitted that these difficulties vanish if we adopt the transcendental standpoint. There is then no longer an independent world: everything is now simply a reflection of our inner activity. However, one cannot inquire into the ground of something that does not exist and we cannot thus assume something outside of it in terms of which it is to be explained.

We cannot start from the world of the senses in order to climb to the notion of a moral world order so long, that is, as we really start with the sense-world and do not surreptitiously introduce a moral order into it.

Our belief in a moral world order must be based on the concept of a supersensible world.

There is such a concept. I find myself free from any influence of the sense-world, absolutely active in and through myself, and hence I am a power transcending all that is sensuous. This freedom is not, however, indefinite: it has its purpose, and this is not a purpose received from the outside but rather one posited by the free self from its inner nature. My own self and my necessary goal are the supersensible reality.

I cannot doubt this freedom or its nature without giving up my own self.

I cannot doubt this, I say – I cannot even think of the possibility that things are not this way, that this inner voice might deceive me and that it requires to be authorized and justified by reference to something external. Concerning this insight I cannot engage in any further rationalizations, interpretations, or explanations. It is what is absolutely positive and categorical.

I cannot transcend this insight unless I decide to destroy my inner nature – I cannot question it because I cannot *will* to question it. Here is the limit to the otherwise untamed flight of reason – here we find the voice that constrains the intellect because it also constrains the heart. Here is the point where thinking and willing are united and where harmony is brought into my being. I could indeed question the insight concerning my freedom if I wanted to fall into contradiction with my own self, for there is no immanent limitation confining the reasoning faculty: it freely advances into the infinite and must be able to do this since I am free in all my utterances and only I myself can set a limit to myself through my own will. Our moral vocation is therefore itself the outcome of a moral attitude and it is identical with our faith. One is thus quite right in maintaining that faith is the basis of all certainty. This is how it must be; since morality, if it is really morality, can be constructed only out of itself and not out of any logically coercive argumentation.

I could question the insight of my moral freedom if I were ready to plunge into a bottomless abyss (if only in a theoretical fashion); if I were ready to forego absolutely any firm point of reference; if I were prepared to do without that certainty that accompanies all my thinking and without which I could not even set out on speculative inquiries. For there is no firm point of reference except the one indicated here: it is founded in the moral sentiment and not in logic; if our rational faculty does not get to it or else proceeds beyond it, the result is that we find ourselves in an unbounded ocean in which each wave is pushed along by some other wave.

By adopting the goal set before me by my own nature, and by making it the purpose of my real activity, I ipso facto posit the possibility of achieving this purpose through my actions. The two statements are identical – to adopt something as my purpose means that I posit it as something real at some future time; if something is posited as real, its possibility is thereby necessarily implied. I must, if I am not to deny my own nature, first set myself the execution of this goal: and I must, secondly assume that it can be realized. There is not here really a first and a second but rather an absolute one: they are not two acts but the one indivisible act dictated by the moral sentiment.

One should note the absolute necessity of what has here been shown. (The reader is requested to grant me for the moment that the possibility of realizing the ultimate moral goal has been demonstrated.) We are not dealing with a wish, a hope, a piece of reflection and consideration, of grounds pro and con, a free decision to assume something whose opposite one also regards as possible. Given the decision to obey the laws of one's inner nature, the assumption is strictly necessary: it is immediately contained in the decision; it is in fact that decision.

One should also observe the logical sequence of the ideas here presented. The inference is not from possibility to reality, but the other way around. Our contention is not: I ought since I can; it is rather: I can since I ought. That I ought and what I ought to do comes first and is most immediately evident. It requires no further explanation, justification, or authorization. It is intrinsically true and evident. It is not based on or conditioned by any other truth, but on the contrary all other truths are conditioned by it. This logical order has frequently been overlooked. A person who maintains that I must first know whether I can do something before I can judge that I ought to do it, is thereby, if he is making a practical judgment, negating the primacy of the moral law and hence the moral law itself, while, if he is making a theoretical judgment, he thereby totally misconstrues the original sequence of our rational processes.

To say that I must simply adopt the goal of morality, that its realization is possible and possible through me, means that every action which I ought to perform and the circumstances that condition such an action are means to my adopted goal. It is in the light of this that my existence, the existence of other moral beings and of the world of the senses as our common stage receive their relation to morality. A wholly new order is thus brought into being and the sense-world with all its immanent laws is no more than the support underlying this order. The world of the senses proceeds in its course according to its eternal laws in order to provide freedom with a sphere of operation, but it does not have the slightest influence on morality or immorality, it does not in any way control a free being. The latter soars above all nature in self-sufficiency and independence. The realization of the purpose of reason can be accomplished only through the efforts of free beings, but because of a higher law this purpose will unquestionably be attained. It is possible to do what is right and every situation is geared to this through the higher law just mentioned: because of this law the moral deed succeeds infallibly and the immoral deed fails just as certainly. The entire universe now exhibits a totally different appearance to us.

This change in appearance will be further illuminated if we raise ourselves to the transcendental viewpoint. Transcendental theory teaches that the world is nothing but the sensuous appearance, given according to intelligible rational laws, of our own inner activity, our own intelligence operating within boundaries that must remain incomprehensible; and a human being cannot be blamed if he has an uncanny feeling when faced with the total disappearance of the ground underneath him. The boundaries just mentioned are admittedly beyond our understanding as far as their origin is concerned. However, practical philosophy teaches that this does not significantly affect anything of practical importance. The boundaries are the clearest and most certain of all things – they determine our fixed position in the moral arrangement of things. What you perceive as a consequence of your position in this moral order has reality and, moreover, the only reality that concerns you: it is the permanent interpretation of the injunction of your duty, the living expression of what you ought to do simply because you ought to do it. Our world is the sensualized material of our duty; the latter is the truly real in things, the genuine primal stuff of all appearances. The compulsion with which our belief in things is forced upon us is a moral compulsion – the only one that can be exerted upon a free being. Nobody can, without destruction of his nature, surrender his moral calling to such a degree that it cannot preserve him, within the limits previously mentioned, for a higher and nobler future state. Considered as the result of a moral world order, this belief in the reality of the sense-world can even be regarded as a kind of revelation. It is our duty that is revealed in the world of the senses.

This is the true faith: this moral order is *the Divine* which we accept. It is constituted by acting rightly. This is the only possible confession of faith: to do what duty prescribes and to do this gaily and naturally, without doubt or calculation of consequences. As a result, this Divine becomes alive and real in us; every one of our deeds is performed in the light of this presupposition and all their consequences will be preserved in the Divine.

True atheism, unbelief and godlessness in the real sense, consists in calculation of consequences, in refusing to obey the voice of one's conscience until one thinks one can foresee the success of one's actions and in thus elevating one's own judgment above that of God and in making oneself into God. He who wills to do evil in order to produce good is a godless person. Under a moral government of the world good cannot come out of evil; and as certainly as one believes in the former, so one cannot believe the latter. You must not lie even, as a result, the world were to collapse and become a heap of ruins. But this last is only a manner of speaking: if you were permitted to believe seriously that the world would collapse, then at the very least your own nature would be self-contradictory and self-destroying. In fact you do not believe this, you cannot believe it, and you are not even permitted to believe it: you know that the plan of the world's preservation does not contain a lie.

The faith just stated is the whole and complete faith. This living and effective moral order is identical with God. We do not and cannot grasp any other God. There is no rational justification for going beyond this moral world order and for inferring the existence of a separate entity as its cause. Our original reason certainly does not make any such inference and it does not know any such separate entity – only a philosophy that misunderstands its own nature draws such an inference. Is this moral world order no more than a contingent entity, something that might not be, that might be as it is or otherwise so that its existence and nature requires to be explained in terms of a cause, so that belief in it requires to be legitimized by showing its ground? If you will stop listening to the demands of a worthless system and if instead you will consult your own inner nature, then you will find that the moral world order is the absolute beginning of all objective knowledge (just as your freedom and your moral vocation are the absolute beginning of all subjective knowledge) and all other objective knowledge must be founded and conditioned by it, while the moral world order itself cannot be conditioned by anything else, since outside of it there is nothing else. You cannot even attempt the explanation [of the moral order] without falsifying and endangering the nature of the original assumption. The assumption of a moral world order is such that it is absolutely self-evident and it does not tolerate any supporting arguments. Yet you wish to make the assumption dependent on such argumentation.

And this ratiocination, how can you succeed with it? After you have undermined the immediate conviction, how do you then proceed to fortify it? Indeed, it does not stand well with your faith if you can embrace it only on condition that it has an external source and if it collapses in the absence of such a support.

Even if one were to permit you to draw this inference and, as a consequence, to conclude that an author of the moral world order exists, what would that conclusion amount to? This entity is supposed to be distinct from you and from the world, it is supposed to engage in activities in the world in accordance with its plans and must therefore be capable of having ideas, of having personality and consciousness. But what do you mean by 'personality' and 'consciousness'? It is plain that when you use these words, you refer to what you have found and come to know in yourself under these labels. The least attention to these notions will teach you that they can be properly employed only if what they refer to is limited and finite. You therefore make the entity to which you apply these predicates into something finite. You have not, as you intended to, succeeded in thinking about God – you have merely multiplied yourself in your thoughts. You can no more explain the moral world order by reference to this entity than by reference to yourself: the moral world order remains unexplained and absolute as before. Indeed, in talking the way you do, you have not engaged in any genuine thinking at all, but you have merely disturbed the air with empty sounds. You could have predicted this outcome without difficulty. You are a finite being and how can that which is finite grasp and understand the infinite?

If faith keeps to what is immediately given, it remains firm and unshakable; if it is made dependent on the concept [of the personal God just discussed] then it becomes shaky, for the concept is impossible and full of contradictions.

It is therefore a misunderstanding to maintain that it is doubtful whether or not there is a God. On the contrary, that there is a moral world order, that in this order a definite position has been assigned to every rational individual and that his work counts, that the destiny of every person (unless it is the consequence of his own conduct) is derived from this plan, that without this plan no hair drops from a head, nor a sparrow from a roof, that every good deed succeeds while every evil one fails and that everything must go well for those who love only the good – all this is not doubtful at all but the most certain thing in the world and the basis of all other certainty, in fact the only truth that is objectively absolutely valid. On the other side, anybody who reflects just a moment and who is candid about the outcome of this reflection cannot doubt that the concept of God as a separate substance is impossible and contradictory. It is permissible to say this openly and put down the idle chatter of the schools in order to elevate the true religion of joyful morality.

[...]

Translated by Paul Edwards
(with minor changes)

25

F. W. J. Schelling, The Ages of the World (Die Weltalter): *The Eternal Life of the Godhead (1815)*

Some of Schelling's most audacious philosophical theology is to be found in a work which was posthumously published under the title *The Ages of the World*. It is a work of Schelling's middle period which, like *Philosophical Investigations into the Essence of Human Freedom* (see section 8), addresses, amongst other things, the tension produced by idealist philosophy between the notion of rational totality (the idea of a fully determinable reality) and the possibility of freedom, that is, of undetermined action. This issue – a pressing question ever since Kant's discussion of the Third Antinomy of Freedom – is considered, however, with specific reference to God's freedom.

It is not possible to summarise the general character of *The Ages of the World*. There are various reasons for this. First, Schelling never completed it: he drafted a number of versions during the 1810s and 1820s – the section reprinted here comes from 1815 – before finally abandoning the project of systematic philosophy. It therefore lacks the logical smoothness of some of Schelling's other works. Second, there is the question of genre. One of Schelling's translators makes the suggestion that *The Ages of the World* is a 'philosophical poem about the rotary movement of natality and fatality, pain and joy, comedy and tragedy within God, that is, within the whole of Being, itself'.[1] It may be that because Schelling's philosophical work at this time was conducted outside academia that he decided to write primarily for himself, as opposed to an audience of students and critics. None of this should make us think, however, that the *Ages of the World* does not contain traditional philosophical questions. Schelling's speculations on God's nature and self-revelation will be familiar territory to any reader acquainted with the broad scholastic and rationalist traditions of philosophy.

Schelling introduces the work with a few polemical remarks against the subjective idealist starting point which he sees as 'an empty misuse of the noble gift of speaking and thinking'.[2] Philosophy – 'science' – must turn to 'objectivity with respect to its object' as an explanatory discipline.[3] The idea of a philosophy which can comprehend the inner and its other in a single system – an objective idealism – is still important to Schelling. As he puts

---

[1] Jason M. Wirth, 'Translator's Introduction' to F. W. J. Schelling, *The Ages of the World* (Albany, NY: State University of New York Press, 2000), p. x.

[2] Schelling, *The Ages of the World*, p. xxxv (*SSW* VIII, 199).

[3] Schelling, *The Ages of the World*, p. xxxv (*SSW* VIII, 200).

it: 'The most supersensible thoughts now receive physical power and life and, vice versa, nature becomes ever more the visible imprint of the highest concepts'.[4]

Schelling is clearly interested – as evidenced in the selected text – in considering God within some kind of predicate theory, a theory required to make sense of the idea of God as both 'freedom and necessity'. A similar problem in the so-called philosophy of God – and which Schelling addresses – is that of how existence can be ascribed to the perfect being given that what is in being is essentially imperfect: 'Supreme Being is for itself groundless and borne by nothing'. Schelling's typically dialectical claim is that God contains an inner antithesis of freedom and necessity, which in some way exhibits itself in our human experience of being, albeit that this antithesis manifests itself as a tension between the 'affirmative' and the 'negative' (a thought already expressed in *Philosophical Investigations into the Essence of Human Freedom*). The same tension, Schelling alleges, has led to one-sided philosophising in which thought rather than being – which are the positive and the negative respectively – has been given systematic pre-eminence.

In a later section of the book – section C of the First Book – the discussions of the original antithesis and unity of God is furthered. Schelling describes the Godhead as simultaneously Yes and No. These are earlier explained as follows: Yes, in that it is 'without change or alteration in itself, not because its purity is sublimated, rather because the Godhead is this highest purity and freedom. The Godhead is this without any movement, in the deepest silence, immediately by virtue of itself';[5] No, in that it is 'an eternally wrathful force that tolerates no being outside of itself'.[6] These two properties are perfectly unified in the 'whole and undivided Godhead'. It is necessary, Schelling thinks, to offer a characterisation of God's attributes as a unified entity since without such an account we could not understand God's actions as the actions of a substantial being: the actions would be God's essence. Hence the need for a theory which explains the predicates (not accidents) of the God substance.

Taking up his long-standing fascination with the question of the historical event of revelation Schelling addresses complex questions about why and how God could have chosen to be revealed in time. The analysis offered by Schelling is extraordinarily abstract. However, he makes a number of claims which are both philosophically daring yet theologically orthodox. Schelling holds that the moment of revelation must be a decision; otherwise God would be without the power of revelation. His notion is that God is revealed – emerges from 'free eternity' – as the Yes and the No, that is, as essentially free and absolute. But, Schelling asks, how can God be both of these at the same time? How can God's unity be conceived? One of

---

[4] Schelling, *The Ages of the World*, p. xl (*SSW* VIII, 205).
[5] Schelling, *The Ages of the World*, pp. 73–4 (*SSW* VIII, 299).
[6] Schelling, *The Ages of the World*, p. 73 (*SSW* VIII, 299).

Schelling's proposals is that since God cannot be precisely Yes and No at the same time – the theory of predication that Schelling seems to rely on excludes this – then God is both *in* (not *at*) different times. These aspects of God are in a simultaneous relation of grounding each other: in the moment of revelation God as absolute was to be understood as the ground of God as freedom.

Schelling contends that God's self-revelation marks the beginning of time, time being contrasted with eternity. Hence we can think of God both as existing atemporally (in eternity) and, through revelation, as existing in time. Schelling goes on to develop this notion of time – or at least to suggest such a development – as revelation as a way of explaining what he sees as time and its epochs. (Hence the working title of the work.)

There is no doubt that Schelling's major theological claims are difficult to grasp. This might be explained by a fundamental tension between his views of God's agency and his simultaneous thesis of God's eternity. Our natural inclination is to see agency as precisely a temporal activity.

THE ETERNAL LIFE OF THE GODHEAD AS THE WHOLE OR THE CONSTRUCTION OF THE COMPLETE IDEA OF GOD[†]

Point of Entry: the Distinction between Necessity and Freedom in God

As with the coming time, God self-referentially [*fürsichtig*] shrouds the point of departure for the past beginning in dark night. It is not given to everyone to know the end and it is given to few to see the primordial beginnings of life and it is given to even fewer to think through the whole of things from beginning to end. Imitation, rather than the inner drive, leads to a research that confuses the senses as if by an inevitable fate. Hence, inner fortitude is necessary in order to keep a firm hold of the interrelation of movement from beginning to end. But they would then like, where only the deed decides, to arbitrate everything with peaceful and general concepts and to represent a history in which, as in reality, scenes of war and peace, pain and joy, deliverance and danger alternate as a mere series of thoughts.

There is a light in this darkness. Just as according to the old and almost hackneyed phrase that the person is the world writ small, so the events of human life, from the deepest to their highest consummation, must accord with the events of life in general. Certainly one who could write completely the history of their own

[†] *SSW* VIII, 207–233. *The Ages of the World* (Albany NY: State University of New York Press, 2000).

life would also have, in a small epitome, concurrently grasped the history of the cosmos. Most people turn away from what is concealed within themselves just as they turn away from the depths of the great life and shy away from the glance into the abysses of that past which are still in one just as much as the present.

All the more so and because I am conscious that I do not speak of something familiar or popular or of that which is in accord with what has been assumed, it seems necessary to me to recollect first and foremost the nature of all happenings, how everything begins in darkness, seeing that no one sees the goal, and so that a particular event is never intelligible by itself but rather that the whole entire transpired occurrence is intelligible. Then just as all history is not just experienced in reality or only in narration, it cannot be communicated, so to speak, all at once with a general concept. Whoever wants knowledge of history must accompany it along its great path, linger with each moment, and surrender to the gradualness of the development. The darkness of the spirit cannot be overcome suddenly or in one fell swoop. The world is not a riddle whose solution could be given with a single word. Its history is too elaborate to be brought, so to speak, as some seem to wish, to a few short, uncompleted propositions on a sheet of paper.

But to speak the truth, it is no less the case with true science than it is with history that there are no authentic propositions, that is, assertions that would have a value or an unlimited and universal validity in and for themselves or apart from the movement through which they are produced. Movement is what is essential to knowledge. When this element of life is withdrawn, propositions die like fruit removed from the tree of life. Absolute propositions, that is, those that are once and for all valid, conflict with the nature of true knowledge which involves progression. Let, then, the object of knowledge be A and then the first proposition that is asserted would be that 'A $=$ x is the case'. Now if this is unconditionally valid, that is, that 'A is always and exclusively only x,' then the investigation is finished. There is nothing further to add to it. But as certainly as the investigation is a progressive kind, it is certain that 'A $=$ x' is only a proposition with a limited validity. It may be valid in the beginning, but as the investigation advances, it turns out that 'A is not simply x'. It is also y, and it is therefore 'x $+$ y'. One errs here when one does not have a concept of a kind of true science. They take the first proposition, 'A $=$ x', as absolute and then they perhaps get, or have in mind from somewhere else in experience, that it would be the case that 'A $=$ y'. Then they immediately oppose the second proposition to the first instead of waiting until the incompleteness of the first proposition would demand, from itself, the advance to the second proposition. For they want to conceive of everything in one proposition, and so they must only grant nothing short of an absolute thesis and, in so doing, sacrifice science. For where there is no succession, there is no science.

From this it seems evident that in true science, each proposition has only a definite and, so to speak, local meaning, and that one who has withdrawn the determinate place and has made the proposition out to be something absolute (dogmatic), either loses sense and meaning, or gets tangled up in contradictions. Then insofar as method is a kind of progression, it is clear that here method is inseparable from the being [*Wesen*] and, outside of this or without this, the matter is also lost. Whoever then believes that they may make the very last the very first and vice versa, or that they can reformulate the proposition that ought only be valid in a particular place into something general or unlimited, may thereby indeed arouse enough confusion and contradictions for the ignorant. But in so doing, they have not actually touched the matter itself, much less damaged it.

God is the oldest of beings – so Thales of Miletus is already purported to have judged. But the concept of God is of great, nay, of the very greatest, range, and is not to be expressed with a single word. Necessity and freedom are in God. Necessity is already recognized when a necessary existence is ascribed to God. To speak naturally, there is necessity insofar as it is before freedom, because a being must first exist before it could act freely. Necessity lies at the foundation of freedom and is in God itself what is first and oldest, insofar as such a distinction can take place in God, which will have to be cleared up through further consideration. Even though the God who is necessary is the God who is free, both are still one and the same. What is a being from nature and what is as such through freedom are completely different. If God were already everything from necessity, then God would be nothing through freedom. And yet God is, according to general consensus, the most voluntaristic being.

Everyone recognizes that God would not be able to create beings outside of itself from a blind necessity in God's nature, but rather with the highest voluntarism. To speak even more exactly, if it were left to the mere capacity of God's necessity, then there would be no creatures because necessity refers only to God's existence as God's own existence. Therefore, in creation, God overcomes the necessity of its nature through freedom and it is freedom that comes above necessity not necessity that comes above freedom.

What is necessary in God we call the nature of God. Its relationship to freedom is similar (but not identical) to the relationship that the Scriptures teach is between the natural and the spiritual life of the person. What is understood here by 'natural' is not simply the by and large 'physical', that is, the corporeal. The soul and the spirit, as well as the body, if not born again, that is, elevated to a different and higher life, belong to the 'natural'. The entirety of Antiquity knows as little as do the Scriptures of the abstract concept of nature.

Even this 'nature' of God is living, nay, it is the highest vitality, and it is not to be expressed so bluntly. Only by progressing from the simple to the complex, through gradual creation, could we hope to reach the full concept of this vitality.

Everyone agrees that the Godhead is the Supreme Being, the purest Love, infinite communicativity and emanation. Yet at the same time they want it to exist as such. But Love does not reach Being [*Seyn*] from itself. Being is ipseity [*Seinheit*], particularity. It is dislocation. But Love has nothing to do with particularity. Love does not seek its own [*das Ihre*] and therefore it cannot be that which has being [*seyend seyn*] with regard to itself. In the same way, a Supreme Being is for itself groundless and borne by nothing. It is in itself the antithesis of personality and therefore another force, moving toward personality, must first make it a ground.

An equivalently eternal force of selfhood, of egoity [*Egoität*], is required so that the being which is Love might exist as its own and might be for itself.

Therefore, two principles are already in what is necessary of God: the outpouring, outstretching, self-giving being, and an equivalently eternal force of selfhood, of retreat into itself, of Being in itself. That being and this force are both already God itself, without God's assistance.

It is not enough to see the antithesis. It must also be recognized that what has been set against each other has the same essentiality and originality. The force with which the being closes itself off, denies itself, is actual in its kind as the opposite principle. Each has its own root and neither can be deduced from the other. If this were so, then the antithesis would again immediately come to an end. But it is impossible *per se* that an exact opposite would derive from its exact opposite.

Indeed, humans show a natural predilection for the affirmative just as much as they turn away from the negative. Everything that is outpouring and goes forth from itself is clear to them. They cannot grasp as straightforwardly that which closes itself off and takes itself, even though it is equivalently essential and it encounters them everywhere and in many forms. Most people would find nothing more natural than if everything in the world were to consist of pure gentleness and goodness, at which point they would soon become aware of the opposite. Something inhibiting, something conflicting, imposes itself everywhere: this Other is that which, so to speak, should not be and yet is, nay, must be. It is this No that resists the Yes, this darkening that resists the light, this obliquity that resists the straight, this left that resists the right, and however else one has attempted to express this eternal antithesis in images. But it is not easy to be able to verbalize it or to conceive it at all scientifically.

The existence of such an eternal antithesis could not elude the first deeply feeling and deeply sensitive people. Already finding this duality in the primordial beginnings of nature but finding its source nowhere among that which is visible, early on one had to say to oneself that the ground of the antithesis is as old as, nay, is even older than, the world; that, just as in everything living, so already in that which is primordially living, there is a doubling that has come down, through many stages, to that which has determined itself as what appears to us as light and darkness, masculine and feminine, spiritual and corporeal. Therefore, the oldest teachings straightforwardly represented the first nature as a being with two conflicting modes of activity.

But in later times, ages more and more alienated from that primordial feeling, the attempt was often made to annihilate the antithesis right at its source, namely, to sublimate the antithesis right at its beginning as one sought to trace one of the conflicting modes back to the other and then sought to derive it from that other. In our age, this was true especially for the force that is set against the spiritual. The antithesis in the end received the most abstract expression, that of thinking and Being. In this sense, Being always stood in opposition to thinking as something impregnable, so that the Philosophy that would explain everything found nothing more difficult than to provide an explanation for precisely this Being. They had to explain this incomprehensibility, this active counterstriving against all thinking, this active darkness, this positive inclination toward darkness. But they preferred to have done away entirely with the discomforting and to resolve fully the incomprehensible in comprehension or (like Leibniz) in representation [*Vorstellung*].

Idealism, which really consists in the denial and nonacknowledgment of that negating primordial force, is the universal system of our times. Without this force, God is that empty infinite that modern philosophy has put in its stead. Modern Philosophy names God the most unlimited being (*ens illimitatissimum*), without thinking that the impossibility of any limit outside of God cannot sublimate that there may be something in God through which God cuts itself off from itself, in a way making itself finite (to an object) for itself. Being infinite is for itself not a perfection. It is rather the marker of that which is imperfect. The perfected is precisely the in itself full, concluded, finished.

Yet also to know the antithesis is not enough if, at the same time, the unity of the being is not known, or if it is not known that, indeed, the antithesis is *one and the same*, that it is the affirmation and the negation, that which pours out and that which holds on. The concept of a connection [*Zusammenhang*] or of anything similar to that is much too weak for the thought that should be expressed here. The merely various can also connect. Precisely that which is set in opposition can only be essentially and, so to speak, personally, 'one,' insofar as it is only the individual nature of the person that is able to unite that which is in conflict. But if one wanted to call everything that is not one and the same a connection, then one would have to say of a person who appears gentle, then wrathful, that the gentle person connects to the wrathful person in them, although, according to the truth, they are one and the same person.

If someone wanted to say further: it is a contradiction that something is *one and the same* and also the exact opposite of itself, then they would have to explain this principle more precisely since, as is known, Leibniz already disputed the absoluteness of this still always repeated rule. Thereupon they might want to consider that a contradiction might not be precisely what one would want.

The authentic, essential contradiction would be immediately sublimated again, or, rather, transformed into something merely formal and literal, if the unity of the being were taken to mean that that which has been set apart are themselves one and the same. Even the most slipshod expression: the Yes is also the No, the Ideal is also the Real, and vice versa, would not justify this imbecilic explanation because in no judgment whatsoever, not even in the merely tautological, is it expressed that the combined (the subject and the predicate) are one and the same. Rather, there is only an identity of the being, of the link (of the copula). The true meaning of every judgment, for instance, A is B, can only be this: *that which* is A is *that which* is B, or *that which* is A and *that which* is B are one and the same. Therefore, a doubling already lies at the bottom of the simple concept: A in this judgment is not A, but 'something = x, that A is'. Likewise, B is not B, but 'something = x, that B is', and not this (not A and B for themselves) but the 'x that is A' and 'the x that is B' is one and the same, that is, the same x. There are actually three propositions contained in the above cited proposition. The first, 'A = x', the second, 'B = x', and, following first from this, the third', A and B are one and the same', that is, 'both are x'.

It follows from itself that the link in judgment is what is essential and that which lies at the bottom of all the parts. The subject and the predicate are each for themselves already a unity and what one by and large calls the copula just indicates the unity of these unities. Furthermore, the judgment is then already exemplified in the simple concept and the conclusion is already contained in the judgment. Hence, the concept is just the furled judgment and the conclusion is the unfurled judgment. These remarks are written here for a future and most highly desirable treatment of the noble art of reason because the knowledge of the general laws of judgment must always accompany the highest science. But one does not philosophize for novices or for those ignorant of this art. Rather, they are to be sent away to school where, as in other arts, no one easily dares to put forward or to assess a musical work who has not learned the first rules of a musical movement.

Hence, it is certainly impossible that the Ideal *as such* is ever the Real and vice versa, and that the Yes is ever a No and that the No is ever a Yes. To assert this would mean sublimating human comprehension, the possibility of expressing oneself, even the contradiction itself. But it is certainly possible that one and the same = x is both Yes and No, Love and Wrath, Leniency and Strictness.

Perhaps some now already locate the contradiction here. But the correctly understood principle of contradiction actually only says as much as that the same *as the same* could not be something and also the opposite of that something. But the principle of contradiction does not disallow that the same, which is A, can be an other that is not A (*contradictio debet esse ad idem*). The same person can be called, for example, good in accordance with their character or in their actions and *as this*, namely, likewise in accord with their character or in their actions, cannot be evil. But this does not disallow that they might be evil in accord with what in them is not in their character or active. In this manner, two contradictory, self-opposed predicates can certainly be ascribed to that person. Expressed in other words this would mean: of two things exactly opposed that are stated of one and the same thing, according to the law of contradiction, if one is in force as the active and as that which has being, then the other must become that which is respectively not acting, Being.

Now, what here should be, actually and in the strictest sense, that which is opposed yet is 'one and the same = x', is the affirming and negating force. It therefore appears that when both *actually* become one, the one or the other would have to become that which respectively does not have Being and is not acting – something like (because this seems to most people to be something hostile) the negating force.

But the original equivalence (equipollence) between both of them now appears between them. Since each, by nature, is equally originary and equally essential, each also has the same claim to be that which has being. Both hold their own weight and neither by nature yields to the other.

Therefore, it is conceded that of that which has been opposed, if they indeed become one, only one of them would be active and the other would be passive. But, enabled by the equivalence of both, it follows that if one is passive, then the other must be so also, and, likewise, if one is active, then, absolutely, the other must also be active. But this is impossible in one and the same unity. Here each can only be either active or passive. Hence, it only follows from that necessity that the one unity decomposes into two unities, the simple antithesis (that we may designate as A and B) intensifies itself into that which has been doubled. It does not follow that in God one force is active and the other is inactive, but rather that God itself is of two different kinds; first the negating force (B) that represses the affirmative being (A), positing it as the inwardly passive or as what is hidden; second, the outstretching, self-communicating being that in clear contrast holds down the negating power in itself and does not let it come outwardly into effect.

This can also be considered another way. That which has been set apart are already in themselves not to be brought apart. The negating and contracting force could not be for itself without something that it negates and contracts, and that which has been negated and contracted cannot be anything other than precisely that which is in itself affirmative and flowing from itself. Hence, this negating power dislocates itself from itself in order to be, so to speak, its own complete being. In turn, that potency which, in accordance with its nature, is spiritual and outstretching, could not persist as such were it not to have, at least in a hidden manner, a force of selfhood. Therefore, this also dislocates itself as its own being and, instead of the desired unity, there has now resulted two oppositionally posited unities located apart from one another.

Should we want to sacrifice one of the two, we would always thereby have given up one of the two principles itself. Because only one is active in it, each of these unities then conducts itself as this one, the first as B, the other as A. But were these equivalent such that neither could, by nature, take second place to the other, then also each of the two unities again maintains the equivalency and each has the same claim to be that which has being [*seyend zu seyn*].

And so then now if both of them were fully apart from one another and without reciprocal contact, then they would be the same as the two primordial beings in the Persian teaching, one being a power insisting on closure and the darkening of the being and the other insisting on its outstretching and revelation. Both do not conduct themselves as one, but as two Godheads.

But it still remains that 'one and the same = x' is both principles (A and B). But not just in accordance with the concept, but really and actually. Hence, 'the same = x' that is the two unities must again be the unity of both unities and with the intensified antithesis is found the intensified unity.

There still seems to be an unavoidable contradiction such that the two unities, having been set apart, should be posited as active and as one. And yet this still admits of resolution such that the unity here demanded has no other but the following meaning. That which has been set apart should be one, that is, a unity of the two is posited, but it is not concomitantly posited that they cease being that which has been set apart. Rather, insofar as there should be unity, there should also be antithesis. Or unity and antithesis should themselves again be in antithesis. But the antithesis is in and for itself no contradiction. It could be no more contradictory that there could be A as well as B, than that just as there is unity, there is antithesis. Again, these are, between themselves, equivalent. The antithesis can as little surrender to unity as unity can surrender to the antithesis.

The antithesis rests on this, that each of the two conflicting powers is a being for itself, a real *principle*. The antithesis is only as such if the two conflicting principles conduct themselves as actually independent and separate from each other. That there should be both antithesis and unity therefore means as much as: that of the negating principle, the affirming principle, and, again, the unity of both, each of these three should be as its own principle, separated from the others. But through this, the unity appears along the same lines with the two principles that have been set in opposition. It is not something like what is chiefly the being. Rather, the unity is just a principle of the being and hence, perfectly equivalent with the two others.

The true meaning of this unity that has been asserted in the beginning is therefore this: 'one and the same = x' is as much the unity as it is the antithesis. Or both of the opposed potencies, the eternally negating potency and the eternally affirming potency, and the unity of both make up the one, inseparable, primordial being.

1) What is Necessary of God = The Nature of God

a) The Triad of Principles in what is Necessary of God or the Nature of God

And here, first after the consummate unfurling of that initial concept, can we glimpse the first nature in its full vitality. We see it, in an equally originary way, decomposed, as it were, into three powers. Each of these powers can be for itself. Hence, the unity is a unity for itself and each of the opposite powers is a whole and complete being. Yet not one of them can be *without* the others also being and hence, only together do they fulfill the whole concept of the Godhead and only that God is necessary. Not one of them is necessary and by nature subordinate to the others. The negating potency is, with regard to that inseparable primordial being, as essential as the affirming potency. And the unity is, in turn, not more essential than each of the opposites are for themselves. Therefore each also has fully the same claim to be the being, to be that which has being. Not one of them can bring itself by nature only to Being or not to be that which has being.

And the law of contradiction, which says that opposites cannot be in one and the same thing and at the same time be that which has being, here, at last, finds its application. God, in accordance with the necessity of its nature, is an eternal No, the highest Being-in-itself, an eternal withdrawal of its being into itself, a withdrawal within which no creature would be capable of living. But the same God, with equal necessity of its nature, although not in accord with the same principle, but in accord with a principle that is completely different from the first principle, is the eternal Yes, an eternal outstretching, giving, and communicating of its being. Each of these principles, in an entirely equal fashion, is the being, that is, each has the same claim to be God or that which has being. Yet they reciprocally exclude each other. If one is that which has being, then the opposed can only be that which does not have being. But, in an equally eternal manner, God is the third term or the unity of the Yes and the No. Just as opposites exclude each other from being what has being [*vom seyend-Seyn*], so again the unity excludes the antithesis and thereby each of the opposites, and, in turn, the antithesis or each of the opposites excludes the unity from being what has being. If the unity is that which has being, then the antithesis, that is, each of the opposites, can only be that which does not have being. And, in turn, if one of the opposites, and thereby the antithesis, has being, then the unity can only retreat into that which does not have being.

And it is not now the case that somehow all three remain inactive so that the contradiction itself could remain in concealment. For that which is these three is the necessary nature, the being that is not allowed not to be, that absolutely must be. But it can only be as the inseparable One of these three. Not one of these for itself would fulfill the whole concept of the necessary being (of the Godhead), and each of these three has the same right to be the being, that is, to be that which has being.

It is thus found that the first nature is, with regard to itself, in contradiction. It is not in contradiction by chance nor is it in one in which it would have been transposed from the outside (for there is nothing outside of it). Rather, it is in a necessary contradiction, posited at the same time with its being and hence, which, more accurately said, is itself its being.

People appear to have a greater aversion for contradiction than for anything else in life. Contradiction coerces them into action and forces them from their cozy repose. When, after a long time, the contradiction is no longer to be covered over, they seek to at least conceal it from themselves and to distance the moment in which matters of life and death must be acted upon. A similar convenience was sought in knowledge through the interpretation of the law of contradiction in which contradiction should never be able to be. However, how can one put forward a law for something that can in no way be? When it is known that a contradiction cannot be, it must be known that it nevertheless in a certain way is. How else should 'that which cannot be' appear to be and how should the law prove itself, that is, prove to be true?

Everything else leaves the active in some sense open. Only the contradiction is absolutely not allowed not to act and is alone what drives, nay, what coerces, action. Therefore, without the contradiction, there would be no movement, no life, and no progress. There would only be eternal stoppage, a deathly slumber of all of the forces.

Were the first nature in harmony with itself, it would remain so. It would be constantly One and would never become Two. It would be an eternal rigidity without progress. The contradiction in the first nature is as certain as life is. As certainly as the being of knowledge consists in progression, it necessarily has as its first posit the positing of the contradiction.

A transition from unity to contradiction is incomprehensible. For how should what is in itself one, whole and perfect, be tempted, charmed, and enticed to emerge out of this peace? The transition from contradiction to unity, on the other hand, is natural, for contradiction is insufferable to everything and everything that finds itself in it will not repose until it has found the unity that reconciles or overcomes it.

b) The Unprethinkable Decision in the Nature of God – The Concept of that which does not have Being

Only the contradiction brings life into the first necessary nature that we have until now only considered conceptually. Just as with the three principles whose irresolvable concatenation the first nature is, such that *each* in accord with its nature is that which has being, but such that if one has being, then necessarily the other does not have being and such that it at the same time still does not befit the first nature to have the freedom to be or not to be, so there is similarly in the first nature also necessitated a decision, even if only one that transpires blindly. If the one has being, then the other does not have being, yet each should and must in the same way be that which has being. With this there is nothing left over except an alternating positing, where alternately now one is that which has being and the other is that which does not have being and then, in turn, it is the other of these which has being and the one which does not have being. Yet, so that it thereby also comes exclusively to this alternating positing in that primordial urge for Being, it is necessary that one of them be the beginning or that which first has being and after this, one of them is the second and one of them is the third. From this, the movement again goes back to the first and, as such, is an eternally expiring and an eternally recommencing life.

But precisely *that* one commences and one of them is the first, must result from a decision that certainly has not been made consciously or through deliberation but can happen rather only when a violent power blindly breaks the unity in the jostling between the necessity and the impossibility to be. But the only place in which a ground of determination can be sought for the precedence of one of them and the succession of the other is the particular nature of each of the principles, which is different from their general nature which consists in each being equally originary and equally independent and each having the same claim to be that which has being. This is not like saying that one of the principles would absolutely have to be the one that proceeds or the one that succeeds. Rather, just that, because it is allowed by its particular nature, the possibility is given to it to be the first, the second, or the third.

It is now clear that what is posited at the beginning is precisely that which is subordinated in the successor. The beginning is only the beginning insofar as it is not that which should actually be, that which truthfully and in itself has being. If there is therefore a decision, then that which can only be posited at the beginning inclines, for the most part and in its particular way, to the nature of that which does not have being.

Precisely the affirmative principle, the authentic being or that which has being (A) as not active, that is, as not having being, is posited in the originary negation. This is not to say that it would, as that which has being, be altogether negated (this is impossible). On the contrary, it is posited as that which has being, but not as having the being of that which has being or, in other words, not as that which has been revealed actually to have being. On the other hand, that which is singularly active in this unity is the negating potency (B), which, as the potency that has been opposed to the being or that which actually has being, cannot be called that which has being, although it in no way because of that is that which does not have being or nothing.

Therefore, whether we might look at what is active in that originary negation or at that which is posited as inactive or passive in it, we will in any case say that the originary negation for the most part shares in the nature of that which does not have being or itself appears as not *having being.*

The concept of not having being, but especially the not being that occurs everywhere in so many forms, has always led the beholder astray and, like a real Proteus, manifoldly brought them into confusion. For just as it is manifest to hardly anyone that actual power lies more in delimitation than expansion and that to withdraw oneself has more to do with might than to give oneself, so is it natural that where they encounter that which through itself does not have being, they rather regard it as 'nothing' and, when it is asserted that it 'is' precisely as that which does not have being, they rather explain this away as the greatest contradiction.

They could have been liberated from this simple grammatical misunderstanding, which also prejudiced a good many interpreters of the Greek philosophers, and from which the concept of the *creatio ex nihilo*, among others, also seems to owe its origin, with this distinction, entirely easy to learn and which can be found, if nowhere else, certainly in Plutarch, between non-Being [*nicht Seyn*] (μὴ εἶναι) and the Being which has no being [*nicht seyend Seyn*] (μὴ Ὄν εἶναι). This lets one also defend the expression "privation (στέρησις)" with which Aristotle indicated the other, the opposed τοὐναντίον, namely, insofar as the negating force, which contracts the being, does not posit that it is-not, but rather that it is not that which has being.

Even the most general consideration must incidentally lead to the concept of that which does not have being. For that which is in each thing the actual Being cannot, because of the antithesis, ever be one and the same with that which has being. Rather, it is, in accord with its nature, that which does not have being but, because of that, it is in no way 'nothing'. For how should nothing be that which is Being itself? Being must after all be. There is no mere Being in which there would be nothing which has being whatsoever (no A without B). That which does not have being is not something that has being against others (objectively), but is something that has being in itself (subjectively). It is only over and against that which mainly has being that it is that which does not have being. But in relationship to itself, it is certainly that which has being. Everything that has being of a humbler rank relates itself, when contrasted with being of a higher rank, as that which does not have being. The same A that, in contrast with another, is that which has being, can appear in contrast with an A of an even higher order as that which does not have being.

So something more or less allows itself expression in our way that Plato already showed in the magnificent dialogue about that which does not have being in which he shows how that which has no being is necessary and how, without this insight, certainty would be entirely indistinguishable from doubt and truth would be entirely indistinguishable from error.

Conceptually, that which has being is always that in which the affirming principle is active and outwardly manifest. But it does not always follow that what has being in accord with the concept is, for this reason, that which indeed really has being. For in an inverted order, or where there is still no order, levelheadedness, and organization, that which in itself or essentially has being can just as well become that which does not have being, when contrasted with what, in accord with its being, really does not have being. Just as the good person suppresses the evil within themselves, the evil person, conversely, silences the good within themselves and posits that what in accord with its being is that which has being is really that which does not have being.

We still want to recall the misuse that another kind of sophistry makes of the concept of not having being. Because Being appears as the highest to blind feeling and because all Being is founded on the closure of the being, sophistry then concludes (if it has not been supplemented too much through this explanation) that Being is unknowable and because to them everything is *Being*, nothing is knowable; all knowing knowledge dissolves Being and only the unknowing one knows. Certainly in itself only that which has being is what is knowable and what does not have being is not what is knowable. But it is still only incomprehensible insofar as and in as much as it is not that which has being. But insofar as it is as such and at the same time something that has being, it is certainly comprehensible and knowable. For that through which it does not have being is precisely that through which it has being. For it is not that which does not have being on account of a comprehensive lack of light and being but on account of an active restriction of the being and hence, on account of acting force. We may therefore look to what is interior and concealed in it or to what is exterior and manifest about it. The former is precisely the essentiality itself but the latter is an active force. Nay, we would like to say more correctly that the latter is the force, the absolute might, which, as such, must likewise be something that has being and therefore must be something knowable.

That God negates itself, restricts its being, and withdraws into itself, is the eternal force and might of God. In this manner, the negating force is that which is singularly revealing of God. But the actual being of God is that which is concealed. The whole therefore stands as A that from the outside is B and hence, the whole = (A = B). Therefore, the whole, because God is that which does not have being (is not manifest) in it, inclines, in accord with its essentiality and in relation to what is other, for the most part toward not being that which has being. This is therefore the beginning, or how we have otherwise already expressed it, the first potency.

Hence, according to the oldest teachings, night is not in general the uppermost being (as these teachings are misunderstood these days), but rather the first that, precisely because of this, becomes the lowest in the progress of the movement. Precisely that which negates all revelation must be made the ground of revelation.

The same thing allows itself to be demonstrated from another angle. A being cannot negate itself without thereby making itself turn inward and therefore making itself the object of its own wanting and desire. The beginning of all knowledge lies in the knowledge of one's ignorance. But it is impossible that the person posits himself or herself as ignorant without thereby inwardly making knowledge into an object of their desire. Positing oneself as that which does not have being and wanting oneself are therefore one and the same. Each being primarily wants itself and this self-wanting is later precisely the basis of egoity, that through which a being withdraws itself or cuts itself off from other things and that through which it is exclusively itself, and therefore is, from the outside and in relation to everything else, negating.

But the power of a beginning is only in wanting in general. For that which is wanted and therefore that which should actually be in accord with the intention is posited as that which does not have being precisely because it is that which is *wanted*. But all beginning is founded on that which is not, on what actually should be (that which in itself has being). Since a being that has nothing outside of itself can want nothing other than simply itself, the unconditioned and absolutely first beginning can lie only in self-wanting. But wanting oneself and negating oneself as having being is one and the same. Therefore, the first beginning can only be in negating oneself as that which has being.

For the beginning really only lies in the negation. All beginning is, in accord with its nature, only a desire for the end or for what leads to the end and hence, negates itself as the end. It is only the tension of the bow – it is not so much that which itself has being as it is the ground that something is. It is not enough for a beginning that now commences or becomes not to be. It must be expressly posited as that which does not have being. A ground is thereby given for it to be. No beginning point (*terminus a quo*) of a movement is an empty, inactive point of departure. Rather, it is a negation of the starting point and the actually emerging movement is an overcoming of this negation. If the movement was not negated, then it could not have been expressly posited. Negation is therefore the necessary precedent (*prius*) of every movement. The beginning of the line is the geometrical point – but not because it extended itself but rather because it is the negation of all extension. One is the beginning of all number, not so much because it itself is a number but because it is the negation of all number, of all multiplicity. That which would intensify itself must first gather itself together and transpose itself into the condition of being a root. What wants to grow must foreshorten itself and hence, negation is the first transition whatsoever from nothing into something.

There is therefore no doubt that if a succession takes place among the primordial powers of life, only the power that contracts and represses the being can be the initiating power. What is first in God after the decision or, because we must assume that as having *happened* since all eternity (and as still always happening), what is altogether first in God, in the living God, the eternal beginning of itself in itself, is that God restricts itself, denies itself, withdraws its essence from the outside and retreats into itself.

The currently accepted teaching about God is that God is without all beginning. The Scripture to the contrary: God is the beginning and the end. We would have to imagine a being regarded as without beginning as the eternal immobility, the purest inactivity. For no acting is without a point out of which and toward which it goes. An acting that would neither have something solid upon which to ground itself nor a specific goal or end that it desires, would be a fully indeterminate acting and not an actual and, as such, distinguishable one. Certainly, therefore, something that is eternal without beginning can be thought as not actual but never as actual. But now we are speaking of a necessarily actual God. Therefore, this God has no beginning only insofar as it has no beginning of its beginning. The beginning in it is an eternal beginning, that is, a beginning that was, as such, from all eternity and still always is and one that never ceases to be a beginning. The beginning that a being has outside of itself and the beginning that a being has within itself are different. A beginning from which it can be alienated and from which it can distance itself is different than a beginning in which it eternally remains because it itself is the beginning.

But the divine nature does not allow that it is just an eternal No and an eternal denial of itself. It is an equally valid part of its nature that it is a being of all beings, the infinitely self-granting and self-communicating being. In that it therefore conceals its being, there thereby appears, by force of the eternal necessity of its nature, the eternal affirmation of its being as it opposes the negation (which is not sublimated but abiding, albeit now receding into the negative). In contrast, the negating force represses itself and precisely thereby intensifies itself into an independent being.

Exactly as when the body collects itself and cools off and a perceptible warmth spreads around it so that it therefore elevates the previously inactive warmth into an active warmth, so too, and with a wholly equal necessity, that originary negation becomes the immediate ground, the potency that begets the actual being. It posits this being outside of itself and independent of itself as a being removed from itself, nay, as a being opposed to it, as that which in itself eternally has being.

Through this, a new light falls upon that originary negation. A being cannot negate itself as actual without at the same time positing oneself as the actualizing potency that begets itself. Hence, conversely, positing oneself as the actualizing potency of oneself and, in turn, positing oneself as not having being is one and the same.

In the first potency (in $A = B$), there was also something that had being (A). But this was posited here as not having being (as passive, as object). In accordance with the presupposition, that which is begot by it is posited as that which has being such that *it has being* [*das Seyende als* **Seyendes**]. It can in this way be called that which has being to the second power (we indicate it by A^2 in which now the negating power, B, disappears). And from this it would be clear that if that originary No is the beginning or the first, than the being opposed to it is the second and the successive being.

That the former can only proceed and that the latter can only succeed can, however, still be looked at in another way. It is natural to the negating force that it represses the being. Once a negating force is posited, it can effect nothing else but the closure of the being. But the negating force is fully alien to the affirming principle in itself. And yet the affirming principle actually has being as that which has being only by repressing the negating force in itself. Furthermore, it would, with regard to itself, never come forth and therefore never elevate to act if the negation of the being had not proceeded. In that it has being, it certainly has it from itself. But that it again has being, that it laboriously proves itself and reveals itself as having being, has its ground in the negating potency. If there were not the No, then the Yes would be without force. No 'I' without the 'not-I' and in as much as the 'not-I' is before the 'I'. That which has being, precisely because it has being from itself, has no ground to desire that it be. But to be negated conflicts with its nature. Therefore, in that it is at all negated, it follows that, excepting that in which it is negated, it is in itself unnegated and in its own purity.

The primordial antithesis is given with these two potencies. Yet the antithesis is not such that it is based on a completely reciprocal exclusion, but only as such that it is based on an opposed relationship, on, so to speak, an inverted position of those first life forces. What in the proceeding potency was the exterior, contracting, and negating, is itself, in the successive potency, the inner, contracted, and self-negated. And conversely, what was there inhibited is what is here free. They are infinitely far from each other and infinitely near. Far, because what is affirmed and manifest in one of them is posited in the other as negated and in the dark. Near, because it only requires an inversion, a turning out of what was concealed and a turning into what is manifest, in order to transpose and, so to speak, transform, the one into the other.

Hence, we already see here the structure for a future, inner unity in which each potency comes out for itself. Hence, the day lies concealed in the night, albeit overwhelmed by the night; likewise the night in the day, albeit kept down by the day, although it can establish itself as soon as the repressive potency disappears.

Hence, good lies concealed in evil, albeit made unrecognizable by evil; likewise evil in good, albeit mastered by the good and brought to inactivity.

But now the unity of the being thus seems torn and hence, each of the opposites stands for and in itself as its own being. Yet they incline themselves toward unity, or they come together in one and the same because the negating force can only feel itself as negating when there is a disclosing being and the latter can only be active as affirming insofar as it liberates the negating and repressing force. It is also impossible that the unity of the being could be sublimated. Hence, facilitated by eternal necessity through the force of indissoluble life, they posit outside and above themselves a third, which is the unity.

This third must in itself be outside and above all antithesis, the purest potency, indifferent toward both, free from both, and the most essential.

From the foregoing it is clear that this cannot be the first, nor the second, only the third, and can only comport itself as having the being of the third potency = A^3.

Just as the originary negation is the eternal beginning, this third is the eternal end. There is an inexorable progression, a necessary concatenation, from the first potency to the third. When the first potency is posited, the second is also necessarily posited, and both of these produce the third with the same necessity. Thereby the goal is achieved. There is nothing higher to be produced in this course.

Yet having arrived at its peak, the movement of itself retreats back into its beginning; for each of the three has an equal right to be that which has being. The former differentiation and the subordination that followed from it is only a differentiation of the being, it is not able to sublimate the equivalence with regard to that which is as what has being. In a nutshell, it is not able to sublimate the existential parity [*die existentielle Gleichheit*].

But we still cannot at all talk here of an ethical relation because we still have only posited blind nature and not an ethical principle. We are taught often enough that the Ideal stands over the Real, that the physical is subordinated to the spiritual, and other such things. There is never a lack of such instruction for us. Indeed, this subordination seemed to be expressed as what was most determined in that we always posited what was akin to the Real as the first potency and what was akin to the Ideal as the second potency. But if one begins thereby to posit as actually subordinated that which ought to be subordinated, what then does one have? One is already finished in the beginning. Everything has happened and there is no further progression.

That originary, necessary, and abiding life hence ascends from the lowest to the highest. Yet when it has arrived at the highest, it retreats immediately back to the beginning in order again to ascend from it. Here we first attain the consummate concept of that first nature (after which all particular concepts, which only had to be posited in order to attain this consummate concept, must again be expelled), namely, that it is a life that eternally circulates within itself, a kind of circle because the lowest always runs into the highest, and the highest again into the lowest.

Hence, it is impossible, by virtue of the nature of the three principles, that each as well as each not be that which has being and therefore they are only thinkable in this urge toward existence as an alternating positing. Hence, now one, now the other, is that which has being. Taking turns, one prevails while the other yields.

Naturally, in this constant annular drive, the differentiation of the higher and the lower again sublimates itself. There is neither a veritable higher nor a veritable lower, since in turn one is the higher and the other is the lower. There is only an unremitting wheel, a rotatory movement that never comes to a standstill and in which there is no differentiation. Even the concept of the beginning, as well as the concept of the end, again sublimates itself in this circulation. There is certainly a beginning of the potency in accordance with its inherent possibility, but this is not an actual beginning. An actual beginning is only one that posits itself as not having being in relationship to that which should actually be. But that which could be the beginning in this movement does not discern itself as the beginning and makes an equal claim with the other principles to be that which has being. A true beginning is one that does not always begin again but persists. A true beginning is that which is the ground of a steady progression, not of an alternating advancing and retreating movement. Likewise, there is only a veritable end in which a being persists that does not need to retreat from itself back to the beginning. Hence, we can also explain this first blind life as one that can find neither its beginning nor its end. In this respect we can say that it is *without* (veritable) beginning and *without* (veritable) end.

Since it did not begin sometime but began since all eternity in order never (veritably) to end, and ended since all eternity, in order always to begin again, it is clear that that first nature was since all eternity and hence, equiprimordially a movement circulating within itself, and that this is its true, living concept.

These are the forces of that inner life that incessantly gives birth to itself and again consumes itself that the person must intimate, not without terror, as what is concealed in everything, even though it is now covered up and from the outside has adopted peaceful qualities. Through that constant retreat to the beginning and the eternal recommencement, it makes itself into substance in the real sense of the word (*id quod substat*), into the always abiding. It is the constant inner mechanism and clockwork, time, eternally commencing, eternally becoming, always devouring itself and always again giving birth to itself.

The antithesis eternally produces itself, in order always again to be consumed by the unity, and the antithesis is eternally consumed by the unity in order always to revive itself anew. This is the sanctuary (ἑστία), the hearth of the life that continually incinerates itself and again rejuvenates itself from the ash. This is the tireless fire (ἀκάματον πῦρ) through whose quenching, as Heraclitus claimed, the cosmos was created. It is circulating within itself, continuously repeating itself by moving backward and again forward as was shown in the visions of one of the prophets. This is the object of the ancient Magi teachings and of that doctrine of fire as a consequence of which the Jewish lawgiver left behind to his people: 'The Lord your God is a devouring fire,' that is, not in God's inner and authentic being [*Wesen*], but certainly in accordance with God's nature.

But this unremitting movement that goes back into itself and recommences is incontestably the scientific concept of that wheel of birth as the interior of all nature that was already revealed to one of the apostles,[1] who was distinguished by a profound glimpse into nature, as well as to those who later wrote from feeling and vision.

This movement can be represented as a systole and a diastole. This is a completely involuntary movement that, once begun, makes itself from itself. The recommencing, the re-ascending is systole, tension that reaches its acme in the third potency. The retreat to the first potency is diastole, slackening, upon which a new contraction immediately follows. Hence, this is the first pulse, the beginning of that alternating movement that goes through the entirety of visible nature, of the eternal contraction and the eternal re-expansion, of the universal ebb and flow.

Visible nature, in particular and as a whole, is an allegory of this perpetually advancing and retreating movement. The tree, for example, constantly drives from the root to the fruit, and when it has arrived at the pinnacle, it again sheds everything and retreats to the state of fruitlessness, and makes itself back into a root, only in order again to ascend. The entire activity of plants concerns the production of seed, only in order again to start over from the beginning and through a new developmental process to produce again only seed and to begin again. Yet all of visible nature appears unable to attain settledness and seems to transmute tirelessly in a similar circle. One generation comes, the other goes. Nature goes to the trouble to develop qualities, aspects, works, and talents to their pinnacle, only again to bury them for centuries in oblivion, and then start anew, perhaps in a new species, but certainly only to attain again the same peak.

Yet this first being never comes to Being since only together do the three potencies fulfill the concept of the divine nature, and only that this nature is so is necessary. Since there is consequently an unremitting urge to be and since it cannot be, it comes to a standstill in desire, as an unremitting striving, an eternally insatiable obsession [*Sucht*] with Being. The ancient saying is appropriate regarding this: Nature strives for itself and does not find itself (*quærit se natura, non invenit*).

Were life to remain at a standstill here, it would be nothing other than an eternal exhaling and inhaling, a constant interchange between life and death, that is, not a true existence but only an eternal drive and zeal to be, without actual Being.

It is clear that the life could never come to an actual existence by virtue of the simple necessity of the divine [nature] and hence, certainly not by virtue of necessity in general.

How or by virtue of what was the life redeemed from this annular drive and led into freedom?

---

[1] ὁ τροχὸς τῆς γενέσεως, *James 3:6* [the wheel of genesis].

Since each of the three principles has an equal claim to be that which has being, the contradiction cannot be resolved through one of the principles somehow
becoming that which has being at the cost of the others. But since the contradiction can also not remain, and since it does so because each of the principles
wants to be that which has being for itself: thus no other solution is thinkable
other than that they *all* communally and voluntarily (then by what would they
be coerced?) sacrifice being that which has being and hence, debase themselves
into simple Being. For thereby that equivalence (equipollence) automatically terminates that did not refer to its essence or its particular nature (by virtue of which
they form more of a gradation), but only such that each of them was driven by
nature in the same fashion to be that which has being. As long as this necessity
continues, they must all strive to be in one and the same locus, namely, in the
locus of that which has being and hence, so to speak, to be in a single point.
A reciprocal inexistence [*Inexistenz*] is demanded because they are incompatible
and when one has being, then the others must be without being. Hence, this
necessity can only terminate if all of the potencies have sacrificed, in the same
fashion, being that which has being. When one of them has being, then all of
the potencies, in accordance with their nature, must strive to be the same. As
soon as this necessity terminates, a confrontation becomes possible, that is, that
each of them enters into its potency. Space opens up and that blind necessity of
reciprocal inexistence metamorphosizes into the relationship of a free belonging
together.

By itself this is certainly illuminating enough. Yet a question emerges: How is it
possible that all of the potencies communally sacrifice being that which has being?

In itself it is clear that nothing whatsoever can give up having being except
before something higher. Just as long as the human heart feels, so to speak, entitled
to selfish desire until its yearning, its craving, that inner void that devours it, is not
fulfilled by a higher good and just as the soul only settles and stills itself when it
acknowledges something higher than itself by which it is made exuberantly blissful,
so too can the blind obsession and craving of the first [nature] only grow silent
before something higher, before which it happily and voluntarily acknowledges
itself as mere Being, as not *having being*.

Furthermore, that renunciation and subsidence into Being should be voluntary.
But until now there has been nothing in that first nature except irresistible drive
and insensate movement. So long as it is not placed outside of this involuntary
movement, there is no freedom thinkable within it. It cannot resist this movement
by itself. Another movement, something incontestably higher, can only withdraw
it from it. And since that involuntary movement is based on the necessity of the
reciprocal inexistence, it cannot be free of this movement except when a cision,
a confrontation, occurs, without it having anything to do with it. The possibility
is then given to it either to accept this cision and thereby redeem itself from the
annular drive or not to accept it and thereby again fall prey to that blind obsession
and craving.

Therefore, in any case, its liberation and deliverance can only come through an Other that is outside of it and wholly independent of it and exalted above it. Since it ought therefore to acknowledge itself as mere Being and not as *having being* before that other, this is not possible without recognizing at the same time its truly having being in that Other.

[...]

Translated by Jason M. Wirth

26

G. W. F. Hegel, Lectures on the Philosophy of
Religion (Vorlesungen über die Philosophie der
Religion): *The Relation of the Philosophy of Religion to
the Current Principles of the Religious Consciousness;
The Concept of Religion (1832)*

Throughout his career Hegel devoted a considerable amount of time to
questions of religion. His earliest (though unpublished) writings, prepared
not long after leaving the Theological Seminary at Tübingen, grapple with
the significance and possibilities of religion, and whilst Professor of Philosophy at Berlin (1818–31) he offered four lecture courses on the philosophy of
religion. The range of material covered in these lectures is perhaps the most
impressive of all of Hegel's lectures: the philosophical considerations of the
concepts of religion, from faith to magic to revelation with intriguing, as
well as informative, accounts of all of the major religious faiths. Although
Hegel's lecturing style was notoriously lacking in elegance it is not difficult
to see, when looking over the pages of these lectures, why it is that visitors
from all over Europe gathered to hear Hegel's thoughts on the philosophy
of religion.

Religious questions are quite central to Hegel's system, and it is not just
the explicitly philosophical-theological writings which reveal Hegel's concern with religion. His works on 'the science of logic' – works of metaphysics – frequently presuppose the possibility of transcendence, named as
God by Hegel. In the first part of the *Encyclopaedia of the Philosophical
Sciences* (first edition, 1817), which deals with logic or metaphysics, Hegel
makes a series of claims about the nature of metaphysical thinking which
suggest that we must presuppose an idea of transcendence. At one important point he argues that 'thinking the empirical world essentially means
altering its empirical form, and transforming it into something universal'.[1]
This is not the specialised activity of philosophy, but an ineradicable characteristic of human thought. So when the empirical world is thought, or
becomes the object of reflection, it is no longer merely empirical but indeed
an object of thought. Hegel describes this thinking as a *negative* activity

[1] G. W. F. Hegel, trans. T. F. Geraets, W. A. Suchting and H. S. Harris, *The Encyclopaedia Logic* (Indianapolis/Cambridge: Hackett, 1991), §50, p. 96 (*HW* VIII, §50, 132).

which brings out 'the inner *import* of what is perceived'.[2] He claims that the negative moment involves the reflective transformation of the material into the spiritual or purely intellectual. In this way the material is allegedly mediated into the spiritual: that is, the being of the world can be explained only as the necessary being of God, Hegel argues. By itself, or independently of God, the world is only contingent being. The idea, then, is that the world is mediated through God in the sense that the world achieves its significance only by reference to its truth in God: 'This elevation (*Erhebung*) of the spirit means that although being certainly does pertain to the world, it is only semblance, not genuine being, not absolute truth; for, on the contrary, the truth is beyond that appearance, in God alone, and only God is genuine being'.[3]

In part of the selection from the lectures reprinted here – the Conception of Religion – Hegel sets out the philosophical framework in which he wants to consider this same question. We can also find a number of further ideas and thoughts which are familiar both from the *Encyclopaedia* and the *Science of Logic* (first edition, in three parts, 1812–16). For instance, he reflects on the problem of 'beginnings' in philosophy: philosophy, unlike other intellectual disciplines, cannot presuppose its 'object' – that is, the thing it sets out to understand – because that would prejudice the outcome of the enquiry. And yet, no beginning is possible unless something is presupposed: otherwise there would be no object of inquiry. In the *Encyclopaedia*, for instance, he writes, 'Philosophy lacks the advantage, which the other sciences enjoy, of being able to *presuppose* its *objects* as given immediately by representation',[4] and the title of an introductory section to the *Science of Logic* – certainly the most intimidating book from the period of German Idealism – asks the question: 'With what must Science begin?' To bring our ordinary knowledge to the level of 'science' means, for Hegel, being able to demonstrate that it comprises a rigorous body of knowledge.

The inquiry begins with what Hegel calls 'ordinary consciousness'. This entails investigation of our ordinary understanding of God and his traditional attributes as well as taking seriously our ordinary 'religious consciousness' in which the nature of God is something we have from conviction. This beginning is, however, 'abstract' according to Hegel. It is a curiosity of Hegel's own terminology that he sees philosophical thinking as 'concrete' and ordinary thought as 'abstract'. The important idea which these terms express is that an item of knowledge remains abstract when it is not understood in its interconnectedness, as it were, with other items: it is simply an isolated piece of knowledge. Concrete knowledge, however, is that which can be considered 'scientific'.

Also in the selection here there are several passages which are significant in any consideration of the religious controversy in which Hegel was

[2] Hegel, *The Encyclopaedia Logic*, §50, p. 96 (*HW* VIII, §50, 132).
[3] Hegel, *The Encyclopaedia Logic*, §50, p. 96 (*HW* VIII, §50, 132).
[4] Hegel, *The Encyclopaedia Logic*, §1, p. 24 (*HW* VIII, §1, 41).

to become entangled. The text seems to suggest straightaway that Hegel was a theist (though virtually every sort of account of God has been attributed to Hegel: theist, atheist, pantheist, panlogicist), but critics argue the need to distinguish between Hegel's convictions and the logical outcomes of his lines of thought. Hegel may unambiguously assert the existence of God, but in his philosophical principle, for instance, that all knowledge be rendered scientific Hegel was seen to cut 'the core – literally the heart – out of Christianity', as Laurence Dickey puts it.[5] And yet for the Young Hegelians, writing in the immediate aftermath of Hegel's death, Hegel's philosophical enterprise was entirely prejudiced by theological presuppositions.

   In the other part of the selection – The Relation of the Philosophy of Religion to the Current Principles of the Religious Consciousness – Hegel shows just how philosophical his approach is when he tackles the notion of 'immediate knowledge'. The critique of immediate knowledge is found throughout Hegel's texts, nowhere more so than in the *Encyclopaedia* where he takes the romantic philosopher and proponent of this position, F. H. Jacobi, to task. There he argues that Jacobi's position is incoherent in that the very notion of faith is a kind of knowledge, and as a kind of knowledge is achieved through a process of education. Education, however, is not a matter of immediate insight.[6]

[5]Laurence Dickey, 'Hegel on Religion and Philosophy', p. 315, in *The Cambridge Companion to Hegel* (Cambridge: Cambridge University Press, 1993), ed. Frederick C. Beiser.
[6]Hegel, *Encyclopaedia*, §67.

III. – THE RELATION OF THE PHILOSOPHY OF RELIGION TO THE CURRENT PRINCIPLES OF THE RELIGIOUS CONSCIOUSNESS.[†]

If at the present day philosophy be an object of enmity because it occupies itself with religion, this cannot really surprise us when we consider the general character of the time. Every one who attempts to take to do with the knowledge of God, and by the aid of thought to comprehend His nature, must be prepared to find, that either no attention will be paid to him, or that people will turn against him and combine to oppose him.

   The more the knowledge of finite things has increased – and the increase is so great that the extension of the sciences has become almost boundless, and all regions of knowledge are enlarged to an extent which makes a comprehensive view

[†]*HW* XVI, 42–54. *Lectures on the Philosophy of Religion* (London: Kegan Paul, Trench, Trübner, 1895), volume I.

impossible – so much the more has the sphere of the knowledge of God become contracted. There was a time when all knowledge was knowledge of God. Our own time, on the contrary, has the distinction of knowing about all and everything, about an infinite number of subjects, but nothing at all of God. Formerly the mind found its supreme interest in knowing God, and searching into His nature. It had and it found no rest unless in thus occupying itself with God. When it could not satisfy this need it felt unhappy. The spiritual conflicts to which the knowledge of God gives rise in the inner life were the highest which the spirit knew and experienced in itself, and all other interests and knowledge were lightly esteemed. Our own time has put this need, with all its toils and conflicts, to silence; we have done with all this, and got rid of it. What Tacitus said of the ancient Germans, that they were *securi adversus deos*, we have once more become in regard to knowledge, *securi adversus deum*.

It no longer gives our age any concern that it knows nothing of God; on the contrary, it is regarded as a mark of the highest intelligence to hold that such knowledge is not even possible. What is laid down by the Christian religion as the supreme, absolute commandment, 'Ye shall know God', is regarded as a piece of folly. Christ says, 'Be ye perfect, as My Father in heaven is perfect'. This lofty demand is to the wisdom of our time an empty sound. It has made of God an infinite phantom, which is far from us, and in like manner has made human knowledge a futile phantom of finiteness, or a mirror upon which fall only shadows, only phenomena. How, then, are we any longer to respect the commandment, and grasp its meaning, when it says to us, 'Be ye perfect, as your Father in heaven is perfect', since we know nothing of the Perfect One, and since our knowing and willing are confined solely and entirely to appearance, and the truth is to be and to remain absolutely and exclusively a something beyond the present? And what, we must further ask, what else would it be worthwhile to comprehend, if God is incomprehensible?

This standpoint must, judged by its content, be considered as the last stage of the degradation of man, in which at the same time he is, it is true, all the more arrogant inasmuch as he thinks he has proved to himself that this degradation is the highest possible state, and is his true destiny. Such a point of view is, indeed, directly opposed to the lofty nature of the Christian religion, for according to this we ought to know God, His nature, and His essential Being, and to esteem this knowledge as something which is the highest of all. (The distinction as to whether this knowledge is brought to us by means of faith, authority, revelation, or reason, is here of no importance.) But although this is the case, and although this point of view has come to dispense both with the content which revelation gives of the Divine nature, and with what belongs to reason, yet it has not shrunk, after all its abject gropings, in that blind arrogance which is proper to it, from turning against philosophy. And yet it is philosophy which is the liberation of the spirit from that shameful degradation, and which has once more brought religion out of the stage of intense suffering which it had to experience when occupying the standpoint referred to. Even the theologians, who are on their own ground in that region of vanity, have ventured to charge philosophy with its destructive tendency – theologians who have no longer anything left of that substantial element which could possibly be destroyed. In order to repel these not merely groundless, but, what is more, frivolous and unprincipled objections, we need only observe cursorily how theologians have, on the contrary, done everything in their power to do away with what is definite in religion, in that they have (1) thrust dogmas into the background, or pronounced them to be unimportant; or (2) consider them only as extraneous definitions given by others, and as mere phenomena of a past history. When we have reflected in this manner upon the aspect presented by the content, and have seen how this last is re-established by philosophy, and placed in safety from the devastations of theology, we shall (3) reflect upon the form of that standpoint, and shall see here how the tendency which, taking its departure from the form, is at enmity with philosophy, is so ignorant of what it is, that it does not even know that it contains in itself the very principle of philosophy.

1. Philosophy and the Prevalent Indifference to Definite Dogmas.

If, then, it be made a reproach to philosophy in its relation to religion that the content of the doctrine of revealed positive religion, and more expressly of the Christian religion, is depreciated by it, and that it subverts and destroys its dogmas, yet this hindrance is taken out of the way, and by the new theology itself, in fact. There are very few dogmas of the earlier system of Church confessions left which have any longer the importance formerly attributed to them, and in their place no other dogmas have been set up. It is easy to convince oneself, by considering what is the real value now attached to ecclesiastical dogmas, that into the religious world generally there has entered a widespread, almost universal indifference towards what in earlier times were held to be essential doctrines of the faith. A few examples will prove this.

Christ still indeed continues to be made the central point of faith, as Mediator, Reconciler, and Redeemer; but what was known as the work of redemption has received a very prosaic and merely psychological signification, so that although the edifying words have been retained, the very thing that was essential in the old doctrine of the Church has been expunged.

'Great energy of character, steadfast adherence to conviction for the sake of which He regarded not His life' – these are the common categories through which Christ is brought down, not indeed to the plane of ordinary everyday life, but to that of human action in general and moral designs, and into a moral sphere into which even heathens like Socrates were capable of entering. Even though

Christ be for many the central point of faith and devotion in the deeper sense, yet Christian life as a whole restricts itself to this devotional bent, and the weighty doctrines of the Trinity, of the resurrection of the body, as also the miracles in the Old and New Testaments, are neglected as matters of indifference, and have lost their importance. The divinity of Christ, dogma, what is peculiar to the Christian religion is set aside, or else reduced to something of merely general nature. It is not only by 'enlightenment' that Christianity has been thus treated, but even by pious theologians themselves. These latter join with the men of enlightenment in saying that the Trinity was brought into Christian doctrine by the Alexandrian school, by the neo-Platonists. But even if it must be conceded that the fathers of the Church studied Greek philosophy, it is in the first instance a matter of no importance whence that doctrine may have come; the only question is, whether it be essentially, inherently, true; but that is a point which is not examined into, and yet that doctrine is the key-note of the Christian religion.

If an opportunity was given to a large number of these theologians to lay their hand on their heart, and say whether they consider faith in the Trinity to be indispensably necessary to salvation, and whether they believe that the absence of such faith leads to damnation, there can be no doubt what the answer would be.

Even the words eternal happiness and eternal damnation are such as cannot be used in good society; such expressions are regarded as $\mathring{\alpha}\rho\rho\eta\tau\alpha$, as words which one shrinks from uttering. Even although a man should not wish to deny these doctrines, he would, in case of his being directly appealed to, find it very difficult to express himself in an affirmative way.

In the doctrinal teaching of these theologians, it will be found that dogmas have become very thin and shrunken, although they are talked about a great deal.

If any one were to take a number of religious books, or collections of sermons, in which the fundamental doctrines of the Christian religion are supposed to be set forth, and attempt to sift the greater part of those writings conscientiously in order to ascertain whether, in a large proportion of such literature, the fundamental doctrines of Christianity are to be found contained and stated in the orthodox sense, without ambiguity or evasion, the answer is again not a doubtful one.

It would appear that the theologians themselves, in accordance with the general training which most of them have received, only attribute that importance which they formerly assigned to the principle and doctrines of positive Christianity — when these were still regarded as such — to these doctrines when they are veiled in a misty indefiniteness. Thus if philosophy has always been regarded as the opponent of the doctrines of the Church, it cannot any longer be such, since these doctrines, which it seemed to threaten with destruction, are no longer regarded by general conviction as of importance. A great part of the danger which threatens philosophy from this side when she considers these dogmas in order to comprehend them ought to be thus taken away, and so philosophy can take up a more untrammelled attitude with regard to dogmas which have so much sunk in interest with theologians themselves.

2. The Historical Treatment of Dogmas.

The strongest indication, however, that the importance of these dogmas has declined, is to be perceived in the fact that they are treated principally in an historical manner, and are regarded in the light of convictions which belong to *others*, as matters of history, which do not go on in our own mind as such, and which do not concern the needs of our spirit. The real interest here is to find out how the matter stands so far as others are concerned, what part others have played, and centres in this accidental origin and appearance of doctrine. The question as to what is a man's own personal conviction only excites astonishment. The absolute manner of the origin of these doctrines out of the depths of Spirit, and thus the necessity, the truth, which they have for *our* spirits too, is shoved on one side by this historical treatment. It brings much zeal and erudition to bear on these doctrines; it is not with their essential substance, however, that it is occupied, but with the externalities of the controversies about them, and with the passions which have gathered around this external mode of the origin of truth. Thus Theology is by her own act put in a low enough position. If the philosophical knowledge of religion is conceived of as something to be reached historically only, then we should have to regard the theologians who have brought it to this point as clerks in a mercantile house, who have only to keep an account of the wealth of strangers, who only act for others without obtaining any property for themselves. They do, indeed, receive salary, but their reward is only to serve, and to register that which is the property of others. Theology of this kind has no longer a place at all in the domain of thought; it has no longer to do with infinite thought in and for itself, but only with it as a finite fact, as opinion, ordinary thought, and so on. History occupies itself with truths which *were* truths – namely, for others, not with such as would come to be the possession of those who are occupied with them. With the true content, with the knowledge of God, such theologians have no concern. They know as little of God as a blind man sees of a painting, even though he handles the frame. They only know how a certain dogma was established by this or that council; what grounds those present at such a council had for establishing it, and how this or that opinion came to predominate. And in all this, it is indeed religion that is in question, and yet it is not religion itself which here comes under consideration. Much is told us of the history of the painter of the picture, and of the fate of the picture itself, what price it had at different times, into what hands it came, but we are never permitted to see anything of the picture itself.

It is essential in philosophy and religion, however, that the spirit should *itself* enter with supreme interest into an inner relation, should not only occupy itself with a thing that is foreign to it, but should draw its content from that which is essential, and should regard itself as worthy of such knowledge. For here it is with the value of his *own* spirit that man is concerned, and he is not at liberty humbly to remain outside and to wander about at a distance.

3. Philosophy and Immediate Knowledge.

In consequence of the emptiness of the standpoint just considered, it might appear as if we only mentioned the reproaches which it casts upon philosophy in order to pronounce expressly against such a point of view, and that our aim, which we do not relinquish, is to do the opposite of that which it holds to be the highest of all aims – namely, to know God. Yet this standpoint has an aspect belonging to its form in which it must really have a rational interest for us, and regarded from this side, the recent attitude of theology is more favourable for philosophy. For with the thought that all objective determinateness has converged in the inwardness of subjectivity, the conviction is bound up that God gives revelation in an immediate way in man; that religion consists just in this, that man has immediate knowledge of God. This immediate knowing is called reason, and also faith, but in a sense other than that in which the Church takes faith. All knowledge, all conviction, all piety, regarded from the point of view which we are considering, is based on the principle that in the spirit, as such, the consciousness of God exists immediately with the consciousness of its self.

a. This statement taken in a direct sense, and as not implying that any polemical attitude has been taken up to philosophy, passes for one which needs no proof, no confirmation. This universal idea, which is now matter of assumption, contains this essential principle – namely, that the highest, the religious content shows itself in the spirit itself, that Spirit manifests itself in Spirit, and in fact *in this my spirit*, that this faith has its source, its root in my deepest personal being, and that it is what is most peculiarly my own, and as such is inseparable from the consciousness of pure spirit.

Inasmuch as this knowledge exists immediately in myself, all external authority, all foreign attestation is cast aside; what is to be of value to me must have its verification in my own spirit, and in order that I may believe I must have the witness of my spirit. It may indeed come to me from without, but any such external origin is a matter of indifference; if it is to be valid, this validity can only build itself up upon the foundation of all truth, in the *witness of the Spirit*.

This principle is the simple principle of philosophical knowledge itself, and philosophy is so far from rejecting it that it constitutes a fundamental characteristic in it itself. Thus it is to be regarded as a gain, a kind of happy circumstance, that fundamental principles of philosophy live even in general popular conceptions, and have become general assumptions, for in this way the philosophical principle may expect the more easily to obtain the general consent of the educated. As a result of this general disposition of the spirit of our time, philosophy has not only won a position which is externally favourable – with what is external it is never concerned, and least of all where it, and active interest in it, takes the form of an institution of the State – but is favoured inwardly, since its principle already lives in the minds and in the hearts of men as an assumption. For philosophy has this in common with the form of culture referred to, that reason is regarded as that part of the spirit in which God reveals himself to man.

b. But the principle of immediate knowledge does not rest satisfied with this simple determinateness, this natural and ingenuous content; it does not only express itself affirmatively, but takes up a directly polemical attitude to philosophical knowledge, and directs its attacks especially against the philosophical knowledge and comprehension of God. Not only does it teach that we are to believe and to know in an immediate manner, not only is it maintained that the consciousness of God is bound up with the consciousness of self, but that the relation to God is *only* an immediate one. The immediateness of the connection is taken as excluding the other characteristic of mediateness, and philosophy, because it is mediated knowledge, is said to be only a finite knowledge of that which is finite.

Thus this knowledge in its immediacy is to get no further than this, that we know that God is, but not what He is; the content, the filling up of the idea of God, is negated. By philosophical knowledge or cognition, we mean not only that we know that an object is, but also what it is; and that to know what it is, is not to know it to the extent of possessing a certain knowledge, certainty, of what it is; but more than this, this knowledge must relate to its characteristics, to its content, and it must be complete and full and proved knowledge, in which the necessary connection of these characteristics is a matter of knowledge.

If we consider more closely what is involved in the assertion of immediate knowledge, it is seen to mean that the consciousness so relates itself to its content that it itself and this content – God – are inseparable. It is this relation, in fact – knowledge of God – and this inseparableness of consciousness from this content, which we call religion. Further, however, it is of the essence of this assertion that we are to limit ourselves to the consideration of religion as such, and to keep strictly to the consideration of the relation to God, and are not to proceed to the knowledge of God, that is, of the divine content – of what the divine content essentially is in itself.

In this sense it is stated, further, that we can only know our relation to God, not what God Himself is; and that it is only our relation to God which is embraced in what is generally called religion. Thus it happens that at the present time we only hear religion spoken of, and do not find that investigation is made regarding the nature of God, what He is in Himself, and how the nature of God must be determined. God, as God, is not even made an object of thought; knowledge does not trench upon that object, and does not exhibit distinct attributes in Him, so as to make it possible that He Himself should be conceived of as constituting the relation of these attributes, and as relation in Himself. God is not before us as an object of knowledge, but only our relation with God, our relation to Him; and while discussions of the nature of God have become fewer and fewer, it is now only required of a man that he should be religious, that he should abide by religion, and we are told that we are not to proceed further to get a knowledge of any divine content.

c. If, however, we bring out what is inherent in the principle of immediate knowing, that is, what is directly affirmed in it, we find it to be just this, that God is spoken of in relation to consciousness in such a way that this relation is something inseparable, or, in other words, that we must of necessity contemplate *both*. It implies, in the first place, the essential distinction, which the conception of religion contains; on the one side, subjective consciousness, and on the other, God recognised as Object in Himself, or implicitly. At the same time, however, it is stated that there is an essential relation between the two, and that it is this inseparable relation of religion which is the real point, and not the notions which one may have concerning God.

What is really contained in this position, and really constitutes its true kernel, is the philosophical Idea itself, only that this Idea is confined by immediate knowledge within limitations which are abolished by philosophy, and which are by it exhibited in their onesidedness and untruth. According to the philosophical conception, God is Spirit, is concrete; and if we inquire more closely what Spirit is, we find that the whole of religious doctrine consists in the development of the fundamental conception of Spirit. For the present, however, it may suffice to say that Spirit is essentially self-manifestation – its nature is *to be for Spirit*. Spirit is for Spirit, and not, be it observed, only in an external, accidental manner. On the contrary, Spirit is only Spirit in so far as it is for Spirit; this constitutes the conception or notion of Spirit itself. Or, to express it more theologically, God is essentially Spirit, so far as He is in His Church. It has been said that the world, the material universe, must have spectators, and must be for Spirit or mind; how much more, then, must God be for Spirit.

We cannot, consequently, view the matter in a onesided way, and consider the subject merely according to its finiteness, to its contingent life, but inasmuch too as it has the infinite absolute object as its content. For if the Subject be considered by itself, it is considered within the limits of finite knowledge, of knowledge which concerns the finite. It is also maintained, on the other hand, that God, in like manner, must not be considered for Himself, for man only knows of God in relation to consciousness; and thus the unity and inseparability of the two determinations – of the knowledge of God and self-consciousness – even presupposes what is expressed in identity, and that dreaded identity itself is contained in it.

As a matter of fact, we thus find the fundamental conception which belongs to philosophy already existing as an universal element in the cultured thought of the present day. And here it becomes apparent, too, that philosophy does not stand above its age as if it were something absolutely different from the general character of the time, but that it is One Spirit which pervades both the actual world and philosophical thought, and that this last is only the true self-comprehension of what is actual. Or, in other words, it is one movement upon which both the age and its philosophy are borne, the distinction being only that the character of the time still appears to present itself as accidental, and is not rationally justified, and may thus even stand in an unreconciled, hostile attitude towards the truly essential content; while philosophy, as the justification of principles, is at the same time the universal peace-bringer and universal reconciliation. As the Lutheran Reformation carried faith back to the first centuries, so the principle of immediate knowledge has carried Christian knowledge back to the primary elements. If, however, this process at first causes the essential content to evaporate, yet it is philosophy which recognises this very principle of immediate knowledge as representing content, and as being such carries it forward to its true expansion within itself.

The want of sound sense which marks the arguments advanced against philosophy knows no bounds. The very opinions which are supposed by those who hold them to militate against philosophy, and to be in the sharpest antagonism to it, upon examination of their content exhibit essential agreement with that which they combat. Thus the result of the study of philosophy is that these walls of separation, which are supposed to divide absolutely, become transparent; and that when we go to the root of things we find that there is absolute accordance where it was believed that there was the greatest opposition.

Part I[†]
The Conception of Religion

What we have to commence with is the question, How is a beginning to be made? It is at least a formal demand of all science, and of philosophy in particular, that nothing should find a place in it which has not been proved. To prove, in the superficial sense, means that a content, a proposition, or a conception is exhibited as resulting from something that has preceded it.

But when a beginning has to be made, nothing has as yet been proved; for we are not yet in the region of result, of what is mediated, or established by means of something else. In dealing with a beginning, we have to do with the immediate. Other sciences have an easy part in this respect, their object being something actually given for them. Thus in geometry, for example, a beginning has been made, for there is a space, or a point. Here there is no question of proving the object, for its existence is directly granted.

It is not allowable in philosophy to make a beginning with 'There is, there are', for in philosophy the object must not be presupposed. This may constitute a difficulty in regard to philosophy in general. But in the present case we do not begin at the point where philosophy has its fountainhead. The science of religion is a science within philosophy; it assumes, so far, the existence of the other divisions of philosophical study, and it is thus a result. From the philosophical point of view we are here already in possession of a result flowing from premises previously established, which now lie behind us. We may, nevertheless, turn for aid to our ordinary consciousness, accept data assumed in a subjective way, and make a beginning from there.

[†]*HW* XVI, 91–101.

The beginning of religion is, similarly with its general content, the as yet un-developed conception of religion itself; namely, that God is the absolute Truth, the Truth of everything, and that religion alone is absolutely true knowledge. We have thus to begin by treating –

A.
GOD.

For us who are already in possession of religion, what God is, is something we are familiar with – a substantial truth which is present in our subjective consciousness. But scientifically considered, God is at first a general, abstract name, which as yet has not come to have any true value. For it is the Philosophy of Religion which is the unfolding, the apprehension of that which God is, and it is only by means of it that our philosophical knowledge of His nature is reached. God is this well-known and familiar idea – an idea, however, which has not yet been scientifically developed, scientifically known.

Having thus referred to this development, which has its justification in philo-sophical science itself, we shall, to begin with, accept as a simple statement of fact the assertion that the result of philosophy is that God is the absolutely True, the Universal in and for itself, the All-comprehending, All-containing, that from which everything derives subsistence. And in regard to this assertion we may also appeal in the first place to religious consciousness, where we find the con-viction that God is indeed the absolutely True, from which all proceeds, and into which all returns, upon which all is dependent, and beside which noth-ing has absolute true self-sustained existence. This, then, is what constitutes the beginning.

This beginning is, scientifically, still abstract. The heart may be ever so full of this idea, still in science it is not with what is in the heart that we have to do, but with what is definitely considered as object for consciousness, and more strictly for thinking consciousness which has attained to the form of thought. To give this fulness the form of thought, of the Notion, is the special work of the Philosophy of Religion.

a. The beginning as abstract, as the first content, Universality namely, has thus, as it were, as yet a subjective standing, implying that the Universal is universal for the beginning only, and does not continue in this condition of universality. The beginning of the content is itself to be conceived of in such a way that, while in all further developments of this content, this Universal will show itself to be absolutely concrete, rich in matter, and full of content, we at the same time do not pass beyond this universality; that this universality, though in a sense we leave it behind so far as the form is concerned, inasmuch as it undergoes a definite development, nevertheless maintains its position as the absolute, permanent foundation, and is not to be taken as a mere subjective beginning.

In so far as He is the Universal, God is for us from the point of view of development, what is shut up within itself, what is in absolute unity with itself. If we say God is that which is shut up within itself, in using such an expression we are thinking of a development which we expect to take place; but the undeveloped condition which we have called the Universality of God, is not in regard to the content itself to be taken as an abstract Universality, outside of which, and as opposed to which, the particular has an independent existence.

This Universality is thus to be understood as the absolutely full, filled up universality, and when we thus say that God is universal, concrete, full of content, we imply that God is One only, and not one as contrasted with many Gods, but that there is only the One, that is, God.

Existing things, the developments of the natural and spiritual world, take manifold forms, and have an infinite variety; they have a being which differs in degree, force, strength, content; but the being of all these things is not independent, but is supported by, dependent on, something else, and has no true independence. If we attribute a being to particular things, it is only a borrowed being, only the semblance of a being, not the absolute self-sustained Being, which is God.

God in His universality, this Universal, in which there is no limitation, no finiteness, no particularity, is the absolute Self-subsisting Being, and the only Self-subsisting Being; and what subsists has its root, its subsistence, in this One alone.

If the substantial element in this its first form is understood in this sense, we may express ourselves thus: God is the absolute Substance, the only true reality. All else, which is real, is not real in itself, has no real existence of itself; the one absolute reality is God alone, and thus He is the absolute Substance.

If this conception is held to in this abstract fashion, it is undoubtedly Spinozism. Substantiality, Substance as such, is as yet not at all differentiated from subjectivity. But the following thought also forms part of the presupposition thus made. God is Spirit, the Absolute Spirit, the eternally undifferentiated Spirit, essentially at home with Himself; this ideality, this subjectivity of Spirit, which is, so to speak, transparency, pure ideality excluding all that is particular, is just the Universality spoken of above, that pure relation to self, what is and remains absolutely at home with itself.

If we use the expression 'Substance', it is implied that this Universal is not yet conceived of as concrete in itself: when it is so conceived of, it is Spirit; and Spirit too always is this unity with itself, even in its concrete inner determination – this One Reality, which we just now called Substance. A further characteristic is that the substantiality, the unity of the absolute reality with itself, is only the foundation, *one* moment in the determination of God as Spirit. The disparagement of philosophy is connected mainly with this way of looking at the question. You hear it said that philosophy must be Spinozism if it is consistent, and that thus it is atheism, fatalism.

But at the beginning we have not as yet characteristics which are distinguished, as One and Another; at the beginning we are only concerned with the One, not with the Other.

In starting from here we have the content as yet in the form of substantiality. Even when we say, 'God, Spirit', these are indefinite words or general ideas. Everything depends upon what has entered into consciousness. At first it is the Simple, the Abstract, that enters into consciousness. In this first simplicity, we still have God in the character of Universality, but we do not remain at this standpoint.

Still, this content continues to be the foundation; in all further development, God never comes out of His unity with Himself. When He, as it is commonly expressed, creates the world, there does not come into existence something evil, Another, which is self-sustained, and independent.

b. This beginning is an object for *us* or content in us; *we* have this object; and thus the question immediately arises, Who are *we*? 'We', 'I', the spirit is itself something very concrete, manifold. I have perceptions, I am, I see, hear, &c., all this I am; this feeling, this seeing. Thus the more precise meaning of this question is, which of these forms of consciousness determines the shape in which this content exists for our minds? Is it found in idea, will, imagination, or feeling? What is the place, where this content, this object has its home? Which of all these supplies the basis of this mental possession?

If we think of the current answers in regard to this, we find it said that God is in us in so far as we believe, feel, form ideas, know. These forms, faculties, aspects of ourselves, namely, feeling, faith, ordinary conception, are to be more particularly considered further on, and especially in relation to this very point. For the present we postpone the search for any reply, nor do we betake ourselves to what we know by experience, observation, namely that we have God in our feeling, &c. To begin with, we shall keep to what we have actually before us, this One, Universal, this Fullness, which is this ever unchangeable transparent ethereal element.

If in considering this One we ask, For which of our faculties or mental activities does this One, this pure Universal, exist? we can only point to the corresponding activity of our mind, the faculty which answers to it, as the soil or substratum in which this content has its home. This is Thought.

Thought alone is the substratum of this content. Thought is the activity of the Universal; it is the Universal in its activity, or operation; or if we express it as the comprehension of the Universal, then that for which the Universal is, is still Thought.

This Universal, which can be produced by Thought, and which is for Thought, may be quite abstract; it is then the Immeasurable, the Infinite, the removal of all limit, of all particularity. This Universal, which is to begin with negative, has its seat in Thought only.

To think of God means to rise above what is sensuous, external, and individual. It means to rise up to what is pure, to that which is in unity with itself; it is a going forth above and beyond the sensuous, beyond what belongs to the sphere of the senses, into the pure region of the Universal. And this region is Thought.

Such, so far as the subjective side is concerned, is the substratum for this content. The content is this absolutely undivided, continuous, self-sufficing One, the Universal; and Thought is the mode of mind for which this Universal exists.

Thus we have a distinction between Thought and the Universal which we at first called God; it is a distinction which in the first place belongs only to our reflection, and which is as yet by no means included in the content on its own account. It is the result of philosophy, as it is already the belief of religion, that God is the One true Reality, and that there is no other reality whatsoever. In this One Reality and pure clearness, the reality and the distinction which we call thinking, have as yet no place.

What we have before us is this One Absolute: we cannot as yet call this content, this determination, religion; for to religion belongs subjective spirit, consciousness. This Universal has its place in Thought, but its localisation in Thought is, to begin with, absorbed in this One, this Eternal, this absolute existence.

In this true, absolute, determination, which is only not as yet developed, perfected, God remains through all development absolute Substance.

This Universal is the starting-point and point of departure, but it is this absolutely abiding Unity, and not a mere basis out of which differences spring, the truth rather being that all differences are here enclosed within this Universal. It is, however, no inert, abstract Universal, but the absolute womb, the eternal impetus and source from which everything proceeds, to which everything returns, and in which everything is eternally preserved.

Thus the Universal never goes out of this ethereal element of likeness with itself, out of this state in which it is together with or at home with itself. It is not possible that God, as this Universal, can actually exist along with another whose existence is anything more than the mere play of appearance or semblance of existence. In relation to this pure Unity and pure transparency, matter is nothing impenetrable, nor has the spirit, the 'I', such exclusiveness as to possess true substantiality of its own.

c. There has been a tendency to call this idea by the name Pantheism; it would be more correctly designated, 'the idea of substantiality'. God is here characterised at first as substance only; the absolute Subject, too, Spirit, remains substance; Spirit is not however substance only, but is also self-determined as Subject. Those who say that speculative philosophy is Pantheism, generally know nothing of this distinction; they overlook the main point, as they always do, and they disparage philosophy by representing it as different from what it really is.

Pantheism, with those who bring this charge against philosophy, has usually been taken to mean that everything, the All, the *Universum*, this complex collection of all that exists, those infinitely many finite things are God, and philosophy is accused of maintaining that All is God – that is, this infinite manifoldness of single things; not the Universality which has essential being, but the individual things in their empirical existence, as they are immediately.

If it be said, God is all this here, this paper, &c., then that is certainly Pantheism, as understood by those who by way of reproach bring forward the objection to which reference has been made, their meaning being that God is everything, all individual things. If I say 'species', that too is a universality, but of quite another kind than Totality, in which the Universal is thought of only as that which comprehends all individual existences, and as that which has Being, that which lies at the foundation of all things, the true content of all individual things.

Pantheism of this kind is not to be found in any religion, and the statement that it is so discoverable is wholly false. It has never occurred to any man to say, all is God – that is, things in their individuality or contingency – much less has it been maintained in any philosophy.

With oriental pantheism, or more correctly Spinozism, we shall make acquaintance later on, under the head of definite religion. Spinozism itself as such, and oriental pantheism, too, contain the thought that in everything the divine is only the universal element of a content, the Essence of things, while at the same time it is also represented as being the determined or specific Essence of the things.

When Brahm says, 'I am the brightness, the shining element in metals, the Ganges among rivers, the life in all that lives, &c.', what is individual is done away with and absorbed. Brahm does not say, 'I am the metal, the rivers, the individual things of each kind by themselves, as such, as they exist immediately'.

The brightness is not the metal itself, but is the Universal, the Substantial, elevated above any individual form; it is no longer $\tau o \pi \tilde{\alpha} \nu$, everything as individual. What is expressed here is no longer what is called pantheism; the idea expressed is rather that of the Essence in such individual things.

All that has life is characterised by the note of time and space; it is, however, only on the imperishable element in this singularity that stress is laid. 'The life of all that lives' is, in that imperishable sphere of life, the Unlimited, the Universal. When, however, it is said that everything is God, the singularity is understood in accordance with all its limits, its finiteness, its perishableness. The origin of this idea of pantheism is to be found in the fact that stress is laid on the abstract not on the spiritual unity; and then, when the idea takes its religious form, where only the substance, the One, ranks as true reality, those who hold these opinions forget that it is just in presence of this One that the individual finite things disappear, and have no reality ascribed to them, and yet they attempt to retain this reality in a material way alongside of the One. They do not believe the Eleatics, who say, the One only exists, and expressly add, and what is not has no existence whatever. All that is finite would be limitation, negation of the One; but that which is not, limitation, finite-ness, limit, and that which is limited, have no existence whatever.

Spinozism has been charged with being atheism, but the world, this All, does not *exist* at all in Spinozism; it has an outward form it is true, we speak of its existence, and our life is to be in it as thus existing. In the philosophical sense, however, the world has no reality at all, has no existence. No reality is ascribed to these individual things; they are finite in nature, and it is plainly stated that they do not exist at all.

Spinozism has been universally charged with leading to the following conclusions: – If all be One, then this philosophy maintains that good is one with evil, and that there is no difference between good and evil, and with this all religion is done away with. You hear it asserted that if the distinction of good and evil is not valid in itself, then it is a matter of indifference whether a man be good or bad. It may, indeed, be conceded that the distinction between good and evil is done away with potentially, that is, in God, who is alone the true Reality. In God there is no evil; the distinction between good and evil could exist only if God were Evil; no one, however, would concede that evil is something affirmative, and that this affirmative is in God. God is good, and good alone; the distinction between evil and good is not present in this One, in this Substance; it is with the element of distinction, or differentiation, that it first enters at all.

God is the One absolutely self-sufficing Being; in substance there is no distinction, no element of difference. With the distinction of God from the world, and especially from man, there first appears the distinction between good and evil. It is a fundamental principle of Spinozism, with regard to this distinction between God and man, that man must have God alone as his chief end. And thus the love of God is law for the element of difference, that is to say, for man; this love to God is alone to be his guide; he is not to ascribe value to his separate existence, to his difference in itself, not to desire to continue in it, but to direct his entire thought towards God alone.

This is the most sublime morality, that evil is non-existent, and that man is not to allow to this distinction, this nullity, any valid existence. Man may wish to persist in this difference, to carry this separation on into a settled opposition to God – the essentially existing Universal – and then man is evil. But it is also possible for him to regard his difference as non-existent, to place his true being in God alone, and direct his aim toward God – and then man is good.

In Spinozism, the distinction between good and evil undoubtedly makes its appearance with reference to God and man – and it appears in it with this qualification, that evil is to be regarded as non-existent. In God as such, in His character as Substance, there is no distinction; it is for man that this distinction exists, as does also the distinction between good and evil.

In accordance with that superficiality with which the polemic against philosophy is carried on, it is added, moreover, that philosophy is a system of Identity. It is quite correct to say that Substance is this one self-identity, but Spirit is just as much this self-identity. Everything is ultimately identity, unity with itself. But those who speak of the philosophy of Identity mean abstract Identity, unity in general, and pay no attention to that upon which alone all depends; namely, the essential nature of this unity, and whether it is defined as Substance or as Spirit. The whole of philosophy is nothing else than a study of the nature of different kinds of unity; the Philosophy of Religion, too, is a succession of unities; it is always unity, yet a unity which is always further defined and made more specific.

In the physical world there are many kinds of unity: when water and earth are brought together, this is a unity, but it is a mixture. If I bring together a base and an acid and a salt, a crystal is the result. I have water too, but I cannot see it, and there is not the slightest moisture. The unity of the water with this material is, therefore, a unity of quite a different character from that in which water and earth are mingled. What is of importance, is the difference in the character of the unity. The Unity of God is always Unity, but everything depends upon the *particular nature* of this Unity; this point being disregarded, that upon which everything depends is overlooked.

What we have first is this divine Universality – Spirit in its entirely undetermined Universality – for which there exists absolutely no element of difference. But upon this absolute foundation (and this we state for the moment as fact) there now appears that element of distinction which, in its spiritual character, is consciousness, and it is with this distinction that religion, as such, begins. When the absolute Universality advances to the stage of judgment, that is to say, when it proceeds to posit itself as determinateness, and God exists as Spirit for Spirit, we have reached the standpoint from which God is regarded as the object of consciousness, and Thought, which at the beginning was universal, is seen to have entered into the condition of relation and differentiation.

Translated by E. B. Speirs and J. Burdon Sanderson

Select Bibliography

The literature on the philosophy of the German Idealists is vast. Great works of scholarship can be found in many European as well as some non-European languages. Any bibliography which is designed to assist the reader must therefore be highly selective. In this case only English language commentaries have been listed as a guide to the reader's first contact point with the existing scholarship on German Idealism.

General Guides and Histories of the Period

Ameriks, Karl (ed.). *The Cambridge Companion to German Idealism* (Cambridge: Cambridge University Press, 2000)

Baur, Michael and Dahlstrom, Daniel O. (eds.). *The Emergence of German Idealism* (Washington, DC: Catholic University of America Press, 1999)

Beiser, Frederick C. *The Fate of Reason: German Philosophy from Kant to Fichte* (Cambridge, MA / London: Harvard University Press, 1987)

Beiser, Frederick C. *German Idealism: The Struggle against Subjectivism, 1781–1801* (Cambridge, MA / London: Harvard University Press, 2002)

Copleston, Frederick. *A History of Philosophy* (New York: Image Books), volume 6 (*The French Enlightenment to Kant*, 1964) and volume 7 (*Fichte to Hegel*, 1965)

Pinkard, Terry. *German Philosophy 1760–1860* (Cambridge: Cambridge University Press, 2002)

Sedgwick, Sally (ed.). *The Reception of Kant's Critical Philosophy: Fichte, Schelling, and Hegel* (Cambridge: Cambridge University Press, 2000)

Solomon, Robert C. and Higgins, Kathleen M. (eds.). *The Age of German Idealism: Routledge History of Philosophy*, volume 6 (London: Routledge, 1993, 2003)

Specific Topics

Ameriks, Karl and Sturma, Dieter (eds.). *The Modern Subject: Conceptions of the Self in Classical German Philosophy* (Albany, NY: State University of New York Press, 1996)

Behler, Ernst. *German Romantic Literary Theory* (Cambridge: Cambridge University Press, 1993)

Beiser, Frederick C. *Enlightenment, Revolution and Romanticism: The Genesis of Modern German Political Thought 1790–1800* (Cambridge, MA / London: Harvard University Press, 1992)

Bowie, Andrew. *Aesthetics and Subjectivity: From Kant to Nietzsche* (Manchester: Manchester University Press, 2003)

Klemm, David E. and Zöller, Günter (eds.) *Figuring the Self: Subject, Absolute, and Others in Classical German Philosophy* (Albany, NY: State University of New York Press, 1997)

Larmore, Charles. *The Romantic Legacy* (New York: Columbia University Press, 1996)

Kant

Kant: Critical German Edition

Gesammelte Schriften, edited by the Royal Prussian Academy of Sciences (Berlin: Walter de Gruyter, 1900ff), 29 volumes

Kant: English Translations (of major works)

Under the joint editorship of Paul Guyer and Allen W. Wood *The Cambridge Edition of the Works of Immanuel Kant*, published by Cambridge University Press, is a series of new translations of Kant's writings. The volumes of this edition to date are:

Theoretical Philosophy, 1755–1770 (1992), ed. and trans. David Walford with Ralf Meerbote
Lectures on Logic (1992), ed. and trans. J. Michael Young
Opus postumum (1993), ed. Eckhart Förster, trans. Eckhart Förster and Michael Rosen
Practical Philosophy (1996), ed. and trans. Mary J. Gregor, intro. Allen W. Wood
Religion and Rational Theology (1996), ed. and trans. Allen W. Wood and George Di Giovanni
Lectures on Ethics (1997), ed. Peter Heath and J. B. Schneewind, trans. Peter Heath
Lectures on Metaphysics (1997), ed. and trans. Karl Ameriks and Steve Naragon
Critique of Pure Reason (1998), ed. and trans. Paul Guyer and Allen W. Wood
Correspondence (1999), trans. and ed. Arnulf Zweig
Critique of the Power of Judgment (2000), ed. Paul Guyer, trans. Paul Guyer and Eric Mathews
Theoretical Philosophy after 1781 (2002), ed. Henry Allison and Peter Heath, trans. Gary Hatfield and Michael Friedman
Notes and Fragments (2005), ed. Paul Guyer, trans. Curtis Bowman, Paul Guyer and Frederick Rauscher

Further Editions of Kant Translations

Critique of Pure Reason (London: Macmillan, 1933), trans. Norman Kemp Smith (*Kritik der reinen Vernunft*, 1781/87)
Prolegomena to Any Future Metaphysics (Cambridge: Cambridge University Press, 1997) ed. and trans. Gary Hatfield (*Prolegomena zu einer jeden künftigen Metaphysik, die als Wissenschaft wird auftreten können*, 1783)
Groundwork of the Metaphysics of Morals (Cambridge: Cambridge University Press, 1997), trans. Mary J. Gregor (*Grundlegung zur Metaphysik der Sitten*, 1785)
Metaphysical Foundations of Natural Science, in *Philosophy of Material Nature* (Indianapolis, IN: Hackett, 1985), trans. James W. Ellington (*Metaphysische Anfangsgründe der Naturwissenschaft*, 1786)
Critique of Practical Reason (Cambridge: Cambridge University Press, 1997), trans. Mary J. Gregor (*Kritik der praktischen Vernunft*, 1788)
Critique of Judgement (Oxford: Clarendon Press, 1952), trans. James Creed Meredith; *Critique of Judgment: Including the First Introduction* (Indianapolis, IN: Hackett, 1987), trans. Werner S. Pluhar (*Kritik der Urteilskraft*, 1790)
Religion Within the Limits of Reason Alone (New York: Harper and Row, 1960), trans. Theodore Meyer Greene and Hoyt Hopewell Hudson (*Die Religion innerhalb der Grenzen der bloßen Vernunft*, 1793/94)
The Metaphysics of Morals (Cambridge: Cambridge University Press, 1991), trans. Mary J. Gregor (*Die Metaphysik der Sitten*, 1797/98)

The Conflict of the Faculties (Lincoln, NE: University of Nebraska Press, 1992), trans. Mary
  J. Gregor (*Der Streit der Facultäten in drei Abschnitten*, 1798)
Anthropology from a Pragmatic Point of View (Carbondale, IL: Southern Illinois University Press,
  1978), trans. Victor Lyle Dowdell and Hans H. Rudnick (*Anthropologie in pragmatischer Hinsicht*,
  1798/1800)
On Education (New York: Dover, 2003), trans. Annette Churton (*Pädagogik*, 1803)
Lectures on Philosophical Theology (Ithaca, NY / London: Cornell University Press, 1978), trans.
  Allen W. Wood and Gertrude M. Clark (*Vorlesungen über die philosophische Religionslehre*, 1817)
Lectures on Ethics (New York: Harper and Row, 1963), trans. Louis Infield
On History (Indianapolis, IN: Bobbs-Merrill, 1963), ed. Lewis White Beck
Political Writings (Cambridge: Cambridge University Press, 1991), ed. Hans Reiss, trans. H. B.
  Nisbet
Philosophical Correspondence 1759–99 (Chicago, IL: University of Chicago Press, 1967), trans.
  Arnulf Zweig
Selected Pre-Critical Writings and Correspondence with Beck (Manchester: Manchester University
  Press / New York: Barnes and Noble, 1968), trans. G. B. Kerferd and D. E. Walford

Kant: General Studies and Introductions

Beck, Lewis White. *Studies in the Philosophy of Kant* (Indianapolis, IN: Bobbs-Merrill, 1965)
Cassirer, Ernst. *Kant's Life and Thought* (New Haven, CT / London: Yale University Press, 1981),
  trans. James Haden
Caygill, Howard. *A Kant Dictionary* (Oxford: Blackwell, 1995)
Chadwick, Ruth F. (ed.). *Immanuel Kant: Critical Assessments* (London: Routledge, 1993) 4
  volumes
Guyer, Paul (ed.). *The Cambridge Companion to Kant* (Cambridge: Cambridge University Press,
  1992)
Henrich, Dieter. *The Unity of Reason: Essays on Kant's Philosophy* (Cambridge, MA / London:
  Harvard University Press, 1994)
Höffe, Otfried. *Immanuel Kant* (Albany, NY: State University of New York Press, 1994), trans.
  Marshall Farrier
Kemp, John. *The Philosophy of Kant* (Oxford: Oxford University Press, 1968)
Körner, Stephan. *Kant* (Harmondsworth: Penguin, 1955)
Kuehn, Manfred. *Kant: A Biography* (Cambridge University Press, 2001)
Walker, R. C. S. *Kant* (London: Routledge and Kegan Paul, 1978)
Wood, Allen W. *Kant* (Oxford: Blackwell, 2004)

Kant: Studies of Specific Topics

Allison, Henry E. *Kant's Theory of Freedom* (Cambridge: Cambridge University Press, 1990)
Allison, Henry E. *Kant's Transcendental Idealism: An Interpretation and Defense* (New Haven, CT /
  London: Yale University Press, 2nd Edition, 2004)
Ameriks, Karl. *Kant's Theory of Mind: An Analysis of the Paralogisms of Pure Reason* (Oxford:
  Clarendon Press, 2nd edition, 2000)
Ameriks, Karl. *Kant and the Fate of Autonomy: Problems in the Appropriation of the Critical Philosophy*
  (Cambridge: Cambridge University Press, 2000)
Aune, Bruce. *Kant's Theory of Morals* (Princeton, NJ: Princeton University Press, 1980)
Beck, Lewis White. *A Commentary on Kant's Critique of Practical Reason* (Chicago, IL: University
  of Chicago Press, 1960)
Beiser, Frederick C. *Enlightenment, Revolution and Romanticism: The Genesis of Modern German
  Political Thought 1790–1800* (Cambridge, MA / London: Harvard University Press, 1992)
Bennett, Jonathan. *Kant's Analytic* (Cambridge: Cambridge University Press, 1966)
Bennett, Jonathan. *Kant's Dialectic* (Cambridge: Cambridge University Press, 1974)
Brook, Andrew. *Kant and the Mind* (Cambridge: Cambridge University Press, 1994)

Cohen, Ted and Guyer, Paul (eds.). *Essays in Kant's Aesthetics* (Chicago, IL: University of Chicago Press, 1982)

Crowther, Paul. *The Kantian Sublime: From Morality to Art* (Oxford: Clarendon Press, 1989)

Friedman, Michael. *Kant and the Exact Sciences* (Cambridge, MA / London: Harvard University Press, 1992)

Galston, William A. *Kant and the Problem of History* (Chicago, IL: The University of Chicago Press, 1975)

Gardner, Sebastian. *Routledge Philosophy Guidebook to Kant and the 'Critique of Pure Reason'* (London: Routledge, 1999)

Gregor, Mary. *Laws of Freedom: A Study of Kant's Method of Applying the Categorical Imperative in the Metaphysik der Sitten* (Oxford: Basil Blackwell, 1963)

Guyer, Paul, *Kant and the Claims of Knowledge* (Cambridge: Cambridge University Press, 1987)

Guyer, Paul. *Kant and the Claims of Taste* (Cambridge: Cambridge University Press, 2nd edition, 1997)

Kemp Smith, Norman. *A Commentary to Kant's* Critique of Pure Reason (London: Macmillan, 1923)

Korsgaard, Christine M. *Creating the Kingdom of Ends* (Cambridge: Cambridge University, 1996)

Longuenesse, Béatrice. *Kant and the Capacity to Judge: Sensibility and Discursivity in the Transcendental Analytic of the 'Critique of Pure Reason'* (Princeton, NJ: Princeton University Press, 1998), trans. Charles T. Wolfe

O'Neill, Onora. *Constructions of Reason: Explorations of Kant's Practical Philosophy* (Cambridge: Cambridge University Press, 1989)

Strawson, Peter F. *The Bounds of Sense: An Essay on Kant's 'Critique of Pure Reason'* (London: Methuen, 1966)

Sullivan, Roger J. *Immanuel Kant's Moral Theory* (Cambridge: Cambridge University Press, 1989)

Sullivan, Roger J. *An Introduction to Kant's Ethics* (Cambridge: Cambridge University Press, 1994)

Williams, Howard. *Kant's Political Philosophy* (Oxford: Basil Blackwell, 1983)

Wood, Allen W. *Kant's Moral Religion* (Ithaca, NY/ London: Cornell University Press, 1970)

Wood, Allen W. *Kant's Rational Theology* (Ithaca, NY/ London: Cornell University Press, 1978)

Yovel, Yirmiyahu. *Kant and the Philosophy of History* (Princeton, NJ: Princeton University Press, 1980)

Zammito, John H. *Kant, Herder, and the Birth of Anthropology* (Chicago, IL: University of Chicago Press, 2002)

Fichte

Fichte: Critical German Editions

Werke, edited by Immanuel Herman Fichte (Berlin: de Gruyter, 1971), 11 volumes

Gesamtausgabe der Bayerischen Akademie der Wissenschaften, edited by Reinhard Lauth, Erich Fuchs and Hans Gliwitzky (Stuttgart-Bad Cannstatt: Frommann-Holzboog, 1962ff)

Fichte: English Translations (of major works)

Attempt at a Critique of All Revelation (Cambridge: Cambridge University Press, 1978), trans. Garrett Green (*Versuch einer Kritik aller Offenbarung*, 1792/93)

Science of Knowledge (Cambridge: Cambridge University Press, 1982), trans. Peter Heath and John Lachs (*Grundlage der gesammten Wissenschaftslehre*, 1794)

Foundations of Transcendental Philosophy (Wissenschaftslehre) nova methodo. (Ithaca, NY: Cornell University Press, 1992), trans. and ed. Daniel Breazeale (*Wissenschaftslehre nova methodo*, 1796–99)

Foundations of Natural Right (Cambridge: Cambridge University Press, 2000), trans. Michael Baur, ed. Frederick Neuhouser (*Grundlage des Naturrechts nach Principien der Wissenschaftslehre*, 1796)
System of Ethics (Cambridge: Cambridge University Press, 2005), ed. Daniel Breazeale and Günter Zöller (*Das System der Sittenlehre nach den Principien der Wissenschaftslehre*, 1798)
'On the Foundation of our Belief in a Divine Government of the Universe', trans. Paul Edwards in *19th Century Philosophy* (New York: The Free Press, 1969), ed. Patrick L. Gardiner (another translation is found in *Introductions to the Wissenschaftslehre and Other Writings*, ed. D. Breazeale) (*Ueber den Grund unseres Glaubens an eine göttliche Weltregierung*, 1798)
The Vocation of Man (Indianapolis, IN: Hackett, 1987), trans. Peter Preuss (*Die Bestimmung des Menschen*, 1800)
'The Closed Commercial State', in *Political Thought of the German Romantics 1793–1815* (Oxford: Basil Blackwell, 1955), trans. and ed. Hans S. Reiss and Peter Brown (*Der geschlossene Handelsstaat*, 1800)
'A Crystal Clear Report to the General Public Concerning the Actual Essence of the Newest Philosophy: An Attempt to Force the Reader to Understand', trans. John Botterman and William Rash, in *Philosophy of German Idealism*, (New York: Continuum, 1987), ed. Ernest Behler (*Sonnenklarer Bericht an das grössere Publikum, über das eigentliche Wesen der neuesten Philosophie*, 1801)
Fichte: Early Philosophical Writings (Ithaca, NY: Cornell University Press, 1988), trans. and ed. Daniel Breazeale
Introductions to the Wissenschaftslehre and Other Writings (Indianapolis, IN: Hackett, 1994), trans. and ed. Daniel Breazeale.
The Science of Knowing: J. G. Fichte's 1804 Lectures on the Wissenschaftslehre (Albany, NY: State University of New York Press, 2005), trans. and ed. Walter E. Wright (*Die Wissenschaftslehre. Vorgetragen im Jahre 1804*)
Addresses to the German Nation (New York: Harper and Row, 1968), trans. R. F. Jones and G. H. Turnbull (*Reden an die deutsche Nation*, 1808)
The Popular Works of Johann Gottlieb Fichte (London: Trübner and Co., 1889), trans. William Smith (reprinted by Thoemmes Continuum, 1999, with an introduction by Daniel Breazeale)

Fichte: Studies

Breazeale, Daniel and Rockmore, Tom (eds.). *New Essays in Fichte's Foundation of the Entire Doctrine of Scientific Knowledge* (New York: Humanity Books, 2001)
Breazeale, Daniel and Rockmore, Tom (eds.). *New Essays on Fichte's later Jena Wissenschaftslehre* (Evanston, IL: Northwestern University Press, 2002)
Everett, Charles C. *Fichte's Science of Knowledge: A Critical Exposition* (Boston and New York: Houghton, Mifflin and Company, 1893)
Henrich, Dieter. 'Fichte's Original Insight', in *Contemporary German Philosophy I* (University Park, PN: Pennsylvania State University Press, 1982), trans. David R. Lachterman
Jalloh, Chernor Maarjou. *Fichte's Kant–Interpretation and the Doctrine of Science* (Lanham, MD: University Press of America, 1988)
La Vopa, Anthony J. *Fichte: Self and the Calling of Philosophy, 1762–1799* (Cambridge: Cambridge University Press, 2001)
Martin, Wayne M. *Idealism and Objectivity: Understanding Fichte's Jena Project* (Stanford, CA: Stanford University Press, 1997)
Neuhouser, Frederick. *Fichte's Theory of Subjectivity* (Cambridge: Cambridge University Press, 1990)
Rockmore, Tom. *Fichte, Marx, and the German Philosophical Tradition* (Carbondale, IL: Southern Illinois University Press, 1980)
Rockmore, Tom and Breazeale, Daniel (eds.). *New Perspectives on Fichte* (Atlantic Highlands, NJ: Humanities Press, 1996)

Seidel, George J. *Fichte's* Wissenschaftslehre *of 1794: A Commentary on Part I*, (Lafayette, IN: Purdue University Press, 1993)

Surber, Jere Paul. *Language and German Idealism: Fichte's Linguistic Philosophy* (Atlantic Highlands, NJ: Humanities Press, 1996)

Turnbull, George Henry. *The Educational Theory of J. G. Fichte : A Critical Account, together with translations* (London: Hodder and Stoughton, 1926)

Williams, Robert R. *Recognition: Fichte and Hegel on the Other* (Albany, NY: State University of New York Press, 1992)

Zöller, Günter. *Fichte's Transcendental Philosophy: The Original Duplicity of Intelligence and Will* (Cambridge: Cambridge University Press, 1998)

Schiller

Schiller: Critical German Edition

Werke, Nationalausgabe, edited by L. Blumenthal and Benno von Weise (Weimar: Böhlhaus Nachfolger, 1943–1967)

Schiller: Translations of Main Philosophical Works

On the Aesthetic Education of Man in a Series of Letters (English and German Facing) (Oxford: Clarendon Press, 1967), trans. Elizabeth M. Wilkinson and L. A. Willoughby (*Über die ästhetische Erziehung des Menschen*, 1795)

On the Naïve and Sentimental in Literature (Manchester: Carcanet Press, 1981), trans. Helen Watanabe-O'Kelly (*Über naive und sentimentalische Dichtung*, 1796)

Essays (New York: Continuum, 1993), ed. Walter Hinderer and Daniel O. Dahlstrom

Schiller: Studies

Beiser, Frederick C. *Schiller as Philosopher: A Re-Examination* (Oxford: Clarendon Press, 2005)

Bowie, Andrew. *Aesthetics and Subjectivity* (Manchester: Manchester University Press, 2003)

Martin, Nicholas. *Nietzsche and Schiller: Untimely Aesthetics* (Oxford: Clarendon Press, 1996)

Reed, T. J. *Schiller* (Past Masters) (Oxford: Oxford University Press, 1991)

Savile, Anthony. *Aesthetic Reconstructions: the Seminal Writings of Lessing, Kant, and Schiller* (Oxford: Basil Blackwell, 1987)

Sharpe, Lesley. *Friedrich Schiller. Drama, Thought and Politics* (Cambridge: Cambridge University Press, 1991)

Schelling

Schelling: Critical German Editions

Sämmtliche Werke, edited by K. F. A. Schelling (Stuttgart: Cotta, 1856–61), 14 volumes. A selection of these volumes can be found in *Ausgewählte Schriften*, edited by Manfred Frank (Frankfurt: Suhrkamp, 1985), 6 volumes

Historisch-kritische Ausgabe. Im Auftrag der Schelling-Kommission der Bayerischen Akademie der Wissenschaften, edited by H. M. Baumgartner, W. G. Jacobs, H. Krings und H. Zeltner (Stuttgart: Frommann-Holzboog 1976 ff)

Schelling: English Translations (of major works)

The Unconditional in Human Knowledge: Four Early Essays 1794–6 (Lewisburg, PN: Bucknell University Press, 1980), ed. Fritz Marti

Ideas for a Philosophy of Nature: Introduction to the Study of This Science (Cambridge: Cambridge University Press, 1988), trans. Errol E. Harris and Peter Heath, intro. Robert Stern (*Ideen zu einer Philosophie der Natur als Einleitung in das Studium dieser Wissenschaft*, 1797)

First Outline of a System of the Philosophy of Nature (Albany, NY: State University of New York Press, 2004), trans. Keith R. Peterson (*Erster Entwurf eines Systems der Naturphilosophie*, 1799)

System of Transcendental Idealism (Charlottesville, VA: University Press of Virginia, 1978), trans. Peter Heath, intro. Michael Vater (*System des transcendentalen Idealismus*, 1800)

Bruno, or On the Natural and the Divine Principle of Things (Albany, NY: State University of New York Press, 1984), trans. Michael Vater (*Bruno oder über das göttliche und natürliche Princip der Dinge. Ein Gespräch*, 1802)

The Philosophy of Art (Minneapolis, MN: Minnesota University Press, 1989), trans. Douglas W. Stott (*Philosophie der Kunst*, 1803)

On University Studies (Athens, OH: Ohio University Press, 1966), trans. E. S. Morgan, ed. Norbert Guterman (*Vorlesungen über die Methode des akademischen Studiums*, 1803)

Of Human Freedom (Philosophical Investigations into the Essence of Human Freedom) (Chicago, IL: Open Court, 1936), trans. James Gutmann (*Philosophische Untersuchungen über das Wesen der menschlichen Freiheit und die damit zusammenhängenden Gegenstände*, 1809)

The Ages of the World (1811–15) (New York: Columbia University Press, 1942), trans. Frederick de Wolfe Bolman (*Die Weltalter*)

The Ages of the World: (Fragment) from the Handwritten Remains, Third Version (c. 1815) (Albany, NY: State University of New York Press, 2000), trans. Jason M. Wirth (*Die Weltalter*)

Clara: Or, on Nature's Connection to the Spirit World (Albany, NY: State University of New York Press, 2002), trans. Fiona Steinkamp (*Clara oder Ueber den Zusammenhang der Natur mit der Geisterwelt. Ein Gespräch*, 1810)

On the History of Modern Philosophy (Cambridge: Cambridge University Press, 1994), trans. Andrew Bowie (*Zur Geschichte der neueren Philosophie. Münchener Vorlesungen*, 1833–34)

Idealism and the Endgame of Theory: Three Essays (Albany, NY: State University of New York Press, 1994), ed. and trans. Thomas Pfau

Schelling: Studies

Beach, Edward A. *The Potencies of the God(s): Schelling's Philosophy of Mythology* (Albany, NY: State University of New York Press, 1994)

Bowie, Andrew. *Schelling and Modern European Philosophy: An Introduction* (London: Routledge, 1993)

Brown, Robert F. *The Later Philosophy of Schelling: the Influence of Boehme on the Works of 1809–1815* (Lewisburg, PA: Bucknell University Press / London: Associated University Presses, 1977)

Esposito, Joseph L. *Schelling's Idealism and Philosophy of Nature* (Lewisburg, PA: Bucknell University Press / London: Associated University Presses, 1977)

Heidegger, Martin, *Schelling's Treatise on the Essence of Human Freedom* (Athens, OH: Ohio University Press, 1985), trans. Joan Stambaugh

Marx, Werner. *The Philosophy of F. W. J. Schelling: History, System, Freedom* (Bloomington, IN: Indiana University Press, 1984)

Norman, Judith and Welchman, Alistair (eds.). *The New Schelling* (London / New York: Continuum, 2004)

Snow, Dale E. *Schelling and the End of Idealism* (Albany, NY: State University of New York Press, 1996)

Tillich, Paul. *The Construction of the History of Religion in Schelling's Positive Philosophy: its Pre-suppositions and Principles* (Lewisburg, PA: Bucknell University Press / London: Associated University Presses, 1974), trans. Victor Nuovo

White, Alan. *Schelling: Introduction to the System of Freedom* (New Haven, CT / London: Yale University Press, 1983)

Wirth, Jason M. (ed.). *Schelling Now: Contemporary Readings* (Bloomington, IN: Indiana University Press, 2005)

Wirth, Jason M. *The Conspiracy of Life: Meditations on Schelling and His Time* (Albany, NY: State University of New York Press, 2003)

Žižek, Slavoj. *The Indivisible Remainder. An Essay on Schelling and Related Matters* (London / New York: Verso, 1996)

Hegel

Hegel: Critical Editions

Gesammelte Werke, edited by the Rheinisch-Westfälischen Akademie der Wissenschaften (Hamburg: Felix Meiner, 1968 ff.)

Werke in zwanzig Bänden: Theorie-Werkausgabe (based on the edition of 1832–1845), edited by Eva Moldenhauer and Karl Markus Michel (Frankfurt: Suhrkamp, 1971), 20 volumes

Hegel: English Translations (of major works)

Early Theological Writings (Chicago, IL: University of Chicago Press, 1948), trans. T. M. Knox

The Difference between Fichte's and Schelling's System of Philosophy (Albany, NY: State University of New York Press, 1977), trans. and ed. H. S. Harris and Walter Cerf (*Differenz des Fichteschen und Schellingschen Systems der Philosophie*, 1801)

Faith and Knowledge (Albany, NY: State University of New York Press, 1977), trans. and ed. H. S. Harris and Walter Cerf (*Glauben und Wissen oder die Reflexionsphilosophie der Subjektivität*, 1802)

Phenomenology of Spirit (Oxford: Oxford University Press, 1977), trans. A. V. Miller (*Phänomenologie des Geistes*, 1807)

Science of Logic (London: Allen and Unwin, 1969), trans. A. V. Miller (*Wissenschaft der Logik*, 1812–16)

The Encyclopaedia Logic (Indianapolis, IN: Hackett, 1991), trans. T. F. Geraets, W. A. Suchting and H. S. Harris (*Encyclopaedia*: Part I) (*Enzyklopädie der philosophischen Wissenschaften im Grundrisse*: Erster Teil. Die Wissenschaft der Logik, 1817/1830)

Philosophy of Nature (Oxford: Clarendon Press, 1970), trans. A. V. Miller; also: (London: George Allen and Unwin / New York: Humanities Press, 1970), trans. Michael J. Petry (*Encyclopaedia*: Part II) (*Enzyklopädie der philosophischen Wissenschaften im Grundrisse*: 'Zweiter Teil. Die Naturphilosophie'*, 1817/1830)

Philosophy of Mind (Oxford: Clarendon Press, 1971), trans. A. V. Miller (*Encyclopaedia*: Part III) (*Enzyklopädie der philosophischen Wissenschaften im Grundrisse*: Dritter Teil. 'Die Philosophie des Geistes', 1817/1830)

Elements of the Philosophy of Right (Cambridge: Cambridge University Press. 1991), trans. H. B. Nisbet (*Grundlinien der Philosophie des Rechts*, 1821)

The Philosophy of History (New York: Dover Publications, 1956), trans. J. Sibree (*Vorlesungen über die Philosophie der Geschichte*, 1840)

Aesthetics (Oxford: Clarendon Press, 1975), 2 volumes. trans. T. M. Knox (*Vorlesungen über die Ästhetik*, 1835)

Lectures on the Philosophy of Religion (London: Kegan Paul, Trench, Trübner, 1895) 3 vols. trans.
E. B. Speirs and J. Burdon Sanderson; also: trans. Peter Hodgson and R. F. Brown (Los Angeles,
CA: University of California Press, 1984–87), 3 volumes (*Vorlesungen über die Philosophie der
Religion*, 1832)

Lectures on the History of Philosophy (Lincoln, NE: University of Nebraska Press, 1985) 3 vols.
trans. E. S. Haldane and F. H. Simson (*Vorlesungen über die Geschichte der Philosophie*, 1832–45)

Hegel: General Studies and Introductions

Beiser, Frederick C. (ed.). *The Cambridge Companion to Hegel* (Cambridge: Cambridge University
Press, 1993)

Beiser, Frederick C. *Hegel* (London: Routledge, 2005)

Houlgate, Stephen. *An Introduction to Hegel: Freedom, Truth, and History* (Oxford: Blackwell,
2005)

Inwood, Michael. *Hegel* (London: Routledge, 1983)

Inwood, Michael. *A Hegel Dictionary* (Oxford: Blackwell, 1992)

Pinkard, Terry. *Hegel: A Biography* (Cambridge: Cambridge University Press, 2000)

Singer, Peter. *Hegel* (Oxford: Oxford University Press, 1983)

Stern, Robert (ed.). *G. W. F. Hegel: Critical Assessments* (London: Routledge, 1993) 4 volumes

Taylor, Charles. *Hegel* (Cambridge: Cambridge University Press, 1975)

Hegel: Studies of Specific Topics

Burbridge, John. *On Hegel's Logic: Fragments of a Commentary* (Atlantic Highlands, NJ: Humanities
Press, 1981)

Desmond, William. *Art and the Absolute: A Study of Hegel's Aesthetics* (Albany, NY: State University
of New York Press, 1986)

Dickey, Laurence. *Hegel: Religion, Economics, and the Politics of Spirit, 1770–1807* (Cambridge:
Cambridge University Press, 1987)

Fackenheim, Emil. *The Religious Dimension in Hegel's Thought* (Bloomington, IN: Indiana University Press, 1967)

Ferrarin, Alfredo. *Hegel and Aristotle* (Cambridge: Cambridge University Press, 2001)

Forster, Michael. *Hegel and Skepticism* (Cambridge, MA: Harvard University Press, 1989)

Forster, Michael. *Hegel's Idea of a Phenomenology of Spirit* (Chicago, IL: University of Chicago
Press, 1998)

Hardimon, Michael O. The *Project of Reconciliation: Hegel's Social Philosophy* (Cambridge: Cambridge University Press, 1994)

Harris, H. S. *Hegel's Development* (Oxford: Oxford University Press), volume I: *Toward the Sunlight
1770–1801* (1972); volume II: *Night Thoughts, Jena 1801–1806* (1983)

Hartnack, Justus. *An Introduction to Hegel's Logic* (Indianapolis, IN: Hackett, 1998)

Houlgate, Stephen (ed.). *Hegel and the Philosophy of Nature* (Albany, NY: State University of New
York Press, 1998)

Hyppolite, Jean. *Genesis and Structure of Hegel's 'Phenomenology of Spirit'* (Evanston, IL: Northwestern University Press, 1974), trans. Samuel Cherniak and John Heckman

Jaeschke, Walter. *Reason in Religion: The Foundations of Hegel's Philosophy of Religion* (Berkeley,
CA: University of California Press, 1994), trans. J. Michael Stewart and Peter C. Hodgson.

Kaminsky, Jack. *Hegel on Art: An Interpretation of Hegel's Aesthetics* (Albany, NY: State University
of New York Press, 1962)

Knowles, Dudley. *Hegel and the Philosophy of Right* (London: Routledge, 2002)

Kojève, Alexandre. *Introduction to the Reading of Hegel: Lectures on the 'Phenomenology of Spirit'*
(New York: Basic Books, 1969), trans. James H. Nicholls

Lauer, Quentin. *A Reading of Hegel's 'Phenomenology of Spirit'* (New York: Fordham University
Press, 1976)

Maker, William (ed.). *Hegel and Aesthetics* (Albany, NY: State University of New York Press, 2000)

McCarney, Joseph, *Hegel on History* (London: Routledge, 2000)

Neuhouser, Frederick. *Foundations of Hegel's Social Theory: Actualizing Freedom* (Cambridge, MA / London: Harvard University Press, 2000)

O'Brien, George D. *Hegel on Reason and History* (Chicago, IL: University of Chicago Press, 1975).

Patten, Alan. *Hegel's Idea of Freedom* (Oxford: Oxford University Press, 1999)

Pelczynski, Z. A. (ed.). *Hegel's Political Philosophy: Problems and Perspectives* (Cambridge: Cambridge University Press, 1971)

Pinkard, Terry. *Hegel's Phenomenology. The Sociality of Reason* (Cambridge: Cambridge University Press, 1994)

Pippin, Robert B. *Hegel's Idealism: The Satisfactions of Self-Consciousness* (Cambridge: Cambridge University Press, 1989)

Rosen, Michael. *Hegel's Dialectic and its Criticism* (Cambridge: Cambridge University Press, 1982)

Solomon, Robert C. *In the Spirit of Hegel* (New York: Oxford University Press, 1983)

Stern, Robert. *Hegel and the 'Phenomenology of Spirit'* (London: Routledge, 2002)

Wood, Allen W. *Hegel's Ethical Thought* (Cambridge: Cambridge University Press, 1990)

Index

Absolute, the, 11, 20–1, 25, 65, 67, 69–74, 83–5, 91, 139, 240, 264, 266–7, 297, 307, 375, 380, 396, 461, 463
Alexander the Great, 323, 341
Ameriks, K., 29
Anaxagoras, 350
apperception *see* self-consciousness
a priori, 8–11, 17, 31–9, 58–60, 65, 69, 73, 96–9, 103, 106–13, 152, 155, 156, 159, 173, 212, 223, 226, 283–4, 295, 298–301, 309–13, 317, 329, 346, 348–52, 356, 358–9, 363, 367, 370–2, 375, 381
architecture, 274–6, 278
Aristotle, 9, 16, 384
art, 18–20, 211–79
    artist, 235, 249–50, 253
    classical art, 269–70, 278
    death of art, 263
    romantic art, 270–2, 276, 277, 278
    symbolic art, 268–74, 278
atheism, 23, 306, 418–19, 424, 461, 464
Aufhebung (sublation), 129, 403
autonomy, 15, 16, 108, 123, 243, 283, 413

Baumanns, P., 14
Baumgarten, A., 16
beauty, 346–52, 361; *see also* art
Beck, J. S., 2, 12
Beiser, F., 4, 61
Berkeley, G., 53
Boehme, J., 399
Burke, E., 244n

Caesar, Julius, 323, 325, 340–1
categorical imperative, 14, 96–9, 103–6, 116, 119, 122
categories, 9–12, 22, 30, 32, 38–9, 56, 82, 110, 331, 345, 346, 384, 391, 453
Cato, 147
Christianity, 194–5, 264–5, 268, 271, 332–3, 394, 411, 414, 414n, 452–4
citizen, 160, 195, 204, 293, 337

civilization, 236–9, 291, 292
coercion, 152–6, 168, 170, 176–8, 183–7
cognition, 83–5, 88, 223
commandment, 18, 452
common sense, 212, 227–9
commonwealth, 158, 160–1, 183, 185–6
concept (*Begriff, Konzept*), 8, 9, 13, 32, 76, 78, 82, 85, 87, 89, 91, 120, 131, 198, 217, 219, 222, 249, 351, 380, 381, 383, 387, 391, 393, 394, 397–406, 460
Condorcet, N. de, 20
consciousness, 13, 61, 62, 77, 81, 86–91, 126, 129, 130, 172, 251–5
constitution, 170, 171, 201, 206, 208, 235, 290, 294, 297–8, 332
constraint, 117–19
contract, 163–4, 188
contradiction, 437–8, 447
cosmology, 11, 384
cosmopolitanism, 292
creation, 143, 144
culture, 230, 236, 289, 292

deduction, 6, 9, 11, 13, 14, 31–3, 40, 42, 56, 57, 60, 98–9, 109, 112, 113, 116–24, 128, 165, 167, 169, 170, 173–6, 178, 184, 188, 252, 298, 255, 301, 315, 368, 384, 423
Descartes, R., 7, 10
desire, 101–2, 130, 134, 136, 214, 217, 225
determinism, 49, 62–3, 95, 138, 141, 306, 461
    predestination, 144
dialectic, 11, 13, 21, 25, 82, 89, 129, 310, 311, 406
Dickey, L., 451
Diez, I. C., 3
Diodorus Siculus, 326
drives,
    formal drive, 241–5
    play drive, 231–2, 242–6
    rational drive, 231
    sense drive, 231, 240–4, 245